Three Faces of Fascism

Three Faces of
Fascism

ACTION FRANÇAISE · ITALIAN FASCISM
NATIONAL SOCIALISM

Ernst Nolte

Translated from the German by
Leila Vennewitz

Holt, Rinehart and Winston
NEW YORK   CHICAGO   SAN FRANCISCO

Contents

Author's Preface to the English Translation   ix

Translator's Acknowledgment   xiii

PART ONE
Fascism and the Era of World Wars

1   Fascism as Characteristic of an Era   3

2   Fascism in Europe (1919–1945)   10
    Fascist Movements   10
    Interpretations of Fascism   16
    First Definition   20

3   Methods and Objective of Study   22
    Criteria of Selection   22

PART TWO
The Action Française

1   The Disparate Roots   29
    Introduction: Revolution and the Political Doctrine   29
    Christian Conservatism: de Maistre and de Bonald   34
    Critical Liberalism: Comte, Le Play, Renan, Taine, Fustel de
      Coulanges   37
    Radical Conservatism: de La Tour du Pin, Drumont, Barrès   48

2   History   54
    Introduction: The Dreyfus Affair   54
    Maurras' Development to 1898   58
    The Action Française to the Founding of its Newspaper   65
    From the Founding of the Newspaper to the End of the War   68
    From the End of the War to the Condemnation by Rome   73
    Condemnation by the Vatican   76

From the Vatican's Condemnation to the Defeat of France   77
Vichy   80
Charles Maurras' Trial, Imprisonment, and Death   84

3 Practice as Consequence   88

Introduction: The Place of Practice and Its Motivations   88
Organization of the Action Française   89
The Leadership   94
The Style   96

4 The Doctrine   100

Introduction: The Hidden System   100
Fear as the Origin   101
State and Sovereignty   103
State and War   110
State and Classes   113
The Enemy as a Whole   120
The Battle   127
The Philosophical Basis   135

PART THREE
Italian Fascism

1 History   145

Fascism and the Action Française   145
How the European Knot Was Tied in Italy   145
Digression on Method   150
Mussolini the Marxist (1902–1914)   151
The War as Revolution   167
Struggle for Social Democracy   178
Nationalism   182
D'Annunzio in Fiume   185
Mussolini's Darkest Year   188
The Socialist Face of 1920   191
Fascist "Re-action"   196
Mussolini's Unexpected Rise and His Last Battle for Coherence 202
The Beginnings of National Fascism   209
National Fascist Totalitarian Development Dictatorship   217
The Last Autonomous Stage (1935–1937)   225
Despotism of Conquest and Satellite State   228
Return to the Origins?—*Repubblica di Salò*   236

2 The Fixed Doctrine   243

3 The Irksome Precursors 247

4 Practice as Premise 250
    Up to the March on Rome 250
    After the Seizure of Power (to 1931) 259
    The Starace Era (1931–1939) 265
    Epilogue 269

PART FOUR
National Socialism

1 National Socialism and Fascism 275

2 The Background: The Race Doctrine 277

3 History 287
    Adolf Hitler 287
    Austria: The Progressive Feudal State 294
    The German Reich: The Feudal Industrial State 298
    War, Revolution, and Peace Treaty 304
    Hitler's Political Beginnings 312
    Teachers and Forces Surrounding the Early Hitler 323
    The Fresh Start (1925–1930) 333
    Appeal to the Masses and Rise to Power (1930–1931) 337
    Single-Minded Seizure of Power (1933) 342
    War in Peacetime (1934–1939) 347
    Levels of War and Degrees of Resistance 354
    Universal Hostility and End 360

4 Practice as Fulfillment 365
    1919–1923 365
    1925–1932 370
    1933–1939 374
    1939–1945 394

5 The Doctrine in Context 402
    Fear and Its Intentions 402
    Unconditional Sovereignty 407
    Eternal War 409
    Absolute Supremacy 410
    Distant Models 414
    Global Struggle for "Recovery" 416
    Nature and Antinature 419

PART FIVE
Fascism as a Metapolitical Phenomenon

The Concept of Transcendence 429
Marx: Philosophical Discovery and Critique of Bourgeois Society 434
Nietzsche: The Prebourgeois Soil of "Culture" 441
Max Weber: The Theoretician of Bourgeois Society before Fascism 446
Outline of a Transcendental Sociology of this Period 450

Appendix A 455

Appendix B 459

Notes 463

Selected Reading List 547

Index 549

Author's Preface to the English Translation

It is surely more than a coincidence that as yet no comprehensive and overall account of fascism has been written.

After 1945, the writings of fascist leaders ceased to go beyond the category of memoirs, a fact which is hardly surprising. While indispensable to a knowledge of the subject, they contribute little to an insight into its nature. The works of the statesmen and military personalities in the opposite camp are bound to contribute even less, despite the high historical level of many such works.

The partisan literature of political writers, almost solely, and for obvious reasons, the work of anti-Fascists, contains virtually all that exists today in the way of insights; but from the very start these writers broke up into sharply divided schools, and by the end of the war the various possible approaches toward arriving at a concept of fascism had already been laid down. The end of the war saw the elimination of the enemy; practically all the new material for analysis originated in Germany, and political developments forced the concept of totalitarianism into the limelight. As a result, further attempts were suspended.

The scholarly exploration of fascism has only been possible since 1945. However, scholars found themselves facing such a wealth of material and such a plethora of possible interpretations that in Italy and Germany they progressed no further than the level of recording historical events from a national standpoint.[1] Historians tend, generally speaking, to emphasize national differences and to regard the concept of fascism with some suspicion, although they find it cannot get along without it or its surrogate.

In the preface to the first German edition it was pointed out that, precisely because of certain shortcomings and exceptional aspects of the author's background, this book has been able to take the step to which none of the three literary categories has so far proceeded. To belabor this today would be an affectation. German historians have admitted the author so wholeheartedly to their ranks that the book may now be regarded, without further explanation, as a work of German historical scholarship. Suffice it to say that the author has traveled a lengthy road—in his eyes more than a mere detour—by way of philosophy to history.

Hence the aim of this book is not description but understanding. Historical understanding, however, is a very different matter from abstract speculation. To understand means to grasp the differentiated within its context. For this reason, National Socialism has not been isolated from the phenomena to which it always claimed to be related, nor has the phenomenon of fascism been separated from the historical period in which it was possible and, for a while, dominant.

At this point the book's underlying assumption should be clearly stated: the fascist era claimed more victims than any era in history, and for this very reason demands the utmost intellectual effort at understanding. This effort is not in vain, even if its results are questioned, and its value is enhanced the more often it is undertaken from a maximum variety of viewpoints and in a maximum number of places.

However much this book may stress thought and hence selection, it also attaches the highest importance to details, provided these are typical and significant. Certain details, such as the young Mussolini's Marxist ideas or Dietrich Eckart's influence on Hitler, are among those sections to which the most study has been devoted. And because historical context is always linked with the sequence of events, the two longest chapters—those dealing with the histories of Italian fascism and National Socialism—differ little from a straightforward historical account.

A very short reading list of related works in English has been appended to this book by the editors as an aid to the English-speaking reader; but no comprehensive bibliography has been collected for this edition, since the very nature of the subject would cause it to assume giant proportions. However, the references in the notes should be of value even to experts in the field, relating as they do to literature which in many cases is unlikely to be familiar to most readers. Where reference is made to translations (not necessarily in English) of well-known works, it is taken for granted that the reader will, if he desires, refer either to the originals or to the accepted English translations, since the addition of English-language references in every case would make the notes unwieldy. For a comprehensive initial orientation on the subject, the reference to three excellent short works should suffice.[2]

It gives me great pleasure to express my gratitude to the translator in the preface to this edition. Leila Vennewitz displays the three cardinal qualities of a mediator between languages: respect for the idea, meticulous attention to each individual word, and a sensitive awareness in interpretation. Furthermore, she took the trouble to visit me and discuss some of the more difficult problems with me. The only major changes in this edition concern passages in the first chapter, some of which were transposed for purposes of clarity while others are now to be found in the appendices.

The originator of the present edition is Thomas C. Wallace, an editor of Holt, Rinehart and Winston, Inc., who undertook its publication long before he could have had any knowledge of the reaction to the book in scholarly circles.

A number of colleagues in the United States have very kindly taken an interest in the translation, and I would like to thank each one of them, particularly Professor Hajo Holborn, Professor Klemens von Klemperer, and Professor Klaus Epstein. Without dwelling on the purely subjective background of the writing of this book, the author wishes to acknowledge with gratitude his debt to Professor Theodor Schieder for his sympathetic interest in the author's work, an interest which began some years ago with the acceptance of a maiden contribution by a wholly unknown author for publication in *Historische Zeitschrift*; also to Reinhard Baumgart of the Piper Verlag for his interest in the book which ensured it of a sound publishing future.

There is no formal dedication, since this book did not originate in any personal relationship with roots in the subject. However, the book would not have been written without the existence and help of my wife. It is in fact her book in a more genuine and intimate sense than any dedication could ever express.

Marburg an der Lahn ERNST NOLTE

Translator's Acknowledgment

The author kindly supplied me with excerpts from his original French and Italian sources of reference, thus enabling me to translate many of his quotations from those languages directly into English.

Robert Freedman's *Marx on Economics* (New York: Harcourt, Brace and Co., 1961) has been valuable as a guide to Marxist terminology; and Dante L. Germino's *The Italian Fascist Party in Power* (Minneapolis: University of Minnesota Press, 1959), has helped me determine English equivalents for common Italian fascist terms.

I am greatly indebted to the following, who have been very helpful in a variety of ways: the author, Professor Ernst Nolte, and his wife, for their keen interest and the knowledgeable aid they have given me throughout; Professor Klemens von Klemperer, of Smith College, Massachusetts, for carefully scrutinizing the translation and supplying many scholarly and expert emendations; Dr. Max Knight, of the University of California, Berkeley, for some invaluable suggestions; Mr. Seymour Barofsky, of New York City, whose thorough professional scanning of the manuscript has resulted in countless technical and stylistic improvements; and Mr. Thomas Wallace, the publishers' editor who has carried the translator through this undertaking from start to finish with his encouragement, fund of knowledge, and seemingly inexhaustible patience. In thanking these helpful people, however, it is not my aim to lay down any part of the burden of responsibility.

Lastly, I wish to express my profound gratitude to my husband, William Vennewitz, whose constant guidance and assistance have been, as always, indispensable.

Vancouver, Canada   LEILA VENNEWITZ
January, 1965

PART ONE

Fascism and the Era of World Wars

CHAPTER ONE

Fascism as Characteristic of an Era

The writer who at the end of the nineteenth century had proposed calling his own time the "era of imperialism" would not have found many to agree with him. Yet the term had been in use for centuries and, in spite of many different interpretations, possessed a relatively clearly defined meaning as to content and scope. This does not apply to the term "fascism," with the result that the phrase "era of fascism" does not find ready acceptance even today.

In 1920 the word "fascism" was known to very few people in Europe, and even Mussolini placed it between quotation marks as being a neologism. In 1923, however, the leftist parties throughout Germany staged an "antifascist day," thereby demonstrating as forcefully against the German, Hungarian, and Bulgarian "Fascists" as against Mussolini's victorious Blackshirts. A particular interpretation of the term was an essential before Hitler's seizure of power—that notorious description of the Social Democrats as Social Fascists, with which the Communist party of Germany repeated the fatal mistake of the Italian Communists in extended and crasser form. But at about the same time the leaders of certain groups of the extreme Right proposed to call an "antifascist congress."[1] A kind of compromise between the former very wide and the latter very narrow definition was represented, after the great about-face of the Comintern,[2] by the commonly held concept of antifascism which made the policy of the Popular Fronts possible and under whose banners the great world coalition finally fought against Hitler and Mussolini, although this coalition had certainly not been formed under these banners. Today the concept of fascism is still one of direct political significance. The question of whether or not the Franco regime can be called fascist touches upon national interests, and a whole series of new developments has led to a notable revival of the term.

To inquire into the nature of the "era of fascism," then, means to add the specific problem of a still much-disputed term—the scholarly discussion of which has barely begun—to the overall difficulty which every periodization entails. On the other hand, it is obvious that the question of fascism cannot be separated from the question of its era, since no universally acknowledged and meaningful concept of the era between 1919 and 1945 exists. Even if the term "fascism" is taken strictly as a name, that is, to describe an isolated phenomenon, the question remains of the extent to which events in Italy were *not*—in spite of their incalculable world-wide effect—epochal. Whichever way we look at it, the common nature of the inquiry into fascism and the era is inescapable, and it is our task to define the concepts and review the facts.

However, the order in which the thematic material is placed is governed by one helpful limitation. Even though fascism existed after 1945 and has continued to exist since that time, and even though it is still capable of arousing bitter conflicts, it cannot be said to have real significance as far as the image of the era is concerned unless the term be stripped almost entirely of its traditional connotation. Thus the very subject of this study precludes any reference to events of the present day.

Hand in hand with this limitation goes a very tangible advantage; for contemporary history, in so many respects at a disadvantage when compared with its older sisters, has at its disposal a virtually ready-made division of eras, enabling us to trace the course of fascism deductively.

To use the term "era of the world wars"[3] and imply the period from 1914 to 1945 would certainly not be valid for all time; but seen from the present day, the dates of August 1, 1914, and May 8, 1945, represent such profound cleavages in history that their epoch-making character has never been denied. What is disputed (aside from how to divide the subsections) is the context into which the epoch is to be placed and the point in time at which the cataclysmic caesura represented by the outbreak of war caused the new constellations to mature and acquire their first self-awareness. The most important of these concepts imply an answer to the question, whether the chronological and formal criterion might not be augmented by a more meaningful one. It should be enough to enumerate three of the best-known of these concepts:

1. The era of the world wars forms part of an age of revolutions and profound social changes, an age of which the most visible starting point was the French revolution.[4]

2. The immediate roots of this era are to be found in the period of imperialism. It was during this time that all the conflicts developed which merely achieved their climax with the outbreak of war.[5]

3. It was not until 1917 that World War I ceased to be simply a conflict of national states. With the entry of the United States into the war and the Bolshevik revolution, the constellation became a universal one: a general state of civil war and the future splitting of the world into two are already discernible in outline.[6]

From each of these definitions and interpretations it is possible to derive the concept of a new type of political phenomenon.

None of the major political trends in Europe had evolved from a war:

liberalism was the expression of the rise of the bourgeoisie; conservatism originally represented the reaction of the threatened aristocratic ruling class; socialism belonged to the proletariat born of the process of industrialization. None of these political doctrines wanted a world war or gave it its unqualified blessing after the outbreak. It was the war that made room for a political phenomenon, which was, so to speak, its very own child, a child which by innate law strove in turn to engender yet another war.

Since 1789, despite all reaction and many political defeats, the social revolution had spread inexorably throughout Europe. It led the bourgeoisie almost everywhere to participate in political power and raised it to a position from which it exerted a determining influence on society; it also provided the bourgeoisie with a new adversary in the shape of the socialistic proletariat. On all sides the newly emancipated class joined forces with the old ruling class against the approaching menace. Although this alliance was only a pragmatic and temporary one, small groups were beginning to transform it into one of principle even before 1914: a historically unique marriage between aristocratic conviction and plebeian reality. At first these groups remained small and unnoticed, but under certain conditions the principle on which they were founded could be of significance for the future since this principle corresponded to a basic characteristic of the social revolution itself: namely, that new auxiliary troops were continually joining the counterrevolution from the ranks of the emancipated, with the result that its face was changing as constantly as that of the revolution.

Before 1914 what was known as imperialism showed itself everywhere to be a compromise between the banal egoism of the national states and the more elusive requirements of the liberal and socialist traditions. Neither Cecil Rhodes nor Theodore Roosevelt nor Friedrich Naumann had any other object in view than to extend their respective "cultural ideas" of their time to the advantage and for the salvation of all peoples within their scope. But was it not implicit in the fundamental nature of this imperialism that it bestow unquestioning approval upon itself?

There is no doubt that the year 1917 represented a cleavage which cut deep into its own time and far into the future. But it is equally certain that the two great powers whose emergence was marked by this cleavage soon withdrew to their own native ground. When the American people opted against Wilson in 1920 it chose two decades of a new isolationism; the skepticism Lenin felt toward the "workers' aristocracy" of the West was soon confirmed. It turned out that the victory of bolshevism in Russia did not prevent its defeat on all the social battlefields of Europe, if it did not in fact actually cause it. Starting not later than 1923, the year of the failure of the last revolts in Germany, the Communist parties were operating everywhere more to the advantage of their enemies' cause than to their own. The Soviet Union became once more an unknown country on the periphery of the world, and Europe was once more the arena of world events. But was it likely that after that fearful interlude the participants should remain quite the same?

The war, the revolution, imperialism, the emergence of the Soviet Union and the United States, were not locally confined phenomena. Neither could a movement which came into being as an outcome of the war, a movement which fought revolution with revolutionary methods, which radicalized imperialism, and which saw in the Soviet Union (and in "Americanism" too, although with less emphasis) the greatest of all threats, be called a locally confined phenomenon, no matter how many differences might be attributable to it due to local conditions. This movement would have found its place in the Europe of the postwar period even if Mussolini and Hitler had never lived. No term other than "fascism" has ever been seriously proposed for it. This word has the drawback of being simultaneously name and concept; it has the advantage of being without concrete content and of not, like German National Socialism, implying an unjustifiable claim. It is not the business of scholarly investigation to invent a new term just because the one commonly used cannot satisfy all requirements.

If, then, fascism can be defined as a new reality which did not exist before World War I, or only in rudimentary form, the obvious next step is to declare it to be the characteristic political trend of an era in which, owing to the withdrawal of the two recently emerged "flanking powers," Europe can be regarded once more as the focal point of the world. Out of four principal powers in this Europe two, as we know, became fascist within ten years, and after ten more years a continent which had become almost totally fascist (or so, at least, it seemed) had torn the two "flanking powers" from their isolation and challenged them to battle.

When a historian speaks of the "era of the Counter Reformation" he does not imply that the Counter Reformation was the dominant force in all areas of the then known world and that it met with no resistance, nor is he obliged to believe that it contained the seeds of the future. He does not even have to regard it as "necessary." In order to describe a period marked by powerful religious elements he simply uses the religious phenomenon which, being central to this trend, represented its most novel and thus most typical manifestation. In the same way, if we are to name an era marked by political conflicts after the most novel phenomenon in the center of events, we cannot do otherwise than call the era of the world wars an era of fascism.

This definition of the era is not new, and so should not be surprising. At various times it has been used (explicitly or implicitly) by leading representatives of the most disparate parties.

At the peak of his reputation and independence during the years 1930 to 1935, Mussolini often said that fascist ideas were the ideas of the age and that within a few years the whole of Europe would be fascist. On all sides he descried, it seemed to him, "fascist ferments of the political and spiritual renewal of the world";[7] he defined fascism as "organized, concentrated, authoritarian democracy on a national basis,"[8] and did not hesitate to claim for it anything in the world that demanded a strengthening of state power and intervention in the economy.

Mussolini's theory of the imminent fascistization of the world undoubtedly seems prejudiced and vague. Yet Thomas Mann's remarks in his essay *Dieser Friede* ("This Peace"), written at the height of the controversy following Munich from the opposite point of view, are very similar. He speaks of the "complete victory" of the "massive trends of the times which can be summarized in the word fascism" and traces them to "Europe's psychological preparedness for fascist infiltration in a political, moral, and intellectual respect."[9] A little later he calls fascism "a disease of the times which is at home everywhere and from which no country is free."[10] And even after Hitler's defeat he speaks (in his discourse on Nietzsche) of "the fascist era of the Occident in which we live and, despite the military victory over fascism, will long continue to live."[11]

This is somewhat reminiscent of the theory expounded by Georg Lukács in his book, *Die Zerstörung der Vernunft*. Here he attempts to describe philosophical irrationalism as an essential component of and background to National Socialism, as the "reactionary answer to the great problems of the past hundred and fifty years."[12] On Germany's path "from Schelling to Hitler" is to be found practically every name of any stature in German philosophy after Hegel's death: Schopenhauer and Nietzsche, Dilthey and Simmel, Scheler and Heidegger, Jaspers and Max Weber. However, in contrast to many attempts at analysis (particularly in Anglo-Saxon literature), Lukács sees the spiritual foundation of National Socialism as other than exclusively German: he regards the evolution in Germany's intellectual and political life merely as the most prominent manifestation of an international process within the capitalist world.

Of course there are many objections to Lukács' ideas,[13] but this much is undoubtedly true: namely, that, beginning with the close of the nineteenth century, a change took place in the spiritual climate all over Europe, a change which was bound to further—although not create—a new political orientation disaffiliating itself from, and indeed directly opposing, the traditional political environment. With no immediate relevance to the political events of the day, the Nietzschean doctrine, which alone permitted the equation of socialism, liberalism, and traditional conservatism, was adopted and developed by a circle of fascistoid authors: the doctrine of the revolt of the slaves and of the impoverishment of life through Judeo-Christian resentment.

A no less convincing proof of the epochal nature of fascism is the fact that it exerted the strongest possible influence on its opponents. This is true not primarily in the narrow sense that it imposed its own traits directly upon them: in this we are often faced with a matter of parallel developments[14] (although they, too, are of great consequence in forming opinion). Fascism forced its adversaries to undertake the most painful self-reappraisal in generations, for it was in their attitude toward fascism that they committed their direst errors and misjudgments.

What was antifascism in its earliest form—the opposition of the Aventine after the murder of Matteotti—if not the alliance of those who before the March on Rome had been unable to agree and had thereby suffered defeat? What did the slogan "antifascist united front" launched by the Communists after 1935 mean, if not the most revolutionary revision of their own tactics of the previous decade? What, on their highest level, was the content of the discussions and writings of German emigrants, if not the most critical self-examination of the German mentality ever to have taken place? And was not this self-examination at times compelled to admit that the very opposition to fascism often bore fascist traits?

The fascist traits which socialist emigrants from Germany[15] could not help observing in Stalin's Russia were not isolated examples. What was left of the spirit of Lenin and Rosa Luxemburg when "militarism and nationalism, the cult of heroes and Byzantinism" occupied pride of place, and world revolution and the international workers' movement were hardly ever mentioned? How were the enormous differences in piecework wages, the reactionary family legislation, the invoking of the traditions of Peter the Great, to be reconciled with the aims of the October revolution? Did not the trials of Lenin's veteran campaigners mean the start of the worst persecution of Communists the world had ever seen, and was not anti-Semitism secretly fostered by the government? A study of the history of the Soviet Union would, of course, have shown that the beginnings of this trend had their roots deep in Lenin's times. Lenin himself had seen to it that criticism of the party was suppressed; he had replaced local spontaneity with a hierarchical superstructure and had ordered police measures against dissatisfied workers. Was Stalin really a usurper, or was he the executor of Lenin's testament? Was Stalinism only the hard husk pressing on the original kernel to protect it from mortal danger, or was it really the complete antithesis that intended to endure? Today we are not inclined to answer any of these questions with a straight Yes or No and thus concede an essential difference between Stalinism and fascism. Nevertheless, Franz Borkenau's thesis is worthy of consideration: he maintains that since 1929 Russia has taken its place "among the totalitarian, fascist powers."[16] And in any case this much may be said with some degree of certainty: that, since the conflict between Stalin and Bukharin, the question of the attitude toward fascism, has, almost more than any other, determined Soviet policy in all its aspects.

Even Roosevelt's America has not escaped similar reproaches. Dorothy Thompson tried to uncover fascist tendencies in the New Deal: Roosevelt was compared with Mussolini as long ago as 1934; and even in 1940 there were still many Americans who hotly attacked the President for his "Caesarism" and his "Führer principle."[17] Roosevelt himself was so far from regarding the accusation of fascism as negligible that he made a point of explaining his attitude.[18]

He did not by any means deny that, in America as well as in Europe, powerful epochal tendencies had brought about the establishment of a "strongly developed leadership."[19] However, it is precisely from this example of Roosevelt that we see how careful we must be not to infer fascism from isolated "fascist" traits. There is no doubt whatever that in his ideas and personality Roosevelt was fundamentally opposed to fascism (and not only to Hitler and the fascism of Germany).[20] Apparently there must be a "fascist minimum" without which the noun would be meaningless and even the adjective "fascist" doubtful. Nevertheless, a careful study of the example of Roosevelt shows that, although fascism was perhaps merely an explosive concentration of principles, most of which were individually necessary, it certainly did not occur as a foreign element in its era, episodic and isolated. Combined with our other considerations and points of evidence, it completes the circle encompassing the thesis that the era of the world wars is identical with the era of fascism.

This only makes the problem of the nature and manifestations of fascism all the more urgent, although it in no way implies a depiction of the era as a whole. Nothing would be more unjustified than to conclude that the other powers of the era, because they cannot be understood apart from their reaction to fascism, constituted no more than this reaction. There is no reason not to suppose that, in the overall relationships of the age, fascism for its part will have to be regarded as being primarily a reaction. Hence the great trends of the age, notably Marxism and liberalism, will always be present in what is to come, and the epochal opponents will keep on appearing, although only in glimpses. Fascistoid thinking, on the other hand, will occupy a good deal of space, if only by one outstanding example, in the form in which it has become a component of fascism. The aim of this study is not to present a picture of the era but a concept of it as far as this can be derived from the nature of fascism. The considerations so far advanced can help to trace the outline of this nature, but they are not sufficient for complete understanding. Detail and clarity are essential to it: without them it is nothing but a soulless diagram.

Up to this point the terrain in which fascism is to be found has been marked out. This terrain now needs to be described in such a way that the multiple nature of the phenomenon clearly emerges. But no phenomenon can be understood if divorced from its surroundings, and the original close affiliation with conservative allies is peculiarly characteristic of fascism. Hence the boundaries that have just been defined must now immediately be recrossed at many points.*

---

* For a further discussion of the application of the term 'fascism,' see Appendix A.

CHAPTER TWO

Fascism in Europe (1919–1945)

Fascist Movements

The year 1919 was a crucial one for fascism, as it was for so many trends of the ensuing decade. Is it a coincidence that the form which was to become the most significant and momentous of all was the first to emerge in embryonic outline from the chaos of the immediate postwar period? For while in the spring of that year Mussolini set up Kurt Eisner as a model for his newly formed Fasci di Combattimento, in Hungary Béla Kun had just taken over the reins of government, and in Germany the combined Reichswehr and peasant-student *Freikorps* overthrew the short-lived Munich Soviet Republic. Of all the revolutionary spasms of that time, this last was the most haphazard, the most doomed, the most idyllic. Triggered by the senseless assassination of the Bavarian prime minister Eisner, who was on the point of resigning, it was the revolt of part of the proletariat under the leadership of a few intellectuals, mostly Jewish and anarchist, in a completely bourgeois city in the heart of a Catholic-agrarian area. By wanton acts of terrorism they managed to injure their own reputation more seriously than their enemies, who for the most part escaped harm.[21] But perhaps it was for this very reason that they aroused so much hatred. And the notion of equating bolshevism with Jewry, and diagnosing both as a deadly disease, took hold more firmly than anywhere else in the mind of the little Reichswehr propagandist Adolf Hitler.

In Hungary the counterrevolution did not bring about the fall of the Béla Kun regime unaided; the advance of the Rumanians sounded the death knell to a revolution which had been just as much a product of national despair and a weapon of national self-assertion as an attack on social traditions. But this was also led mainly by Jews, and the ideas of the young officers who got together first in Szeged differed little from those of their Munich comrades. In 1919 Julius Gömbös was already calling himself a "National Socialist." The numerous patriotic organizations that arose soon afterward can in many aspects be compared to the patriotic groups of Bavaria. Gömbös headed the most important of them as "supreme leader," and in the unfavorable climate of the Bethlen era he wrote pamphlets on international Jewry and founded the new "Party of Racial Defense."[22]

More successful in their external battles, but not really a factor of internal political significance, were the first Austrian *Heimatwehren* of 1919. It was only by degrees that they lost their supraparty position, and not until 1927 did they take the road known as "Heimwehr fascism," which was to become one of the elements of Austro-fascism.

In Poland, too, the threat from outside the country—although it came from Bolshevik Russia and, in contrast with Bavaria and Hungary, actually did represent a deadly threat—did not lead directly to the development of fascist trends. The popular anti-Semitism of the National Democrats and the authoritarianism of the legionaries, who had founded the state, had not yet been joined, so that for some years an extremely liberal parliamentary regime could prevail, until the rebellion of May 1926 brought Pilsudski to the helm.

In Italy the Fiume enterprise of Gabriele D'Annunzio (in September, 1919) marked an important stage on the road of early fascism. The basic traits of its style and symbolism were developed in Fiume, not Milan, and it was here that the poet's socialistic romanticism gave early definition to what was later to become corporatism.

In 1919 in northern Anatolia, Mustafa Kemal Pasha began his struggle for Turkey's heartland in the revolt against his own government and the foreign powers.[23] Although his national defense dictatorship really only belongs on the periphery of this study of fascism, its brilliant success was an encouraging stimulus for all opponents of the Treaty of Versailles.

Also from 1919 stem the rudiments of what was later to become in Rumania the Iron Guard, a student association founded by Codreanu with the object of offering partisan-type resistance to the Red Army invasion he feared was imminent.

In 1919 war and revolution in Europe were more closely contiguous than ever before or since, and that year signaled the starting point of the first fascist parties. Their development progressed at varying speeds, but the years 1922 and 1923 were crucial way stations. During these years the first two fascist parties entered the spotlight of history and world-wide interest; it was chiefly these two which were to keep the world in suspense: one of them achieved a momentous victory, the other suffered a still more momentous defeat. At the end of October, 1922, Mussolini's Blackshirts conquered the capital with their curious "March on Rome," and barely more than a year later Hitler ran impetuously against the reluctantly drawn sword of a government that until then had been consistently friendly and favorably inclined.

A third event from this period is worthy of mention, although it took place in a corner of Europe. On June 9, 1923, the government of the peasant leader

Aleksandr Stamboliski—called by his enemies an "agrarian Communist"—was overthrown in Sofia, and the new government of Tsankov steered a bloody course of oppression against the smoldering peasant resistance and in particular against the Communist party. By June 23 the Comintern had issued an appeal to the workers of the world, calling upon them to protest against the crimes of the "victorious Bulgarian fascist clique."[24] Thus in 1922–23 the world saw not only the emergence of the two principal fascist movements under the sign of what was, compared to 1919, a strangely altered battle front, but also the first official appearance of that polemical and universal interpretation which was so vital to the further development of fascism.[25]

From then on fascist movements mushroomed in Europe. In most cases it is hardly possible to say to what extent independent causes or the influence of Mussolini's shining example stood godfather at their birth.[26] It is enough merely to list those groups, parties, and movements which failed to achieve power, or to achieve it unaided. The regimes themselves require a closer scrutiny, as do those countries in which a comparatively uniform trend toward fascism is discernible.

In many cases the splinter groups are the easiest to identify: isolated in their countries, they often looked for a substitute in their boundless admiration for Mussolini and Hitler. Perhaps it is doing an injustice to Léon Degrelle's Belgian Rexists, to the Finnish Lappo Movement, or to the Flemish National Solidarists, to include them here—the Danish National Socialist party of Fritz Clausen, the Francists of Marcel Bucard, the various forms of Swiss fascism, and many similar manifestations in most of the countries of Europe were scarcely more than clumsy imitations.

Possessed of independent roots, and for a short period also of some weight of their own, were the French groups—which, incidentally, greatly enlivened the fascist picture with their diversity and intellectual level (Brasillach, Drieu la Rochelle), and which also, as is generally believed, came closest to seizing power in February, 1934: Georges Valois' *Faisceau*, Pierre Taittinger's *Jeunesses Patriotes*, Colonel de la Rocque's *Croix de Feu*, Jacques Doriot's *Parti Populaire Français*, and finally Marcel Déat's neosocialist splinter group. The British Fascists also had a face of their own. The first of the British groups was constituted as early as 1923, and by 1926 British fascist groups were said to have at least half a million members. The best-known of these was the British Union of Fascists, founded in 1933 by Sir Oswald Mosley, who had been the youngest minister in the Labor party cabinet and in the eyes of many, a future prime minister. The foreign-sounding party label did not prevent it from enjoying a spectacular, albeit short-lived, rise.[27] The Estonian Association of Freedom Fighters must not be overlooked, the only one of all the fascist groups to succeed in legally obtaining the absolute majority vote of the people, but which the government nevertheless brought to its knees by means of a *coup d'état*.[28]

It was not so much their own strength as foreign aid and the chance happenings of war that allowed some of these parties to get into power. Quisling and his *Nasjonal Samling* gave the world a familiar example of this. Their place could have been taken with equal justification by Mussert and the Dutch National Socialist party. German aid also enabled the Iron Guard to come to power (partially and temporarily)[29] in Rumania, and Szálasi's Arrow Cross party in Hungary. Mussolini made the Ustasha leader Pavelić the *Poglavnik* of the Croats. The picture in Tiso's Slovakia is not quite so clear. The Pétain regime was subjected to violent criticism from the Right, and no external influences affected its establishment. Doriot's Sigmaringen power was merely a shadow play and a farce.

The regimes are another matter; they were typified mainly by the independence of their development, even when they did not remain unsupported. They are outlined here in an order determined by the extent of fascism's disaffiliation from the original alliance with conservative or even liberal forces.

The most striking example was Hungary, where the relationship between the extreme Right and the state, and hence the problem of its form, was revealed in three paradigmatic stages. The policy of fulfillment and renunciation of the Bethlen era may well be compared with the Weimar Republic, the government of Gömbös with the earliest period of Hitler's chancellorship, when the conservatives appeared to have tamed and "contained" their drummers, and the rule of Szálasi with the latter period of National Socialism. Certainly the contrasts were consistently less violent to the extent that, in a country where for eighteen years the flags had flown at half-mast, the general desire for revision of the peace treaty was taken just as much for granted as counterrevolutionary sympathies. The clash of principles, the spark from which fascism first catches fire, was absent. Moreover, Horthy himself was considered to be one of the "men of Szeged." And even Count Bethlen could not seriously be called a (democratic) liberal. Finally, the Hungarians grasped the fact which the National Socialists would never admit: that the fulfillment policy was an inevitable stage on the road to reform. For all practical purposes a Left did not exist, which was why the transition from Bethlen to Gömbös was not in the least comparable to the change-over of January 30, 1933, in Germany. Nevertheless, Gömbös, the man of the people and the supreme commander of MOVE (Hungarian Association of National Defense),[30] was a completely different type from the liberal-authoritative aristocrat Bethlen, and the Jews in particular faced the prospect of his government with some trepidation. But Horthy did not die, like Hindenburg, nor did he let himself be stripped of power, like Victor Emmanuel. Instead he firmly tied the prime minister's hands, and Gömbös was even obliged to renounce his anti-Semitism more or less explicitly. During this period, however, Hungary found its way into the camp of the emerging Axis, and following on his election victory of 1935, Gömbös addressed the assembled crowds in balcony speeches just like his models in Rome and Berlin, with whom he shared a spiritual origin dating from 1919. Horthy's position, true, continued to remain so strong that he was able to consider summarily dismissing Gömbös, and it was only the latter's sudden death that prevented a possible trial of strength. However, if we wished to deny outright the similarity of the Hungarian with the German situation during the first months of 1933, we would have to regard the fascist nature of National Socialism as being rooted in the personal energy of Hitler, the senility of Hindenburg, and the irresponsible actions of von Papen and Hugenberg.

That Horthy would have voluntarily allowed fascism to assume power in the unmistakable guise represented by Ferenc Szálasi's Arrow Cross party is quite inconceivable. Although Szálasi was a former officer, Horthy was bound to feel an aversion for everything he stood for: the mysticism with which he stead-fastly believed in his mission of saving Hungary, and through Hungary the world; his desire to win the support of the poorer classes and the, at times, emphatically "proletarian" character of his movement; its violence and ruthless propaganda methods; and even the "Hungarianist" program itself, which went beyond the *restitutio in integrum* of old Hungary. Thus it was only under the most dubious circumstances that Szálasi became leader of the government: that is, in the shadow of the violent German reaction to Horthy's armistice offer of October 15, 1944. But he began at a point where Mussolini left off: after the occupation of a country by the enemy and with the unmistakable signs of ultimate defeat. The face of his regime, therefore, took shape solely under the iron necessities of the struggle of despair and did not to any notable extent show spontaneous or typical features of its own.

The "moral dictatorship" set up by Pilsudski in Poland in 1926, with the aim of leading the country to "recovery" (*Sanacja*) by abolishing the "abuses" of the parliamentary system, relied principally on the army. The core of the army consisted of his own legionaries, and even if Pilsudski himself never infringed on the multiplicity of parties and a fairly extensive freedom of expression of opinion, his successors took some forceful steps in the direction of an authoritarian, one-party dictatorship of soldier-statesmen. However, the marshal's regime constantly met with resistance from the Left and with criticism by an organized force on the extreme Right.

If the wholesale suppression of parties and freedom of the press is to be regarded as a sufficient criterion of fascism, it would be necessary to call the "king's dictatorship" of Alexander I in Yugoslavia fascist. But Yugoslavia, even more than Hungary and Poland, lacked the popular movement and the potential single party, a much more distinctive characteristic.

Originally this was also lacking in the Portugal of Salazar, and it has remained to this day an artificial structure. For at bottom the *Estado Novo* is simply a military dictatorship which was lucky enough to find an outstanding civilian who simultaneously strengthened and transformed it.[31] Both the state party of the *União Nacional* and corporatism were and still are merely the means of this strengthening and transformation; they have no independent origin or autonomous will.

In Spain, on the other hand, even before Franco's military revolt there were militant formations of the extreme Right that showed typical rivalry-similarity with the Left. The name of the first of these groups gives us a sufficient clue: *Juntas de Ofensiva Nacional-Sindicalista* (JONS). In February, 1934, it combined with the *Falange Española*, founded by José Antonio Primo de Rivera, and the radical nature of its program (nationalization of banks and the elimination of large landed estates) aroused a great deal of suspicion from the old Right. The outbreak of war, however, cut off its chances of independent development: all the outstanding leaders fell, and in April, 1937, Franco combined the movement—not without some resistance—with the radical-traditionalist units of the Carlist *Requetes* to form the new state party under his leadership: the *Falange Española Tradicionalista y de las JONS*.[32] In its heyday the Falange in Spain played quite a different role from the *União Nacional* in Portugal, yet it is reasonable to suppose that its conservative allies—army, church, and landed gentry—were always stronger than it was, since they were able to maintain a leader from their own ranks at its head.

Austrian "Heimwehr fascism" managed to put the state on a new footing from top to bottom, but Austro-fascism, which finally succeeded the parliamentary system, was not the same thing, and although Starhemberg might be said to have been more of a Fascist than an aristocrat, this would not be true of either Dollfuss or Schuschnigg.

In fact, of all the fascist movements and trends it was only with Italian fascism and with German National Socialism that a truly popular movement achieved victory, relatively unaided, and swept its leader to the position of supreme head of state. Only here did violent confrontations with the conservative forces continue right up to the final days of the regime and often develop into overt hostility with each side bent on destroying the other. But this view, which considers the relationship of fascism to the traditional system of leadership and code of norms, is not the only one from which a comparison of the different forms of fascism is possible, nor does it permit striking antitheses. For Mussolini had first to turn from a republican into a monarchist before he could embark on the March on Rome, and even during the period of his greatest power he could never contemplate the abolishment of the monarchy. Almost more palpable was the restriction of power which Hitler underwent when he had to allow the major conservative force, the army, a measure of independence of which there continued to be characteristic evidence up until July 20, 1944. Even National Socialism was never the sole determining force except as a trend; and it is this orientation which is the common denominator of all types of fascism, not the particular measure of their success, which continued to depend on a number of chance factors.

It is a peculiarity of the study of history to be concerned with individuality and thus to emphasize the necessity of description. It makes us more keenly aware that such terms as liberalism, parliamentarianism, monarchism, are not fixed quantities but can mean different things in different circumstances. Yet the historian does not for that reason abandon them. That is why he will also insist on the broadest possible empirical basis for the study of fascism. He is in a position to do so since he is familiar with diffuse entities of this kind. For example, nineteenth-century socialism encompasses a vast number of manifestations, and the pupils of Fourier and Saint-Simon were not without reason bitter enemies. Yet there is no question but that a fundamental kinship existed. And just as the historian must protest the exclusion from socialism of all those who do not acknowledge the idea of a phalanstery, so he must object to the narrowing *a limine* of the concept of fascism merely on account of isolated distinguishing marks.

Interpretations of Fascism

One thing, however, the historian cannot do by himself: he cannot evolve a concept on his own authority. He always finds it prefabricated—coined by either supporters or opponents. If he were merely to follow his own bent, he would never exhaust the examination of the smallest of such a term's manifestations, for the associations are endless, and the differences finally lead back to the intangibility of the *individuum ineffabile*. Even the "complexity" (although not the immeasurability) of the phenomenon is only apparent to discerning observation. The original interpretations of political trends, however, are always formed, before objective study forms them, in the confrontations of social existence itself. Applied to a given phenomenon they represent a conception rather than a description. But if the historian has to assume these conceptions rather than initiate them, he will still place them in critical association with each other and with the description, so that in principle it can transcend its premises.

The primary condition for this is the complete and unprejudiced review of conceptions. If the objective study of fascism is made possible by the fact that the phenomenon may be regarded as "dead," this signifies a considerable advance, always assuming that the number of conceptions is not subject to chance increase but is a matter of conclusive necessity.

The oldest of these conceptions is the socialist one. It is, so to speak, older than fascism itself. When in October, 1914, after a hard struggle with his conscience, Mussolini went over to interventionism, he definitely wanted this to be understood as socialist interventionism in favor of attacked nations. His attempt to make the party fall in step with the new line failed however, and when three weeks after resigning as editor of *Avanti!* he established his own newspaper, his former colleagues kept on repeating in his former newspaper the inexorable question: *Chi paga?* (Who is paying?) It is true that this question could not be unequivocally answered then, nor can it be now, but it determined the basic outline of the socialist interpretation up until our own day. Yet it undoubtedly did Mussolini an injustice if it implied that it was for financial reasons that he carried out the best-substantiated of his political changes of course; it did, however, reveal an incontestable truth, by associating Mussolini's lack of means with the high cost of publishing, in the thesis that, at least objectively, he must be a pawn in someone's game and that this game was primarily an antisocialist one. This interpretation was painfully confirmed for the Socialists when their positions of power and their organizations, which only a few months earlier had spread fear and trembling throughout the bourgeoisie, were wiped out during 1921 and 1922 by the Fascists with the open support of agrarians, the big bourgeoisie, and even the state. The view that fascism is a secondary phenomenon derived from one of the two fundamental social realities (the bourgeoisie as against the proletariat), is the basis of all socialist interpretations. Within this framework they range from a primitive theory of agents[33] to a large number of diversified theories which attempt to work out the possibilities and limitations of a subjection of the original content by means of what has been deduced.[34]

However, the attitude of liberalism, even in the case of Italy, does not absolutely confirm this theory. It is true that, until the March on Rome, the *Corriere della Sera* under Luigi Albertini supported not so much fascism as Mussolini, but it then very soon adopted a stance of sharp opposition. It is also true that the three most respected liberal politicians—the former prime ministers Giolitti, Orlando, and Salandra—hesitated, even as late as the crucial date of January 3, 1925. But an organ of the stature of *La Stampa* had opposed fascism unequivocally from the very beginning, and its editor, Luigi Salvatorelli, found in the term *Antirisorgimento* one of the most effective formulas for the battle with the state party. This term virtually contained the idea of "totalitarianism," and it achieved canonical status when Farinacci and Mussolini deliberately adopted it for the Fascist party in 1925. Leading Italian writers, as distinct from many non-Italian authors, have always strongly emphasized this totalitarian character of Italian fascism; Giuseppe Antonio Borgese followed in the footsteps of the Latin-liberal tradition of regarding Germany as the paragon of modernity and freedom to such an extent that even in 1935 he saw greater chances for freedom and resistance in Germany.[35]

However, the term "totalitarian" was actually evolved by German and American authors as a result of the twin experience of National Socialism and bolshevism. Its interpretation ranges from the political to the metapolitical-metaphysical. The first contrasts the totalitarian state with the liberal-constitutional state and regards it as distinguished by a number of basic features (such as the existence of an ideologically oriented single party) which suspend civil and spiritual liberty.[36] The true nature of the totalitarian state would therefore be a system of uniformity, artificially and compulsorily set up, which presupposes the diversity of the liberal era and hence must oppose it, if necessary by terroristic methods. According to this interpretation, rule by a conservative group must also be totalitarian rule if it forcibly suppresses all other parties and opinions.

A classic formulation of the second interpretation was given by Peter Count Yorck von Wartenburg when addressing the People's Court: "The essential element is ... the total claim of the state on the citizen involving the elimination of his religious and moral obligations toward God."[37] According to this conception, then, a politically total rule would not actually be totalitarian if it permitted freedom in man's prepolitical and metapolitical relations to other individuals and to God. In its further extension this interpretation is inclined to regard certain features of total claim as denoting totalitarianism's true essence: in terrorism, which proceeds with extreme harshness against the familiar and the traditional; in universalism, which aims at world domination; in perversion, which demands those very things which are contrary to the laws of God and humanity.[38]

How easily this conception allies itself with Christian and conservative beliefs, how greatly it exemplifies the tempering of traditionally antagonistic opinions, is plain to see.[39] However, the specifically Christian-ecclesiastical attitude toward fascism is a separate chapter, and a strange one. For the fact that in most European countries the churches encouraged fascism to a sometimes very considerable degree is something which their adversaries have repeatedly emphasized and which it is hard to deny. Yet it would probably be fairer to speak of an early ambivalence. For even Codreanu, whose allegiance to the church was closer than that of all fascism's founders and whose views had an affinity to those of the Rumanian Orthodox tradition, complained bitterly that, with few exceptions, the clergy did not support the Iron Guard. In Italy and Germany there were also many examples of negative utterances and actions on the part of the clergy even during fascism's preliminary stages. The policy of the Curia, however, remained favorable despite all reservations, the Lateran Pact and the Reich Concordat being well-known instances. Neither pact was able to prevent the early outbreak of violent disputes, primarily concerning the education of the young. In June, 1931, the encyclical *Non abbiamo bisogno* ("We do not need") was directed against Mussolini, as was in 1937 the far better known pronouncement against Hitler, *Mit brennender Sorge* ("With burning anxiety"). Neither achieved the desired goal, but in Italy good relations were nevertheless maintained. Actually a Christian confrontation of uncompromising severity existed only toward National Socialism, and this showed itself less in theoretical works than in testimonies from the death cell and the concentration camp.[40] Moreover, where it found expression in theory, no effort was made specifically to designate National Socialism, which was merely cited as an example of the dangers threatening from secularization and often mentioned in direct association with older antiecclesiastical trends. In any case, the crux lies in the early approval of the churches, even when—and especially when—this approval was attributable to sympathy for a "historic battle of resistance to bolshevism,"[41] for, indeed, the inner relationship between National Socialism and bolshevism presents the central thesis.

The inner kinship of what appeared to be antagonistic is also central to the conservative conception, which, of course, took the longest time to evolve. Although it is true that evidence of conservative mistrust is to be found in the preliminary stages, it is equally true that the revolution in Italy and Germany could never even have taken place without conservative collaboration. Perhaps nothing is quite as characteristic as the fact that in England even in the late twenties the number of profascist conservative writings was legion.[42] Long experience,[43] both bitter and profound, was necessary before a change could be wrought. The best example is probably that of Hermann Rauschning, the only high-ranking National Socialist who later became an out-and-out enemy of the regime. His book, *The Revolution of Nihilism*,[44] offers concrete and significant insights into the nature of the new phenomenon which could not easily have been obtained by a socialist or a liberal. It goes far beyond that kind of conservative attitude which finds the plebeian traits of fascism distasteful.[45] But when it comes to tracing ideological backgrounds, both versions unite in making Hitler the final logical conclusion of Rousseau's starting point, and the fascist revolution the continuation of the French revolution.[46]

By this time the essential fact has been clearly brought out that it was precisely this experience of fascism and its hostile proximity to bolshevism that caused the traditional ways of political thought to develop new fronts and new issues. The most significant differences to emerge were, first the political and metapolitical interpretations, and second the opposing views which flowed from them: fascism is either specified, or more or less equated with bolshevism. The socialist and political-liberal conceptions form the first group; the trans-political-liberal, the Christian, and the principal version of the conservative conception form the second. The democratic-socialist interpretation is the specifying one; the Communist interpretation (in turn identifying fascism with a certain stage of capitalism) is alone in postulating complete antithesis. Even the political-liberal interpretation tends to equate fascism with bolshevism—actually the central thesis of all the other conceptions.

The picture is materially supplemented, however, if we include some more recent interpretations which, although taking a narrower view, still regard the subject as a whole.

First there is the Jewish interpretation, which is based on the most appalling of all human experiences. Nothing is more natural than that this conception should bring the whole weight of this experience to bear in favor of a distinction between National Socialism and fascism. Generally speaking, the anti-Semitic nature of almost all other fascist movements cannot deflect the horrified eyes of the world from National Socialism.[47] Accordingly, the distinction between National Socialism and bolshevism ought to be the next logical step, and very often it is. However, when the nature of Stalinism is seen in its terroristic lust for destruction in contradistinction to the world conspiracy, especially to the Trotskyist one, the equation between fascism and bolshevism can be made here too, and the link with the liberal-conservative conception established.

On the other hand, the psychoanalytical method of observation clearly supports the specifying interpretation. It looks primarily at the style and methods of fascism: the unshackling of primitive instincts, the denial of reason, the spellbinding of the senses by pageantry and parades. It sees all this as the emerging of archaic complexes which are older than nationality. This accounts just as much for the international character of fascism as its antithesis to the much more rational Marxism.[48]

Sociology is, with its basic idea of class structure, a further counterweight to the prevailing equating interpretations. By and large fascism and communism do not recruit their supporters from the same class substratum. This is a point of view, therefore, which, although discredited by the exclusiveness of its claim in the Communist interpretation, cannot be entirely ruled out.[49]

It can hardly be sufficiently emphasized that none of these interpretations has been dreamed up in an ivory tower. Indeed, the chief among them are the fruits of grim ordeals which often brought death to many thousands of human beings. We cannot, then, summarily dismiss one or indiscriminately align ourselves with another. When those of us who come after have access to living experiences from a distance only, we must try to compensate for this deficiency by attempting to co-ordinate the revelatory forces generated by these methods of observation. The demarcation of each will then automatically become apparent.

First Definition

Superficial though it may be, this survey of the phenomenon and its interpretations to date enables us to arrive at a preliminary definition which will serve as a guide and at the same time be subjected to study and demonstration within this analysis.

Neither antiparliamentarianism nor anti-Semitism is a suitable criterion for the concept of fascism. It would be equally imprecise to define fascism as anticommunism, but it would be obviously misleading to use a definition which did not adequately stress, or even entirely omitted, this basic criterion. Nevertheless, the identifying conception must also be taken into account. Hence the following suggests itself:

FASCISM IS ANTI-MARXISM WHICH SEEKS TO DESTROY THE ENEMY BY THE EVOLVEMENT OF A RADICALLY OPPOSED AND YET RELATED

IDEOLOGY AND BY THE USE OF ALMOST IDENTICAL AND YET TYPICALLY MODIFIED METHODS, ALWAYS, HOWEVER, WITHIN THE UNYIELDING FRAMEWORK OF NATIONAL SELF-ASSERTION AND AUTONOMY.[50]

This definition implies that without Marxism there is no fascism, that fascism is at the same time closer to and further from communism than is liberal anti-communism, that it necessarily shows at least an inclination toward a radical ideology, that fascism should never be said to exist in the absence of at least the rudiments of an organization and propaganda comparable to those of Marxism. It enables us to understand the extent to which there can be stages of fascism: according to the evolution of the ideology and the predominance of one of its two chief components, the pseudosocialist or the elite—that is, race—element; according to the degree of determination in, and the more or less universal nature of, the will to destruction; and according to the energy of execution. The decisive factors, however, are starting point and direction, for this concept is a "teleological" one, and even the most marked differentiation of stages does not do away with the unity of its essential nature.

Finally, this definition enables us to make concrete distinctions and identifications: neither the Pan-Germans nor Stoecker's Christian Socialists come under it; on the other hand, there is no reason to maintain that every opponent of Hitler in his party or in the other groups of the extreme Right was a non-Fascist.

CHAPTER THREE

Methods and Objective of Study

Criteria of Selection

The first question, then, is that of method. This is relatively easy to determine, since the chief consideration is the development of the concept of the era. We cannot make use of historiography in the ordinary sense, nor of typology.* Hence two things are required: limitation, which permits the examination of detail; and penetration, which does not impose a definition of the phenomenon from the outside but allows that phenomenon to speak for itself in the fullest possible terms and takes its self-image seriously. This method may be called the phenomenological. Fortunately there can be scarcely a doubt as to which of the numerous types of fascism are to be selected; the obvious choices are the two best known and most successful—Italian fascism and German National Socialism. Such limitation, however, does not imply that other forms of fascism are of no significance; on the contrary, it places them on a footing which enables them to be properly understood. Hence the main objective is to put hasty judgment aside and try to let Italian fascism and National Socialism speak for themselves.

A number of factors favor this approach. The principle of selecting from a plethora of utterances is the first to claim our attention. In a leadership movement, only the leader can make binding statements. Of course, it would be foolish to omit all reference to Gentile and Rocco, Farinacci and Grandi, Rosenberg and Himmler, Goebbels and Ley, but the basic pattern must be derived from the writings and speeches of Mussolini and Hitler. Practically all the material is now available: a firm foundation has been provided for posterity by the recent publication in Italy of Mussolini's *Opera Omnia*; and since the appearance of *Hitler's Table Talk* (American edition: *Hitler's Secret Conversations*), *Politische Testament* (*The Testament of Adolf Hitler*), and *Hitlers Zweites Buch* (*Hitler's Secret Book*), we also have a solid basis for Hitler,

* See Appendix B.

especially as we now have access to a number of unpublished earlier speeches. Moreover, many invaluable secondary documents have come to light, in particular the diaries of Count Ciano, minutes of various conferences, and the like. In short, it is possible today, in the case of both Hitler and Mussolini, to present on the strength of virtually complete documentation a comprehensive picture of their ideas, and to let them speak for themselves in a way that, due to the fragmentary nature of their utterances, they themselves perhaps never realized.

There are, of course, two obvious objections. Is Hitler to be allowed to "take the floor" again so many years after his death, after the entire world was forced to go to war in order to silence forever the hoarse voice of the raging demagogue? The assurance should hardly be necessary that a totally different picture will emerge from his utterances when taken collectively than from a speech made on the occasion of, say, a national holiday or the annual appeal to support the Winter Aid program. Here the "word" is not the random utterance made from motives of expediency, but the meaning of the whole, a meaning which is only partially and fragmentarily present in such an occasional utterance. And Mussolini's voice must always be listened to at the same time. It is here in this counterpoint of the hidden dialogue between the two fascist leaders that one of the principal distinguishing marks of fascism is disclosed.

The second objection is more serious. Is it worthwhile, is it not after all misleading, to build a structure of ideas out of ideas which are not ideas at all? Are not Hitler's "ideas" an aggregate of vulgar phrases lacking in both originality and discipline? Was not Mussolini merely a semieducated opportunist who was fond of dressing up his journalistic notions with what were at best a few philosophical rags?

This verdict is too harsh, arising as it does from an academic concept of originality which can have no place in politics. It is correct that Mussolini's thinking was mercurial, fragmentary, and often liable to fluctuation. But if we proceed, as today we must, from his Marxist youth, we cannot fail to perceive a continuous and highly significant thread, and we are forced to admit that never has the path of any outstanding European politician been more closely and variously affiliated with the intellectual evolution of his time. Moreover, it is of inestimable advantage to let Marxism—fascism's chief opponent—find its voice and come to life within the framework of fascism. It is equally correct that, for nearly every thesis of Hitler's, numerous parallels exist in the popular literature of German politics. Seen collectively, however, these ideas form a structure of staggering logicality and consistency.

The presentation of Mussolini's and Hitler's ideas must therefore be made central to the sections devoted to Italian fascism and National Socialism, and this must be done so minutely, and they must be allowed to speak for themselves so fully, that there can be no suspicion of merely strengthening a preconceived theory with the aid of a few well-chosen quotations. At this point we are at once faced with a primary and highly significant difference. Hitler's ideas can and must be presented systematically: they remained almost unchanged from 1924 on and are in essence not dependent on the vicissitudes of the political history of National Socialism; whereas Mussolini's ideas are simultaneously cause and effect of the history of Italian fascism. Hence the history of Italian fascism must be shown in closest conjunction with the history of Mussolini's intellectual development. A systematic chapter does not need to be very long and is concerned solely with the *Dottrina del fascismo* of 1932. However, our chief interest in the history of National Socialism lies not in its details but in the extent to which it assumes curious and generic (radical fascist) aspects when seen against the backdrop of events in Italy.

Equally characteristic differences are disclosed by a third chapter in each section (not necessarily in numerical order) which aim at tracing the relationship to the "precursors." This necessarily occupies considerable space in the section on National Socialism. But we must not enumerate those oft-cited and purely hypothetical "precursors of National Socialism" such as Fichte, Arndt, or Treitschke, whom Hitler himself had probably never even read. Instead we must limit ourselves strictly to the more prominent racist writers and augment this by a description of the intellectual climate of the first postwar years in Munich, the central figure of which, among those surrounding Hitler, was Dietrich Eckart.

Mussolini had no forerunners, and his evolution as a Fascist did not stem from a body of tradition. For him the decisive factor continued to be the early influence of a philosophy of life which, however, merely caused a curious coloration of his Marxism. In later years he acknowledged only Alfredo Oriani as a precursor, a writer of the late Risorgimento of hardly more than provincial significance. He always found it difficult to establish a convincing relationship with the powerful national tradition of the Risorgimento, and the short chapter dealing with precursors of Italian fascism is concerned mainly with his contradictory efforts to untie this knot.

Meanwhile we may ask: Does not this method of observation lay too much stress on the ideological aspect of fascism? Does it not overlook the fact that we are concerned with real movements springing from real social causes? Besides, is not ideology of a secondary and instrumental nature in fascism?

To begin with, it is highly debatable whether "ideology" in the fascist sphere really means the same thing as it did to the nineteenth-century critique of the term. It is very doubtful whether the distinction between the "real" and the "ideological" has any absolute validity, and it is presumably unavoidable that the critique of ideology is itself subjected to criticism. The extensive chapters on history are aimed at doing justice to the complexity of human motivations; however, only blind prejudice could deny that in Hitler's case the most powerful of these motivations was the existence of certain basic concepts.

That is why the enormous area of practice may without arbitrariness be reduced to the few essential traits which are most closely allied to the "ideology." From among the countless punitive expeditions undertaken by the Italian Fascists we need only cite a few as typical examples; from among the copious volumes of the *Reichsgesetzblatt* (official publication of Reich statutes), only a few hundred pages are of more than cursory interest. But here again we encounter an important and characteristic difference between Italian fascism and National Socialism.

In Italian fascism, practice represents the premise of the idea, although it is a practice determined by interests and theories. In National Socialism, practice represents the fulfillment of the idea, and without such practice the idea would have neither weight nor authenticity. In both cases, practice manifests itself as organization, style, and leadership impulse, and these are the directions in which it is to be pursued. Here again the selection of the paradigmatic permits us to resort to a variety of details. Here again, insight into each separate example prevents us from making the common mistake of regarding National Socialism as a progressive and analogous intensification of Italian fascism—in many areas fascism actually remained the unsurpassed teacher. But here again we are faced with that fulfillment which accounts for National Socialism being so often regarded as a phenomenon *sui generis*.

Tradition, history, practice, and system are thus the areas in which the phenomenon presents and expresses itself. No longer do we have an idea intervening from outside to set the phenomenon in motion. As in the case of the typological method, it is the phenomenon's own impulse which becomes perceptible and evident.

But we must turn to a serious shortcoming. The fact that the "intellectual climate" within which fascism and National Socialism grew up cannot be portrayed in detail is unavoidable. Such writers as Oswald Spengler and Carl Schmitt, Gottfried Benn and Ernst Jünger, are complex figures, and their relationship to fascism is obscure and in any case ineffective. If our study is not to degenerate into the uncertain and the inconclusive, we must limit it strictly to outright political phenomena. But fascism is also underestimated as a political phenomenon if we allow it to originate with World War I, out of nothing or at best a few literary precursors. The political constellations of the postwar period were anticipated by two decades in the politically most advanced and turbulent country in Europe when the conservative groups in the Dreyfus affair suffered a serious defeat and saw the state in the hands of leftist-oriented forces, which elsewhere in Europe were still in a situation of hopeless opposition, whereas at the same time liberal and socialist ideas had reached a crisis and the war was casting a shadow that for receptive minds was sufficiently noticeable. The Action Française was the first political grouping of any influence or intellectual status to bear unmistakably fascist traits.[51] The fact that it appeared as the latest form of the oldest counterrevolutionary movement—French legitimism and royalism—is its most revealing characteristic, for those modern traits which cannot be traced to this tradition stand out all the more clearly. It goes without saying that its monarchism is not enough to distinguish it irrevocably from fascism: Codreanu and Mosley, De Bono and Ernst Röhm, were also supporters of the monarchy. However, it is not intended as a proof of positive equation with fascism if one long section is devoted to the Action Française and placed at the head of this study. It will probably show that the Action Française should be called early fascism and that from certain points of view it is even more closely akin to National Socialism than to Italian fascism.

The precursor here is not the narrow world of anti-Semitic writers, but the great and significant tradition of French counterrevolutionary thought in all its manifestations. That which in National Socialism seems narrow, in Italian fascism too limited to a particular period, stands revealed here on a broader horizon. The curious *volte face* in liberal thought to be found in Renan and Taine offers more than a mere substitute for the lack of German fascistoid authors. In this *volte face*—more convincingly because more hesitantly than in the case of Nietzsche—we can grasp that change which, intellectually speaking, anticipated the era of the world wars by nearly half a century.

The history of the Action Française forms a symptomatic component of the history of a country which from 1789 to 1919 was always politically a few steps ahead of the rest of Europe.

In spite of all its doctrinal rigidity, the system of Maurras' ideas is of an extent, acuteness, and depth without parallel in the Germany or Italy of that time.

The practice of the Action Française anticipates, in the clear simplicity of the rudimentary, the characteristic traits of the infinitely cruder and more wholesale methods used in Italy and Germany.

Seen by itself, the Action Française is not an epochal phenomenon. Yet it is, as it were, the missing link demonstrating fascism as a stage in an overall and much older struggle. Only by including it in our scope can this study rest on a proper foundation and we ourselves be justified in undertaking a final appraisal of the scene.

The final appraisal will not be simply a philosophical appendage. Rather it is intended to grasp in general terms what has always been an element of the matter itself. Maurras was not guided primarily by political motives, and the metapolitical element in National Socialism found expression in a way which will never be forgotten. Hence the last chapter, by making "fascism as a meta-political phenomenon" its object and preparing the ground by an analysis of certain problems as posed by Marx, Nietzsche, and Max Weber, becomes an integral part of the phenomenological study. Only thus can the era be related to the age, and fascism to the phenomena of bourgeois society and bolshevism, and only in this broadest of all contexts can it be seen what, in the ultimate analysis, fascism and its era really were.

The Action Française

CHAPTER ONE

The Disparate Roots

Introduction: Revolution and the Political Doctrine

If fascism is a form of anti-Marxism designed to exterminate its opponent, it cannot be satisfied with the mere political defeat of a recognizable party: it must expose the "spiritual roots" and include them in its condemnation. It is a curious fact that Italian fascism and German National Socialism fell far short of fulfilling this obligation. By invoking the superiority of action, Italian fascism spared itself the consistent evolution of a doctrine. Fascism has therefore at times been described as "unideological" in nature, representing in its day a typical antithesis to the constant efforts of Marxism to establish a relationship with a great and tangible intellectual tradition. In this vital point, therefore— their relationship to the past—Marxism and fascism are not commensurable.

This deduction goes too far, although it does contain a germ of truth to be demonstrated later on. At a very early stage Mussolini instructed the thinkers and journalists of the regime to regard fascism as the categorical and wholesale denial of the French revolution, and it was precisely this denial that formed the daily bread of the National Socialist polemic. However, the struggle against the revolution, the most radical offshoot of which was held—by supporters and opponents alike—to be Marxism, had a long prehistory in Germany, as well as in Italy. From Adam Müller to Paul de Lagarde, from the von Gerlach brothers to the Social Darwinists of the turn of the century, the developers of anti-revolutionary thought omitted hardly a single one of the arguments which Hitler later utilized.[1]

But Hitler was not familiar with the traditions on whose soil he stood and was thus incapable of giving broad expression to his ideas. Throughout his life his great wish was to devote himself solely to the formulation of his doctrine once his political projects had been carried out. This wish is proof that National Socialism was neither a complete doctrine nor a mere absence of doctrine, but a possibility that never came to fulfillment. The same applies to Italian fascism.

This is why the intellectual significance of fascism as a total phenomenon cannot be adequately grasped merely by studying its two principal manifestations.

Charles Maurras[2] must, therefore, be included in the study of fascism; of him alone can it be said that he absorbed the whole stream of counterrevolutionary thought since 1789, transformed it, and gave it new shape for his time and his political party. Only by including him can fascism be compared with its chief opponent; only thus can it be clearly seen that the concept of "anti-Marxism" must be understood in a truly broad sense.

Marx looked upon himself as the heir to German philosophy, English national economy, and French socialism. Maurras defined his forerunners with equal clarity and devoted scarcely less time to their study. The men he mentions most often are: de Maistre, de Bonald, Comte, Le Play, Renan, Taine, and Fustel de Coulanges.[3] These men present the oldest and most important line of European counterrevolutionary thought, a line of greater independence and proximity to events than the political philosophy of the German romantics and their successors, who were inspired by Burke and were more removed from the experience of revolution. This line is also more varied and more complete in its literature, especially if we include those contemporaries of Maurras whom he sometimes referred to as his *maîtres*: de La Tour du Pin, Drumont, and Barrès.

As far as Maurras is concerned, the question remains whether and in what sense it is permissible to speak of a uniform trend of thought, whereas in the case of Marx's precursors there can be no doubt as to a basic agreement among them despite their differences. Although Marx interpreted and carried through Hegelian philosophy, French socialism, and the English national economy, single-mindedly and forcefully, it cannot be claimed that he stripped even one of the elements of its central meaning (insofar as this was political).

It is somewhat different when Maurras chooses Comte's law of three stages as the object of his critique. His relationship to his teachers is always one of conscious selection, although he never stated the nature of this selection, either in context or principle, nor did he offer his opinion as to the various basic differences among his teachers. In 1907 his colleague Louis Dimier published a book called *Les Maîtres de la Contre-Révolution au XIXe siècle*, the title alone suggesting the existence of a series of essentially homogeneous thinkers whose common characteristic is the "reactionary" trend.

The incompleteness of this view will shortly appear. The precursors divide into three distinct groups; as the principle of selection becomes clearer, some significant conclusions can be drawn as to the nature of the Maurras doctrine.

For Dimier the fixed point in relation to which all the thinkers named are agreed is the French revolution. But this fixed point is not enough to allow the differences to become apparent.

The French revolution is itself only one element in a total revolutionary movement which, according to long-established opinion, begins with the Renaissance and culminates in "modern times." In its day this movement was regarded as a "coming of age" and yet during the periods of its greatest impact it also gave rise to self-doubts. It took place in the most varied fields and as a totality has been given a host of names. To reiterate the familiar, the most important antitheses to which it gave expression may be recapitulated somewhat as follows: freedom of science versus dogmatic obscurantism; the rule of reason versus the rule of tradition; tolerance versus oppression; progress versus reaction; technology versus traditional routine; spontaneity versus rigid authority; self-determination versus despotism.

The movement as a whole has been called among other things: Enlightenment, technologization, liberalism, secularization, industrialization. Each of these names implies a certain interpretation and moves on its own level. Is it perhaps a system composed of alternating and mutually supporting strata? Does Enlightenment in the literary field correspond to secularization in religion, to liberalism in politics, to the rise of technology in economics? This is the obvious interpretation, but it evades the issue of the underlying common characteristic.

If the definition of the whole is debatable, the relationship of the individual elements is likewise unresolved. Is political liberalism essential to freedom of science? Is technological progress equivalent to moral progress? Is self-determination identical with the rule of reason?

Yet one central idea continually emerges: the concept of liberty, and it is the nebulousness of this idea that renders it so useful. Thus, in preliminary terms, the whole may be called the process of emancipation directed against an old world and liberating entire areas from a state of traditional dependence, while the corresponding process in politics may be called liberalism, which opposes an *ancien régime* and aims at releasing the individual from age-old dependence. Let us therefore in a broad sense call all those who are in basic agreement with both movements—regardless of variations of emphasis—liberals.

It is highly typical of the magnitude of the process, of its complex and heterogeneous nature, that not one of the great thinkers of the seventeenth and eighteenth centuries is not in some way closely associated with it, while not one of them undertakes to formulate all its aspects in a uniform and radical manner. Althusius, for instance, was the first systematizer of the doctrine of popular sovereignty and the right to resist, yet as a fervent Calvinist he was a long way from accepting the principle of religious freedom. Bodin, on the other hand, was a champion of absolutism in political doctrine only, while in the area of religion he demanded tolerance and laid the foundation for the doctrine of natural religion.

Perhaps John Locke produced the most all-embracing definition of the spirit of the Enlightenment, but he remained far removed from the accuracy of Bacon's insight into the scientific-technical future, and his letters on tolerance excluded the toleration of Catholics and atheists.

Montesquieu created for the European continent the doctrine of the division of power, yet at the same time he emphasized the importance of natural conditions, of climate, soil, and national character to such an extent that the universal character and liberal nature of the doctrine were impaired.

All these thinkers were much too close to the old world and the *ancien régime* to be able to—or want to—develop the consequences emanating from their original ideas in all their breadth and depth. They were prejudiced and to that extent moderate liberals; they were all philosophers, speaking mainly to their own kind.

The great historical significance of Rousseau is that he was a thinker whose ties with the old world were weak and, in his own eyes, always suspect—a man who as a writer wielded a magnetic and immensely far-flung influence. In him we see for the first time the radical and enthusiastic liberal. With Rousseau it is already apparent that radical decision also includes the selection of certain elements of the whole trend and the rejection of others.

A definite one-sidedness is already evident in the fact that Rousseau eliminates the idea of progress and interprets historical movement as decadence (*Discours sur les sciences et les arts*). In his view the chief instrument and manifestation of this decay is science. Tolerance fares no better at his hands; for it is inherent in the consistent nature of his political doctrine to deny tolerance even to Christianity, since it trains men to be inhabitants of a world beyond rather than citizens.

Both starting point and goal of his thought is liberty, its original presence in each human being and the loss of it in society. The study of this enigmatic relationship is the object of his second *Discours* (*Discours sur l'origine de l'inégalité parmi les hommes*). There can be little doubt that here, from a philosophical point of view, Rousseau presupposes the derivation of human nature, by means of one single principle—that of liberty—from a hypothetical prehuman original state, comparable to Condillac's famous thought experiment with the marble statue. If the starting point is called *liberté originelle*, or *naturelle*, it is clear that we are not yet dealing with human liberty but rather with its roots, which go back beyond the distinction between good and bad, happiness and unhappiness, possession and nonpossession.[4] These distinctions and hence human existence (that is, social existence) only become possible with the restriction of *liberté originelle*. The loss of it is therefore not decadence, but the essential factor in all decadence *and* all progress. Rousseau emphasizes that the original state never existed, that it is lost "forever."[5]

This first ontological construct inevitably leads to a second: What would be the nature of a state of society which on a higher plane once more produced that *liberté naturelle*? Since human and social conditions must mean restriction and dependence, a form of dependence would have to be found the nature of which would no longer be particular but total, and which in its very totality would coincide once again with the nature of original liberty.[6] If each person surrenders himself completely, that is, uniformly, to the law of the *volonté générale*, total obedience is equivalent to total liberty, since each human being no longer faces another human being, or a chance institution, but only the universality of his own self. Clearly this construct is in the Kantian sense an idea, just as the derivation of humanity was transcendental philosophy. Rousseau is obviously laying the foundation for the framework of the dialectic.

But he does not avoid that subreption which is the tempting fruit in the desert of transcendental philosophy. He discovers "natural liberty" and "social liberty" to be actually existing human conditions, one among the savages, the other among the Spartans and Romans and even in the city-state of Geneva, so that the abstract construct at once becomes a concrete "primitivism." From this subreption flow the most powerful of his influences: the call of "back to nature," the belief in "natural goodness," the definition of liberty by equality, the phrase "compulsion to liberty," and the idea of "virtue." From this subreption flows that enthusiasm Rousseau feels and inspires: the feeling that he represents and champions the limitless in the limited, the universal in the particular, salvation where there is no salvation. Doctrines which in the past had long been familiar and widespread now gained new potency: the doctrine of popular sovereignty, the mandatory nature of public authority, the right to resistance and revolution.

Thus Rousseau became the "Father of the French Revolution," and all the hatred which it aroused found in him a favorite target. But we must distinguish between the elements of the revolution which have merely a random association with Rousseau's name (such as the idea of "popular sovereignty," or "sovereignty of the people," as opposed to the "divine right of kings") and those which in fact would have been scarcely conceivable without him: above all, for example, the Jacobinic "compulsion to liberty." If the revolution as a whole is a challenge to liberal thought, it is an even greater challenge to the enthusiastic liberalism of Rousseau and the Jacobins. Without doubt the radicalization of a liberal beginning, this "compulsion to liberty," menacing and unfamiliar as it is, occupies such a prominent position in the total process that from then on it was capable of splitting political thought into parties. That all future "enthusiastic liberalism" (that is, almost all socialism) will accept it as a governing principle, goes without saying. For "critical liberalism," on the other hand (liberalism which has become critical of itself and has come to believe that "liberty" is something more than one of various ways of life and that the relation between liberty and its realization constitutes a problem of incomparable delicacy and difficulty), it provides the constant incentive for discussion and self-examination. For "Christian conservative" thought it represents chiefly a means of refuting liberalism as a whole by its "fruit." The position of "radical conservatism" can also be deduced from its relation to it, a position which we will define in the course of our study.

Christian Conservatism: de Maistre and de Bonald

When Joseph de Maistre uses his famous expression "radically evil" to describe the French revolution and imputes a "satanic character" to it,[7] what can this mean except that it is to be totally condemned, in all its manifestations and in all its roots? The devil is the perverting element (*diabolos*): the revolution aspires to overthrow the very foundation of eternal order, the rule of the authority of God and of the temporal authorities stemming from it, and to replace the *regnum dei* with a *regnum hominis*. By dint of repeated attacks and brilliant, profound, and provocative formulas, de Maistre attempts to prove that this undertaking runs counter to both reason and nature. When he calls war "divine,"[8] he firmly confronts the peace-loving optimism of all liberal thinkers with the incomprehensible, superhuman reality which man feels is his unjustifiable lot because he is denied the power of controlling it. When he extols the executioner as the "bond" of all human society,[9] he is endeavoring to banish to the realm of insubstantial dreams the conception of the state as developed by the age of the Enlightenment. But he also attacks the divine nature of the revolution directly: human reason, that "trembling light,"[10] which is incapable of creating order among men because it engenders discussion rather than the faith which is essential to human existence. Hence it is absurd for the servants of the revolution, the scholars, to claim that they can evolve rules for life, from which, by virtue of their analytical approach, they are irretrievably remote: "They have the natural sciences to amuse them; what do they have to complain about?"[11] The aristocracy and the clergy are the administrators of the essential truths; in defending these truths through the Inquisition, they did right. For without the authority of the binding element, all existence crumbles into nothing. That is why Voltaire, the great champion of tolerance, is by the same token the protagonist of decay and destruction: "That which our miserable century calls superstition, fanaticism, intolerance, etc., was a necessary ingredient of French greatness."[12] De Maistre also does not hesitate to give liberalism the ultimate slap in the face: he praises Aristotle for having recognized that certain men are destined by nature to be slaves.

In so doing he reaches back beyond Christianity to find the ideal way of life in ancient times. But the reason he gives is far from ancient: "Man is too wicked to be free."[13] The protoreality of original sin is enough to condemn to failure the illusory dreams of the Enlightenment. If man were by nature good, he would in fact need neither authority nor punishment. But in reality he *is* otherwise: "Unimaginable combination of two differing and incompatible forces, a monstrous centaur, he feels he is the result of some unknown offense, some abominable miscegenation which has vitiated man in his innermost essence."[14]

And this incomprehensible creature lives in an incomprehensible world, under an "occult and terrible law which demands human blood."[15] In his efforts to substantiate as solidly as possible the necessity of authority and rule, de Maistre shows us a world which raises doubts as to whether it is ruled by the Christian fatherly goodness of God or, as seems more likely, the bloodthirsty barbarity of the Indian Shiva. The dividing line between de Maistre's gloomy Jansenist theology and brutal naturalism seems exceedingly fine throughout. He gives himself away when he says that "invincible nature"[16] will right matters in France and lead to the restoration of the monarchy.

In spite of his iridescent conception of nature, his conception gives him the tremendous advantage over Rousseau of being able to draw on experience, for Rousseau's *état de nature*, like his *liberté naturelle*, is an unverifiable quantity: not only metaphysical truth, but actual experience shows that a republic is impossible in a large state. In this way the adversary is deprived of one of his most effective weapons (the appeal to "nature" and "empiricism"); his metaphysical premises are exposed and attacked head-on.

Can we still call this Christian conservatism? Is not de Maistre actually closer to Nietzsche than to Bossuet, since he anticipates Nietzsche's formulas almost word for word?[17] Is this not a naturalistic nationalism which, strangely enough, reveals some remarkable similarities with his antagonist Rousseau?[18]

Doubts become still more serious when we consider the explanation de Maistre offers for the origin of the "great conspiracy"[19] of modern times. Protestantism is for him the beginning of the "revolutionary monster,"[20] the revolt of mere individual reason which destroys blind respect for authority and replaces obedience with discussion. Its fruit is the philosophy of the Enlightenment, whose icy breath kills all religion, every "exquisite emotion," every "sublime *élan*."[21]

Does not de Maistre at this point come quite close to Maurras' words: "Beneath the cross of this suffering God, night spread out over the modern age"?[22] He needed, so it seems, to take only one more short step: to see in Protestantism the reawakening of the true, original, anarchistic Christianity, which could only become the protagonist of authority in the enforced form given it by imperial Roman paganism.

But perhaps this step is not so short after all. In any case de Maistre is a long way from taking it. In spite of his utterances regarding France's greatness and the value of national dogmas, the fact remains that his heart belongs completely to the unity of Christian Europe. He sees the great battle of the age as the "fight to the death between Christianity and Enlightenment."[23]

The object of his *Considérations sur la France* is to recognize the rule of Providence in this stupendous happening. He counters Bacon with the classic objection of Christian philosophy—that it is absurd to look for causes in nature alone, since nature as a whole is merely an effect. There are enough indirect turns of phrase to show that, in spite of the provocative thesis on slavery, his conservatism is not without that "liberalism" which forms an ingredient of

Christianity itself.[24] The fact that his conservatism is extreme does not necessarily make it "radical." Radical conservatism casts doubt on its own historical
roots, because it believes it can see in them a connection with the enemy.

But neither is de Maistre a theocrat. For him, as for the whole *ancien régime*,
state and church remain distinct although closely linked entities. It was Hobbes
and Rousseau who had suggested "reuniting the two heads of the eagle,"[25]
and who thus prepared the way for a secularized theocracy—in other words,
"totalitarianism."

De Maistre is a reactionary. But the dazzling complexity of his personality
and thinking conceal *in nuce* some of the most modern evolutionary trends.

The basic features of this Christian conservatism become even more apparent
with Louis de Bonald, who of the two men is the less brilliant but the more
systematic thinker.

He attempts to deal with society "as the natural scientist treats of the quantitative relationships ... between physical objects."[26] He makes a point of
placing his efforts on a parallel with Kepler and Newton, with the result that we
find the eighteenth-century idea of social physics undergoing a surprising transformation. For if nature is governed by eternal, immutable natural laws, ought
not society then to be subject to an "eternal, universal, necessary order"?[27]
But how could nature—society's sole legitimate lawgiver—require the qualities
inherent in nation-states: that mobility and variability which is so very much
the stigma of a man who tries in wanton pride to detach himself from nature?
"The most marked characteristic which distinguishes natural power from the
power which is not natural, from human or popular power, is, I do not say the
duration, but the stability of the one, the mutability of the other; for there is
stability in nature, mutability in man."[28]

If, however, this stability also finds expression, as is "natural," in human
existence, it manifests itself as heredity: that is to say, in a natural society the
three original social functions, which de Bonald calls *pouvoir, ministre, sujet*,
must be the birthright of certain families.

Thus de Bonald, in proceeding from the concept of nature of the natural
sciences, which he identifies with the Christian conception of eternal divinely
ordained order, finally derives all the features of the *ancien régime*, including
the hereditary nature of professions, the "inalienability of property,"[29] and
so forth as "natural" preconditions of true society; he strips the enemy of his
favorite social concept and turns it into the herald proclaiming kingship by the
grace of God.

Of course he is bound to accept the presence of two very serious difficulties.
"Natural society" has actually been destroyed, or at least shaken to its
foundations, by a *philosophisme ignorant et perfide*.[30] Although the idea of the
"internal enemy"[31] may make sense politically, it seems meaningless in a philosophical deduction, for how could all-powerful nature have an enemy? Here

de Bonald is faced with the basic difficulty of all Christian conservative thought: that of explaining the illegitimate power of the enemy in all its limitless facticity. De Maistre had spoken of the "satanic" nature of the revolution and tried to define its place in the plan of Providence. De Bonald appears to assume the protopower of denial which must finally deny itself: "[Atheists] ... deny the effect after having denied the cause, ... deny the universe, deny God, deny their very selves."[32] In either case, adopting the concept of the natural entails the concept of the antinatural and the crux of explaining it.

Apart from this difficulty, however, de Bonald is more successful and convincing than de Maistre in his efforts to ensure a place for the Christian concept of God, for, in spite of all his expounding of the *forces destructrives* of man when left to himself, he does not draw quite as gloomy a picture of the world as does de Maistre. Even according to orthodox Christian doctrine, God is believed primarily to be also the "creator of nature," therefore He is by no means entirely denaturalized. Hence de Bonald regards God as the source of all natural power, the sole sovereign from whom all power emanates: "Remove God from this world, and there is no other reason for duty than violence, because there is no longer any other claim to power."[33] But a new difficulty arises when it is a matter of defining the nature of Christian society as opposed, say, to pagan society. For in that case it can only be characterized by its unconditional loyalty to the "law"; the evangelical, liberating, emancipatory nature of Christianity can at best be noted and admitted,[34] but within the framework of this mode of thought it remains unverifiable.

Thus there are three main traits characterizing this Christian conservatism: the rejection of the revolution in its roots and all its manifestations, the rivalry with it over the conception of nature, and the difficulty of returning to Christianity from the convenient idea of "naturalism."

Critical Liberalism: Comte, Le Play, Renan, Taine, Fustel de Coulanges

Regardless of Auguste Comte's predilection for referring to de Maistre, the atmosphere in which his ideas exist is different in every respect from that surrounding the great reactionary.

What is his law of three stages, the doctrine of the progressive supplanting of the theological (fictitious) and metaphysical (abstract) stages by the scientific (positive) era, if not the essence of the historical philosophy of the Enlightenment? (Indeed, it is to be found as early as Turgot and Saint-Simon.) Does not his postulate, that a reasonable and peaceful mode of government must be evolved, correspond exactly to the liberal theory of government? Does not his remark, that revolutionary ideas have become so powerful and are taken so much for granted that even their opponents are forced to make use of them, justify revolution in its deepest existence?

Seen from the viewpoint of historical philosophy, his positivism is in fact an attempt to grasp the revolutions in human history and to appoint himself the voice of the greatest and most far-reaching of all revolutions. Human existence is by nature revolutionary since it is a continual evolution. What evolves is the specifically human, the capacity for abstract thought, reason. Since reason is essential to all human behavior, all revolutions, although the various fields overlap and exert a reciprocal influence, are primarily spiritual. The transition from the theological to the metaphysical stage, which replaced the gods as the living, active forces of nature by abstract and lifeless entities, was such a revolution. Such a revolution—the scientific—is the transition from the metaphysical to the positive stage, which replaces the absolute by the relative, and the chimerical, the speculative, the nebulous, the fluctuating, by the factual, the useful, the definite, the precise, to move finally from purely negative criticism of the existing to the positive organization of the new.[35] The culmination of this stage will mean the supremacy of morals emancipated from theology and metaphysics, uniform education of all classes, the political unity of Western Europe as mankind's advance guard working with a deep sense of brotherhood toward the development of the backward races, reverence of mankind as the *grand être*—in short, the *regnum hominis*, envisaged by Bacon and rejected by de Maistre as satanic.

How was it ever possible to detach Comte from this unmistakable atmosphere and place him among the "counterrevolutionary thinkers"? The explanation lies clearly in the fact that Comte was severely critical of the French revolution. Comte called the revolution a "negative" phenomenon which could criticize and destroy, but not construct. For it sprang from Protestantism, the purely critical character of which is implicit in the very name. And finally it gave rise to the era of senseless social strife in which the heartless selfishness of the employers and the blind utopianism of the workers were of equal folly. Critical anarchy is responsible for the attacks on the nature of marriage, the inability to grasp that it is not the individual but the family which represents the social unit.

He regards Rousseau as the originator of the revolutionary utopia, which is actually metaphysics: the secularization of the doctrine of the Fall, a sinister attack on the ideas of progress and civilization. To the same kind of visionary primitivists belong those who refuse to acknowledge the inescapable nature of the division of labor and who dream of social conditions in which it is abolished. The only reasonable positivist reaction against fatal specialization is that which strengthens the sense of the universal.

For Comte the revolution is a "critical" era which he contrasts with "organic" eras, not the least of which are the Catholic Middle Ages. The positive age will have several features in common with this medieval period: stability of social conditions, and the independent existence of spiritual power.

There are three ways of finding Comte's "counterrevolutionary tendencies" in this critique. Marxists will see in it an attack on its basic and esoteric doctrines (abolishment of division of labor and of alienation, the rise of the "whole man"). But it would first have to be proved that Marxism alone is revolutionary and that it is revolutionary in all its elements. Until that is done the use of the term "counterrevolutionary" is not convincing. In any case, it is a matter of a divergence of opinion within the revolutionary school.

Political liberals, in the narrowest sense, might feel some concern over Comte's apotheosis of a stable condition of society, his dislike of the parliamentary system, above all his conception of "spiritual power," which seems to smack of a new kind of theocracy. But from Fichte via Hegel to Marx, the great historic thinkers have, independently of their party affiliation, thought of the present as strife and of the future as stability. And the independence of spiritual power is the very antithesis of theocracy. Its task is to preserve the West's most valuable achievement, the distinction between the spiritual and the temporal. The term "spiritual power" is admittedly misleading. For Comte it is not a question of the *existence* of this power—it can, for instance, take the form of the rule of the press—but of its independence, authority, and modernity. In other words, expressed in modern terms its only task is to be a safeguard against totalitarian and ecclesiastical tendencies or the corrupting power of a venal intellectual class. Despite the singularities evinced by Comte's later development, in its beginnings even his doctrine of spiritual power (in a higher sense) is thoroughly liberal in nature.

Finally, anyone who wishes to use Comte for "reactionary" purposes must disregard the most obvious fact of all: the positive significance of the "negative" in a philosophy which is in fact, although not in name, dialectic. Only willfulness, which tries to usurp rather than understand, can fail to grasp the meaning of Comte's own words: "It is our task to bring to completion the far-reaching spiritual undertaking begun by Bacon, Descartes, and Galileo, then revolutionary upheavals will be a thing of the past."[36]

Comte is the first critical liberal. In the midst of the total process, which he endorses, he criticizes the claim to absolutism of certain manifestations of the revolution: that is, he criticizes enthusiastic liberalism. Maurras isolated this dialectic element and used it as an absolute to serve the purposes of counterrevolutionary thought. This speaks for the incisiveness of the critique, but not necessarily for the validity of the separation.

That Frédéric Le Play might also be called a critical liberal is not at first sight readily understandable. This outstanding social thinker, who exerted an enormous influence in France, is hardly known elsewhere except as the originator of the doctrine of *autorités sociales*, of *hommes d'élite*,[37] on whom all social salvation depends and in whom the chief claim and self-awareness of the French "notables" were reflected. A number of characteristics justify numbering Le Play among the Christian conservatives. He, too, speaks of the "false dogmas of the revolution,"[38] and stigmatizes the "terrible levelers"[39] who with *pouvoir paternel* have attacked divine law, the most natural of all hierarchies. The statute of the *Code Civil* which deprives the testator of testamentary freedom, signifies a perpetual hostile attack on the stability and order of social relationships. It destroys the clan (*la famille-souche*), that type of patriarchal family around which family property accumulates like the shell around the oyster: germ cell of authority, continuity, and health in the life of the nation. It divides society into isolated and envious individuals who base their "hopes" on the death of the progenitor and carelessly tear the work of a lifetime to shreds. The restoration of paternal authority and hence of testamentary freedom is the demand constantly reiterated in the first volume of Le Play's principal work, *La réforme sociale en France*, first published in 1864.

According to Le Play, the father is the model for both the landowner and the industrial employer. Just as it is a father's first duty to subdue the original sin of his offspring,[40] so it is the duty of property owners and employers to guide the *imprévoyance* of their subordinates, for whose welfare they are responsible and from whom in return they may expect obedience and respect. Reform of life can only mean the restoration of an *ordre moral* in which these natural relationships are taken for granted.

Side by side with these highly conservative, "paternalistic" features there are in both Le Play and de Maistre conceptions and emotions which give the impression of being more modern, although they stem directly from the underlying conception: the aversion to *littérateurs*, the recalling of "our former greatness,"[41] the emphasis on the value of the clan in terms of population policy as a bulwark against the "decay and paralysis of the race,"[42] the proud reference to the "peasant imbued with the national spirit."[43]

All these "reactionary" features are in fact to be found in Le Play. But in order to assess them correctly it is essential for us to look at his life.

Le Play did not belong to the landed aristocracy, like de Bonald, which might have made it possible to regard his paternalism as a reflection and sublimation of his own position in life. Instead, like Comte, he was the product of one of the great technical colleges of Paris, he was himself a professor at the *École des Mines*, and as a young man he was the chief mining official under Napoleon III. Councilor of State and Senator, Commissioner-General of the Paris Exhibition of 1867, he was one of the great technologists and executives of the nineteenth century. Traveling tirelessly year in year out, a fanatic for detail, a master of compromise, a promoter of scientific teamwork, Le Play could draw on "observation" and "facts" with far greater authority than de Maistre, de Bonald, or even Comte. His book on the European worker, first published in 1855, is based on an immense amount of empirical research and a vividness of presentation unparalleled in social research up to that time. From the seminomads of the Urals, to Turkish blacksmiths, miners from the Harz Mountains, blade manufacturers from Solingen, watchmakers from

Geneva, cutlers from Sheffield, and ragpickers in Paris, he takes individual examples to depict ways of life and working conditions down to their smallest details.

Thus it is incorrect to say that Le Play is a reactionary because he is not acquainted with modern and industrial conditions. Indeed, we see on closer inspection that the reaction of his doctrine derives from his admiration for England, the most advanced *peuple-modèle*. Here he finds that stability of the *ordre moral*, that power of custom, that faith in the Bible and the Ten Commandments, which he so sorely misses in the turbulent unrest, the revolutionary *tabula rasa*, the skepticism, of France. Here he encounters a leading class which, "attached to the soil, incorporated in the people, identified with all the country's interests,"[44] has managed to avoid those mistakes which have caused the downfall of France's aristocracy: the mania for privileges, the arrogance, the absence of a function in society. Here he discovers a lively regional life such as had long since been killed in France by bureaucratic centralism; and all this is permeated and upheld by the spirit of liberty. Tolerance, free discussion, private initiative, are clearly the basic requirements in England for the unprecedented well-being of the nation.

It is the picture of liberal England, therefore, and not a nostalgia for the French *ancien régime*, which leads Le Play to his reactionary conclusions—one more proof that great care must be taken in using the word "reactionary." Reaction and progress are indeed often related and sometimes even identical. In the eyes of the theoretician of absolutism, the English parliamentary system was bound to be reactionary, a relic of the Middle Ages. Yet it became the protagonist of modernity. It is England that teaches Le Play the French error of "confusing the spirit of liberty and the spirit of the revolution,"[45] and it is England that makes it clear to him that "[the French revolution] is more closely bound . . . up with restraint than with liberty."[46] These are the underlying theses of critical liberalism. In the light of these theses, Le Play's other ideas also acquire a new look.

In point of fact the clan is not an anachronistic "patriarchal" community. Its task is rather to combine the advantages of the patriarchal system with those of the new *famille instable*. By *autorités sociales* Le Play does not mean simply "notables," but rather those men in authority who have resisted the powerful temptation toward decadence and dereliction of duty. The revolution is not the satanic cause of all France's ills; it has merely carried on the mistakes of the *ancien régime*. Hence Le Play is far removed from the favorite demand of the true reactionary: the demand for the restoration of the corporations. On the contrary, *liberté de travail* is in his view "one of the few advantages of our era of instability and antagonism."[47]

His critical liberalism is the precondition for those of his ideas which represent new and vital contributions to social theory. There is first of all his theory of the accidental nature of the proletariat.[48] Admittedly, he did not lack that perception or feeling for the whole forsaken mass of humanity,[49] which during the same period led Marx to his theory of the essential and eschatological nature of the proletariat. But, in contrast to Marx, he was convinced of the quality and indispensability of the European leading class, and he regarded it as a utopian idea that the proletariat could lift itself up without its help. Forty years before Bernstein, but conforming to the tradition of French socialism and also to Comte, he thus devises the image of a reformism whose aim is to serve liberty by making revolution superfluous.

Finally there is his theory that bureaucracy is the most intimate threat to the future of Europe, that it tends to complicate business, to carry government intervention further and further, to stifle private life and private initiative to an ever-increasing degree.[50] This is the point at which Le Play's theory most often shows wholly modern characteristics.

His influence was considerable. The *Unions de paix sociale* which he founded did not, to be sure, directly achieve very much against the growing social antagonism; but a (liberal) Le Play school arose, and it is impossible to imagine the evolution of Catholic social doctrine without his books or his journal, *La Réforme Sociale*. One of the most enthusiastic contributors to the journal— some years after the death of the master—was Charles Maurras.

Ernest Renan represents a turning point in the development of French critical liberalism. The element of criticism emerges in more plastic and varied form; for the first time the possibility arises of critical liberal thought turning against liberalism itself.

Renan was liberal from deep inner necessity, and he never failed to describe himself specifically as a liberal. In Protestant countries, criticism of the Bible did not necessarily preclude loose ties with the church, but when the young theologian of the St. Sulpice seminary took up this criticism, it meant a complete rupture with the Catholic Church. His liberalism, therefore, began by being merely the preservation of his own independence and his own course, the battle against the intolerance of the church and the church's hostility toward emancipation, the faith in the transforming and corrective power of science, the hope in a free, individual, undogmatic Christianity, and the belief in the superiority of the Protestant nations and their freedom-loving principles. His early work, *L'Avenir de la science*, is typical of nineteenth-century "faith in science." His great work on the origins of Christianity (in particular his *La Vie de Jésus*) made him among Catholics the most hated man in France. A brilliant career, which soon led him to a chair in the Collège de France, gave him the status of spokesman for intellectual France.

However, even before 1870 his ideas on revolution reveal some surprising emphases and shades of meaning and give some indication of the potential development of this sensitive spirit. It is, of course, quite according to tradition for him to separate liberalism and revolution, to defend Turgot and Montesquieu against any and all accusations, and to reserve blame solely for the "actual so-called revolutionary school," "which was associated chiefly with Rousseau and which gave the French revolution its final character, that is to say, its tendency toward abstract organization, without taking either former rights or liberty into account."[51] In the same way, he remains within the scope of traditional thought when he admires the Germanic world, its science and its virtue, and that feudal spirit which gave birth to it. And it is equally natural that he should prefer the Greek philosophy of Socrates and Plato to the narrow, fanatical spirit of prophetic Judaism. But one discordant note makes itself heard: to achieve perfection, Christianity must move further and further away from Judaism, "in order that the spirit of the Indo-European race predominate in its bosom."[52] Religion as an expression of race? Is this the influence of Count Gobineau, with whom Renan was linked by family ties? Is it not reminiscent of Nietzsche when Renan says in 1864 that all advanced culture is in certain respects an out-and-out aristocratic affair?[53] Would the young Comte have agreed to the statement that, although it was no longer possible to believe in the supernatural, religion remained a necessity? "The day it [religion] disappears, the very heart of mankind would shrivel up."[54] For this reason Renan's famous critique of the revolution in *Questions contemporaines* (1868) is more extensive, more dramatic, and more effective than anything comparable, regardless of how little its content goes beyond Le Play, for instance. It gives one the impression that this man might be capable of attacking the very core of the revolution.

In point of fact, a year later he expounds the surprising thesis that the great virtue of a nation consists in enduring *traditional* inequality. According to him, the monarchic system is for specific reasons a necessity for France. The liberal party in France does not realize that every political structure must have a conservative basis. Yet in the fluctuating and tension-filled relation between liberalism, republicanism, and democracy, even this represents an extreme but nonetheless feasible constellation.

It was the Franco-Prussian war that brought all the contradictory possibilities of Renan's thoughts and feelings to full maturity. As late as September 15, 1870, he wrote an article appealing for reason and moderation. His French and liberal self-esteem remain unshaken, albeit driven very near to that radical, democratic position from which he had until just then remained aloof: "Democracy does not want war, does not understand war. The progress of democracy will be the end of the reign of those men of iron, survivors of another age, whom our century has watched in terror emerge from the bowels of the ancient Germanic world."[55]

But only a few months later, after the final defeat, the Paris Commune, and the loss of Alsace-Lorraine, Renan draws quite a different picture in *La Réforme intellectuelle et morale*. Prussia was victorious because it had remained in the *ancien régime*; *ancien régime* means the preservation of virility, the virility of a people is founded in its blood, the blood of the aristocracy, which stands at its head. This aristocracy had once been Germanic everywhere: obstinate, proud, inaccessible, it had been the procreator of all great things. France, on the other hand, had got rid of its aristocracy in the revolution, thereby committing suicide in a very real sense. Yet in England too, "this peaceful and thoroughly Christian school of economists"[56] was pushing aside the aristocracy; in English public opinion the resurrected Celtic spirit, which is "more gentle, more pleasant, more human,"[57] was making itself felt. Only in Prussia had the elements of strength been preserved: the aristocracy, the hierarchy, the harsh treatment of the people. France was bound for hopeless extinction if it was unable to save itself by a reform "along Prussian lines."[58] However, the main obstacle in the way of a reform of this kind, besides retrogressive Catholicism, was democracy, which is responsible for France's political and military weakness and which fails to grasp "the superiority of the aristocrat and the savant,"[59] and indulges in feeble dreams of a universal state of peace. Such a condition, however, should it ever come about, would entail the direst threats to morals and intelligence.[60]

This has long ceased to be an "internal liberal" critique[61] of the narrow-mindedness, the brutality, the fervor, of the revolution: it is the despair of liberalism itself, the apotheosis of counterrevolution in principle, a symptom of the new alliance between abdicating intellect and triumphant force.

From now on there are many such symptoms in Renan's work. Almost without effort, and with more emotion than thought, he anticipates the great topics of the next half-century and thus also a large part of the far-reaching criticism of liberalism: the essential injustice of nature and society, the separation between *verum* and *bonum*, the lowest and highest of men, the fatal quality of progress and the perpetual presence of inequality. But at the same time this astonishing personality, appearing between Marx and Nietzsche, can pursue theses of the Enlightenment to their most radical and blasphemous conclusions: "Reason . . . after having organized mankind will organize God."[62]

In spite of all this, Renan remains a liberal to the very end. His famous speech of 1882 (*Qu'est-ce qu'une nation?*) is one long panegyric of human liberty and its power even over the natural conditions of individual existence, such as race. In an address to a Christian-Jewish society in 1883 he said: ". . . Judaism will render services in the future. It will serve the true cause of liberalism, of the modern spirit. Every Jew is a liberal. He is a liberal by nature."[63] And even in his last statements he shifts the emphasis of his earlier criticism from the revolution to the revolutionaries, and calls the revolution a natural phenomenon in harmony with what is desired by the "nature of things."[64]

The strange, well-nigh incomprehensible vacillations in Renan's thought are not *merely* an isolated phenomenon. They are also an indication of the fragile nature of all liberal thought, that is, of the essential weakness of all liberal thinkers.

Hippolyte Taine was a less rich, varied, and sensitive spirit than Renan. But his work also signified the typical progress of one impulse of the emancipatory movement in the eighteenth century: of that science which became increasingly materialistic and naturalistic the more it was obliged to remain armed against possible usurpations on the part of the miraculous and the lawless. Taine's famous (or infamous) statement, that virtue and vice are products like vitriol and sugar, belongs in this context, as does his claim to be able to develop a human botany in his research. A more modern note is struck by his explanation of causes: race, environment, and moment are the causes of all human manifestation; but race means the "innate and hereditary positions" and is the primary and richest source of historical events.[65]

Until 1870 Taine could be regarded as the prototype of the nonpolitical savant whose sole faith is in science. Then came the war and, above all, the Commune, to subject his existence as a natural scientist to the acid test. He wrote his great work on *Les Origines de la France contemporaine*[66] and painted a fuller and more accurate picture of the revolution than any known description up to that time. In a work covering six volumes, the revolution is mercilessly dissected—but the dissector also stands revealed. What is exposed is not a telescopic lens, far above the human level, merely reflecting that which is, but a human being, assessing, fighting, aspiring. The images he uses betray the stages and divisions of this struggle. He attempts to describe France's great metamorphosis as that "of an insect shedding its skin."[67] But then he goes on to depict the *ancien régime*: its exploitative nature, its inconceivable inequality, its inhuman hunting laws, but above all, a mental outlook which allows the aristocrat to regard the peasant as belonging to another species, and sees the king as the private owner of a great domain, not the mandatary of the people— an outlook which enabled Louis XVI in the midst of the revolution to give more thought to his hunting and the number of animals killed than to political events. Taine comes to the conclusion that the central point of government is the central point of evil: "Here is the peak of the public abscess, and here it will burst."[68] Indeed, the first volume is an excellent exposition of the vital question: Are there social conditions which differ so radically from the subsequent condition that transition by mere reform is unthinkable? If an affirmative answer can be given to this question, then the next—and for the critical liberal crucial—problem arises: In proliberty revolutions, which antiliberty elements can, actually and morally, be considered inevitable and acceptable, and which not? Taine contents himself with reference to England's supposedly organic evolution. But then the same man who has so excellently presented such a number of factual reasons proceeds to search for the causes of the revolution in purely nonfactual manifestations, and finds them in the eighteenth-century scientific and "classical" spirit, which, with a preposterous *petitio principii*, he calls "poison." Despite his efforts to rescue himself by the sophistry that each of the two elements is beneficial and dangerous only in combination, it remains a fact that this theory of his casts doubt upon the whole emancipatory movement. The incompatibility of the images indicates the incompatibility of the concepts: either the court and its usurpation of all the lifeblood of the nation represents the abscess, in which case any point of view can only be judged according to whether it acknowledges or denies the abscess; or the classical spirit with its fondness for abstractions is the causative poison, and in that case the *ancien régime* is justified in its basic character. Taine's fear—which is actually his fear of the Commune—is so strong that he prefers the second thesis: any kind of government is better than the eruption of the domestic barbarians. Whereas he begins by depicting the French aristocracy as a dead and useless branch on the tree of society, as time goes on he compares it with a costly essence, and the main accusation he levels against it is that too much refinement and culture had prevented it from girding itself for a determined resistance.[69]

In three powerful volumes he describes the torrent of mud which the revolution brings in its wake; he is continually horror-struck at the barbaric monster in man which pierces the thin veneer of reason and ferociously raises its bloodthirsty paw. And suddenly he sees the revolution as the abscess feeding off the body of society, with a festering discharge of the most noxious passions and the basest motives. The sins of the aristocracy are now quite forgotten, and all Taine's sympathy is directed toward it, toward the "cultured, kind, trusting minority,"[70] persecuted by the brutal masses but in reality the nursery for the nation's political leadership.

Taine's real hatred, however—the "natural scientist's" absurd and uninhibited hatred—is aimed at the Jacobins. These are neither barbarians nor children, but mediocre minds filled with a few abstract ideas, which have reached a state of exaltation. Using a biological image, Taine tries to present them as being in a state of puberty, but the phenomenon outgrows this inoffensive metaphor. The abstraction emerges more and more as the archenemy of life; an "absolutist principle" seems to be at war with reality and to have taken possession of the Jacobins, in whose heads it exists as a "monstrous parasite."[71]

From Taine's severe and substantial criticism of the Jacobins' primitivist conception of men and government, of their despotism, their totalitarian tendency toward the subjugation of the soul, it is quite clear that this is the criticism of a liberal: like a dangerous wolf, the state must be kept at bay. But on the whole it is debatable whether with Taine's work critical liberalism has won its battle against the revolution. In his work, a highly unscientific partisanship is all too clearly apparent; political postulates are indicated which transcend the boundaries of traditional liberal policy: alliance of the new with the old elite, armed civil resistance to the threat of the mob, distrust of humanitarianism as a debilitating and possibly even life-inimical force.

Shortly before his death, Hippolyte Taine paid a visit to the young Maurras, one of whose publications had caught his eye. At his death he demanded a Protestant burial. Thus, symbolically, the two poles emerge between which critical liberalism moved in Latin countries.

It might be supposed that the ground of critical liberal thought has now been sufficiently covered, were it not for the fact that Maurras—for reasons not immediately apparent—also counted among his forerunners Fustel de Coulanges, the great historian who in some ways, however, contrasts oddly with the four pioneering thinkers.

The reason is not to be found in Fustel's famous work, *La Cité antique*, with which he joined the ranks of the rediscoverers of the religious and cultural foundations of life in ancient times. This rediscovery took place entirely within the spirit of liberalism and not without a horizon of practical and relevant considerations: "We have deluded ourselves as to liberty among the ancients, and for this reason alone liberty among the moderns has been jeopardized."[72]

It is also hard to find adequate explanation in Fustel's wartime essays, in spite of the ardent patriotism that pervades them and the important token they offer of the profound perturbation of the French spirit in the face of Prussian-German reality.[73]

What was significant to Maurras, however, was the *Institutions politiques de l'ancienne France*, in which Fustel hoped to uncover a long-neglected truth which would at the same time render his country an important service. His subject is that proud self-appreciation of the French aristocracy, taken by the revolution and given negative form: the aristocracy, so the revolution claimed, were the descendants of the Germanic conquerors; its blood was of a different kind and it ruled by virtue of conquest. Fustel regards this revolutionary doctrine as one born of hatred which will go on engendering new hatred; he believes he can show that the principles on which it is based are illusory. According to him, it is but a latter-day explanation of the class antagonism between aristocracy and bourgeoisie; it is entirely mistaken to imagine that the Germanic invasion had been a race war.

Fustel's thesis remained disputed by scientific inquiry, but it is easy to see what it must have meant to Maurras. He might have felt justified in extracting and isolating the counterrevolutionary aspects of Renan's and Taine's doctrines from their context: their doctrines were obviously nothing but an acute form of the "Germanism" of the two thinkers and pointed in the direction of Gobineau and Nietzsche. In other words, they were the very antithesis of an anti-German French nationalism. It was only with Fustel's exposition that Renan's and Taine's "counterrevolutionary" theses were deprived of their Germanophile poison; he was the indispensable factor enabling Maurras to dissect the two most ambiguous representatives of French liberalism for the purpose of making them his forerunners.

Radical Conservatism: de La Tour du Pin, Drumont, Barrès

Was this method of dissection also necessary in the case of Maurras' immediate predecessors and contemporaries, de la Tour du Pin, Drumont, and Barrès? That they are not liberals, even in the broadest sense, is clear enough. But why should they be regarded as a special group of radical conservatives and thereby separated from the Christian conservatism of de Maistre and de Bonald? Can we deny the Marquis de La Tour du Pin—who, like his friend Albert de Mun, is prominent in every history of the Catholic social movement—his roots in Christian traditions and his sincere Catholic conviction, even if later on, unlike de Mun, he did not join the Ralliement and finally became a contributor to the newspaper *Action Française*? Was not Edouard Drumont, the originator of organized anti-Semitism in France, also a man of profound Christian feeling? And had not even Barrès a more spiritual relationship to Christianity than Maurras?

However, the question here is not of personal faith but of existing public conditions and the individual's position in them.

De Maistre and de Bonald had personal experience of the revolution, but scarcely of the republic as the institutionalized revolution. In 1871 France found itself with a republic just as fortuitously and unintentionally as it had in 1792, but until 1885 no Napoleon had appeared on the scene to provide the transition to a normal form of government. The republic proved durable but by no means stable. The insecure structure became a proving ground for the modern relationship between politics and economy, and it was not only to conservatives that the manifestations were repugnant. It was the aristocracy that intrigued against the First Republic; in the Third Republic it was the masses who shouted down the parliamentarians with the cry, À *bas les voleurs!*

De Maistre and de Bonald were familiar with the rabble, but not with an organized workers' movement whose goal was the complete overthrow of the existing order of society and which was further from, and at the same time closer to, the conservatives than was bourgeois radicalism.

For de Maistre and de Bonald, the revolution was "satanic," but so far there had appeared no one to associate it negatively with a familiar phenomenon, as Marx had done on a popular level with his indictment of "the capitalists."

Under the conditions of the republic, therefore, radical conservatism tended to take the wind out of the sails of the workers' movement by emphasizing its own battle against the bourgeois world, and by substituting the hate-image of the capitalist with its own hate-image, the Jew. It was by nature rabble-rousing and anti-Semitic. Its very radicalism gives it a more modern look. The final direction radical conservatism would one day take had not yet been decided, but its state of tension with the bourgeoisie, which had long since become the modern conservative force, is obvious, and the consequences of its anti-

Semitism harbored a conflict with the old conservative force of which it was a radical offshoot.

The guiding principle of all de La Tour du Pin's efforts is "the break with liberalism, in religion, in economy, in politics."[74] This "break" signifies the return to the corporative social structure of the Middle Ages, that is, the uniting of property owners, managers, and workers of a branch of industry to form corporations which preclude class struggle, possess officially recognized functions, render competition intrinsically impossible, abolish private judicial rights in labor relations, and endow each member with an official character. It is remarkable what an inward affinity this proposal—which Le Play would no doubt have called "reactionary"—reveals with socialist ideas and concepts. It does not aim only to dull socialist postulates by partial fulfillment: elimination of the antagonism between capital and labor, of the commodity nature of labor, and so forth. By resorting to the patristic idea and labeling capitalism "usury," de La Tour du Pin arrives at the doctrine of the value of labor and surplus value, at the theory of exploitation and social polarization, at the condemnation of all idleness, at the demand for "co-ownership" on the part of the proletariat[75] in the tools of production. It is his familiarity with the world of labor and the infectious power of its spontaneous ideas that makes de La Tour du Pin turn so sharply against the social egoism of the property-owning classes, with the result that unmistakable signs of an internal conservative conflict begin to emerge. But it may already be assumed at this juncture that in the final analysis this conflict is fictitious. For from a political point of view, corporatism is clearly intended to deprive the individual of his democratic participation in sovereignty and to lead him from the plight of the citizen to the secure existence of a co-worker. Because of this common intention, a unity can be restored which would have suffered from pure consistencies. And the same applies when in 1898 de La Tour du Pin takes up an old anti-Semitic theme and maintains: "It is the Jewish idea which has led the rich to exploit the poor by means of the modern form of usury, capitalism; the poor to hate the rich by means of the proletariat."[76] It is already possible to foresee on whose back conservative unity is to be restored. It will not be long before the thesis is advanced that the revolution was the work of the Jews, and that the false ideas of liberty and equality were essentially Jewish in nature and incompatible with the Christian spirit and Christian civilization.[77] But how long can this midway position be held? Are there not already signs of a new and more serious internal conservative conflict in which the issue is no longer one of material interests but of the consistency and purity of the specific conception?

It is to Édouard Drumont's credit that he did not evade the more difficult of the two issues; it was to his shame that he persisted in the unsophisticated outlook of his early days.

It would be wrong to present as a rabble-rouser and a violent agitator the man whose two-volume work, *La France juive* (1886), made history and, in one readily verifiable sense, denoted the start of the Dreyfus affair.[78] He was actually a shy, extremely cultured writer and journalist who had achieved some prominence with his sensitive book on old Paris[79] and who, as he admits himself, would have preferred to spend his life in libraries or monasteries. It would be equally wrong to form too simple and undifferentiated an idea of anti-Semitism. There are Christian, liberal, democratic, and socialist forms of anti-Semitisms, all of them a long way from being radical anti-Semitism. There must be one method of judging the anti-Semitism which sees itself faced by a Jewish group that appropriates all the advantages of emancipation without assuming its disadvantages, and another method of judging a form of anti-Semitism which swiftly and skillfully takes for its target a Jewish group in the process of disintegration. Anti-Semitism in Germany after 1945 takes one form, "the same thing" in the France of 1886 takes another.

The number of Jews at that time was, to be sure, not very large. But the number of German-Jewish names in banking especially, but also in the intellectual professions, was legion. The activity of Jews as agents in almost every important transaction and upheaval was particularly striking: in the Panama scandal, the negotiating role—although by no means the initiating one—of two Jews of German origin caused the greatest public scandal. Moreover, this role coincided with a period of profound unfathomable changes which threatened the status of every individual, every profession, every people, and which could have been felt nowhere more strongly than in France—a country that, unlike the others of Europe, was not equipped with the apparently solid armor of traditional forms of government.

Drumont was therefore merely expressing a general sentiment when he said: "They [the French] feel caught up in something disquieting and obscure."[80] And it is not the calculation of the demagogue but the transparency of a highly personal and moral conviction when he postulates: "In our era of universal lies, one must speak the truth."[81] The truth which he believed he discovered was that the Jews were not simply the manifestations of present unrest but its cause: "As soon as you attack the Jew, you engage in hand-to-hand combat with reality, you pit yourself against your true enemy."[82]

Thus, from feelings that merit attention and insights that are partially accurate, there arose the first modern anti-Semitism worthy of serious literary consideration, which was to be absorbed all too quickly, to a greater or lesser degree, by every radical conservative endeavor of the day as its most vital component.[83]

Yet *La France juive* is a shapeless work: a chronicle of historical events, culture, manners and modes, and society, in one vast collection of barely verifiable anecdotes—an orgy of Parisian gossip devoid of either plan or firmly structured thought. Nevertheless, it contains nearly all the themes of subsequent forms of anti-Semitism: from the contrasting of the creative, idealistic, justice-loving Aryan race with the parasitic, exploiting, cunning Semitic species, via the friend-foe Jewish brothers—the capitalist and the socialist—to undisguised threats of murder and the announcement of impending revolution. This revolution is to wipe out the work of the other revolution in which the Jewish spirit and Jewish people destroyed the happiness of old France (although the pickings remained scanty indeed). As with de La Tour du Pin, the image of old France approaches the idyllic, it might even be said, the paradigmatic, whereas all liberal criticism of the revolution had also been a criticism of the *ancien régime*.

Drumont's book shows *élan* and stature, it is a criticism of modern civilization as a whole, a civilization which has impoverished and degraded man and robbed life of its poetry and truth. And then at times he knows exactly why the Jew can play an important role in this society: "At a time when one lives only by the intellect, he [the Jew] has the necessary daring, the boldness of the intellect."[84] However fond he is of denouncing the "modern Judean civilization," his book as a whole must lead to the conclusion that it deals with fundamental characteristics which could not possibly have been created by a handful of Jews.

In fact Drumont's indictments of the conservatives and the bourgeoisie become increasingly bitter. It might even seem that by 1889 (*La fin d'un monde*) Judaism was no more than a secondary phenomenon for him, included in the larger and equally odious world of the bourgeoisie. Here French socialism probably receives the highest accolades ever accorded it up to that time by a conservative writer. Drumont calls the socialist goal "very noble," the work "very necessary,"[85] and specifically states that socialist ideas are the inevitable outcome of the reality of the modern world. Moreover, he adopts the socialist conception that the revolution was a bourgeois undertaking to the detriment of the people, and he goes one better by stating that in the Paris Commune the proletarian element was very noble, while the bourgeois element had been barbarous. It will remain "the eternal crime of the conservatives"[86] that they participated in the shameful reprisal actions after the Commune. He predicts: "These victims of the bourgeoisie [such as the small shopkeepers who had been ruined by the competition of the department stores] will soon form the advance guard of the socialist army."[87] As early as 1889, therefore, Drumont brings to a climax, although only verbally, the revolutionary antibourgeois element in radical conservatism.

It would be easy to prove that this turnabout was not to be taken very seriously and was the result of frustrated love rather than a growing understanding. But it cost Drumont the confidence of the French bourgeoisie forever. Even at the time of his greatest journalistic triumphs, during the Dreyfus affair, indeed when he was elected deputy for Algiers in 1898, he never had the slightest chance of political success.

However, it speaks for the seriousness of his emotions that he did not lead the second internal conservative controversy in the same general direction as his successors. He sided with the minor clergy against the bishops and openly attacked Rome: the "new church" had, he claimed, abandoned all the teachings of the church fathers concerning matters of interest and money and had allied itself with the "Jewish system."[88] This did not help him to make friends. But he brought to light a further characteristic of radical conservatism: potential universal hostility. By his example he demonstrated to all who came after him that the friendship of the mighty must on no account be imperiled if political influence and power are to be achieved.

When Drumont died in 1917 he was lonely, deserted, and forgotten. But at the end of World War II the two most opposite and talented figures of the Maurras school, Bernanos and Brasillach, recalled Drumont (quite independently of one another) as the father of a French National Socialism.

Maurice Barrès did not essentially enrich the two basic characteristics of radical conservatism, the pseudorevolutionary antibourgeois trend and anti-Semitism, thereby avoiding their potential inherent conflict. He conducted his early election campaigns on the platform of a national socialism, interpreting socialism as the endorsement of economic changes and the transformation (*changement*) of the upper classes; as a reporter during Dreyfus' appeal trial, he formulated some memorable anti-Semitic phrases ("That Dreyfus is capable of treason, I deduce from his race"[89]). But this is not where his importance lies.

In some ways de La Tour du Pin and Drumont had been internationalists. They found themselves facing an international phenomenon and had visions of world-wide alliances for their own side. For Barrès, who was born in Lorraine and whose childhood memories were filled with images of the Franco-Prussian war, the great neighbor state to the east was the chief enemy. To that extent he was the father of French nationalism; to that extent he represented merely a transitional step toward the "integral nationalism" of Maurras, who succeeded in uniting both trends with the thesis, "The revolution comes from Germany." Barrès had to keep his distance from Maurras, in spite of their personal friendship, because in Barrès' eyes (following in Taine's footsteps), nationalism was the "acceptance of determinism."[90] He could therefore not consent to the strange refashioning of the fatherland which Maurras undertook, to the elimination of the revolution from the nation's history. It is true that Barrès emphasizes the national character of the revolution to the utmost, but since he tries to embrace *all* the nation's history with the same affection, he cannot sympathize with Maurras' stern narrow-mindedness, especially as this was incompatible with his own remarkable sensitivity. This explains why he was afraid Maurras would create "hard little souls"[91] and why he asked whether Maurras did not want to "enslave";[92] that is why his book, *Les diverses familles spirituelles de la France,* may be broadly understood as the climax of his life's work.

But, as with Drumont, so with Barrès we find traits which seem "more modern" than the Maurrassian doctrines. "The soil and the dead," "blood and soil," "uprooting" and "rooted in"—as to content these expressions can easily be deduced from Taine and Le Play, but as formulas and indications of an atmosphere they are a symptom of something new. They led to the battle against the intellectuals as the "logicians of the absolute"[93] who no longer feel a spontaneous identification with the indigenous group,[94] and thus to one of the most fascinating phenomena of the twentieth century: the battle of intellectuals against intellectuals. A relativist irrationalism—obviously a position of decadence—glorifies instinct and blood and thus creates one of the most remarkable characteristics of future fascism. Nor is Barrès ignorant of the concept of race: "A terrible consequence for certain people: the question of race has opened up."[95]

Although Barrès' idea of race is thoroughly French and he regards it as a historical and vigorous group-unit, could he ignore the fact that Taine had already formulated the idea much more naturalistically: as the mysterious primal cause behind all manifestations of life? Did he not suspect that this concept contained the definitive potential of radical conservatism, a potential which was never fully realized and was in sharp contradiction to the Barrès type of nationalism?

Conservatism is too broad and nebulous a concept for it to remain undifferentiated. There is no clearer picture of its significance at any given time than that provided by its attitude toward the revolution, its logical and historical prerequisite. But it never becomes identical with that mode of thought—critical liberalism—which, while combating the revolution, cannot help acknowledging it as one of its consequences.

France was the land of revolutions. It was inevitable that it should also become the land of the counterrevolution. But there are at least three fundamentally differing trends in the intellectual counterrevolution. Each had to undergo a radical amputation before it could become one with *the* counterrevolutionary doctrine, the Maurrassian ideology and the Action Française. The new conservatism consists simply of old ingredients and is therefore completely conservative. But it only acquired *these* components by the iconoclastic destruction of what had formerly been homogeneous. In this sense it is revolutionary. Revolutionary reaction—this is the underlying characteristic of fascism. Even on the initial level of its relation to its roots, the Action Française displays this distinguishing mark.

CHAPTER TWO

History

Introduction: The Dreyfus Affair

The story of the Action Française begins with the Dreyfus affair. This most bloodless of all revolutions,[1] however, also gave rise to socialist participation in the government,[2] to the separation of church and state, and to the *de facto* subordination of military to civil power. The distinction between socialism and communism,[3] the birth of Zionism,[4] and the formation of the final intellectual consequences of anti-Semitism[5] are all more or less obviously associated with this affair. Indeed, there is some justification for the view that, in France, the Dreyfus affair marked the beginning of the twentieth century, while elsewhere in Europe it did not begin until World War I.[6] It would be strange if the conservative party, defeated but by no means destroyed in this struggle, had *not* precipitated a new pattern of thought pointing the way toward the future of postwar Europe.

In the same way that the Action Française is insignificant when viewed apart from the horizon of "fascism," so the Dreyfus affair[7] is incomprehensible if it merely represents a lawsuit in which some wicked people persecute an innocent man, and some brave people appeal to the public and eventually free and rehabilitate him. Rather, the Dreyfus affair ceases to be a purely legal matter at a precise moment in time. This moment in time was determined by an act of the future founder of the Action Française. To some extent, therefore, the Dreyfus affair and the Action Française stand in a mutual cause-and-effect relationship.

Certainly the Dreyfus affair was one of the strangest and most dramatic legal cases of all time. But it did not start out like that, nor did it maintain that level throughout.

Neither the arrest of Captain Dreyfus, despite the extraordinary circumstances surrounding it, nor his sentence to life imprisonment on Devil's Island, despite the questionable evidence on which the sentence was based, was sufficient in itself to constitute an "affair." They represented a miscarriage of justice, possibly even a gross violation of justice. The determination of the Dreyfus family to effect a rehabilitation was necessary to create the affair, even though at first only in a negative sense. In association with some influential Jewish friends the delicate business was approached as if it were a dubious financial transaction. They went to work furtively, bought documents illegally, made large donations to newspapers, and did not even avoid the appearance of attempting to bribe important persons. Was it any wonder that the public began to be alarmed, that there were rumors of a Jewish syndicate which was conspiring to liberate the traitor with every means at its disposal?

Yet the "syndicate" was completely innocent of the fact that the case finally became an affair in a positive sense. On the contrary, this new development could be attributed to the alertness of a sincere officer who, as the new head of the Intelligence Bureau, discovered the real author of the documents in question and maintained the genuineness of his discovery in the face of all opposition. But the rumors of a syndicate offered the best possible support to that opposition, and Colonel Picquart, the real hero of this affair, seemed to be pursuing a lost cause.

There is no doubt that Zola's famous letter, "J'accuse," appearing in Clemenceau's paper *Aurore* (January 13, 1898), marked a turning point. It transformed the legal matter into a public affair in its full sense. It summarized all that the "syndicate's" investigations had brought to light over the years, and enough dubious and suspicious material existed to put the General Staff in an awkward position. But this letter did not yet turn the affair into a true political issue, the kind that sets great masses of people in passionate motion against one another. The details were too numerous and the hypotheses too bold to convince the masses. Moreover, it was not hard to ascribe discreditable motives to both Zola and Clemenceau.

In the summer of 1898 public opinion and parliament were still almost unanimously opposed to the appeal and hostilely inclined toward the handful of "Dreyfusards." No convincing "new evidence" had been brought forward; the only thunderclaps which the so-called syndicate had been able to produce were the rustlings of papers; the sudden flash which casts a new and ominous light on the nocturnal landscape was lacking. When it finally struck, the Dreyfusards were as surprised as everyone else.

Early in September, 1898, the public learned with astonishment and alarm that on August 30, on the orders of Minister of War Cavaignac, Lieutenant-Colonel Henry, Picquart's successor as head of the Intelligence Bureau, had been arrested. It was reported that he had admitted having forged a secret document classified by the minister of war. The next day he had committed suicide with a razor blade in his cell on Mont Valérien.

Paris, France, the world, held its breath. It was patently obvious that this was the new evidence needed for the appeal, and it was in truth very decisive evidence. Henry had played an important role in the affair right from the start. If *he* admitted his guilt—and how else was his suicide to be interpreted?—the whole edifice of the accusation of Dreyfus must be shaken to its foundations. An immediate appeal was the least that could be demanded now. And in fact, according to expert witnesses, for forty-eight hours there was not a soul in Paris who did not believe that an appeal was inevitable.

Then in the midst of the confusion and consternation, a newspaper article appeared which altered the situation. Its author was Charles Maurras,[8] a thirty-year-old writer hitherto known only in limited circles. The article was entitled, "The first blood." It looked at things in a way which no one had thought or dared to look. It summoned the colonel as a "blood witness": "This blood smokes, and it will cry out until its spilling is avenged, not by you, who have yielded to a noble despair, not even by the troublesome coterie at the Ministry, but by your chief executioners, whom I publicly name: the members of the Syndicate of Treason. In the state of confusion in which the national parties find themselves, we have not been able to give you the great funeral which your martyrdom deserves. We should have flourished the bloodstained tunic on our boulevards, as well as the bloodstained blades, we should have borne the coffin in a procession and worshiped the shroud as if it were a black flag. It will be to our shame that we did not attempt this. But patriotic feeling, although diffused and multiplied against itself, still incapable of action, has nevertheless been resuscitated."[9]

For the rest of his life, Maurras' opponents accused him of having glorified the person of Henry and of having represented his forgery as a *faux patriotique*.[10] In actual fact, what Maurras did was of far greater and direr significance. He submitted a reinterpretation of extraordinary scope. No thinking person could mistake the issue: either Henry considered himself guilty, or his superiors considered him guilty. If Henry had been of one mind with himself, his brother officers, and his superiors concerning the status of an ultrasecret document, he would not have needed to carry out such a pathetically clumsy forgery and would, if necessary, have been able to brave all the storms of public opinion. Whoever took the guilt from Henry's shoulders transferred it to his superiors. And indeed Maurras did not shrink from accusing the *coterie ministérielle*; but was he not the very one to cut the ground from under his defense of the army and the former ministers? It was possible to regard the Dreyfusards as capable of bribing deputies and inciting soldiers to mutiny; but to regard them as sufficiently powerful to place a razor in the hands of the head of the Intelligence Bureau, without him being conscious of having committed a serious crime, was to credit them with superhuman powers, of which there is no evidence.

At the same time Maurras endowed this desperate claim with its myth, the most occult and sinister of all myths: that of blood. Shed by the hand of the enemy, unexpiated, not only does it cry out for revenge, but it is also the first drop in a sea of blood that a treacherous and dangerous attack, both from without and within, will demand of France. A blood spell destined to unite the clan for the *dernière bataille*[11]—this is what the myth-creating eye of Maurras, the so-called rationalist, beholds.

Yet at the same time he plunges onto a path which is hardly the predestined one for the lyricist and the *Félibre* (one of a group of then modern Provençal writers), the friend of Moréas and Mistral, and the literary critic and storyteller. To his dying day he will have to vindicate the article which he always claims to regard as "the best, in any case most useful act" of his life.[12]

There can be no doubt that this article was a lie, and that Maurras had no illusions about that. But it was not a lie in the ordinary sense. Had there been an appeal at that time and in those circumstances, the Dreyfus affair would have concluded as a purely legal matter, presumably without any significant political consequences—but for the army, it would have meant an enormous loss of prestige and respect in the eyes of *everyone*. Maurras could not seriously believe that the behavior of all branches of the army had been blameless in the affair. But he was sufficiently convinced that the very life of France was threatened both from within and without, and that in every respect the army represented the ultimate guarantee of France's existence. To this extent the Dreyfusards, particularly if Dreyfus was innocent, were dangerous enemies. They were trying to drag the army before a tribunal in whose judgment it could not possibly pass muster: that of the individual who insists on his human dignity. If one were to follow up all the letters of treachery in an army, sheer reading would prevent one from taking action. Clemenceau forgets this, and since he limits himself to the case of Captain Dreyfus he must have been bribed by the syndicate, even if he has never received a sou for his paper. Maurras' underlying thought process can be reduced to the following formula: Justice kills what is vital.

That is why in a deeper sense his lie is for him the truth. With the legal affair becoming a political affair—indeed the focal point of all French politics—army and church find themselves exposed to fiercer attacks and greater dangers than had ever been thought possible; but the conservative element among the people, the only one which really counts, closes its ranks all the more solidly around the threatened institutions, thus ensuring their survival.

A lie which the intellect sees for what it is but which is at one with the deeper motivations of life, may be called a living lie. There are living lies not only of the individual, but also of a class, an era, or a historical trend. Maurras' article on Henry represents the living lie at the core of the French army. In politics its result was the Action Française, and it was no accident that the Action Française enjoyed more sympathy in the army (and the church) than anywhere else.

The living lie of a, morally, profoundly threatened army marks the start of Italian fascism: the lie that the battle of Vittorio Veneto decided the world war.

The living lie of a, morally *and* factually, profoundly threatened army is one of the preconditions for German National Socialism: the legend of the stab in the back.

This common factor must be kept in mind as pointing up the inadequacy of the categories of a mere history of ideas.

Meanwhile, it would be doing Maurras an injustice to believe that he, too, could find a simple and arrogant solution in collective expediency to the problem of truth. For him, truth and reason remain linked. This explains how, for him, the living lie of the Henry article can become the continuing spur and driving force behind justification and rationalization.

Barrès once said that Maurras had evolved his theory "in conformity with his instincts."[13] Barrès is thinking, rightly enough, of a level below reason, but he overnaturalizes it by using the word "instinct." A metaphor seems more appropriate: just as a tree which has been cut produces rosin to close the wound, and the deeper the cut the more rosin is produced, so Maurras weaves over the living lie of his "best, in any case most useful act," a web of theories which justify, explain, and substantiate. It is true that they seldom refer directly to that article—most of them probably stem from earlier beginnings and more recent experiences—and it is true that they combine to form a structure of imposing consistency. At times one might believe that the great goal had been achieved, that of writing a *Contre-Encyclopédie* and even of countering the envied and hated doctrine of Karl Marx with a work of comparable stature. To a certain extent this ideology *is* the political movement of the Action Française. In fact, within the space of twenty-five years two of the most typical and intellectual personalities of their wartime generations (Erneste Psichari in 1913, and Robert Brasillach in 1937),[14] called him the outstanding political thinker of his time. But when in 1945 Maurras, an old man of seventy-six, faced the revolutionary court at Lyons, infinitely more guilty toward his country than Dreyfus but from a formal and legal point of view equally innocent, he called out, after the verdict was pronounced depriving him of freedom and civil rights for life: *C'est la revanche de Dreyfus!*[15] No matter how far he had advanced beyond his beginnings, he was still their prisoner, and perhaps this was really the revenge of that living lie—that to the end of his days he never succeeded in understanding it, hence himself and the role he had played.

Maurras' Development to 1898[16]

Who was Charles Maurras? What course did he follow before he stepped forward at the age of thirty into the front line of French politics, to remain one of its most remarkable figures for the next half-century?

His development is in some aspects highly individual, in others typical of his generation, and as a whole so complex that it cannot be described with a few sociological or psychological formulas.

To begin with, it is not quite accurate to say that Maurras came from a lower middle-class family. Admittedly, his father was only a local tax collector, and living conditions at home were cramped. But his maternal grandfather was mayor of the old port of Martigues, in Provence, and there were numerous ties linking the family with the broader and freer existence of seafaring people, shipowners, and sea captains. As a boy, Charles' first and dearest wish was to become a naval officer, and later he liked to think that it was only the fact of his deafness that led him to literature, philosophy, and politics. As in countless French families, the father was a nonbeliever, the mother devout; but even she inclined to some degree toward liberal ideas. Within the wider family circle there was a considerable variety of political belief, and Maurras rightly said that it was not due to family tradition that he arrived at his political doctrine. However, one important reservation must be made. His mother, of far greater influence in his upbringing than his father, who died young, had seen her own mother faint on hearing the news of the revolution of 1848, and horror of the revolution left a permanent mark on her son. This fundamental bourgeois fear of revolution is perhaps the most important element in Maurras' make-up; it provides a remarkable similarity with Nietzsche and a marked antithesis to the proletarian Mussolini.

This fear was preceded by another terrible fear. When the Franco-Prussian war broke out, young Charles Maurras was barely two and a half. Fixed forever in his earliest memories were the terror and excitement of those days. When he asked who were the Prussians that everyone was talking about, he was told: "Wicked men, barbarians wearing spiked helmets."[17]

Side by side with this dual terror, the consolation and charm of books filled the imagination of the precocious boy. Homer fascinated him, especially the *Odyssey*; the glory and grandeur of the Greek gods lighted an inextinguishable flame in him.

After the death of his father in 1876, the little family moved to Aix-en-Provence, where Charles attended the Collège Catholique, which was run by priests. He made swift and intensive inroads into the spiritual world. Lamenais' ideas on revolutionary theocracy took hold of the twelve-year-old boy like a fever. The next wave to engulf his interest was that of the romantic poets,[18] Musset and Baudelaire, and later Verlaine.

Then came disaster, the incomprehensible, the irrational misfortune. At the age of fourteen his hearing began to deteriorate progressively; he became practically deaf and could no longer follow lectures. He had still been dreaming of becoming a naval officer; this possibility now vanished as did the more concrete prospect of a normal course of study. A young abbé, who later became a bishop and for whom Maurras always retained the utmost respect, became interested in him. However, it was not religion but philosophy that occupied first place in his mind. The magnificent, hopeless gloom of Lucretius' poem "On the Nature of Things" gripped his gloom-encircled soul; confronted brutally with the origin of evil, he looked for and found in Kant nothing but skepticism, and still more intensive and desperate was his meeting with the "sinister" Pascal. In short, Maurras lost his faith, and his physical disaster was followed by the profound upheaval and transformation of his spiritual life.

Then came a surprising turn. In 1885 Maurras, then seventeen, went to Paris and, unprepared and inexperienced as he was, gave himself up entirely to literature. He became a regular contributor to various Catholic and conservative periodicals. But this was the accidental result of some letters of introduction. His mental and spiritual state was anything but settled, and for years the most disparate elements existed side by side within him. In later years he spoke of a period of anarchy; but it is impossible to define the boundaries of this period clearly. It was probably more of a substratum, an ever-present contingency over a number of years, but never for a moment did it turn into sympathy for the political movement of anarchism or of the revolutionary parties. Therefore it is not correct when Maurras says: "Literature led us to politics."[19] On the contrary, politics, that is, the counterrevolutionary position on the nonroyalist Right, was the least affected by his crisis. It was in literature that he overcame his crisis, and it was then that Maurras, with his good grounding in the classics, discovered a new synthesis which in turn formed the basis for his political theory. However, regardless of the passionate single-mindedness with which Maurras at first devoted himself to philosophy in Paris, he was denied any comparable success: "In esthetics, in politics, I have known the joy of grasping original ideas in their most lofty evidence, but in pure philosophy, no."[20]

His encounter with Comte marks the end of his philosophical search. Here he met with a thinker whose philosophy renounced God and all metaphysics but who nevertheless promised to salvage and vindicate that human "order" which Maurras, even in the hours of his deepest despair, had never questioned. But although Maurras found a spiritual home in positivism, he first eliminated all elements which might still be considered metaphysical in Comte—the law of three stages, the concept of progress, the religion of humanity—to retain merely an *empirisme organisateur*, which cannot seriously be called a *philosophical* home.

From among all these impressions of the first ten years, a few experiences stand out which finally became basic to Maurras' spiritual and political development. Some of these are quite new, others relate strikingly to childhood impressions, confirming and radicalizing them.

During the very first days of his stay in Paris, he was "struck, moved, almost hurt,"[21] to come across so many foreign names on the boulevards, names which were distinguished by the abhorrent letters "K" or "W" or "Z". Therefore it is an esthetic impression that causes him to take the first step toward his later anti-Semitism, as well as the naïve confusion and xenophobia of the young provincial in the metropolis, rather like Hitler's experiences twenty years later in Vienna. During the following year he no doubt read, like everyone else, Drumont's *La France juive*, and the Panama scandal must have provided him, like so many others, with material for new insights. Yet his anti-Semitism is far from being intransigent or a matter of principle: in 1889 he voted in an election for the first time in his life for General Boulanger's adviser, the Jewish Senator Naquet, and in 1895 his first book (*Le Chemin de Paradis*) was published by the Jewish firm of Calmann-Lévy.

Meanwhile the cardinal experience of his childhood was confirmed and strengthened when he met with vivid reminders of the 1871 Commune. Characteristically, only the thought that the Louvre had been in danger agitated him,[22] and this thought filled him with apprehension and horror both for the past and for the future. Unlike Drumont, he disregarded the mass shootings, the terrible repression. Nietzsche's reaction had been very similar. This evidently accounts for the basic feeling, common to both men, that culture consisted of "apple peel over glowing chaos"[23] and "a tiny lost island in the sea of endless chaos."[24] This feeling was strengthened yet again when Maurras was told soon afterward that, at the time of the Commune when attempts were being made to save the Louvre, a voice from the crowd was heard shouting: "Let it all burn, why not? All the better! ... Down with the slaves of the dead, long live life and its flame!"[25] Not only was barbaric ignorance at work, therefore, but a false philosophy and its diabolical lust for destruction. How was such a terrible thing to be countered except by a new doctrine of the preciousness of all that is fragile and of the essentially preserving nature of man? In retrospect Maurras called this story "the starting point of the reflections which were to lead me to where I now am."[26] But there is no doubt that even at that time a living phenomenon served to strengthen the impression of history: the propaganda of Marxism, which he soon came to consider "German and Jewish."[27]

Once again his provincial origin had a political consequence. What had once been the breath of life to him, his native Provence, became in Paris something he sorely missed. This nostalgia drove him to learn the Provençal language and to approach the *Félibres* who were trying to carry on and further the work of Mistral in Paris. Finally—in Petrarch's valley at the Spring of Vaucluse—he met the master himself: and it was then that the meaning of the Latin expression *multa renascentur* became clear to him. Unlike the *Félibres* in Paris, however, Maurras and some of his friends were not content with a mere esthetic and folklorist program; they made far-reaching political demands: decentralization of the government, restoration of the old provinces, official recognition of the Provençal language—indeed, there was some talk of "sovereignty" for the provinces, and certain government quarters began to be alarmed. There is no denying that Maurras began with a program (which he never actually disavowed) that *appears* to run completely counter to all fascist endeavors. But again it must be realized that his aim was a reaction not only against uniformity as such, but against Jacobinic uniformity. Thus when all appeals directed by him and his friends at the country and local traditions met with unshakable indifference, the idea gradually ripened that necessary reform could be instituted "from above."

Once again it was probably the reawakening of his childhood experiences, of his love of Homer and the shining world of his gods, which finally enabled him to take a firm stand in the realm of esthetics too: that of neoclassicism and its inclination toward the eternal, the essential, the enduring, as against the romantic blandishments of the ephemeral and the fashionable; of its attention to meaning, syntax, and orderliness of expression, as against the romantic emancipation of words and picturesque sound-portraits; of its sense of simplicity and clarity, as against the rambling, agitated, confused style of the romantic. Maurras' friend and master in this development, Jean Moréas, and the *École Romane* founded by him are known today only to the history of literature; Maurras' own great critical works on the romantic era date from the time after 1898.

From this period of change only one book is still known, the artistic merit of which is disputed but whose political and ideological importance are very great: *Le Chemin de Paradis*, published in 1895 but written partly in 1891. Outwardly it is nothing but a series of "myths and fables," about Phidias and Crito, about Sybaris, about Arles during the late antiquity, about fishermen and seafaring people. The preface sets out the purpose of the fables: to demonstrate the need for harmony by showing the destructive power of the narrow-minded and the extreme, of unbridled lust or fanatical religions. But the preface also states directly what Maurras means by fanatical religions: chiefly, monotheistic Christianity which destroys the living harmonies of classical paganism and under whose emblem—the cross of a suffering god—night has spread over the modern age.[28] This night, however, is due mainly to the unrest and revolt of masses of slaves who during ancient times and the Middle Ages had their place, their order, their purpose, but who now move restlessly, aimlessly, unhappily under the leadership of fools who refuse to acknowledge that "inhumanity does not begin with shed blood but originates in the disturbance which is knowingly brought to the hearts."[29] In the famous story *Les Serviteurs*, the slaves who were separated from their masters in the underworld and did not know what to do with themselves understood this. "The souls of men have not all been drawn from the same source. The daughters of potter's clay will not rise to the rank of those whom the gods begat in beds of purple." The book abounds in remarkable epithets, whether the infinite is called an *obscène chaos*, or whether the subject is the "Hebrew Christ," the madness of the antislavery congress, or the "poor Protestant and neo-Christian geese."

Nevertheless, the outstanding fact is not that Maurras arrived independently at formulas of radical conservatism which are ordinarily associated with

Nietzsche, but which were in the air ever since the original—that is, Christian—conservatism appeared to have become outmoded and inadequate; rather, the decisive factor is that Maurras calls his view "sufficiently heathen and Christian to merit the beautiful title of Catholic."[30] To him Catholicism is merely Christianity divested of its poisonous content by its Roman-heathen form. Maurras therefore takes that radical and pseudorevolutionary conservatism which in its pure form, as developed by Nietzsche, can only exist on a literary level and turns it into a politically active quantity. If Maurras succeeds in giving it modern methods and in preserving as a mere means the old tree in whose root system the new plant is growing, then he has created an entirely new political phenomenon for which there is as yet no name.

But at the same time there are indications of a profound and crucial ambiguity. In line with its innate character, the new party is dedicated to the battle against the universal revolt of the slaves, hence it must be equally universal. In this context Nietzsche had dreamed of a future "party of life," whose goal would be "the destruction of all that is degenerate."[31] But was there some international manifestation in whose protection and shadow the new entity could grow? Neither Catholicism, science, nor industry was a suitable starting point. What was available was the only group which was empowered to act and was unmistakably aware of itself, but which, of course, was not universal: the nation. The paradox might remain hidden for a while. At some time or other it was bound to come to light.

The fact that to Maurras the *object* of politics might be his own nation was already inherent in his most important childhood experiences. The national enemy, Germany, had indeed never ceased to preoccupy him.[32] And one day, in 1894, he read the recently published translation of Fichte's *Reden an die deutsche Nation*. It acted on him like a thunderbolt. Now he understood the enemy. What had obscurely oppressed him became coherent, the dark doors opened: he held the key (*j'en tenais la clé*).[33] This was the heart of the mysterious creature: the German obsession with "I," the intoxication with self, the monotheism of the national "I." This was the sinister threat; and from that day forward, on every platform to which he had access, his comments are to be heard on the preacher-philosopher of Berlin, his work, his action.[34] It is at one and the same time example and promise, henceforward Maurras' dearest wish is *une troupe de jeunes Fichte*,[35] and the German rebellion against Napoleon becomes for him a model and a standard—although a totally misleading standard, for the analogy with Nietzsche's "revolt of the slaves," and hence the specific distinguishing mark of the century, is entirely absent from Fichte.

One last, completely new experience enhanced the importance of the "nation" in Maurras' mind. In 1896 he attended the first Olympic Games in Athens as a reporter for the *Gazette de France*. He observed the harmony of the opening ceremony, but he also observed the delirium, the unbridled passion, of the crowd during the contests when it came to urging on or cheering a compatriot.

Was not Baron de Coubertin's noble idealism a "cloud," while the irrational behavior of the masses was reality? Was not the peaceful contest, which disclosed such abhorrent traits to the observer, actually the proving ground for warlike conflict? There in the Pan-Athenian stadium the competing nations stood revealed to Maurras as the fundamental reality of the age. This graphic experience was to remain with him for a long time as something much more powerful than his theoretical horror of revolution which, after all, he was never to see with his own eyes.

Yet at the same time he saw how small France was in the world, how it was surpassed by Germans and Englishmen. His classically educated mind was flooded with analogies: did not France resemble Athens weakened by democracy in the face of the barbarian power of Philip of Macedon? Had it not once, under its kings, been the leading power, had it not set a standard for the world?

Maurras returned to Paris a passionate opponent of democracy and a determined supporter of monarchy. His years of apprenticeship were over. At last he had "found his harbor."[36] But it was still to be seen whether he would serve his country as a writer or as a politician. It was the Henry affair which first drove him out onto the high seas aboard a man-of-war.

We are now in a position to summarize Maurras' youthful development as a whole. In it, social, national, religious, esthetic causes and motives blend indistinguishably. Neither his bourgeois fear of revolution, nor his national sensibility, nor his esthetic impulse toward the finite and the perfect, nor the loss of his faith, can be isolated or looked to alone for elucidation. This complicated medley of factors does not achieve direction and completion until faced with the challenge of events. In Athens Maurras perceived the truth, even if perhaps only part of it. Not until he had finally become a man did events cease to shake him: from then on, he used them instead merely to confirm his theories.

However, one further crucial fact remains to be considered: Maurras—for whatever reasons—did not, like his school friend Henri Bremond, become a theologian, although for the gifted son of a Catholic family, educated at an ecclesiastical college, this would have been a natural course. Nor did he find a home in philosophy, as his teacher Renan did at certain times. Also, he was not satisfied with being just an author, like his opponent André Gide, since literature, while not shirking political issues, does avoid lasting political involvement. Politics became for him the most extreme and vital "synthesis." Thus he ran the whole gamut which distinguishes the Occident as a self-secularizing society. This sets him clearly apart from all the random short-term politicians who are only outwardly affected by the contexts of social evolution as a whole. Not every ideologist is in this sense an "integral politician." But integral politics is perhaps the most ambiguous and dangerous manifestation of the European trend. Looking back Maurras said of the Henry affair: "I entered politics like a religion."[37] Seen in this way, Maurras can only be compared with Marx. For both men, politics cannot be separated from theology, metaphysics, and esthetics, even when the proponents themselves deny the connection. This must be borne in mind above all else when we turn from Maurras' inner development to political events.

The Action Française to the Founding of its Newspaper

To call Maurras the founder of the Action Française is not literally correct. It is true that the Henry article transformed and greatly accentuated the Dreyfus crisis, which was apparently on the verge of being resolved. If, in the eyes of their opponents, the Dreyfusards had hitherto been members of a conspiratorial syndicate, they were from now to be charged with a criminal plot that seemed to threaten state and society, indeed France itself. Vice versa, the supporters of the appeal now expressed rage and indignation at being confronted by people who dared to justify a forgery. The warring parties ceased to be opponents, they became enemies, with no quarter given or expected. But Maurras was not alone in seeing what now had to be done.

The main battle lines had been drawn. All those who supported army and church, the whole powerful group of the conservative bourgeoisie, were ranged solidly against Dreyfus. All those who were anticlerically inclined, especially the masses of the socialist workers, gathered in the opposing camp. An astonishing about-face had taken place: in 1894 Jaurès had attacked the government in the Chamber because its class justice had not sentenced the rich Captain Dreyfus to death; the originator of the affair, General Mercier, was an anticlerical republican; Leo XIII's Ralliement policy had split the Catholics into two groups, one progressive and one reactionary. But now the fine nuances disappeared: society became polarized in two hostile blocs accusing each other of criminal plots. The decision must be handed down by the "intellect," by the ever-important French intelligentsia. It appeared to be siding more and more with the Dreyfus cause. The university professors and elementary school teachers declared themselves almost to a man in favor of Dreyfus, the *enseignement secondaire* still hesitated. Clemenceau joined Reinach in founding the *Ligue pour la défense des droits de l'homme* and had published a *Manifeste des intellectuels*. Support of Dreyfus appeared to be in itself an intellectual act: thinking people and individuals versus cold-blooded reasons of state and the blind frenzy of the masses. If this impression were to gain the upper hand, the cause of the Dreyfus opponents was lost.

What must be done, therefore, was to gather together the anti-Dreyfus intelligentsia, and Maurras took an important part in this. On December 31, 1898, the *Ligue de la patrie française* saw the light of day. The result was overwhelming. Almost the entire Académie Française joined, and within a very short time there were a hundred thousand applications. It seemed that France's intellectuals did not after all side with the traitor and against the father-land!

But the League's declaration was a half-hearted affair of little consequence, shaped by a host of considerations for conflicting views.

Of an entirely different caliber was the manifesto published a few days earlier (December 19, 1898) in the newspaper *L'Éclair* by the young writer Maurice Pujo in the name of some friends. It bore the title "Action française" and set out with vigor to combat the *considérations humanitaires*, the "anarchists," the abstraction of the *droits de l'homme*, the parliamentary system, and individual-ism. It ended with the demand that internally France be "organized" and externally it become as strong as it had been under the *ancien régime*, without, of course, reverting to "forms of the past."[38]

Thus two trends toward an anti-Dreyfus rally existed side by side: the one academic, many-faceted, successful; the other radical and full of initiative, championed by unknown young men.

When the second group was finally constituted in the summer of 1899 under the name "Action Française," it was with the legitimate conviction that the great *Ligue de la patrie française* was not equal to its task. Maurras had been in touch with this new group since January, but he never hesitated to give credit for its founding to Maurice Pujo and, above all, Henri Vaugeois.[39]

Vaugeois was professor of philosophy at the Lycée in Coulommiers; like Pujo, his background was one of radical liberalism. Both men had been members of the *Union pour l'Action morale*, a center of Kantian and Protestant ideas which naturally enough very soon adopted a position on the Dreyfus side. Vaugeois and Pujo rebelled, but their leftist origin remained apparent for a long time.

Vaugeois was moved by the desire to reconcile progress and stability, to unite the truth of the monarchy with the truth of the republic to form a higher, third, entity.[40] He was not without sympathy for revolutionary socialism, yet he opened the first issue of the "little gray review," *Action Française*, with an article entitled "Réaction d'abord."

Within two years he let himself be convinced by Maurras that monarchy was the indispensable condition and culmination of the required reaction, that only the basic struggle against the principle of republic could avert the deadly dangers manifested by the Dreyfusards. Vaugeois was not the only one to surrender to Maurras' tireless and fanatical powers of persuasion: in 1899 Maurras was possibly the sole monarchist in the group; by 1903 the entire Action Française was monarchist. To this extent, then, he can rightly be called its founder.

The Action Française was constituted, almost to the day, simultaneously with Waldeck-Rousseau's government—simultaneously, that is, with the politi-cal triumph of the Dreyfusards. This triumph was accentuated and confirmed from year to year: in 1906 Clemenceau was to become prime minister and

Picquart minister of war. The Action Française was at first merely a small group of young intellectuals, quite without influence, whose sole asset was a tiny review and who met regularly for long discussions in the Café de Flore: its members had varying intellectual backgrounds—they included positivists, Spinozists, one Protestant, a few practicing Catholics. But they were fanatically convinced that it was their task to found a new political doctrine and that thereon depended the salvation of the state. Indeed, they stood at the cross-roads of ideological directions and political opinions.

The Dreyfus affair had been chiefly significant for the fact that segments of the population and positions which had formerly been united were now divided, and those which had formerly been divided were now united. Ever since their birth during the French revolution, the concepts of "nation" and "fatherland," and of "humanity" and "human rights," had belonged together. In the Dreyfus affair, however, the *Ligue de la patrie française* and the *Ligue pour la défense des droits de l'homme* faced each other in opposition, although in actual practice the mutual hostility was mitigated by the fact that Clemenceau did not cease to be a patriot, nor did Barrès deny his close ties with the revolution. But, ideologically speaking, dissociation was now on the agenda, especially as the socialists had long been pressing forward in the opposite direction. It was clear that the new nationalism would not become complete, "integral," until it dissociated itself entirely from the ideas of the French revolution. However, in France the counteridea to revolution since the execution of Louis XVI had been that of the monarchy (not the empire, which was regarded as plebiscite democracy). Only a monarchistic nationalism, therefore, would be an integral, that is, antirevolutionary nationalism, although for that very reason not, in the ordinary sense of the word, conservative.

By the same token, the affair brought about the uniting of convictions, trends, and parties that had been hitherto mutually unsympathetic or even hostile: atheists and assumptionists on the one hand, bourgeois radicals and socialists on the other. It cannot be denied that the young men of the Action Française brilliantly discharged their duty of digesting, justifying, and radicalizing the experiences of the Dreyfus affair and thus creating for the Right a coherent ideology adapted to modern requirements. They invented nothing, but they analyzed the system of "counterrevolutionary" doctrines and frequently combined its elements in new syntheses of far-reaching consequences. It has been rightly said that, in the years preceding World War I, nowhere was there an intellectual political general staff of such high caliber as in the youthful Action Française.

Maurras, Vaugeois, and Pujo were joined by Jacques Bainville,[41] a marvel of precocious intelligence, and Léon Daudet,[42] son of the novelist, a rhetorician and polemicist of unbounded vitality; Louis Dimier[43] wrote his book on *Les Maîtres de la contre-révolution au XIXe siècle*, in which he attempted to claim even Proudhon among the forefathers of the Action Française. Pierre Lasserre[44] followed up Maurras' studies of the romantic period and made a name for himself as a literary historian. The most active of all, however, was Maurras. As early as 1899 the little gray review published his essay, *Les Monod peints par eux-mêmes*,[45] in which he traces the history of a Protestant family and advances the thesis that liberalism is the ideological disguise of the will to power of certain groups which in themselves could not be less liberal. Out of this essay grew the famous doctrine of the *Quatre états confédérés: Juifs, protestants, franc-maçons, métèques* (Jews, Protestants, Freemasons, aliens), which divided the French into two groups and denied one of them the right to call itself French. In 1900 there followed *L'Enquête sur la Monarchie*: in an enormous range of questions, answers, and comments, the "neoroyalist" doctrine was developed and substantiated. The short work, *Les Amants de Venise, George Sand et Alfred de Musset*, made the romantic era and especially the romantic idea of love the object of an attack of enduring effectiveness. *L'Avenir de l'Intelligence* offered the intellectuals the alternative of entering either into an enslaving alliance with abstract and cosmopolitan financial powers, or into a liberating co-operation with the aristocracy of blood. The first completely political polemic was directed against Marc Sangnier and the beginnings of Christian Democracy, and attacked both mercilessly as being excrescences of the revolutionary spirit, and more or less openly challenged the ecclesiastical authorities to intervene (*Le dilemme de Marc Sangnier*, 1906). In 1906 the little group dared to do what no party had ever undertaken: it founded a kind of party college, *L'Institut d'Action française* (including what was provocatively called the *Chaire du Syllabus*). It thereby emphasized its intellectual character and underlined its claim to have evolved its own, entirely new doctrine. The year before had seen the founding of the *Ligue d'Action française*, the basic organizational structure of its supporters. By its very name it renounced any claim to be a "party" and ranked itself in the tradition of the great mass and street movements such as Déroulèdes' League of Patriots.[46] In their oath of loyalty, the members swore to further the cause of the monarchy *par tous les moyens*.

At the beginning of 1908 the Action Française could hardly be said to be a political force, but it did represent an intellectual potential of considerable effectiveness whose influence made itself felt throughout France as well as here and there in Italy.

From the Founding of the Newspaper to the End of the War

With the founding of the daily paper in March, 1908, the Action Française entered upon a new phase. It could now no longer be ignored. For the next twenty years it marked the position of the extreme Right in France, and its daily newspaper, with Léon Daudet as editor-in-chief, was the most aggressive and vociferous political organ in the country. Although isolated by its royalism, it was precisely this feature that caused it also to be feared. The republic could still by no means be sure of the army. In 1910 it was possible for Maurras, together with two high-ranking officers (although they remained anonymous), to carry on in full view of the public a detailed discussion of the possibilities of a coup against the regime (*Si le coup de force est possible*). These were the Right's counterpart to *Réflexions sur la violence*; and even though they became less well-known than Sorel's famous essays, they are actually of far greater significance for their time. They are aimed unmistakably at the seizure of political power; they present the first outlines of a blueprint for the March on Rome, while Sorel's violence is at bottom quite unpolitical and is aimed at maintaining alertness and vigilance and at countering the degeneration of capitalism.

It is true that a helpful general, like Monk, for whom Maurras was keeping so anxious a look-out, never materialized. Nevertheless the new violence did not remain purely verbal.

During the winter of 1908–09 a series of public lectures was announced at the Sorbonne, to be given by a Lycée professor by the name of Thalamas, who was said to have "insulted" Joan of Arc. At the first lecture a group of the newly formed *Camelots du Roi* (street vendors of the king) appeared, led by Maurice Pujo; they drowned out the professor with catcalls and bombarded him with various objects; finally one of the group jumped onto the rostrum and brutally slapped the defenseless professor. For the next few weeks the course had to be given under police protection. But the *Camelots* were always finding new ways of creating a disturbance. They started brawls under the windows of the auditorium, got into fights with students who did not share their views, and bewildered the police with silent marches. Pujo made his way with some of his companions into another auditorium, dismissed the astonished professor, and gave a speech in praise of Joan of Arc. The punishments were minor—they were regarded partly as martyrdom and partly as adventures. On the next-to-last day of the course, using a strategy requiring military precision, they managed to enter the auditorium, in spite of the heavy police guard, and beat up the lecturer on the rostrum. Both state and university yielded: the course was not completed.

This was no longer a students' prank, despite all its *opéra bouffe* features. And this violence was not an isolated case.

Right up until the war, the Action Française carried on a fierce campaign against what they called the illegal rehabilitation of Dreyfus by the Court of Appeal in 1906.[47] In the midst of a session a *Camelot* shouted "Traitors!" at the judges of the highest court in the land. The Comédie Française wanted to put on a play by Henry Bernstein. But he had been a deserter. So the Action Française used force to prevent the performance. All over France statues of the most prominent Dreyfusards were destroyed or mutilated. The police either could not or would not protect them. A waiter who sympathized with the

Action Française slapped the president of the republic on the street. With keen logic Maurras proved in his paper that, viewed correctly and with insight, the head of state had been the aggressor in the incident.

It is impossible to ignore the fact that in all these frivolous, or apparently harmless features, the basic structure of fascist violence was becoming clearly discernible: it is organized, not elemental; brutal, not wildly passionate; it aims not merely to wipe out the enemy but to subject him to physical humiliation and moral defamation; it even attacks, immediately and directly, the very cornerstones and shrines of bourgeois life—justice, science, and art—whenever they seem to jeopardize a higher interest; it always comes *post festum*, when the enemy's first wave of attack has subsided; it represents revenge and "a punitive expedition" rather than a means of survival; it incurs no great risks and occurs only with a certain amount of condonation on the part of state and police.

In their interrelationship these elements are without parallel; they cannot be compared with either the completely different violence of the Left or with the turbulent, instinctive, and anarchistic mass movements of the Boulanger crisis, or with anti-Semitic agitation.

A further unprecedented element was introduced into politics by the Action Française with its attitude toward religious issues. It is true that secular parties had long been attempting to improve their position by supporting the Catholic Church—the most typical example was the anxious way in which the anti-clerical bourgeoisie (led by Thiers) gave ground under the impact of the revolution, and the promulgation of the proecclesiastical school law (*Loi Falloux*) of 1850.[48] But it was totally without parallel for a political group headed by atheists and agnostics to go all-out in praise of Catholicism as France's most valuable basic element, and with skill and determination to defend the "Syllabus"—the church's declaration of war on modern society, which even good Catholics were not very readily disposed to discuss.[49]

But the church was engaged in a stubborn and difficult battle against modernism, and it had few allies. The Vatican was the only world power actually to take the Action Française seriously as far back as 1910. Maurras had friends in high places among the Roman and French hierarchy.[50] Pius X himself did not conceal his sympathies; when he granted an audience to Maurras' mother, he said to her of her son: "Je bénis son œuvre."[51] The condemnation of the Sillon—the forerunner of the Christian Democratic movement, founded by Marc Sangnier—was a joint effort. Maurras had laid the groundwork with his ceaseless polemics; the Vatican completed it. There are many places in the papal document on the Sillon which seem to justify the question of whether the phrases were not lifted almost verbatim from Maurras. When Maurras triumphantly published the document in an appendix to his book on Sangnier, he overlooked one important fact: the Sillon was also condemned because in it Catholics collaborated with unbelievers. Was not the Action Française in a similar situation?

It was, in fact, condemned. If it had friends in Rome, it also had powerful enemies, and nothing was less surprising than that. One could accuse Marc Sangnier of whatever one liked, but of one thing there was no doubt at all: he was a fervent and sincere son of the church. But Maurras had put forward theses concerning Catholicism toward which the church was bound to be increasingly sensitive, particularly since they were perceived as mere organization forms and political trends from a more secular point of view. The result was that the Index Congregation condemned several of Maurras' books. Pius X signed the decree, but withheld publication for a later date. He is said to have called Maurras' first books *Damnabiles, non damnandus* (worthy of condemnation, but not condemned).[52] This clearly meant that the church regarded the Action Française as a valuable although impure means to an end which it did not want to relinquish until it had served its purpose. But was not the church a tool in Maurras' hands also? Thus even in those halcyon days an enormous ambiguity casts its shadow over the relation between the Action Française and the Catholic Church.

Also ambiguous, and moreover unsuccessful, was the attempt at an alliance with another great power, syndicalism—a young power, barely constituted but unusually promising. Circumstances favored a resurrection in a new form of the original nationalist-socialist ideas of Henri Vaugeois;[53] the precipitating factor was the collaboration on the newspaper *Action Française* of the highly gifted son of the working class, Georges Valois.[54] The hostility of both movements—the nationalist and the socialist—toward the republic provided the basis and starting point. With Maurras as chairman, supporters of the Action Française and students of Georges Sorel joined together to form the *Cercle Proudhon*, which brought out its own *Cahiers*, whose first statement contained a strange mixture of socialist and nationalist ideas: "Democracy is the greatest error of the past century ... in economics and politics [it] permitted the establishment of the capitalist regime which destroys in the state that which democratic ideas dissolve in the spirit, namely, the nation, the family, morals, by substituting the law of gold for the laws of blood."[55]

Sorel's favorite student, Édouard Berth, later advanced the thesis that *fascisme avant la lettre*[56] was made in the *Cercle Proudhon*. This is an exaggeration. Fascism is more than an aggregate of theoretical convictions; it is a system of a certain consistency, a certain unity of doctrine and practice or organizational form and mode of behavior. No fascist system has been anticapitalist except in a verbal sense, but each has contained, unsuccessfully, a genuine nationalist-socialist tendency. Therefore the failure of the *Cercle Proudhon*—already foreshadowed by Maurras' open dislike of Proudhon and by his clinging to the paternalistic corporatism of de La Tour du Pin—is even more characteristic than its existence, interesting and significant though this may have been.

For the Action Française there were more important things than obscure social-political experiments. At the head of these stood preparation for war.

In 1908 Clemenceau and Picquart held the reins of government, but the era of Poincaré and Barthou was dawning. The public was becoming increasingly alarmed at the neglect of armaments on the part of the government of the victorious Dreyfusards, who, indeed, could not have desired the strengthening of an army which, even at the height of their power, they had been unable really to reform. The *Action Française* incessantly discussed the unfavorable comparison of military expenditures in Germany and France; incessantly it waged war on Jaurès and his "Germanophilia," his pacifist and humanitarian "clouds," and pointed to the loyal and nationalistic nature of the German Social Democrats; Léon Daudet campaigned with frenzied violence against German-Jewish espionage in France.[57] In 1910 Maurras published his book, *Kiel et Tanger*, which has become possibly his best-known work, a penetrating analysis of international politics and an impassioned demand for continuity and determination in foreign political action.[58] When the three-year conscription period was introduced in 1913, the *Ligue d'Action française* and the *Camelots du Roi* went out onto the streets and smashed all attempts at active leftist resistance.

In all fairness it must be admitted that these war preparations on the part of the Action Française did not originate in a liking for war as such, and did not have the unleashing of an attack as their goal. Nor was it a case of an isolated warlike expression: "The reawakening of French pride"[59] was the work of many men and many trends. There is no better indication of its suprapersonal nature than Péguy's evolution from a fundamental antimilitarism to the terrible words: *Jaurès sur la charrette*.[60] But it was basic to Maurras' doctrine that war is an eternal factor in human existence, and an intellectually heightened vision had made him prepare for the onrushing disaster, while Jaurès was still trying to prevent it. When war broke out, Maurras could say: "I saw it and predicted it." But he could only say this like the prophet who announces impending lightning, and plants an oak tree before it strikes.

On July 31, the day of the German mobilization, a deranged fanatic shot and killed the great socialist politician who saw the destruction of his life's dream—that the French republic and the German empire might remain in accord until the world-saving alliance of the socialist democracies of France and Germany could be established—and who nevertheless clung desperately to a last hope. Maurras always denied that he had had Jaurès shot, claiming that the assassin had been a follower of Marc Sangnier.[61] But Sangnier was not the man to have imbued the assassin with such deadly hatred, and in the eyes of the socialists Maurras remained, morally at least, the murderer of Jaurès. And with this, the Action Française's hour of triumph deprived it forever of the chance to enter into a positive relationship with the great masses of the people.

However deeply the war affected the Action Française, and however much it promoted the releasing of intensive energies on the part of those who stayed behind, it nevertheless marked a pause in the political history of the Action Française. Drawn into a political truce, the Action Française no longer had any policy of its own, although it pursued the common policy more relentlessly than any other party. Its share in the war propaganda was considerable. Among other things Maurras published a collection of essays from the years 1890 to 1905 entitled *Quand les Français ne s'aimaient pas—Chronique d'une renaissance*; reminiscence, warning, challenge—all were implicit in the title. But of far greater influence on public opinion was the appearance of Bainville's *Histoire de deux peuples*, which, like all Bainville's books, was distributed through very large printings and contributed, almost more than any other work, to the undermining of the revolutionary-democratic-socialist viewpoint and to the strengthening of the conviction that the dismemberment and impotence of Germany were indispensable to France's peace and greatness. Above all, however, the Action Française hunted down traitors. It consistently regarded socialists with distrust, and it did in fact succeed in instigating the great espionage affair concerning the socialist newspaper *Le Bonnet Rouge*, thereby eliminating one of its most detested enemies, the "anarchist" Vigo-Almereyda. When a changed Clemenceau finally took over the government, it became clear that Jacobinic and "integral" nationalism were capable of excellent mutual understanding in the hour of danger. The Action Française extended considerable aid to the dictator when he used dubious methods to get rid of some of his former political friends (Caillaux, Malvy); throughout his life Clemenceau remained full of sincere admiration for the Action Française. Maurras, never particularly bashful when it came to self-appraisal, said later that Clemenceau had carried out the policy of the Action Française and thereby —that is, by antidemocratic and monarchistic methods—achieved victory.[62] To a degree this is no doubt correct. But Maurras did not ask himself whether, in the final analysis, that form of constitution was not the stronger which in certain circumstances was able to transform itself into its very opposite while its opponents seemed destined to remain unaltered, similar only to themselves.

From the End of the War to the Condemnation by Rome

After the allied victory—which seemed to many people a French victory—the reputation of the Action Française was at its zenith. No one could deny or belittle its participation in the triumph. Even its position—on the extreme Right within the now decidedly "rightist"-oriented country—was bound to ensure that its influence would be considerable.

Yet there is little doubt that the end of the war sounded the death knell for development in the direction that the Action Française itself was inclined to regard as paramount. A monarchist restitution could have come out of a defeat, but the victorious republic seemed to refute Maurras' theses so palpably that a royalist restoration never again became a real possibility. Royalism, therefore, paralyzed the strength of its position and became an insurmountable barrier excluding the Action Française from any participation in political power.

Furthermore, even the overall significance attributable to the Action Française as the paradigm of a supranational trend was now forfeited. Its younger cousins in Italy and Germany were developing (in more favorable circumstances) with astonishing energy and soon left it with only a place in the shade. What did it signify, after all, that Léon Daudet now and again tyrannized the Right in parliament and frantically called for a court indictment of Briand? At the same time in Rome a successful antiparliamentarian ironically congratulated parliament on the fact that he had not commandeered the chamber as quarters for his victorious Blackshirts. What, after all, did it signify that in 1925, when some followers of the Action Française were assassinated or killed in brawls, Maurras threatened the minister of the interior (a Jew) by open letter that he would shoot him down like a dog if the police did not take effective protective measures?[63] Soon the world would be witnessing very different instances of unpunished defiance of government authority. And what, finally, did it signify when, led by the Action Française, the law students at the Sorbonne used force to impose their will on the minister of the interior in a minor issue? What had fifteen years earlier been the first rumblings of distant eruptions and had thus had a legitimate claim on public interest, was in the stormy postwar period a trivial event of purely local significance. Without a doubt, the Action Française was losing ground because it was no longer advancing.

Yet it would be mistaken to regard the Action Française as being merely a local French phenomenon for the rest of its existence. The situation in which it functioned remained of a paradigmatic nature; and the fact that they were mainly intellectual situations, remote from considerations of national-political objectives and responsibilities, makes their analysis all the more valuable. The Action Française still had to contend with the following issues:

1. The victory of its own people over the hated archenemy. This is a situation which never confronted Mussolini's Italy, or only (in 1940) in an incidental and spurious way, and one which National Socialist Germany experienced momentarily after its initial successes in the Soviet Union.

2. The resistance of conservative forces, in the shadow of which it had grown up. In similar situations, Mussolini was ousted, Hitler triumphed.

3. The fact of being drawn into the center of gravity of a stronger power, at once related and hostile: the fate of Italy after 1935.

4. Its own victory, which from start to finish coincides with the nation's defeat. This is an exaggerated foreshortening of the character of both fascist and National Socialist rule. (Although Italian fascism was preceded by the Italian victory in World War I, its point of departure was an interpretation

which regarded the result of the peace negotiations as a defeat; the end of Vichy coincided with what the world in general regarded as the victory of France, but, according to Maurras, it constituted the nation's defeat, and in fact it was a defeat of that part of the nation which was represented by Pétain.)

5. Its own glaring and hopeless defeat. It is the final stage of the Action Française, of Italian fascism, and of National Socialism, and *only* of these three among all the trends which can in a broad and provisional sense be called "fascist" and regarded as original phenomena. This issue is faced only by the Action Française, because only the head of the Action Française (who, like Hitler and Mussolini after him, had long *been* the movement) survived the defeat. Mussolini was for a short time in a comparable situation during the *Repubblica di Salò*.

Its confrontation with the nation's triumph in 1918 contained the seeds of its future defeats. From the very first day, the Action Française had protested vehemently against the use to which the government and the allies wanted to put the victory bought at the price of so much French blood. It believed that "the bad treaty" rendered France's sacrifice useless in that, although it harassed and tormented the defeated enemy, it did not strike at his very mainspring, his national entity. To France's undoing this entity was declared by democratic tradition to be inviolate, but out of it must necessarily grow the great war of revenge. Jacques Bainville's *Conséquences politiques de la paix* contained a masterly popular analysis and political prophecy. (In National Socialist Germany this book was translated as an example of the French desire to annihilate. The fact was overlooked that, on the contrary, it was evidence of the strength of a tradition which did not regard the desire to annihilate as the highest law of the land and which thereby preserved Germany's national existence.) As always, Maurras expressed himself more violently and more radically.[64]

He demanded the immediate partition of Germany into its twenty-six states and did not hesitate to regard a *bolchévisme bienfaisant*[65] as desirable for Germany. He denounced what he called the Germanomaniac feelings of the French socialists, radicals, and Jews, proposed measures which included the transformation of Germany into a military colony, and missed no opportunity of emphasizing that the partition of Germany was the *only* way of preventing a war of revenge being waged with overwhelming ferocity. This intelligent man was dazzled and defeated by his own mania: did he not realize that he was paving the way for France's defeatism, self-doubts, and moral disarmament against the impending moment when the unreality of the partition plans was to become evident? Was he not aware that he was giving advice which was factually and morally impossible for France to implement, but which virtually anticipated Hitler when he shouted in a frenzy before the Geneva Conference: "Act, act, act, before the windbags get together!"[66]

Condemnation by the Vatican

Maurras had no sense of his own inconsistency. Even after 1925, when German unity was assured and its political and economic rise were well under way, he did not switch to a policy of alliances, of collective security, or even reconciliation with Germany. His idea was still to rely entirely on France's strength, and to regard the Action Française as the chief pillar of this strength. This partially explains his behavior during the worst internal shock ever experienced by the Action Française: its condemnation by the Vatican.[67]

The history of this condemnation is fraught with many obscure features, despite the quality of inevitability inherent in the events themselves. Seen in detail, the letter of the Archbishop of Bordeaux, Cardinal Andrieu, to the youth of his diocese, marking the first stage of the condemnation, is anything but a masterpiece of a fair, thorough analysis. Seen as a whole, however, it defines the point at issue with perfect clarity: "Catholics by calculation, not by conviction, the men who lead the Action Française use the church, or hope at least to use it; but they do not serve it, since they reject the divine message which it is the church's mission to propagate."

Indeed the church found itself in a very strange position vis-à-vis the Action Française. The latter did not espouse an anticlerical doctrine to be condemned from without in open conflict, like liberalism and socialism, nor was it a sect in the bosom of the church itself, representing deviationist doctrinal opinions. Where doctrine was concerned it was almost impossible to come to grips with it. The well-known demand, *politique d'abord*, did not necessarily have to be interpreted axiologically. The equally well-known (and ill-famed) postulate, *par tous les moyens, même légaux*, could be rendered harmless by distinguishing between the terms "illegal" and "illegitimate." With a polite gesture the whole supernatural doctrinal edifice of the church was left unmolested; what radical hostility toward Christianity appeared in Maurras' early writings could be regarded separately as mere private opinion. The church, then, was in an awkward position. It was continually having to fight unbelievers who were fighting the church; in this case it was confronted by unbelievers who supported the church and whose support it had long accepted. It now had to pay for Pius X's distinction between *damnabilis* and *damnandus*. If it abstained from condemnation for reasons of policy, would not final condemnation then have to be regarded as policy pure and simple?

This accounts for the church's difficulty in disembarrassing itself of these new friends. This accounts for the condemnation taking place in stages and for its final formulation being based on events which took place during this very process.

In the first place, in September, 1926, Pope Pius XI sent a letter to Cardinal Andrieu congratulating him on his initiative. In it he emphasized the ambiguous atmosphere within the Action Française which threatened to alienate the faithful "imperceptibly" from the true Catholic spirit; the faithful were not permitted to follow the leaders of the Action Française "blindly" in matters of morals or faith.

It still seemed as if it might be possible to come to terms. Jacques Maritain, a rising star in the firmament of neoscholasticism and a long-time admirer of Maurras, made some proposals for mediation in his book, *Une opinion sur Charles Maurras et le devoir des catholiques*, which were welcomed by a number of bishops. But between the *Osservatore Romano* and the *Action Française* there arose a polemical controversy in which Maurras, who never minced words, saw the whole problem solely in its political aspects and vehemently denounced what he called a German-Briandist conspiracy to "dupe" the Holy See. Thereupon the papal address of December 20 pronounced the unequivocal condemnation: "Catholics are not permitted to adhere to the school of those who place the interests of parties above religion and make religion the servant of those interests."[68]

Now it became apparent what the hierarchy and two thousand years of wisdom meant to Maurras when they contradicted his own insight and his own will. The reply is as unequivocal as the papal declaration: "The father who demands of his son that he kill his mother or, what amounts to the same thing, that he have his mother killed, can be listened to with respect; he cannot be obeyed. ... We shall not betray our country. Non possumus."[69]

This reply was as redolent with bad taste and total lack of respect as it was of boundless self-conceit. It was the final rupture. From now the *Action Française* became "the most anticlerical newspaper in France"[70] and one which did not shrink from attacks on the person of the pope himself. The church drew the final line in March of the following year: the French episcopate almost unanimously approved the pope's action,[71] the unrepentant members of the Action Française were threatened with the church's direst punishments. A series of individual tragedies followed: many instances of furtive disobedience within the church, and, above all, within its orders; but on the whole the operation was successful. The church proved itself to be the only established and con-servative power capable of breaking with its neoconservative friends on its own initiative, and of freeing itself from the dangerous parasitic plants which had grown up in its shade and from its own roots. (When the Count of Paris did the same thing in 1937, the monarchy had long ceased to have any independent strength.) The unsatisfactory and ultimately brutal elements of the process of condemnation were the price the church had to pay for its long hesitation and waiting.

From the Vatican's Condemnation to the Defeat of France

Thus once again the situation of the Action Française underwent a profound change. If royalism, its teeth drawn since 1918, prevented it from extending over the entire Right, so the condemnation deprived it, if not of its whole body of Catholic followers, at least of a coming generation from among young Catholics as well as of a powerful moral support. New rightist organizations shot up; the example of victorious Italian fascism was a stimulus. But the Action Française was the least able to profit by this example since, as the older organization, it had itself set the example for fascism. To many lively young minds, the Action Française now seemed an ancient, rigid, desiccated relic. What did Maurras' masters—Renan, Taine, Comte—mean to the world of youth? This world felt liberated by Bergson, fascinated by Gide, inspired by Proust. Had not positivism become dusty and obsolete? Was not Maurras closing his eyes to all that was vital and mobile in literature and life?

Georges Valois left the Action Française and, following in Mussolini's footsteps, founded his *Faisceau*. Pierre Taittinger's *Jeunesses Patriotes* had an overwhelming mass success. During the thirties Colonel de la Rocque's *Croix de Feu* entered the spotlight. Astonishing successes were achieved by the *Parti Populaire Français* under the inspiring leadership of Jacques Doriot, a renegade from communism.[72] The former socialist Marcel Déat took his first independent steps on the Right. Finally there arose under the Popular Front regime the *Cagoule*, a terrorist organization which was founded by an erstwhile supporter of the Action Française and which had the temerity to deride its origin as "Inaction Française." All these movements[73] display more fascist traits than the Action Française itself, if the basic characteristics of fascism are taken to be turbulence, uniforms, military maneuvers, and an expression of determination, in the manner of Mussolini, on the face of a dynamic leader.

In the midst of this young new world the Action Française stood like some random monolith from ancient times. It cannot, of course, be seriously maintained that it had become old and inert: it triggered the Stavisky scandal, had its due share in the attempted rebellion of February 6, 1934, and its League was dissolved in 1936 by Léon Blum along with all the other Leagues. But it no longer held the position of the extreme Right in the political world and had ceased to have a monopoly on impassioned speeches and violent gestures. As one among many it saw itself confronted by the crucial problem of what attitude to adopt toward the most successful movement of its own kind— toward fascism and later toward National Socialism. Admittedly there were but few who took the easy path of the newly formed little group of Marcel Bucard's Francists, who in 1934 sent Mussolini and even Hitler telegrams expressing their solidarity.[74] But the Action Française had the most difficult task of all, for it alone was not an imitator.

In his diaries, Bainville had unreservedly welcomed the victory of fascism because to him it meant the defeat of the revolutionary socialist and Communist forces.[75] Maurras expressed himself with greater caution. He regretted that the *idées justes* had not triumphed in France but instead had now led to the strengthening of Italy[76] (whose national unification he had always declared to be a disastrous result of Napoleon III's foolish policy). But he did not hide the fact that he felt sympathy not only for the salutary ideas of fascism but also for its champions, the Italian nationalists, for whom the Action Française had indeed often been a model and a stimulus. However, he was apparently prevented from giving all his sympathies because of the person of Mussolini himself, who, as a former revolutionary, always remained suspect in his eyes.

The ambiguity became manifest when Italy conducted its colonial war against Ethiopia. Together with the entire rightist press, Maurras plunged into a fierce opposition of the sanctions decided upon in Geneva. When a hundred and forty leftist deputies demanded a further tightening of sanctions, Maurras publicly and explicitly threatened them with death.[77] He always claimed that national motives alone, and no preference whatever for the fascist ideology, were the determining factors for him. Only France's alliance with Rome could have subdued Hitler; only the ideological blindness of the Left could have overlooked this fundamental postulate of national policy. But the so-called Manifesto of French Intellectuals[78] of October 4, 1935, published in a roundabout way by the Action Française and also signed by Maurras, speaks another language. Here an out-and-out preference for the social system of Italy and an undisguised aversion to all forms of "antifascism" are voiced. The war against Ethiopia is not only accepted, it is specifically vindicated as being the struggle of civilization against barbarism.

There is one still clearer proof that national interest was not the sole decisive factor in Maurras' attitude. When the Spanish civil war broke out, he supported Franco without reservation; he made a personal visit to Spain, long before the French republic had assumed relations with the rebel military regime. His report[79] of his journey is an enthusiastic, mythologizing paean of praise. This enthusiasm obviously does not spring from national considerations. At that very moment France was being threatened (regardless of opinions on causes and desirability) on two fronts by countries with related systems. To encourage the rise of a third related system on the third and last frontier bordered on treason. His enthusiasm sprang from a social, wholly supranational emotion—from the joy of seeing the "powers of darkness" overcome by the champions of "light."

However, toward Hitler and Germany Maurras knew no such ambiguity of emotion and thought. As early as 1933 he had issued warnings, later on he called National Socialism an "Islam of the North."[80] In 1937 he published a book called *Devant l'Allemagne Éternelle*, the preface to which contains some valuable insights,[81] although, generally speaking, it is merely a collection of earlier articles. This is yet another example of that narcissism by which his own history was becoming his main concern. No matter how often the *Action Française* printed its *Armons, armons, armons!*, its opposition to Hitler remained strangely weak and ineffectual. The reason was obvious: in order for Maurras' opposition to be imbued with strength and energy, he would have had to join forces with "antifascism," which he actually detested as an enemy of society no less than as the enemy of the nation. The result was a paradox at once typical and tragic: Germany's oldest and bitterest enemy was pursuing a policy which in practically all respects was tantamount to a support of Hitler.[82] He is against an alliance with the Soviet Union, he not only delivers up Czechoslovakia but defames it; he is against living up to the obligations toward Poland since it is in any event beyond aid. His *Que pouvez-vous pour la Pologne?* is a worthy counterpart to Déat's famous *Mourir pour Dantzig?* Together with the entire French Right, out of hatred for the internal enemy Maurras pursued a policy of cowardice and defeat. But Déat, Doriot, and Laval later acknowledged that their chief concern was that of social order and cultural traditions (strange as this acknowledgment may sound coming from them). Maurras never ceased to detest Germany as intensely as he detested communism. And that is why by the eve of the war the defeat of Maurras was already the most certain defeat of all.

Vichy[83]

It is characteristic of this defeat that it bore the illusion of victory.

Although the Pétain regime was the fruit of defeat, it was in no way comparable to any of the quisling governments which proliferated in Europe, all of which were stigmatized by their remoteness from the true feelings of the country concerned. On the contrary, Marshal Pétain's assumption of responsibility met with his country's almost unanimous approval: in fact the view was practically universal in France that the military defeat was equivalent to the defeat of the parliamentary system. How else than under the pressure of overwhelming public opinion could Laval have managed to induce the vast majority of deputies to make the voluntary renunciation which ensured not only legality but a new kind of legitimacy to the Pétain regime? For several months everyone in France was talking about democracy and parliamentarianism the way, forty years earlier, Maurras had been talking almost alone. Marshal Pétain had always been sympathetically inclined toward Maurras' ideas, now his immediate environment consisted of men who were Maurras' pupils.[84] Soon after taking over the government he called Maurras *le plus français des Français*, and Maurras in turn extended Pétain his full and enthusiastic support. René Benjamin said at the time that France had two great men: one was the power of action, Pétain; the other the power of thought, Maurras. Maurras did not hide his jubilation at the triumph of his ideas: "When will this agave blossom finally burst through the hard shell? Sometimes it needs less than twenty-five years. Ours needed forty years. But here it is at last."[85] In almost complete disregard of the cautions necessitated by defeat, he spoke of Pétain's appearance (using a literary metaphor) as a *divine surprise*.[86] Indirectly it became quite clear that he was prepared to welcome the defeat if it meant the triumph of his ideas. For now his country would find its way back to its own identity and at last embark upon a swift ascent.

This was the hope that gave the *Révolution nationale* its initial impetus and its initial optimism. In the land of the oldest tradition of counterrevolutionary thinking it would be possible—and Maurras was not alone in this belief—to endow the national rebirth with that conservative, moderate, and reasonable character which fascism and National Socialism transcended to the point of the extreme and the radical. But even the brief upsurge of Vichy and the "national revolution" sufficed to show the true state of affairs regarding two of Maurras' basic ideas: monarchy and federalism.

Pétain became the object of all the elemental monarchistic emotions still existing among the French people: women held up their children for him to touch, the provinces of France ceremoniously presented their savior with gifts.

And Maurras did not dissociate himself: he led the country in this total surrender to the person of Pétain. The man who criticized the pope and offered resistance to his king when their ideas seemed to him mistaken, now preached blind submission when Pétain led France onto the path of collaboration, a path which almost inevitably meant France's ultimate downfall.[87] The man who for forty years had championed the House of Bourbon, now uttered no word of protest when Pétain and Laval agreed to give the Count of Paris a cool reception. The man whose best-known early work outlined to the intellectuals their liberation through an alliance with the aristocracy of blood, now spoke in words of the most grotesque self-emasculation of mind and spirit in favor of the most hackneyed military regime. Thus the old suspicion is borne out that Maurras' monarchism was no more traditional and genuine than his Catholicism. Because of this, as early as 1931 Waldemar Gurian defined it as "Caesarism freed of its momentary character."[88] This is not entirely correct because Bonapartism was also a Caesarism of this kind. Maurras' monarchism is better described as a Caesarism detached from its revolutionary origins (and thus capable of appearing all the more "revolutionary" in the present age, determined as this age had been for the past hundred and fifty years by the traditions of the French revolution). If this definition is correct, the distance separating it from fascism and National Socialism is once again considerably diminished.

The same applies to federalism, that oldest and most respected item in Maurras' program. The fact that steps were taken to restore the former provinces filled him with deep satisfaction. But for the time being these steps were without practical significance. Of the utmost practical significance, however, was the fact that government regulations deprived the organs of local administration of all independent status, that henceforward the mayors of even small towns were appointed by the central government, that the tremendous administrative power of the prefects was further increased. And in the face of all this Maurras was not merely silent: he welcomed it, he actually stated that the principal points of his earliest federalist program had been illusory.[89] He slapped his face with his own hand and proudly displayed the red mark for all to see.

Other fallacies were exposed one after another as the star of Vichy and the "national revolution" began to set. It must have been clear to every thinking person that, at the very latest with the occupation of all France by German troops in November, 1942, an independent French existence was a thing of the past, even in name. The clandestine rebuilding of a national armed force in which Maurras, misled by the analogy of Germany in 1813 and 1918, had placed such great hopes, turned out to be completely ineffectual. Pétain virtually left all governmental power in the hands of Pierre Laval, and Laval was firmly counting on a German victory, as were Déat, Doriot, and the other collaborators, while increasingly large segments of the population joined the Resistance and the French schism assumed its newest form.

Maurras continued to publish the *Action Française* in Lyons. As if France were still an independent state, he preached a steady and unswerving devotion to the long since powerless Maréchal, and persisted in his hatred of the English and the Jews. Around him the atmosphere had become cold and lonely: Jacques Bainville had been dead since 1936, and Léon Daudet changed very much before he died in 1942; the most gifted of the younger ones were now "traitors" and collaborators: Drieu la Rochelle, Lucien Rebatet, Dominique Sordet, Robert Brasillach.[90] He was the only one, it seemed, who remained what he had always been. But circumstances having intrinsically altered, features were now exposed which had hitherto been concealed.

The first to be uncovered was the true nature of his anti-Semitism. He had always claimed that his *antisémitisme d'État* differed essentially from the German *antisémitisme de peau*; he was concerned, so he said, not with the destruction or even the exclusion of Jews, but with turning pernicious and illegitimate masters into useful servants of the common weal.

But when Vichy's first laws affecting Jews made them second-class citizens, and barred them from all access to public office, Maurras doubted the wisdom of letting them retain even their money.[91]

When the Jews in occupied France were forced in May, 1942, to wear armbands with the Star of David, this provoked silent and bitter indignation among nearly all Frenchmen, but Maurras did not deem the German *antisémitisme de peau* worthy of protest or even of silence. On the contrary, he regarded it as a suitable opportunity to rid France, too, of the "Jewish scourge."[92]

When in 1944 a Jew proposed that some of the Eastern European Jews under threat of extermination be settled in deserted French villages, he was so indignant at the thought that *ce qu'il y a de plus crasseux dans les ghéttos de l'Europe centrale* might come to France that he named the Jew in question publicly and in such a manner that he was bound to fall into the clutches of German or French authorities.[93]

So much hardness of heart and coldness of thought make it unlikely that between Maurras' and Hitler's anti-Semitism the basic difference existed which Maurras was always so keen to emphasize.

Above all, however, it was during those years of supreme test that the true nature of Maurras' nationalism was revealed, that is, of his motivation and his real as opposed to ostensible aim.

Immediately after the capitulation, Maurras had proclaimed the watchword: *Unité française d'abord*, the routine formula of traditional nationalism. But it very soon became clear that powerful forces were at work to dissolve it. In the very first days after Pétain took over the government, Maurras had been obliged angrily to break off relations with his pupil and colleague Dominique Sordet because Sordet wanted, instead of the halfhearted and hesitant support of Germany by France which was now inevitable, a sincere and determined co-operation, thus paving the way for collaboration. At about the same time he had to brand as treason the famous appeal of General de Gaulle, of a man who had been far from unsympathetic toward the Action Française. No attitude could have been more correct and legitimate if it were a case of the problems confronting a sovereign and independent state; no attitude could have been more blind and foolish in a case of life and death in a conquered country in the throes of a confrontation between two mighty blocs where there could be no compromise either politically, militarily, or ideologically. The best and most moving aspect of Pétain's activity, his desire to protect the French people, to remain with them as a living consolation, as a hostage prepared to sacrifice himself,[94] sprang not from political but from humane motives. He could not defend himself against becoming a pawn of German policy. Maurras, on the other hand, became precisely this on his own initiative. Of course, he continued to attack the collaborators, among whom were so many of his most outstanding pupils, but here censorship obliged him to exercise caution and discretion; on the other hand, the *Action Française* inveighed long and loudly against Englishmen, Jews, and Gaullists. This made it in a twofold sense an asset to German policy: it advocated highly desirable foreign political ideas, and corresponded exactly to the directive given to Abetz, that of sowing discord among the French. Maurras was no less subject than anyone else to the overriding law of the extraordinary situation, which Pierre Laval had once put into words with the apt remark: "There are two men who can save our country at this moment; and if I were not Laval I would like to be General de Gaulle."[95]

Perhaps Maurras' error is more tragic and more deserving of respect than Laval's obsequious insight, but only for a limited period. Why, even in 1943–44, did he have to persist in his campaign against the *communo-gaullistes* although nobody could seriously doubt any longer that the small, "traitorous" secession of 1940 had become France's sole hope of liberation and all the *gloire* of French history had meanwhile attached itself to its banners? Why did he so passionately oppose the invasion, when France was feverishly awaiting the liberation forces and did not count the inevitable sacrifices?

The grounds for his opposition to Gaullism and the Resistance were presumably social. Because to him the Resistance was primarily a social danger,[96] he opposed it to the bitter end, although obviously national interest had, at least for the time being, become inseparable from it.

His hostility to the invasion (especially that from the south), his absurd accusation that, out of hatred for France, the Anglo-Saxons had desisted from the possible landing in Germany itself, is at first sight incomprehensible. The answer is to be found by looking at certain places in some of his very early writings, where he reviews the blood-and-soil novels of Émile Pouvillon and presents the dubious thesis that the firm foundation of all patriotism is the love of one's own native place, one's own church tower.[97] Evidently it was this local patriotism which caused him to give priority to the stones of his native place over the honor of his country.

For fifty years Maurras had claimed that he represented the *pays réel* as against the *pays légal*. When this distinction finally assumed tangible shape, when a regime vanished like smoke before the will of the nation, he was the ultimate defender of the powerless *pays légal*. For fifty years he had been the foremost figure of nationalism. But the nation's hour laid bare the roots of his nationalism: the one was supranational, the other prenational.

He was truly an utterly defeated man when early in September, 1944, he hid from the troops who were marching into Lyons and a few days later was arrested.

Charles Maurras' Trial, Imprisonment, and Death

This brings the history of the Action Française to a close. No issue of the paper ever appeared again; no political organization bears this name. But as an epilogue, Maurras' trial, imprisonment, and final years are inseparable from it.

From its very outset the Maurras trial[98] showed extraordinary similarities with the Dreyfus trial. Like Dreyfus, Maurras was brought before a special tribunal outside the ordinary administration of justice: a revolutionary court took the place of a court martial. Moreover, no motive whatever could be found for the crime of which Maurras was accused—*intelligences avec l'ennemi en vue de favoriser ses entreprises*. The indictment itself was compiled hastily and carelessly; the most copious incriminating document, a collection of quotations from the *Action Française*, was prepared by a man of doubtful integrity and contained so many inaccuracies that in places it is tantamount to a forgery. Of the weightiest accusations—that in his paper Maurras had denounced French members of the Resistance by name or with so little concealment that they were arrested by the militia or the Gestapo and in some cases killed—only the first half turned out to be warranted; the second and more serious half could not be proved with certainty. The old man of seventy-five, against whom the entire press was conducting a violent campaign, defended himself with a strange mixture of pride, independence, and insolence. He called the public prosecutor "Monsieur le procureur de la femme sans tête" (that is, the republic), dashed to pieces Claudel's very superficial indictment, described his political evolution with monotonous verbosity, and remained completely unshaken and devoid of self-doubts.

However, he was not facing judges desirous of objectivity, but enemies whose purpose was an act of political annihilation. He was sentenced to life imprisonment and *dégradation nationale*. There is no doubt that juristically this was a miscarriage of justice, since no *intention* to collaborate could be proved and, moreover, certain documents in his favor were withheld from the court.[99] All this had a great deal of similarity with the Dreyfus case. But the overwhelming difference is that in a metajuristic sense the indictment was correct; that, seen objectively, Maurras did collaborate with the enemy, and that the sentence was the expression of a higher justice. It excluded him from that France which from the very beginning he had dismissed from *his* France.

Did Maurras mean with his cry, *C'est la revanche de Dreyfus!*, that he wanted to go over these strange and confusing circumstances once again in his mind? Would it not have been natural for him now, in the light of this parallelism, to ponder the problem of the guarantee of rights in the state and the multiple threats to them? Could one not expect from him, a man who was more than just a politician, something more than memoirs and vindications? Was there to be no final reckoning with half a century of political experience and thus with himself—a redefining of that part of his own thought which was enduring, and of that part whose weakness had been exposed by failure?

Although his years in prison proved to be the richest period of Maurras' literary productivity, they contained nothing of all that which might have been anticipated. The inflexibility of old age and the peculiar rigidity of Maurras' classicist thought combined to produce an almost frightening phenomenon best typified by processes of nature: the crystalline hardness of flint, the fertility of the tropical jungle, ever renewed but ever the same, the monotony of falling raindrops.[100]

Maurras discourses; he discourses ceaselessly on his life, which also means on the story of the Action Française, and for the historian this is often very revealing. But even the most interesting sections bear the mark of a monomaniacal narcissism which cannot shake off either Thalamas or Marius Plateau,[101] and which imprints the stamp of the absolute on persons and events that are at best significant as symptomatic manifestations. Thus the central idea of his book, *Le bienheureux Pie X., sauveur de la France*, is that Pius X condemned Marc Sangnier, Marc Sangnier had been a kind of Christian Jaurès, Jaurès had wanted to destroy France, hence Pius X was the savior of France. This thesis implies the existence of two others (and is obviously intended to imply them): Maurras paved the way for the salvation of France, and the present Christian

Democracy would lead to communism. The first thesis is doubtful, the second incorrect. They are wrapped up in a highly partisan presentation of history.

In those places where Maurras' historiography is not self-glorification, it is self-vindication. He justifies the continued publication of the *Action Française* after November, 1942, by saying that it was intended to prevent worse things from happening.[102] But all those whom Maurras called "traitors," headed by Laval, have claimed this argument and had good reason to do so.

He seeks to justify his policy before World War II by a whole series of conjunctives, an idyllic world history of unrealities,[103] culminating in the supposition: *If* the forces of democracy had followed my advice and had avoided war in 1939 ... , France's prestige would have increased enormously, and Hitler would soon have voluntarily offered himself up for execution.

As for his nationalism—this he explains by the most insincere argument of all: nationalism is so far from being outmoded that even the U.S.A. and the Soviet Union are national and nationalistic phenomena.[104] Yet this was the very thing of which he continually accused the French revolution—that it had aroused a national awareness among all peoples, thus sacrificing France's unique priority. The most naïve argument of all backfires on its originator: if the Soviet Union is nationalistic, then nationalist *ideology* in Maurras' sense is a *quantité négligeable*; then conceivably even the struggle against Jaurès was superfluous and foolish.

Ultimately, therefore, it is not surprising that in the fundamental matter of the Action Française's relation to fascism and National Socialism, Maurras has little to say that is pertinent and nothing that is revealing. In typical propagandist fashion he tirelessly reiterates the thesis that National Socialism is a Hitlerism and as such a new form of Fichteanism: in other words, the exact opposite, the very antithesis, of the Action Française.[105] Hence he claims that denazification must mean de-Germanization, or it will amount to nothing.[106] The second thesis throws light on the actual value of the first. It is the outright expression of the inclination (if not personal, at least factual) toward genocide, which links him with Hitler.

As for fascism, he does not deny a certain ideological kinship for the period up to 1943, but he immediately takes the contrasting attitude toward the problem of centralism and raises it as an insurmountable obstacle in this temporary marriage.[107]

A quite different impression is gained, however, by recalling some of his books written during the period of triumph (1940 to 1943). Here he does not hesitate to place the Action Française, fascism, and National Socialism in one positive parallel;[108] here he uses the term fascism in its broadest sense;[109] here he claims for the French counterrevolutionary tradition (that is, for himself) an ideological leadership vis-à-vis not only the Portuguese and the Italians but also the Germans.[110]

In March, 1952, the president of the republic released Maurras on account of his great age. As if to carry through the similarity with the fate of Dreyfus up to the very end, a revisionist movement had meanwhile grown up in his favor (led by the former Dreyfusard, Daniel Halévy); but Maurras accepted his freedom without insisting on prior rehabilitation. He never saw Paris again, however, as he had to go to a clinic in Tours. The Catholic Church had never forsaken him, so now they sent him a priest who did not shirk the last uphill struggle.[111] He died, on November 16, 1952, reconciled with the church, reconciled perhaps even with the Christian God: there is a beautiful poem of his in *La Balance Intérieure*, his last collection of poems, which bears out this assumption.[112]

It must have been more than accidental that his end differed so greatly from the death of other leaders of fascist movements. Maurras was the first man in Europe who as a thinker and a politician drove conservatism beyond the limits dividing it from incipient fascism. But his environment, mode of life, and level of thought prevented him from burning all his bridges behind him. He did not succeed in destroying the conservative power, on which he leaned, as Mussolini destroyed the monarchy and Hitler destroyed the army. In spite of all his intellectual extremism, he nevertheless *also* gave new form to age-old insights of the conservative tradition in a manner both brilliant and convincing. That is why it was not merely for him personally that a way back remained open: the history of his ideas also did not come to an end with his death. Freed from his personality and rid of their most radical features, they still form an element of the present day in his own country[113] as well as far beyond its borders, thereby constituting a root of the future.

CHAPTER THREE

Practice as Consequence

Introduction: The Place of Practice and Its Motivations

Political practice *can* be the consequence of a doctrine. The Action Française is an outstanding example of this. Doctrine *can* be the ultimate formative power, but it can be also be adroitly flourished and manipulated by a completely self-centered individual, or it can be the immobile pillow under the head of an organization which has grown complacent.

But the union of doctrine and practice does not mean they are identical. On the contrary, their relationship harbors a remarkable diversity.

It is possible for doctrine to outweigh practice to such a degree that the latter becomes a mere consequence. Practice is thus denied all the countless compromises which generally go to make up the "history" of a party and the day-to-day existence of politics. This practice knows nothing of the many roads that lead to Rome: it knows only the one, laborious road, one which, however, opens the way to paradise.

The best example is Marxism. Never before had a political movement declared war so uncompromisingly on *all* existing conditions. Never had a radical declaration of war met with such a response. Never was there a great thinker and writer who showed such a will to fight and such a talent for organization as Marx. But the only reason he was able to carry out his "union of theory and practice" so smoothly was because it hovered in the void beyond reality and had no need of compromise. However, when youthful Marxism was faced by its first really significant political act, and the amalgamation of the Eisenach group and the followers of Lassalle into the Social Democratic party was being arranged, Marx wrote his ruthless *Critique of the Gotha Programme*, which unhesitatingly placed the purity of doctrine ahead of political expediency. But Bebel went his own way, and it was with this very inconsistency that he created the conditions necessary for a mass party and for a new stage in consistent policy which, despite all reformism, remained officially valid until the outbreak of the war in 1914. It was not until forty years after its founding that the German Social Democratic party ceased to be a paradigm for the priority of doctrine.

The opposite alternative is that of practice as premise, of which the best example appears to be Italian fascism. Fascism in Italy in 1919, in its earliest form and in line with Mussolini's own development, was a revolutionary nationalist-socialist movement whose domestic political program was one of extreme radicalism. But it did not meet with success until, after the failure of the socialist attempts at revolution, it became the protagonist of "reaction" and of the allegedly still threatened order. Ideological justification followed but slowly and hesitantly in the vigorous footsteps of practice. Finally the "priority of action over theory" actually became one of the cardinal points of Italian fascist doctrine.

But even if this interpretation required neither correction nor reservation, the question must arise of whether this is an underlying trait of all fascist movements, or whether such a sharp difference exists that it is legitimate to separate Italian fascism completely from the Action Française and from National Socialism. For as far as the Action Française is concerned, it is obvious that, in its view, doctrine was of primary significance, and whatever opinion we may have of Hitler's *Weltanschauung*, he unquestionably regarded it as the most important element in his political activity. Yet to Maurras and Hitler doctrine and practice never possessed that unbroken unity that they did to Marx and the young Mussolini. It was only in their earliest days that they could risk presenting their doctrines openly and unreservedly; they were soon forced to subterfuge and caution out of consideration for their allies. And Mussolini for his part had much to hide: namely, the fifteen Marxist years of his active life. In all forms of fascism, therefore, in complete contrast to Marxism, the relation between doctrine and practice is complex and obscure. It is not easy to distinguish between consequence, premise, and opportunistic adaptability.

This is why the study of practice is so important. In the case of the Action Française it is very difficult because of the scarcity of material, but it, too, promises disclosures of a particularly interesting kind. The organization and fighting methods of the Action Française can no more be interpreted as consequences of World War I than can its doctrine. Until 1914 they were clearly defined in their basic outline. Although, compared to what came later, they may seem unimpressive in their proportions, they nevertheless have the unique significance of the rudimentary and the initial.

Organization of the Action Française

By the very choice of its name, the little group founded by Vaugeois and Pujo let it be known that it was determined on a course of political activity and did not intend merely to represent a group of intellectuals. Its modest beginnings and Maurras' role in them have already been discussed, as have the initial successes: the founding of the *Ligue d'Action française*, the setting up of the *Institut d'Action française*, the founding of the daily paper, the earliest deeds of the *Camelots du Roi*. The close relationship between the chief components of the organization and the rapid expansion of each of them characterize the course of events until the outbreak of war.

From the start, the daily paper was entirely at the service of its political organizations: under the heading *Ligue d'Action française* it announced all coming events; a roll of honor listed the wounded and the arrested; and considerable space was devoted to the lectures at the *Institut d'Action française*. By the same token, the League could be regarded as a kind of sales organization for the paper, this object being implicit in the name *Camelots du Roi* (street vendors of the king).

The *Camelots* were not the only branch of the League; there were also the *Étudiants d'Action française*, the *Dames royalistes*, and the *Jeunes Filles royalistes*.

The newspaper did not long remain the sole journalistic tool at the disposal of the Action Française. The *Nouvelle Librairie Nationale*, under the management of Georges Valois since 1912, published numerous books of the school and the *Revue critique des idées et des livres*, a kind of philosophical, belletristic subsidiary of the newspaper.

But there were also other channels through which the influence of the Action Française spread. Before the war, for instance, a group of sympathizers bought up the well-known Catholic paper *L'Univers* and gave it a new direction. Perhaps it was an exaggeration to say, as did one of Maurras' bitterest opponents in 1928: "After the war Maurras and his school had complete control of everything vaguely or closely connected with French Catholicism, and directed it as they pleased,"[1] but the statement contained a grain of truth. And even in the few years preceding 1914 the Action Française had achieved an organizational expansion and intellectual penetration which in comparable circumstances is unique.

The formation of its own trade unions, however, was something it never attempted. It never went beyond a certain flirting with syndicalism, and the *Cercle Proudhon* remained, more than any other of the organizations of the Action Française, a group of intellectuals which never achieved any practical significance.

Among all these bodies, three principal ones deserve closer study: the *Institut d'Action française*, the first party college of the Right; the *Camelots du Roi*, the first "storm troopers"; and the *Nouvelle Librairie Nationale*, the first party publishing house.

Unlike subsequent party colleges, the *Institut d'Action française* possessed neither its own building nor full-time lecturers. All its meetings took place in the rented rooms of the building of the Sociétés Savantes;[2] occupants of the "professorial chairs," most of which had been named after the movement's forerunners, consisted of the principal contributors to the *Action Française*. Yet very few institutes of this kind have had such a high intellectual level.

Maurras himself held the "Chaire Sainte-Beuve." In the "Chaire Rivarol" Louis Dimier gave the lectures which were published in his book on nineteenth-century counterrevolutionary teachers; the chair of Léon de Montesquiou was named after Auguste Comte and dedicated to the study of "the reactionary in positivism." In the "Chaire Maurice Barrès" Lucien Moreau lectured on his *Philosophie du nationalisme français*; and the "Chaire du Syllabus," always occupied by priests, was devoted to the discussion of the true relation between state, church, and politics. Finally, the occupant of the "Chaire Amouretti" was the most brilliant lecturer of all: Jacques Bainville.

Students and leaders of society right up to the cardinal[3] crowded into these lectures. A few salaried employees and workingmen, probably members of the *Camelots du Roi*, were also present. These were not mass meetings, but their influence on the nation's educated class and, through many ramifications, on the *réveil de l'orgueil français*, was considerable.

The *Camelots du Roi*[4] started out in the most meager and anonymous way imaginable. A young man (Henri de Lyons) had collected a few friends who sold royalist newspapers at church doors, without, however, attracting the attention of the Action Française leaders. Some time later a young student (Maxime Réal del Sarte) interrupted a session of the Supreme Court and hurled violent abuse at the judges on account of what he called the unlawful rehabilitation of Dreyfus. In the ensuing uproar a number of students went to his aid. The two groups then amalgamated through the agency of Maurice Pujo, who as a member of the *comités directeurs de l'Action française* took over the political leadership while Sarte and Lyons formally headed the combined group as president and secretary respectively. The young group won its first spurs through the "Affaire Thalamas," and by dint of stubbornness, discipline, and precise planning—as well as ruthlessness and brutality—it introduced a new note into the turbulent riots and demonstrations of the Latin Quarter. The price of these battles was many days of imprisonment, which were carefully totaled and triumphantly published in *Action Française*. Hero worship and the spell of bloodshed had existed in the Action Française before the *Camelots*; witness the bloodstained handkerchief of one of the students who had been wounded in a clash with socialists, which had been preserved in the editorial room as a precious relic.[5] But now the *Camelots* started assembling a veritable collection of trophies and later decorated a hall in the new building of *Action Française* with captured flags and emblems of their opponents, as well as other mementos.[6] After the victory a vigorous reorganization was undertaken, the *Camelots du Roi* joined the *Ligue* officially; unworthy members were removed by "purging"; the first regular committee of nine members was constituted;

strict regulations were issued regarding membership, and, in Maurice Pujo's words, the *Camelots*, "students, minor employees, workers, united in brotherhood in their great task, [became] a body of knights without fear and without reproach."[7]

Thus the *Camelots* regarded themselves as a kind of order, classless in origin,[8] hierarchic in structure, soldierly in spirit. They were the elite troops in the acts of violence which occurred during the "holy war"[9] waged by the Action Française against the French republic, in the disruption of theatrical performances, the demolition of statues, and the attack on Briand's ministry of justice. In the idyllic prewar days, this war was not, of course, without its humorous and harmless features; no deaths were reported on either side. Nevertheless, there is reason to doubt the correctness of Dimier's opinion: "The *Camelots du Roi* were greatly dreaded at the time, fear went before their name."[10] By 1911 their reputation had already penetrated as far as the Italian provinces to the young Mussolini, whose then Marxist heart overflowed with angry contempt.[11]

Nothing provides a clearer picture today of the spirit of the *Camelots* than their long-forgotten songs. The *Camelots* were born out of indignation over the methods of justice; they had grown up before the barriers of the courts, amid catcalls, riots, and the receiving of their sentences, and that is why they sang:[12]

> Long live the Camelots of the King, mother mine,
> Long live the Camelots of the King!
> They care not a fig for the laws of the land,
> Long live the Camelots of the King![13]

Where in Christian-conservative Europe of those days could such a deep-seated aversion to law and order have found its voice except, perhaps, among the anarchists? But in no socialist or anarchist song do we find such a rabid hostility to ruling forms of government as in the refrain:

> Long live the King, down with the Republic.
> Long live the King, the tramp will soon be hanged![14]

Nowhere in sedate and reasonable prewar Europe is there evidence of such personal animosity for a political opponent as in the image of parliament being thrown into the Seine:

> Briand will swim as he always does,
> And Jaurès will drink till his belly is full.
> And the members will sink from sight like the carcasses of dogs.[15]

However, it would be a mistake to regard the *Camelots* as out-and-out enemies of the state. When obliged to do so, they managed to get along very well with certain republicans, notably the conservative nationalists.

When Barthou presented parliament with plans for a three-year conscription period, the *Camelots* took part manfully in the street riots and then even appropriated for themselves the honor and glory of having been responsible for the success of the legislation. In any case Pujo now proudly referred to his men as *Gendarmes supplémentaires*.[16] Flouters of the law as auxiliary police: a strange union with more than a hint of things to come!

It is hardly surprising that in the official "Battle Song of the *Camelots du Roi*" hostility toward state and authority retreated markedly in favor of relatively safe anti-Semitism with its mass appeal. Maurras—together with Pujo—composed the song: there has scarcely ever been an instance of a respected author devising such a concoction purely from motives of political fanaticism:

> The Jew having taken all,
> Having robbed Paris of all she owns,
> Now says to France:
> "You belong to us alone:
> Obey! Down on your knees, all of you!"
>
> *Refrain:*
>   No, no, France is astir,
>   Her eyes flash fire,
>   No, no,
>   Enough of treason now.
>
> Insolent Jew, hold your tongue,
> Behold your King approaches,
> And our race
> Runs ahead of him.
> Back to where you belong, Jew,
> Our King will lead us!
>
> *Refrain:*
>   One, two, France is astir,
>   Her eyes flash fire,
>   One, two,
>   The French are at home.
>
> Tomorrow, on our graves,
> The wheat will be more beautiful,
> Let us close our ranks!
> This summer we shall have
> Wine from the grapevines
> With royalty.
>
> *Refrain:*
>   One, two, France is astir,
>   Her eyes flash fire,
>   One, two,
>   The French are at home.[17]

The *Nouvelle Librairie Nationale* was not strictly speaking an Action Française enterprise. It did not have a monopoly on all Action Française writers, nor did it receive financial aid during difficult times.[18] Yet the term "central publishing house" is not unjustified, for, unlike such firms as Flammarion and Grasset, which also published Maurras and his friends, the *Nouvelle Librairie Nationale* based its entire program on the Action Française. It also published the bible of the new school: the *Enquête sur la Monarchie*. Around the *Nouvelle Librairie Nationale* a publication list developed of monumental single-mindedness, and yet of astonishing wealth and startling diversity. Side by side with de La Tour du Pin's standard work, *Vers un ordre social chrétien*, stands Bainville's *Bismarck et la France* (1909); and beside *Précis de l'affaire Dreyfus* we find Valois' *Enquête* on the monarchy and the working class; series on the history of the French revolution, military problems, and matters of nationalism, allowed experts and lesser-known authors to express their views. Regional authors contributed to the series *Les pays de France*, and even novels indicated their ideological stance by their subjects. The Institute's lectures were published here, and the careful cultivation and documentation of the history of the Action Française (*Les étapes de l'Action française*) began at a very early date.

After the war Valois displayed superlative skill in expanding his own empire and that of the *Nouvelle Librairie Nationale* by publishing successful collected works (*Les Écrivains de la Renaissance française*) and by establishing promising new publishing firms (*La Maison du livre français*). His rupture with the Action Française in 1925 put an end to this development. But this did not eliminate the previous success; the great potential for publishing enterprises of this kind in the twentieth century had been revealed. And the foundations were all laid before 1914.

The Leadership

However many offshoots the Action Française managed to produce, the newspaper always remained the operative center. And by the same token the determining factor within the movement was not the director, not the polemicist, not the mass orator, but the superior intellect—Maurras himself. Although his responsibility for the monarchism of the Action Française could not be doubted, it was equally certain that in 1905 he was not yet undeniably the supreme leader. He began by writing in the daily paper more often than not under his pseudonym "Criton." But because of the appearance of the *Enquête* in book form, the attacks made on him by some theologians, and the publication of *Kiel et Tanger*, his prestige mounted steadily. Years before the war he was already the undisputed *Maître*, possibly even the *Chef*. But he gave no "orders." All decisions were made by a group known as the *Comités directeurs* [Board of Directors] *de l'Action française*, in which the *Comité directeur* of every important organization was represented, usually by the president and secretary. Resolutions were passed by a majority vote after detailed discussion, but were always announced as being unanimous. This ostensibly democratic principle of committee and majority, which shows up strangely in an organization dedicated so completely to "authority," was nevertheless radically modified by two circumstances. On the one hand, the boards of the various organizations were not elected by the members of the organization in question; rather, the candidates "appointed themselves on the basis of services rendered."[19] This clearly constitutes a very imprecise method of appointment, permitting plenty of latitude from above. Furthermore, it soon became impossible in the general board to undertake anything which ran counter to Maurras' will. His "jealousy of authority"[20] was notorious and often allowed a good deal of scope for personal rancor. For instance, he kept as prominent and influential a member as Georges Valois out of the *Comités directeurs* for many years because he "did not care" for him.[21]

The fact remains that, in the early history of fascism and National Socialism, democratic methods still played their part, and that there, too, the editorial office of a newspaper was the first headquarters of an embryonic movement. After World War I the *Führerprinzip* became more and more of a determining factor in the Action Française. When, following on the assassination of Marius Plateau, a demonstration of sympathy for the murderess was organized by political opponents, Maurras *ordered* "the principal ones among these shameless persons to be beaten and purged."[22] Two years later, in his "Letter to Schrameck," Maurras pointed out to the minister that in the Action Française his (Maurras') orders were unconditionally obeyed and that there would not be a moment's hesitation in spilling the "dog's blood" of a Jewish alien even if he were among the highest dignitaries of the republic.[23] Moreover, the Vatican's condemnation, which undoubtedly put an end to the political chances of the Action Française, turned Maurras—its principal target—into a charismatic leader among its faithful followers, and the sole hope of a France persecuted from without and within by enemies and false friends. Daudet's book, *Maurras et son temps*, in its fulsome praise of the "great man" and his "mission," scarcely lags behind corresponding Italian and German panegyrics. But it is doubtful whether this can be regarded purely as a further development of the original era of the Action Française, or whether it does not to a large extent already represent a reflection of conditions outside France.

On the other hand, it was after World War I that the strongest doubts as to Maurras' qualities of leadership were voiced. The great movement of desertion from the Action Française—starting with Drieu la Rochelle and continuing with Dimier, Valois, Bucard, Brasillach, Deloncle up to Rebatet—did not, after all (with the single exception of Georges Bernanos), go toward the Left or the Center, but toward the Right in the direction of what was generally known as French "fascism," toward unfettered authority and a determined will to power. That he was a great political teacher, but "not a leader," was the criticism first publicly leveled at Maurras by Valois,[24] and one which met with increasing support on the radical Right. Valois maintained that, in moments calling for decision, he had heard Maurras discuss useless theoretical distinctions by the hour, and for the rest of his life Maurras never found an opportunity of rebutting these doubts other than theoretically and polemically.

The political failure of the Action Française is not solely due to objective circumstances; it also derived from a "crisis in leadership." Its organizations, impelled by a strong and confidence-inspiring sense of leadership, functioned excellently so long as it was a case of disseminating beliefs in a conventional as well as unconventional manner and of arousing respect among its opponents for its own doctrine and existence. But these impulses broke down whenever it was a matter of shaking the opponent internally as well, and of imbuing potential friends with unlimited confidence in a capacity for victory. This breakdown was not just an individual occurrence; it was eminently French and bourgeois.

In intellectual France there was no one who could have dismissed Maurras as a mere fanatic or semiliterate Carbonaro. In contrast to Germany, this fact was essential to his success. But at the same time it rendered Maurras incapable of those primitive simplifications which are the daily bread of the agitated masses. The compactness of his system did not allow him to make the opponent's legitimate demands his own and ostensibly transcend them. In Germany Hitler did not merely *play the part* of a man of the people, to some extent he *was* one. For here there still existed old democratic demands which were not yet realized (unification of the Reich, Greater Germany, and so forth). In France the *only* dream for the great masses was that of socialism. But this was too remote from any attempt at realization for it to become, as in Germany and Italy, an object of hatred for the masses. Anti-Semitism by itself was not enough. And Maurras—an outstanding intellect, a member of the middle class—was as little suited to become a man of the people as were circumstances in France to promote his transformation. And although Daudet was a greater orator and far less intelligent, he was much too fond of the good life and beautiful women to be able to take the master's place.

It is intensely characteristic that the few real "leaders" of French fascism—headed by Jacques Doriot—did not emerge from the circle of impatient renegades of the Action Française, but rather from the rigid and not particularly "French" discipline of the Stalinist Communist party.

The Style

Style is the visible essence of a political phenomenon. It is not merely a composite resulting from doctrine, organization, and leadership impulse: over a period of time it becomes the framework from which no new initiative can emerge without destroying the whole structure. A political movement can more readily deny parts of its doctrine, make changes in leadership, or modify the organization, than arbitrarily transform its style. The more original the trend, the more unmistakable the style. It is the living past. It cannot therefore be set apart merely as one component. To understand a doctrine requires above all reason; to have a grasp of an organization is a matter of will; to recognize its style requires above all else discernment. Style may be manifest in a *single* photograph, while in thousands of speeches it may only be present in vague outline. Since the style of the Action Française was one of an organization centered entirely around a newspaper, it would obviously find its chief expression in the literary style of the leading editors.

Maurras' own style was anything but serene. How could it have been when his doctrine asserted that, whereas the majority of Frenchmen were *imbéciles*, the country's political leaders were a band of unpatriotic traitors and profit-hungry intriguers? Even when his polemic remains relatively dispassionate, the words he uses expose icy abysses. In 1915 he was still calling Clemenceau *l'adversaire du pays ... l'ennemi de toute sagesse et de toute raison.*[25] Not infrequently, however, his style becomes intensely personal and defamatory, especially in the case of former political friends: when the Pretender's political agent spoke out against the Action Française in 1909, he became a "bandit" and a friend of the Jews; when Georges Valois left the Action Française in 1925, Maurras did not consider it beneath his dignity to put forward the most pernicious accusations (for example, that as a young man during his stay in Russia Valois had been a police informer),[26] accusations which, if they were correct, were bound to discredit Maurras himself. By and large, however, Maurras' style is one of utmost restraint when compared with that of Léon Daudet. The novelist's imagination provided Daudet with such a wealth of disparaging, caustic, and scornful epithets and adjectives that, just as the medieval Romans took their building material from the Colosseum, whole generations of polemicists and pamphleteers could afterwards draw on Daudet as an inexhaustible reservoir of inspiration—except where, as in a great many cases, the expressions were untranslatable. A political opponent from the Christian Democratic camp by the name of Denais turns up as *Pied-Denais* (*pied-de-nez*), Monsieur Georges Hoog as *Katal-Hoog* (catalogue).[27] A learned man of the stature of Georges Goyau is called *petit tartufe Goyau, pleurnichard* (sniveler), *nain moral et physique* (moral and physical dwarf), *plat pied en toute saison* (flat-footed all year round).[28]

It is not surprising that, to Daudet, Briand is *le traître*; but even the most conservative of the republican statesmen does not fare much better: Delcassé is *le gnom de Fachoda*; Millerand is *le défenestré*, Poincaré *le pleutre.*[29]

A man who wrote like that, who had his battle groups sing "The tramp will soon be hanged!", must have either complete power or none at all. For such a man the area of compromise and negotiation was out of bounds.

However, the Action Française was driven by its premises not only to an absolute policy but also to useless and meaningless outbursts which cannot in any sense be called policy. Late in the fall of 1923 Daudet wrote: "I had applauded the disappearance of Matthias Erzberger (one less!), that of Rathenau (again one less!). I shall likewise applaud the disappearance of Ludendorff, of von Seeckt, and I applaud the German famine."[30] It is difficult to imagine a more utterly blind delusion. But perhaps it is not after all a delusion; this furious outburst of hatred demonstrates that Daudet had no faith in the relatively feasible solution to partition Germany, and gave way to uncontrolled emotions of no practical significance except that they provided avalanches of grist to the propaganda mills of the other side.

Violence on the home front, however, was not limited to the verbal. It has been shown that in the initial undertakings of the *Camelots du Roi* the basic traits of fascist terrorism were already clearly discernible. There is no ignoring how smoothly the songs fitted into the pattern. What was lacking were certain postwar features: mass demonstrations in uniform, premilitary training, dedication of banners, and parades. Also absent was that deadly seriousness which comes only when men offer their lives for a cause. In its place was much youthful enthusiasm, a cheerful confidence in their cunning ruses—as, for example, when, shortly after they were formed, the *Camelots* managed by an ingenious telephone maneuver to have their arrested comrades released "by the minister himself."[31] Even after the war they still clung to this style. Their private intelligence service tapped the chief telephone lines, and when Léon Daudet was arrested in 1927 after a dramatic siege of the *Action Française* building, the master stroke was once more successful: a telephone call from "the ministry" ordered the warden of the Santé to release Daudet immediately. and somehow the check back was mysteriously switched through to the same "ministry," so that the prisoner had the pleasure of escaping with official blessing. The government mobilized enough police reinforcements to cope with an attack on the Élysée Palace; in spite of this, Daudet made his getaway to Brussels, and all France laughed at the escapade.[32]

It must be admitted that the saga of the Action Française had its humorous side. But the fact remains that the new style, "a judicious combination of brains and brawn,"[33] was something quite without precedent, and that this groping, incomplete quality was the very thing that testified to its originality. If France was spared the whole desperate bitterness of Germany's and Italy's social strife until 1942, it is nonetheless true that this strife was anticipated in France by the Dreyfus affair at a time when in Germany and Italy the impending earthquake was as yet barely perceptible.

True, no photograph exists exposing the character of the Action Française as dramatically and graphically as is so often the case with pictures from the Italian fascist and National Socialist era. A group of peaceful citizens, the *Comités directeurs* of the Action Française are walking in the procession in honor of Joan of Arc, among them Maurras, short, gray, and unobtrusive, carrying an umbrella.[34] But do not Marx and Engels in their frock coats look in photographs like harmless citizens? Was not Marx, when his daughter wanted to get married, the image of a worried bourgeois father? Taken by itself, a photograph can be as misleading as style: the total political phenomenon is manifest only to the total view.

CHAPTER FOUR

The Doctrine

Introduction: The Hidden System

The stronger the element of doctrine in a political movement, the less it is grasped in its totality when the historian restricts himself to unearthing the spiritual roots, recounting the history, and expounding the practice. Doctrine must be examined for its own sake—in its entirety and with its claim to truth, a structure which is more fully accounted for by origin and history than a living person is explained by the character of his parents and the vicissitudes of his life. This method of observation[1] is generally regarded as systematic, as opposed to historical, and it presents no difficulty where the system has been asserted by the thinker and the thing itself steps forward. A systematic presentation of Hegelian philosophy needs merely to follow what Hegel has already outlined in masterly fashion. A reflected glow from that period of systematic (that is, well-ordered, encyclopedic) thought still shines over Marx—but what discrepancies, leaps, and gaps there are even with him!

Das Kapital presupposes throughout an anthropology whose rudiments he described in unpublished early works; a discussion of the materialism of natural science is foretold in the *Introduction to the Critique of Political Economy*, but it never takes place; the relationship between science and productive forces is at best indicated as a problem in the broadest generalizations; the most important chapter on the classes was never written. Nietzsche even made a virtue of the lack of a system, and yet he could not suppress the wish to write a "crowning work." Anyone who wished to live and think face to face with reality had to write as aphoristically as Nietzsche, or be as great a servant of expediency as Lenin or Mussolini.

Maurras was also a servant of expediency. The enormous number of his articles bears this out; still more his books, the great majority of which are mere collections of articles. What he claimed to be the "Counter-Encyclopedia," the five-volume *Dictionnaire politique et critique*, was compiled by a pupil; of the book which might best be called his crowning work, *Mes idées politiques*, only the introduction had been written systematically and at leisure. However, Maurras is not for an instant to be mistaken for a journalist. The word "system" in its Greek origin means "placing together." Everything Maurras wrote fits together and has an unmistakable identity. In this sense, an original, all-embracing, compact system of feeling and thought underlies all his utterances. It is ever-present, but only by implication; and even lengthier works as a rule develop only certain aspects in detail. Maurras is an unsystematic systematizer, and in this he resembles all the outstanding thinkers of his era.

An attempt to reconstruct this hidden system might be made by following the example of Hegelian philosophy and placing Maurras' views on nature, man, history, civilization, and so forth, side by side on the ascending steps of universality and trying to deduce one from the other. The result would be something amounting to a traditional philosophical system. But it is no accident that Maurras himself did not evolve any such system. What must be aimed for is not a system in the sense of a *pictura mundi*, but rather the systematic quality of his thought.

Fear as the Origin

We shall take Maurras' "basic emotion" as the main thread of our study. The merest glance shows that this basic emotion, present in even the most subtle intellectual operations, is fear. At first sight it has little in common with the much-discussed central concept of existentialist philosophy. Maurras' fear, or dread, is not metaphysical and does not imply a "slipping away of being in the whole." In accordance with the usual meaning of the word, Maurras feels fear for something and of something. He fears the objects and conditions of the past and present world. Since the emotion is being continually translated into thoughts, certain manifestations are rationalized and justified, others criticized and rejected. The net result is a comprehensive doctrine of political good and political evil in which the main emphasis is on the intimidating and hate-inspiring enemy, an enemy which Maurras pursues to its very earliest historical manifestations. Instead of a historical philosophy, the outcome is a prescription for practice, an appeal for political struggle. Fear has been an underlying element of the intellectual history of Europe for the past hundred years. Perhaps it has never been so dominant as in Maurras' case: it is hard to find a clearer example of those admixtures and concretizations which make dread as questionable an emotion as it is legitimate.

The existence of beauty brings forth Maurras' undisguised fear. For it is in Maurras' nature to equate beauty with the fragile and the threatened. If a thing as such is a miracle in face of the delirium of the "original confusion"[2]—which to the son of Martigues is ever apparent as the gloomy stagnation of the swamp and to the reader of Lucretius as the senseless whirling of atoms—how much more do mystery and unfathomable mercy constitute the beautiful and the enduring! Did not a Venetian bomb suffice to demolish that supreme example of beauty, the Parthenon? Is not the Parthenon threatened just as much today as at any hour of its existence? "Any inadvertence—the greedy earth, the deep sea, children's destructiveness, human ignorance, the damp hot climate—could all too easily reclaim and wipe out this treasure."[3] Maurras does not believe that beauty is situated in the inmost heart of the world and hence invincible; for him it springs, as it were, from a random chance of being and can only endure as long as the world's primeval brutality does not turn against it. Fear for what is beautiful and fear of its destruction are therefore inseparable from his existence: "For if long ages, methodical and persevering effort, almost divine intentions, are required to build a town, to set up a state, to found a civilization, there is nothing easier than to destroy these frail structures. A few tons of powder quickly reduce half the Parthenon to ruins, a colony of microbes decimates the population of Athens, three or four base ideas systematized by fools have managed quite well during the past hundred years to render a thousand years of French history useless."[4]

We see, then, that to him beauty consists not only of temples and statues but of social phenomena: states, peoples, religions. But if Maurras regards temples as being threatened by the destructive forces of nature, the enemies of beautiful ideas appear to be other ideas which are evidently comparable, in the parallelism of his sentence, to elementary inhuman forces.

This constitutes an important metabasis: the commensurable is interpreted by the image of the incommensurable. An interpretation of this kind cannot be called thought: it is the direct expression of emotion, and it is emotion which sees all order within the state threatened by the assault of the "barbarians from the depths" with their paradoxical battle cries of freedom and equality. Again it is emotion which regards France as hemmed in, repressed, crushed between Anglo-Saxons and Germans, northern Slavs and southern Slavs, Islam and China: "What can little France do among all these giants? ... Can it have any other fate than that of ancient Greece?"[5] And it is still emotion when the young man of letters traces foreign influences in syntax, word sequence, and style, and comes to the conclusion: "the very foundation of our ethnic and linguistic personality has been ruined or is threatened with being ruined."[6]

Whenever he mentions the monarchy, fear is the underlying factor: "France needs the monarchy, if ... it does not satisfy this need, ... this will be the end of France."[7] The possibility that this end might be a reality, that the "Jewish" ideal of a mankind no longer divided into nations was far from being a mere dream, is so deeply embedded in Maurras' emotions that the most powerful arguments he can think of must always first be employed in allaying his own doubts. There was a Jaurès in Maurras too, and he had to write vast quantities in order to drown out that powerful voice. But what was cause for an optimism on a planetary scale for the great politician from Castres, becomes for the lyricist from Martigues a nightmare of fear: "An imperceptible degeneration has come to Florence, to Italy, to this whole planet, which day by day becomes colder, uglier, and more barbaric."[8]

This trend toward ugliness in the world is due to the increasing dissolution of those "beautiful inequalities"[9] which make beauty beautiful, the state strong, the people healthy: the victory of the swamp and its catabolic, dissolving, concealing power. "Curiosity is curious about everything, tolerance is tolerant of everything, the one or the other to an equal degree. All things receive, if they remain in a state of mutual balance, a uniform value, an equivalent price. The primary and the secondary, the more valuable and the less valuable—the torch of freedom will never distinguish among all these things."[10]

For Maurras, the swamp, the power which destroys life and beauty, and liberalism, the dominating thought pattern of the modern age, are identical. And at this point it becomes clear that in his fear—a fear which may seem purely political—Maurras is in the last resort concerned with himself and mankind: "Should the liberal lie spread over the earth, should anarchism and universal democratism spread the 'panbéotie' announced by Renan, should the barbarians from the depths, as predicted by Macaulay, appear at the appropriate time, then man will disappear as a human being, just as he will have disappeared in the form of Frenchman, Greek, or Latin."[11]

State and Sovereignty

Déesse France. In the dark night of barbarism a "chosen kingdom" (*royaume choisi*), a "shining island,"[12] the greatest of nature's realities, is holding out;[13] the *patrie*, the *Déesse France*, as Maurras calls France (borrowing a phrase from André Chénier), a unique treasure without parallel in human history.[14] These epithets are enough to suggest the primary characteristic of Maurras' nationalism: above all else it is esthetic. France corresponds first and foremost to what is beautiful, it is the "wonder of wonders,"[15] the unique creative heritage that makes a human being of a human being, and an artist of an artist.

But this nationalism is also metaphysical. It established itself in a vacuum which was once filled with metaphysical convictions regarding the absolute. As a goddess, the *patrie* becomes the final absolute, thus simultaneously satisfying the age-old need for worship and the modern desire for security and demonstrability. There were few people who formulated this well-known process as early and as clearly as Maurras: "For those who think naturalistically but who wish to bring order into their thinking, a Goddess France presents none of the difficulties inherent in other formulas. It satisfies reason, for, since it represents the fatherland, it resides, as Sophocles would say, in the great laws of the world. Yet this god who is so rational is by no means abstract. One sees and touches France. It has a body, it has a soul: its history, its arts, its charming natural beauties, the magnanimous society of its heroes. But since the goddess may perish, she appeals to our devotion; and since her superhuman life may nevertheless be extended infinitely, she shares in the eternal majesty. ... Among such diverse spirits, only one good could exist: the cult of the fatherland."[16]

Every goddess is absolute in her sphere and demands absolute devotion; this is an intrinsic part of her nature. Because Maurras' nationalism is absolute, his first political demand is one of absolute sovereignty for his country. This accounts for his deep dislike of any system of alliances which would transcend the cool chess game of a superior intelligence. He has a deep-seated fear that France might become a "dependent nation" and thus have to cease being a goddess. Here also lie the roots of his hostility toward a unified Germany: the political weight of seventy-six million Germans was forcing France into an irrevocable alliance with the Anglo-Saxons in which it was the weaker partner.

The postulate of absolute sovereignty drove Maurras to a decisive step which makes the distinction between his nationalism and that of the Jacobins quite clear. The latter had never differentiated between nation and mankind: the revolutionary formation of the nation out of the ruins of the *ancien régime* is itself an element of human progress, and it is up to France as the most advanced nation to bring this message to all peoples. Without this achievement on France's part and without this message, the nation would indeed be nothing: Jacobinic nationalism is not narcissistic but missionary. It is here that Maurras draws the fateful dividing line: "Monsieur Hervé is a patriot; only he believes that, politically speaking, there are greater interests than national interests and that above the fatherland exists the human race. ... We will swear, by God: fatherland *and* mankind. But if events say: fatherland *or* mankind, what is one to do in that case? Those who say ... 'France first' are patriots, those who say: 'France, but ... ,' are humanitarians."[17] This dissociation of fatherland from mankind is of the utmost significance. It is the guiding principle of fascistic nationalism, which is always antihumanitarian and narcissistic. Maurras did not develop this principle to its final extreme: as a rule he tried to mitigate and conceal it. But by so doing he does not eliminate it. And if his nationalism is not Jacobinic, it is also not "legitimate." A legitimate nationalism would be loyalty to the person of the king and the blood royal, an emotion essential to patriotism. To Maurras, however—and here he is quite Jacobinic—the king is the "functionary" of the nation,[18] and he regards heredity as a matter of political expediency. Maurras' nationalism is without precedent in history. He is the first to conceive of nationhood as a privilege, and to deny other peoples the right to nationality. He is the first to transform, while fully conscious of what he was doing, the Kantian categorical imperative into the pseudoabsolute imperative of *France d'abord*: "If you want France to live, you must want this or that."[19]

The fatherland refashioned. However, the Goddess France is certainly not the country as it appears to the eye, with its factories, taverns, schools, and its millions of people. When Maurras speaks of the *Déesse France*, he is thinking of the "most perfect society" Europe has ever known, the society of the *ancien régime* and of the "first city of the world,"[20] the Paris of the eighteenth century. While Taine had at least tried to point out the unchanging features of the past with his phrase *esprit classique*, Maurras specifically rejects this and works out a mythological history of ancient France[21] which merely proved how France had meanwhile moved away from the *ancien régime*. A historical chart in which he sets out to contrast the consequences of monarchy and republic approaches an infantile naïveté: under the monarchy *ordre et progrès* constantly prevailed, under the republic *désordre et diminution* with equal regularity.[22]

The inevitable result of letting himself be led astray by history was the refashioning of the fatherland. Whatever failed to correspond to the immaculate image of the goddess had to be exposed as "un-French" and, if possible, traced to a foreign source. This chiefly applies to the "so-called" French revolution and its "allegedly" French ideas. The fact that the majority of Frenchmen supported these ideas is immaterial. For just as the hunting field may have to be protected from the hunters, so France is not identical with the French population: "The revolutionary disorder, based on an individualistic philosophy, numbers, furthermore, almost as many accomplices as there are mediocre and envious people, fools and scoundrels, in France. And of those there are plenty. If a generous elite does not intervene, ... the curing of this national ataxia can be regarded as a beautiful dream, but as only a dream."[23] Like a sculptor, Maurras blithely chips away from his statue of the *patrie* the bits of national history that do not correspond to the harmonious image of his goddess. Like a surgeon, he amputates one limb after another from the living body of the nation, leaving intact only the heart, the *élite généreuse*.

The result is a profound cleft within the nation, comparable to that schism produced by Marxism. Liberalism is excluded by Maurras in its entirety, just as it was by Marx—indeed, even more uncompromisingly. Three large mutually opposing groups are formed, of which each rejects the other two and declares them to be related.

Trotsky tells the story of how, while walking with Lenin in London, Lenin pointed to Westminster Abbey and said: "That is *their* [the bourgeois'] famous Westminster."[24] In much the same way Maurras uses a dissociating pronoun: "Now that it has become a satellite state in a system of superior powers, your republic is less able than ever to resist exterior forces and their movement."[25] Maurras' goddess is a martial goddess. She cleaves history, divides the people of the nation, and her battle cry is: "Civil war." Indeed, says Maurras, a force which resulted in an "antinational government" would deserve to be received like the army of the king of Prussia.[26] As the goddess is known only to the elite, and only the elite knows the actual meaning of "national" (that is, of

itself), the life of society becomes a state of cold war, and only the strength of
the elite can determine the moment at which the hot civil war begins against
what it considers to be the antinational government. This is precisely what the
refrain of the "Battle Song of the *Camelots du Roi*" says:

> Long live the *Camelots du Roi*,
> They care not a fig for the laws of the land.[27]

The Look of Envy. Since the goddess is so little to be identified with the everyday
fatherland, it is impossible to understand another characteristic of Maurras'
nationalism, one which also distinguishes it strikingly from Jacobinic nationalism: the look of envy which he is constantly directing toward other nations and
other parties. More than all others, imperial Germany fills Maurras with envy
as much as with fear and hatred: its discipline, its industry, its order, are in his
eyes the pattern for a better and a stronger France.[28] Maurras attributes these
qualities to the difference in forms of government and declares the Germans to
be mere imitators of France. This thesis is, of course, not entirely incorrect:
the national and centralist monarchy of the Hohenzollerns was presumably
more closely related in character to the Bourbon monarchy than to the German
tradition of the "Reich." But the explanation is nonetheless manifestly inadequate: this type of monarchy was neither a possession nor an invention
of France. Moreover, what Maurras admires most in German politics is the
very thing which proved the most disastrous mistake of the German empire,
its naval policy and the authoritarian-demagogic methods by which it was
pursued and popularized.[29] Thirty years later he will also not deny Hitler his
envious admiration of German political methods, "division of labor, economy
of means, energy of attack,"[30] at the very time when these methods were on the
point of bringing about the most astounding result: the destruction of his own
state.

But Maurras had not yet had his fill of examples of the paradigmatic enemy:
on countless occasions (like Drumont before him) he recalls the memory of the
German *Tugend-Bund* (League of Virtue); he desires a "troop of young Fichtes"
for France,[31] and not the least of the accusations he levels at the republic is
that it renders impossible the Bismarck policy of government *against* parliament
and public opinion.[32]

But he looks enviously toward England too: "All those countries which have
resolutely maintained these 'relics of the past'—tradition, authority, subordination of the masses to natural leaders—manufacture more products than we do,
sell them at better prices than we do, even produce more children than we do.
Look at monarchist and feudal Prussia, at aristocratic England with its
community life."[33]

This is not a masterpiece of political analysis. He does not ask whether the
"relics of the past" are similar in England and Prussia and have a corresponding
relationship to social movements. But Maurras is obviously not concerned

primarily with the analytical quality of his statement: he seeks to beat and to chastise, to heap the whole responsibility for France's lack of progress on the revolution. Maurras counters the abstractions of the revolution with an equally abstract method of observation, a method which is interested only in the formal aspect of state structure and equates monarchy with monarchy, aristocracy with aristocracy, and the masses with the masses.

But if the France of his day lacks determination, direction, and will power, the champions of the goddess are also aware of a serious deficiency in her early days and cast envious looks at their political enemies at home. Recalling former times, Maurras says: "[There is] absolutely no common political education. The enemy possesses the language of the ... revolution. We have neither a nomenclature, nor a method, nor corresponding intellectual resources."[34]

Maurras' nationalism is therefore not only esthetic, metaphysical, and narcissistic: it is primarily and emphatically reactive. For this reason, too, the missionary streak is lacking in him, and Maurras was fond of making a virtue of this deficiency. But his claim to propound political truth is continually at odds with this self-limitation, and it is with a curious mixture of regret and pride that Maurras followed the victorious advance of "his" ideas in Italy.

Critique of Democracy. Maurras' chief claim to truth concerns his critique of democracy: no other part of his work has had such an effect.

Democracy is the wasting disease from which the goddess suffers, the deadly threat to her existence. One has only to open one's eyes to perceive this truth. It is an empirical fact that France has sunk from the position of the world's leading power—a rank it occupied in the eighteenth century—to one which is now barely more than secondary.

It is an empirical fact that in France matters are openly discussed which in other states are the concern of secret resolutions. It is a fact that parties are subject to influences beyond control, not least to those from abroad. The face of democracy is not beautiful, its gait not steady, its hand not firm. It is the disease which makes of the goddess the very antithesis of herself.

Democracy is the form of government which offers public interest neither abode nor voice. It believes that public interest will spring automatically from the forces and pressures of private interests, instead of which the state becomes the prey of the blind greed of countless individuals: "Public interests have no resonant voice. But private interests bark from morning till night."[35] The idea of "government" is thereby actually abolished; democracy is not really a form of government but a kind of anarchy. The rule of the sum of individual spontaneity means the paralysis of the spontaneity of the common weal and its voice. That is why Maurras calls the French republic a "constant conspiracy against the public weal."[36] This, of course, shows to what extent Maurras' empiricism is based on general assumptions. To have such a view of democracy one must be at the opposite end of the scale from its basic conviction that public interest has its main abode in the heart of every single citizen and thus cannot be particularized once and for all in one "voice."

For Maurras' abysmal pessimism—which sees even the monarchy as a guarantee of public interest only because the trivial private interests of the monarch *must* be identical with public interest—the republican *vertu civique* does not even merit serious discussion. The people's representatives can no more have this virtue than can the people themselves. Their "regime of wind-bags"[37] paralyzes the activity of a government whose counterpart in Berlin is a *gouvernement de l'action*; their most vital interests—those of re-election—compel them to flatter the banal instincts of the masses and "to neglect reality for the sake of outward appearance."[38] Outward appearance in its most concentrated form is *l'opinion*, public opinion. It is inconstant, vacillating, temperamental, superficial—in all things the antithesis of truth. But it has the power of the lie, for what opinion does the individual absorb more greedily than the one which makes out that he is the victim of injustice, that he is being exploited? To create this opinion is precisely the business and *raison d'être* of radical politicians in a democracy: "Let us repeat that democracy is the great creator, the stimulator, the promoter, of that collective movement known as class struggle."[39] The outward appearance (which is not necessarily "false") that injustice exists in society overlooks the cardinal truth that the area of peace as represented by the nation in the planetary struggle is the greatest essential and the greatest blessing for even its poorest inhabitant. But class struggle weakens the rampart separating the abode of peace from the outer turmoil by undermining even military discipline. Maurras has never quoted anything by Rousseau or Marx with the same deeply felt horror as these lines by Pottier:

> If these cannibals insist
> On making heroes of us all,
> They will soon find out that our bullets
> Are for our own generals.[40]

There is good reason to believe that this is where the very core and origin of Maurras' critique of democracy lie. We shall return to this later. In any case, his practical-political critique is summed up in a demand as naïve as it is radical: "There is only one way to improve democracy: to destroy it."[41]

The practical-political point of view, however, is not the only one. It is frequently joined by a kind of psychological definition aimed at demonstrating the "antihuman" nature of democracy. A typical epithet, as striking as it is repulsive, is, for example, the apodictical phrase: "Democracy is forgetting."[42] Is this merely an image, a transference of category, to which only the artist may be entitled? The meaning becomes clear when one looks at the thesis: "The flourishing state resembles the human soul, *sui conscia, sui memor, sui compos* (aware of itself, remembering itself, in control of itself)."[43] This truly Platonic parallelism of the structures of soul and state already contains the rejection of democracy not in its consequence but in its premise, since in the end it is organizational and likens human beings to cells in reference to their aims. Nevertheless its analytical value may be considerable. That a modern democracy does not usually favor tradition—that is, the uniform grasp of tradition—is obvious. It remains to be asked whether in certain situations forgetting can be more important to man and state than remembering. To Maurras, however, remembering means above all the authority of a solid interpretation of political experiences, the rule of a long-standing traditional style in politics. Because democracy lacks this style, it resembles the barbarian in a famous passage in Demosthenes (a passage which Maurras claims was responsible for his political thinking): In a fist fight the barbarian reacts only to the blows dealt him by his opponent, whereas he himself has no idea of how to seize the initiative. It follows that Wilhelm II is actually the monarch of the Third Republic, for it is always his actions that dictate its reactions. In this respect the republic is like a woman: it lacks "the male principle of initiative and action."[44] Yet the final goal of Maurras' interpretation is the total banishment of "the irresponsibility, anonymity, unconcern, instability"[45] of the parliamentary regime from the sphere of human activity, and all he will allow is a comparison with an irrational animal: "The Third Republic has at its center no organ capable of assuming this task, neither intelligence nor will power nor sense of leadership—nothing human."[46]

Maurras brings yet a third big gun to bear on democracy: a point of view no longer limited to empirical statement of fact or graphic comparison, but essentially unanswerable—the logical-metaphysical standpoint. According to this, organization can only mean the creating of inequalities and aristocracies; democracy with its leveling tendency is necessarily a destructive force, equality being sterile and even deadly. Time and again Maurras returns to the incompatibility of progress and equality: "All progress complicates, creates differences, differentiates."[47] This is indeed an irrefutable argument as long as it is based on the concept of mechanical equality, and as long as the potential distinctions within the individual himself are taken into account as little as are the various areas in which "equality" can occur. But Maurras, it would appear, has always the most primitive opponent in mind, and so he arrives at the great metaphysical and mythicizing drama of the famous sentence from the *Enquête*: "Democracy is evil, democracy is death."[48]

His critique is a political-empirical critique of the weakness of democracy (that is, of the democratic state), a psychological critique of the antihuman nature of democracy, a logical-metaphysical critique of the absurdity of democracy. There can be no doubt whatever that in its absolute form it is untenable. Two facts form an insuperable barrier. One is the very existence of Maurras' critique—the absurd needs no criticism. The second is that the genesis of his critique is so readily understandable, so patently obvious. From 1899 to 1914 France was the only true mass democracy in Europe. Caught between a severe political defeat of the conservative forces and World War I (for which it urgently required these forces), its very foundations assailed by anarchism, Marxist socialism, and revolutionary syndicalism, agitated by anti-Semitism, mourning its lost provinces, in a perilous foreign political situation, helpless in the face of the unprecedented fusion of politics and economy—it would have had to invent a Maurras if he had not already existed. But, aside from his claim to absoluteness, much of Maurras' critique of democracy remains valid, merely because, of course, criticism is a necessary part of democracy and hence renders even the worst enemy worthy of attention and his most radical opinion useful.

It would no doubt be interesting to examine the actual relevance of Maurras' critique. But it is more important to outline its philosophical-political significance by looking at his two most hated enemies: Rousseau and Marx.

Strangely enough, in the matter of democracy these two men seem to agree almost word for word with Maurras. Do we not find in the *Contrat Social*: "there is no regime as subject to civil wars and internal unrest as democracy or the people's regime because there is none which tends so strongly and continuously toward change of form"?[49] And does not Marx specifically confirm Maurras' thesis that democracy is the "instigator" of class warfare when he maintains "that it is in this most recent form of government of bourgeois society that the class war is once and for all to be fought"?[50] This agreement is indeed a strange proof of the old saying that extremes meet. But Rousseau and Marx, of course, being enthusiastic liberals, are aiming in exactly the opposite direction with their critique of democracy. In Rousseau's opinion, every state is "lost" in which the citizens hand over their social rights and obligations to representatives, instead of always gathering in the market place, like the *politai* of ancient Greece, to exercise their sovereign rights; in other words, he criticizes representative democracy because its abstract nature is opposed to the primitivism of his ideal—freedom of the people.[51] Marx, the heir to the Hegelian doctrine of evolution, regards bourgeois democracy as *still* being the state, as *still* representing oppression; indeed, to him it is the most severe oppression because it is the most recent form. The fundamental problem of the difference between public and private interest is solved for both men in the model of either a remote past or a radically altered future, by the fusion of the general and the particular in the bosom of either the universal being or the reborn human being. Thus the two trends, after meeting for an instant, immediately diverge again toward opposite ends of the pole, and it remains doubtful whether they are capable of tempering and teaching one another.

State and War

Défense Nationale. In Maurras' view, the internal weaknesses of democracy are related to the problem of the defense of the state. It is, of course, possible to imagine a state which, though possessed of absolute sovereignty, does not need to make outward use of it because it is not threatened. Even in Thomas More's Utopia this is only approximately the case. In the world as we know it the most important of all rights of sovereignty is "the right over peace or war."[52] But democracy always forgets "the first duty of the state: to hold itself in readiness for the tragic constellation."[53] It refuses to acknowledge the vital connection between state and war, and even less the fact that the statehood of a state increases in proportion to its determination to be prepared for war. Only on this condition can it preserve peace. How could democracy acknowledge this law in view of its own obvious inferiority in the central sphere of the state? "Through the ages military and diplomatic operations have been subject to three conditions: speed, continuity, secrecy. Through the ages the assembling of large numbers of people could be neither very speedy nor very safe nor very discreet. That is why through the ages it has been kings, leaders, who have conducted diplomacy and war. Through the ages parliamentary democracies have understood no more about war than they have about diplomacy."[54]

Soldier-King and Border Areas. The man who is skilled in war is the king. In Maurras' view he is "absolute master" of his army, his navy, and his diplomacy.[55] He is the united will of the nation, so independent of all subordinate impulses (of which democracy is always a pawn) that he can plan and desire at the longest possible range. Maurras devoted the best known of his books, *Kiel et Tanger*, to an attempt to prove that a republic is incapable of those virtues of foresight, continuity, and determination without which national survival is impossible in the modern world. That is why he prints the following eternal and fundamental law of political existence in capital letters: "THUS THOSE PEOPLES WHO ARE GOVERNED BY THEIR MEN OF ACTION AND THEIR MILITARY LEADERS WIN OUT OVER THOSE PEOPLES WHO ARE GOVERNED BY THEIR LAWYERS AND THEIR PROFESSORS."[56]

The meaning of monarchy to Maurras is perfectly clear: it is a military kingdom; in *L'Avenir de l'Intelligence*, Maurras already frankly equates *royauté* with *gouvernement militaire*. The soldier-king is the leader of his people in war and into war, the absolute supreme commander who, like Richelieu, prepares for war by stirring up civil war in the enemy's country,[57] and who then knows the right hour at which to strike. It could not be said of war waged by such a man, as Maurras said in 1920 after what was, after all, the victorious war of the republic: "Instead of submitting to it, we ought to have chosen it, begun it at our own hour, at our own moment, and in our own interest."[58]

This might seem to make Maurras too much the warmonger, the forerunner of Hitler. Was not peace the highest task of politics? Did he not constantly condemn Napoleon, the supreme soldier-king? But for Maurras, the master stroke was the wholly advantageous peace, the Richelieu-type treaty modeled on Münster and Osnabrück. Besides, he did not condemn Napoleon for waging wars but for exhausting French vitality in useless campaigns for the sake of principles which were bound to be disastrous for France. Although Maurras' monarchism contains a reactionary idyllic element, its fascist quality is much more significant; it was above all a "call for a leader," the leader of the counterrevolution and sovereign of war: "We lack the man at the helm; we lack him, the man, and that's all."[59]

Admittedly, "defense" is Maurras' primary concern. But this defense does not exclude offensive action and a policy of annexation; on the contrary, it renders them indispensable. France must not border directly on the enemy, it must surround itself with quasi-colonial areas, border areas, which bear the traces of its spirit and constitute vital defense barriers. Although he obviously does not envisage colonization areas and "living space," he is thinking of more than zones of cultural influence: he sees (during the war) *des Alsaces possibles*[60] along the lower reaches of the Moselle, provided France does not despair of its vitality. And after the war he worked out a detailed plan (*La Part du Combattant*) designed to make the individual French soldier the financial beneficiary of the war and to turn the Saar territory into a kind of military colony.[61]

In the absence of the king, the army is his deputy: the precious guarantee of national existence. The cult of the army was for Maurras the chief motivation in his attitude toward the Dreyfus affair, the reason behind his opposition to Jaurès and Marc Sangnier. To him this cult is the hallmark of conservative France. He claims that, among even the most modest members of the lower middle class, the sword is the most hallowed sign: symbol of both honor and nobility.[62]

In 1905 we find him using a very remarkable expression when he describes the army as *ce précieux faisceau de forces nationales*.[63] The army is indeed the *faisceau* (*fascio*: bundle, sheaf, union). If it is headed by a soldier-king as envisaged by Maurras it becomes the paradigm of "fascist" society.

Critique of Pacifism. One "prejudice" stands in the way of Maurras' views: the belief that the era of European war was at an end and that outside of Europe the colonial powers could reach an amicable understanding.[64] This "prejudice" was based on Saint-Simon's belief that the industrial age was directly opposed to the military age; but it was also the burden of Napoleon's testament, the conviction of Auguste Comte, and the axiom of all European liberalism until the deep cleft made by the Franco-Prussian war. The reasons which Maurras advances to oppose it have been confirmed by experience: industrial competition would give rise to industrial wars; colonial rivalry was bound to engender colonial disputes.[65] But it is quite plain that his reasons are grounded in a more comprehensive conviction, a conviction which believes itself to arise out of insight into eternal laws: material wealth, since it is divisible, must produce envy and hatred and ultimately war; the greater the wealth, the more certain the war. This is how, in *Anthinéa*, he explains the grim, gloomy face of Florence in the midst of the sweet serenity of the surrounding countryside. War is "destined to live as long as humanity."[66] But war is not only eternal: it is also good. Without "this beautiful crossfire of hatred and love,"[67] man's lot would be nothing but a vegetating existence. Life and war are identical and good. And here again Maurras is closer to Rousseau and Marx with his critique than to some of his teachers and paragons—in this case, for instance, Comte.[68]

Of course, Maurras proved too much. For his empiricism also encounters the revolution, and his axiomatic method also justifies social war. Hence by means of complicated maneuvers he has in turn to restrict the right of war. It is the essence of civilization, he says, to channel warlike instincts and turn them outward, against external enemies. Class war is blasphemous, since it violates the nation's sphere of peace. Although wars are terrible, they are creative, while the days following upon social revolutions are gloomy (mornes).[69] All these arguments are obvious sophisms or petitiones principii. But they reveal the ambivalence of Maurras' (as well as of the fascist and conservative) attitude to war. Maurras is at the same time a national warrior and a social pacifist. The reason he opposes Jaurès so bitterly and so desperately is not only because Jaurès disarmed France and delivered it up to German attack, but because he believes Jaurès and his ilk forbid war between state and state and yet they cold-bloodedly prepare it between house and house.[70] The bourgeois pacifism of Saint-Simon and Comte, which applied equally to national and social conditions, is swept brusquely aside by Maurras; of far greater importance to him is the quasi-pacifism of the socialists, diametrically opposed to his own pacifism. The clairons (bugles) of the défense nationale are mingled with the more sonorous instruments of the défense sociale: "In France one may state the axiom, 'No army, no public order.' The radical, socialist, and Communist masters will then be masters of all."[71]

State and Classes

Défense Sociale. Again, it is theoretically possible to imagine a state which is sovereign and martial but internally classless. Again, modern reality is otherwise. It follows that even a nationalist movement must, like any other party, have an internal political program and a definite social relevance, even though it may, more than any other party, be inclined to hide this aspect under moral postulates and, compared to the demands of foreign policy, to keep this program in the background. Since a nation is the sum of its differences, every far-reaching political decision entails power shifts among the various groups. Even a nationalist seizure of power under the banner of "national unity" cannot eliminate these differences; to the problems of internal policy with which it is faced, it offers a certain solution which is henceforth beyond discussion. Maurras' doctrine, which did not become the official state ideology (or only partially and belatedly), offers an incomparable opportunity of studying the "class nature" of the movement.

Generally speaking, Maurras' statements on this subject are quite elementary and spontaneous. "Ah, let us defend ourselves against the barbarians!"[72] These barbarians are not the Germans or the Russians: they are the "barbarians from the depths," the "enemies at home" who would start their socialist or anarchist revolution "tomorrow" if the army did not prevent them.[73] But he is not thinking merely of a brand of revolutionaries and the crowds which follow them. Even the movement that later became the Popular Front is far from being the "Left" which Maurras has in mind. For the past twenty-seven years, so he stated at the beginning of the century, the forces chiefly represented by the National Assembly of 1871 and forming the nation's elite, had been regularly defeated and governed by the forces of the enemy.[74] All republicans, all liberals, were therefore regarded by Maurras as "Reds," champions of "egalitarian barbarism," and a barricade had to be raised against them. Over and over again, and with no false sense of discretion, he names the strata on which he wishes to rely. At the top are always the church and the officers' corps (*l'armée*), in other words, not classes in the true sense. They are followed by "landed gentry, peasants, old aristocracy, old and new bourgeoisie."[75] The last definition is the broadest and is obviously imprecise.

In *L'Avenir de l'Intelligence* Maurras had already banished cosmopolitan "finance" from the national bourgeoisie, and no doubt one must also eliminate the anticlerical urban petite bourgeoisie, which had been the real pillar of the revolution. It is of great significance, however, that Maurras can attempt to drive a wedge not through this class as a whole—a class of such vital importance to France—but through that section of the intelligentsia which could be considered the voice of that class. For he divides the freethinkers into anarchists and bourgeois, and proposes an alliance between the latter and the Catholics on account of their common love of social order and stability. "I do not maintain that it must necessarily come to this; but if it does not come to this, we are lost."[76] In other words, Maurras pays the utmost attention to the relatively classless intelligentsia, and this is natural, since after all he regards socialism not as a spontaneous class movement of the workers but as a phenomenon artificially created by revolutionary intellectuals. Yet it is quite plain that Maurras has some unmistakably "bourgeois" reactions. All through his life he regards socialism primarily as "looting" (*pillage*), and he believes that the Jews are chiefly attracted by French "fortune": "They want to denationalize us in order to plunder us."[77] He even lets slip the dubious remark that the two most powerful forces in man are religious faith and the sense of property.[78] He quite logically sets out the unity of the three *défenses*: "religious defense plus (and not minus) social defense plus (and not minus) national defense."[79] To paraphrase Maurras' own words, this can only mean "national defense, but ... "; and for this limitation he has not even the excuse that he is concerned with ideas. Again a specific feature of Maurras' monarchism is exposed: plebiscite Caesarism with its revolutionary origin is suspect because it favors *défense nationale* too much, whereas monarchy guarantees the unity of the three *défenses*: "To patriots, to Catholics, to traditionalists, to men of order, we say: If you wish to preserve such of your possessions as still remain, if you wish to avoid the excesses of opposing evils, then create the monarchy, which will syndicate the defense of all that you love against all that you hate."[80]

This might be interpreted as a remarkable confirmation of the Marxist thesis of class roots and class interests. It is a fact that history knows of no case where a leading class has voluntarily renounced what may be called its essential privileges for the sake of the fatherland. But these privileges always remain associated with the guidance and the life of society. Whether they are actually superfluous or harmful is decided by the degree of indignation and resistance they engender. It is doubtful whether a truly leading class can have a mere class interest at all. It is a sign of the strength of Maurras' social self-awareness when he states: "But I am not a moderate, says Sangnier, I am a revolutionary, an antibourgeois. This pathetic defense does not deceive the masses. ... One should never deny the class of one's origin, class consciousness is one of the factors of national consciousness."[81] But Marc Sangnier's attitude is more typical of that profound schism within the bourgeoisie itself, a schism which is perhaps the most striking stigma of European history in more than a century. For communism (before the consolidation of the U.S.S.R.) is almost as much of a nonentity as fascism once one imagines it deprived of its bourgeois element.

The Schism in the Bourgeoisie. It is a mark of the power of this schism that Maurras, despite the strength of his social self-awareness, was to become one of its most outstanding representatives.

De Maistre was antiliberal because he was a Catholic and an aristocrat, Maurras is antiliberal although he is an unbeliever and a bourgeois, and yet he does not deny his origin, thus paving the way for a situation in which bourgeoisie and liberalism can no longer be equated. It is true that he cannot help admitting that the bourgeoisie is related to liberalism, and he does not hesitate to reproach the bourgeoisie on this account: it is "the disputatious class, the most individualistic and the most divided of the whole nation."[82] The "energetic minority" which has been called upon to save the country would destroy itself if it gave itself up to discussion.[83] To this extent, therefore, this minority is antibourgeois and is opposed not only to the liberals but also to the "old conservative world which was always the headquarters of an insurmountable lack of political understanding,"[84] and to this extent it can look with sympathy toward the Left, toward the syndicalists. Even the Reds speak only "of the aristocracy of labor, of the will of the elites, of their rights, of the necessity of forcing this will upon the majorities."[85] Georges Sorel, his pupil Édouard Berth, Maurras' follower Georges Valois—all worked toward this rapprochement between royalism and syndicalism, while Maurras himself took the *Cercle Proudhon* under his wing, and no less a person than the man who was later to be the Duce of fascism observed these attempts with all the indignation of a Marxist heart. But if the trend toward mass agitation, the veering toward the Left, is typical of radical conservatism, Maurras did not allow it very much scope and generally even avoided using the Saint-Simon term "producer" on which the Italian nationalists were trying to build up their success. By and large he contented himself with the alleged classlessness of the *Camelots* and in social problems invoked de La Tour du Pin (whom, not without reason, he named more often than he quoted). For the rest he left no doubt that he was concerned not with destroying the bourgeoisie but with strengthening it. And if some doubts remained regarding the nature of his social and internal political views, one look at his early writings was sufficient to throw light on these.

The Reactionary Soil. For these writings develop, with complete clarity, the doctrine of the revolt of the slaves, a doctrine which can no more be ascribed solely to Nietzsche than its antithesis, the doctrine of dialectical progress, can be ascribed to Hegel. The doctrine of the revolt of the slaves is the radical negation of the emancipatory process in its practical aspect; it inevitably involves the rejection of "modern ideas," and is almost always nostalgic for the archaic, and it never fails to culminate in a search for the cause of evil. Generally speaking, Maurras does not see things as radically and unpolitically as Nietzsche, but in the practical assessment of emancipation there is scarcely any difference. "How many men do we know who, born to be slaves, would regain their peace inside the *Ergastule* [slaves' prison] from which modern history has been foolish enough to banish them!"[86] The word "banish" (*exiler*) is a good indication of the gap between the optimistic and lofty concept of liberty of Hegel and (say) Marx, and the esthetic and pessimistic naturalism of Schopenhauer and Hartmann as translated baldly by Maurras into sociology. The direct link between the Greek mythological wording of *Le Chemin de Paradis* and modern reality appears in another passage from its preface: "Anyone who arouses the first concupiscence in the mind and bowels of a primitive person, who reduces the venerable privilege sometimes possessed by those fortunate people, that of dying without having lived, must be greeted by the contempt of man."[87] This may sound at first like a pious indictment of *concupiscentia*, but a footnote makes it clear that the sense is highly topical and political. Without further comment, it quotes a statement of Lassalle's to the effect that the German worker must be taught to realize how unhappy he is.

Even this wording conceals Maurras' real thoughts if one interprets them as an objection on his part to Lassalle wanting to create a false awareness. His esthetic-cosmological concept of order is required to provide the key. Seen thus, order exists as rank, hierarchy. It would be easy to grasp his concept and easier to defend it if it were merely a question of everything in "its" place according to its greater or lesser capacities. This is a rough picture of the Catholic doctrine of order. But it presupposes a different world picture from that of Maurras, the reader of Lucretius. It is not an inevitable corollary of their nature that atoms, the "fathers of the world," are divided into those which are shut away forever in the dark heart of things and those which are "fortunate" enough to revel in the light. The fate of every atom is mere "co-incidence," but it is only out of this coincidence that the unique and happy constellation of beauty and perfection can grow. "The whole world would be less good if it contained fewer mysterious victims whose sacrifice contributed to its perfection."[88] Quality is rank: it is this mechanistic assumption that gives Maurras' doctrine of order its unmistakable flavor. Although Maurras' statements frequently assume the usual "organic" scale in which order and beauty are normal and victorious, one is always conscious of his underlying fear that beauty and order, which are *not* in the nature of things, must perish if their accidental nature and their injustice are acknowledged. It follows that workers really are "victims." But when they acknowledge this, it means the end of "beautiful inequalities." Hence democracy is to be regarded as that form of government which is not prepared to sacrifice anyone and hence allows everyone to have his say. It is precisely for this reason that it is *le mal et la mort*.

Whatever the interpretation and the reasoning may be, there can be no doubt of the "reactionary" quality of Maurras' social views. The demand for peaceful labor relations and co-operation among the classes is reactionary from the standpoint of Marxism; the preservation of a hereditary aristocracy will also be described as reactionary by conventional liberalism. But the desire to reinstate as the axis, as the "strong main body" of the state's leadership, a hereditary aristocracy which was overthrown long ago and which has virtually disappeared from political life is reactionary in a more general sense.[89]

Every radical conservatism, however much it may incite the masses, reveals obvious reactionary traits. Nevertheless, the reasoning is generally clear enough to average human understanding, and even if Maurras goes further than usual in the matter of hereditary aristocracy, his arguments are quite simple: "The evil which must be eliminated is competition: competition of earnings, competition of talents or ambitious aspirations."[90] Although this applies primarily to the ruler, it also essentially concerns the leading class, whose quality consists in its rank. Maurras even extends this principle downward and arrives at some very far-reaching conclusions: by means of the triple play of physical, political, and economic heredity, nature produces a businessman or a diplomat with greater ease and at less cost in a race of businessmen and diplomats than in a race of winegrowers or soldiers.[91] Although certainly correct in many cases as an empirical statement, as a principle and postulate in a society such as the present one it is grotesquely reactionary. It may be maintained that a corporative, noncompetitive society with a hereditary monarchy and aristocracy means a "better," or at any rate more tranquil, existence than capitalist competitive society with all its unrest; but not even the most skillful pen can demonstrate that it means "progress." Maurras has to pay the price of never really developing a doctrine of society. By invoking de La Tour du Pin and Le Play (two irreconcilables, moreover), he has always felt justified in devoting his attention exclusively to governmental and political forms. De La Tour du Pin's anticapitalistic corporatism is, of course, compatible with Maurras' hereditary aristocracy; but how the dynamics of the capitalist social structure are supposed to tolerate the age-old repose of an (essentially) noncompetitive aristocratic class as its political head remains unexplained. For in actual practice Maurras never manifested an anticapitalist attitude beyond his anti-Semitic aversion to "finance." In fact after *Enquête* he hardly ever returned to this pivotal question of hereditary aristocracy, and in its place he put forward the more nebulous concept of the elite. He never achieves a clear solution to the problem (so difficult for every radical conservative) of an aristocracy exempt from the people's sovereignty and from intellectual and economic competition and thus, to a certain extent at least, hereditary.

His polemic against the abolition of the *Décret de Messidor sur les préséances*, which was proposed by Clemenceau in 1907 and was responsible for the defining of the precedence of civilian over military authority even on the lower levels, was also quite plainly reactionary. But even though during his long life-time Maurras never saw the reinstatement of a hereditary aristocracy either in France or elsewhere, he might have flattered himself for a brief moment during the Vichy period that he had finally triumphed over Clemenceau after all.

Similar treatment can be extended to a third reactionary theme. The idea that "for woman the single goal [*fin*] is man"[92] is deeply rooted in popular sentiment, and in the majority of cases it is doubtless true. Yet it contradicts one of the most remarkable phenomena of modern times: the emancipation of women.

Ambiguity of Defense. All three themes are reactions to similar and universal processes: the retreat of heredity, the threat to the social precedence of the military, the undermining of the unconditional juristic domination of the man. There was no more urgent task than to make the resistance to these and similar manifestations as international as they themselves were. In all countries their political form of expression—democracy—did not lack for sympathy and support for similar aspirations, and the socialists had even managed to create an international organization. Hence the stronger the element of *défense sociale* became in nationalism, the more it was bound to tend toward an alliance of all threatened interests on an international level. In France, however, this obvious assumption did not apply. On the contrary, it was the most demagogic and, from the conservative aspect, the most questionable trend—that of Drumont—which worked with the greatest vigor toward an anti-Semitic International. Maurras remained aloof from all tendencies toward an *Internationale Blanche*, apparently because, by the use of a doubtful thesis, he ascribed the revolution to Germany, thus overemphasizing the national element to a degree not necessarily inherent in the basic structure of this thinking. But to him, too, the Jew, along with the German, remained the prime cause of evil, and even he could not readily identify one figure with the other. Hence the trend toward an international alliance with similar social forces remained as an undercurrent to his ideas, and he did not hesitate to express this when after the war France was in a position of military and political hegemony over the continent of Europe. In his view, the Treaty of Rapallo, dangerous though it might be, opened up positive aspects; the entire European counterrevolution could now join together in resistance to it.[93] The practical demand was as follows: "There is one road to salvation, ... there is only one: the International of Order, proclaimed by the French army in Berlin."[94] The more removed the possibility of the French army marching on Berlin, the further Maurras also moved away from that idea which for a moment had seemed to him the only appropriate answer to the universal revolutionary threat. But he never lost sight of it entirely. And hence he was wrong in dismissing as "traitors" those of his pupils who declared themselves in favor of the "International of Order" proclaimed in Paris by the German army. They had decided to extricate themselves from an ambivalence which challenged Maurras just as much as any other thinker of radical conservatism and fascism.

Critique of Socialism. Maurras' critique of socialism lacks the acuteness, trenchancy, and acrimony of his critique of democracy or pacifism.[95]

It is true that from the very beginning socialism forms the darkest foil to Maurras' social philosophy. It also supplies the background to his critique of democracy. Those who desire democracy in government, he says, must also desire it in industry, that is, they must have socialism: communism is no less than the logically extended republic. But throughout all this the black sheep is socialism, for whom liberalism and democracy are to be made responsible in order to discredit them. The blackness of the sheep is assumed—but not proved or analyzed. The arguments consistently reflect the social structure of France which, despite all political agitation, remained firm and strong and which never offered any real opportunity for Marxist revolution until 1944. Although (after 1914) Maurras did once say that Marx, not Rothschild, was the greatest Jew of the nineteenth century,[96] the section on Marx in the *Dictionnaire politique et critique* betrays a picturesque ignorance. His contribution to the fundamental critique of Marxism is limited to casual remarks without much content. His emphasis of the role of the democratic republic is merely a shift of emphasis in Marxist concepts: "Do you wish to put an end to socialism? Attack the elective system, your plight stems from that and will only come to an end when it does."[97]

A more original and significant fact is that Maurras did not take the internationalism of the Marxist movement very seriously. He soon regarded the

German Social Democrats as rabid nationalists and believed that only the French socialists were internationally minded. Even here he was mistaken, as future events showed. The "critique of facts," which he pursued in 1902, was more powerful than he imagined: "And I in turn will add that, far from forming a vast economic community among the nations in which all members are to be united, the European worker profits from the economic progress of his own country, just as he benefits from the economic deficiencies of rival countries."[98] Maurras' critique of socialism, then, is only significant insofar as it involves the discovery of the reality of the proletariat, which at that time was breaking forth on all sides and which only a few years later was to lead Lenin to form his doctrine of the workers' aristocracy—a discovery which, however, only acquires its tragic and moving emphasis when viewed against the background of Marx's and Engels' theses and aspirations. But if it is true that this critique cannot be called the focal point of Maurras' work, it is equally true that all signposts point toward it. No doubt anti-Marxism is only the potential background, as it were, to Maurras' antiliberalism, but already in his case one element cannot be separated from the other.

The Enemy as a Whole

Democrats, pacifists, socialists, are enemies—they are not *the* enemy. The enemy is a complex of enemies and causes which, although often varying in phenotype, are imbued with one uniform spirit. The examination of this tissue, the clarifying of its elements and interrelationships, constitutes the most striking part of Maurras' efforts. The attempt to define the spirit of the enemy in its primordial meaning is the very heart and soul of his philosophy. No related doctrine attains the trenchancy of Maurras' doctrine of the enemy, none is very far removed from it. In some cases a different stand is taken, or the actual philosophy may be neglected, but the basic description is the same.

Present Enemies. The tangible enemies of the present day are like icebergs, whose main bulk remains beneath the water. They form three ranks which at first sight appear to be quite far apart.

The first rank is composed of exponents of certain political doctrines. Liberalism, democracy, socialism, communism, anarchism, are varying manifestations of the same essentially individualistic revolutionary idea. They are linked together in a coherent chain which makes it possible to trace the absurdity of its most radical link, anarchism, to its beginnings, liberalism. To Maurras this theoretical coherence is more important than an empirical examination of the actual behavior of these forces. According to him, democracy obscurely reveres anarchy, the franker, bolder, and purer expression of itself:[99] Kropotkin's ideology is latent in Montesquieu's assumptions.[100] This is why *Kiel et Tanger* is aimed more at the moderate republicans (who in their

practical attitude were highly conservative) than at the "Red" radicals surrounding Clemenceau; this is why he claims to detest Mirabeau and Sieyès
more than Robespierre and Saint-Just. The doctrinarian, motivated by principles, hates more than anything else blindness toward ideological coherence;
he thereby eliminates for his party the important chance of achieving co-
operation with the conservative wing of the liberals. The predominance of the
ideological standpoint in the formation of even practical-political friendships
is one of the chief criteria for distinguishing radical conservatism from the
empirical-opportunistic variety.

The second rank seems to be of an entirely different kind. "Jews, Protestants,
Freemasons, aliens" are not primarily political entities. They can be traced back
to the sphere of Catholic dogma and only there do they have tangible meaning.
When Maurice Paléologue visited the Vatican during the Dreyfus affair, pity
for France was expressed there because it allowed itself to be ruled by "Freemasons, Protestants, atheists and Jews."[101] Maurras replaces the atheists by
the incongruous term *métèques* (aliens) and creates with his *Quatre États confédérés* a new political concept, one which might be acceptable to the positivists
but which brought in its wake all the hatred of religious warfare. Since the
Dreyfus affair it had been possible to advance many empirical reasons for this
concept which were convincing not only to Catholics. Those things which spoke
empirically against it were less obvious and were speedily dismissed, and the
propaganda was facilitated by a further simplification. For the four terms are
not of equal weight. Maurras did not emphasize the problem of the *métèques*
too greatly, for there were plenty of sons and grandsons of immigrants among
the best men of France. He also avoided becoming involved with the obscure
history of the Freemasons (in whose annals it would have been possible at one
time to find Joseph de Maistre). The chief accusation leveled at Protestantism
is that it was "Jewish"; in other words, the attack is of necessity concentrated
on the Jews—a characteristic not inherent in the Catholic series of "Freemasons, Protestants, atheists, Jews."

The third rank is composed of two neighboring nations, the Germans and the
English, together with the most remote and abstract power in the world, high
finance. The juxtaposition seems odd, but it is substantiated in many ways. For
instance, Maurras maintains after World War I that France's sovereignty is
being attacked by a "combination of Anglo-Saxon finance and Judeo-German
finance."[102]

It is not surprising that here, too, Jewry must provide the connecting link,
but Maurras is a long way from identifying finance with Jewry. His attack on
world finance is the most sporadic of his battles: it often subsides for years, only
to start up again suddenly. It reached its peak during Maurras' youth, in
L'Avenir de l'Intelligence. Here he tries to prove complicity between international finance and international revolution and claims that personal and
"national" wealth are the target of both.[103] He regards London and Frankfurt

as the headquarters of international finance, thus providing the link with the two most inimical nations.

England is the land where the Bible reigns, where the parliamentary system was born, its naval supremacy represents a standing threat to France's colonial possessions. Germany is the home of the Reformation, the birthplace of Kant, the robber of Alsace-Lorraine. Both are Germanic, that is, barbaric, countries, hostile to sunshine and clarity, as remote from the discipline of Rome as from the moderation of Greece. The more the liberal school had made paragons of them, the fiercer became Maurras' contempt and hatred for them. But his contempt is accompanied by paradoxically envious looks toward power and prestige, population strength and discipline, industry and prosperity.[104]

One important distinction, however, must not be overlooked. The English invasion took place five hundred years ago, the German invasion in the immediate past. If England gave the world the parliamentary system, Germany developed socialism. If England took the French colonies in America, German unity was born of France's defeat and hung like a sword of Damocles over the heads of yesterday's conquered. If England sent travelers, Germany sent its Jews. The scales of aversion sink in favor of England, and Germany reigns supreme on the horizon of hatred.

Thus from each rank one element comes to the fore, and the three combine to form the vanguard of the enemy of today—anarchism, Jewry, Germany: "The barbarians from the depths, the barbarian from the East, our Demos flanked by its two friends, the German and the Jew."[105] They are the protagonists of a European and planetary conspiracy against Catholicism and France; in their combined efforts a "diabolical plan" comes to fruition. But plan and conspiracy are not an invention of the day, their historical roots reach deep into the past until they become indistinguishably intertwined.

The Historical Roots. It is surprising to note that Maurras finds those roots which are closest to the present to be in the romantic era. In Germany the romantic era is considered the literary embodiment of the conservative and reactionary spirit. Nostalgia for the Middle Ages seems just as much an invention of this era as a sense of history and respect for historical data. But in France it is less easy to overlook the fact that the romantic era is inconceivable without Rousseau, and it is here that those other elements soon make themselves felt: the lawlessness of romantic subjectivity, the romantic fondness for innovations, the hostility toward a classical tradition which, in contrast to Germany, was also a political tradition. It was with the heirs and successors of the romantic era that the young Maurras fought his first literary battles, and in these skirmishes it was already apparent how closely related esthetic and political categories were in his mind. For example, he charges a symbolist author with being a theoretician of the anarchist republic in the field of art, with never writing two words which are not at each other's throats and which do not accuse each other of infringing on the sacred rights of their individuality.[106] He writes his *Les Amants de Venise, George Sand et Alfred de Musset*, to show the *hubris* and sin of unfettered individualism exemplified by the erotic licentiousness of George Sand, who betrayed the beloved poet with an Italian doctor almost under his very eyes when he was ill. The real product of the romantic era was, to Maurras, corruption. And corruption was the product of the father of the era, who was also the father of the revolution—that *misérable Rousseau*. The attack on Rousseau runs like a thread throughout Maurras' work: more substantial than his criticism of Marx, more violent than his polemic against Kant, more tireless than his diatribe against Chateaubriand. According to Maurras, Rousseau, lacking any intellectual or moral resources, filled with the resentment of an "indignant and aggrieved sensibility," had arrived at the capital of the civilized world "like one of those false prophets who, spewed out of the desert, wrapped in an old sack, girded in a camel skin and his hair filthy with ashes, paraded their melancholy lamentations through the streets of Zion."[107] It is always the Rousseau of "back to Nature," the advocate of the infallibility of one's own conscience, the defender of the people's sovereignty, whom Maurras has in mind. He as much as ignores Rousseau, the appealer for civic unity, the teacher of an inviolable *religion civile*, the enemy of the parliamentary system. It is the attacker, not the attacked, that Maurras always sees in individualism. This is characteristic of the situation in which he writes—a situation which, of course, does not exist solely in the battle against the *mystique dreyfusienne*[108] as a synthesis of the romantic era and the revolution, but which in its most universal form is common to conservatism and fascism.

The main target of romantic and revolutionary individualism is that spiritual, moral, esthetic discipline, that vested order of reason and taste, which has come down as Greece's most priceless heritage by way of Rome to France. Maurras' classicist humanism leads him to draw the dividing line in eighteenth-century thought very much as the liberal school does, yet in a quite different sense. He separates Voltaire and sometimes even Montesquieu from Rousseau, not as different trends in the same movement, but as diametrically opposed representatives of a "classical" and a "revolutionary" spirit. He is therefore obliged to destroy the spiritual unity of the century and to purchase the immaculateness of his classical era at the price of the incomprehensible fact that one single man, and a foreigner to boot, could undermine its self-confidence and steer the age toward revolution.

It is true, of course, that Maurras did not regard Rousseau as an isolated individual. It was no coincidence that he had been born in Geneva and was a Calvinist. But the spirit of Protestantism which he stands for is utterly foreign and extraneous to the Roman-classical-Catholic spirit. Maurras apparently derives his interpretation of the Reformation as "the revolt of the individual against the species" from Comte, but he overlooks the close and vital bond existing for Comte between the "negative" spirit of Protestantism and the preceding era, and he overlooks to an even greater extent the positive aspect of this negative quality: its progressive spirit. Violent and undialectical comparisons dominate Maurras' thinking in all its dimensions. In the same way that he separates the revolution from the eighteenth century, so he separates Protestantism from the late Catholic Middle Ages. If the Reformation signifies nothing more than the "unleashed tumult of spiritual life,"[109] if it is nothing but an anarchistic attack on the civilization of Rome, then it must have its roots beyond Rome, in a barbaric, anarchistic, anti-Roman phenomenon. By taking over the self-interpretation of Protestantism while reversing its emphasis, he finds this phenomenon in early Christianity. This is actually a form of Jewish prophetism, whose anticivilization and primitivistic nature had been described by Renan. The anticivilization element combines the "Hebrew desert" with the "Teutonic forests": the prophet's cry awakens in the Teuton the unfettered raging of his instincts, Biblicism and Teutonism unite in modern barbarism. Thus the familiar liberal thesis that liberty and democracy originated in ancient Germany acquires a new and unfamiliar emphasis. Democracy, born in the Teuton forests, rightly drew its sustenance and strength from the Christianity of the Jew Jesus who—again according to Renan—was an anarchist visionary: "The fathers of the revolution are in Geneva, in Wittenberg, and in more ancient times in Jerusalem; they derive from the Jewish spirit and from varieties of an independent Christianity which were rampant in Eastern deserts and Teutonic forests, in the various focal points of barbarism."[110]

This Judaism, however, far from being a mere distant historical root, is to be found unchanged in all its freshness in the modern world: "The Jew, a monotheist and fed by the prophets, has become an agent of the revolution."[111] (Nor was Maurras by any means the originator of this thesis. It had been presented in France—with different emphasis, of course—by Bernard Lazare, and in Germany by the outstanding neo-Kantian, Hermann Cohen.) If Rome had succeeded in rendering the "poison of the Magnificat"[112] harmless, if medieval society had been able to restrict and exploit the Jews, Protestantism and the revolution have torn down the barriers, and the rebellious barbarian stands menacingly within the walls of a deeply convulsed society.

Maurras once presented this Manichaean black-and-white image in the form of a historical tale from the early days of his native Provence (*L'Étang de Marthe et les Hauteurs d'Aristarchê*):[113] The Phocaeans, the founders of Marseilles, were led by a cultured Ephesian lady, Aristarche, who faithfully nursed the worship of Artemis and Athena on the heights of the newly founded city and transplanted Greek culture, "the taste for the perfect, the cultivated, the complete," to the new Greece. Centuries later Marius the Roman brought his Syrian soothsayer Martha to that part of the world. Repulsed by the Greek inhabitants, whose city religion naturally excluded the "free priests and the wandering priestesses," she settled in the marshes, close to the con-

fusion primitive, in order to practice her magic arts, communicate with the spirits, exorcise, drive out and call up devils, and make herself indispensable to the primitive people in the vicinity. "She confused the heart of man. She isolated him, led him astray. She was welcomed as a benefactress." Then in a great vision Maurras links up this first barbaric invasion of his country with all subsequent barbaric incursions and finally declares: "All the great periods of distress in history—for our own Occident as a whole as well as for its little market towns—are accounted for by the emanation of this same Jewish and Syrian miasma."

Nature and Significance of the Doctrine of the Enemy. This is something more than a most remarkable reversal of liberal historical thought: the imagery betrays its unprecedented character despite the adoption of familiar elements.[114] The age of the Enlightenment had always depicted its relationship to the preceding era of blind religious faith by contrasting light with darkness. The battle against darkness can be carried on grimly, obstinately, even fanatically: but by its very nature it proceeds without acrimony and without despair, for it seems that darkness must of necessity precede light and finally yield to it. "Miasmas," "leprosy" (*la lèpre anarchique et juive*),[115] "microbes,"[116] are insidious, unassailable, lethal enemies of the healthy body; unlike light and darkness, the enemies are incommensurable and resistance to them is grim and desperate. This unmistakable mentality becomes as clear with Maurras as the quite extraordinary direction which the struggle will later take in the field of practical reason.

The enemies are great in number, but one among them stands out, the one who furnishes the world conspiracy with its spiritual background and its most gifted personnel: the Jew. However, since it is almost impossible to grasp him directly, he must be attacked in that power with which he has most closely allied himself. That power is Germany. Although even before 1914 Maurras always associated Jewry and Germanism, now after the victorious ending of the war he makes use of every opportunity to denounce Germany as the center of world revolution: Germany is the "stem and root" of Russian bolshevism;[117] German Jews are the masters in Moscow;[118] Berlin is the head of the worldwide conspiracy whose branches cover Moscow, Bucharest, Tiflis, Ankara, Athens, and Tunis.[119] There is only one effective way to eliminate this world threat: destroy German unity, which is desired chiefly by Jews and socialists, and restore those "German liberties" (the situation during the period following the Peace of Westphalia) which had for so long ensured the peace and well-being of Europe.[120]

There can be no doubt as to who is the enemy in Maurras' eyes. It is the emancipatory process itself in all its manifestations. Maurras undertakes the same reassessment of the course of history that led Nietzsche to his concept of the *Attentat*, but he has none of Nietzsche's nonpolitical radicalism: archaism, the repudiation en bloc of Christianity, the Dionysian cult. His "humanism" is exaggerated to the point of radical classicism,[121] but it leaves the way open to the (somewhat foreshortened) Periclean Athens; his Catholicism is anti-Christian, but it does not quite bar the way to the true Rome;[122] his classicism may appear rigid, but it allows him to remain in positive contact with the rationalist-universalist philosophy of Europe.[123] That which on the intellectual level appears as a tempering of the hostility to history toward which every radical conservatism tends, is precisely what makes his political effectiveness possible. (Hitler achieved this by keeping silent.) As a politician Nietzsche could at best have established a sect, although there is no doubt that his thinking defines a border line which practical politics can approach asymptotically.

It would be easy to pick holes in Maurras' theses: they are there for all to see. But with all their weaknesses these theses demonstrate that the contrary axioms of the liberal theory of history could no longer be taken for granted. A profounder critique would be one which pointed out that the contrary theories exhibit the same elements but give them a contradictory interpretation. Whether this is a sign of weakness or necessity can only be established by examining the philosophical significance of the two doctrines. For the time being, all that is required is the pragmatic presentation of the relevance of Maurras' doctrine to the French self-image.

It is easy to underestimate the difficulty of France's intellectual position since the middle of the eighteenth century. This difficulty arose from the fact that France was the most progressive of the Catholic countries. The entire body of liberal thought, however, regarded "progress" as synonymous with "anti-Catholic," and took it for granted that the Reformation had been the essential precursor of freedom of thought. This accounted for the curious Germano-philia, which was actually nothing but the despair of liberal thinkers over France's Catholic past and present. The revolution did not do away with the tormenting problem. It succeeded too well, and yet did not succeed enough for friend and foe not to have been filled with gnawing doubts. France, it seemed, was too progressive to be Catholic, and too Catholic to be truly progressive.

Joseph de Maistre's eyes were turned toward Rome, Michelet pinned his hopes on Germany, whose democratic revolution was to give the French progressive party its final consolidation. It was clearly the mission of critical liberalism to moderate violent contrasts and to enable France to achieve a new self-respect on the soil of a new synthesis. Comte contributed notably in this direction, but Renan and Taine, under pressure of events, developed a nationalism which actually radicalized and embraced their Germanophilia as a vital element, the result being a highly dubious synthesis of the Catholic and the progressive trend. Maurras ignored any such synthesis; by rejecting Germano-philia he also eliminated liberalism, although he retained the positivist interpretation of Catholicism. By so doing he consolidated one of the two opposites on another level and infused it with new young life. He thus restored France's self-respect as a Catholic and Latin power, but at the cost of refashioning, that is, crippling, his own country, and at a moment when for the first time a reconciliation with the other side had become possible.

The Battle

Intellectual Struggle and "Purging." To paint a picture of the enemy which renders him as hideous and repulsive as possible may constitute a victory, but it does not do away with the necessity of fighting for each position. When Voltaire called the church *l'infame*, the battle had scarcely begun.

The opponent whom Maurras challenged was formidable. The enemy's claim to represent *the* "modern point of view" had hardly yet been disputed. "Progress, liberty, science" was not merely the inscription above the literary side door to the spacious palace of Europe: it was blazoned across the political and official main entrance. But fissures and cracks had long been visible in the splendid edifice of the liberal continent. They had first begun to show in the differences between Voltaire and Rousseau and had really come to light in Marx's critique of Hegel, whose system had been the most impressive and consistent definition of Christian-Protestant ideas of liberty. When the inhabitants of the newly built servants' wing ran up their own flag and began to speak threateningly of storming the rooms of their masters, those who lived in the central portion were inclined to view with greater sympathy the ramparts of the oldest section, which till then they had derided for their inconvenience. Some even decided to move and eagerly widened the old embrasures in order to be able to mount new weapons in them.

This, then, might be a picture of the battle of the various trends in liberalism and conservatism. Maurras' strongest resource in the intellectual battle, however, was his ability to turn his enemies' weapons upon themselves.

They had prided themselves on the critical and scientific spirit and had dedicated it to the battle against obscurantism and superstition. Now in defending tradition Maurras boasts of his method as being the most modern and the most appropriate: "The critical spirit, the positive methods of science, a naturalism stripped as much of all antireligious as of all religious intentions— these are the essential causes of recent intellectual events."[124]

Republicans and democrats had always claimed "progressiveness" as their hallmark. But Maurras gives their principle of equality a purely abstract interpretation, deduces from biology the law that all progress complicates and differentiates, and comes to the conclusion: "This democratic republican principle is therefore in direct opposition to the scientific laws of all progress."[125]

"Unity of theory and practice" was declared by the socialist party to be its own special achievement. But was it really invented by Marx? "I have never been able to make much out of this distinction between action and contemplation. That comes to us from the Orient. The master of Western philosophy said: To know, in order to foresee, so as to make provision; to induce, in order to deduce, so as to construct."[126]

The parliamentary regime considers itself "modern" as against the "reactionary" monarchies. Maurras says: "The parliamentary system, according to Montesquieu a product of the Teuton forests, is a barbaric machine, too slow and too cumbersome to respond to the conditions of the new order. This Merovingian chariot must make way for the automobile."[127]

"Unity of the nation" was the battle cry of the French middle class against the arrogant aloofness of the aristocracy. "Classlessness" was what the proletariat demanded from a privileged bourgeoisie. But the Action Française boasted of a "proud youth recruited from all classes in the land."[128] In this way it lays its claim to the future and relegates its enemy to the side of the moribund and the rigid; all over the world, it said, the old republican attitude was dying out.[129]

This seizing of the enemy's weapons is often contrived and by no means altogether convincing. It always bears the stamp of reinterpretation. At this point we come up against the fundamental fact that it is not just a case of determining which realities are to be subclassified under which incontrovertible concepts: rather, it is precisely this relation to the primary concepts of progress, liberty, and science that is ambiguous. A few examples will bear out the forced nature of this reinterpretation.

For instance, Maurras deals with Marx's confrontation between capitalists and proletarians, but reinterprets it to give it exactly the opposite meaning by calling the rich the "active and fortunate producers" and the poor the "greedy consumers."[130]

It is not surprising that he tries to imbue the conservatives with a new self-respect by saying: "You were treated as stragglers, and you stood for progress."[131] For if progress had till then necessarily been thought of in terms of the future, with Maurras it acquires a new and surprising relationship: "To the radicals who say 'We do not wish to go back to the past,' the evidence replies that behind, in the past, there were advantages, ... superiority, progress."[132]

It is obvious that Maurras isolates only certain subordinate elements of the great emancipatory concepts of liberty, progress, and science with the positive intention of being better able to deny the overall meaning.

The meaning of Maurras' federalism[133] is to provide a climate for individual spontaneity, to create "liberties" within a local setting which are concrete and feasible. The revolutionary concept of liberty, however, with its gigantic demand that each individual be responsible for the whole (its highest philosophical exposition is Kant's categorical imperative) is to him the greatest threat of all. The demonstration of the fatal quality and the absurdity implicit in this interpretation of liberty is the pivotal theme of his entire life's work.

He sees "progress" primarily as differentiation, the establishing of inequalities. But the important thing is not so much empirical differences as the atmosphere surrounding and defining them. A king is a king and different from the people; but whether slaves kiss his feet, or subjects show their devotion, or fellow citizens shake his hand, is a difference of the utmost significance. Progress in the liberal sense is emancipation, "progress in the knowledge of liberty," which is synonymous with the progress of the unity of the world. And Marx's position is not so far from this Hegelian definition as might appear. To Maurras, however, this rising and intelligible historical line of liberal thought is "a barely secularized Messianism."[134] But Messianism is Oriental and mystical. The effrontery of Jewish chiliasm has spared neither the secret of the grave nor the secret of the cradle, yet in three thousand years of speculation it has deceived only itself and the simple-minded.[135] And just as he criticizes the determinism and rationalism of the idea of progress, so he also criticizes its vision of a goal: centralization and unification are not by any means predetermined. All through the universe there is a superabundance of disintegrating tendencies.[136] But the critique of the component parts is clearly also intended to include a critique of the basic concept: that such a thing as progress of liberty exists and, moreover, that it is the *unum necessarium*.

Maurras ascribes a "scientific character" to his natural laws of social existence. But his attitude toward science is far from being positive. "There exists today a kind of scientific fanaticism which threatens to spell the doom of science: it would blow up everything in order to test an explosive, it would ruin a country to extract an interesting document from the archives and bring it to light. This anarchistic and revolutionary system derives from a metaphysical source. ..."[137] These extreme examples reveal his obvious intention: to attack the supranational objectivity of science whose lifeblood is that ruthlessness which refuses to subordinate itself to anything else and is in that sense indeed "anarchistic."

It is only logical that Maurras very soon began to make demands that science submit to a national cleansing process. Even before the Dreyfus affair he denounced the historian Gabriel Monod as a "German outpost at the university"[138] and vociferously demanded the elimination of German influence in the academic field: "The end of this kind of university scandal will mark our rehabilitation."[139] Naturally the war gave great impetus to this "intellectual police action"[140] and to the "purge"[141] which paved the way. Even the most harmless and well-worn lines of international scientific communication, the system of "correspondents" in the great scientific institutions, were attacked with vindictive arguments: Why was the Institut de France permitted to retain as correspondents the colleagues of the arsonists of Louvain and Reims?[142] But it is not only against the Germans that he calls for police action. In his earliest political essay he demands that the theoreticians of political anarchy be watched, and that this surveillance should also include religious sects inclining toward anarchy. He does not actually say "anarchism": he obviously means everything to the Left of the positivist conservatives. This three-quarter totalitarianism he calls "the most complete spiritual freedom."[143]

Power and Inferiority of the Enemy. But Maurras does not manage to hide the universal hostility which makes it impossible for him and his movement to enter into an alliance with any but stronger powers or suicidal ones. His dislike of England was scarcely less than his dislike of Germany, but he also opposed the Russian alliance before both World War I and II. For America—"nebulous aggregate of population"[144]—he felt little but contempt, and even his espousal of Mussolini's cause before World War II was bound to appear suspect in Italian eyes, coming as it did from a man who had consistently disparaged Napoleon III because the emperor supported the idea of Italian unity. Was not Maurras' ire over the foreigners in Paris aimed not only at the "Russian, Galician, and Rumanian Jews, revolutionaries all of them,"[145] but also at the harmless Italian restaurants in the heart of the city?[146] He did, to be sure, try to ally himself with (real or pretended) separatist forces in Germany; but it soon became all too clear that he regarded the Bavarian and Rhineland Catholics merely as coldly manipulated tools and a long way from being fellow soldiers in a great and common cause. How the alliances with the pope and with the pretender to the throne ended is well known. His only ties which—so it seems—remained sincere and free of ulterior motives were those with the army. Yet there are probably very few men who have been as outspokenly critical of high-ranking officers and army functionaries as Maurras.[147]

The facts of the overwhelming strength of the external enemy and the weakness of his own country remain to torment him; they cannot be explained away by any intellectual deduction, any desperate calumniation. The strength and arrogance of the internal enemy, the steady defeats of "order" and "tradition," remain constant. Maurras was no stranger to doubt and perplexity, even despair, in the face of these facts, although his cultural self-confidence was never shaken. There would seem to be nothing left for him but the usual cultural pessimism or the extolling of rejuvenating barbarism, but Maurras extricates himself by a thesis of remarkable boldness: the enemy, despite unfavorable natural conditions, is powerful by virtue of sound principles of organization which, however, properly belong to France and the classical tradition. Thus he makes the enemy's superiority ground for an enhanced French pride: "Not because they broke with Rome, but because they plagiarized certain great Roman and French ideas, did London and Berlin become powerful."[148] The handful of Jews, Protestants, Freemasons, and aliens come face to face with forty million Frenchmen who are atomized by the laws of revolution, yet they themselves in collective unison penetrate and dominate the sand pile at will, like iron bodies.[149] This interpretation enables Maurras to stress the essential inferiority of the enemy. The German race (*race boche*) is "one of the most depraved,"[150] the German nation is "bad by birth, has come off badly, is in every respect badly equipped, with a heavy spirit and a base heart."[151] Even his most serious comments on the Germans never fail to add gratuitous insults to his potential insight: "Eternal candidate for civilization, the German only becomes civilized when he does not feel powerful; the idea of his weakness is the condition for progress toward perfection."[152]

The internal enemy fares no better. The booklet *Les Monod peints par eux-mêmes* contains a curious chapter headed "The Monod state peoples France with apes and madmen."[153] Here Maurras tries to prove—half jokingly, as he admits—that the Protestant Monod clan exhibits unusually numerous instances of mental illness and physical ugliness.

In a violent diatribe against Clemenceau he calls the leader of the Dreyfusards "Attila's revenge" and as an added proof cites his physiognomy: "Those Hun's whiskers, that nose, that Mongol skull!"[154]

If even a doctrine emphasizing as strongly as Maurras' does the "formal" character of politics, approaches so closely to a race doctrine (quite apart from its anti-Semitism), how strong must be the inclinations of the radical-conservative mentality toward this simplest of all ideologies![155]

The Elite to the Rescue, and the Supported Revolution. The democratic republic is more than an existing fact, a bad existing fact: it is above all a method by which foreigners rule France. Maurras regards it as axiomatic that within this framework the French elite cannot achieve supremacy, this elite being the antithesis of the people, of the masses. If the people are delinquent, distracted, and frivolous, in France there exists an elite which understands and does not forget.[156] Of whom does this elite consist? Maurras provides the simple answer: the best. "The best, in all the arts, professions, and classes; the best officers; the best philosophers; the best writers; the best administrators."[157] The first half of this definition is possibly an imitation of Saint-Simon's famous parable and perhaps not a very successful one; the second half expresses something concrete and revealing: namely, this elite is primarily an alliance between the officers' corps and the "national" intelligentsia.

This elite exists, but it is not yet aware of itself. It does not yet realize that its numerical weakness and its constant defeats under the democratic system constitute no objection to its political potential. For the natural relationship is this: "Will, decision, enterprise emanate from the small number; consent, acceptance, from the majority. It is to the minorities that virtue, boldness, power, and conception belong."[158]

But one condition needs to be fulfilled. Unity of will and doctrine are the first essential to the power of the minorities.[159] The French elite is still a long way from this unity. To create it is the task of an elite within the elite—the Action

Française. It must concentrate its propaganda on the "active classes" (among which he once also named "the workers in large-scale industry")[160] and instill in them the conviction that it is only the monarchy which, as the antithesis of the democratic republic, can conquer once and for all the anti-French forces and which, combined with the serviceable segments of the old aristocracy, can form from the elite that new aristocracy which will be the strong framework and the ruling class of a new France: "This boon—let us create it! This determined minority which will make history, which the masses will follow."[161]

The legitimacy of this minority consists in its inner strength (*force*). It does not allow itself to be duped by the democratic distinction between might and right. Like all monarchies and aristocracies it knows "that the world belongs to power, that is to say, to quality."[162] It knows that power is "good in itself."[163] Hence it does not desire to establish the monarchy otherwise than *par la force*.[164] But power is not muscular strength or the blind threat of a purely material force. Power is above all organization. Since democracy is by nature unable to organize itself, it is powerless, even though it may have the support of millions of votes.

The overcoming of a powerless government by a determined and well-organized minority is a kind of revolution. Despite his deep-seated aversion to the term, Maurras does not shrink from using it in this connection and from speaking of "conservative revolution,"[165] "revolution for the king."[166] Radical reaction is revolution against the revolution. What it is *not* is a blind and elemental popular revolt. It aims from the outset at the focal points of power. The praise which Maurras accords Guesde and his Marxists is highly typical: they were not intimidated by the apparently insuperable difficulties which a country of small and medium-sized property holdings such as France presented to the socialists; they had chosen "the good method" and striven above all for the winning of power as they were rightly of the opinion that what today seemed impossible would then become possible. Maurras is convinced that: "Faced by a group of resolute individuals who know what they want, where they are going, and where to break through, the rest gives way, yields, is led, and carried away."[167]

At this time, during the first decade of the century, European socialism's classic Marxist concept of revolution (the rising, led by the avant-garde, of the "huge majority" of the masses, proletarianized by industrial evolution) was supplanted by two extreme theories—reformism, and Blanquist-inclined bolshevism. In conservatism two very similar trends were occurring, and they could only really come to fruition in France since it was only in France that conservatism was not in power. While the Ralliement policy supported the idea of a republic in principle, the Action Française was the chief proponent of the use of violence in opposing those principles. Its position can be termed a conservative Blanquism. But there is one vital distinguishing mark between Blanquism of the Left and of the Right. The latter relies on elements of established authority, and its original trend goes so far as to limit itself to educational efforts toward the "French General Monk,"[168] toward the "revolution from above,"[169] and for the rest to leave the overthrow of the republic entirely to a military coup. Maurras' ideal "conservative revolution" was always the restoration of the Bourbons in 1814, for which feminine perseverance and cunning had been just as essential as Talleyrand's diplomatic skill. History's great hours are determined not by mystical necessity but by the will and resolution of individuals: "A small squad, four men, a corporal, can gain control over a whole regime if they have properly chosen the moment and the point of attack."[170]

But in his *Si le coup de force est possible*, Maurras discusses a second possibility. Actions of mass violence may be indispensable in modern times, and a "Monk" or nationally minded prefects are replaced by "somewhat reckless and daredevil 'partisans.' "[171] But an uprising does not yet signify the actual seizure of power. Here again, the aid of those holding key positions in the police, in politics, or in the army, remains decisive: "One relies on the master of the minute or the second, on the possessor of any segment of public power, during one of those days of ebullition and tumult when, as Drumont says, there is electricity in the air."[172]

Maurras' apparently unbridled voluntarism ("Anything can happen, so one is capable of anything. All that is required is the will. One should desire the utmost, and reality bursts forth.")[173] is therefore not without limitation after all. For one thing, a difficult and somewhat obscure relation exists between it and the theory of society's natural laws; for another, it is moderated by that attitude of respectful courtship toward established authority which later paid off as an essential ingredient of the successful "revolution" of the popular leaders, Mussolini and Hitler.

The Vision of the Future. The product of the conservative revolution, the monarchy, is by no means the idyllic pattern which many of Maurras' utterances appear to depict so fondly:

At home it means: "Restoration of the army, consolidation of public opinion, punishment of traitors, silencing of those with a mania for political parties, resurrection of authority."[174]

Abroad it means: "A diplomatic system ... a general plan of action in Europe and elsewhere ... unity, stability ... secrecy ... the ability to grasp the offensive at a given moment, to survive defeat or victory without revolution."[175]

To judge by these words, it might look like a good conservative program. But only at first sight. This monarchy is not a living and reconciling tradition. It is an "innovation" and can be understood by the great bulk of the people only as the most recent and emphatic expression of *défense sociale*. And if that is how it is understood, that is what it is compelled to be.

It is in no way reconciled with the liberal trends of the preceding century, in other words "constitutional." On the contrary it is, as Maurras has stated repeatedly, "absolute." This absoluteness must inevitably entail absolute hostility.

In foreign policy it does not acknowledge the most important result of the revolution: the crystallization of the principle of nationality. Its ultimate aim is the reduction of its principal neighbor to a state of weakness and partition, a state which centuries ago had actually been achieved by a French monarchy. But a central aim cannot be hidden. It can at best be denied, and this monarchy is capable of many subterfuges since it has a "general plan of action" and can wait patiently for the favorable moment; but in the long run it will not deceive its victim, it will only force him to the uttermost exertion.

Hostile to the outcome of history, hostile to its neighbors, basically hostile to its own people, this state will have to live in a condition of constant mobilization. The soldier-king will turn the state into an armed camp. The "traitors" will be many, and every punishment must act as a deterrent.[176] "Consolidation" of public opinion will inevitably mean its total manipulation.[177] The war, which is unavoidable, will be a life-and-death struggle, and it will not be possible to count on reliable allies since this state has never learned to value, honor, or cherish anything other than itself.

How insubstantial, when confronted by the reality of these implications, are the fine speeches about the free and spontaneous life of the provinces, about the security of existence in a state which has eliminated competition in politics! Within the framework of its essential conditions, although not by intention, Maurras' doctrine of state is fascist through and through.

Despair over the Unique. But now the subjective motivation underlying Maurras' political thought, insofar as it is *only* political, is also definable. It is his despair over that which is unique in recent European history.

Certainly Maurras would never have become a political thinker had it not been for socialism and the anarchist trend in democracy. We do Maurras an injustice if we regard him as *only* a champion of bourgeois class interests. This criticism comes all too easily if we overlook how unstable, how threatened, and how threatening the political system of the Third Republic actually was. It is a self-deception not to acknowledge how much naïve optimism and enthusiastic utopianism were exposed in the democratic-socialistic movement of the time.

Yet all this was merely an extreme and early form of that which stands out in all modern European history: the cry of the tormented is not stifled; even the radical adversary has his say; even antisocial utopia turns out to be the vehicle of an unprecedented progress. This historically unique development is not "good" and not "beautiful"; it is inexpressibly hard when it isolates individuals and makes them feel powerless; it is ugly beyond measure in that it ousts, drains, and destroys all traditional beauty. But the good and the beautiful are not historically unique: they were the rule up to the beginning of the new Europe insofar as they were synonymous with the simple and the "natural."

Technical progress and economic development have long ceased to be unique. But the fact that they are taking place within the framework of political institutions, which appear to be weakness itself, is without parallel in the history of the world.

In 1901 Maurras said to his vision of "Monk" in an imaginary conversation: "General, give us a king such as the other nations have."[178] At that time it was only the French political fate which seemed unique. Maurras despaired of it. But in reality the kings and their kingdoms were not as strong, united, and resistant as Maurras imagined. They, too, already bore the mark of that uniqueness on their brows. Even if they were not destroyed by it, they yielded to it to such a degree that France became merely one country among many. But the more unmistakable and universal this unique element became, the deeper and more widespread became the despair which it engendered. Maurras was simply one of the first to put a very common reaction into words.

The Philosophical Basis

Eternal Nature. We have seen how in his political thinking Maurras contemplates the threat inherent in his primordial fear and how he evolves a therapy. However, his entire thinking is permeated at the same time by certain philosophical convictions that now need to be examined. We are concerned with three levels which do not, of course, represent differing stages in time, as if there had originally been only one undefined fear which then found articulation in political thinking and was finally resolved in a philosophical conception. On the contrary, the fear is constantly being interpreted, and this interpretation confirms and intensifies the fear. The philosophical interpretation in turn forms part of Maurras' earliest work. Nevertheless, in a systematic study it is permissible and desirable to separate these levels, since only thus can we arrive at that summary which Maurras scarcely ever attempted.

The idea of "nature" is fundamental to Maurras' conception to an extent far beyond mere political polemic and "disarming" of the enemy (that is, using his weapons against him). He sees nature, in what seems to be an entirely Platonic sense, as a unity of immutable laws of existence: "As long as what is, is, the laws of existence succumb neither to the ravages of time nor to the oscillation of the universe. That our world is not eternal, that its materials pass away, evidence tells us this; but that its form endures, that its essential relations are fixed, and that they exist as long as it does, the evidence for this is no less clear."[179]

The doctrine of the immutability of essence applies also, and above all, to human nature. This immediately gives rise to a sharp conflict between Maurras and the historical philosophy of German idealists and Marxists who, although far from abandoning "eternal necessity," nevertheless wish to regard it primarily as a complex of evolutionary laws and thus get away from the "static" quality of Platonic philosophy. They tend toward the idea of the "transformation of human nature" and hence attach such extraordinary importance to history, since history constitutes the area of the transformation. What Maurras offers in its place seems to be either banality or *petitio principii*. According to him, history knows no essential changes: men steal, kill, and rape in an airplane as they do in a carriage or an automobile.[180] The great material and moral laws of human nature could not have been changed "by virtue of 1789 or 1848."[181] Now, of course, one is justified in asking whether Hegel and Marx really tried to envisage a transformation *of* human nature or a transformation *in* human nature. However, Maurras does not evolve his contradiction along the lines of fundamental considerations, but hastens instead toward concrete applications which throw a harsh light on the questionable nature of his interpretation.

Just as it is impossible for black to be simultaneously white, so it is impossible for "anarchy" to contain foresight and wisdom, for egalitarianism to be a match for nature.[182] The laws of the Consulate violated all the laws of nature and regarded the differences among Frenchmen as nonexistent, without, however, having actually been able to eliminate classes, for "what system could eliminate nature itself?"[183]

It is consistent with this alleged immutability that "blood" must play an important role as the most vital of all substances: "As long as men are begotten by blood, and blood is shed in battle, the truly political order will be administered by blood. ... States (as states) are dependent upon hereditary leading strata."[184]

There is no doubt that either all these "laws" must be formulated so abstractly and generally that they lose their political application, or that they are mere statements made during a given political situation. This becomes quite evident when Maurras gives a lively description of the spontaneous and unconditional acceptance by Englishmen of their government and king and adds the postulate: "One ought only to imitate here, not England precisely, but the true nature of the universe."[185]

In the area of human relations, Maurras' ontological basic principle, "the tendency of being to persevere in being,"[186] means primarily: self-preservation of the "natural" groups which within themselves are necessarily differentiated. Maurras would like to unite this self-preservation so indissolubly with the nature of the universe that he has recourse to a Greek or even Oriental image which is in sharp contradiction to the entire traditional European understanding of history: "The great wheel that turns and turns has made no progress, although nothing halts it."[187]

The Antinatural. But is Maurras a true Platonist? Where is the delight in beholding the divine and harmonious cosmos? Where is the profound confidence in eternal laws? Maurras' life is one long impassioned struggle in order to preserve something perishable which no inviolable law can secure from moral danger, which no turn of the everlasting wheel can bring back. His life is a grim, fear-ridden struggle against the "antinatural." For Plato the antinatural does not exist. Plato recognizes the principle of *chora*, in which ideas must of necessity attain only partial realization. He deals with sin and guilt, error and death. But he knows nothing of an active principle inimical to beauty, order, and truth. Yet this is precisely where Maurras' thought leads. He uses the term *dénaturé* in a purely derogatory sense, attempting in this way to express a condemnation: democracy, as a denatured state, is a denial of eternal laws, its call for liberty and equality is against nature, which requires subordination and hierarchy.

However, a glance at some of Maurras' less stereotyped phrases is more revealing. In a very early article reviewing Émile Pouvillon's "blood and soil" novels, he remarks that for the past hundred years French testamentary laws have been contrary to nature and the deepest instincts of the peasants, instincts which, however, these laws have been unable to destroy.[188]

He regards monarchy primarily as a "regime of flesh and blood, animated by a human heart, illumined and guided by human reason."[189] It is the antithesis of the denatured "anonym" of democracy.

France, Hervé, and Jaurès are not real enemies of the *patrie* to Maurras. "They have simply more or less detached themselves."[190] Patriots, alarmed by this detachment, will restore natural order by subordinating all their political ideas to the existence and salvation of the nation.

In these instances, then, "natural" means for Maurras the primitive instinct of the individual (the desire that his property endure, for instance), the personal character of the apex of the group, the unconditional allegiance of the individual to his group.

But whatever evaluation is arrived at, one thing is certain: even such fundamental "natural" realities are not to be taken for granted, nor are they impervious to attack. In the realm of humanity, something *exists* which renders even the primitive instincts of the individual uncertain; the anonymity of the exercise of power in the republic *exists*; intellectuals who strive for a point of view beyond their group *exist*. The antinatural exists. Above and beyond any obvious Platonism there arises the essential question in Maurras' philosophical thought: What is the true nature of the antinatural?

Monotheism. Maurras never had any doubts as to the most prominent indication of the antinatural in man. For man, his state, and his world, the greatest danger is not plague, famine, or war; it is his own heart, which is capable of dedicating itself to a single absolute and thus of transcending and destroying the beautiful unity of the manifold, its true domain. This basic conviction is already quite evident in *Le Chemin de Paradis*; it is a certainty even at the point where it is merely cautiously formulated as a query: "It is a case of knowing whether the idea of God, of a single god, present in the consciousness, is always a beneficent and politic idea. ... If, in this naturally anarchist consciousness, the feeling is allowed to germinate that it can establish direct relations with the absolute, infinite, and all-powerful being, then the idea of this invisible and distant master will quickly deprive the consciousness of the respect it owes to its visible and nearby masters: it will prefer to obey God rather than men."[191]

Thus the inmost meaning of Maurras' battle against liberty and equality is revealed. Liberty is not an empty idea: it is the primordial capacity of man's very soul to turn the gaze away from being and toward the invisible, non-being. It is not refuted by a demonstration that the invisible is an illusion. It is detachment itself and is indeed "anarchy" insofar as all rule is being and visible and as such can be transcended. This liberty, however, also means equality, for every man is as such defined by it, and it cannot by nature be split up into degrees and steps, however much differences may become palpable in real life.

Liberty puts everything, as it were, in brackets. If, however, primitive instinct and group allegiance are "natural," then that which puts them in brackets is "antinatural." Maurras is fighting the aggressive reality of history because it represents the ultimate threat to beauty, being, and the finite. There is no hope of destroying the antinatural, but it must be "channeled" if finite and natural human existence is to remain possible: "The delicate nature and the difficulty of the task ... consist, then, in rendering harmless the infinite and absolute principle which ... is introduced into human relations. Perhaps the solution is to be found in the establishment of terrestrial authorities whose task it is to channel, reactivate, and moderate this formidable intervention of the divine. This is what Catholicism does."[192]

What are the ideas and forces which have aroused and developed man's most mysterious potential, freedom toward the infinite?

First of all comes Jewish prophetism, which in a way is the "inventor" of monotheism. But Greek philosophy is also not without blame. Maurras praises Aristotle because he refused to reduce the universal to the One. Without specifically saying so, he thus rejects Parmenides and the Eleatics, who reduced the entire visible world to "appearance" in honor of the One and solely existing Whole.

Then comes Christianity in its very essence: the glad tidings of the heavenly Father, man's only Lord. Maurras has made little effort to hide the fact that he really wants to attack Christ and regards Catholicism as un-Christian precisely because, to him, Catholicism is the incomparable masterpiece of pagan and secular wisdom which by a hierarchical system of mediators makes the church the spokesman of man and eliminates both Father and Son.

The encapsuled poison was not released again until the advent of Protestantism, and one look at Milton beside Shakespeare (that "clear child of the Renaissance")[193] is enough to reveal what has happened: "Gloomy preachers have darkened the world and have clouded man's gaze."[194] German idealism merely represents the ultimate stage of Christian monotheism. Kant's ethic is hostile to the world and to man. "There *are* duties. Pagan wisdom seems to be in complete agreement with the Catholic Church. I fear that your austere duty, in the singular, is either very inhuman or very base ... if ... without discrimination and without circumspection it tries to control this troubled ocean of our human situations."[195]

The romantic religion of love is destructive, "the gloomiest and narrowest of human monotheisms."[196] Science is destructive, when it does not adjust to the service of higher interests; its system "consists of replacing the God of the Jews by curiosity, inappropriately known as 'science,' set up on an altar as the focal point of the world and accorded the same honors as Jehovah."[197]

These spiritual entities are not only older than the phenomena against which Maurras directs his political attack—the French revolution, liberalism, democracy, German nationalism, socialism—they are more universal in meaning, and only in the light of this meaning can we understand what in the final analysis these phenomena are. They are secularized monotheisms and thus a deadly threat to human existence, which has its being in the natural rhythm of the manifold and the beautiful. In their totality and unity with their roots, they are the negative intention of primordial fear: the enigmatic quality which in man himself sets out to destroy man.

Thus Maurras' oft-repeated comforting assurances vanish into unreality, assurances that humanity does not change, that whatever perishes returns. But against their true background appears that real philosophy of Maurras which is not speculation but artistic and political action, the fruit of a desperate passion for the finite, the here-and-now, the being: "This is the mystery of art. Art which unties also ties up. Art which liberates also excels in winding the chains which, hard or soft, hated or blessed, with or against our will, maintain us as true citizens of our world and acclimatize us to its suns."[198]

But only once did Maurras attempt to expound this philosophy and to superimpose it over the apparent ontology of being and form. This occurred very early, in connection with the review of a book by Jules de Gaultier with the fanciful title of *Le Bovarysme*. Under this heading Gaultier, connoisseur and popularizer of German philosophy in France, evolves a mixture of transcendental philosophy and psychological analysis which uses the term "Bovaryism" to indicate "the capacity for discontent and insatiability,"[199] and to clarify such phenomena as alienation, deracination, misunderstanding. On the whole Maurras agrees with him and expresses his own opinion as follows: "There exists in us—there exists in everything, even in the tiniest atom—an extraordinary tendency to emerge from ourselves. Call it the Spirit of the Eternal Migration, if you need spirits as in the *Arabian Nights*; but is it not, properly, Love itself?"[200] This is what he called antinatural, the very element of being, self-destruction of form, the reverse of that *tendance de persévérer dans l'être*, the fatal excess in the heart of what exists which the thinking entity, man, can support in extreme "monotheistic" delusion, the true basis of primordial fear in which the Occidental certainty of transcendence[201] is confirmed and at the same time reverts radically to the negative.

But even without this fortuitous interpretation, the meaning of Maurras' thought can now be defined in its broadest significance. That which arouses his fear, the fundamental capacity for distinguishing between being and that which is, between God and world, between "ought" and "is," can be understood philosophically as transcendence. Through the centuries it has been understood under a variety of names as the ultimate hallmark of human nature as such, until in the nineteenth century its association with the progressive and fundamental changes in human life became evident, and finally an anxiety, which was by no means *exclusively* political in nature, began to replace an excessively optimistic acceptance. What Hegel called "progress in the awareness of liberty" became for Nietzsche "total degeneration." But if Nietzsche[202] formulated his conception in a nonpolitical radicalism, Maurras, independently of him, was the first to transform his conception into word and deed in political reality. Maurras represents the literary and political resistance to transcendence,[203] and at the same time the unconditional defense of the autarchic, martial, aristocratic state of the *ancien régime* as a pattern for France at all times.

Failure and Tragedy. But did this grim campaigner belong at all to the world for which he was fighting? It has been pointed out that, with his vehemence, his narrow-mindedness, and his intolerance, he was the very opposite of a man of the *ancien régime*. His nationalism has been the subject of analyses which reveal a close relationship with Jacobinic nationalism (not altogether justifiably, as has been shown). It should not be overlooked, so it has been said, that, as a human and political type, he belongs completely to the democratic age of the powerful press and the supremacy of *l'opinion*. But the strength of these observations might possibly be impaired by saying that in war the enemy and the terrain rightly determine the cut and color of the uniform. However, there are more incisive and weighty factors to consider.

Maurras' nationalism, too, is a form of monotheism. It is true that he tried specifically to contrive a formal contrast between it and monotheistic German nationalism. The *hubris* of the latter aimed at making its own nation a *peuple-dieu*,[204] while Maurras' doctrine contained a variety of positive references to the Latin cultural field. These references are not convincing, however. Even if Maurras does not regard France as a *peuple-dieu*, he certainly sees it as a *peuple-humanité*,[205] and he often took pains to clarify the meaning of the expression *France d'abord*. No estheticizing sophism regarding the difference between *dieu* and *déesse* can disguise the fact that in his eyes neither a god nor a goddess existed besides and independently of the Goddess France.

His attitude toward the *unité de conscience* brings us even closer to the fractured core of Maurras' thought and emotion. He believed that this precious possession, the unity of faith among his people, had been lost, and that this fact had to be endured.[206] With all the force at his command, he always maintained the right of his heterodoxy vis-à-vis Catholicism. Any number of difficulties would have been avoided if the leader of the Action Française had made even only a formal avowal of Catholicism. Why was "Paris" not worth a Mass for *him*? There is only one convincing explanation: not only did he acknowledge a basic consequence of a development which he always described as "disastrous" (thus diminishing the value of his protest against all other results), but in the obstinacy with which he defended his heterodox convictions he stood squarely on the shoulders of Protestantism.

A model of the conservative tragedy: in the heart of the man who, of all Europeans, fought transcendence with the most vigorous and effective words, this transcendence never ceased to live on. But as a conservative tragedy the most paradoxical of all syntheses is the beginning of fascism, and this remains one of its basic characteristics even at that point where it can no longer be called a tragedy.

PART THREE

Italian Fascism

CHAPTER ONE

History

Fascism and the Action Française

The relationship between the Action Française and fascism must not be regarded as one of cause and effect. Direct influences do exist,[1] but by the same token even Italian nationalism—which of all the elements of fascism had the most contact with the Action Française—is not to be genetically deduced from it. On the other hand, they are certainly not merely parallel phenomena. If it is true that the practice of a small political group hardly bears comparison with that of a victorious mass movement in the twenty years of its unrestricted rule, it is also true that the precise, self-contained doctrine of the Action Française, and the often wavering, continually evolving doctrine of Italian fascism, do not move on the same plane. For the same reason the relationship cannot be considered one of design and realization. Perhaps only in the area of practice, organization, and style can the rudimentary design be perceived in the completed edifice. The doctrine of the Action Française as against that of fascism should rather be looked on as attracting, but not originating, the movement of the less coherent, less logical doctrine. Hence the Action Française is to fascism—however much both are simultaneously practice and theory—what philosophy is to life: just as life is more colorful, rich, and complex, so it is also less equipped with, and more needful of, direction.

How the European Knot Was Tied in Italy

In Italy the relationship between national state and antifeudal revolution, which was basic to the internal constitution of all European states, had been quite different from that in France. In France the revolution followed the national state; in a sense, the revolution endangered the state by destroying its solid foundation through the elimination of its state-forming power, the monarchy, and by jeopardizing its outward supremacy by proclaiming the principle of nationality. In Italy the national state was the result of the revolution, and in spite of all internal tension, the motivating factors of this revolution never disintegrated as they had in France. Gioberti as Sardinian prime minister in 1848 was no Mirabeau, and Mazzini as triumvir of the Republic of Rome was far from being a Robespierre. The people as a whole were never really aroused, and what were called *moti popolari* were directed against the foreigners who for centuries had obstructed Italy's path to unity. No royal assassination struck terror and discord into men's souls, yet the triumph of Cavour and Victor Emmanuel opened up a freer path for the future than the French revolution had been able to do. The prerevolutionary leading class did not, as in France, continue to play a prominent role in spite of its defeat. Papal administration in the church state disappeared forever, as did that of the Bourbons in Naples. No bond of continuity linked the officers' corps of the new state to that of the old, although for decades the "black aristocracy" of Rome continued to regard the House of Savoy as infamous brigands. With his *non expedit* the pope had removed himself and his followers more thoroughly from political life than the bloodiest work of the guillotine could ever have done; on the other hand, the state was astute enough not to jeopardize the authority of the church in the life of the people.

In France the *ancien régime* and the various revolutionary factions split up in hatred and yet remained associated in an inconclusive battle, whereas in Italy they lived side by side as more or less good neighbors, either no longer associated or not yet separated. Admittedly Mazzini and Garibaldi had wanted to fight not for the Savoy monarchy but for a democratic republic; but they put up with the fact that their victories and defeats benefited the opponent, who was nevertheless fighting on their side, and they did not die as outcasts in irreconcilable hatred like most of the German revolutionaries. On the other hand the liberal Count Cavour and the semibourgeois royal house did not need to outlaw the bourgeois revolutionary party, as happened in Germany: the creation of the national state by a double-headed revolution gave the nation a unity and spiritual consistency which neither France nor Germany possessed.

Thus the Italian Risorgimento was the last successful spiritual and political trend in Western Europe to have a continuous and positive link with the great emancipatory movement. Both Mazzini and Gioberti agreed that the law of life is progress, that this progress is to be regarded primarily as the trend toward the equality of all people in liberty, that it is only within this trend that the principle of nationality can find justification. And however much the two most outstanding thinkers of the Risorgimento diverged from each other in the metaphysical substantiation of these principles, they approached each other again in the criticism of certain manifestations of the French revolution: its individualism, its hedonism, its emphasis on rights instead of duties. In this sense the Risorgimento is the first and only political victory of critical liberalism in Europe.

But it was a highly precarious victory. Had not Gioberti himself written a book in 1843 on the *primato morale e civile degli italiani,* basing his proof largely on the existence of the church? Yet can primacy be compatible with equality, and might not pride in the church override service to the church? Do we not find in Mazzini the concept of *mare nostro,*[2] as well as a very dubious reference to natural boundaries when he deals with border disputes?[3] Does not this theory that Austria must be destroyed by the liberation of its oppressed peoples bear the unmistakable mark of duplicity? If Taine and Renan bowed and turned before the pressure of new realities, we also find in Gioberti and Mazzini a few rudimentary indications of new trends.

Another point to be considered is that, if the politically active bourgeoisie revealed such an unbroken relationship to liberalism, it was only because it was conscious of being the undisputed protagonist of the change-over and because there was no imminent popular rebellion threatening its position. The Commune was not, as it was in France and Germany, experienced as a deep divide: if there were riots in Rome in 1870, their aim was to demand the new monarchy's annexation of the leonine city.

For Italy as for all Europe, the entry of the masses into politics and the testing of liberal ideas was to be the problem of the coming decades. The sons of the heroes of the Risorgimento solved it skillfully but unspectacularly, with a slowness of pace that could only have been called wisdom if it had been able to preclude the unforeseen. The franchise was expanded very gradually, and it was a long time before Italy entered into rivalry with the great powers over colonial territories. The defeat at Aduwa in 1896 represented the first serious injury to youthful national pride as well as the moral defeat of one of the last survivors of the Risorgimento, Francesco Crispi. At the same time it kindled the beginnings of nationalism, even if at first this occurred more in the minds of individual men (notably Enrico Corradini) than in the visible form of publications or organizations. But its significance cannot be even remotely compared to what the defeat of 1871 meant for France.

At roughly the same time, socialist and anarchist agitation met with their first successes. Severe repressive measures availed little, and the general strike of 1904 generated such alarm among the bourgeoisie that Pius X virtually revoked the *non expedit,* thus opening up the way for the formation of a Catholic mass party whose ideological attitude toward the Risorgimento was bound to be more negative than that of the socialists. However, it was precisely the association of socialism with liberalism that led the first nationalists to look askance at their party of origin and consider the possibility of an alliance with the Catholics. Although this unrest was far milder than that caused by the Dreyfus affair in France, it had greater prospects inasmuch as it was directed primarily against the socialists and only secondarily against democrats and liberals.

But by this time socialism had already become a card in Prime Minister Giovanni Giolitti's political game. His aim was to strengthen the reformist wing of the Socialist party and then draw the PSI into the government as bourgeois democracy's left wing. In 1910 he seemed to be on the verge of success. The revolutionary faction surrounding Costantino Lazzari had sunk to insignificance, the only remaining point of dispute between Filippo Turati and Leonida Bissolati was the timing of collaboration. Moreover, the prime minister had made such excellent diplomatic preparations for the planned colonial campaign in Libya that, as far as could be judged, it would be possible to conduct it without seriously impairing the political and intellectual stability of the country. Hence the intended introduction of universal suffrage did not appear to entail any danger.

If Giolitti's plan had succeeded, he would have brought Italy in one leap to the forefront of political developments in all of Europe and simultaneously completed the great task inherited from the Risorgimento. In looking back, observers might have found no more convincing example of historical determinism.

But the war roused more resistance in the Socialist party than Giolitti had envisaged, and at the party conference at Reggio Emilia in 1912 the hitherto totally unknown[4] party secretary of Forlì, Benito Mussolini, succeeded in having the right-wing reformists led by Bissolati and Bonomi expelled from the party, thus creating a definite ascendancy for the revolutionary faction. Shortly afterward he became managing editor of *Avanti!*, and it was mainly due to him that the Socialist party, now again unquestionably antigovernment, emerged as the chief gainer from the first general elections in 1913. Thus Giolitti, although he won the war, had lost the real, the political, battle. He had actually set the course that was to lead him and Italian liberalism to their downfall, because the victory of the intransigent Socialists had resulted, on the opposing side, in the strengthening of the nationalists and conservatives led by Salandra, and because the first disturbance to the peace of Europe had proved impossible to control and therefore became one of the prime causes of World War I. But this whole development, at least in its early stages, was by no means inevitable. It was to a marked degree the result of a "temperament" and would presumably have taken a different course had this temperament been absent.

However, why it should have taken this direction and no other, why it was able to arouse emotions and to convince, will become clearer from a number of contingent circumstances, and not least from a study of the intellectual climate as a whole. Here, too, the unforeseeable has an important place. The fact that the survivors and descendants of the Risorgimento employed bitter words of reproach during the colorless period of transformation and the Giolitti era, that in the face of the triumph of a hardhearted positivism they turned nostalgically to former times and antiquity, is as readily understandable as that this criticism was not directed in principle against the liberal character of the century.

It is true that Alfredo Oriani, whom Mussolini saw with doubtful reasoning as Italian fascism's sole precursor, sang the praises of the heroes and warriors of old, but he never went so far as to condone war per se, nor did he ever forget that Garibaldi was "a warrior who did not like war."[5] It is also true that Giosuè Carducci condemned the wretchedness of the times and attributed its beginnings to that day when "a red-haired Galilean mounted the steps of the Capitol,"[6] yet the old republican was far from using the theory of the revolt of the slaves to place his paganism in a polemical and reactionary relation to the social movements of his time.

But it was impossible to foresee that a man with almost no associations with the Risorgimento, Gabriele D'Annunzio, should achieve a position of the utmost influence over Italy's intellectual youth. For Italy's younger generation he was Nietzsche and Barrès rolled into one. He eluded the difficulties inherent in his concepts through the captivating melody of words, of which he was a master like Baudelaire or Rilke. He was far removed from the philosophy and the agony of Nietzsche, but, like him, he praised "the terrible energies, the sense of power, the instinct for battle and domination, the abundance of productive and fructifying forces, all the virtues of Dionysian man, the victor, the destroyer, the creator."[7] Like Barrès he proclaimed the fatherland as far back as the early eighteen nineties; but all he ever saw in the nation was the most desirable scope for his own personality, whereas the objective aggregate of experience such as underlay the work of the Frenchman, who had looked at the defeat of 1870, was foreign to D'Annunzio.

D'Annunzio was in fact a Dionysian man of modern and highly original stamp, more so than almost any other man in Europe. His influence in Italy was incalculable. If the common European endeavor around the turn of the century toward rejuvenation often took on a more markedly irrational character in Italy—in spite of contrary native traditions—than in France and Germany, this was in great part attributable to D'Annunzio.

The oldest of the Florentine avant-garde publications, *Leonardo*, founded early in 1903 by Giuseppe Prezzolini and Giovanni Papini, devoted most of its attention to this change in the intellectual climate: the defeat of positivism, the rebirth of spiritualism, the reawakening of faith and mysticism. Its program was the formulation of a vague pressure, and finally it opened up its columns to magical idealism and the occult.[8] The young contributors to *Hermes*, led by Giuseppe Antonio Borgese, paid homage to an esthetic imperialism; while in *Regno* (in which Pareto often appeared), expansion of life was the watchword of Corradini's nationalism, not the defense of traditional values as in the *Action Française*.

Clarified and matured, but not abandoned, all these beginnings appear in *La Voce*, Prezzolini's and Papini's second and more important publication founded in 1908. The chief thing to be clarified is nationalism: it is detached from Corradini's Roman imperial rhetoric, removed from its sharply anti-socialist objective, and led to a more mature understanding of social phenomena. It is not surprising, therefore, that the journal opposes the Tripolitanian war. The philosophical basis is also clarified in detail, although not formally defined, by Benedetto Croce and Giovanni Gentile, who at the time scarcely suspected their future antagonism and closely co-operated to make their journal *Critica* a subtle organ of intellectual rejuvenation. Also clarified is the relationship to futurism and syndicalism, to Giolitti and Bergson, to Barrès and Maurras.

Nevertheless when world war broke out, the desire for the "new," for "action," was for *La Voce* and most of its contributors more powerful than considerations of expediency or obligation. In combination with all "young" forces, it worked toward that decision which set Italy apart from all other European nations: the decision to enter the war voluntarily. And Prezzolini went to Rome as political correspondent of the only daily newspaper which was founded for the specific purpose of bringing about intervention: the *Popolo d'Italia* of Benito Mussolini.

Digression on Method

The "rejuvenation movement" as such was not the source of fascism but merely its precondition, and it also produced some of its principal opponents: Giovanni Amendola, leader of the Aventine opposition; Gaetano Salvemini, the first of the antifascist historians; Giuseppe Antonio Borgese, the outstanding poet, literary historian, and political writer. The springs of fascism were: the nationalists led by Enrico Corradini, the legionaries led by the D'Annunzio of the Fiume enterprise, and the former Marxists who had split off from the Socialist party and were led by Mussolini.[9] These three groups gave Italian fascism the leaders, the ethos, and the ideas. Hence it is impossible to understand fascism without a look at the nature of Italian nationalism, the events in Fiume, and Mussolini's socialist period. Of these three elements, Mussolini's development is at one and the same time the least familiar and the most important. Thus, for this period, and even more so for later times, Mussolini's intellectual biography must be our principal guideline. It also offers the inestimable advantage of presenting us with that very Marxism which as the cause of middle-class alarm became the main precondition for fascism.

This does not mean that fascism is identical with "Mussolinism." Yet even when Mussolini appeared to be excluded from the fascist movement for a few months between 1920 and 1921, nothing could be settled in the party which did not in the end obtain—or compel—his consent. This applies, of course, still more to the period of his rule.

We should not ignore the objection that there can be no "intellectual biography" of Mussolini, that with his superficial education and what was at best a journalistic flair, he sometimes sought to cover up his strivings for power with a veneer of incoherent thoughts, while in actual fact he was merely led by arbitrary contingencies.[10]

But it would be manifestly unfair to judge Mussolini by the standards of Benedetto Croce or even of university scholarship. It is true that his love of Greek philosophy always turns out to be an unhappy one when he displays it in any form other than the wholly abstract,[11] but the oft-repeated claim that the only work of Marx he had read was the *Communist Manifesto* is as false as the argument that he knew scarcely anything of Nietzsche beyond his "Live dangerously."[12] His command of contemporary philosophy and political literature was at least as great as that of any other contemporary European political leader. So it would seem best not to cast doubts on Mussolini's sincerity without good reason, and not to be skeptical in our approach to his self-interpretation.

The great difficulty remains of containing a widely ramified historical phenomenon within the narrow circle of a single life. Interpolations and hindsight will be unavoidable, and the serious problem of periodization permits no completely satisfactory solution. There were no such difficulties in the case of the Action Française, because political history and the significance of the doctrine could be separated relatively easily and Maurras did not experience any notable personal development. But Italian fascism *is* its history, and this history is indissolubly linked to the biography of Mussolini.

Mussolini the Marxist (1902–1914)

To call Mussolini a Marxist is to evoke surprise,[13] even today. Friends and foes alike have generally credited him with a mere vague revolutionism, a feeling which had been widespread in the Romagna since papal times and which after 1870, due to the activity of Bakunin's emissaries (with whom Mussolini's father Alessandro soon established contact) had assumed an anarchist character. The determining factor for Mussolini, it was said, was his lower middle-class origin; to this he owed his legacy of protest which, because it was ambitious, was of a purely personal nature.[14] His father was a small property owner and a farrier (*fabbro ferraio*) and his mother a schoolteacher. But if the family were badly off, this was due mainly to the father's political ardor, which too often kept him from his work. But then, where in all Italy at that time were there, in the strict Marxist sense of the word, proletarians; where in all Europe did a socialist leader emerge from this class? At the time his son was born (1883) Alessandro was no more an anarchist than his revered model Andrea Costa who, although

Bakunin's secretary in former years, had meanwhile come a great deal closer to the German Social Democrats and to Marxism.[15]

Reliable reports, and reminiscences of Mussolini himself,[16] depict the sturdy lad as a kind of gang leader disporting himself on the slopes around Forlimpopoli and in the gorges of the nearby river. At the age of ten he was separated from the other schoolboys at mealtime in the Salesian College at Faenza and made to eat with a few others of his kind at the "poor table." There is no reason why rage at injustice should not become a legitimate starting point for lasting socialistic feelings.

If Mussolini was continually being called *duce*,[17] even in the early stages of his socialist period, this fact did not necessarily predestine him to be the "Duce of fascism." The fact that from childhood on he possessed the temperament of a *condottiere* is a precondition for his later life,[18] but it is not sufficient to determine its direction. A second, equally important motivation in his life is the fact that from his earliest days his father filled him with socialist ideas and introduced him to socialist literature. It is not the tales of heroic deeds or imperialist dreams,[19] invented or adapted by fascist biographers, that reflect the spiritual atmosphere of Mussolini's youthful years, but a simple report such as the following, originating from Mussolini himself in 1912: "We acknowledge our heresy. We cannot conceive of a patriotic socialism. Socialism is truly of a panhuman and universal nature. Ever since our earliest years, when socialist manuals large and small passed through our hands, we have known that there are only two fatherlands in the world, that of the exploited and that of the exploiters."[20] The early possession of a political faith (*fede*) is no less decisive for Mussolini than the psychic disposition to be a *condottiere*.

Throughout his life Mussolini was a *condottiere* in possession of a faith or in search of a faith. The relationship between the two basic elements is what constitutes his history. The only time they were wholly united was during the first and longest period of his political activity, dedicated entirely to service in the Socialist party.

Mussolini only practiced his profession of elementary, later high school, teacher of French language and literature for a very short time; even during his emigration period in Switzerland he was already living chiefly as a propagandist and as a contributor to socialist journals. During his second sojourn abroad, in the Austrian Trentino (1909), he was secretary of the *Camera del Lavoro* and editor of a weekly paper. After his expulsion he was secretary until 1912 of the provincial federation of Forlì and publisher of the weekly journal *La Lotta di Classe*. The congress at Reggio Emilia brought him into national prominence; as managing editor of *Avanti!*, he was, although not the "Duce," probably the party's most influential, colorful, and compelling personality. In spite of the objections and misgivings he often caused and of the dubious nature of many of his theses—not only in the eyes of his opponents—we can detect no consistent trend away from the party. No less an event than World

War I was required to bring about a rupture that was certainly not a personal whim.

No other period in Mussolini's life was so uniform, or so shaped by the idea and the preaching of a doctrine. It is the only period in which it is possible to make a comprehensive analysis of his ideas, instead of merely setting down chronologically, and psychologically explaining, his unorthodox and confusing utterances (such as those resulting from his preoccupation with Nietzsche).

Mussolini himself undoubtedly wished to be regarded as a Marxist. Whenever possible he extols the memory of the "father and teacher"[21] who alone represents the "compass" of the proletarian and Marxist movement. Even the master's most disputed doctrines, the theory of progressive pauperization, for example, finds in him a stout defender,[22] and there is scarcely one concrete political decision which he does not justify by invoking Marx. Even in his demand for Italy's entry into the war he uses Marx as a key witness.[23]

His Marxism is, of course, neither theoretical nor philosophical. Unlike Lenin, he never undertook extensive economic research, nor was he ever interested in the differences between Hegelian and Marxist dialectics. But the basic elements of the doctrine which have practical relevance emerge with great clarity in Mussolini's thought: the doctrines of class warfare, final goal, and internationalism.

Class warfare between capitalists and proletarians is to Mussolini as to all Marxists the fundamental reality of the time and its universal characteristic; it has priority over all other warfare and even determines what seem to be independent intellectual attitudes. Its origin is the separation of the means of production and producers in bourgeois society, a separation which must necessarily result in a clash between capital and labor.[24] The proletarians produce wealth, yet are excluded from it.[25]

The aim of class warfare is the expropriation of the bourgeoisie and collectivization of means of production and exchange. The enemy of the proletariat in class warfare is primarily the state as the "Defense Committee" of the ruling classes.[26] The army is primarily an internal political means of oppression, hence antimilitaristic propaganda (carried on by Mussolini to the point of glorifying desertion)[27] is a necessary part of proletarian class warfare. The characteristic of class warfare is violence, where possible, for "a class does not give up its privileges, even when it is forced to do so."[28]

Attempts have mistakenly been made to attribute Mussolini's concept of violence to Sorel. His relations with Sorel were not nearly as close and cordial as was later claimed. There was, of course, a time when he called him "our master."[29] But when Sorel made the famous switch to Maurras, Mussolini broke vituperatively with the "pensioned bookworm"[30] and did not refer to him again until 1914. It is not Sorel but Marx whom he calls "the magnificent philosopher of working-class violence."[31] It cannot be denied that Mussolini soon acquired the reputation of a *barricadero* and a Blanquist. His reputation was due less to certain theoretical convictions than to his temperament, when he conducted an anticlerical campaign of unparalleled fury in the Trentino, or when he pursued social warfare between farm laborers, sharecroppers, and property owners to the point of bloody excesses in the Romagna, or when he was the only prominent Marxist to defend the wild popular uprising of the *Settimana Rossa* (Red Week) in 1914. Wherever it was a matter of taking a theoretical stand he remained well on the Marxist track: he demanded that the Italian proletariat become less of a people and more of a class;[32] he violently opposed the syndicalists' mania for general strikes;[33] and he called continually for "preparation." His antiparliamentarianism, therefore, does not indicate anarchist and syndicalist abstention (that is, election boycott). For him, as for Marx, class warfare takes many forms. What is indicative is not that he is in favor of violence but that he insists on letting violence have the last word.

But the class war saw itself threatened. Within the party itself, the "socialism of the lawyers," with its preference for parliamentary procedure and its emphasis on spontaneous development, was leading toward the "complete rejection of Marxism"[34] and thus to decadence. The "emigrants of the bourgeoisie"[35] were seeking to replace class warfare with class collaboration; the pragmatism of daily work threatened to supplant revolutionary zeal: "If class collaboration is permitted, scruples fall. One goes further. Into the Quirinal, into the government. But Karl Marx is relegated to the attic."[36]

Thus Mussolini's position in the European clash between revolutionists and reformists was one of the utmost clarity and success. Nowhere else in Europe were socialists so close to official (not merely, as in the France of the Dreyfus affair, unofficial) participation in the government. Mussolini's victory in Reggio Emilia was not only over Bissolati and (indirectly) over Turati, but above all over Giolitti. If communism is described as the splitting off of the intransigent wing from the reformist section of the Socialist party which is willing to co-operate, Mussolini may with good reason be called the first and, from one standpoint, only European Communist; for in all the other European countries this rift occurred under the influence of Russian bolshevism, which formed in 1902 as well as in 1914 in entirely different circumstances. In any case at that time Mussolini laid the foundations not only for Italian postwar communism (he boasted of this paternity as late as his first chamber speech as a Fascist deputy in 1921),[37] but also for the impotence of the embryonic Social Democracy led by Turati, and this impotence was perhaps the most immediate cause of the fascist victory.

His "voluntarism," which some have mistakenly tried to play off against his Marxist orthodoxy,[38] is only the theoretical expression of his intransigence. For this voluntarism is directed polemically against the evolution theory of the time and corresponds precisely to Lenin's battle against the doctrine of "automatism": "This conception banned will and violence from the world, it denied the revolution. Yet Marx, when speaking of a 'revolutionary evolution,' taught us to distinguish between slow economic evolution and the sudden collapse of the political, social, and juridical superstructure. Positivist evolutionism had banned disasters from life and history, but behold: modern theories belie the overtaxed *Natura non facit saltus*."[39] When Mussolini says "will," we see that all he means is "dialectic." When he speaks of "idealism," he is thinking of the independence of political awareness and will as opposed to the pressure of direct economic interests. Terms that sound alike can have very different meanings. To Engels "idealism" means a definite epistomological position; to Lenin, a position of the theory of cognition. To Mussolini the same term is a weapon in the struggle against trends in syndicalism which strive for the establishment of an independent position vis-à-vis the Socialist party: "Union as such is not strength. ... Union becomes strength only when it is conscious. The worker who is merely [economically] organized becomes a petit bourgeois who only obeys the voice of his own interests. Any ideal demand finds him deaf."[40] "Revolutionary idealism" alone can prevent the Socialist party from degenerating into "a kind of corporatist and egoistic workers' trade-unionist movement [*operaismo*]."[41]

Here again, then, Mussolini thinks along exactly the same lines as Lenin, who had spoken of working-class "spontaneity" and the "trade-unionist consciousness" which only the knowing will of the professional revolutionists could set on the right track. Mussolini, too, wanted the party to be an "organization of warriors, of soldiers."[42]

Mussolini participated with equal vigor in the dispute over the method of class warfare. What made this dispute necessary was the fact that nowhere in Europe in 1914 did conditions display that "maturity" which according to Marxist doctrine was essential to the proletarian revolution: namely, the polarization of society into a small number of exploiters and the "enormous majority" of the industrially exploited. Marx himself had been by no means disposed to wait idly for "economic prerequisites" to mature: he had written to Engels, for example, about the possibility of supporting the proletarian revolution in Germany by a second Peasants' War.[43] This proposal, born of impatience, is nothing but an anticipation of the Bolshevik answer, their victorious prescription: alliance of workers and peasants. In a doctrinal sense, of course, it remains a paradoxical and temporary alliance: even Lenin up to the time of his rule did not wish to call such a revolution a socialist one.

No less than Marx and Lenin, Mussolini grasped the importance of propaganda among the peasants. The system prevalent in northern Italy, by which labor and profit were very unequally distributed among property owners, sharecroppers (*mezzadri*), and day laborers (*braccianti*), offered singularly favorable conditions. By supporting the *braccianti* to the hilt and declaring the total abolition of sharecropping to be his next goal, Mussolini made the province of Forlì a stronghold of socialism and pushed the hitherto dominant republicans into the defensive. But he intends to make use of democratic institutions solely "in order that our hour shall come sooner,"[44] and he works among the *braccianti* because the revolution must break out "simultaneously in the towns and in the country."[45]

The socialist revolution is the deciding factor in class warfare because it eliminates it. But for this very reason it cannot be a peaceful transition. The utmost intensification of class warfare is essential to its elimination: "Instead of deluding the proletariat as to the possibility of eradicating all causes of bloodbaths, we wish to prepare it and accustom it to war for the day of the 'greatest bloodbath of all,' when the two hostile classes will clash in the supreme trial."[46]

In this sense, Marxism and disaster consciousness are for Mussolini identical.[47] Just as Lenin's sober language becomes dynamic and forceful when he speaks of the revolution,[48] so Mussolini is capable of images of great power and penetration: "When we begin the great symphony, our orchestra will have instruments of steel."[49] And if Marx and Engels are afraid that a war—that penultimate and by now almost outmoded form of disaster—might delay the revolution, Mussolini on the eve of the world war expressed the confidence: "With the unleashing of a mighty clash of peoples the bourgeoisie is playing its last card and calls forth on the world scene that which Karl Marx called the sixth great power: the social revolution."[50]

Rarely has a political doctrine ever frightened so many people, endowed so many people with what was till then a totally unknown self-confidence, as the doctrine of the revolutionary class war of the proletariat. Rarely has a doctrine ever had such overwhelming success in its early stages, such a stubborn series of failures in its continuing realization. Born originally of a philosophical construct, it seemed to correspond to the historical process as long as no new relative condition of social stability had been reached, and it always became powerful again wherever exceptional events jeopardized this condition. Otherwise it became apparent all too soon that "the proletariat," while it might permit a uniform conception of itself, possessed no uniformity whatever as a political phenomenon. The two basic components of the conception were already proving contradictory. For Marx, the purpose of the proletariat was on the one hand to render the bourgeoisie superfluous and on the other to sweep it away in a storm of indignation. Marx overlooked the fact that the "proletariat," in the sense of the "propertyless" class, differentiated within itself in a highly differentiated society and no longer stood in revolutionary opposition to conditions of which it had itself become a part; while the "proletariat" in the sense of the "manual labor" class, which retained its revolutionary outlook, stood outside society and was therefore incapable of leading it.

He also neglected to write a "phenomenology of the proletariat" (the chapter on "classes" in the third volume of *Das Kapital* was never written); generally speaking, Marxism had no idea of how to cope with the true state of mind— that is, a state of mind determined not by the economic situation alone but by a whole complex of historical conditions—of the various groups of the "proletariat." It was like a Chinese puzzle: scarcely had the hitherto reactionary masses got rid of the influence of the priest and veered toward the revolutionary doctrine than they were already drifting into the "bourgeois," or Social Democratic, camp. This trend also had to be called "reactionary."

All over Europe the revolutionary party was caught between two "reactionary" fires, and nowhere did it find itself in undisputed possession of the proletariat, yet it urgently needed this possession, since every serious revolutionary threat was bound to unite the "bourgeoisie" (of which likewise no concept of practical relevance existed) into a single compact bloc. The inevitable result was the emergence of such questions as: What was the proletariat "actually"? Who represented it? How was the tendency toward the bourgeoisie within the proletariat itself to be explained? Where was an alliance, so essential to victory, to be sought? Marx's and Engels' reply to the first of these questions was the rather vague concept of the "avant-garde"; the tendency toward the bourgeoisie was something they noted as an English phenomenon rather than something they tried to explain;[51] and they took for granted that in the "democratic revolution," the "progressive section" of the bourgeoisie would be their allies.[52] However, they never asked themselves the obvious question, whether a party which, from the outset, loudly proclaims itself to be the future gravedigger of its allies is a fit partner in an alliance.

Lenin allotted the avant-garde the role of organization core of the professional revolutionists, chose the peasants as his partners in an alliance, and attributed the entrance into the bourgeoisie of a section of the working class to the fact that imperialist monopolistic capitalism had succeeded in some Western countries in "bribing" a "workers' aristocracy" by turning over to them some of their excess profits. Naturally these replies could not but lead to a profound transformation of Marxism: the spontaneity of the masses had to be replaced by the authority of leadership, the international struggle between capitalists and proletarians had to become the struggle between exploited and exploiting people, the victorious revolution must cease to be anything but a prelude to the decisive clash of the two unequal partners.

Indeed, international Marxism before World War I did not lack for problems. Mussolini's answers were mainly in the form of practical actions rather than theoretical considerations: struggle against reformism, syndicalism, undialectical positivism. To this extent they may legitimately be placed on a level with Lenin's words and actions.

However, there are two significant characteristics which distinguish him from Lenin. Nowhere in Mussolini's writings do we find a parallel to that staggering statement: "The doctrine of Marx is all-powerful because it is correct."[53] On the contrary, he claims to be against an "idolatry" of Marx";[54] he is prepared to enter into a discussion with his opponents on the subject of "The Living and the Dead in Marxism";[55] he gives consideration to the idea, expressed by Prezzolini, that Marxism might be a reflection of the special conditions in England;[56] he seems to admit the existence of a "new, young, industrial, daring" middle class as distinct from the decayed old conservative bourgeoisie.[57] In contrast to this is his view that the social struggle in Italy was often only *prelotta-di-classe*, a preliminary class struggle.[58] But is it possible, taking Marxist premises as a basis, to justify leading the "people" to war against a bourgeoisie that has only just assumed its industrial task and function?

Mussolini does not raise this question. But filled though he was with Marxist faith, he was not a dogmatizer whom *nothing* can deflect from the course on which he has embarked. Equally open to doubt and astonishing insight, this man will not be proof against a severe attack on his *fede*.

It appears possible to separate his fundamental impulses, for to Mussolini's power of insight is added an extraordinary impressionability, which does not allow him to cut himself off from or remain indifferent to intellectual trends or exceptional events. This clearly emerges when he interprets class warfare with the aid of categories which, although not a priori un-Marxist in meaning, flow from a different intellectual world and atmosphere.

Thus he sets off—abruptly, that is undialectically—the "small, determined, bold nucleus," which is supposed to be the real protagonist, against "the mass which, although numerous, is also chaotic, amorphous, and cowardly."[59] He frequently speaks of the *élite proletaria*, which he looks upon as the dynamic minority forming an opposite pole to the static masses. He sees it as the group of the "strong," the "heroes," who are capable of victory. The revolution, "with the swiftness of lightning distinguishes between the strong and the weak, between the apostles and the artisans, between the courageous and the cowardly";[60] *before* its "historic day,"[61] revolutionary idealism has the power to will and imagine it and hence serves "to distinguish organization from organization, and cattle from human beings."[62]

Certainly all this is not said in the sense of Pareto,[63] whose theory of the cycle of elites is directed against the idea of the classless society; certainly it would be foolish to overlook the fact that with this phraseology Mussolini is not far removed from the *feelings* of Marx, Engels, and Lenin. What do Marx and Engels despise more than the "drooling impotence"[64] of "Communists by sentiment"?[65] Did not Lenin write the harsh words: "An oppressed class which does not strive to gain a knowledge of weapons, to be drilled in the use of weapons, to possess weapons, an oppressed class of this kind deserves only to be oppressed, maltreated, and treated like slaves"?[66]

Indeed, Marxism is far from being unwarlike, unheroic, tenderhearted, philanthropic. But it will never become an ideology of victors, of heroes, of the hard, of the young. Nor will it do so in Mussolini's case. Nevertheless, the change in terminology reveals that instability which may lead to surprising developments.

Like the young writers centered around *Leonardo* and *La Voce*, Mussolini could not avoid the influence of that powerful universal European trend of thought which, anticipated in large part by Nietzsche, had shot up, as if by spontaneous generation, in innumerable places in a variety of contradictory forms: the "life-philosophy." Mussolini did not hesitate to invoke it specifically: "The classic conception of revolution finds in today's trend of philosophic thought an element of vitality. Our conception rejuvenates. Reformism, on the other hand, the wise and duly evolutionary, positivist, and pacifist reformism, is henceforth condemned to decrepitude and decay."[67]

It is the spirit of this so-called life-philosophy (albeit not only this spirit) which causes Mussolini to say that socialism must once again become "movement, struggle, action,"[68] it must rid itself of the "idyllic, arcadian, pacifist conception" of the reformists;[69] it is this spirit which causes him to utter, more often almost than anything else, Guyau's words: *Vivre, ce n'est pas calculer, c'est agir.*[70]

This is far from being un-Marxist. For Marxism is also a kind of "life-philosophy" and is concerned with the struggle of expanding life against the immovable bonds which it temporarily needs. But Marxism centers its conception of life not, like Bergson, on the idea of the "creative development" of biological life but, like Hegel, on the perfectible rise of history seen as "transcendental."

The dividing line becomes clear when Mussolini states: "He who says fecundation says laceration. No life without shedding blood."[71] The idea of the classless society cannot be derived from the conception of biological life. Classless society means the transition from the realm of necessity into the realm of liberty. It is in fact antinature, if "nature" is to be understood as the rule of the principles of organic and animal life. Indeed, nothing is easier than to deduce the eternal and natural necessity of war from the essence of "life."

It is true that Mussolini approaches those logical "life-philosophy" conclusions which as a Marxist he is not at liberty to appropriate. But he never oversteps the bounds. There is no doubt that the main principle of reformism, Bernstein's "Movement is all, the goal is nothing," is an inevitable conclusion of this approach. It is his unshakable clinging to the final socialist goal, to the *finalità*, which never quite permits Mussolini, despite all his proximity to the new trend, to become its disciple.

The final socialist goal is not a freely conceived ideal: it is the outcome of a fatality which is independent of the comings and goings of individual human beings. If Mussolini did not emphasize this element as often and as strongly as the founders of "scientific socialism" had done, a ready explanation is to be found in the altered intellectual climate. The opposition had long ceased to represent utopianism and the philosophy of liberty: instead it now comprised positivism and the "bourgeois" doctrine of evolution. Why carry coals to Newcastle? Nevertheless the concept of necessity remains for Mussolini an obvious requirement, and wherever he formulates this concept he does so radically.

The ideal is merely the meaning of the historical process itself, revealed in the enlightened will of an exceptional class. This meaning transcends the move-ment of its realization in that it leads to a condition (a form of movement) which differs in principle from all former conditions. Mussolini is therefore defending socialism's chief characteristic when he says, in attacking the reform-ists: " 'We are not concerned with aims,' shouts Bonomi. 'For us movement suffices.' But what kind of movement? Delirium tremens is also a movement."[72] The sum total of socialist aims, which alone makes it possible to define the "natural process" that produces them, is always described by Mussolini in a highly orthodox manner.

Socialism is first of all "the transition of means of production and of exchange to proletarian collectivity,"[73] thereby removing the absurdity of private appropriation of the products of collective labor.[74] Without the slightest reservation Mussolini upholds the demand for the "expropriation of the bourgeoisie." This remains for him the prerequisite to an "association" which excludes classes.[75] Only a classless association can bring about the "happiness" of all mankind, because it represents the "society of the free and equal."[76] It signifies the "final disappearance of the exploitation of man by man"[77] and thus the end of the "prehistory of mankind": "The bridge between animal man and humane man, the bridge between prehistory and history, the bridge leading mankind from the struggle for life to an affinity for life, will be built by socialism!"[78]

If Marx's image of the future is strangely diagrammatic and colorless, he was undoubtedly motivated by the fear of being led astray onto the paths of such excessive dreamers as Fourier. His dryness is the expression of his respect for the unknown. Where Mussolini does augment Marx's outline with some vivid colors, it is to express a keen sense of the dawning world of technology. He enthusiastically greeted the first attempts at flight by Latham and Blériot because they proclaimed a "quickening of the rhythm of our life."[79] Although he interpreted the event from a strictly Marxist point of view as being a "sign of peace" and as proclaiming the end of the "fratricidal domination of man over man,"[80] a strange new note becomes audible when in the same breath he praises the pilots as a *futura razza di dominatori* and *spiriti inquieti*. In many places it is possible to detect a shift in emphasis which seems to lead away from Marx's fundamental humanistic feeling to an enthusiastic recognition of the new technical world as such. Mussolini no longer speaks of man's domination of the machine; instead he describes socialism as a society "in which life will become more intense and frenetic, ruled by the rhythm of machines."[81] The hope that leads him on is not a wondrous blossoming of art in the society of the future; rather he predicts, as an out-and-out technocrat, the downfall of the Muses— "the pale inhabitants of Parnassus"—in the new world of nature-dominating titans.[82]

But this shift in emphasis can be attributed more to the character of the times than to the person of Mussolini.

A similar situation exists regarding the meaning of the ideal, a question which Marx never specifically posed. But then he did not find himself confronted by reformists. He could still believe that the situation of the proletariat did not permit of "ideallessness" (that is, an exclusive concern with the present). For Mussolini it was the possession of the ideal that distinguished the revolutionary from the reformist: "It is the ideal—it is our final goal—that gives us an unmistakable stamp. ... "[83] Only the ideal permits and justifies resistance to those sirens of immediate expediency who call mockingly: "Ignore the gospels, descend from the clouds, hold fast to reality."[84]

This is precisely the meaning of ideallessness: the adapting to "reality," to the conditions of the moment. One may flatter oneself that one can master and alter these conditions: in actual fact one becomes their slave, one surrenders to their inexorable law. That is why Mussolini, in his paper, attacked Bissolati's speech at the party conference in Milan as lacking "any emphasis on the future."[85] That is why after the outbreak of the Libyan war he depicted with unparalleled animosity the renegade who justified this war and who was now committed to a course of consenting to all realities of this society. He takes as an example Paolo Orano (twenty-five years later he was to be commissioned by Mussolini to initiate the fascist race ideology): "Paolo Orano finds the Italo-Turkish war 'beautiful, good, clarifying, well-nigh sacred.' Paolo Orano feels it necessary to concur with tartarinesque Italian nationalism. ... Paolo Orano swallows with the ingenuous grimace of the experienced farceur all that he has said and written against militarism during the fifteen years of his subversive activity, and raises his voice in a hymn of praise to the murderous scimitar. ... Before long Paolo Orano too will be a great philosopher, honored and recognized by the powers of the monarchy. I leave him lying in the cemeteries of spineless men."[86]

The fact that Mussolini emphasizes the "ideal" with a vigor unknown to Marx and Lenin does not, however, place him outside the framework of Marxist orthodoxy. The unclear form which Marx gave his being-consciousness statement avenges itself everywhere in Marxism; and if Marx and Lenin dramatically show "idealism" the door, it finds its way in again through the back door under such disguises as "revolutionary ardor" or "determination of the working class."

The difference becomes apparent when Mussolini claims that what divides the parties is not a table of laws but their mentality;[87] it becomes unmistakable when, again resorting to "life-philosophy" categories, he seems to detach "faith" from all reality, indeed, even to declare it as the foundation of all reality: "And is socialism perhaps reducible to a theorem? We want to believe in it, we must believe in it, mankind has need of a creed. It is faith that moves mountains, because it gives the illusion that the mountains move. Illusion is perhaps the sole reality of life."[88]

Thus emerges the myth, the late-European myth, which presupposes the existence of skepticism by the desire to overcome it. But in Mussolini's case it does not spring from the restlessness of the unbeliever seeking a faith as a sick man seeks medicine. Instead Mussolini transposes his basic conviction into the myth or the "illusion" in order to move it out of the reach of scientific critique. Half a century of history and critique had not passed over Marxism without leaving its mark. Yet Marxism had displayed a vitality which no scientific doctrine was ever able to approach. To paraphrase Sorel's words, Marxism might be called the last faith in Europe. But it reached a crossroads when it began to be aware of this characteristic. At this crossroads, like Sorel, stood Mussolini; but Lenin and Kautsky made their decision too.

Once again Mussolini comes close to the border line where Marxism ends and "life-philosophy" begins, when he says: "Every finality is an act of faith."[89] This very confidence most clearly reveals the possibility of a sudden change of course: "What life, what enthusiasm, what force in our ranks!"[90] What would happen if one day, more life, more enthusiasm, more force were to be found in the ranks of others? Would intensity of faith then become the measure of validity? If some other party showed the greater "vitality" in street fighting, would its cause then be the right one?

Here again Mussolini approaches the border line, but he does not overstep it. Isolated utterances must be seen in relation to the whole; then we see that his Marxism is solid enough to cope with these sallies toward the border line. Neither his concept of class warfare nor that of socialist finality stands alone: there is always his internationalism, and only the mutual penetration of the components gives us the whole.

Like class warfare or finality, internationalism is more than a political program item. It is contained in the reality of conditions no matter how often the mere reality of the day may hide it. Industry, trade, science eliminate borders. Even the bourgeoisie has no native land: "In the economic field, capitalist activity has broken through the boundaries and everywhere imposed its production methods; in the cultural field, the internationalism of thought has long since been achieved."[91] In his earliest stages Mussolini drew from these premises the conclusion that war—at least in Europe—had become impossible; but soon (like Lenin) he demanded that war be transformed into civil war. A transformation of this kind cannot represent an isolated occurrence: the socialist revolution must be an international one.

In the idyllic Europe of the beginning of the century, few men attempted any reasoned criticism of the pacifist conception, in which both liberalism and socialism concurred: of these, mainly Maurras and Corradini, with their disciples, fell within Mussolini's scope of knowledge. Mussolini followed the development of nationalism with great attention, and without any furtive sympathy. He saw in it the betrayal of the bourgeoisie of its own creation, a bourgeois means of distraction for the purpose of delaying the socialist revolution. He was astute enough to realize that the nationalists' hymns to war had an internal political and class warfare meaning. He took issue with "loudmouthed" Italian nationalism immediately after it made its first public appearance in 1910; no one could have done so with greater disdain or contempt: "Monarchy, army, war! Behold the three spiritual, ideological light-houses around which have gathered the moths—the stragglers—of Italian nationalism. Three words, three institutions, three absurdities!"[92]

Bourgeois nationalism is associated with all the old worn-out forces of society. These are to be the first to be removed. Their stronghold in Italy is the Vatican, the *vecchia vaticana lupa cruenta*, as Mussolini says with Carducci.[93] But without the support the Vatican receives from the feudal-clerical imperial power of Austria, it would be powerless. Mussolini's abiding and profound aversion to the "imperial pact" of the *Dreibund* is therefore sufficiently explained by his Marxist background; there is no need to have recourse to *ex eventu* alleged Irredentist feelings of which there is no evidence in his public activity.

He counteracts bourgeois betrayal with the proletarian answer. This consists first and foremost in resisting the blandishments of the bourgeoisie and in recognizing "the smoke screen of patriotic romanticism"[94] for what it is: a weapon of the class enemy. In the eyes of proletarian antipatriotism, the father-land is "a deceitful fiction whose time has run out."[95] The proletariat overcomes "the concept of the fatherland by a different concept, one of class."[96] Again Mussolini invokes Marx who with his battle cry of "Proletarians of the world, unite!" has become a "destroyer of the old patriotic ideology."[97]

But moral resistance is not enough. The bourgeoisie is not content with propaganda. It proceeds to action, and that means to war. For Mussolini there is no doubt as to the answer of the proletariat: "In case of war, instead of hurrying to the frontier we will unleash rebellion at home."[98] Thus when the war in Libya began, he made a serious attempt to turn his words into deeds. The province of Forlì was almost the only region in Italy where the war met with resistance (admittedly little more than noise) from the people. That Mussolini was among those chiefly responsible is certain, although his actual share in the events may have been a matter of dispute. Undoubtedly the failure was a bitter disappointment to him. But he did not give up: "I will create the antiwar feeling which is lacking today."[99] Although one illusion collapsed, he looked ahead to the next "historic day" when the bourgeoisie desires not merely to conduct a colonial enterprise but to light a world conflagration: "Then, however, we hope to be prepared."[100]

It is indeed a desperately difficult matter to try and argue away Mussolini the internationalist, or to regard him merely as an ardent nationalist in disguise. Nevertheless, fascist literature devoted itself tirelessly to this task; but despite all manner of stratagems, from the repetition of unverifiable stories to outright falsifications, it never succeeded in drawing even a halfway convincing picture of Mussolini's socialist epoch.[101]

The difficulty, the "borderline" element, in Mussolini's internationalism does not lie where all the panegyrists and apologists try to find it. It is to be found in the abstract radicalism and naïve youthfulness of his internationalism. At nineteen he proclaimed: "Socialism knows no nationality";[102] the young teacher of French language and literature in Oneglia writes: "The oppressed have no fatherland: they regard themselves as citizens of the universe";[103] the editor of *La Lotta di Classe* following in the footsteps of Hervé calls the national flag a "rag to be planted on a dunghill";[104] and a little later, in words which sound like treason, he opposes the patriotic enthusiasm of the Libyan war: "We proclaim loud and clear that the Arab and Turkish proletarians are our brothers, while our irreconcilable enemies are the Turkish as much as the Italian bourgeois, without subtle distinction or hypocritical consideration."[105] As the managing editor of *Avanti!*, he fiercely opposes a French socialist's idea that a socialist state must also be military in character: "We are of the opposite opinion. We believe—in view of the economic, political, cultural interdependence of the nations and the steadily growing proletarian internationalism —that, when the socialist revolution breaks out in one country, either the others will follow suit or the proletariat will be strong enough to prevent the national bourgeoisie from any armed intervention."[106]

What stands out sharply and pregnantly against these naïve utterances is not some obscure rhetoric about the grandeur and glory of Rome, but one of those simple insights of which Mussolini was always capable: "Italy is still fragmented as in the time of Giusti. There are no national problems, but only regional problems, not a national policy, but only a regional policy."[107] His faith in Marxist internationalism and his insight into the immaturity of Italian conditions still stand side by side in unproblematical unity; but will a dubious unity be equal to a serious test?

It is, therefore, quite untenable to call the early Mussolini a revolutionary syndicalist, a follower of Sorel, let alone Pareto. That he was a Marxist is beyond doubt, yet it seems legitimate to cast doubts on the orthodoxy of his Marxism. We must of course realize that only a very small minority of Marxists occupy an unassailable position. Has not even Lenin been accused over and over again of "Blanquism"? Are not the Frenchman's impatience and political violence to be found ultimately in Marx himself? Strangely enough it was precisely the Italian socialists who were fond of accusing Mussolini of incoherence, confusion, and intellectual inferiority, without realizing what light they were thus throwing on themselves since, after all, they had allowed themselves to be led by this man in crucial years and not much later to be completely defeated by him. It is always easy to select isolated quotations and arrange them effectively; it is more just, and not toward Mussolini alone, to present his Marxism as a whole in order to come to a conclusive judgment. So we must ask: (1) What position does Mussolini assume within the framework of Marxism as a whole? (2) Where do we find the beginnings of a possible estrangement? (3) Are these beginnings merely external?

As far as the attitude toward class warfare is concerned, both reformist and revolutionary views are to be found in Marxism. We have only to remember that Marxism is a thought system that was evolved by its two protagonists over a period of fifty years, and that Engels' foreword to Marx's *Class Struggles in France* is the very Magna Carta of reformism, worlds apart from the *Communist Manifesto*'s spirit of the barricades. But even in *Das Kapital* itself, revolutionary protest stands shoulder to shoulder with the affirmation of lengthy reform work. We might call the will to revolution the spirit of Marxism; the exhortation to be patient and wait for circumstances to ripen, the meaning of Marxism.

As for finality, by comparison with the utopians Marx is a cool realist who plunges rash, exaggerated hopes into the icy waters of resisting, tumultuous reality; beside the mere practicians, however, he is a believer imbued with impatience, who hopes in the near future to see the realization of the "quite other," the new aggregate state of the world.

The abstract internationalism of the *Communist Manifesto* is far from being Marx's and Engels' last word on the problem of contradictions in the world and the significance of the nations. The articles in the *Neue Rheinische Zeitung* during the revolution of 1848[108] give an entirely different picture. They are permeated through and through with the passionate conviction that the large and progressive nations have a greater right than the "little nations," that the theory of the brotherhood of nations is nonsense if it disregards the different levels of civilization among the various peoples. And from Marx's essays on British rule in India[109] it is still possible to deduce that his "nearest will" would have to affirm colonial compulsion, while only his "furthest will" could oppose all forms of oppression.

Mussolini decides in favor of the spirit, the faith, the furthest will, as against the meaning, the realism, the "nearest will," of Marxism, and in so doing makes the equivocal unequivocal. However this choice is neither random nor arbitrary, nor merely personal: it is the choice of "leftist" Marxism as such; it is also the choice of Lenin and Rosa Luxemburg, of Trotsky and Liebknecht, of Guesde and Hervé. It corresponds far more to the mood of Marx's life, far less to actual conditions as they existed in Western Europe at the beginning of the twentieth century, than does its antithesis.

Undoubtedly the beginnings of a possible estrangement from Marxism are much more marked in Mussolini's thought than in Lenin's. They stem, as has been shown, from the adoption of certain categories of the "life-philosophy." Thus we find that with Mussolini the Marxism which had become unequivocal has in the same breath become ambivalent again. That which for Marx and Lenin had been an obvious, unspecified element in the cause—bravery and strength, courage and heroism, vitality and separateness—becomes for Mussolini independent and self-aware, it even tends here and there toward general concepts which are no longer compatible with Marxism. ("No life without shedding blood"—does that mean no life without war and political revolution?)

That which Marx and Lenin regard as scientific insight into the necessary course of history and its self-elevation in the realm of liberty, represents for Mussolini a "faith," and this faith tends in turn to become a mere element in the advancing *élan vital*. The abstract radicalism of his internationalism is finally linked so curiously with an unproblematical enthusiasm for the progressive power of technology that here too an estrangement does not appear impossible.

This potential estrangement finds its sharpest expression in Mussolini's preoccupation with Nietzsche.[110] Although this preoccupation was sporadic in nature and frequently encapsuled, as it were, for years, Mussolini's impressionability leads him not only to attempt a series of interesting and questionable syntheses of Nietzsche's and Marx's thoughts but to place the totally incompatible side by side. He, the very man who countless times extolled the various stages and epochs of emancipation, does not hesitate to present Nietzsche's concept of the "revolt of the slaves" with obvious sympathy. He actually seems unaware of the fact that he is bringing the two opposite interpretations of history—the Hegel-Marx "realization" and the Nietzsche-Maurras *Attentat*—into a paradoxical and untenable proximity. This is undoubtedly an extreme state of affairs, the first and most radical example of the kind of things that could continue to "coexist" so mystifyingly in Mussolini's mind.

On the whole, however, the adulteration of Marxism by thought processes of different origins is not an isolated occurrence. As long as Marxism forms part of a complex and varied society, an analysis which also involves synthesis remains an element and criterion of its vitality. A comparison of the writings of Gramsci and Stalin makes it clear what Marxism owes to liberal society, whose sharpest and most perspicacious critic it was. Mussolini's penchant for Nietzsche may show to what degree of jeopardizing Marxism such an analysis may lead.

But this jeopardizing is more than an external one. It is capable of saying something about the object itself. The ideas of the freely developing individual who is no longer subject to division of labor and exploitation and of the peaceful universal association of industrially producing human beings were, after all, by no means inventions of Marxism. They had already been unfolded in all their clarity by Fourier and Saint-Simon. Nor was it Marxism which produced the insight into the fundamental significance of class warfare or the thesis of the conditioning of consciousness by social station. Marx found all that in bourgeois French history. The only thing peculiar to Marxism is the "proof" that class warfare must from inherent necessity end in a classless society.[111] Marxism too is a synthesis of the great dispassionate designs of the age of Enlightenment with the realities and necessities of the nineteenth century, just like Hegel's "Prussian" state philosophy, Comte's critical idea of progress, and Mazzini's national idea of humanity. It, too, cannot avoid a potential disintegration into its elements. When Mussolini interpreted it with "life-philosophy" categories, he laid the foundations for a dissociation which was only waiting for a catalyst.

The War as Revolution

This catalyst was the war. It subjected Marxism in every country to an acid test, and in no country did Marxism emerge—inwardly or outwardly—unscathed. In Mussolini it encountered not an "editor" of *Avanti!*,[112] who played "no leading role,"[113] but the most influential and at the same time the most self-willed personality of that European socialist party which of all parties found itself in the most difficult situation and which was the only one able at first to act according to prewar ideas.

The fact that the socialist International proved incapable of preventing the war by a general strike is not to be attributed simply to "failure." The reason was that the countries of Europe did not regard themselves as socially homo-geneous, and it was mainly the Marxist doctrine which had contributed toward emphasizing the differences.

The French socialists had good Marxist reasons to regard the war as an attack by a feudal military power on a progressive, albeit bourgeois, democ-racy. As a result they had no compunction about becoming soldiers of the *patrie*, and the best-known of all antimilitarists, Gustave Hervé, took this step with the greatest possible show of determination. For them no abyss opened up between the demands of reality and their socialist conscience.

For Lenin and Trotsky, on the other hand, there was from the very beginning no question whatever but that the Tsarist monarchy must be defeated, for all Marxists looked on Tsarism as the most reactionary and medieval power in Europe. In accordance with their convictions they came to a remarkable decision against "reality," which even a man like Georgi Plekhanov had not been able to shun, and they needed all their revolutionary determination to carry it through. Thus they did not really remain "apart from the bloody world of the war"[114] which according to Lenin spared only the "petty conditions of a few minor states,"[115] leaving them to the indifferent enjoyment of their insignificance.

The German socialists were in the most ambivalent situation. Reactionary in comparison to the Western democracies, progressive when placed next to Russian autocracy, Germany found itself in what was to Marxist eyes an untenable middle position. Marx's solution to the dilemma had been to revolu-tionize Germany and then to have Germany wage war against the Eastern enemy of European liberty. But the German Social Democrats felt their conscience to be salved by carrying out half the plan, and the disappointment generated by their behavior among all European socialists has actually never been overcome. Even Rosa Luxemburg's and Karl Liebknecht's "No" did not satisfactorily solve the dilemma and approached the abstract negation of pacifism. Nevertheless it permitted them to fight and finally to die for their cause.

Italy was bound by the *Dreibund* to the Central Powers. This meant that at the start of the war there was a danger of Italy being drawn into it. Mussolini was the only leading socialist in Europe who resolutely threatened his government with rebellion,[116] and indeed the declaration of Italian neutrality soon followed. But this lone triumph of Marxist orthodoxy in the European disaster was dubious enough: even if he was not actually playing the government's game, his motives certainly did not cause him to run counter to public opinion. The securing of neutrality drove the socialist ship into windless corners full of brackish water. This neutralism was bound to become indistinguishable from bourgeois pacifism and have the practical effect of allying itself with the Austrophile Catholics and Giolitti's conservative bourgeoisie against the most active forces of the remaining Left, which were all urging war, whether for reasons of friendship toward French democracy or as a result of Irredentist strivings for the Trentino and Trieste.

How could such a situation have been tolerable to a man like Mussolini, whose first reaction to the war had characteristically been to regard it as a judgment on the struggle between revolutionaries and reformists: "What is happening today proves to us ... that those predictions on which evolutionary, gradualistic, possibilistic, and positivist reformism based so many of its hopes were vastly exaggerated. The possibility of war remains, and history is full of the unforeseen."[117] If, however, revolution proved impossible as the answer to potential war, then war itself was the form of revolution in this period. Not every war, of course, especially not war for war's sake, but this particular war inasmuch as it seemed destined to further prorevolution developments. Even the most principled Marxist could hardly withdraw with a clear conscience from this war into an ivory tower of abiding truths. For Marxism had always recognized the national war of defense. Was one not, as a Marxist, at liberty— under an obligation, even—to go to the aid of a victim of aggression? But the national war of liberation also had its place in Marxist doctrine. Was not Austrian rule in the Trentino and Trieste the last heritage from the period of Italy's servitude? Not to resist evil had never been a Marxist maxim. Did not a German victory threaten democratic freedoms in all Europe?

A Marxist such as Mussolini, who wanted "to make history, not endure it,"[118] to whom, more than any other, deed and action had become characteristic values, could not stand aside and quietistically withdraw into a corner as a mere spectator. For a Marxist who took a concrete and historic view of himself (as Marx himself had undoubtedly always done), the decision to intervene on the side of the Entente was *possible* in the Italian situation. For a Marxist who had been influenced by "life-philosophy" and Nietzsche it was *necessary*.

All Mussolini's premises culminated in the decision which he took in October, 1914, and which he substantiated with the last words he wrote in *Avanti!*: "We have had the unique privilege of living in the most tragic hour of the world's history. Do we wish to be—as men and as socialists—passive spectators of this grandiose drama? Or do we wish to be ... its protagonists? Let us not salvage the 'letter' of the party if this means killing the 'spirit' of socialism!"[119]

But Mussolini did not readily give up even the letter of the doctrine. The months of August and September were a time of wrestling with himself, and there is no doubt this was a solemn and serious struggle. He who at other times attached so much importance to being right or having been right, was now not afraid to confess his doubts and difficulties openly: "I am not ashamed to admit that during these two tragic months my thinking has known vacillation, uncertainty, and trepidation."[120]

The attempt has been made to cast doubt on Mussolini's struggle with his conscience and the importance of his decision by claiming that at the beginning of the war he showed sympathy for Germany and that it was not until after the Battle of the Marne that, with the skilled perception of the opportunist, he threw in his lot with the winning side. There is no documentary evidence of this. From the very first moment he ranges himself unequivocally against Austria and Germany on account of their "rapacious" ultimata to Serbia and Belgium; shortly afterward he passionately attacks the "unprecedented and rapacious events" in Belgium and soon finds that the German threat is no mere phrase. By September 5—that is, before the end of the Battle of the Marne—the outcome of the war in favor of the Entente was in his eyes a certainty, because of the Anglo-French-Russian agreement not to enter into separate treaties.

His rejection of war was not based on humanitarian considerations but again on the principles of the revolutionary faction, which held that war was the most extreme form of class collaboration[121] and that even the war against Austria was not compatible with socialist principles. As early as August 16 he commented on an intransigent letter by Amedeo Bordiga:[122] although basically in agreement with it, he distinguished between *logica pura dei principi* and *posizione storica del socialismo*, a distinction aimed at justifying the attitude of the Belgian socialists and substantiating the different estimations of the "*Junker* regime" and of French democracy.[123]

He evidently wished to get rid of his own doubts and difficulties when he polemicized violently against the *delirium tremens nazionalista*, against those professional warmongers who in July were still in favor of the *Dreibund* and who wanted war for war's sake.[124] Indeed, on September 22 he published, in the name of the directorate, a radical manifesto against *the* war and on his own initiative introduced a kind of members' poll which probably contributed more than almost anything else toward setting the party on an unconditional antiwar course.

Yet in the meantime his misgivings about the lifelessness of pure principles had increased, and "reality" reached out to him with a thousand arms. Those patriarchs of socialism whom he most revered were openly in favor of Italy's entry into the war: Amilcare Cipriani, Édouard Vaillant, Pyotr Kropotkin. The "young ones" of his own generation were also working toward intervention: Gaetano Salvemini, Giovanni Amendola. In *La Voce* Prezzolini apostrophized him as follows: "Dear Mussolini, either hound or hare. But you still have time to run away. Come out, out of this ambiguousness. Let your warlike soul emerge entire."[125] Everyone who sympathized with France, and hated Germany and Austria, as he did, had long since joined the camp of the Entente.[126] Garibaldinian legions were already fighting on the French front. There were increasing grounds for fearing that the maintenance of absolute neutrality might deprive the party and Italy of their freedom of movement and represent a calculable advantage for the Central Powers. One seems to hear the cry of a drowning man when he writes on October 13: "Who would dare maintain today that the Socialist party has not made tremendous concessions to historical and national reality. ... What more did they want? That we become the court jesters of the 'democratic' war? That we suddenly throw all our convictions onto the rubbish heap merely because a new reality surprised us?"[127]

The historical reality retained the upper hand, but it was clear that Mussolini was still hoping to bring it into a new relationship with his principles. On October 18 appeared his article "Dalla neutralità assoluta alla neutralità attiva ed operante," which restated and combined all the arguments of the preceding months and which should have led to a reorientation of the party.[128] The party would henceforth no longer have held an unassailable position in the "absolute" but instead would have paid tribute to the "iron necessity of space and time." However, the fact that Mussolini had no intention at all of betraying his principles, that, on the contrary, he merely wanted to render them more flexible and "historic," can be confidently assumed. But why was it he who led the party to make the most irreconcilable statements? What effect was it bound to have if the perhaps unavoidable adjustment to reality was actually introduced with the recommendation for a war of aggression?

Indeed, this article was the last which Mussolini wrote as managing editor of *Avanti!*. The very next day the directorate of the party met in Bologna, and Mussolini's standpoint did not find a single supporter; although the way to reconciliation was left open for him, he resigned immediately as editor of *Avanti!*. The statements he made on this occasion permit a deep insight into his motives: "I would understand our absolute neutrality if you had the courage to carry it through to the end, and that means, to provoke insurrection; but this you reject a priori because you know you will meet with failure. Then say in all sincerity that you are against war ... because you are afraid of the bayonets. ... If you want, if you feel like it, I will stand at your head: neutralists outside the law ... very well, a decision must be made. But absolute neutrality within the law, from now on this has become impossible."[129]

No cogent reason is advanced. There is no mention of democracy, of Italy's necessities of life, of the unredeemed territories. The impossibility of radical coherence leads the revolutionary onto a path which he must share with his bitterest opponents. He evidently hoped in spite of everything to draw the party or large sections of it to his side. Not many days were needed to show him how mistaken he was. On October 25 he wrote to his friend Torquato Nanni: "I tried to open up the blind alley which the party had got into, but in the clash I fell."[130]

Mussolini was not the man to subordinate himself to party discipline. But he might have been expected to keep silent or at least not to write anything against the party, and he evidently did make such a promise to his colleagues in the party leadership. But he could not bring himself to hide what he felt to be the truth, and within a few weeks an abyss of misunderstanding, contempt, and hatred opened up between him and his former friends which was never again to be bridged.

Toward the end of October, apparently, it occurred to him to create his own organ, and by November 15 the first issue of *Il Popolo d'Italia* had appeared. Nothing was more natural than for the Socialists to suspect a "sellout" and a "betrayal." It seemed impossible that a man completely without means should be able within a few days to conjure up a daily newspaper unaided and out of nothing. It was true that while still managing editor of *Avanti!* Mussolini had had a few conversations with the editor of a Bologna paper which was considered the organ of the agrarians, and it was from this man that he obtained valuable aid in technical problems. But where the capital came from has to this day never been satisfactorily explained. It was not long before there were rumors of French funds, but this could never be proved.[131] The most likely hypothesis is that certain government departments saw to the obtaining of funds, for there were many circles in Italy which were interested in a weakening of the Socialist party. There is no doubt, then, that Mussolini, in allowing a newspaper to be created for him, became a card in some game. But there are absolutely no grounds for assuming that money, his own newspaper, were the *motive* behind his going over to interventionism. But this was what *Avanti!* hinted when, after the appearance of the new paper, it kept reiterating the question: *Chi paga?* Within a few weeks the onetime darling of the party had become *venduto alla borghesia* and a *transfuga* who merited the "righteous hatred" of the Italian proletariat.[132] When on November 24 Mussolini faced the members' assembly of the Milan section, which had to decide the matter of his expulsion, his speech was swallowed up in a storm of curses, whistles, and threats. The Socialist party morally lynched the "traitor"; not a single one of Italy's socialist papers stood by him; he had been unable to bring over to his side even a small section of the party. It was his first and most momentous defeat. He was alone.

But he had good reason for believing that he was a victim of injustice. The hardest won decision of his life concerned an issue which actually split all socialism into two camps, and it was the very "spirit" of Marxism from which a good deal of justification for his decision can be derived. In his eyes this decision must have seemed not only misunderstood but slandered when it was attributed to a base opportunism. How dared they call him a "renegade"? The man who goes over to the enemy is the man who no longer wishes to endure the trials and tribulations of his own position and looks forward to a better life on the other side. What was unendurable in Mussolini's position? What was he to gain by going over? With that touching naïveté which shows how very much socialism was a "world apart," Mussolini later asked whether at twenty-eight he had not possessed all his heart could desire. To a socialist, the editorship of *Avanti!* was worth more than the bourgeois prime ministership. His former comrades did not understand Mussolini.

Neither did Mussolini understand the attitude of his former friends. He had little feeling for the humanitarian tradition of socialism (not always identical with the Marxist tradition) that is compelled to reject as monstrous a way of thinking which was prepared to sacrifice hundreds of thousands of young lives for the sole purpose of "having been there." All he saw was lack of revolutionary zeal and personal cowardice. Out of this mutual misunderstanding there arose a polemic of utmost vehemence and often rank hostility, a polemic in which the groundwork was laid for the socialist conception of Italian fascism and the fascist conception of socialism. In any case, the estrangement was now a *fait accompli*. Mussolini was now a general without an army, a believer without a faith.

However, a small group of men to whom he was *duce* soon rallied round him again. By October, while Mussolini was still wrestling with himself, interventionist *fasci*, led by such men as Filippo Corridoni, Michele Bianchi, Massimo Rocca, and Cesare Rossi,[133] had emerged from the ranks of the syndicalists and socialists. In December they joined forces with Mussolini's followers to form the *fascio d'azione rivoluzionaria*, the germ cell of fascism. The only vital item on their program was the intervention on the side of the Entente; for the rest, Mussolini set up a postulate which it was not easy to achieve: "To reaffirm socialist ideals and review them in the light of the criticism under the present terrible lesson of facts."[134]

In other words, Mussolini is assuming no less a task than an up-to-date revision of socialism, leaving its "ideals" intact, but adopting a new relationship to a new reality. This is a good Marxist undertaking. But will Mussolini be equal to it, being not a cool, impersonal thinker, but standing exposed to all impressions of the hour? Can he retain his *fede* if he lets go the hand of the powerful spirit and abandons the guiding principle of which until now not even his boldest escapades have lost sight?

His very first endeavor in his own newspaper proves how slippery is his ground. The fact that at the moment it might be more revolutionary to want war than not to want it, that Marx had called upon the proletariat to assist in the solution of such bourgeois tasks as national unification, that one could not judge the war of the aggressor (Germany) and that of the victim of aggression (Belgium) by the same standard—all this is maybe granted by the socialist point of view. Yet it is surely an excessively "absolute" conclusion to say, "Life is that which is relative; the absolute exists only in cold and sterile abstraction."[135] This conclusion is stranger still if it prepares the soil for the re-emergence of ancient "eternal verities" which were the very thing socialism had wished to destroy, if it says, for example, that the usual explanations for war are inadequate: "there is the insuppressible discord of the peoples but also something else which we cannot hide from ourselves, and that is that man is a warlike animal, perhaps the most warlike animal in all zoology."[136] As chief witness he cites Proudhon who, he says, described war as "divine." But Mussolini does not know that this famous remark stems originally from Joseph de Maistre, and he takes no account of the fact that thought systems are like heavenly bodies, that they are centers of gravity with a far-reaching power of attraction which give the individual little scope for the exercise of free will. Mussolini, of course, only wishes to deny Marx where the latter is "outmoded," in order to return to Mazzini, Proudhon, Bakunin, Fourier, and Pisacane,[137] but it is very much open to question whether the planet which has become a comet will be free to determine its direction. From now on we can no longer divorce Mussolini's thinking from his life and subject it to systematic observation. This does not prevent us, however, from tracing certain primary motives at the various stages of his life.

The war years were the only period in Mussolini's life which was not in the true sense political. After the intervention, the *fasci d'azione rivoluzionaria* quickly lost their cohesion; when Mussolini returned from the front in 1917,[138] he remained till the end of the war merely a journalist, and one whose influence is hard to assess.

However, this apolitical period was the result of the second great political victory of his life. Although the interventionist currents were numerous and varied and became considerably stronger during the winter of 1914–15, in spite of German counterefforts,[139] intervention would never have been achieved in the face of resistance by Giolitti and the parliamentary majority if during the "radiant days" of May the masses of the war-minded minority had not taken to the streets in some large Italian cities and imposed their will on the resisting nation. D'Annunzio in Rome and Mussolini in Milan were the focal points of noisy and enthusiastic demonstrations. Mussolini, backed by the endless applause of gigantic crowds, threatened the head of state: "If you, O Monarch, do not resort to Article 5 of the Statute and declare war on the enemies of European civilization, if you refuse, well then, you will lose your crown."[140] This was, of course, an empty threat, for the king's government had just signed the London Pact. Thus, for the first time in modern Europe, through the combined action of the head of state and a mass minority, the violation of a parliament and hence the exclusion of the majority took place; a "qualitative" principle appeared to replace the "quantitative" one.

But although Italy entered the war in accordance with Mussolini's will, and although the war finally ended as he wished, his inner course during this period is nevertheless marked by a series of defeats. Hostility toward Germany steps to the fore as his dominating motive. Unrequited love and a surprisingly strong sense of national weakness combined to produce an emotion of genuine sincerity. To the runaway pupil, Marxism is German and Prussian, actually nothing more than Pan-German domination; no one, he feels, has demonstrated as clearly as the German Social Democrats that "everything which is treason, disgrace, deceit, is genuinely German."[141] Here Mussolini shows himself to be well acquainted with the *Sozialistische Monatshefte*, and he levels almost exactly the same accusations against German revisionism as were later leveled at fascism, and he does not neglect to attribute the heresy specifically to Marx and Engels: 'militarist and imperialist 'revisionism' links up again with Marxism and can invoke its founders, the aforesaid Marx and Engels, who were fanatical nationalists and convinced militarists."[142] The Germans held the Italians in subjection for centuries and were now about to rob them of their soul by means of German *Kultur*.[143] They exploited Italy economically and by dint of Pan-German theories even claimed its poets and leaders for the Teutonic race; and they looked down arrogantly on its people as a lesser race of mere *mandolinisti*. Mussolini does not shrink from a personal confession of guilt: before the war socialism had been—*mea culpa, mea culpa, mea maxima culpa*—a powerful trump card in Pan-Germany's game.[144] In ceaselessly demanding the declaration of war against Germany he is carrying on a war against his own past and for the benefit of his future as defender of Latin culture and as a follower of Mazzini. As a result, all the commonplaces of war propaganda take on a highly personal coloration.

Hence it was logical that in 1915 he declared himself unequivocally against Japan's entry into the war: Europeans must cope with the Germans on their own, or German arrogance would become even greater.[145] But two years later he wrote an article entitled "Avanti, il Mikado!" in which he suggested that Japan intervene in Europe by marching through Russia which had just become Bolshevist. Then in 1918 he pinned all his hope on the Americans. But did this not mean that in its deepest and most spiritual sense the war had been in vain?

As if to drown out this question, his attacks on the Germans become increasingly virulent. He calls hysterically for measures against the *quinta arma*[146] which Germany carries on so skillfully within the nations: "that vast, oblique, subterranean, terrible organization ... which threatens to paralyze—from behind—the nations of the Quadruple Entente";[147] without a qualm he stigmatizes the socialists as being internal allies of the enemy, criminals of the treacherous "stab in the back";[148] without hesitation he outlines the program of civil war: "Bombs in the hand against the Germans and their friends in Russia and other countries."[149]

Yet obviously he does not wish to be confused with those who combine animosity toward the Germans (albeit in a much less pronounced and personal way) with hostility to the socialists, that is, with the nationalists. So he resumes the old duel that he began in 1910 and continued in 1914 immediately before he went over to interventionism.[150] The starting point for him is the first Russian revolution. Francesco Coppola, "with all the rage and despair of a man who has drunk of de Maistre and become intoxicated with him," had regarded the revolution as responsible for the collapse of the Russian army. Scarcely had the first reports of the Brusilov offensive arrived when Mussolini wrote an article attacking him entitled "Bandiere Rosse." It also betrayed many of Mussolini's secret hopes and emotions: "Here we see events loudly refuting the reactionary thesis of Zimmerwald.... The red flags planted on the Galician trenches have the highest symbolic value. It is the revolution which does not fear war, it is the war which rescues the revolution. The flags with the imperial eagles: they will not withstand the red flags of the revolution. THE RED FLAG WILL RISE on the palace at Potsdam too when the armies of the revolution and of the Western democracies have shattered the Germany of the Hohenzollerns and of Scheidemann."[151]

This is obviously the deepest and most cherished dream of the Jacobinic socialist that Mussolini still was: to head the revolutionary armies and to defend and spread the revolution. Yet even in Russia this dream did not become reality; the disastrous activity of "German agents" headed by Lenin nipped it in the bud; in this regard Francesco Coppola proved to be right.

But Mussolini does not yet concede defeat. His next attack is against Enrico Corradini, who had put "democracy" on trial and made it responsible for all the weaknesses in the Entente's conduct of the war.[152] Does Corradini intend, Mussolini asks, to set up Germany and Turkey as models? Was Tsarism then *not* a "parasitical regime"? On no account does Mussolini wish his criticism of democracy to be confused with that of the nationalists. They criticize democracy as such; Mussolini demands dictatorship as a means, but democracy as a goal. Clemenceau is to him the ideal democratic dictator, and on no one does he bestow such acclaim during the final phase of the war, in no one does he place so much confidence. But he also regards Lloyd George and Wilson as democratic dictators.

This phase of the duel remained for the time being undecided, and in certain minor matters Mussolini was already noticeably approaching nationalist terminology and thinking during the war, as in the question of the "great power,"[153] for example, in the Adriatic problems, and in the new assessment of Catholicism as a positive political power which had tamed the mysticism of early Christianity to Latin clarity.[154] We are obviously concerned with an analysis that offers many possibilities of synthesis.

However, the most personal and intense instance of Mussolini's coming to grips with Marxism is his confrontation with Lenin and the Bolshevik revolution. During his stay in Switzerland, Mussolini had had contact, if not with Lenin himself, with men around him; he had read some of Lenin's writings;[155] Angelica Balabanov, Mussolini's former tutor, was now with Lenin in Russia. At the beginning of the war the Russian had come to a decision which was diametrically opposed yet at the same time closely related to his own. But it is typical of Mussolini's prevailing interests of the moment that, like his dialogue with Marxism, even the duel with Lenin appears at first as merely one further aspect of the struggle against Germany.

Lenin emerges at first as a mere shadow, barely visible against the joyously welcomed light of the February revolution. But it was not long before the "infamous treason perpetrated by extremists in the service of Germany" began to cause Mussolini serious concern.[156] Above all he sees the threat to the Entente which Russia's withdrawal from the war would cause, and he consoles himself with the thought that half a million Americans are worth more than five million muzhiks.[157] But beneath these external political overtones the unmistakable jealousy of the frustrated revolutionary keeps on cropping up, a jealousy which finds a moment's brief satisfaction when, after Lenin's flight following the July events, he is able to pronounce Lenin a "revolutionary made of hemp" (*rivoluzionario di stoppa*).[158] But the agitation of the Leninists goes on, the Russian armies continue to crumble; and from this Bolshevik experience Mussolini draws a conclusion which leads inevitably to significant "totalitarian" consequences: "The moral of the Russian events is clear: he who attacks the moral health of the army is guilty of treason, and he who tolerates the attack is an accomplice of the traitor."[159] Immediately prior to the victory of the Bolshevik revolution, however, he is led by a strange pride to claim (wrongly) a kind of paternity for himself: he had been the first, he maintained, to preach Blanquism, which had led on the one hand to intervention and on the other to Leninism.[160] At the moment of the upheaval itself, though, he produces much more naïve and emotional explanations: "Hindenburg has not gone to Petrograd simply because Lenin—alias Ulyanov, or, to use the true baptismal and race name, Ceorbaum—has returned to Petrograd. With today's revolt of the Maximalists, Germany has conquered Petrograd without firing a shot. The other three gentlemen forming the Bolshevik tetrarchy have these names: Apfelbaum, Rosenfeld, Bronstein. We are, as anyone can see, in the midst of authentic Germanism."[161] Truly an extremely strange ambivalence of judgment and emotion: it ranges from a sympathy which almost amounts to an identification to that naïve mythicizing indignation which Maurras and Hitler (and not they alone) displayed.[162] It will stay with him till he dies, although later on his reasonable and considered judgments will gain the upper hand for some time.

At first, events appeared to provide a wealth of confirmation for the thesis that Lenin had "sold out." The peace of Brest Litovsk seemed above all to confirm for Mussolini that his behavior had been correct when he parted company with socialism, that he had correctly assessed the socialists when he pronounced them cowards. Although by this time Mussolini is a revolutionary only within the limitations of the well-worn courses of war, the peace of Brest seems to set the seal on his triumph over Lenin, who had become a counterrevolutionary: "A peace that murders the revolution, that is Lenin's masterpiece!"[163]

But affairs in Moscow take a different course from the one that might have been assumed from these premises. A mere six months later Mussolini was admiringly contrasting "Lenin's brutal energy" with the apathy of the Italian bourgeoisie which, he said, was unwilling to assume its historical responsibility.[164] And he is not very convincing when he takes over articles on Soviet terrorism from Turati's *Critica Sociale* and uses the grist of humanitarian indignation for his own mill, a mill that always ground much coarser grain. However, in order to cope intellectually with these events, Mussolini suddenly invokes Karl Marx again, this time to serve as star witness against an "untimely" revolution.[165]

The duel with Lenin did not turn out as Mussolini desired and expected. The falsest accusation of all, however, was that, for Lenin, violence was not the exception but the prevailing system. Was it not Mussolini himself who had always equated revolution with war? Did he not conduct a tireless campaign in his paper for the totalization and intensification of the war? He ceaselessly takes the field against Germans remaining in Italy and German property, he demands concentration camps and confiscation; he wants to put workers in uniform and have foreigners distinguished by a badge; *inquadrare* becomes his favorite word; he ruthlessly demands all-out attacks on German cities and even justifies assassination: "I for my part approve of assassination—inasmuch as it helps me to conquer."[166]

All this does not bode well for the historical position Mussolini has adopted to replace the Marxist[167] one—that of Mazzini. It is in the spirit of Mazzini that he desires to operate: Italy must place itself at the head of those nations which are struggling for their freedom.[168] Undoubtedly he is more convincing than the nationalists, who demand the annexation not only of Fiume but of all Dalmatia and whose main concern seems to be the creation of a hereditary enmity toward the neighboring Slavic nations. With his socialist origin, Mussolini has no feeling whatever for that fixed gaze in the direction of coastal strips, rocky islands, and Venetian lions; his new friends had even to force him to turn his attention toward Fiume.[169] But finally he too wants Dalmatia as far down as Narenta, and it becomes very doubtful whether his friendship with the oppressed peoples of the Hapsburg empire can withstand the inevitable postwar conflicts of interest.

It is only natural for him to give vent to pseudoreligious emotion when the bells finally peal out victory and the Italian flag waves over Trent and Trieste. It is only natural for him to believe he had triumphed over the "red and black priests"[170] of neutralism, who were "creeping about dejectedly" while the masses and the workers were celebrating victory. But in the confusion of collective triumph was he not forgetting too soon the spiritual defeats which his disoriented path had cost him, was he not overlooking too readily the arguments which could be brought *against* him?

Struggle for Social Democracy

At the end of the war Italy undoubtedly found itself in a better position than any other European power of the Entente. The nationality principle had rewarded its most loyal offspring with a cornucopia of gifts: not only were the furthest Italian-language borders reached everywhere, and Trent, Trieste, and Pola won, in addition these borders were all unassailable—and Austria, the age-old enemy of national existence, was completely destroyed. Henceforth there stretched between the Alps and the sea the most contained and trouble-free national region of Continental Europe. How different was the position of France, still faced by the enemy along open borders, an enemy which had scarcely been seriously weakened and whose national existence was protected by the nationality principle! How different even was the position of England, which had no idea of how to cope with the crisis in its empire, a crisis which the war had rendered incurable!

Any shadows cast over this picture of Italian external affairs were simply due to the fact that it had not been possible or thought desirable to adhere to Mazzini's commandments. In the Treaty of London the Italians were granted the greater part of Dalmatia, but they had to relinquish their claim on Fiume. Although Dalmatia, the eastern Adriatic coast, was a region rich in historic memories from the time of Venetian rule, the number of Italian inhabitants was relatively small and limited entirely to the coastal towns. Fiume, on the other hand, was preponderantly Italian (although far from being *italianissima*), but for the whole Croatian hinterland it was a vital port, and its own interests pointed to a symbiosis.[171] Nevertheless, when Austria collapsed it was occupied, like Dalmatia, by Italian troops, and Yugoslavia, not yet constituted, had only words with which to resist. It is not hard to understand that Italy now laid claim to Fiume; but it is easier still to understand that, with this blatant infringement of an existing treaty and a much-vaunted principle, it did not exactly meet with a sympathetic ear at the peace conference. Why did it deny the Yugoslavs the very thing it claimed for itself in South Tirol? Why did it not consider an exchange, which would have been the most obvious solution of all? Was not the impression inevitable that Italian policy was being laid down by the nationalists, to whom the nationality principle was a mere pretext and who were guided solely by motives of power and prestige? (They had no intention, however, of letting things come to a war—according to their doctrine, the only valid criterion of irreducible questions of power; they preferred an exaggerated display of moral indignation vis-à-vis the Allies.) This tension in foreign policy overshadowed all events in Italy until and beyond the Treaty of Rapallo.[172]

Yet in actual importance it was but a poor shadow in comparison with political conflicts at home.[173] The dispute between interventionists and neutralists had never been suspended or overcome in the hour of common need and common determination; the war, which was supposed to "create" or "confirm" the nation, had in fact split it more deeply than ever, since it had itself been the product of a cleavage not unlike civil war. If the interventionists could point to the war as the highest confirmation of their will, the former neutralists could equally well object that the gains might have been achieved without war, that the enormous losses had been too high a price, and that in any event those who bore the immediate and sole responsibility for the death of seven hundred thousand young men should be punished. Even if these accusations were derived from an "unheroic" mentality, they were bound to find their mark with the interventionists at a point of deep-seated uncertainty and self-doubt. For despite the undeniable fact that the Italian armies had fought well, they had not achieved any convincing successes; they had not even managed to conquer as much as Austria had been prepared four years earlier to give up. Thus it could not even be claimed that Italy had contributed notably to a containment of hostile forces: the Austrian defense position in the Alps was too favored by nature for the use of mass armies there. It was therefore necessary, if Italy's own moral personality was to be saved, to seize upon the battle of Vittorio Veneto,[174] an encounter which had merely given the *coup de grâce* to the abandoned army of an already crumbling state, and to describe it falsely as the decisive battle of the world war. But the resistance met with in Paris was more easily explained by the phrase *vittoria mutilata*, which closed its eyes to the treaty text and the true situation in Fiume[175] and offered a convenient clear-cut schema to sensitive consciences. Thus two lies transformed the content of "true" interventionism into a coin of topical politics, and the task of circulating this coin was assumed primarily by the nationalists.

But the former neutralists were not content with discussing the past either. The socialists must have seen their belief confirmed that only a radical change in the social structure could cut the ground forever from under the feet of the forces of intervention. But there was no agreement as to what form this change should take. The majority of the party were victims—in words, at least—of the disastrous misconception that the party must take Lenin's revolution as its model. Those who held this belief were deluding themselves in nearly every point where delusion was possible: the structure of their own party, the nature of society, the degree of dependence on the state, the character of the people. But they had considerable initial success because they managed to gain influence over the as yet unorganized force which was to be the decisive one.

This third force was the enormous bulk of peasants, members of the middle class, and workers, who had fought through this first democratic war in the history of Italy and who now brought back to their native land not so much memories as the will to far-reaching reform: reform of the agrarian structure, of the army constitution, of labor legislation, of election methods. But their determination would inevitably be lost and dissipated if it did not join hands with an already organized political group. Only a minority could have been willing, with the nationalists, to glorify the war instead of transforming it into tangible social results. But not very many turned with enthusiasm to the Leninists: the masses are not inclined to a radicalism which makes strong doctrinal demands. The majority supported the general mood of discontent, known as revolutionary, participated in the innumerable strikes, land seizures, and so forth, but did not achieve any political will of their own. If it had been possible to detach the reformist socialists (headed by the leaders of the large trade-union organizations) from their ambiguous and inwardly insincere association with the Leninists in the Socialist party and to bring them together with these masses, then presumably the great reform party of Social Democracy would have been born, which would have been capable of initiating far-reaching social changes from below as well as protecting them from above.[176] Those apparently destined to undertake this task were the leftist interventionists, who were equally removed from the nationalists as from the Leninists.

Here lay Mussolini's political potential in 1919, and it was in fact in this direction that his political will was moving. But this will was burdened by the past and weakened by that sensibility which was unable to elude the emotion of the moment. That his insight was bound to lead him onto this path is beyond question. His critical analysis of Marxism, begun during the war, caused him to alter his views so radically and so widely that we find ourselves asking how these gradualistic theses can be compatible with his restless temperament. He is now convinced that capitalism still has a long life ahead of it; hence, that class co-operation is the order of the hour. Whereas he once spoke of *giornata storica*, today he sees "that world economy, so extraordinarily complex, is not to be changed by 'coups de main.' "[177] He regards the separation of bourgeoisie and proletariat as naïve; in the highly differentiated and individualist societies of the West a revolution such as Lenin's is not possible. (This explains why he stated as late as April, 1919, that Italy was in no way threatened by bolshevism.)[178] With sharp and accurate perception he criticizes the tactics of the Socialist party,[179] which fills the masses with expectations they neither can nor wish to realize; he declares it to be his task to bring this party "to reason." It is not hard to see where Mussolini believes this "reason" to lie: it is the reformism, once so bitterly attacked, of Turati (who, to be sure, lacks the courage of his convictions) and the model of the French CGT under Jouhaux.

Fascism, which was founded on March 23, 1919, at a poorly attended meeting in Milan, mainly of former leftist interventionists,[180] wishes to be regarded as the beginning of a national socialism, germ cell of social democracy, or perhaps merely its midwife. For it is envisaged as a temporary, loose association, without dogmas and *finalità remote*, pragmatically intent on the carrying out of certain tasks.[181] These tasks are those fundamental social changes which Leninism jeopardizes by linking them with untenable dogmas: republic, agrarian reform (*la terra ai contadini*), abolition of the senate, confiscation of church property, partial expropriation of capital, economic councils (*Consigli nazionali*) side by side with a political parliament. In any case Mussolini is still very much aware at this point that a "revolution" must affect property rights, and youthful fascism not only frequently cites Kurt Eisner[182] as a model for its program, but points pridefully to the *carattere popolare e sovversivo* of the founding meeting.[183]

Nevertheless, there were many good reasons even at that time for not trusting to the revolutionary character of this "antiparty," and it is hardly due to coincidence or inability that Turati, D'Aragona,[184] and Buozzi[185] did not wish to trust themselves to this helper.

Mussolini's extraordinary mobility in the Adriatic question must have been enough to arouse misgivings. Following some unfriendly remarks in the French press, the oppressed peoples of the Hapsburg empire, who until that very moment had been allies, became for him *queste tribù* against whom he musters Italy's three-thousand-year-old culture to do battle;[186] whereas those Italians in favor of a compromise solution he attacks with increasing ferocity as "renunciation politicians" (*rinunciatari*). With excessive speed the man who toward the end of the war stood godfather to the Italian "League of Nations Movement" and enthusiastically acclaimed the American president, goes over to a spiteful anti-Wilsonism. In a violent onslaught of rage against "the supreme council of wolves, foxes, jackals in Paris"[187] he abandons himself to the theory of the proletarian peoples, although he presumably knows what Corradini's intention had been when he established it, and assuredly does not overlook the fact that the same objections can be leveled against this theory as against the "naïve" theory of the proletarian class.

Thus if in a remarkable phase of his duel with Lenin, he accuses his great opponent of reintroducing capitalism into Russia, it must seem especially suspicious to the allied democratic anti-Bolsheviks to see Mussolini using the myth formulations of anti-Semitism: according to this, joint efforts of Jewish bankers in London and New York and their racial brothers in Moscow were hindering the victory of the White armies in an act of vengeance against the Aryan race and Christianity.[188]

These and similar deviations from the principal course are no doubt chiefly attributable to the fact that since the end of the war Mussolini had been in a truly desperate position. For years he had controlled the masses; now practically no one listened to him. All the antipathy now being openly hurled at the detested war found its chief target in him. It glorified the Socialist party, for which he was *the* Judas and traitor. He no longer had any foothold among the masses; hence all political plans which might have been worthy of him remained nebulous, while the only contact that remained for him was with a military and political demimonde. At the war's end he allied himself with the Arditi, a special body of men who, with dagger and hand grenade, performed bold exploits but were exempt from the drudgery of life in the trenches.[189] The Arditi and their friends involved him in a very ugly demonstration against Leonida Bissolati, who had dared to support an exchange of Dalmatia and Fiume and to doubt the usefulness of the Brenner border; in short, against the very man who ought to have been his most important ally in the struggle for "social democracy."[190] In April the same men entered the *Avanti!* building after a street battle and set it on fire. Mussolini sought to justify the incident in his newspaper[191] after he had already declared civil war on the "slanderers": "We shall defend the dead. All the dead, even if we have to dig trenches in the squares and streets of our cities."[192]

The parliamentary elections of November, 1919, finally made him realize his position. Negotiations over a leftist bloc failed because of the danger of incurring the people's wrath by using his name. Isolated, he received barely five thousand votes out of more than two hundred and fifty thousand. Throughout Italy the Socialists celebrated an overwhelming victory. With one hundred and fifty-six representatives they had become the strongest party; in a coalition with the Popolari they would have had an absolute majority. No one so much as mentioned Mussolini now. Politically speaking, he seemed to be defunct.

But two months previously Gabriele D'Annunzio with a few hundred volunteers had occupied Fiume, and when the Socialists used the opening session of parliament for an empty gesture, nationalist crowds in the streets of Rome organized a hunt of Socialist deputies and manhandled many of them. While Mussolini's star seems to be declining, two new heavenly bodies appear on Italy's political horizon: nationalism and D'Annunzio.

Nationalism

Italian nationalism is no younger than French nationalism; but whereas the latter started from an internal political event which generated the highest degree of international concern, for Enrico Corradini[193] it was the very limited national defeat at Aduwa that prompted his transition from literature to politics. The internal political conflict was not as marked as in France; Corradini had been a liberal, which is why the formative process took longer than in the neighboring country. But when the first issue of *Il Regno* appeared in November, 1903, Corradini and his friends immediately fell upon socialism as the chief adversary with much greater single-mindedness, but they were also much more naïve in adopting its conception of problems and its terminology.

The foreword itself to *Il Regno* leaves no room for doubt: the journal is intended as a voice "against the baseness of the present time. And above all against that of ignoble socialism. ... In place of any ordering of noble ideas, the wrath of the basest instincts of greed and destruction has been laid down."[194] But this demarcation of the front entails a second one: the front against a bourgeoisie that does not defend itself, against an ideology out of which the "evil plant of socialism" has grown. In other words, with surprising frankness this nationalism declares itself, from the outset, to be the mouthpiece and advocate of that section of the bourgeoisie that despairs of liberalism because it does not feel sufficiently protected from socialism—one might say: of that bourgeoisie that took Mussolini the Marxist seriously and was afraid of him. At first Corradini quite plainly regarded as an internal political recipe that which was going to become more and more the basis of the doctrine: the emphasis on foreign policy, the glorification of war. The bourgeoisie, he said, had never realized that its salvation lay precisely in what socialism most hated—in a policy of expansion and imperialism.[195] Hence the Russo-Japanese war was welcomed joyously as a proof of the "modernity of war." No less a man than Vilfredo Pareto provided the most clear-cut definition of the new doctrine and its assumptions: the bourgeoisie, he said, had come to believe that it could lead the people at will through elections; but now the people—or rather, a new elite of the people which was using the intellectual proletariat that had foolishly been created by the bourgeoisie itself—were moving toward the conquest of the state and above all toward the possessions of the bourgeoisie. "Only a war in which many nations were involved and which was of fairly long duration could interfere with the regular course of the phenomenon. It could, however, alter that course if the stupidly humanitarian feelings of the bourgeoisie were to change and make way for virile feelings. But of this there is not, at least at present, the slightest indication."[196] What is remarkable at this point is not that the bourgeoisie as such expresses its class interests overtly, but that it required decades before the incompatibility of liberalism and the Marxist theory of class warfare found polemical expression and was extended to the dual opposition of this theory; and it is still more remarkable that a section of the bourgeoisie should adopt the assumptions of its opponent to such an extent that it loses all "world view" of its own, regards war as the sole solution, and shows a tendency to deny its own historical roots.

Corradini keeps entirely to the mode of thought and terminology of the opponent when he makes the famous distinction between "proletarian" and "bourgeois" nations[197] and declares that nationalism desires to be for the whole nation what socialism has been for the proletariat. Thus the threat to the bourgeoisie is removed in that the exploitation concept is shifted one step higher. Even so, it remains a concept of far less rational content and far less clear-cut appeal than the Marxist conception. Nor is it extended to call for the solidarity of all proletarian nations in the struggle against an exploiting bourgeoisie of nations. For Corradini's dream is imperialism, and his ideal is Rome. Hence he prefers the matching concepts of static and dynamic, or old and young, nations, with their stronger biological connotation. For all Italian nationalists, the model of a dynamic nation was Germany, and Germany's "world revolution" against the saturated and conservative nations of the West was observed with satisfaction and admiration. The inner logic of the doctrine would have required that the two dynamic nations unite in the world war so as to replace moribund wealthy impotence with their youthful and imperial strength. Yet, after starting out loyal to the *Dreibund*, the nationalists later went over to the side of the Entente. This is justified by Francesco Coppola[198] with the tortuous explanation that, beside the stronger dynamic nation, Italy could have only played a secondary role, while among senile nations it had a better chance of extending its own power[199]—a stupid (and during the war very damaging) argument on the part of a clever man, but the characteristic expression of a desperate situation, of a daydream of world power and unrestricted autonomy, for which the elementary prerequisites were lacking and must inevitably be lacking even more as time goes on.

But perhaps this was the very reason why no other European country so enthusiastically acclaimed the war as a healing, hallowing, and ontological power; and after all, Italy was the only country to enter two world wars without being compelled by necessity to do so. Not even in Hitler's Germany were the identification of right with might, the ridiculing of *umanitarismo cristiano o democratico*,[200] the reduction of history to an amoral struggle of isolated peoples for the breadbasket, ever pursued to a greater extent than in the Italian nationalism of Corradini, Coppola, and their friends.

Greatly as they exceeded the men of the Action Française in ruthless "modernity," they nevertheless lagged far behind them in their depiction of the "history of decay," even though the commonplaces of conservative thought, from antiindividualism to antiparliamentarianism, were manipulated by them with virtuosity (by some, such as Alfredo Rocco,[201] with a good deal of emphasis, by others, such as Francesco Coppola, with less). It is noticeable, however, that Enrico Corradini does not even hesitate to criticize the Risorgimento,[202] and his formulation of historical anti-Semitism is as sharp as Maurras': "Rome was carried by the eagles of its will to the Roman empire, to the Pax Romana; Judea could only dream. ... The first socialism is in the Bible. The first justice of the lowest is in the Bible. The first violence of the meek against the violent, the first arrogance of the humble against the arrogant, are in the Bible. ... The prophet is the revolution."[203] Corradini's philosophy is restricted to "organic" metaphysics of the eternal laws of life which man can and must not infringe; his classicist estheticism shows traces of still being linked to the concepts of "civilization" and "mankind."

Seen as a whole, Italian nationalism is a somewhat younger and much coarser brother of the French, a boxer as compared to a fencer, free of the prejudices of a long and cultured background—but also, seen objectively, free of its despair and cruelty. But it is precisely the sturdier and less logical nature of Italian nationalism, combined with the influence on it of Marxist terminology and mode of thought, that make possible a meeting with heretical socialists. For the nationalists do not hesitate to acknowledge a "positive side" to liberalism, democracy, and socialism, and to speak soon and emphatically of "revolution," indeed at times to proclaim national democracy or even national socialism as their ideal. Their concept of the *produttori* is just as much a potential point of contact as is their will to solve the problems of the proletariat by the conquest of settlement colonies. Even among the founders of the weekly periodical *L'Idea Nazionale*, which in 1911 replaced the defunct *Il Regno*,[204] there was a former revolutionary socialist: Roberto Forges-Davanzati. The Libyan war brought quite a number of socialist intellectuals closer to nationalism. At that point, of course, the nationalists were still regarded as mere auxiliary forces of Giolitti and the liberals; but with the world war they assumed their own, unmistakable position, and in the postwar period nationalism, faithful to its traditions, became the spearhead of the imperialist and antisocialist trend. Nationalists created their storm troop divisions (the *squadre azzurre*) and reigned supreme in the streets of Rome. With Luigi Federzoni[205] nationalism also represented the extreme Right in parliament. But it was bound to appear doubtful whether the nationalists would achieve direct contact with the masses. They pinned their hopes on the memory of the war and on problems of foreign policy that the war had left unsolved. And when the news arrived of D'Annunzio's coup in Fiume, *L'Idea Nazionale* gave him its unqualified support. Mussolini did the same in Milan. Thus Fiume brought together the two elements which were to be each other's destiny.

D'Annunzio in Fiume

At the end of the war Fiume had been occupied by Italian troops, joined later by French and English contingents: the Allied occupation corresponded better to the unclarified situation. Not that there was the slightest possibility of the city being simply handed over to Yugoslavia or becoming the victim of a Croatian coup; but uncertainty bred mistrust, and it was above all the nationalists who were interested in exploiting this mistrust against the government of Francesco Saverio Nitti, whose internal policy they feared more than anything else because it aimed ultimately at constituting Social Democracy. The agitation in Fiume led to incidents; as a result of a unanimous decision of the Allied command, some Italian divisions had to leave the city and were for the time being stationed quite close by, in Ronchi. There a number of officers conspired to seize Fiume, and they asked Gabriele D'Annunzio to assume command.

During the war D'Annunzio, as had been his dream, added to his fame as a poet his fame as a warrior. He had been decorated with the Gold Medal, Italy's highest and rarest decoration for bravery, he had lost an eye, and by the end of the war he held the rank of lieutenant colonel. Yet what he had actually been was not a soldier but a kind of privileged adventurer in assorted uniforms who in a Venetian palace thought up the most daring exploits and carried them out on land, on sea, and in the air. He was honored as the nation's greatest poet, but also as the man who in May, 1915, had made a vital contribution to Italy's entry into the war. Thus *one* man in Europe, over and above the disciplined and confined dying of the masses, carried on the war as the supreme adventure, the gigantic confirmation of his own powerful ego. It was in him that all those whose mentality and situation permitted a similar outlook found themselves confirmed, chiefly a large number of young officers. For master and disciples alike, the end of the war meant the same: the end of ecstasy, the beginning of a workaday world. For D'Annunzio and his followers, Fiume offered a unique opportunity to continue living the "great" life.[206]

It is hard to believe that "patriotism" was the primary motive of these men. They were not, after all, defending a forlorn corner of their native soil, at the cost of loss and sacrifice, from the onslaughts of the enemy: they saw to it that the troops of their own army retreated without bloodshed, and deserted in order to parade about.

Legally speaking, it was in fact with a group of deserters that D'Annunzio set out from Ronchi on the evening of September 11 against Fiume. But the march of these deserters was supported in many ways by the regular army, and in Fiume the commanding general, after a short tussle with his conscience, embraced the great poet with tears and left the field to him. It was the first demonstration of what oaths of loyalty and allegiance were in future actually to mean to their champions. France and England submitted to the affront and withdrew their contingents. It was the first successful bluff in postwar Europe, and it would not be the last. For over a year D'Annunzio ruled Fiume as *comandante*. Never in the world's history has there been a more impressive farce or one with greater implications for the future.

The government in Rome ordered a blockade of Fiume, at the same time keeping it supplied through the Red Cross. Italian troops encircled the city and remained on the friendliest terms with D'Annunzio's legionaries. Half the population were hostile toward the Comandante,[207] yet in front of his palace one delirious public demonstration followed another; the *gagliardetti* (triangular pennants) vanished when the *salvatore* appeared, the legionaries' daggers flashed and the death skulls on their insignia threatened. In the dialogue between speaker and masses, excitement mounted until it became a paroxysm, and to the question *A chi l'Italia?* a thousand voices echoed back like thunder *A noi*. Did that not explode all traditional ideas? "Here is life bursting forth! Here is life on the rampage!"[208]

Indeed, the legionaries and the daughters of the city paid homage to life and the unique hour in endless promiscuity.[209] D'Annunzio saw the dawn of a new age where life would be fuller and more beautiful: "Versailles means decrepitude, infirmity, obtuseness, deceit, betrayal, and cruelty, which look out on the world from eyes dilated with fear; Ronchi means youth, beauty, daring, cheerful sacrifice, broad aims, profound newness. ... The newness of life is not in Odessa, it is in Fiume, it is not by the Black Sea, it is by the Carnaro."[210]

This newness of life was simply the reawakening of the oldest culture. For as the champion of Rome and its three-thousand-year-old mission, the soldier-poet was keeping watch against the advancing barbarism of Slavic tribes that have no history: "Were we not to hold it [Postumia], the flood of Balkan tribes, the flood of Slavic barbarism, would advance to within twenty kilometers of the walls of Trieste."[211]

But D'Annunzio's deep cultural awareness does not prevent him, in his wrath against the powers of Versailles—who tolerate him but have not recognized him—from proclaiming himself the leader of the crusade on behalf of all oppressed peoples: "It is the new crusade of all the poor and impoverished nations, the new crusade of all poor and free men, against the nations which usurp and amass all wealth, against the predatory races."[212]

True, all that entered the port of Fiume was now and again a ship they had been lucky enough to capture; true, the wharves and factories were more or less at a standstill—nevertheless, D'Annunzio presented his city with a new political and economic constitution, later known as the *Carta del Carnaro*, which was drawn up mainly by the syndicalist Alceste De Ambris, and which, if it is modern to mix, is certainly the most modern of all constitutions. From the medieval past it took the names of its two houses (*Consiglio degli Ottimi*, *Consiglio dei Provvisori*) and the importance of autonomous corporations; it denounced the parasites and, like anarchosyndicalism, praised the producer; it aimed at establishing a popular government as envisaged by Rousseau, and interpreted much like Rousseau the unqualified power handed over "in danger" to the Comandante; like the age of Enlightenment, it emancipated women, and, like the ancient *polis*, introduced a cult of the state. For the first time in a modern constitution, music becomes an *istituzione religiosa e sociale*, for a great people not only makes God in its own image, but also composes a hymn for its God. A "circular building," to be built shortly and to accommodate at least ten thousand people, is to serve for the celebration of the new faith. Thus old and new become the element of the new world which is destined to triumph victoriously over capitalism and socialism.[213]

This program obviously contains some points (in particular the merely conditional recognition of property) which must render it suspicious in the eyes of conservatives. In fact D'Annunzio came more and more into contact with revolutionaries, headed by Errico Malatesta,[214] while some of his young officers developed into virtual Communists. With the plan for a "march on Rome" was linked the will to a republic, and all this made some of the most loyal friends in Rome increasingly uneasy. Since with the Treaty of Rapallo D'Annunzio had become a serious debit item in Italy's foreign policy, and since he made his situation still worse by foolish provocations, the end of the adventure was rapidly approaching. Shortly before Christmas of 1920, Giolitti gave the regular troops the order to attack. The first few dead provided D'Annunzio with the concept of *Natale di sangue*, but when the first shells from the battleship "Andrea Doria" roared over the great square which had so often heard the cry *Italia o morte* and struck the Comandante's palace, the poet left his city[215] and went to Lake Garda, where for a few years he still remained a political power, then became an exalted memory, and finally died as a burden.[216] His legionaries scattered throughout Italy in 1921; the majority swelled the ranks of the Fascists, although many of them could not forgive Mussolini for being a "traitor."

Mussolini's Darkest Year

Neither reaction is surprising. On the one hand the Fascists adopted the "style" of the Fiume enterprise with far fewer qualms than the nationalists; on the other, for the leader of the Fascists the year of D'Annunzio's great adventure meant the darkest year of his political career, and his loyalty to the Comandante was not exempt from doubt.

Throughout this time Mussolini seemed to be little else than D'Annunzio's personal journalist in Italy. Immediately after the march on Ronchi he declared that Fiume was now the seat of "his" government, and henceforth he and the Fascists would obey it alone. (The government in Rome let pass this treasonable utterance just as it had the phrase *quel porco di Nitti*.)[217] He desired to be one of D'Annunzio's legionaries: "Disciplined soldier ... at the disposal of the Comandante."[218] And although at first he used to address the poet in personal letters as *Mio caro D'Annunzio*, he soon adopted a more formal address and assured the Comandante: *Sono il vostro soldato*.[219]

How little this subordinate role suited Mussolini can be seen from the fact that the anarchistic and individualistic streak in his character emerged more strongly in this period than in any other. Fascism had become for him the "refuge of all heretics, the church of all heresies,"[220] and he was groping his way back to a thinker who was at times important to him in his younger days, when he said: "Leave the way open for the elemental forces of individuals, because there is no other human reality apart from the individual. Why should Stirner not become topical again?"[221] There is no better description of the desperate mental state, no clearer example of what was apparently a permanent trait in the future restorer of the concept of state, than the following outburst of April, 1920: "Down with the state in all its types and personifications. The state of yesterday, of today, of tomorrow. The bourgeois state and the socialist one. For those of us who are the doomed of individualism, all that remains for today's darkness and tomorrow's gloom is the henceforth absurd but ever consoling religion of anarchy!"[222]

But the Protestantism of this heretic "of both Vaticans, in Moscow and Rome," is expressed mainly in the form of a paganism which, because of its contempt for all "theologies" and all "Christianisms," sees modernity primarily as "nature" and has apparently finally abandoned Marx in favor of Nietzsche: "We who deeply loathe all Christianisms, from that of Jesus to that of Marx, look with extraordinary sympathy on this 'new impetus' to modern life, in the pagan forms of the cult of strength and daring."[223] The result is a sense of crisis that sometimes resembles that which possessed Hitler: "The world today bears strange analogies with that of Julian the Apostate. Will the 'red-haired Galilean' conquer yet again? Or will the Mongolian Galilean of the Kremlin be victorious? Will there be a successful 'revaluation' of all values, as there was in the twilight of Rome?"[224]

But myth formulations and Nietzschean radicalisms are always quickly "encapsuled" in Mussolini's mind; they do not prevent him from making sober political analyses and examining whatever problems are relevant to him at the moment. Hence his criticism of the Socialist party remains unchanged and shrewd: it is obstructing one's own path to antagonize the middle classes to no purpose, repel the war veterans, and try to dress Italians in the blouse of the Russian muzhik; it is foolish to glorify the manual laborer blindly; the deceptive union of revolutionaries and reformists would result in mutual crippling; indeed, he even speaks of "Turati's and our opinion."[225] Generally he argues entirely as a "functionary" of socialism; this is still his interpretation of his interventionism, for he claims to have been the one who made the present situation possible, who brought about the fall of the stage setting "which was hiding the city of Utopia."[226] The Socialist party must now have the courage to hoist the flag of collaboration; for it is its duty to complete the bourgeois revolution in a country whose problems are presocialist and whose forces of production are in a rudimentary state.[227]

It is fascinating to watch how this man, on whom these insights were forced by circumstances, in the same breath depreciates them, as again and again he expresses his contempt for them, the contempt of his "temperament," which never ceases to take full credit as the founder of Italian communism: "You do not have the temperament for the 'historic day' or the 'bloodbath' of Mussolini's memory. Do what you can do, and stop pretending to be lions when you are rabbits, and cease talking about the barricades when all you understand is how to go to the polls."[228] Typical of this mixing of elements is the form given to his relationship with Lenin. Now he no longer denies Russian Communist heroism and the will to fight, but he has ceased to admit that they are fighting for the Communist society. Bolshevism, he says, is revealing its capitalistic, warlike, nationalistic face, and Lenin is the greatest of all reactionaries in

Europe. The fact that some Communists now declare that he too has "sold out," is noted by Mussolini with the utmost satisfaction: "That is a little bit our revenge."[229] Horror and admiration fight in him when he says (and actually he never got beyond this assessment): "Lenin's attempt is a vast, terrible experiment in vile bodies. Lenin is an artist who has worked with human beings as other artists work in marble or metals. ... There has been no masterpiece. The artist has failed. The task was beyond his powers."[230]

If sympathy is mixed with aversion in his attitude toward Lenin, his sympathetic movement toward the nationalists is constantly being retarded by resistance. Although Mussolini, like the nationalists, applauds the captains of industry, and in the midst of revolutionary verbalism accepts with pride the term "reactionary," he nevertheless wants a distinction made between his freedom-loving and democratic antibolshevism and that of the nationalists, and he objects to the national movement being confused with one part of it, the Nationalists.[231] When the Treaty of Rapallo is signed, his positive evaluation diverges radically from the indignation of *L'Idea Nazionale* over the "betrayal." Unlike *L'Idea Nazionale* he supports a peaceful policy vis-à-vis Yugoslavia and stresses the demand: "This ambiguity between nationalism and fascism—which has arisen in some centers—must cease."[232]

At the same time this attitude constitutes a breach, never quite healed, with the legionaries, who accuse him of *minimalismo adriatico*—and all attempts at appeasement have little effect. Mussolini's comments on the *Natale di sangue* sound conspicuously reserved. By the end of 1920 he has regained his political independence.

Nor was the drought of that year always of equal intensity. Admittedly the first few months saw him at the nadir of his political career. The accusations leveled at him by two former editors of his newspaper, because he used money collected *pro Fiume* to finance the small private army which protected the *Popolo d'Italia*, would almost have finished him off morally, and it was only D'Annunzio's generosity that saved him. In those days he spoke of the "remnants of fascism,"[233] and felt he was lucky to be "still on his feet."[234] But about the middle of the year, fascism achieved its first great successes in Trieste and Venezia Giulia in a ruthless struggle that was simultaneously a nationality and a class war. On August 21 he was able to speak of "fascism's hour," even though he still believed in its merely temporary nature.[235] As the seizing of the factories by the workers (of which, incidentally, he very much approved)[236] drew to a close, he was welcomed as a savior and was able to make a great speech in "purged" Trieste, the "cradle of fascism."[237] On October 20 he spoke for the first time of fascism existing above the bourgeoisie and the proletariat, saying that it might become the *forza dominatrice* of the nation.[238] But it required the events in Bologna and the Po valley (which evidently came as a surprise to him too) to bring him back, after December, within a few months to a position of influence and power in high politics. This advancing wave of fascism coincides with the ebb of the socialist tide, which reached its peak in the seizing of the factories and then petered out exhausted and disillusioned.

The Socialist Face of 1920

It is a fact that even D'Annunzio's enterprise would not have met with nearly such a strong response had it not offered a number of influential men and newspapers a unique opportunity to distract attention from more important events or to create new hope in respect to them. For this year was indeed the heyday of the Socialist party and of those social movements of which it had made itself the advocate, movements whose interests it often completely ignored yet for whose excesses it was often held responsible. The year 1919 had moved quite clearly in the direction of far-reaching political and social changes, and this direction was confirmed by the result of the elections of November, 1919, and identified with certain parties, that is, with the Socialists and the Popolari. If these parties had joined forces they would have had a parliamentary majority and been able to put through almost any change—except "the revolution."

What does "revolution" mean in this case?

Any process can be called revolution which leads by extralegal means to a change in the highest political leadership. In this sense, the forcing of intervention in 1915 may be called a revolution. But it only brought about that which would in principle have been legally possible, and it left untouched the political structure of the country. In a more drastic sense we can speak of political revolution only when it causes a change in the political system, that is, when no possible configuration within the system can coincide with it. In this sense fascism brought about a revolution, but it did not do so all at once—we cannot really speak of a "fascist state" before 1926.

Since Marx we have been accustomed to apply the term "revolution" only to those upheavals which cause a fundamental change in the economic structure as well, and thus in matters of property and ownership. But Marx himself by no means denies that a change of this kind may be a long-drawn-out process, and he therefore does not hesitate to call the bourgeoisie as such "revolutionary." Revolution can, of course, coincide with a political overthrow, thus fulfilling the fourth and apparently highest conception of the term.

Such a political-economic revolution is neither logically nor historically an impossibility: the French revolution was of this type, and so was the Russian. But all that the Italian socialists could think of was a revolution of the proletariat against the bourgeoisie. Its inevitability had been foretold by Marx, and no prediction is more compelling than that which signifies the elimination of the class which manifestly monopolizes the social wealth and the management of labor, and its replacement by abstract and collective direction of labor and property in a more universal society. Yet no prediction has proved more incorrect during the course of a century, if "proletariat" is taken to be a definite group, typified by manual labor, in contrast to all the "rest" of society.

In the hundred years since the *Communist Manifesto* there has been no single instance of the proletariat—as seen in these terms—defeating "the" bourgeoisie. Nor *could* it succeed in doing so. For "bourgeoisie" must not be equated with one of its manifestations—with the one described by Thomas Mann, for example. The concept of bourgeois-capitalist production methods must be seen in sufficient breadth to include every type of rationalized and collectivized production of which the distinguishing feature is ownership—largely private—of the means of production by an undetermined number of people. In principle it excludes neither a certain amount of planning nor the complete absence of property on the part of any particular group. The proletariat in the Marxist sense, whose rise appears for a time identical with the rise of society itself, in turn assumes a negative relationship to this development as soon as a definite and relatively high proportion of technical and intellectual labor becomes necessary in the day-by-day production process; those who perform this work do not fit into any Marxist category, and the social movement is producing them in rapidly increasing numbers. Even in its most random and imperfect national individuality, bourgeois society will become the more indestructible the further it proceeds beyond the starting point of this development, as long as the proletariat persists in its isolation.

The "proletarian" revolutions in Russia and China are no exceptions to this rule. The technical and intellectual cadres of industrial society need not be brought to the fore via the bourgeois-liberal path; but once they are there the "proletariat" cannot prevail against them. It may be possible for an antifeudal agrarian revolution to be led by a proletarian nucleus; the results will be remarkable, but will certainly not correspond to the Marxist image.

Moreover, it is not permissible to speak of a "proletarian nucleus" without qualification. For scarcely anywhere has it occurred to the proletariat to regard itself as anything but a section (admittedly an underprivileged section) of bourgeois society; it was bourgeois intellectuals who first provided it with a coherent faith in its world mission. The result is: revolution in the Marxist sense is the impossible revolution.

This certainly does not imply the absurd thesis that everything must always remain as it is, or even that a sweeping upheaval is not possible.

As far as Italy is concerned, the questions to be asked are as follows: (1) Was Italy already so bourgeois that the proletarian revolution was bound to be considered impossible? (2) Was Italy still so agrarian-feudal that a proletarian antifeudal revolution was possible? (3) Was the socialist leadership in its background and mentality able and willing to endure the rigors of such a revolution? (4) Was the chosen moment, after a war which, although victorious, was not really "desired," a favorable one?

The fate of the Italian revolution resides in the fact that all these questions must be answered with "No," and most particularly the third one.

At the party conference at Leghorn (January, 1921), which resulted in the secession of the Communists, Costantino Lazzari, one of the chief Maximalists, criticized the *Ordine Nuovo* group on the grounds that he had never read anything about "humanity" or "brotherhood" in that paper.[239] It was a touching remark, typical of that spirit of bourgeois humanity which more than any other determined Italian socialism and which had prompted the reaction of the young Mussolini.[240] In contrasting vein, even Filippo Turati, shortly before the March on Rome, expressed the hope that the factions of socialism which were now divided would nevertheless collaborate to weave a "shroud for bourgeois society."[241] All these men were not revolutionary enough to desire blood and disaster, and not reformist enough to break with familiar thought patterns.

But perhaps this was merely the mirror-image of the objective situation. It may be said, in anticipation: The socialists maintained that they desired the impossible revolution, and renounced the possible one; Italy, the country with the oldest bourgeoisie in Europe, was sufficiently bourgeois to resist even a serious proletarian attempt at revolution;[242] it was not sufficiently bourgeois to face it without fear and panic.

Since Mussolini was unable to make the possible revolution with the Socialists and Popolari (and only *with* them was it not a chimera), he made the total political revolution with the nationalist bourgeoisie, and this revolution was at the same time the successful counterrevolution.

But these propositions are only the anticipatory extract from a long and involved history.

We must begin with the fact—basic to the whole postwar development—that the leadership of the Socialist party, unlike public opinion, did not identify itself with the demand for a constitutional assembly, but instead declared its immediate aim to be: "The formation of the Socialist Republic and the dictatorship of the proletariat."[243] These words remained constant over and above all the movements which, after the turmoil of 1919, were combined, utilized—and forgotten—by the Socialist party in its spectacular rise in political power.

But how diverse these movements were!

In Turin a group of highly qualified workers, centering around Gramsci's *Ordine Nuovo*,[244] devoted themselves very seriously to the problem of factory management through the producers themselves, the basic problem of the socialists. Here the idea and practice of *Consigli di fabbrica* grew and were tried out; but they were foolish enough to make all too frequent use of the Russian word "soviet."

A unique school of politics and sense of responsibility for social classes browbeaten for centuries was provided by the administration of the socialist communes. But the new mayors and councilors not only aroused the inevitable ire of the dispossessed notables, they also frequently allowed themselves to become unnecessarily provocative. It was usually the red flag rather than the tricolor which fluttered above the municipal building, crosses and pictures of the king were hurriedly removed from communal rooms, and here and there stamps and emergency currency were issued with the sign of the hammer and sickle. In the small community of Poggibonsi the tricolor was even burned on a funeral pyre.[245]

Agricultural conditions in the Po valley represented class warfare at its bitterest, yet not in the revolutionary sense. The surplus population and the system of *bracciantato* (day labor) were bound to lead either to the complete impotence of the ruthlessly exploited day laborers, who were only employed for a few months at a time, or to the land workers combining and trying to fight collectively for adequate wages and equal conditions for all. It is not surprising that the "leagues" of the *braccianti* were highly tyrannical organizations: unconditional discipline offset the weakness of their position. They tried above all to put into effect the principle of the *imponibile della mano d'opera*, that is, the landowner or tenant farmer was obliged to take a certain number of laborers whether or not he could use them. Vice versa, the individual laborer could only dispose of his labor with the consent of the league. Anyone breaking through the solidarity was ruthlessly boycotted: no shopkeeper would sell him bread, no carpenter would do him a hand's turn, no doctor dared visit his house. The monopolistic hold of the leagues over labor sometimes went so far that a tenant farmer would have to pay a *taglia* (tax) because he had put to work a son who was not a member of the league. Nothing was more natural than that this system should have caused enormous resentment and bitterness not only among the property owners, and that increasingly vocal demands were made to the authorities for restoring and safeguarding "freedom of work."

Yet another sphere consisted of the network of producing and consumer co-operatives which had been built up over decades with much determination and energy—and nowhere more outstandingly than in Ravenna by the deputy Nullo Baldini,[246] who had been a kind of pupil of Alessandro Mussolini and had carried the young Benito in his arms.[247] This was the only large-scale attempt in all Europe to develop within the capitalist social order an organism which could hollow out this order from within and which, after the training of new leadership groups, could eventually eliminate it. It was an attempt which sprung from a purely reformist spirit but, with its *Camere di Lavoro, Case del Popolo*, and cultural groups, it represented in all its institutions a revolutionary creation: a state within a state, one which the great masses saw as their true home.

Again, of an entirely different nature were the turbulent strivings of the land-poor southern Italian peasants to start an attack on the latifundia. This constituted a powerful revolutionary movement, but one which was more or less ignored by the Socialist party since it was almost without influence on these "backward" masses.

Yet were not the urban masses also backward? Did not the party regularly lose its grip on them whenever one of the innumerable high-cost-of-living riots took place? Did not these masses reveal a hypersensitivity which responded to even the most trivial provocation to go on strike? In any case the absurd resistance to the introduction of daylight-saving time, or the obstinate refusal to make their contributions to the newly created social insurance, showed that they were a long way from being "educated" masses in the Marxist sense rather than being merely intoxicated by revolutionary slogans. It was not the masses as such which undertook the celebrated occupation of the factories at the end of August, but the working-class elite, which was organized in the metal workers' union (FIOM). The occupation of the factories had not been intended as a political-revolutionary act;[248] nevertheless, this unprecedented event has rightly been regarded as the ultimate climax of the revolutionary movement. Mussolini had been one of the first to applaud this type of "productive strike."[249] It failed because of an inadequate conception of "production": the top technical personnel did not take part (which was not at all surprising); delivery and sales came to a standstill, international reactions were inevitable. As head of the government Giolitti moved very cautiously, he avoided any use of force, and finally negotiated an agreement guaranteeing the workers rights that were hitherto unheard of, which buried all revolutionary hopes forever.[250]

After September 25 all that was left to the Italian proletariat was to defend the rights and gains won so laboriously during the preceding two years. The only way to defend them was to exert influence on the government. But the party continued to talk about the "revolution" as if nothing had happened: it is just as difficult to adjust convictions and modes of thought to altered circumstances as rights and forms of property. In spite of the bloc formation of the bourgeois parties, the communal elections of October 31 placed a third of the Italian communes and provincial administrations in socialist hands. The party was still a giant—but his knees were now paralyzed. The tragedy was that he went on talking as if he were still the fastest runner. Yet the feet of those who were to carry him out were already at the door.

It is true that, seen as a whole, the revolutionary movement had been remarkably bloodless. But in its complexity, in its confusion, and above all in its grand words, it had alarmed so many people and damaged so many interests that an incalculable reservoir of rage, hatred, revenge, and contempt was bound to accumulate. Errico Malatesta saw things correctly when he said: "If we do not go on to the end, we shall have to pay with bloody tears for the fear we are now causing the bourgeoisie."[251] This prophecy came true all too soon. For Malatesta, however, the grimmest feature was that men of whom he had once thought highly had a considerable share in it.

Fascist "Re-action"

The question of the significance of fascist action in the defeat of socialism has been answered in contradictory terms by the opposing parties. Fascism claimed to have conquered the Bolshevik revolution and saved Italy. But there is little to be said for this answer. Mussolini's early utterances, the only relevant ones, do no more to confirm it than do the facts themselves. The antifascist thesis is obviously much more accurate: that fascism gave the *coup de grâce* to the revolution *after* its failure.[252]

Various undisputed facts corroborate this: in October, 1920, the number of Fascists throughout Italy was still only one hundred and ninety, but by the end of the year there were eight hundred.[253] Mussolini declined to take part in the communal elections because he foresaw a glaring defeat. No fascist action whatever resulted during the occupation of the factories. Thus if it is true that the occupation of the factories was the climax as well as the last chance of the revolutionary movement, the antifascist thesis is absolutely correct. And from an objective standpoint there is indeed the highest degree of probability for this opinion.

Seen subjectively, however, matters looked different. In November, 1920, it was still impossible in Bologna to bury a corpse or employ a worker without a license from the *Camera del Lavoro*. Even during this period many socialist municipal administrations tried to replace dealers and artisans by city-owned concerns, and at this late hour there was still no lack of revolutionary speeches in Italy. That powerful sections of the middle classes should in many regions still feel that their most vital interests were being threatened is understandable. They did not reflect on the danger to the state, they saw the danger to themselves. To expect them to see that the disappearance of the danger to the state would sooner or later entail the disappearance of the danger to themselves, would be unreasonable. If we wish to obtain a picture of the severity and agitation of the struggle which took place during the next few months, we must not take Mussolini's articles as a basis, for they always address the socialists in the voice of mentor or mocker; rather, we should look at the impassioned utterances published by the young Dino Grandi[254] in the *Assalto* of Bologna: "Get away from us! Do not touch us! Spare us the effort of spitting in your ugly faces!"[255]

It is highly probable that the antifascist argument is correct, yet the fascist interpretation is understandable, for there is another aspect from which the two opposite "absolute" theses require differentiation. On the one hand we must consider the remarkable differences in the situations in the various regions of Italy, since historically these regions were much more individualized and more deeply divided from each other than in any country in Europe. While in Trieste and Friuli, fascism had achieved victory *before* the seizing of the factories, the regions of southern Italy (except for Apulia) and the islands were scarcely aware of its existence right up to the time of the March on Rome. But this is not to say that in the various principal towns or areas socialist violence had been dominant until September, 1920, to be succeeded all of a sudden by fascist violence. In Milan a discharged officer calmly shot a red flag to shreds on the street right after the end of the war, and some young rowdies tugged Serrati's[256] beard;[257] in April, 1919, the *Avanti!* premises were burned down. This did not alter the fact that during these critical months the Fascists did not move, and that in July, 1922, the red flag was still waving over the city hall of Italy's second largest city. In Siena the *Casa del Popolo* was destroyed in March, 1920, but halfway through 1922 the "Reds" successfully defended the city of Parma against a whole fascist army.[258] In short, instances of fascist violence occurred very early on, as a warning, a sign, a hope, for many; but, by the same token, important socialist positions of power were still in existence in 1922.

Nevertheless, when the battle broke out in full force at the end of 1920, it was determined by the preponderance of one particular party in a way that could not but cause consternation and often indignation. Everywhere the Fascists were the aggressors. Socialist acts of violence, allegedly the reason for reprisals, were for the most part merely a reaction to attacks by Fascists. On all sides fascist violence aimed systematically and methodically at the destruction of the enemy, while socialist resistance was incoherent and sporadic, and tired rapidly. The basic outline of events is clear, although their depiction by both parties differs widely in emphasis and elucidation.[259]

One of the chief advantages of the fascist *squadre d'azione* consisted in the fact that they had at their disposal men who were all experienced in battle and not particularly squeamish, former Arditi or discharged officers. These were joined mainly by high school and university students. It is remarkable to note, using Chiurco's figures, for example, how powerfully these two groups delineated the face of early fascism. It was not the "bourgeoisie" as such that formed this front, but two highly special strata of the middle classes, strata which are typified by an "impetuosity" which can be defined equally well both positively and negatively (idealism, contempt for death, spirit of sacrifice, and brutality, cynicism, contempt for human beings). Their opponents were undoubtedly all more "bourgeois" in outlook than they, and this can also be defined both positively and negatively. Mussolini spoke very early of the fascist leopard which could do as it pleased with the lazy cattle of the socialist masses.[260]

The targets of the squads were all socialist institutions, no matter whether they were affiliated with revolutionary or reformist factions: *Camere di Lavoro*, *Case di Popolo*, socialist communal administrations, and so forth. They were looted, burned down, forced to liquidate: often scarcely a trace of them remained. What means did the socialists have to counter these *spedizioni punitive* on a comparable level? The *fasci* were often without proper headquarters—and to that extent they were nothing. But since they were to be regarded as the extended arm of the middle classes, indeed of the state, they were in that sense everything.

These expeditions could always rely on the financial backing of powerful circles and the tacit, not to say practical, consent of the authorities. The fact that the agrarians supplied the trucks and paid for the gasoline, that the industrialists regarded the Fascists as the "legitimate defenders" of their interests, is one of the main theses of the socialist argument, and it is confirmed by the Fascist Chiurco.[261] It is, of course, a thesis of supreme banality; what really requires explanation is why a large section of the middle class did *not* support the Fascists and soon came to be regarded as a hostile power by the Fascists. The attitude of the state and the authorities is another matter. Only too often the Carabinieri searched the *Case di Popolo* for arms before an attack by Fascists and then left them to their fate, and this remains, like many similar events, an object of astonishment to the impartial observer, even when he takes into account that the socialists had done little to win the sympathy of the police.

These attacks were carried out by co-operative means, "trucks and telephone," as it was known.[262] When a Fascist was murdered in some town by unknown hands, within a few hours trucks loaded with armed Fascists came rumbling in from all the neighboring towns for a "punitive expedition."[263] The socialist communities, on the other hand, allowed themselves to be overpowered one after another by the enemy, without even attempting a joint action. Mussolini's observation proved correct—that the simple folk clung most tenaciously to their bit of earth and at best paid lip service to internationalism. The nationalists, accustomed to using the telephone and communicating over long distances, showed themselves more flexible and more powerful than the internationalists, who saw and loved only their own little corner.

So within a few months a few hundred squads of young men, supported by almost all the established forces of society, in a ruthless, naked class war destroyed with fire and sword in the principal regions of Italy all those hard-won institutions in which the process of the people's self-education had taken place, but which, after the attempted impossible revolution, seemed to large sections of the middle classes an intolerable threat. The story of this struggle is one of infinite and depressing monotony. It is enough to look at the beginning, a few typical examples, and the shift in emphasis which soon ensued and which was obviously essential to the continuance of fascism.

The systematic fascist terror began as a nationality war in Trieste and Friuli. Here socialism was somewhat loosely identified with "the Slavic race," because the party had retained its principles of organization from the Austrian era: that is, it did not exclude Slovenes, and it defended international peace just as vigorously as it carried on inter-class warfare. However, Yugoslav circles laid claim to Istria, Friuli, and Trieste; a final settlement had not yet been made, and the national and social defense of the Italians, who were superior in every respect, developed sufficient explosive power to destroy almost entirely the whole network of socialist institutions in the country, whether *Camere di Lavoro* or cultural groups. Since the authorities were completely on the side of the Fascists, these "punitive expeditions" (there were sufficient incidents to supply pretexts) often assumed the character of campaigns of troops and citizens' militia against Slavic villages on the Carso, in Istria, or in the Gorizia area. The destruction of the Hotel Balkan in Trieste, the headquarters of the Slovene organizations, by a joint action on the part of Fascists and police was the climax of this campaign. Long before the end of the year, socialists all over Italy had started collecting for the "victims of fascism" in the Venezia Giulia. But this was a fringe area of Italy with exceptional conditions. The decisive breakthrough in a vital area was not achieved by fascism until six months later with events in Bologna.

Bologna might have been called the Red capital of Italy. An important industrial city, as well as the center of the Emilia with its innumerable leagues, Bologna came into almost unlimited socialist possession immediately after the war. The communal elections of October, 1920, further confirmed this supremacy. But in the meantime a *nucleo nazionalista* and a *fascio* (under Arpinati) had been constituted. The socialists had become uneasy. Riots were feared for the opening session (November 21) of the newly elected city council. It is highly typical of the situation that the socialists, instead of requesting government protection, occupied with their own guards and defended the city hall, the Palazza d'Accursio, which was decorated with the red flag. This proved fatal. For when the Fascists actually tried to penetrate into the crowded square in front of the building and fired off a number of shots, the inexperienced guards lost their heads and in panic tossed their hand grenades into the crowd. In the commotion of the council meeting shots were fired by an unknown hand from the public seats at the "national" minority, and a lawyer, Giulio Giordani, who had been wounded in the war, was killed. Then the most remarkable thing happened: although the main responsibility for the events obviously lay with the Fascists, although the eight dead and sixty wounded in the square were all socialists or socialist sympathizers, the death of the Nationalist deputy brought all the hatred, all the resentment, all the indignation, which had been accumulating for years in the middle classes, to a primitive outburst of extraordinary violence. All those who until that moment had dared only to clench their fists in their pockets, now streamed toward fascism. Day after day new storm troops were formed, night after night socialist bases fell and burned, from one moment to the next the victors of the elections became hunted animals. The purged city also liberated its hinterland, the punitive expeditions drove out in long truck columns, forced the leagues and municipal administrations to liquidate, and restored the principle of "freedom of work." Those taking part, however, and evidently a large section of the population as well, believed that all this was merely the reply to a wanton crime.

The bloody deed of Empoli, which enabled Italian fascism to make its final breakthrough in Tuscany, was of a similarly complex and ambiguous nature. The rumor that truckloads of Fascists were approaching had caused a commotion among the inhabitants of this stronghold of agitation and had resulted in a general, although very rudimentary, arming. When two trucks loaded with men actually did drive into the town they were received with a hail of stones and shots. The first truck managed to get away; as for the occupants of the second truck, their desperate assurances that they were not Fascists but army technicians in mufti were of little avail; the enraged mob descended upon them without listening and beat them to death with sticks and stones. It seemed as if furies had sunk their teeth in the flesh of their victims, one wounded man who fled was discovered, and when he asked for a glass of water he was clubbed to death and thrown into the Arno. Here too, then, fear of the Fascists bred a panic of violence, which in turn enabled violence by the Fascists—which was much more far-reaching and purposeful—to achieve victory in an atmosphere of sympathy.[264]

The same situation applies more or less even to the act of terrorism in the Diana Theater in Milan (March 23). A bomb planted by anarchists caused terrible destruction, blowing some twenty innocent spectators to pieces and wounding many others. It appears that the bomb had been intended for the police headquarters as a protest against some scandalous cases of distortion of justice favoring the Fascists, and that some misinformed young men took the murder weapon into the theater in a moment of confusion.[265] But at such a moment who asks about motives and circumstances? One saw only the horribly mutilated innocent bodies—and nothing was easier to understand than that.

This, then, was what socialist violence was like: brought out essentially by fascism, which had set out to overcome it, sporadic, at best wild, never planned, flanked by individual terrorism and the atrocities of the mob (the *teppa*). The Socialist party was not directly responsible for the deeds of the anarchists and the mob, but it was blamed for them; and even though liberal society is almost insensitive to theoretical questioning of its existence, even though it can transform practical threats into stages in its development, it is still, like any other society, horror-struck when it sees the dregs of society emerge. If state violence, properly applied, achieves a maximum of effect with a minimum of actual implementation, the violence of the Italian socialists led with a minimum of reality to a maximum of false and evil appearance and gained nothing at all.

Fascist violence was totally different in character, as can be shown by three early examples. In April, 1921, the leader of Florentine fascism, Marchese Dino Perrone Compagni, wrote a letter to the mayor of a small town in Tuscany, pointing with seeming courtesy that the commune was no longer to be presided over by an individual such as himself. Therefore he advised the mayor to resign by a certain date, otherwise he would have to bear *ogni responsabilità di cose e di persone.* Were the mayor to apply to government authorities, the ultimatum would expire four days earlier.[266]

That the marchese was not joking was something everyone knew. One might have expected him to use the services of a go-between to convey his demands and threats to the mayor. As an aristocrat he disdained such devious methods. He signed his full name and address and used the official letterhead of the *fascio* of Florence. It did not even seem to enter his mind that the letter was a criminal offense and a mockery of government authority.

One of Italy's most famous "squadrists," Sandro Carosi, entered a workmen's café with some companions, drew his pistol and with a broad smile forced one of the men present to stand against the wall with a cup on his head: he was going to prove his marksmanship. But the bullet entered the man's head and killed him—in mock despair the marksman bewailed his unsteady hand. The newspaper reported the occurrence under the headline *Uno sfortunato Guglielmo Tell*, and justice saw no reason to intervene.[267]

The mayor of Roccastrada refused to resign. After an agony of waiting, trucks of Fascists arrived on July 24. A number of houses were set on fire, the peasants fled into the fields. Finally the Fascists left, the inhabitants returned. But within a few minutes the engines roared again, the brakes screamed, the Fascists jumped down ready for action, it was too late for another escape. On the way back a "squadrist" had been killed by a bullet from an unknown hand, and the wrath of the gods broke over the unfortunate village. Summary executions and brutal arson transformed the peaceful little place not into a battlefield but into a scene from Dante's *Inferno*.[268]

The violence displayed here is that of injured and threatened higher classes—from lower middle class to aristocracy—cynical, systematic, purblind, devoid of any human relationship to its own people. This is why fascism was regarded by all serious contemporary observers of its beginnings as a manifestation of "re-action," as *Jacquerie borghese*,[269] waging a victorious war of desperation on its class enemy.[270]

But this sociological classification is inadequate. It was no mere coincidence that fascist methods made the greatest impression on the young, who in turn developed and refined them. For them these methods must have meant the "transcending" of middle-class society, something they yearned for in a blend of idealism, desire for adventure, and blind urge to action. Here presumably is to be found the answer to the difficult question of why such men as Grandi, Balbo,[271] De Vecchi,[272] De Bono,[273] Ciano,[274] turned to fascism rather than to nationalism, to which by reason of their background they stood closer. That which was more nebulous, less rigid, must have appealed to the young as being more promising, and to the former legionaries of D'Annunzio it presented a greater affinity to their social projects. But there was also the element of chance. Had Mussolini emigrated after the elections of 1919, as for a short time he apparently planned to do, those powerful emotions and feelings would certainly not have remained nonexistent, and it is more than likely that they would have joined forces with nationalism.

But explanations based on the psychology of generations and similar considerations do not exhaust the nature of fascist violence. It contains something of original evil, of cynical contempt for human beings, and diabolical delight in the humiliation of another human being, of a dark love of force for its own sake. We must never lose sight of this "prebourgeois" trait.[275]

It was first revealed at a very early stage in the peculiar hostility of this movement toward the state, a hostility which contrasted very strangely with the movement's practical dependence on the organs of the state and with its theoretical glorification of the state. Close scrutiny shows that this hostility was not limited to an antagonism toward a particular form of state; rather it was revealed as being directed at the state per se insofar as the state constituted an impediment to its will: in other words, at legality in general. For this, too, three examples may be cited.

At the beginning of May, 1920, Fascists in Citadella Veneto demanded the release of arrested comrades. A clash ensued during which three Fascists fell. Thereupon the Fascists killed the official responsible.[276]

In July, 1920, a group of five hundred Fascists set out for the antifascist stronghold of Sarzana in order to liberate Renato Ricci,[277] who was incarcerated there. They advanced on the handful of Carabinieri sentries at the entrance to the town with the cry of "Viva l'Italia! Viva il Re! Siamo fascisti!" The sentries fired when their order to halt was not obeyed. The Fascists, taken completely by surprise, fled in panic, leaving a few dead behind, their retreat was barred by anti-Fascists, and without the renewed intervention of the Carabinieri scarcely a single one would have escaped with his life. But the *Popolo d'Italia* denounced the *capitano* of the Carabinieri as if he were a criminal, and the Fascists actually managed to make the loyal man a target of a successful campaign.[278]

In Modena Fascists protested against government measures. Discussions with a commissar ensued. Understandably enough, he had no intention of showing the *gagliardetti* the usual deference and taking off his hat to them.[279] A Fascist struck the irreverent covering from the commissar's head, the indignant official drew his pistol and fired. The incident expanded, and seven Fascists fell. Thus seven new "martyrs" could be consecrated and free rein given to a disproportionate indignation. That in the person of a minor official the state itself was being abused and raped did not seem to occur to anyone.

Mussolini's Unexpected Rise and His Last Battle for Coherence

It is highly probable that such an explosive event as the rise of Italian fascism during the months around the turn of the year 1920–21 was not the "work" of one man. Mussolini followed the metamorphosis of his creation not only with astonishment but also with alarm, and with a disapproval that first became steadily sharper and then slowly ebbed away. It was not, as legend would have it, that Mussolini led fascism to the threshold of victory in 1921: a new fascism shaped for itself a Mussolini after its own measure and image.

Even the earliest manifestations of this fascism go beyond what Mussolini had originally desired. At the end of November, 1920, he wrote: "Fascism breaks forth irrepressibly in every corner of Italy, while the proletariat, nauseated, disillusioned, 'massacred,' begins to disband."[280] Two years before he had wanted "to fight many a good fight still"[281] side by side with the proletariat that had taken part in the war; now he had to admit that the proletariat had remained in the hands of his enemies, and that the awakening of fascism ran parallel with the capitulation of the proletariat. At the same time he dug the grave for the principal fascist myth before it had properly evolved: "Bolshevism is lying prostrate in its death throes, mortally wounded."[282] Does that not sound exactly as if he would like to call an alarmed "Halt, enough!" to the "spontaneous, irresistible movement"?[283] The *fasci* should be purged, he said, too many people had come in on the "wave of success." The man who had from his early days sung the praises of *violenza* now made one appeal after the other to his pupils about the proper understanding of force: it should be chivalrous, only a reply to crime and challenge, never an end in itself. One should not deny socialists the right to political manifestations. It was a genuine revolution to have dissuaded the Socialist party from its tyrannical claims to hegemony and to have made it one party among other parties. In dealing with the socialists one must be able to divide the innocent from the criminals, the men of honor from the scoundrels.[284] Fascism must not, as socialism had once done, lose its "sense of moderation," otherwise its victory would be lost.[285]

But did he really have any influence on the course of events? When on April 3 the Fascists of "liberated" Bologna staged an enthusiastic welcome for him, he had to admit in addressing the public, half overcome, half uneasy: "sometimes I can feel that the movement has already overflowed the narrow confines I had assigned to it."[286]

What are the confines and hence the "aims" which this new fascism, which conquered whole cities and overthrew firmly entrenched positions, had transcended? Presumably it is no less than the fundamental nature of the first fascism itself. This first fascism, which shared its concrete program with the socialists, was to be an instrument, a flexible little weapon, in the hands of the renegade socialist leader who at times considered himself the only socialist in Italy since the start of the war.[287] With this instrument he intended to get a new grip on the bloated Socialist party horse which was galloping off in the wrong direction, and to guide it toward his own hard-won view.[288] The new fascism was obviously more than a temporary association for a specific purpose. But there is no evidence that at that time Mussolini wished to regard it as anything more than one new party among the others. For the time being his influence consisted chiefly in his interpretation of the phenomenon. Here the original conception is expressed just as much as the rudiments of a new (albeit not wholly unprepared) self-image.

When Mussolini asks: "Without the beatings, the revolver shots, and the arson of the Fascists—when would the terrible drunken Russian frenzy of Italian bolshevism ever have evaporated?" he is obviously not claiming that fascism saved Italy by repulsing a "social-communist" general attack; what he means is that the force of fascism has saved socialism from straying onto a path foreign to its nature. So he goes on: "Fascism has therefore assisted the cause of Italian socialism."[289] He is therefore still speaking as a "functionary" of socialism, as the "whip of Social Democracy," in the same spirit in which he passes judgment on the Socialist party congress at Leghorn and the party split: "Will it be the beginning of wisdom?"[290]

In keeping with this spirit is the positive interpretation he gives to fascism: in its concrete aspects, its program is similar, he says, to that of the Socialist party; he wishes to carry out the only revolution possible in Italy—the agrarian.[291] Whatever the socialists have to say about the background and financing of the punitive expeditions he refutes as *turpiloquio* ("obscene language") and in this way arrives at a peculiar method, full of deception and self-deception, of justifying the fascist enterprises: they were the merited reply to "calumnies." But how little the squad leaders asked the Duce for his opinion, or even kept him informed, is shown with striking clarity by the involved, semi-ironical comment which Mussolini made (in July!) on the punitive expedition against one of the Popolari newspapers in Treviso: that the Fascists did not even inform their newspaper was proof of a special and complex mentality transcending the framework of the old parties.[292]

It was no doubt this feeling of impotence vis-à-vis the primitive, combined with the impossibility of discussing concrete matters with the socialists, that caused him soon to escape into the myth: fascism represents the common interest; it has proceeded from a "profound need of this our Aryan and Mediterranean people who, at a given moment, felt itself threatened in its vital areas of existence by a tragic folly."[293] The ancient culture, Rome's imperial claim to rule, is reawakening in fascism, it is its task to lead Italy to the reconquest of the world, which was once its possession.[294]

All this tends directly toward nationalism, but with the difference that not one of the distinguished gentlemen of *L'Idea Nazionale* was ever capable of such coarse, plebeian language as Mussolini used, for example, in his election speech on the Piazza Belgioioso early in May, 1921.[295] Certainly not one of them would ever even have dreamed of thinking that, although one was against all forms of bolshevism, if one had to choose one would prefer that of Lenin, because it was of gigantic, barbaric, universal proportions.[296]

But outbursts of temperament on Mussolini's part are always mere symptoms, signposts; never do they represent the ultimate and decisive word. Scarcely had the new elections of May, 1921 (instituted by Giolitti in the vain hope of critically weakening the parliamentary positions of socialists and Popolari), swept him into parliament with a triumphant number of votes and, for the first time since 1914, returned him, as leader of the faction of some thirty-five Fascist deputies, to a serious position of political power, than he plunged into his final battle for coherence and continuity with his beginnings. This battle brought him three of the most serious defeats of his political career and was a vital factor determining his entire subsequent existence.

On his arrival in Rome he granted the *Giornale d'Italia* an interview in which he stated that fascism must on no account be confused with nationalism, its leanings were republican, and hence the faction would not take part in the opening session of parliament, the so-called *seduta reale*, representing as it did a dynastic manifestation. The leading forces of the nation were Popolari, socialists, and Fascists, and collaboration among them was not inconceivable.[297]

It was not surprising that the interview caused a tremendous stir. It was a real slap in the face for all those who had voted for fascism because they wished to see socialism destroyed and conditions stabilized according to conservative ideas. Fascism as the catalyst of, the dreaded Socialist-Popolari coalition against which the Vatican and large-scale industry, dynasty, and army, were working so energetically: in spite of all reservations[298] this was one of the most provocative ideas it was possible to utter, especially as it contained a direct threat to the monarchy.

For Mussolini the commotion was an occasion to direct "clear words to the recruits." To many new Fascists, he said, the history of fascism was evidently unknown; he, Mussolini, would not permit "the distinguishing characteristics of that fascism which I founded to be so altered that they become unrecognizable."[299] If words had any meaning, then the phrase "republican leanings" also meant something, and it was no mere coincidence that the symbol of fascism was the Roman and republican lictor's bundle. He was prepared to defend these ideas against all comers; he would not abandon coherence, even if everyone else thought differently; for he was a leader who led, not a leader who followed.[300] But he very soon found himself on the defensive: although he cried *Fascisti della vigilia, fascisti dell'azione, difendete il fascismo!*[301] he sensed just as little sympathy among the republicans, socialists, and Popolari as among the nationalists and liberals. So he plunged into outbursts of furious, wholesale hostility,[302] and yet still placed too much confidence in his faction. At the decisive vote it turned out that, in this question which he himself regarded as the crucially important one, the majority of the group was against him. It was Mussolini's first grave defeat in the struggle with the new fascism. But he bowed to it and contented himself with compromises designed to conceal the scope of its significance.

However, it is highly improbable that he was fighting a battle here for the coherence of a political dogma. He had no qualms about admitting that in parliament the Fascists, together with Salandra's National Liberals, formed the "national Right," and his first chamber speech revealed a strongly marked antidemocratic and antisocialist accent (not least, no doubt, in order to emphasize the triumph of the "heretic" whom "these had excluded from their orthodox church" and for whom they presumably felt a "secret nostalgia").[303] But it is also unlikely that it was a mere tactical chess move aimed at ensuring freedom of movement toward conservatives and nationalists. Mussolini's punctual thinking and feeling contain some key areas which never cease to be of vital concern to him, although not even these reveal an inflexible constancy. Among them is presumably his republicanism and certainly an instinctive attachment to *socialismo pensante*, to the men of honor among the agitators, in short, to the great chance—missed repeatedly—of 1919, and ultimately to the memories of his childhood.[304] In any case, during the summer of 1921 he behaved exactly as was to be expected, and there is little reason to believe in those tactical motivations which he soon had to use in order to appease his angry followers.

The effort to "make peace" (*pacificazione*) between the Fascists and socialists has little in common with lordly chess moves and far more with a life-and-death struggle. Mussolini specifically and with unmistakable words starts it off by surrendering one of the strongest trump cards of his party, the myth of the necessary struggle against the Bolshevik menace: "To say that a 'Bolshevik' danger still exists in Italy is to confuse certain vague fears with reality. Bolshevism is conquered. More than that: it has been abjured by the leaders and the masses."[305] Force has achieved its aim: in the area of bourgeois rivalry, fascism must now prove that it can be a life enzyme of the future Italy. This future Italy was not imagined by Mussolini as "fascist" at all; in a chamber speech he cited the three great forces which in sincere collaboration must lead the country to a happier destiny: a self-improving socialism, the Popolari, and finally fascism[306] (evidently also to be improved). It was still the same old plan, adapted to circumstances—the constitution of a three-armed Social Democracy—and it was as far from realization as ever, yet still not far enough not to endanger powerful sympathies for fascism.

Moreover, practical measures were not long in coming; a strict order went out to all *fasci* forbidding them to undertake further punitive expeditions against economic organizations and corporations. Mussolini inveighed bitterly and violently against the change in fascism: "The fascism of recent times in certain areas has no resemblance at all to the first one ... that was a movement of defense of the nation, not purely and simply a repressive organization for the defense of certain private interests."[307] With these hard and explicit words is combined in the most remarkable way his unmistakable sympathy for Turati and his men, whose entry into the government is to infuse new blood into the ruling class.[308] Thus Mussolini is still a long way from the idea that rejuvenation is not a political and sociological problem, but quite simply a biological one, so that conditions in a factory might be called renewed or even revolutionized the moment the impulsive youngest son takes over the management from the cautious father.

But what would the young and old "squadrists" say to all this, equally removed as they were from unrealizable political ideas on the one hand and socialist memories of childhood on the other, and whose entire political self-confidence depended on the conviction that they had to fight the internal war with fire and the sword for the survival of their threatened native land?

They protested, they won supporters, they mutinied. They called a conference in Bologna without even a *pro forma* invitation to Mussolini, and threatened to secede. Dino Grandi proclaimed the Emilia as the "cradle of fascism"; "agrarian" fascism, the "new Fascists," picked up the gauntlet and it became apparent that they controlled the principal areas of Italy: Emilia, Romagna, Veneto, Tuscany, Umbria. Balbo, Grandi, Farinacci, Arpinati, Calza-Bini, Bolzon were against Mussolini; secret meetings seemed to be preparing the way for a palace revolution.[309]

Mussolini was obviously surprised at the violence of this reaction. Although at the signing of the "peace treaty" (on August 3, 1921), he had confidently stated that, with the wand of his faith, his courage, his passion, he would either correct fascism or make life impossible for it,[310] his statement soon contained undertones of dark defiance: that the Emilia wanted to secede was a matter of indifference to him; the goals of fascism had for the most part been achieved. If fascism was no longer liberation but tyranny, no longer the guardian of the nation but the safeguarding of private interests and of the most opaque, unfeeling, pitiless castes in Italy, then it was no longer *his* fascism. "Fascism can get along without me? Of course, but I too can get along without fascism."[311] A week later he resigned from the executive: "He who is defeated must go."[312]

However, in reality it is not here that his defeat lies, but in the fact that his separation was only partial. He shrank from making the second crucial break in his political career. Not that he had no clear perception of the terms of the alternative. He knew that this crisis was not a matter of a mere problem in evolution; he knew it meant the end of one political concept and the beginning of another.

Perhaps it would have been possible at this moment in time to separate Mussolini from fascism. But the socialists restricted themselves to a short-sighted triumph,[313] and the Right did everything in their power to keep Mussolini on their side. There were, after all, many points in Mussolini's temperament, philosophy of life, and even insights (for instance, that the world was moving "toward the Right") which facilitated his taking this step. Was he still thinking of battle when he requested that the national congress planned for early November take place in Milan rather than Rome? The refusal was a further defeat and revealed the situation to him in all its grimness. But meanwhile Balbo and Grandi had realized how incapable fascism was of getting along without Mussolini: his superior experience, his newspaper, his personality which held the masses spellbound. Thus, pursuant to Grandi's thesis, the congress buried the peace treaty without a struggle, and accepted according to Mussolini's will the transformation of the "movement" into a party; the two antagonists embraced, and not long afterwards the acclamation of the marching masses elected Mussolini as Duce of fascism,[314] of that new fascism which had little in common with the old movement beyond the meaningless name. The party which *wished* to dominate Italy had at last conquered the man who *could* rule the country.

For Mussolini this meant, more than anything else, the moral capitulation to nationalism. The idea of the nation being the fixed point and the highest criterion (strange though this absolute may appear in Mussolini's loudly proclaimed "relativism")[315] was merely one common starting point which did not exclude diametrically opposite views on all concrete matters. Nationalism can be defined as that political movement which aims at solving the foreign and domestic political difficulties of the bourgeois national state which arise at a certain point in capitalist evolution by taming instead of accepting the masses, and which tries to consolidate this taming by the utmost accentuation of the foreign political problems of the isolated nation, as well as by categorically rejecting those ideologies which have accompanied the rise of the masses. Up to now Mussolini had wanted nothing of all this. He had wanted to help create Social Democracy as the spontaneous expression of the masses which were penetrating the state, he had been in favor of a sensible solution to the problems of the Adriatic, he had seen himself and his actions in terms of the secular process of democratization. After the Congress of Rome he learned very quickly to abjure all this and to become increasingly at home in the ideas of the Right: "It is believed, for example, that war must lead to revolution. The opposite is likely ... a great restoration."[316] But who was it who had based the most momentous decision of his political existence on this false thesis? Is this not a case of Mussolini slapping Mussolini?

Whose is the thesis of the "trial of the nineteenth century," whose mockery that of the ideas of the Encyclopedists? Is this not far closer to Maurras' mode of speech and thought than to that of Mussolini the Jacobin, the acclaimer of the Commune? Is not the speech about the "betrayed brothers of the Adriatic"[317] precisely the one that Mussolini had hitherto been at pains to tone down, albeit laboriously and tortuously?

It is only logical that Mussolini should now try (by invoking a thesis of Coppola) explicitly to deny the old form of fascism and its "primitive armor" which made it appear a leftist movement. To demand a return to its origins was, he claimed, "infantile."[318]

The Beginnings of National Fascism

The Congress of Rome marks the end of the story of the unfamiliar Mussolini, of the orthodox and later heretical socialist, and thus at the same time the end of unfamiliar fascism. However, it would not be enough to say the new element consisted solely in the fact that Mussolini had now gone over to nationalism. The change-over of such a man is not without its effect on the cause with which he identifies himself, especially when this change-over is the expression of a supraindividual change in situation. Nationalism as it was known up to that time was represented mainly by men who, by their background, upbringing, and outlook, belonged unquestionably to the middle classes and the national tradition, whose cause they were therefore able to carry on with no internal rupture. Mussolini and his friends, on the other hand, could never unmake their early days on the far side of the barricades, with the result that their new nationalism was marked by denials and circumscribed by desires not experienced by their forerunners. In addition there now appeared the nationalism of the few radical ideologists, who did not shrink from its extreme antitraditional consequences. The alliance of these three groups constitutes national fascism, and it is its history which begins with the Congress of Rome.

In its basic outline this history is well known and to depict it yet again *in extenso* is not our task. It might seem to render its prehistory obsolete and superfluous. But only from a study of the prehistory can we understand the ultimate and most characteristic form of Italian fascism, the *Repubblica di Salò*, and only when seen in the spotlights of beginning and end does "normal" national fascism move into the range of an autonomous critique. For in the Mussolini of this early period is to be found not only that which moderates national fascism but also that which accentuates it: that is, the tendency to see fascism as a synthesis as well as the rudiments of a political race doctrine. It is only from these particular aspects that we shall sketch the familiar history.

The year 1922 was the year of the fascist seizure of power and its preparation. This preparation was a dual one. On the one hand it was supported by "squadrism," beside whose new enterprises all previous actions paled. Mussolini ceased to try and control the squads: on the contrary, he supported them with the demand that force be resorted to on a grand scale to paralyze the enemy's vital centers. Entire regions were now subject to the control of the squads, who adopted the habit of simply "expelling" those persons who fell into disfavor, especially socialist leaders, with the result that even deputies, among them Giacomo Matteotti, had to take up residence in other cities as "refugees." Towns were "conquered"; Mussolini himself spoke like a general in enemy territory: "Rimini in our hands means the arm of the pincers which we lacked to squeeze the Emilia and the Romagna, and fascist Rimini is

simultaneously the bridgehead for penetration into the neighboring province. ...
The provinces will not long resist our fateful advance."[319]

There is something incredible about all this. The government permitted a
party army to conquer and terrorize the country. Not only did it not prevent
these actions, usually it even legalized them subsequently by, for example,
sanctioning the resignations of socialist municipal administrators which had been
brought about by beatings, shootings, and castor oil. Yet action by Fascists was
by no means directed only against the "social communists" (an identification
which Mussolini had declared inadmissible as late as 1921);[320] the Fascists also
struck at the Popolari, the democratic liberals, and the state itself. During the
summer of 1922, for instance, many tens of thousands of Blackshirts occupied
Bologna and camped for days, like an army, in the city streets to compel the
recalling of the prefect. And the state actually yielded.

Was it the state that was so weak (or so very much an accomplice)? Was it a
crisis of the parliamentary system? For threatened interests to cling to each
other is in this system the most natural thing in the world. That on this occasion
threatened institutions were unable to form a coalition cannot be regarded as
normal. The "squadrist" actions in the streets ought, on their own, to have
resulted without question in the formation of an antifascist cabinet, composed
of socialists, Popolari, and democrats, which by July, 1922, would undoubtedly
have been capable of putting an end to fascist terror. But Mussolini's masterly
parliamentary skill was able twice to prevent such a government from forming,
and thus Italy found itself facing the crisis of 1922 under a government whose
leader (Luigi Facta) was a man of inferior stature and excessive optimism,
and whose members (anti-Fascists and pro-Fascists) worked to produce a
mutual paralysis.[321]

The only reason Italian fascism was able to win out was that the forces for
which the liberal state is both a *sine qua non* and also a framework within which
they compete, did not combine soon enough. They acted like people who do not
appreciate the air they breathe because all their attention is focused on dividing
up a cake.

This comparison, of course, has a flaw. The cake might represent the
antagonism of Giolitti and Nitti, the hostility of Don Sturzo for Giolitti, even
the opposition of the Vatican to an alliance between the Popolari and the
socialists: but more significant was a concern for their own existence, in comparison to which the fear of fascism seemed less important. The Communist
party expressed itself at that time as follows: "If the bourgeoisie actually does
go all the way and throttles Social Democracy in the white reaction, it will
prepare—let this not be taken for a paradox—the best conditions for its swift
defeat at the hands of the revolution."[322] If the Communists displayed such
incredible blindness, such a staggering overestimation of their own resources,
would not false confidence then substantiate the insubstantial quality of the
fear? And on the brink of their own grave the *Maximalisti* also continued to

talk as if they were still in the year 1912 and at the party congress of Reggio Emilia. So the dying man brandished his cardboard sword and achieved his final victory by driving his assistant into the abyss. Mussolini the Marxist had done the essential groundwork for Mussolini the Fascist.

In the eyes of the liberal parties Mussolini's "old fascist" past turned out very much to the advantage of Mussolini the fascist parliamentarian. His desire to lead fascism by legal means to collaboration with the state, that is, to participate in a coalition government, seemed so sincere that even such a mediocre politician as Facta had hopes of being able to capture and tame fascism. Probably the reason for the success of Mussolini's tactics was that he actually had not yet made his decision and hence by comparison with a man like Balbo could justifiably be considered a moderate.

But people did not take the trouble to realize that the urge for a "faith," the intoxication of greatness, and the logic of consistency, were working in Mussolini, and that the day could not be far off when by comparison with him Balbo would be considered a moderate. Was not the Duce and the demigod already visible when he dramatically proclaimed: from the future fascist schools and universities the nation's new and ruling class would issue,[323] fascism would last for at least a hundred years,[324] it is now merely in its earliest stage, like Christianity at the time of Christ?[325]

Events were triggered by Italo Balbo's march on Ravenna in the last days of July, 1922. Not content with militarily occupying a city with thousands of "squadrists" and illuminating it with the fires of the "social-Bolshevist dens," the *Condottiere* demanded and obtained from government authorities trucks and gasoline—ostensibly for withdrawal, actually to invade the surrounding countryside with a "fire column" and leave a trail of burned-out houses and beaten-up individuals.[326] As a reply to this, the *Alleanza del Lavoro* (in which reformists, *Maximalisti*, anarchists, and Communists were combined) called a general strike. This was to be a "lawful" one, to remind the government of its duty to protect democratic freedoms. It was the most natural and yet the most thoughtless decision that could have been made. It reminded the nation, with great emphasis, of the innumerable and pointless strikes of the most recent past; the championing by the *sovversivi* of the state, to which they continued to deny their political collaboration, seemed incredible; the last weapon against a possible fascist attempt at an uprising was surrendered, and the adversary was handed an invaluable excuse to prove himself the preserver of order. And indeed the mobilized Fascists put an end to the general strike all over Italy shortly before its announced termination, subdued the last strongholds which were still offering resistance, and destroyed what remained of the *Camere di Lavoro* and socialist institutions. Police and Fascists worked together almost everywhere. It was the Caporetto of the socialists.[327]

The only thing now standing between fascism and Rome was the army, and possibly an energetic government, one which had not yet been formed. Once again the preparations ran on two tracks, and once again Mussolini kept all possibilities open for himself.

He had the high command of the fascist militia divide Italy into zones like a military terrain, and the government made no move. Immediately before the March on Rome he held a great rally in Naples: the president of parliament sent a welcoming telegram, schools were given a holiday, and Mussolini's absolutely unequivocal speech was listened to by all government and civic authorities seated in places of honor.[328]

Of greater importance was the political groundwork. Mussolini negotiated simultaneously with Giolitti, Nitti, and Salandra, allowing each to hope that *he* would be the one to incorporate the unruly but promising national force of fascism into the state; he won the capitalists by promising to deprive the state of all economic functions; he got rid of D'Annunzio by masterful maneuvering;[329] he gave the Vatican his "most loyal assurances";[330] above all, he reassured the army and the monarchy by protestations of loyalty: "One must have the courage to be monarchist."[331] In a series of great speeches he presented the nation with his ideas, which are best summarized in the famous words from his speech at Udine: "Our program is simple: we wish to govern Italy."[332]

There were two circumstances which led to the decision for a solution by force: first, the now apparently inevitable take-over of the government by Giolitti; second, Facta's plan to stage a great national rally in Rome on November 4, Victory Day, with a speech by D'Annunzio as the climax, aimed at paving the way for a general pacification and reconciliation. On the first point Mussolini remarked at the crucial session of the innermost executive on October 16: "Giolitti must be prevented from taking over the government. In the same way that he gave orders to fire on D'Annunzio, he would also give orders to fire on the Fascists."[333]

There are thus two very strange motivations prompting this "national revolution" to march on the capital: (1) the desire to prevent the "revolution" from becoming a revolution (in which shots are fired); (2) the wish to forestall a national demonstration of reconciliation.

And the "March" itself was unique. Throughout most of northern Italy the Fascists occupied public buildings and sometimes barracks; scarcely anywhere did the authorities offer resistance. Where they did, the insurgents fell back more or less without fighting. On the whole the revolution proceeded in an atmosphere of great cordiality: in Trieste fascist leaders happened to be sitting with the general and the heads of the administration drinking champagne when the news of the "mobilization" arrived, and jokes were exchanged in the best of moods about the necessity of now having to shoot each other.[334] But why, after all? The local proclamation culminated in such phrases as: *Viva l'Italia! Viva il Re! Viva l'Esercito!*[335] Or: *Nel nome di Dio, della Patria rinata, del Re Vittorio, di tutti i morti per l'Italia.*[336] The Fascists and nationalists (a reliable witness such as Chiurco attached the utmost importance to the joint action of

Black- and Blueshirts)[337] were in many places under the command of former officers; one of the commanding *quadrumviri* was a general. It had been agreed and taken for granted that Blackshirts did not shoot at *grigioverdi* (field-gray uniforms); reciprocity was expected and obtained. The banner headlines of the *Popolo d'Italia* of October 28 proclaimed: *Tutte le caserme di Siena occupate dai fascisti. I grigioverdi fraternizzano con le Camicie Nere.*[338]

Thus the March on Rome could begin under favorable auspices. The *quadrumviri* Bianchi, Balbo, De Bono, and De Vecchi set up their headquarters in the Hotel Brufani at Perugia directly opposite the prefecture; a police lieutenant and ten men would have been enough to deal the fascist revolution a mortal blow, but the high government official found it compatible with his duty to hand over his power. So the columns marched on the capital: from the north, the Tuscans under Marchese Perrone Compagni and General Ceccherini; from the east, two army columns under Giuseppe Bottai and Ulisse Igliori,[339] the reserves were waiting near Foligno and were under the command of General Zamboni. They were less than forty thousand men, miserably armed, some only with clubs, without a single cannon, altogether much more like story-book robber bands than an army. On October 28–29, 1922, all divisions halted some thirty to forty kilometers outside Rome—some of them were stopped by a handful of Carabinieri—the whole lot unfed and inadequately equipped, worn out by continuous rain, waiting for the order to attack which never came.

For meanwhile Rome was being conquered in the salons of the Quirinal. When the first reports of the uprising arrived on the evening of the 27th, the Facta cabinet could think of nothing cleverer to do than to resign. But even this excessively weak government, which was now only provisionally in charge, had enough feeling for the nature of the state to decide upon and proclaim a state of siege. The little king, who once before, in 1915, had bowed to the mob, did not have this feeling. He thought of his family (was not his cousin, the Duke of Aosta, striving for succession with the aid of the Fascists?), and he feared for his safety (the highest-ranking officers of his army had told him that one hundred thousand Fascists were marching against the seven thousand men of the garrison of Rome—actually it was twenty-eight thousand soldiers, under the command of an antifascist general of Jewish origin, and from a military standpoint the Fascists had no chance whatever against them).[340] Besides, he did not care for this parliament, and most of all he was afraid that after a break with the Fascists the socialist revolution would rear its head again.

So the incredible happened: the king refused to affix his signature to the decree: the state of siege had to be revoked. As a result, not only the country but—paradoxical though it may sound—also Mussolini was at the mercy of caprice. For it seems more than likely that he had never until this moment thought of becoming head of the government himself, not to mention a "totalitarian" government. He probably had a Salandra-Mussolini solution in mind, like the nationalists in Rome and also all the fascist intermediaries

(Grandi, Ciano, De Vecchi, Marinelli). But in the new circumstances, whether by his own incentive or (as some reports have it) under the pressure of radical collaborators, he was no longer prepared to be satisfied with that, and from Milan he let it be known that he demanded complete power. He already had it, after all, since it had been surrendered in Rome, and this time the king could no longer refuse to sign. On the evening of October 29 Mussolini took the night train to Rome and arrived there long before his legionaries, who on the following day entered the city, paraded, and were able to prove their unslaked warlike courage by destroying "subversive" newspapers.[341]

Thus the March on Rome was really a comedy, but a comedy where laughter dies away when we see how the knot is tied.

The cabinet which Mussolini formed was a "cabinet of national concentration" with an extreme right-wing orientation,[342] but a long way from being a one-party government. Mussolini took over the presidency, the ministry of the interior, as well as—temporarily—the foreign ministry; all other important ministries were filled by nationalists, liberals, and supraparty conservatives (such as the "Duca della Vittoria," General Diaz, and the "Duca del Mare," Admiral Thaon di Revel); the Popolari were also represented. The Fascists got most of the undersecretary positions.[343]

The hopes with which Mussolini was welcomed were high and sincere. For nothing had paralyzed his adversaries more than the belief that he alone was capable of simultaneously crushing the Communists and controlling fascist extremism. Furthermore, no one doubted that the form of government must undergo a change which would create conditions of clear majority in parliament and give the head of state greater authority. The fact that such qualified men as Orlando, Giolitti, and Benedetto Croce supported Mussolini at this moment cannot possibly be attributed to faults of character on the part of these blameless men. After the turmoil of the past years the desire for stability had become overwhelming, and people felt justified in regarding the violence of the change in government as merely a slight flaw which was not too great a price to pay for the return of order and security.

In the first year and a half of Mussolini's government there actually was a great deal which lived up to the expectations of the liberals and the conservatives. In his first chamber speech the young prime minister solemnly beseeched God's help in his great undertaking, even the left-wing deputies joined in the cry *Viva l'Esercito!* Strikes ended as if by magic,[344] trains suddenly ran on time, bureaucracy's leisurely pace was transformed under the eyes of the dynamic leader into hard work and enthusiasm, and when the first sod was turned for a new highway Mussolini proclaimed: "The entire nation must become a wharf, a factory."[345] No one disputed his proud assurance at the beginning of 1924: "The whole rhythm of Italian life has been accelerated,"[346] any more than it could be denied that Mussolini solved the chief problem of foreign policy, Fiume-Dalmatia, in a moderate and circumspect manner. At home neither special tribunals nor emergency laws were introduced, and the newspapers of the opposition continued to appear.

In fact it is hardly possible to doubt that in those days Mussolini still saw the *fascio* of the nation as an articulated unit with its own internal tensions, and that his idea was merely to tame the opposition, not eliminate it, and that to that extent he was sincere in his intention of "returning to the constitution." But he had neither his people nor his opponents nor his own impulsive nature under control, and least of all the inherent logic of a system.

One cannot, as the liberals demanded, conquer a state with armed, utterly unconstitutional bands and then disband them as if nothing had happened. Mussolini's uncontrolled outburst in the midst of the otherwise controlled first chamber speech was to enhance the squads' self-confidence: "I was able to turn this dull gray assembly hall into a bivouac for the maniples."[347] That is why the squads were institutionalized, turned into the fascist militia, a party army, which swore allegiance only to the party leader, not to the King, and yet was regarded as an organ of the state. But is it at all possible to speak of state in the liberal sense once its chief mainstays are torn from under it (the forming of the political will in the free play of opinions, uninfluenced by the effects of force)? And Mussolini made it quite plain that he intended to stay in power whatever happened, and he even substantiated this theoretically with Pareto-like formulas.[348] Hence the elections of April, 1924, were already a farce, even though they secured an unexpectedly strong majority for fascism which cannot be attributed solely to terror. Although the atrocities of the "squadrists" (as, for example, the terrible, wholly arbitrary murders in Turin in December, 1922)[349] could be regarded as spontaneous acts and regrettable lapses, it was impossible to overlook the fact that for Mussolini these were also a political card which he desired to keep up his sleeve so as to be able at all times to threaten his enemies with the unleashing of the Blackshirts.[350] Not only, then, was the militia the legalized infringement of the constitution, it actually stood for legalized illegality. Its existence was thus aimed not only at the liberal state but basically at the very idea of the state.

There was good reason to suppose, therefore, that the second important constitutional change of these early years, the metamorphosis of the "Fascist Grand Council" into an organ of state, would lead not to a nationalization of the party but to a "partialization" of the state.

After all, the course of Mussolini's thinking would have been reason enough to cause the liberals some anxious speculation. Not only did he barely hold back on the idea of a people without living space and its inevitable expansion (though he did so with a statesman's caution), and publicly confirm fascism's ideological capitulation to nationalism,[351] he adopted ideas on freedom, the state, and human nature[352] which were more reminiscent of de Maistre and Maurras than of Corradini, and he increased the confusion by not hesitating to refer positively to Lenin and bolshevism.[353]

All the uneasiness, all the doubts, all the misgivings which were strangely combined in the Italian people with approval and hope, were transformed into one single cry of indignation and horror when the news of the murder of the Socialist deputy Giacomo Matteotti spread through the country. It was by no means the worst of the "squadrists' " acts of violence, and Matteotti was far from being the first deputy to die; but in his courage and nobility this man had become the symbol of the opposition,[354] and a short time previously Mussolini had uttered statements that indicated at least his moral responsibility. Overnight almost the whole of Italy became antifascist. Party badges disappeared as if by magic, the newspapers shrieked their accusations against the "regime of murderers"; alone and despairing, Mussolini sat surrounded by the empty antechambers of the Palazzo Chigi, and many of his opponents believed, not without reason, that a dozen determined men could have arrested the "criminal" at that moment without any difficulty. It was a wonderful reaction doing the highest honor to the country and its people, shining like a bright light before the dark portal of the next two decades. But it was a tragic destiny that it should be this light which was in some ways to be the source of that darkness.

Only a few days before the murder Mussolini had made an important speech in the chamber aimed at persuading the opposition, in apparently sincere words which did not spare fascism, to collaborate: he had no intention, he claimed, of abolishing parliament, but the opposition must be "sensible," it must not oppose for the sake of opposing.[355]

It would no doubt be wrong to interpret these words as Mussolini's conversion to the parliamentary system; but it is legitimate to assume that from his stronger position he wanted to resume the old coalition ideas of 1921 and did not wish to hand himself and the country over to fascist extremism. Hence there is no reason to doubt the sincerity of his lamentations: "Only an enemy who had spent long nights thinking up something diabolical could perpetrate this crime which strikes us today with horror and wrests cries of indignation from us. ... I could say without false modesty that I had nearly reached the end of my labors, of the completion of my work, and then this fate, this bestiality, this crime—not irreparably, I believe—disturbs this process of moral reconstruction."[356]

But the damage was beyond repair. For six months the opposition remained on the Aventine, the sights of their (moral) machine guns trained on Mussolini. From Mussolini came numerous almost imploring offers: he did not desire a general leveling of minds, for an Italy brought to such a state would be intolerable; the opposition could exert influence on fascism and correct it if it stayed close to it; but if it continued to fire at it from outside it would force Fascists to close ranks and adopt an unconciliatory tactic.[357]

There are indications that Mussolini was thinking at that time of resigning and proposing Filippo Turati to the king as his successor;[358] but for other reasons it is also not unlikely that he was thinking of 1919 during that period.

It is natural enough that the Aventine did not trust a man who spoke with equal sincerity, but with opposite meanings, according to whether he was facing the Senate or a gathering of Blackshirts. What his "true" face was has never been ascertained.

Mussolini did not fall, because he was supported by king and pope, by Senate and industry, who feared the new confrontation with socialists and Communists. But one of Mussolini's possibilities was gone forever, and among all the possibilities it was precisely that one which had been least based on his *fede* and his temperament, and most on his insight: that of being the head, not the dictator, of a social democracy. But even in the famous speech of January 3, 1925, which "clarified the situation" and marked the final acceptance of fascist totalitarianism, the undertone of sorrow, of despair even, is—paradoxically and yet understandably enough—just as discernible as the firmer ties with the monarchy and the conservative forces.[359]

National Fascist Totalitarian Development Dictatorship

It was only now, more than two years after taking over the government, that the total seizure of power occurred. Even that was not carried out according to a preconceived plan: it took some years to be completed, in fits and starts, and was given a new thrust by each of the attempts to assassinate Mussolini. The last of these (the one at Bologna) had the greatest consequences and has given rise to many questions; to this day they have not been convincingly answered.[360] The establishment of "fascist Italy" may be said to date from the beginning of 1927; the ensuing years served to stabilize the regime, and the Lateran treaties made an important contribution to this. A severe test of endurance was the world economic crisis which, however, thanks not least to the newly developed technique of governing, was survived without serious damage. Nevertheless, it was one of the causes leading to the colonial war against Ethiopia. Had it been the only cause, this war would have signified not the end of an era but its culmination, which was what Mussolini had intended.[361] But since many factors had altered Italy's position and Mussolini's mode of thought, it is possible to fix the end of this period at the beginning of 1935. After a transitional period of some two years Mussolini found himself in a situation differing radically from the foregoing one, even though to all but the sharpest eyes the glory of its beginnings hid the wretchedness of its end.

The most significant event of this second-longest and presumably also second-happiest era of Mussolini's political existence was without doubt the institution of what is known as totalitarian rule. After January 3, 1925, Mussolini ceased to oppose the *ripresa totale, integrale*[362] of fascist action which his extremists had so long been demanding. "Squadrism" raised its head powerfully once more and argued with its opponents after its own fashion.[363] Farinacci, the newly appointed secretary-general, set to work with all the vigor of his fanaticism to *smatteottizzare* (eradicate Mateotti-ism), to glorify the *intransigenza rivoluzionaria* of fascism, to threaten the opponents with the *terza ondata* (third wave), and quite simply to call all anti-Fascists un-Italian.[364]

Soon the opposition lost all freedom of movement; at first the Fascists were content with ruthless sequestration of opposition newspapers, but after the attempted assassination at Bologna all newspapers inimical to the regime were banned, a supreme special tribunal was set up, the sentence of *confino* (banishment to remote islands) became a preventive measure wielded by the prefects at will, without (practically speaking) any opportunity for protest or control.[365] Where else but on rocky islands were even potential enemies to live, since Mussolini's *feroce volontà totalitaria*[366] had long since denied all parties their right to existence and aimed at turning the nation into a "granite" or "monolithic block"? Had he forgotten that only two years earlier an Italy without opposition, without the struggle of social and spiritual forces, seemed "intolerable" to him? Opposition was foolish and superfluous, he now said, in a totalitarian regime such as the fascist state; he could find the essential opposition in his own breast and in the resistance of objects.[367]

For just as the opposition is within him, so is the state within him. The oft-quoted formula: "Everything inside the state, nothing outside the state, nothing against the state" (*Tutto nello Stato, niente al di fuori dello Stato, nulla contro lo Stato*) is not to be interpreted in the traditional manner as an antithesis between state on the one hand and particularity of an individual or collective on the other; rather, it distinguishes the state by the fact that it cannot be sharply divided from the party or put in opposition to the party. State apparatus and party apparatus are instruments of government in Mussolini's hands, with the party—because of its greater modernity as well as its ideological dignity—gaining greater significance from year to year.

The body of laws which consolidated the "Mussolinization" of the state were the so-called *Leggi fascistissime*: not by accident were they created by Alfredo Rocco.

The *Leggi di difesa*[368] introduced special jurisdiction, made loyalty to the regime a criterion in the selection of civil servants, deprived emigrants of citizenship, banned secret societies, and made administrative action possible against not only undesirable political acts but also intentions, thoughts, and speech.

The *Leggi di riforma costituzionale*[369] made the head of government the superior of the ministers, turned parliament into a party congress, identified for all practical purposes executive with legislative power, raised the Fascist Grand Council to the most powerful organ of the state.

The *Leggi di riforma sociale*[370] constituted the "corporative state," about which innumerable books have been written and yet whose nature can be described succinctly by a single sentence of Mussolini's: "We control the political forces, we control the moral forces, we control the economic forces, thus we are in the midst of the corporative fascist state."[371] Corporatism is the system of the party state which puts its labor force at the disposal of its leader as a "mass which obeys."[372]

In their totality these laws give Mussolini a position without parallel in constitutional history. It can even be compared with Hitler's position. Since the Grand Council had to be "consulted" in matters of succession, yet Mussolini was the only one who could summon the Grand Council and decide on its agenda,[373] the Duce had control of the monarchy even in its most vital interests, quite apart from the fact that the king had no more power of initiative than parliament. Even the supreme command of the sovereign over the army became a mere nominal right, no different from the theoretical possibility of refusing his signature and hence the "sanctioning" of a law. Hindenburg had a great deal more power vis-à-vis Hitler than the Italian king beside Mussolini. The only thing Mussolini dared not touch was the institution of monarchy, and death would not come to his aid as it did for Hitler. Although it is without doubt correct that the court could provide an almost unassailable center of crystallization for antiregime forces which were capable of emerging at the proper moment, it was only very much later that this possibility became a reality, and, relatively, much later than July 20, 1944, in Germany.

Stranger and more significant was the relationship of fascism to the Catholic Church, that is, to a moral power of the first rank which, itself "totalitarian," seemed bound to collide violently with any other totalitarian claim. But one must not confuse totalitarianisms. The word "totalitarian," in the sense of laying full claim to, and obligation on, a human being, is applicable to every religion, every outlook on the world and on life, even the liberal. But only in the eyes of liberalism is this form really purely formal—that is, not ultimately concretizable, and hence Kant's categorical imperative is its classic formulation. It leaves religions free, tolerates them, because it does not regard truth as demonstrable or personal freedom as definable. The only reason it is non-totalitarian in the material sense, and appears to abandon man to the mere whim of his moods, is because, from a formal point of view, it is more totalitarian, that is, more inexorable, than other ideologies. In an analogous sense Western Christianity is also liberal. By distinguishing between God's sphere and the emperor's, it leaves many possibilities open to political man; but it lays unyielding claim to his soul for its path to salvation. The ancient world never knew this kind of separation, this kind of freedom, even the *polis* was ideally a completely totalitarian unity of the spiritual and the political.

Hence the liberal, partial totalitarianism of the Western church is in theory compatible with a totalitarianism which only lays total claim to political man, the "body," provided it acknowledges the "soul," that is, the religious, divine derivation of man (and as often as not this virtually means: "does not deny" the soul).

We must begin, then, by distinguishing between preliberal or religious totalitarianism, and postliberal, or political, totalitarianism. Within the political species there are two totalitarianisms: one is compatible with the religious form, and the other (perhaps only seemingly) is compatible with it. From this follows the first criterion of the difference between Communist and fascist totalitarianism.

This difference becomes quite clear in Mussolini's development, which in the postwar years follows a plain course from former anticlericalism and hatred of religion to deep respect for the church. This development cannot be regarded as merely opportunistic; in embryonic form it is inherent in Mussolini's old convictions as to his "life-philosophy" and is linked inevitably with his new conservative thinking. His first speech in the chamber already contains an expression of his reverence for the church; from then on he never ceased to seek its favor, and the Lateran treaties were the crowning conclusion. By leaving the "care of souls" entirely to the church he was able to define with that much greater vigor the areas to which he laid claim *in maniera totalitaria*: the education of the citizen which he immediately defined more precisely as "martial education."[374] The ecclesiastical negotiators may well have had a suspicion that with a man like Mussolini the distinction was false and baseless, since for him the whole weight fell entirely on the side to which he was laying claim. But he did not "deny," and so the church gave in.[375] Yet in his most solemn official statements Mussolini's potential antagonism was patently obvious, as, for instance, when in his great chamber speech on *consciliazione* he produced the radical-conservative commonplace about Rome's taming of the Christian revolt of slaves, or interpreted the Catholic nature of the fascist state as follows: "The fascist state lays full claim to an ethical character: it is Catholic, but it is fascist; even above all, exclusively, essentially fascist."[376]

It is true that the papacy retained a far greater independence toward Mussolini than did the monarchy, but it too did not represent any serious restriction of Mussolini's power; its resistance was limited to encyclicals (*Non abbiamo bisogno*) and achieved no practical relevance until the final period of the war.[377] Here a surprising objection might indeed be raised. It might be said that Italian fascism lacked two of the most important generic traits of all political totalitarianism: terror, which compels uniformity of political behavior, and a well-defined ideology which sets its stamp on all life of the mind and spirit.

As for terror, it is not absolutely essential that its aim be the physical destruction of the adversary, let alone that it be directed at apolitical population groups (such as kulaks or Jews). For one thing, fascism came to power with the aid of such a powerful terror that later action became in a way superfluous; and for another, it attacked the opposition's political-intellectual leading class even after the fascist victory no less ruthlessly than was the case in Germany, for example.[378] And since it achieved victory in the face of much stronger and more determined resistance, its measures were bound to produce much more widespread terror, although, of course, this terror affected almost exclusively those classes of the population which sympathized with socialism and communism and hence were barely heard in the foreign press.

As for ideology, the assertion that the deed preceded the doctrine is an indication of the inadequacy of fascism's spiritual consistency. But after 1932 every new party member was given, in addition to his membership card and a rifle, a copy of Mussolini's *Dottrina del fascismo*; and the intention of the center of power to make the ideology supreme is more important than the extent of its realization at any one time.

In 1927, therefore, Italian fascism displayed the chief generic traits of political totalitarianism as well as the specific characteristics of national fascist totalitarianism: the function as instrument for the infallible hand of the founder and leader, potentially hostile reliance on conservative social forces. However, in order to advance to the particular, the aims of whatever totalitarianism is under review must also be considered.

Although the term "national fascism" appears at first to describe a method (the unification of the nation in a bundle of energies), it also indicates the goal: the nation is the object of all its efforts as well as their subject. In a very wide sense it is concerned with the "welfare" of the nation. It goes without saying that "welfare" can be interpreted in many different ways and with many different assumptions. Mussolini's chief concern during the first totalitarian period was the exerting of every possible effort to bring Italy to a level of development which other nations had already reached. As there can be no objection to this goal on principle, the rule of this one man, however unlimited it may be and however much its methods may be disputed, cannot be regarded as despotism; it should be defined as a totalitarian national fascist development dictatorship.

For after all there was more to fascism than *only* castor oil and truncheons; it also meant, once victory had been achieved, the enthusiasm of reconstruction, the zest of going to work, in which many of the best energies of youth's urge to action found an abode. That Italian life needed a profound renewal, that Italy must at last become a modern state, that there must be an end to bureaucratic dilatoriness, had been repeated much too often during the past thirty years for this new outlook not to have also inspired fascism.

Bold words are sure to find an echo in young hearts—and was not Mussolini's promise, "In ten years, my comrades, Italy will be unrecognizable,"[379] truly a bold one? The wave of enthusiasm which engulfed the man on the threshing machine who caught the sheaves wrested from the swamp land was not the artificial product of a skillful stage manager, much less the result of terrorism. Mussolini's opponents were correct, of course, when they pointed out that Italy had always been the land of remarkable reclamations (*bonificazioni*), that the cultivation of the Pontine Marshes was a minor achievement compared with the reclamation of the Po Delta during the previous century.[380]

Never before, however, had these essential undertakings entered so much into the forefront of national consciousness, never had they been linked so closely with other works in a national upward surge (for example, the building of roads, the development of the aircraft and automobile industry, etc.), never had the state in the person of its leader identified itself with them to such an extent.

Every totalitarian dictatorship must be founded on some necessary, incontestable factor which it perhaps merely annexes, perhaps exceeds to a dangerous degree, but which for the time being disarms the objections of its opponents and elicits the approval of the masses. In Russia at the end of 1917 this necessity, which none disputed, was peace and the agrarian revolution; in Germany in 1933 it was the revision of the peace treaty; in Italy it was the reclaiming of fallow land, the opening up of backward areas by the building of roads, irrigation, and so forth. Mussolini could be sure of not being contradicted when he said in 1928: "In an Italy which has been completely reclaimed, cultivated, irrigated, disciplined, that is to say, a fascist Italy, there is room and bread for ten million more people."[381] In words like these there was an echo, for those who had ears to hear, of the dialogue of the young socialist with the nationalistic dreams of settlement colonies in Libya—of that Libya in which, after fifteen years, less than a thousand peasant families had settled.[382] There was good reason to assume that in practical effectiveness Mussolini still stood a good way to the left of the imperialistic martial joys of the nationalists. Did he not proudly say on the occasion of the dedication of Littoria: "This is the war we prefer"?[383] Does not the "development dictatorship" itself, with its eyes on the future, its irreverence for the past, and its concern with practical tasks, stand to some extent "to the Left"?

The interpretation which Mussolini gives to his actions and to the Italian situation appears more often than not to confirm this view. Italy, he claimed, was a young capitalist country which, unlike England or America, could not afford to waste its energies and capital in strikes, lockouts, and other labor disputes; the thing to do was to "regain in a few years the time lost in half a century" by means of the wheat battle (*battaglia del grano*) and similar efforts.[384] In the future Italy must no longer be "backward." During the world economic crisis he expressed the very realistic, entirely unheroic hope that it would be precisely Italy's less developed economic system which would allow her to offer better resistance. A great deal of evidence points to the fact that in fascism (which for this very reason, according to Mussolini, was not an "article for export"),[385] he saw merely a concentration of energy which, in these particular circumstances and at that particular time, was indispensable to the more rapid development of a backward country.

If we visualize the Mussolini who, as the topmost and hardest-working civil servant in the country accomplished an amazing quota of work every day,[386] who granted judicious interviews to French, English, and American news agencies, who carried on "European" conversations with Emil Ludwig, we must admit that it is not surprising that people spoke of him as being a good, "paternalistic,"[387] sensible dictator.

But those who saw only that Mussolini had to overlook or minimize that other and no less genuine manifestation: the Mussolini who reviewed his troops from a white Arab horse with the eyes of a Caesar, or who addressed his Blackshirts from a tank turret, engulfed by the roar of a thousand voices shouting *Duce, Duce, Duce*; the Mussolini who put the *Impero* above all else, and who even in those days had ceased to have colleagues but only underlings whom he never asked to sit down. They had to disregard the opinions not only of socialists and Communists but also of the foreign ethnic groups who were kept in a similar state of fear by the mailed fist of the regime: the South Tiroleans and the Slavs. These people were not only, like numerous other minorities in Europe, the victims of various forms of injustice, but unmistakable words from the lips of the Duce[388] announced to them the planned destruction of their ethnic individuality. And finally they had to ignore (and yet what was more obvious?) the deep-seated onetime Marxist who had stood on an equal level with Lenin and who could not be satisfied with being the leader of a counterrevolution and the hard-working prime minister of a medium-sized and backward country, that Marxist who had retained his inclination for concrete social analysis—but also his need for universal perspectives.

How else can we explain the fact that Mussolini ascribes the dignity of a world salvation to the corporative economy, although he had defined its instrumental and exceptional nature, as well as its dependence on the capitalist world system, with sufficient clarity? "As the past century has seen the capitalist economy, so will the present century see the corporative economy. There is no other way, my comrades, of overcoming the tragic conflict of capital and labor, which is a focal point of the Marxist doctrine that we have overcome. Capital and labor must be placed on the same level, each must be given the same rights and duties."[389] This thesis also takes the form that fascism, having created equality vis-à-vis the law, was now creating equality vis-à-vis labor; it is reiterated much too often for us to regard it as mere social demagogy. Although the Mussolini of the final period was to pronounce a crushing sentence on the correctness of this thesis in its factual sense, its mere existence proves how far from gaining undisputed supremacy in Mussolini's mind was the conservatives' favorite thesis of fundamental inequality. In any case, it is possible to derive universal perspectives very easily from it: outside of fascist principles there is no salvation, Europe and the world could not help but become fascist.[390] The fact that as a result Italy would necessarily forfeit its preferred position did not worry Mussolini; unlike Hitler, he did not believe the new way of life must be jealously guarded as a privilege. (There was, of course, also in National Socialism a universal trend, namely in its race doctrine; it is in fact a hallmark of national fascisms as against nationalisms.)

Also pointing toward the universal is Mussolini's harking back to the Roman tradition. He pursued this theme with still greater vigor, and it led him to the antithesis of "Rome or Moscow." However, that this was not an unproblematical antithesis propounded in the manner of Maurras or Hitler is shown by the fact that Mussolini followed the fluctuating fate of European communism with close attention, and that with a highly characteristic satisfaction—although not entirely without apprehension—he referred to a book which asserted that the latest developments of communism in the Soviet Union were merely a "triumph of fascism."[391]

In any event, he continued to be no less the former comrade of Lenin than a son of the wolf, and both operated in the same direction—that of regaining a political faith which he had reluctantly renounced between 1918 and 1925; and he could not be satisfied with undertaking peaceful and mediocre cultivation in a medium-sized country: "Fascism is not only a party, it is a regime; it is not only a regime but a faith; it is not only a faith but a religion. ..."[392]

Every faith contains the idea of a supreme act which reveals man's true self to himself. Even during his Marxist period this was never, for Mussolini, labor liberated from its alienation, but the revolution. If after 1914 this specific war was identified in his eyes with the revolution, after 1920 its place was taken by war *as such*, although this place was not especially accentuated. Even the development dictator did not make it any too clear that it was here, and not in some opinion or other regarding the relation between capital and labor, that the heart of his *fede* lay; but it cannot be maintained that he was at pains to conceal it: "I do not believe in perpetual peace, indeed, I regard it as degrading and negative toward the fundamental virtues of man which only emerge into the light of the sun in bloody efforts."[393] It was probably more than a distracting maneuver in the face of economic crisis when he made strikingly belligerent speeches in Leghorn and Florence in 1930, envisaging the nation as a projectile, and offering the prospect of liberation from imprisonment on the Mediterranean.[394] And presumably it was more than a reply to the events in Austria when in 1934 he called for the transformation of Italy into a *nazione militarista* and *guerriera* or foretold the sending of punitive expeditions across the frontier.[395]

The most unremitting and passionate involvement of all those years was directed toward one problem, which achieves its full meaning only in this context: the demographic problem. Mussolini followed statistics ceaselessly, apportioned praise and blame to towns and districts according to the level of surplus births, noted not without satisfaction the "aging" of the other European peoples, yet uttered cries of alarm about the jeopardizing of the white race. From the antithetical relationship between fertility and industrialization he quite happily derived reactionary conclusions: he wanted to "ruralize" Italy. At the same time, in spite of the world economic crisis, he put a stop to emigration. He was haunted, as it were, by the notion that the *patria* might lose men, "that is, future soldiers."[396] Just because fascism began by being a "development dictatorship" we must not ignore the fact that its deepest and quite overt trend had always been in the direction of war.

The Last Autonomous Stage (1935–1937)

It was, however, a trend that at first seemed remote from any possibility of realization. The idea of a war against France and England for supremacy in the Mediterranean was out of the question for Mussolini, nor did he desire it. Although he may have expressed himself in favor of a revision of treaties and now and again have addressed threatening or contemptuous words to the Western powers, he still remained from 1922 to 1935 completely within the scope of "Western civilization." It was surely more than flattery when in an interview with a Paris newspaper in 1927 he distinguished between levels of cultural and human proximity and placed the Italians closest to the French, while the Germans found themselves placed behind the English and very close to the Russians, who were divided by an "abyss" from the Italians.[397] The direction of his gaze toward London and Paris, the preponderance of French and English works in his reading, fully confirm this estimate. And he certainly did not go so far as to create an ideological gulf between fascism and the West: on the contrary, with the utmost naturalness he claimed as being fascist all those trends in Western countries which tended toward strengthening of government authority, restriction of strikes, control of economy. This was the basis for his popularity among all the conservative classes of Europe; fascism seemed to be an autochthonous recipe guarding against the crumbling of Western culture, far removed from the alarming excesses of German National Socialism. It was either overlooked or not known that Mussolini's education and mode of thought were Western on a broad surface level only, while their roots were German—Marx and Nietzsche.

The natural synthesis of a development dictatorship and war would have been a colonial undertaking on a large scale. But the world had been parceled out, the old colonial powers hung onto their possessions only by dint of great effort, and Mussolini had no hope whatever of obtaining their consent. However, the situation changed when National Socialism came to power in Germany. Italy's value for the Western powers, and hence their willingness to make concessions, rose as if by magic. But had not that event wrought too fundamental a change in the situation for it to be exploited politically?

Mussolini was more keenly aware than most of the Western statesmen of the unique and menacing nature of National Socialism. This is how he described it in 1934: "One hundred per cent racism. Against everything and everyone: yesterday against Christian civilization, today against Latin civilization, tomorrow, who knows, against the civilization of the whole world ... drunk with a stubborn bellicosity."[398] Shortly afterward he combined ridiculing of the allegedly pure Germanic race with a remarkable insight into certain unavoidable consequences of this race doctrine (which at the same time he declared to be "Jewish"): "We shall see whether Nazism succeeds in making a pure-blooded 'herd.' According to the most favorable hypothesis ... one needs six centuries of racial marriages and not less of racial castrations."[399]

If these utterances are correct, it follows that National Socialism is merely the most radical form of that "Germanism" which was the object of his aversion during his youth, against which he went to war, and which, even after victory, he continued to observe with lively mistrust.[400] It then becomes inevitable, insofar as "Western civilization" remains the supreme concept, that another world war be waged and this time brought to the radical conclusion which the socialists and Wilsonites prevented on the earlier occasion.[401]

But in those days Mussolini could still believe in this concept of civilization. After fifteen years of national fascism this became difficult or impossible. Thus we find side by side in the same man two incompatible languages, the languages of two different phases in his development. For the founder of fascism is quite obviously filled with pride at the sight of a great nation won over to "his" principles: "Behold another great country which is creating the unitarian, authoritarian, totalitarian, that is, fascist state, with certain emphases which fascism has dispensed with since it operated in a different historical milieu."[402] And the grounds for pride are joined by grounds for admiration. In an article appearing anonymously on February 26, 1935, in the *Popolo d'Italia*, he noted with surprise and emotion the success of the National Socialist campaign for increasing the birth rate: "The fact is that the German nation has responded to the appeal ... proving that Germany does not want to die by voluntary extinction like the miserly senile old peoples of the West but that it has faith in its future."[403] Since nothing during the past ten years had occupied Mussolini's mind as much as the "demographic" problem, and nothing had disappointed him as much as the failure of his attempts to solve it, it is very probable that this is the crucial motivation for his rapprochement with Germany. But even when it was a matter, not of the contrast between the higher and lower levels of civilization but of the struggle between the virile and the decadent peoples, it was essential to choose, to place oneself on the correct side in a life-and-death struggle which was bound to make all other adjustments subordinate and temporary.

But Mussolini did not choose: instead he utilized the opportunity to execute a "maneuver" in the narrowest national interest—the conquest of Ethiopia. For there is no doubt that he intended to exploit the predicament of the Western powers in order to force their consent. This meant, of course, surrendering his freedom of action. Success must lead to an alliance with England and France, for only with their consent was it possible to retain the new colonial territory. Even a total victory in alliance with Hitler would have canceled out the value of the sacrifices and efforts of the Ethiopian campaign, since it would have put at Italy's disposal far more suitable areas in closer proximity to the mother country. The conversations in Rome with Laval in January, 1935, as well as the Stresa agreements were part of the maneuver. He did not, it is true, obtain a formal consent, but he must have had reason to expect toleration.[404] Thus there took place something very similar to the events of 1921 to 1922: just as Mussolini's "squadrists" then had crushed an unarmed opponent with the benevolent neutrality of governmental power, so between October, 1935, and May, 1936, his armies and marshals, with all the resources of technology and a ruthless conduct of war,[405] conquered a helpless country which did not even have a single fighter plane, while some of the great powers hesitatingly applied "sanctions," the success of which they themselves dreaded. It was the last colonial war in European history and perhaps for that very reason its most brutal and deliberate act of conquest, the founding of an "imperium" whose origin bore no resemblance to that of the envied British empire. Mussolini accompanied the war at times with the old talk of a "civilizing mission," at times with the more modern postulates of "vital necessity." When on May 9, 1936, he proclaimed "the reappearance of the Imperium on the fateful hills of Rome" (*la riapparizione dell'Impero sui colli fatali di Roma*),[406] the frenzied acclamations of his enthusiastic people swelled to an apotheosis.[407]

Was there ever a more privileged favorite of fortune than Mussolini? In 1921 the internal paralysis of a conquered opponent led to the victory of fascism; in 1922 the isolation of the individual local party leaders (*Ras*) created for him a dominating position to which his performance on behalf of the party did not entitle him; in 1935 it was the approaching world storm which enabled him to gather in the last colonial harvest before it was too late.

But just as in 1920 his enemies had lacked the insight into the exigencies of the hour, so now it was lacking in him. He made gains which a few years earlier would never have been dreamed of. Now was the time for consolidation and defense. His insight could not but tell him that the only way to preserve the new position was by making Italy one of several partners, with himself unique and solitary. The duality with a much stronger, less satisfied country as well as a far more logical and single-minded man of his own type was bound in the long run to bring ruin to himself and his state, regardless of the glory it first appeared to promise.

But this insight wore civilian dress, and Mussolini had left that behind long ago. The most powerful sides of his nature contradicted this insight: his faith in life and in war as life's supreme test, the intoxication of greatness, of always trying the impossible, the love of grand perspectives. It is not likely, of course, that he seriously believed in his self-made myth of the "iniquitous siege";[408] the Western powers did not make the way back particularly difficult for him, nor did he at first fail to drop hints and offers. Italy, he said, had now become a conservative country, a rapprochement with the Western powers was not only desirable but necessary.[409] But it could not be accomplished from one day to the next, and patience had never been one of Mussolini's virtues.

Starting with the middle of 1936, the visits of high National Socialist dignitaries in Rome multiplied: Frank, Schirach, Himmler, Göring, von Blomberg. There was no doubt that their uniforms were infinitely more appropriate to the atmosphere of a mass fascist rally than the unobtrusive apparel of Western statesmen. Mussolini gave the *Völkischer Beobachter* his first interview, and as in the old days with the nationalists the link was established via the bridge of antibolshevism. Very early on, without any real necessity, he spoke of a "Rome-Berlin Axis"[410] and gave unmistakable hints of potential claims on the Western powers, especially France. Now at last he was on the same track as the Italian nationalists, whose ultimate goal had always been the world-dividing alliance with dynamic Germany against the decadent rich nations of the West. But (starting with the Moscow trials) he was able to see this goal in terms of perspectives which were less familiar to the nationalists and which represented his own most personal triumph: "Lenin's star, now extinct, declines toward a horizon in a sea of blood vainly shed, while the fructifying dazzling sun of Rome rises higher and higher in the sky."[411]

Thus he no doubt believed that, in the glory of his incomparable prestige, he could confidently undertake the journey to Berlin. But this journey marked for all time the last autonomous stage of his path.

Despotism of Conquest and Satellite State

This journey made a profound and indelible impression on Mussolini. Devotion was something he was familiar with, but that a minister (Goebbels) should keep his arm outstretched in salute throughout his whole speech was new to him; waves of popular acclamation had always surrounded him, but the German seriousness of enthusiasm moved him more deeply than the volatile nature of his own countrymen; he had often taken part in maneuvers, but the force and precision of the exercises of the most powerful army in the world put all that had gone before in the shade; flattery, sympathy, friendship had been extended to him often enough by foreigners, but the sincere esteem[412] of a man like Hitler was for him a new and overwhelming experience. This style of foreign policy appealed to Mussolini's "temperament" as nothing had ever done before, and without a second thought he turned a maxim of personal ethics into a principle of the relations between the two states which differed so fundamentally in their interests: "To speak clearly and openly and, when one is friends, to march together to the end."[413]

The significance of this choice was not hard to discern. This was no alliance of two development dictatorships aiming at mutual support and safeguarding. If Hitler's hegemony had its popular basis in the "national" problems of vanquished Germany, he had nevertheless expressed his will to conquer new *Lebensraum* in Eastern Europe so early and so often, and yet met with so little real resistance, that his system could be called (to use a term from his early speeches) a "totalitarian geopolitical dictatorship of conquest."[414] True, Italy also had its territorial aspirations beyond its borders. It was no accident that the problem of Dalmatia had been the first cause of Italian disillusionment after the war, and the nationalists had also always had their eye on Tunis, Corsica, and Albania. But all these ambitious desires never found firm support among the Italian people, and Mussolini himself was more of a stranger to them than were some of his followers. The alliance with Germany forced him irresistibly onto this geopolitical path; but since both sides of the new policy met with little popular or even party sympathy, his system of rule must henceforth be called a "totalitarian geopolitical despotism." The structure of Italian fascism contained no method of preventing ór even controlling such a remarkable transformation of foreign political aims. A great many of the most important members of the Grand Council—not to mention the king—were hostile to the pro-German policy from the very beginning, but beside the *fondatore dell' Impero* they counted for less than had the last Sardinian member of parliament beside Giolitti. And while Hitler's geopolitical inclinations show the unde niable grandeur of the colossal and the historically unique, the diaries of Count Ciano reflect the depressing picture of a petty desire for "booty" by which Mussolini's impulsive spirit was now possessed.[415]

But the geopolitical element by no means exhausts the content of Hitler's policy. Easily recognizable only in the most superficial aspects, this policy was founded on the will for a sweeping cure of a "world sickness" in which Hitler believed to have discerned the real cause of the threat to Germany. Hitler always concealed this aspect of his thinking with much greater care, although not completely: it is this side which makes it possible to speak of his system as being in essence a "totalitarian despotism of salvation," "salvation" meaning the saving of the Germanic, that is, Aryan, race from injurious and in the end deadly influences.[416] Hence in its negative effect Hitler's hegemony must necessarily be a "despotism of destruction." It is evident that this doctrine of salvation is merely the mythicizing interpretation of a primary emotion—fear. There remains the question of who is afraid of whom.

All that can be found of this fear in Italian nationalism as well as in Mussolini is a few traces, in the same way that we also find in him rudiments of anti-Semitism and a political race doctrine. But on the whole Mussolini's "life-philosophy" is the faithful expression of a politically youthful, homogeneous, unthreatened nation.

Yet even here Mussolini's impressionability cannot escape the stronger will and the more impassioned thinking. The summer of 1938 marked the beginning of the fascist race policy. In spite of there being little reason to bestow special praise on Mussolini's "humanity,"[417] we must say that, although he surpassed

Corradini, he never went as far as Hitler, in that he did not isolate and mythicize the Jewish question or strive for anything beyond the political exclusion and separation of the Jews. In this he coincided with Maurras.

Yet it is more than merely a case of imitation. As so often happened with Mussolini, under certain circumstances one element came into play which had previously been combined with others and was thus relatively concealed. As a young man Mussolini had already, and not without sympathy, quoted Nietzschean phrases concerning the antithesis of Jews and Rome,[418] and after the war there were more than a few instances of anti-Semitic phrases flowing from his pen, usually in connection with the polemic against bolshevism.[419] In 1934 his anti-Germanism took on an anti-Semitic note, and even before his journey to Germany there was a quarrel with an Italian Jewish periodical.[420]

However, his utterances against anti-Semitism are more frequent and more pronounced, and not only in his talks with Emil Ludwig. Personally, Mussolini had much cause for gratitude. In his Marxist period as well as during the fascist time, Jewish women had played an important role in his life: Angelica Balabanov and Margherita G. Sarfatti. He had had a very high opinion of Sonnino and Luzzatti. The founder of Roman fascism was a Jew (Enrico Rocca), also the theoretician of corporatism (Gino Arias); moreover, there had been quite a number of Jews among the early Fascists.

On the other hand we cannot overlook the fact that the number of Jews among the opponents of fascism was considerable: Treves, Modigliani, Carlo Rosselli, and others. Thus from the autonomous development of Italian fascism two insights can be gleaned regarding the problem of the relationship of national fascism to Jewry: (1) Jewry and national fascism do not necessarily have to be hostile to each other; (2) In spite of the participation of Jews—who, considering their small number in Italy (seventy thousand) were extraordinarily active—in intellectual and political life no appreciable anti-Semitism developed in Italy.[421]

As a matter of fact, the starting point of the fascist race policy was not the hatred of Jews but the fear of a "race of half-breeds" in the *Impero*.[422] Immediately after the conclusion of the campaign very strict regulations were put into force, for "without a clear, definite, omnipresent race consciousness empires cannot be maintained."[423] It is in this context that Mussolini declared the laws affecting Jews, and so he felt entitled to declare all those who had spoken of foreign influences as "poor fools" (these included king and pope).[424] But this legislation did not deny its model, the Nuremberg legislation, and it can hardly be claimed that it was much milder. The fact that in its economic "discriminations" (the ban on employing one hundred or more persons, owning more than fifty hectares of land, and so on) it made an exception of the families of war veterans and fascist "veteran campaigners," legionaries of Fiume, and so forth, related to a state of affairs which did not exist in Germany in that form; but even the sons of fallen Fascists were not allowed to marry Italians or attend any

Italian school. In order to emphasize native roots and national dignity still more strongly, a further ban was added prohibiting all civil servants (in the widest sense) from marrying foreign women of any race.[425]

The unpopularity of these measures in Italy can be seen from Ciano's diaries.[426] And the same invaluable documents reveal a Mussolini who has become boastful, cynical, undisciplined, making the most far-reaching decisions on impulse.[427] It is not even necessary to resort to these intimate documents, however. Events and speeches become more and more uniform and ritualistic, ideas become more and more shallow and insignificant. The man who in his youth evolved a highly symptomatic and yet unique version of Marxism, who was one of the first to recognize the new needs of the workers' movement, who seemed for a time to be the spiritual leader of all novel and youthful trends in Europe, this man now merely repeats the few formulas which his new friends manipulate with far greater skill—the rights of the young and prolific peoples, the danger of bolshevism, the harm done by criticism, and the priority of the (politically) faithful agrarian masses.

Of all the outstanding totalitarian personalities of the era, Mussolini was not the man with the deepest thoughts but he was probably the one with the most thoughts; he was not the most outstanding, but he was the most human; he was not the most single-minded, but he was the most many-sided. Thus to a certain extent he was the most liberal. Of them all he was the one who lost the most through his own system. Hitler and Lenin remained exactly as they were, since from the outset they represented only their own fixed convictions. Mussolini was the only one to represent both systems in himself. There is no need to waste time examining the effect of fascism on the spiritual life of Italy, since it was so well able to make a dupe of its leader.

Nevertheless it seems risky to allow Mussolini's "despotism" to begin with his journey to Germany. Although his behavior during the *Anschluss* of Austria gave rise to widespread anxiety in Italy, even practiced observers were unable to detect any clouding of the relationship between Duce and people during Hitler's return visit in May, 1938. By investing himself as well as the king with the rank of a *Primo maresciallo dell'Impero*—a step without parallel in constitutional history—he placed the *fondatore dell'Impero* on almost the same footing, from the point of view of protocol, with the *Re Imperatore* and made even the figurehead, which was all that the king was anyway, appear a challenge.[428] During the intervention in Spain he seemed to be the guiding spirit, Hitler only an auxiliary. And the days of Munich became the outward climax of Mussolini's entire life. His intervention made the conference possible, he was the sole participant to speak all the negotiating languages; for the first time in the history of Italy, so it was bound to appear, Italy provided the leading personality of a great European congress. On his return to Italy he was welcomed by millions upon millions—some of them even on their knees—who, deeply and sincerely moved, looked on him as the savior of peace and of Europe.

Yet the glory was false and the triumph without foundation. Mussolini, the man who wanted to establish the complete autonomy of his native land and thus break the gentle bonds of the Mediterranean partnership with England and France, was to be conscious all too soon of having surrendered himself and his people to a far more incisive heteronomy.

Two anonymous newspaper articles were perhaps the earliest and clearest indication of the change-over. On September 15, 1938, in a "Letter to Runciman" he defended Hitler's demands on Czechoslovakia, and added: "If Hitler laid claim to the annexation of three and a half million Czechs, Europe would have reason to become agitated and aroused. But Hitler has no such intention."[429]

He spoke in the tone of a bosom friend and initiate and no doubt felt himself transported back to the times when he was fighting for the right of self-determination and displayed a lively sympathy in the establishing of Czech legions in Italy.[430]

Only a few months later Hitler established a protectorate over seven million Czechs as if they were a barbaric colonial people, without any thought of asking Mussolini for his advice. Yet in the *Giornale d'Italia* Mussolini justified this arrogant step of his ally and even specifically declared his solidarity. That it could not but be fatal for the weaker partner to ally himself with the more powerful one above and beyond all principles (except perhaps for those of personal friendship and collective vitality) did not occur to Mussolini. There was no one who had either the courage or the constitutional position to point this out to him, least of all his son-in-law Ciano.[431] Indeed, in May he concluded the "steel pact" which in Article III provided with remarkable simplicity for each partner to render all possible military support to the other as soon as that one became involved in a war. In other words, it contained something so unconditional as to make a mockery of all the traditions of diplomacy, and showed more clearly than many other things that only in an unreal sense was it now possible to speak of a relationship between two national states. In reality it was the alliance of two political creeds for the supreme act and content of their *fede*: for war.

But although in this way Mussolini once again made the distinction between Italy and fascism which in 1922 had been his point of departure,[432] on the highest and most momentous level, national fascism nevertheless remained much too closely linked to its starting point—the nation—for it to be able to create the genuinely unconditional solidarity of the true and universal creed. Whereas Mussolini often allowed himself to be guided in his words and deeds by blind jealousy, Hitler had no intention of permitting his ally even the right to be heard when it came to starting the war.

National fascism was incapable of bringing forth a judicious coalition of nations or of creating the unconditional solidarity of an encompassing *Weltanschauung*. This was the wound of its war; thus not only did it soon destroy the weaker partner, it also gave the stronger one no serious advantage beyond his own strength.

The course taken by events is well known: Italy's initial *Nonbelligeranza*, which dealt a blow to Mussolini's prestige and self-confidence from which he never recovered, the precipitate intervention against France which brought little honor and barred forever the way back to the Allies, the campaign against Greece, which was a jealous answer to German action in Rumania and which turned out to be one of the worst failures of the entire war,[433] the fluctuating struggle for North Africa which brought Italy's panzer divisions either to the bottom of the sea or under German command, the participation in the overrunning of the Soviet Union, which finally destroyed the confidence of the Italian people in Mussolini because they understood it even less than the war as a whole, and finally the Allied landing in Sicily on July 10, 1943, which met with almost no resistance and dealt a mortal blow to the regime.

Only one event in this connection merits special attention. This is the occupation of Yugoslavia in April, 1941, during which Italian troops, freed at last from the Albanian bridgehead, fulfilled only a subsidiary function. But while Yugoslavia was only a secondary theater for Germany, it suddenly became apparent that for Italy it meant something quite different. To the surprise of the uninitiated it turned out that for twelve years Mussolini had been keeping a number of Croatian separatists—among them Ante Pavelić—in readiness and now immediately used them against the conquered country so as to split it in two. But Mussolini forced the newly independent Croatia to drink from the poison cup by not only annexing large parts of Dalmatia but even incorporating the Lyublyana area into Italy, and thus from the start weakening Croatia to the position of a mere party state of Ustasha. Thus toward the end of his life Mussolini at last even solved the "Adriatic problem" (although without much contribution on his part). Moreover, he did so in the most radical sense by destroying the troublesome neighbor, that is, by turning its national territory into "defense areas" and satellite states. Even after World War I Mussolini's thoughts had traveled momentarily in a comparable direction,[434] but D'Annunzio and the nationalists had blown the Adriatic trumpets of war much more frequently and loudly than he. After the March on Rome he had carried on a policy of reconciliation toward Yugoslavia. Nevertheless, the desire to reincorporate into fascism the territories which had once been Venetian had remained alive; by intensifying this trend now Mussolini added to his fascism a basic characteristic of national fascism which had hitherto been lacking. National fascism, as we have shown, is distinguished from nationalism by, among other things, the fact that it demands the destruction of a neighboring state whose very existence appears to threaten its own position of power and the historic remains of its past dominant status in the area. What Germany was for Maurras, Russia was for Hitler and now Yugoslavia for Mussolini. But he too drank of the fatal poison in this most counterhistorical of all his intentions. The new provinces became a steady drain on Italian blood and Italian prestige; here were laid the cornerstones of that state which alone after the war deprived Italy of some of its most beautiful cities and most desirable areas.

The nub of the tragedy lay in the nature of national fascism itself which allowed Italy to have neither allies nor comrades—at the very utmost, the appearance of both. However, it is not in events that this tragedy finds its sharpest expression and its fulfillment, but in Mussolini's emotions and thoughts. For we cannot dismiss out of hand the hypothesis that a swift German victory would have also meant the triumph of the Axis. In either case though, Mussolini would have been defeated.

It does not speak well for Mussolini's resilience and adaptability that in this unprecedented situation he let himself be guided, without closer scrutiny, by old ideas. The reason he gave to himself and others for the entry into the new war is exactly the same as that of 1914: Italy could not stand aside from an event of such magnitude. He ignored the fact that totally different historical situations can necessitate totally different decisions, that the concrete conditions for those former considerations no longer existed. Yet this time, in complete contrast to 1914, he soon undertook a petty calculation,[435] and not even the undignified, satellite-type phrases which he already had to use in 1940[436] made him realize the difference existing between the early years of the era and the latter ones.

First there was always the handy arsenal of his "life-philosophy," second the carelessly applied formula from his revolutionary past: "It has never happened that the conservative spirit triumphed over the revolution, and it will not happen now either."[437] But not only up to 1914, even up to 1935 his thinking did not in any way lead to the premises that Berlin and Tokyo represented the ideas of the future as against Moscow and Washington.[438]

Furthermore, the war so casually begun was also badly conducted. Mussolini's vision was more acute than that of those of his people who attributed every misfortune to "betrayal," for after all betrayal itself is to a certain extent a symptom of the betrayed. In December, 1940, he remarked to Ciano that the Italians of 1914 had been superior, and that that did not redound to the credit of the regime.[439] Indeed, had it been worth depriving the people with the oldest culture in Europe of the lightness, the special idiom, the dignity and variety, the weakness and colorfulness of their life, if twenty years of totalitarian *inquadramento* had not even been able to generate the martial achievements to which the much-criticized prewar regime had given birth?

What Mussolini was finding fault with was, of course, precisely this "too little." Hence the more the masses isolated fascism, the more the war years saw desperate efforts to step up ideological indoctrination, to reinforce the influence of the party, and to create an army of defenders-of-the-faith. The man who had once been a relativist and a heretic gave a high party functionary

(Carlo Ravasio) the specific command "to be responsible for the orthodoxy of the party,"[440] and the savior of Europe, the enemy of bolshevism, set up the Communist *fede* as a model with greater vigor than ever before, thereby proclaiming his lifelong duel with Lenin as lost. In Russia, he admitted, half the soldiers were fighting fascism because of their Communist beliefs. Their loyalty to their faith was stronger than their love for their country. There could be no other explanation for Russian achievements and resistance.[441]

Was Mussolini conscious of his defeat—his defeat by Hitler and Lenin, Roosevelt and Turati? Was he trying to withdraw from the game by cautiously shifting the responsibility onto others? At least his behavior, during the final weeks before July 25, 1943, does not exclude such a supposition. He appeared totally unaware of the secret talks which the king was conducting with fascist and prefascist politicians, he appeared not to notice the rumblings in even the highest ranks of the hierarchy. No one could force him to summon a session of the Grand Council; he did it of his own accord. He knew the order of the day which Grandi had prepared, and according to the statutes he could have refused its acceptance in the agenda. He would have had no difficulty in having the entire Grand Council arrested after the session. He did none of these things.

On the other hand, there is little reason to believe that he acted with the deliberate intention of putting an end to his political game. Instead he seems to have acted in one of those deeply enervated moods of depression that not infrequently overtook this man of action. In the heated ten-hour discussion, which Mussolini followed with mere surprise and lethargy, those who had created and led the "squadrist" army for fascism, and who for twenty years had been treated by Mussolini like lackeys, expressed much of their pent-up anger and resentment. Nevertheless, the intention of the order of the day was by no means to depose Mussolini, a step which the Grand Council was constitutionally not empowered to take. All it demanded was the reinstatement of normal (that is, fascist) constitutional life and the resumption by the king of the supreme military command which Mussolini had usurped.[442] Mussolini displayed little knowledge of human nature when he blindly put his trust in the amicable feelings of a king whom he had so often severely wounded. His arrest brought down the imposing edifice of fascism like a house of cards; even the elite troops of the militia did not lift a finger: the party, so long isolated, disappeared from the life of the nation as if it had never been. No abyss opened up; life seemed to go on without interruption—and so, of course, by order of Badoglio, did the war.

Mussolini apathetically let himself be taken from place to place, his thoughts occupied with death and the dead; for a female admirer he autographed a photo with the words: *Mussolini defunto*.[443]

Return to the Origins?—Repubblica di Salò

But this defunct man was forced to rise from the dead. Hitler's friendship liberated Mussolini to bear witness—scarcely with pleasure but certainly of necessity—to himself and against himself. The law pursuant to which the new state was to begin its existence was outlined by Mussolini in his very first speech after his liberation over Radio Munich, on September 18, 1943.

The disgraceful betrayal by the monarchy of its "faithful servant" would now, Mussolini said, without question lead Italy back to those older and purer republican traditions of the Italian unification movement typified by the name of Mazzini. Return to the origins (twenty years ago he had called them "infantile") was now to be his motto; pursuant to the principles of these origins, the new state was to be national and social in the highest sense of the words. It would destroy the parasitical plutocracy and at last make labor the master of the economy. The traitors, in particular the faithless members of the Grand Council, were to be exterminated. A new armed might was to be built up around the formations of the militia.[444]

But Mussolini did not cite the preamble to this law: the occupation of Italy by the Germans. Could such a program be implemented by a man and a party who now no longer possessed even the appearance of independence? The new head of state was not even allowed to enter his capital; in the villas on Lake Garda, strictly guarded by the SS, the republican government took up its quarters, a government to which the most important and best-known men of fascism no longer belonged, since efforts were being made to stage a great treason trial against them, although the legal basis for such a trial was more than scant.

The only ones who stood by Mussolini were stubborn fanatics,[445] and they managed, in conjunction with the Germans, to see to it that Mussolini was not permitted to spare even the father of his grandchildren.[446] Thus once again fascism freed itself symbolically from those men who had changed its face in 1921, and this took place just as much against the irresolute will of Mussolini as that first metamorphosis. Thus the character of fascism as it had been in 1921 —its resemblance to a foreign army on native soil—re-emerged in yet more horrible distortion. How was the war on the side of the National Socialist Germany, a war which had never been popular, now to form the basis for a union of regime and people? The militia divisions, quickly re-formed from mercenaries and convinced Fascists, remained civil war formations—the *Repubblica Sociale Italiana* never possessed a real army.

But this time they were not borne up by feelings of enthusiasm and confidence in victory; the steady, although painfully slow, advance of the Allied front was accompanied by growing partisan activity, by strikes, by elusive but unremitting propaganda activity on the part of the internal enemy in the cities. This time it was the Fascists who provided targets for "punitive expeditions," which were very often of an insidious kind: in the summer of 1944 one of the victims to fall was Giovanni Gentile, who a year before had been the last person publicly to defend Mussolini. If twenty years earlier "national feeling" had supported and championed the Fascists, this feeling now turned with equal vehemence against them and identified them more and more with the German enemy. Hitler encouraged this propaganda to an extraordinary degree by the measures he took: he appeared to make its theses the very foundation for his actions by obviously regarding as null and void his assurances as to the inviolability of the Brenner frontier; indeed, he quite clearly considered himself Austria's successor and made preparations for the detachment of Trieste, Gorizia, and the Adriatic coast.[447] The gains of World War I were lost. This meant that one of the things dearest to Mussolini's heart was affected; but he did not even dare to make a firm protest. In Italy as in all Europe, national fascism proved to be the most untrustworthy of all the nation's children.

On this precarious basis, amid this universal disintegration, Mussolini threw himself heart and soul into the attaining of a goal that some have unjustifiably made out to be a mere demagogic concession—the goal of socialization.[448] Yet in substantiating this goal he cut the ground from under his own feet as well as from under all his previous achievements.

The essential task now, he declared in the first cabinet council of the Republic, was to define the place, function, and responsibility of labor in a truly modern national society.[449] Did this mean that for two decades fascism had not allocated a suitable place to labor, that, in spite of all fascist chronology, Italy had not been a truly modern state? Mussolini did everything to avoid this inevitable question and to stress the continuity of the fascist revolution, particularly the great significance of the *Carta del Lavoro*. It was only the encounter with a hypocritical monarch that had caused the fascist revolution to deviate from its course (*ha deviato il corso della rivoluzione fascista*);[450] the king and Badoglio were rejecting the progressive legislation of the Republic today "in order to preserve unchanged their own selfish class privileges."[451] Mussolini might have been reminded of the fact that it was that very encounter with the king that had made the fascist revolution possible in the first place; and it could be asked with equal justification what kind of a revolution that was which had permitted the leading classes to preserve their selfish privileges for twenty years and which had allowed itself to be perverted in its intentions by the "active resistance of the capitalists."[452]

The practical measures of the fascist era had spoken a language it was impossible to misunderstand. The allocation of all direction (*gestione*) of business enterprises exclusively to the owners had not been a "concession" within the *Carta del Lavoro* but, in many vague and fine-sounding words, its very essence. This determination had solved a much-disputed ideological question by wiping out the ground gained during the "Bolshevist" years of

1919–20. Now, however, in 1943, the principle was established that labor must enter into the core of the productive mechanism and actively co-operate in it, and consequently participate in the *gestione*. The *Consigli di fabbrica* were restored, and the workers were guaranteed the right to choose their representatives by secret ballot. Yet the abolition of these dangerous institutions[453] had signified precisely one of the most crucial totalitarian measures after January 3, 1925.

The dualistic structure of the fascist syndical system, which by means of various associations placed employer and employee side by side and then united them by state organs, had not been a minor defect of corporatism but its much-admired intrinsic nature. Of course, Mussolini's opponents had always pointed out that the pretended equality was merely an apparent one, and that in actual fact it led to an unlimited hegemony of the self-represented capitalists over the employees. With a stroke of the pen and even some specific words[454] Mussolini now acknowledged those critics to have been right: a joint trade union of labor and technology (*Confederazione generale del lavoro e della tecnica*) replaced the former institutions, capital as such was excluded from trade-union representation.

This was bound to lead ultimately to the nationalization of capital, and Mussolini pursued this trend so tenaciously that at the end of March, 1945, all enterprises with more than a hundred workers or a capital of a million lire were withdrawn from private initiative. More significant still is the fact that Mussolini stressed the importance of the "most thorough transformation of the positions in which the producers find themselves in the enterprise,"[455] the hegemony of bureaucracy must be avoided, for example by the introduction of profit participation. In 1921–22 fascism had crushed the overflowing spontaneous energy of the people and for twenty years had kept it under interdiction in the straitjacket of a system which for this very reason enjoyed such widespread sympathy in the world. It was this spontaneous energy that Mussolini was now trying to call forth and encourage once again, although his way of going about it was certainly very halfhearted. He cited as noteworthy that one of the deputy mayors of Milan was not a party member. A law relating to *consulte comunali elettive* was aimed at cautiously airing the armor plating of state authority at one point and at rounding up those who were unaccustomed to any political activity for the purpose of responsible collaboration (in a way reminiscent of Maurras' *libertés*). Mussolini even considered permitting an opposition party, but he was unable to implement this plan because of the resistance of Farinacci and other extremists.[456] He continued to insist, however, that the single party must be "controlled" by other loyal groups. He even specifically abandoned the ideological claim to totality: "abjurations, ideological renunciations, genuflections, gestures of cowardice are required from no one."[457]

It was in this manner that Mussolini now desired at last to create the state of the "producers," a state in which no one possessed rights who did not work but in which no worker was excluded from political life. These were very strange demands for the autocratic Duce of authoritarian and militaristic fascism who in the footsteps of the nationalists had so thoroughly tamed and disciplined the masses but who had always refused to "accept" them. On the other hand, these demands were not strange for the onetime Marxist and the whip of Social Democracy who had not completely renounced his old ideas until January 3, 1925. It is this early Mussolini who gives the following definition of the *Repubblica Sociale Italiana*: "It will be the republic of the Italian workers, and it has already begun on the determined realization of all those postulates which for forty years were inscribed on the flags of the socialist movements."[458] In other words, he declares the RSI to be not the continuation of fascism but the realization of a forty-year socialist activity (from 1880 to 1920) in which he and his father had played such a big part.

Mussolini's opponents have spoken of the demagogy of the man to whom no other path remained but the wooing of the workers once the mainstays of his power—monarchy, army, industry—had deserted him. If we look at Mussolini's life as a whole we cannot share this opinion. The periods which are separated by eighteen years of fascism run too smoothly into each other, periods whose fundamental outlooks influenced even this fascism in the form of a moderation of its more radical potential. But does this justify us in saying, as has actually on occasion been said, that in his heart of hearts Mussolini always remained a socialist?

Such a statement suffers from the assumption that the term is unequivocal. For Mussolini was never a socialist in the academic sense: his impressionability, his temperament, led him even in his Marxist period to the very brink of what was permissible. Although in an external sense his Marxism prepared the later fascism as its complement and precondition, closer scrutiny reveals that it was inclined toward a sudden swing to fascism, and it is here that the uniquely symptomatic significance of the person of Mussolini lies. The most accurate comment we can make is that certain basic socialist feelings were from his early youth a definite legacy of his spirit: too weak to set him on the fixed course of a coherent life, too strong to avoid becoming powerful again at any time, in appropriate circumstances.

But even during this final period they do not by any means crowd out the points of the "fascist" disposition of his thought. The core of these points of disposition is shown once again to be the experience and glorification of war, of war per se: war is the great testing ground of the peoples, in it is revealed their inner composition. He brutally contrasts the German and Russian heroism at Vitebsk and Stalingrad with the shameful behavior of those Italian soldiers who surrendered Pantelleria without a struggle.[459] What else can he have in mind than the "corrupting elements which derive from those four million slaves whom Rome to its misfortune carried within its womb"?[460] For it was of those that he spoke, threateningly and accusingly, shortly before his fall, thereby at the end of his life also adopting *in toto* Hitler's political race doctrine. Yet this was simply an elaboration of those Pan-German theories he had disputed in his youth,[461] and it signified the rending of the nation, the discovery of which had once been the second great experience of his life.

All that was left to do now was to determine the race whose intellectual leadership had unleashed the great revolt of the slaves and which bore the responsibility for all the world's ills: he would then be walking entirely in Hitler's footsteps. It was no mere chance that at least until the beginning of the war Mussolini had kept aloof from this thesis. After all, his whole existence was a single living refutation of this theory. It is true that during the war he did, like Hitler, speak of the world sickness caused by demoplutocracy and Judaism, a sickness which must be cured by fire and the sword.[462] Yet the measures of his final period, only as sporadic utterances,[463] indicate that Mussolini's most recent views could exist side by side with the renascent former ones, just as his fascination with Nietzsche had once existed side by side with Marxist radicalism. Thus an *Ispettorato Generale della Razza* was created and entrusted to Giovanni Preziosi, who might be called the Italian Rosenberg. The only reason Mussolini and Preziosi were spared having to answer the question of whether they would not shrink from the final practical consequences was because they had no autonomy in this field.

How powerful "fascism" had remained as an element in Mussolini is also shown by his final attitudes toward communism. They were frequently filled with a note of triumph at the victory of this "antiliberal and antidemocratic" doctrine, but more than anything they revealed sheer, unconcealed envy of the standardized newspaper and standardized radio. However, all this is merely a reflection of ultimate defeat; a deep insight into the mysterious proximity and distance between Mussolini and Lenin is not discernible in Mussolini himself.

Finally, the new myth, which Mussolini undertook to create at a very early stage, operated entirely according to traditional fascist ideas. The dire position into which the king had brought the monarchy and the country, first through collaborating with fascism and then through the delayed capitulation, offered an excellent starting point for apologia and attack. It was to this that Mussolini's last book [464] and numerous articles in *Corrispondenza Repubblicana* were dedicated: nostalgia for fascism would grip the masses soon enough, and a longing for the days "when the flag of the *patria* waved from the Alps to the Somalian equator and the Italian people was one of the most respected people on earth."[465] His strange preoccupation with self, which had gone on increasing through the years and which prompted him to make the absurd claim that the antifascist parties in southern Italy were imitating the socialization program of the RSI,[466] led him to attempt, in the face of all his mistakes, his failure, his complete collapse, to bind the Italians even for the future to the most foolish of all fascist maxims: *Mussolini aveva ragione*[467] (Mussolini was right).

We must accord utmost value to the statements which Mussolini made shortly before his death. For a year and a half he had been little more than a prisoner; now at last he spoke quite openly to a few close friends, and what erupts from him with the greatest force is his hostility toward the Germans. At first it is, of course, a hostility toward those who opposed his plans for socialization, who ignored his proposals, who without either political or strategic imagination carried on a war which under his leadership, he felt, would have been won.[468] But from his criticism of the present emerges an earlier aversion, a deeper criticism, directed at the German "nature" as such, and ultimately at the anti-European and unimaginative "will to power" which he had stigmatized as long ago as 1914. In the face of fascism, not to mention the first and most powerful champion of the orientation to the north, the reasoning certainly seems strange: "How in fact could one speak of a united Europe with an explosive and unsatisfied Germany?"[468]

But this is not the only memory which seemed to have been forgotten only to rise again in force. More surprising still is the following idea which, in the midst of a "testament" of apologia, he confided to a journalist on April 30, 1945: "If the vicissitudes of this war had been favorable to the Axis, I would at the moment of victory have proposed world socialization to the Führer, that is: frontiers of an exclusively historical nature ... uniform currency ... the real and radical abolition of all armaments. ..."[470] It is not our task here to examine what Mussolini had in mind when he made these naïve statements and whether he may have made them for some definite purpose. The very fact *that* he made them shows that the internationalism of his youth was not after all simply a whim which vanished without trace, that the *finalità* of Marxism had evidently lived on in him, although unconsciously.

But in glaring contrast with this pacifist trend is the much more passionate, more frequently reiterated conviction that only the warrior was a man,[471] while no mention is ever made of an idea.

It was precisely three ideas, however—hostility toward Germany, Marxist socialism, the inevitability of war—which in their incompatibility touched off the first and most momentous conflict in Mussolini, that of 1914. Thirty years later they still stand side by side in his spirit, less reconciled than ever, although transformed. These are the ideas which in the hour of death entwine once again and pervert each other.

After the collapse of the final negotiations, he said a few despairing and courageous words, in the courtyard of the Milan prefecture, to the handful of Blackshirts and senior functionaries who were still with him: "We shall reach the Valtellina to take up our positions for the last desperate defense: to die with the sun in our faces, our eyes turned to the mountain peaks, the last smile of our native land."[472]

But after that he did not show much determination. In the end he and his men joined a German column going north along Lake Como. They were stopped by partisans near Dongo, the Germans were allowed to continue, the Italians were arrested[473] without offering any resistance. Finally a suspicious-looking man was pulled down from a German truck—someone had thrown a German military greatcoat around him and put a steel helmet on his head. It was Mussolini. War laid hands on the enemy of the Germans in German garb, and the warrior neither tried to resist nor sought a defiant death. Someone called out to him from the crowd of partisans: "Why did you betray socialism?"[474] All the elements which had determined his life returned to confront him, and he failed every one of them.

The final hours passed in apathy and sleep. The death he died was little else but a murder, and yet it was a subtle mercy. He died the death of warriors and revolutionaries, although he had actually been neither. But the fact that his intellectual and nervous sensibility detected and experienced war and revolution as the basic reality of his time long before they emerged in force, renders all the more representative a man who traversed all the political ideas and positions of his age. Of these, fascism was the most important for the world, but hardly the closest to his own heart.[475]

CHAPTER TWO

The Fixed Doctrine

The history of fascism must be viewed simultaneously with the history of Mussolini's intellectual development. Only in this way does its doctrine emerge in its wealth of variation, its contradictions, its insights derived from living experience, but above all in its constant interplay with concrete political situations. However, it must not be ignored that Mussolini himself attempted a definition, in an article in the *Enciclopedia Italiana*.[1] This article was later reproduced innumerable times as *Dottrina del fascismo* and was always given canonical status.

We cannot attempt a thorough description and interpretation here; it is enough to select a few basic characteristics to show to which type of interpretation of fascism this alleged ideological foundation belongs.

The section on history offers an important verifiable clue. Here, to describe his early development, Mussolini refers to Sorel, Péguy, Lagardelle, to Olivetti's *Pagine Libere* and Paolo Orano's *Lupa*. The Mussolini we find here is the "revolutionary syndicalist," that romantic and fashionable figure whose hazy, nebulous shape was the very thing to delight the middle-class world of Europe. There is no mention of intransigent Marxism, not even of those men who had a marked influence on the young Mussolini: Nietzsche and Bergson. This is the Mussolini who did his best to suppress the only more-or-less reliable description of his youth—the book written by his former friend Torquato Nanni—because it "was not really necessary at that time for everyone to know my past as an iconoclast."[2] If we substitute "Marxist" for iconoclast it is easy to understand why for twenty years no one was permitted to borrow the bound volumes of *Avanti!* or *La Lotta di Classe* from Italian libraries. Fascism might be described as that movement which lacked the courage to acknowledge its real prehistory. The less courage displayed, we might continue, the nearer the interpretation in question approaches the academic pattern.

The nature of this pattern consists in applying traditional concepts of academic philosophical discussion (form, matter, self-awareness, fulfillment, freedom, state) to fascism. The result is that the historical essence and the compromise nature of fascism vanish in the beauties of an a priori construction, while by the same token it is stripped of all that is unfamiliar and threatening and is introduced to the cultural establishment as its own youngest offspring.

This is quite clearly the pattern when Sergio Panunzio says: "Just as there is no material without form, and form without material is empty, so syndicalism cannot be understood without corporatism, and the latter cannot exist without the former."[3] Giovanni Gentile's definition is similar in essence: "Fascism does not face liberalism as the system of authority faces the system of liberty, but rather as the system of true and concrete liberty faces the system of abstract and false liberty."[4]

It is enough to cite a single sentence from the *Dottrina* for its proximity to this pattern to become strikingly apparent: "The fascist state ... is form, inner law and discipline of the whole person. It permeates will and intellect. Its principle, the central inspiration of the human personality dwelling in the civic community, penetrates to the depths and settles in the heart of the man of action as well as of the thinker, of the artist as well as of the scientist: as the spirit of the spirit."[5]

Those are certainly fine and impressive words. But they testify as little to the specific form of the fascist state, to its relationship to the peculiar reality of the party, to the concrete situation of the intellectual aspect of man within his reality, as does the steady rain to the manifold activities in the room against whose window it is pattering. In adopting the Hegelian terminology via Gentile —infinitely more so in this work than anywhere else in his writings—Mussolini succeeds in producing a remarkable mystification, but he also separates fascism from its real spiritual significance (to be found in its relationship to Marx and Nietzsche) and restricts it to an earlier stage of the history of ideas. But this stage is lopped off too, robbed almost entirely of its relation to the concepts of civilization and freedom, with the result that actually all that remains is the founding of the strong state and the rejection of anarchy.

Wherever Hegelianism prompts Mussolini to express original tendencies, it appears only as the terminological guise of his "life-philosophy" ideas: thus the "spiritualistic" antithesis as against the economic materialism "of so-called scientific or Marxist socialism," which crudely contrasts the voluntarism of the youthful Mussolini with the merely popular conception of Marxism; thus also his refusal to eliminate the demoliberal nineteenth century from history in favor of de Maistre. "There is no going back" is one of the few phrases to which Mussolini remained faithful in every period of his life, and so he found easy access here to the Hegelian concept of synthesis. One cannot hold fast to this concept if one rejects the concept of "progress," nor can one overlook the fact that there is an innate tendency among Fascists to reach much further back into the past than only shortly before 1789. Mussolini is not told this by Giovanni Gentile but with all the greater conviction by Adolf Hitler, who wrote to him in 1941: "It often seems to me that in these fifteen hundred years the evolution of mankind has only suffered an interruption and is now once again about to return to former paths."[6] Nevertheless, there are already hints of Mussolini's hostility toward history wherever he speaks his own language without pretension. This occurs mainly in the section in which he attacks pacificism and which takes off from the romantic notion that only war places man on his own before the alternatives of life and death, thus leading him to the supreme test.

It is fascist style unadulterated by any philosophical formulas when Mussolini writes: "This antipacifist spirit is transported by fascism into the lives of individuals as well. The proud squadrist motto 'I don't give a damn' is an act of a philosophy which is more than stoical, the epitome of a doctrine which is more than political: inherent in it are the discipline to fight, the acceptance of dangers; it is a new style of Italian life."[7] It is not quite clear, however, how these maxims (if they are to be more than a mere ideology of boxing) are to be reconciled with the inevitable "everyday security" of the life of the citizen, with the opaque rationality of the modern world. But then Mussolini does not take seriously the contradiction between the subject of large-scale war, the state, and a superimposed system which deprives the state of freedom of action and autonomy: "That which is called crisis can only be resolved by the state and within the state."[8] Not many years later the world economic crisis was to show him how wrong he was. But it must be admitted that he knew how to transform the exigencies of this crisis into popular enthusiasm for the conquest of the *Impero.* Other "typically fascist" phrases—the need for a population policy, the state as will to power and rule, imperialism as a proof of vitality—also occur again and again in the less official writings, essays, and speeches.

Content and polemics, however, are only given their precise definition in the *Dottrina* by the commonplaces of conservatism. Before 1920 such expression and terms do not occur at all in Mussolini's writings, or, if they do, then only in isolated instances, whereas they are the very mainstay of this work.

Accordingly, fascist man does not lead a life apart from all others, independent, self-indulgently following the whim of the moment: instead he personifies "nation and *patria,* moral law which links individuals and generations together in tradition and vocation."[9] The stressing of the value of "tradition in memories, in language, in customs, in the rules governing social life"[10] sounds rather strange coming from the lips of the man who wanted to make Italy "unrecognizable" in ten years and whose dearest wish was the uprooting of three centuries of the Italian tradition of "servitude." Equally strange to those familiar with his development and temperament must have been the phrase "against all individualistic abstractions with a materialistic base, of the kind typical of the eighteenth century, and against all utopias and Jacobinic innovations."[11] It was precisely those familiar with his past, however, who were least able to overlook the fact that his criticism of a quantitative concept of democracy harmonized perfectly with some of his oldest ideas, although in such a way that this criticism is shifted here into a different context and is hence altered in meaning. When he stresses "the irremediable, fertile, and beneficent inequality of men,"[12] it sounds quite different from when in his youth he praises the *élite proletaria*, and it is just as surprising when he looks to Germany to substantiate his critique of liberalism, "the doctrine which seems foreign to the German spirit."[13] Yet still more characteristic of this work is the fact that there is only one writer from whom he quotes at length: neither Marx nor Nietzsche, neither Sorel nor Pareto, but Renan, to whom he ascribes a "premonition of fascism." The gist of the quotation concerns that fear vital to the self-criticism of liberalism—"vulgar democracy must, it seems, lead to the extinction of every refined culture and every higher discipline."[14] But there is in fact virtually no evidence for this fear in all the rest of Mussolini's works up to this time. Here lies one of the main differences in his mentality as compared to Maurras and Hitler, and presumably the chief reason for his lack of anti-Semitism. Nevertheless, his adoption of conservative commonplaces should not be underestimated. It is a sign of the altered political and intellectual climate, and, in conjunction with Mussolini's impressionability, it is an indication of that evolution which will bring him closer to Maurras and even to Hitler.

The *Dottrina del fascismo* is not nearly as basic to the understanding of "fascism" as the *Enquête sur la Monarchie* or *Mein Kampf*. Its core is that vague "life-philosophy" of which Italian fascism may under certain aspects be taken to be the political expression, insofar as this philosophy is fixed and actuated by the far older conservatism. This explosive duality is swathed in the ceremonial garb of Hegelian terminology. However, this terminology is more than a mere superficial decoration since it is highly appropriate to the circumstance that both "life-philosophy" and conservatism appear without their most radical implications: the concept of the revolt of the slaves, the basic emotion of fear, and the motivation of anti-Semitism. The *Dottrina del fascismo* is a typical example of the compromise nature of Italian fascism and especially of its conservative academic interpretation; the beginnings of a more radical development are to be sought not in the fixed product but in the sum of its history.

CHAPTER THREE

The Irksome Precursors

If it were permissible to make the relationship to precursors the sole criterion in comparing political trends, it would be impossible to imagine a greater contrast than that between the Action Française and Italian fascism. On the one hand a continual quoting and invoking; on the other a brusque dismissal of "old philosophers and senescent young philosophers in search of precursors and pioneers."[1] Here, eyes turned proudly toward a long series of famous names; there, unremittingly, only the verbal praise of a single author of merely local importance. Here, profound knowledge; there, at best a few superficial backward glances.

However, it is no use trying to explain this situation by saying simply that we are comparing a forward-looking dynamism with a static way of thinking addicted to the past. The young Mussolini was also "dynamic" and yet was possessed of a very alert and extensive historical awareness. The reasons why Italian fascism is in an even more difficult position in relation to its precursors than to its own early history are to be found in the nature of the Italian national tradition.

In Italy there did not exist two mortally opposed currents of thought: the only politically fertile tradition was the Risorgimento which, although complex in itself, was felt to be primarily a unity. Only an absurdly reactionary, that is, temporal, Catholic party would have been able to adopt a position of open hostility to the Risorgimento. Every other party, even nationalist and fascist, had to find accommodation in its ship. But, like Scylla and Charybdis, a truth and a necessity threatened the ship and its passenger, and both were formulated by Mussolini with great clarity.

On July 14, 1918, in Genoa, Mussolini celebrated the storming of the Bastille and said of the heroes of the Risorgimento: "They were all ... the heirs to the immortal ideas of the French revolution."[2]

Shortly after January 3, 1925, he addressed the following directives to the management of a fascist periodical: "We must fight democracy above all in its social and philosophical principles which derive from the overexploited French revolution."[3]

A lesser dilemma follows the first and basic one. Were not Mazzini and Garibaldi republicans? What attitude were the now monarchic Fascists to adopt toward this republicanism? Perhaps the ever-increasing glorification of ancient Rome was simply an attempt by the Fascists to forget the stranglehold which drove them to an impossible denial, thereby forcing them to maintain a position of compromise without greatness.

There are three ways of dealing with such a dilemma. The conflict can be reinterpreted as a dialectic relationship of evolution, by saying, perhaps, that only in fascism had the immature "democratism" of the Risorgimento grown into "true" democracy. The validity of the first of Mussolini's two sentences can be questioned, and it can be claimed that actually the Risorgimento had nothing to do with democracy and liberalism. And finally, the conflict can be accepted and the irksome but valuable connection dissolved.

All three possibilities are to be found in Mussolini's thinking, at least in rudimentary form. The simplest one, at any rate the most suitable for major speeches, appears to be the first.

No antithesis exists between Garibaldi and the Blackshirts, but rather a "historical and ideal continuity," he declared in December, 1923,[4] and soon afterward he persuaded the militia that it was making the dream of the Risorgimento come true.[5]

Before all the world Mussolini maintained this claim in the great chamber speech on the Lateran treaties: "Not only do we not deny the Italian Risorgimento, but we complete it."[6] On this occasion the attempt "of certain Catholic circles" to put the Risorgimento on trial encountered sharp disapproval. Mussolini implied that the weakness of the Risorgimento was that it represented the work of tiny minorities. Fascism is thus made to appear a kind of repetition of the Risorgimento on a higher and more extensive level.[7]

The unveiling of a monument to Anita Garibaldi in 1932 offered an opportunity for a solemn reaffirmation of this thesis. Before the massed Garibaldians in their red shirts Mussolini declared: "The Blackshirts who knew how to fight and die during the years of humiliation, are politically also on the ideal line of the Redshirts and their leader."[8]

That there must be many aspects contradicting this interpretation is clearly shown by the fact that Mussolini had to call upon no less a person than the *Quadrumvir* De Vecchi to head the authoritative periodical *Rassegna storica del Risorgimento*, with specific instructions to look at things "through fascist eyes."[9] The periodical, he declared soon after, was a professorial meeting-place of the old days; "from many points of view" fascism was the continuation of the movement which in the nineteenth century had unified the *patria*, and was destined to endow it with power in the twentieth.[10]

It becomes evident here that Mussolini does not really consider "continuation" to be "evolution" but that he is closer to the second possibility and is inclined to separate the "aspects" of the Risorgimento. This is quite according to Maurras' method, and since it is applied again to representatives of critical liberalism it promises equal success. For instance, Mazzini's passing criticism of France and of the individualism of the revolution is emphasized out of context in order to erase the memory of his far more fundamental affinity to the "world" of the French revolution. It is in this sense that Mussolini maintains that Mazzini and Garibaldi were not liberals, that the Risorgimento had nothing to do with liberalism and democracy.[11]

But the potentially hostile implications for the Risorgimento must not be overlooked when he calls liberalism and democracy "two imports that we have digested badly";[12] for after all, it was hardly the pope and the Bourbons who financed these imports. To a movement that aspires to be the "complete, categorical, definitive antithesis" to the whole world of the French revolution,[13] the proximity of the Risorgimento must be irksome and compromising.

Hence there were good reasons for Salvatorelli's term "Anti-Risorgimento" becoming a key word in antifascist polemics.[14] And there was a fascist faction which made no attempt to disarm this accusation by subtle differentiations, but instead radicalized it and made of it a virtue. Curzio Malaparte's concept of ascism as "Counter Reformation" follows this trend,[15] the title of Asvero Gravelli's[16] periodical *Anti-Europa* speaks for itself, and Giulio Evola[17] goes back furthest of all: for him anti-Semitism and anti-Christianism are essential to the liberating return to "pagan imperialism."

This is a form of common European radical conservatism, which is an ingredient of all forms of fascism and which is somewhat in evidence also in Mussolini.[18] However, in Italy it existed mainly on a literary level. In the majority of his official utterances, the Duce was closer to that other pole of fascist ideology, to Giovanni Gentile's academic interpretation that fascism, "in harmony with the teachings of Mazzini, is the most perfect form of liberalism and democracy."[19]

Both these poles should be borne in mind when trying to plumb fascist ideology. But there is nothing specifically Italian about them; and if Mussolini's punctual thinking remained dependent on them as ideological guides, it is also true that their expression in the reality of fascist Italy was completely dependent on the will of the Duce and his trend of thought of the moment. It was not in its theory that the Fascist party exerted its strongest impact on Mussolini, but in the basic structure of its practice.

CHAPTER FOUR

Practice as Premise

Up to the March on Rome

The fact that fascist thinkers so frequently proclaimed the priority of action over doctrine is merely the reflection of the strange circumstance that, apart from Mussolini's opinions and intentions, Italian fascism always remained tied to certain primary actions. These were not commanded by nor did they derive from a firm organization, but they nevertheless revealed a certain outward appearance which evolved far more autonomously and convincingly than any doctrinal position. To some extent, therefore, in fascism, practice actually preceded the organization, not to mention the motivation of a central direction. But it goes without saying that this practice was not an *actus purus* but rather the reaction to certain situations on the part of a group of people thinking and feeling along the same lines. The situation which generated Italian fascist practice was the revolutionary unrest of the postwar days in Italy, or "bolshevism." This ferment threatened economic, moral, and intellectual positions which cannot be adequately described as "bourgeois." For it presented a multiplicity of aspects and could still be regarded as a phase of the antifeudal revolution. Consequently the parties of the middle classes sought to differentiate, to exploit, to direct. The least bourgeois fringe areas of the middle classes, on the other hand, former officers or elite soldiers and students, were by nature most inclined to identify everything revolutionary as Bolshevik and to eliminate it by frontal attack, although in such a way that they laid claim to the "actual" and "true" revolution for their activities.

Thus by the practice of its beginnings fascism is far more in line with an undifferentiated antibolshevism than Mussolini's convictions warrant, and certain characteristics of its practice constitute an element which is the least dependent on its history but in turn determines this history more than any other.

More typical of fascist practice, of greater consequence for the fascist future than the carefully prepared programmatic founding assembly of March 23, 1919, were the spontaneous events which occurred three weeks later in Milan.

On April 15, following upon a general strike of protest, two large rallies took place, that of the striking workers in the arena, and a counterdemonstration of "patriots" in the cathedral square. In agreement with the unions and the Socialist party, the workers resolved to resume work the following day; the anarchists withdrew from the meeting as a sign of protest; some young fellows and the usual rabble joined them, and they marched on the square. A few hundred patriotic demonstrators, most of them war veterans, met them head-on; these determined and experienced fighters quickly gained the upper hand over the confused and helpless mob, and four dead and thirty wounded were left lying in the street. Trained not to leave a victory unexploited, the demonstrators now marched on the *Avanti!* building, attacked it, destroyed furniture and machinery, and set fire to the rest. Victory was achieved, the enemy destroyed, but the victory celebrations were still lacking. So the column— "officers and soldiers of all arms, students, workers"[1]—marched behind the black flag of the Arditi and a few Italian tricolors to the headquarters of the *Popolo d'Italia*. There were shouts for Mussolini; when he appeared on the balcony the crowd gave him a "delirious ovation" and was not satisfied until he spoke a few words.

These events were clearly not organized, since at first they merely represented the reaction to an unpredictable action on the part of the adversary. But the immense advantage for the "patriots" consisted in the fact that the military sense of order and subordination was still as alive in them as the habit of counterattacking. In other words, it was something different from the disorganized spontaneity of most of the socialist and Communist demonstrations. There were undoubtedly a few men who immediately took the lead, the chief among them being the former Arditi captain, Ferruccio Vecchi,[2] who later boasted that his first work had not been a book but a deed—the destruction of the *Avanti!* Yet within this limitation it is permissible to speak of a spontaneous action of the crowd. There is no proof that Mussolini organized the demonstration or was even involved in it. But his newspaper had made itself the mouthpiece of the Arditi, and so his name became indissolubly linked with the first radical counterrevolutionary deed in Italy.

Reaction which goes far beyond its immediate cause and feels the need of singing its own praises and elevating itself—that is the basic manifestation of fascist practice: punitive expeditions with songs and banners.[3] It can dispense almost entirely with organization, and entirely with a central guiding impulse; but it requires accurately circumscribed prerequisites for it to function properly.

Not that organization was entirely absent from early fascism. The founding assembly had been content with appointing a *Guinta esecutiva* (including Mussolini, Vecchi, Michele Bianchi, Mario Giampaoli). Within a short time reports were assembled from propagandists who endeavored to cover all Italy with a network of *fasci*. Two commissions were appointed to promote this work, a *commissione propaganda e stampa* (including Mussolini, Marinetti, Bianchi) and a *commissione amministrativa* (of which the most important member was Giovanni Marinelli). The Guinta was soon replaced by a central committee, having an executive commission and a secretary-general (the first being Umberto Pasella). Ties between headquarters in Milan and the individual *fasci* throughout the country were loose; for the time being the lack of organization was made into a virtue, and the diversity in *fasci* and lack of statutes were proudly contrasted with "rigidly constructed and interwoven organizations."[4] At the first national congress in Florence (October, 1919), the number of Fascists was given as forty thousand, that of the constituted *asci* as one hundred, that of those in process of organization also as one hundred. A whole year later the number of *fasci* was no higher, although since the summer of 1920 Mussolini had spoken of a "proud development" of fascism; these figures should therefore be regarded with caution. In any case, the progress of fascism in the year and a half after its founding, in spite of some initial successes, was limited, the organization rudimentary, a central direction hardly existed, and there were no statutes whatever.

Fascism's only significant and striking position of power was the *Popolo d'Italia*; as late as mid-1920, Italian fascism, like the Action Française, was a movement centering entirely around a newspaper and one in which the managing editor of the paper held a dominating position which was not anchored institutionally within the framework of the party. The second factor to enhance Mussolini's position was that the Milan *fascio* was far and away the most important; the *fascio* of Ferrara, for example, had only forty members in the summer of 1920, and to the ordinary citizen it was no different from other clubs and small groups.

Generally speaking, fascism vegetated along almost to the end of 1920, with no strong organization, no noticeable leadership, no impressive style. The style was the first to show a remarkable evolution, but the impetus did not come from the ranks of the Fascists. It was from D'Annunzio's Fiume enterprise that they derived their *élan*, their fire, and their formulas. In the *città olocausta* the shared experiences of the Comandante and the many thousands of legionaries generated a new style of living and speech.

During the war the poet had already coined the battle cry *Eia, eia, eia, alalà!*; to this he now added the suggestive question addressed to the crowd: *A chi Fiume?* (or, *la forza? l'Italia?*), which was always followed by a unanimous *A noi! Gagliardetti* were carried in front of the legionary units, skulls and crossbones threatened from the black shirts of their uniforms. They all saluted with raised arms, wore daggers, and in their songs announced to the enemy government in Rome that they would storm the Quirinal with daggers and hand grenades, or else they sang:

> Our Bersaglieri with Ceccherini as our leader
> Will go to Cagoia [Nitti] and give him a bad time.[5]

Their armed units had disquieting and evocative names: *Disperata, Me ne frego*, and other similar ones. Chanting in unison they assured the Comandante of their loyalty and devotion:

> Whenever the Comandante desires,
> Wherever the Comandante desires!
> One for all, all for one.[6]

During great rallies, almost the entire population crowded into the square in front of the Comandante's palace (sometimes in formation so that their colored clothing spelled out letters for the benefit of aerial photos), and the poet's intoxicating words drove citizens and soldiers into a state of almost Dionysian ecstasy, so that the cry *Italia o morte!* echoed from a thousand voices over the gulf to the besieging troops on the opposite shore.

The Fascists were not long in appropriating these elements, and within the larger scope of the state as a whole and the social struggle they rendered them effective as never before. At the same time the revolutionary movement gave fascism its great chance. But the signal victories over the retreating enemy were not achieved along the lines of the spontaneous events in Milan. This was the hour of the local organizers.

Early May, 1920, saw the establishment of the first "action squads" (*squadre d'azione*) in Trieste, and with them fascism made an all-important discovery. The most suitable members of a *fascio* were combined into small units, equipped more or less primitively with weapons, and according to a prearranged plan put systematically into action against the "internal enemy." The directorate of the Trieste *fascio* (including Giunta), at that time the strongest in all Italy, was in charge of the whole operation. But when the actions spread rapidly throughout the whole area of Venezia Giulia, the individual *fasci* were quick to support each other without waiting for specific orders. It was here in this border zone with its nationality conflicts that the fascist squads were definitely regarded as citizens' militia and auxiliary police; this meant that their aggressive character was especially emphasized and, of course, it facilitated obtaining arms for them. Each *squadra* had its name, chosen with much care and devotion: *Disperata, Disperatissima, Lupi Neri*, and so on; each did its best to have its own *gagliardetto*, which it very soon began to regard as an object of worship (hence the demand for respect from fellow citizens). The favorite symbols on the *gagliardetti* included the lictor's bundle and the death's-head (*teschio*).

Many photographs exist of such squads (especially in Chiurco's books). They usually show a group of ten to twenty-five stern-faced men; more often than not they hold cudgels and attempt in some way to indicate uniform clothing. War veterans are plainly in the majority, but quite young faces constantly show up too. Professional men and officers are represented with conspicuous frequency, and often the total impression is that of a German students' corps. In the face of these pictures, Mussolini's aspiration to declare fascism a movement of the Left remains a mystery.

In a very similar manner the militant fascist movement in Bologna, and later in the other regions of Italy, arose and became a reality. In every case it could not get along without organization; but this organization was undertaken by the local chiefs without consulting Milan. Here the groundwork was laid for the powerful position of the *Ras*, some of whom retained their local power intact until the end of fascism (the prime example being Farinacci[7] in Cremona). Bologna made the black shirt popular—originally it had simply been the work shirt of the *braccianti* in Emilia, of those day laborers whose leagues had been destroyed by punitive expeditions and whose leaders had been killed or crushed. Bologna was also the first city[8] to celebrate the fascist victory with a demonstration in massive style, and it felt that the only proper way to crown this demonstration was by the presence of the man who alone of all Fascists already possessed a reputation: Mussolini. This demonstration of April 3, 1921, already exhibits all the characteristics of the fascist style and is hence worth looking at more closely.

In celebration of one political party, the flags of Italy flutter from every window in Bologna's main streets. According to reports which, though undoubtedly biased, are not untrustworthy, great masses of people with happy faces parade through the streets from early in the morning. War veterans proudly wear their decorations. The sound of marching columns echoes unceasingly. From all sides songs are to be heard, and the cry of *Evviva l'Italia*. One train after another, filled with out-of-town Fascists, enters the station, while bands play a welcome. In the afternoon a great column is formed to fetch Mussolini. Twenty decorated automobiles form the head, followed by a battalion of three hundred cyclists flanked by motorcycles with sidecars. Next come four battalions on foot, each company bearing the name of a national hero and hailed enthusiastically by the crowd. When Mussolini's train enters the station, the sounds of "Giovinezza" ring out, all the *gagliardetti* and flags are waved in his honor. From ten thousand throats an *Alalà* soars to the sky. With a maneuver of lightning swiftness the *Compagnia Mussolini* surrounds the car in which the Condottiere and those accompanying him take their seats. Rank upon rank of units of Fascists join the procession. From every house, from every sidewalk, bursts forth the wild enthusiasm of the people. Mussolini is hailed as *Duce* and *Salvatore d'Italia*. The great bell resounds from the Palazzo d'Accursio, and in the wide square, standing in the car, Mussolini reviews his marching troops.[9]

It would be ridiculous, of course, to assume that "all" Bologna welcomed Mussolini in this manner; not many months before the majority had voted Socialist. But it would be even more ridiculous to believe that the terrorist actions of a few hundred men could have created a complete "climate" of enthusiastic approval. Deep feelings must have been wounded—and not only powerful interests threatened—for a party to encounter so much applause which six months earlier had been known to only a few people. Bologna had been Italy's "Moscow": here in the presence of the mayor the "Soviet" had been proclaimed, here the national flag was not permitted to wave. Now on the heels of the impossible revolution of the proletariat came the possible counter-revolution of the threatened. In it the fascist style was formed, and it was never more genuine. Here in elemental force the wave surged up on which fascism was to ride and which it was later constantly forced to evoke artificially. For this style has its own laws. The party which desires to make use of it must never again lag behind it.

And that is why an acute observer might have told Mussolini in advance that he was bound to lose his fight with Grandi and the other *Ras*, because a party of this kind can never be satisfied with being one of many and merely making its opponent "see reason." However, Grandi might also have seen that this style positively demanded *one* man on whom all honors must be heaped and in whom all faith must be placed. If Grandi was right with his trend toward totality, so was Mussolini with his emphasis on the party (although this was not developed until later), that is, to central direction and discipline.

The first noteworthy results of Mussolini's influence as a leader were the program and statutes of December, 1921, which were ratified by the Congress of Rome. They are also the still incomplete but basic essentials for the development of the Duce's party. For this reason they too merit attention.

This *Statuto-Regolamento Generale del Partito Nazionale Fascista* named as the actual organ of leadership the central committee which was composed of party leaders and a representative from each region in Italy. It was regarded quite democratically as the "direct expression of the will of the organized," by whom it had been elected at the national congress. It culminated upward in the head of the directorate and in particular in the secretary-general; while down-ward each regional representative watched over those provincial units which were contained in each region. The directorate was composed of eleven members including the secretary-general.[10] The statute says nothing of rank within the directorate, nor does it mention a "Duce"; in practice, of course, Mussolini's name was always mentioned first, and the fact that the faithful Michele Bianchi was secretary-general confirmed his position of power.

The building stones of the organization were the individual *fasci*, which could be formed as sections of the party wherever membership numbered twenty or more. They also had a directorate and a political secretary. They were under orders of strict discipline; but the regulation, frequently emphasized, that the formation of *fasci* had to be reported is an indication of the degree of independence they had hitherto enjoyed. Within one province, all *fasci* had to unite in provincial federations. These also had a directorate and a political secretary (the latter subsequently becoming the famous *federale*, corresponding to the German *Gauleiter*).

The most typical feature of *fasci* structure is the fact that they were identical with the *squadre di combattimento*, at least nominally. Each *fascio* formed one *squadra* (or more) from among its members. The dividing of "squadrists" into *principi* and *triari* (reserves) took place according to differences in age and physical ability, although in principle there was no difference between the party and its fighting units; thus the Italian Fascist party was from the very beginning far more thoroughly militarized than the German NSDAP. The squads were at first also organized "from below," according to democratic principles: the members elected their commanders. Each squad had its own *gagliardetto*; squads were ultimately subordinate to an *Ispettorato Generale* within the office of the secretary-general. (This resulted in a strange duplication in the party command; the most conspicuous instance of this was during the March on Rome.)

Another very strange phenomenon within the framework of the single *fasci* was the so-called *Gruppi di competenza*. These included those who were engaged professionally in the principal public institutions (railway, postal service, street-car system, power companies, waterworks, and so forth), as well as other specialists. The ulterior motive was, of course, the breaking of strikes; for this institution there is likewise no parallel in the National Socialist party.

The women (*Gruppi femminili*), the students (*Gruppi universitari*), and the youth (*Avanguardie giovanili fasciste*) belonged directly to the party, which was not the case in Germany. Taken as a whole, the *Statuto-Regolamento Generale* is undeniably that of a party which intends "to govern Italy." If in the original manifestation of fascist practice the trend toward expansion and evolution was unmistakable, it also suggested an organization which assumed tasks that would normally be the concern of the state alone. No great perception is required to foresee that the democratic components of this statute were relics of its chaotic beginnings and would soon have to make room for the expanded rights of the leadership.[11]

The area in which this development first became obvious was the "military sector." The *Direttive per l'organizzazione delle squadre fasciste* of early 1922 still corresponded to the statute and merely augmented it in many details.[12] However, the emphasis was already wholly on the hierarchic structure, which with the use of Roman terms corresponded largely to that of the army. Each *squadra* (from twenty to fifty men) was divided into *squadriglie* of four men under a *caporale*, four squads formed a *centuria* under the command of a *centurione*, four centuries were a cohort under a *seniore* (major), and finally from three to nine cohorts formed a legion commanded by a *console* (colonel). Of critical importance is the fact that all ranks were elective, except that senior officers could only be elected by other officers.

Within a few months the *Regolamento di disciplina per la Milizia fascista* (early October, 1922)[13] laid much greater stress on rank and eliminated elective status entirely. The members of the militia were obligated to a "blind, respectful, absolute obedience" toward their superiors. They were required to carry out their duties with "profound mysticism" and were instructed specifically to strive for absolute justice, "also outside of, and always within, the written and formal law." What absolute justice meant could be seen in the fact that all were condemned who, out of false humanity, did not proceed against Italy's internal enemies on the basis of an eye for an eye, a tooth for a tooth, and that traitors were threatened with "the most severe sanctions." Thus this group of armed men created their own moral and penal laws and set them up with barely veiled emphasis against the laws of the state. It is not surprising that they had their own decorations (gold medals, decorations for wounds, and so forth) and salutes (such as, to the *gagliardetti*), that the high command had its own *fogli d'ordine* (official gazettes), and that it finally divided Italy up publicly into military zones. In such a climate the democratic election of leaders could no longer flourish, hence the specific statement: "The chiefs are chosen and assigned to the units of the fascist militia by the higher ranks. ..."[14]

Such was the state of affairs shortly before the March on Rome. Nothing seems more obvious than that a state which sees a parastate organism growing within itself must either cut it out or be conquered by it, like someone with cancer. But the strange thing was that a general stood at the head of this organization, and the state itself had donated its lifeblood to the organization by encouraging its officers to take a leading part in it, or at least not preventing them from doing so.[15]

The difficulties encountered by Italian fascism in expanding in the trade-union field were naturally infinitely greater. It is true that Mussolini had proclaimed a *Sindacalismo Nazionale* at a very early stage, and that he had many friends among the leaders of the smallest of the three trade-union organizations, the *Unione italiana del Lavoro*, in particular Edmondo Rossoni; but as late as the latter part of 1921, fascism had almost no success to show in this field, until Rossoni left his old organization and devoted himself wholly to constructing a fascist syndicalism. Far more revealing than the speeches at the congresses was the creation of the first fascist syndicate.

The scene of this story, as told by Chiurco,[16] was the village of S. Bartolommeo in Bosco in the province of Ferrara, which at the beginning of 1921 was still Red. Here, after his return from the front, Alfredo Giovanni Volta, a war veteran and the son of a landowner, had been boycotted by the local League; however, he had entered into battle with the League and sent it a formal "declaration of war." He began by forming a combat group with some other veterans. Pressure by the boycott forced this group to dissolve. Somewhat later Volta replaced it by a monarchist group called *Patria e Libertà*. This also fell victim to the League's animosity. The young man's third attempt was the founding of a *fascio*. Meanwhile the general situation had changed, word of the deeds of the Fascists had spread throughout the country, dissatisfaction with the League came to light. Now the law itself proceeded vigorously against the *Capolega*, Volta and his followers triumphed: the League was turned into a *Sindacato fascista*, retaining its headquarters, its hierarchy, its personnel; only the flag and the leadership were changed.

Similar events occurred in 1921 in countless places. The fascist offensive removed the executives of the local trade-union organizations, and the leaderless masses put themselves, so to speak, under the "protection" of the Fascists, whose only remaining task now was that of *inquadramento*. History makes the conditions necessary for fascist syndicalism abundantly clear. Fascist syndicalism was the result of a battle waged by nontrade-union forces; it presupposed the passivity of the organized from the very start, a passivity which was achieved in the militia only after bitter fighting.[17]

Fascism showed a great deal more imagination in the development of its style. Mussolini had long ago stressed the importance of the "choreographic and picturesque side."[18] That which in April, 1921, in Bologna had still to a great extent been a spontaneous upward surge following upon extraordinary events, was a year and a half later in Cremona a well-staged theatrical performance, capable of being repeated at any time, with uniforms (even for women), solemn consecration of flags,[19] parading of columns with raised arms before the saluting Duce, roll call of the fallen (*Appello dei martiri*), and finally the glorification of Mussolini (*nostro amato capo e maestro*).[20] The degree of calculating knowledge and cool manipulation of emotional material already in existence in the top leadership is evident from a remark made by Mussolini at about that time: "Democracy has deprived the life of the people of 'style': that is, a line of conduct, the color, the strength, the picturesque, the unexpected, the mystical; in sum, all that counts in the soul of the masses. We play the lyre on all its strings: from violence to religion, from art to politics."[21]

Of course, Mussolini was by no means the inventor of this side of the picture. He did not even, as did Hitler, design badges and flags. What was at the bottom of this position of leadership which, after the great crisis, he managed to re-create for himself in such a short time, and which permitted him in the summer of 1922 to issue orders of a very far-reaching kind to the *Ras*, although he was only nominally the creator of the movement and delivered major speeches to the people on relatively rare occasions only? Apart from an unaccountable personal superiority and his ability to fascinate, there are three main reasons: his capacity of managing editor of the oldest and most important party newspaper, his leading role in the party's parliamentary faction, and the purely local ambitions of most of the *Ras*. It would be quite wrong to imagine the leadership motivation which flowed from Mussolini to the party as total or even merely dictatorial. Centralization was inherent in the force of circumstance itself, and in its practical implementation it was largely the work of Balbo and

Bianchi. Every outstanding event of the year 1922 was planned and directed by others, including even the March on Rome.

If we consider the scope already achieved by the organization in the meantime (*scuola di propaganda e cultura fascista* in Milan, cavalry and air force units, local fascist secret police, and so on), we are justified in maintaining that, at the time of the seizure of power, Mussolini could certainly be regarded as the supreme commander of his party, but that the party was nevertheless more powerful than he, since owing to its structure it was moving in a more clearly recognizable and totalitarian direction.

After the Seizure of Power (to 1931)

Although it might be claimed that October 28, 1922, was not a crucial date for Mussolini's political concepts, it is nevertheless true that for the party the March on Rome meant the beginning of a new period. The processes which determined the party over the next few years can be most readily described as detachment, expansion, and hierarchization.

The party detached itself from groups with which it had hitherto lived in a certain symbiosis, for instance the Freemasons. It is a proof of the "national" character of Italian Freemasonry as well as of fascism's initial proximity to liberal thinking that, according to trustworthy reports, fascism was supported by the Freemasons with large sums of money, and that, at least until 1923, no less than five Freemasons were members of the Fascist Grand Council.[22] But friendship with the church was more important, and thus Mussolini could demonstrate political coherence to himself in the required manner by decreeing early in 1923 the incompatibility of membership in the PNF and Freemasonry. The Grand Council members in question yielded. For the once powerful Italian Freemasons, this decision amounted, practically speaking, to a sentence of death.

The liberals, who had supported fascism so staunchly, were very soon forced to make a choice. Giovanni Gentile, who had entered Mussolini's government while still a liberal, soon went over to fascism; the great majority of those liberals who in the 1921 elections had been elected on the roster of the *blocco nazionale*, were not renominated in 1924; the few remaining candidates could only be looked upon as figureheads and fellow travelers. The three influential ex-presidents, Giolitti, Orlando, and Salandra, did not, it is true, go over to the opposition until after November 1924 (although not to the Aventine);[23] but to all intents and purposes Italian fascism's separation from its liberal foster parents was complete by 1924.

Relations with the nationalists were clarified still earlier and even more radically. Although we are justified in speaking of nationalism's ideological victory over the still undefined and groping fascism, the nationalists' organization was nevertheless taken over lock, stock, and barrel in a fusion (at the beginning of 1923) which was nothing less than an annexation. Not even *L'Idea Nazionale* continued to exist; a short time later it was merged with the *Tribuna*.

1923 also saw the elimination of a partnership which in this case consisted only of government collaboration—that with the Popolari. Even before the murder of Matteotti, the Fascist party had extricated itself from most of those vague relationships which were typical of its youth: it had acquired unmistakable contours.

Naturally this process of detachment was not a total one, nor, on account of the preconditions, was this possible. Hand in hand with it went a marked orientation toward the stronger and older social forces: the monarchy (the army), the church, major industry. This orientation does not signify a loss of independence, rather it manifests a willingness to compromise. The willingness to compromise was quite plain at all stages in the chief areas of fascist expansion.

The establishment of the militia (*Milizia Volontaria per la Sicurezza Nazionale*, MVSN) sprang from one of the most inexorable needs of the fascist regime;[24] at the same time it represented a truly alarming advance into an area which seemed to be the preserve of the army. Beside the few hundred thousand soldiers there was now a (nominally) greater number of armed and organized men, with their own supreme command and their own uniforms, men who, moreover, swore allegiance only to the party leader and the head of government. However, the army was reassured by the fact that almost all the militia officers were army reserve officers, and more importantly the regulations provided for the "absorption" of the militia into the army in the event of mobilization. Hence the militia was an invaluable means of taking care of supernumerary officers, particularly as it displayed only minor efforts toward having its own officer-training courses and, most important of all, it was not housed in barracks. The rudiments of an independent and potentially dangerous development seemed insignificant. There were, for instance, the *Moschettieri di Mussolini*, a unit which saw to guarding the Duce, but there were also in growing numbers the *Battaglioni CCNN* (*Camicie Nere*), which in the early days were at the disposal of the military command as a kind of light-infantry unit. Two legions of professional Blackshirts fought in Libya as a *Milizia Coloniale*; in addition a whole series of special militia were set up (*Milizia Forestale, Stradale, Confinaria, Ferroviaria, Postelegrafonica, Portuaria, Universitaria*).

The reason why the beginnings of a trend which might threaten the army did not emerge more strongly until the early thirties is to be found, on the one hand, in the basic conditions of the peace period (in National Socialist Germany there were likewise until the outbreak of the war only the rudiments of the *Waffen-SS*), and on the other, in the effects of the Matteotti crisis, which forced Mussolini to require the militia to swear allegiance to the king and to put a commanding general of the army (for the time being) at its head. Hence, although the form of the militia was the outcome of a dual compromise, it soon became clear that it was far more than an auxiliary political police for the suppression of revolutionaries.

Fascist syndicalism was also ambivalent. Rossoni had appropriated the old plans for creating *sindacati misti* (mixed syndicates) and as a result wished to combine employers and employees in one single great *Confederazione*. For obvious reasons the industrialists, who had organized themselves in the *Confederazione dell'Industria* with great skill and power, were against this proposal. Mussolini decided in their favor. Practically speaking, fascist corporatism meant forcing the employees to accept fascist functionaries as their representatives, and welding this representation with the virtually unaltered representation of the industrialists by means of government intervention. That this placed all the advantages on the side of the employers is not hard to see. And indeed nothing was heard of any resistance from their side, whereas the fascist employees' syndicates had to be promoted with the most extraordinary devices, for example by distinguishing between "legally recognized" and "*de facto* existing" organizations, while only the legally recognized (that is, fascist) trade unions were given the right to conclude collective agreements binding on all. Thus compulsion and inducement[25] were forged into a weapon which not even the once powerful CGL was able to withstand. In this way Mussolini freed Italy from all labor disputes. Why would the industrialists not have supported him? And yet the system which seemed so convenient, which dried up not only the source of social unrest but also the wellspring of progress and control within capitalist methods of production, also contained immediate grave dangers for the captains of industry. For in actual fact it was not "the state" but the party, and ultimately Mussolini, to whose power of arbitration they were subjected. Hence the struggle among the various influences did not cease, although it was withdrawn from the public eye. There was always a left wing in the party, and Mussolini seldom refrained from "antibourgeois" utterances. Only the war deprived the more observant industrialists of an answer to their apprehensive question, whether they had not driven out the devil with Beelzebub.[26]

It is not impossible that Mussolini's yielding to the church had to do with a change in his beliefs, although his basic lack of religious faith can scarcely be doubted.[27] Already a necessary condition to the seizure of power, this yielding was accentuated by Gentile's school reform which handed over the elementary schools largely to the church, and it was completed by the Lateran treaties. But Mussolini did not yield in the matter of training outside the schools; this was claimed *in toto* by the Fascist party: he tolerated no Catholic boy scouts outside of the *Balilla*. Nor did he give way in the question of church participation in the fringe areas of political life (Catholic Action), although he left it to the party secretary Giurati to issue dire threats and to revive "squadrism" for a short time.[28] Under these circumstances it is hard to say who benefited the most from the Lateran treaties: if on the one hand the situation was such that even extremists did not equate *fascistizzazione* with de-ecclesiasticization, on the other the church presented no obstacle to the party's claim to embrace and educate the entire population along fascist lines. Not even during the stormy periods of the Matteotti crisis did the party desist from taking measures to develop its most recent organizations such as the *Balilla* and *Dopolavoro*.[29]

By early 1927 the party had got rid of all competitors on the political scene, and its organization was more or less stablilized. Around the hard core of the Fascisti and, in party eyes, of equal status, were the women's and youth organizations (*Fasciste, Avanguardisti, Balilla, Giovani Italiane, Piccole Italiane, Universitari fascisti*); these were followed—likewise directly dependent on party leadership—by the *Associazioni nazionali fascisti* (*pubblico impiego, insegnanti, ferrovieri, dipendenti industrie stato, postelegrafonici*); the outermost circle consisted of various trade unions, *Opera nazionale Dopolavoro, Istituto nazionale fascista di cultura*, and other similar bodies. These circles embraced virtually the entire population. The number of male party members at that time was slightly over eight hundred thousand. The significance of this figure is best seen from the fact that before the war even in the largest cities of Italy political associations seldom had more than a hundred members, and that even the Socialist party in its heyday after the war numbered hardly more than one hundred thousand members. It remained for fascism to create the first mass party organized from top to bottom.

The development of the internal structure of the party in the years after the March on Rome followed exactly the same course taken by the militia when it underwent its earlier transformation. On October 13, 1923, the Grand Council laid down new regulations[30] amounting to a complete hierarchization and centralization. Provincial secretaries did continue to be elected by local congresses, but now they required the Duce's ratification. In the same way the National Council (of the provincial secretaries) retained a certain right of proposal in regard to the party directorate (*proporrà una rosa di nomi*),[31] although the choice of the five members and hence of the secretary-general remained the prerogative of the Duce. Of even greater importance was the regulation that the directorate was not permitted to make any political decisions of importance without the Duce's prior authorization.

The leadership constitution was finally laid down in the statute published on October 12, 1926, which, to judge by its content, belongs among the *Leggi fascistissime*.[32] The preamble is typical and curious: it still calls fascism *una milizia al servizio della nazione* and defines the state of war as the norm of fascism, "primarily in order to crush those who stifle the nation's will; today and forever, to defend and develop the power of the Italian people."[33] The "original manifestation of fascist practice" is clearly to be retained, and even at that time the question must have leaped to the mind of the observer as to where the Fascists were to find that opposition which, in overwhelming reaction and to their own glory, they were supposed to crush. This statute stabilizes a powerful and mindless instrument which in the hand of its master can seek out stronger opponents than a few "social-communist dens" or a weak liberal state.

The provincial secretaries and their assembly, the National Council, lost all independent status; they were now appointed by the secretary-general of the party and became henceforth mere intermediate authorities. The entire stress now shifted to the Grand Council and thus to the Duce as its president. The Duce summoned the Grand Council and was free to choose a portion of the members as he pleased. Since those who were ex officio members of the Grand Council were also appointed by Mussolini by way of other channels, he actually directed the supreme organ like a puppet show, and it was not surprising that the party secretary soon started off the sessions with a kind of roll call and the members sprang to their feet shouting *Viva il Duce!*"[34] Hence, the fact that the Grand Council appointed the secretary-general (later, Secretary of the Party), the vice-secretaries, and the rest of the members of the party directorate, was an empty formula which, incidentally, was not to be accorded a very long life. The chain of command was now quite unequivocal: the Duce appointed (practically speaking) the party secretary, who summoned the provincial secretaries, who in turn appointed the secretaries of the individual *fasci*. The secretaries for their part had absolute authority over each directorate; only the name "secretary" recalled the early days, as did the regulation that the Fascists must be granted *ampia facoltà di discussione* at major assemblies. But these assemblies took place once a year, and apart from discussion participants had neither functions nor rights. Not right but duty was to be the Fascist's magic word, hence the new Fascist swore an oath of unqualified devotion: "I swear to follow without argument the orders of the Duce and to serve with all my strength and, if need be, with my blood the cause of the fascist revolution."[35] The extent to which the party identified itself with the state and even with the *patria* is shown by the most interesting and most ominous regulation in the statute, namely that anyone expelled from the party was a "traitor to his country" and must be removed from political life.

But in the next draft of the statute (of December 1929),[36] this regulation was changed in that the expression *vita politica* was replaced by *vita pubblica*. That could only mean what the boycott of the leagues had meant—the boycott against which fascism had gone to war on behalf of freedom of work and freedom of the human being—although on a far more universal scale. Never had there been anything comparable in civilized countries. But since the world had been accustomed to equate "terror" with mass murder, the Europe of that time failed to realize either the terroristic nature or the unprecedented quality of the formula.[37]

For the rest, this statute and the ensuing organizational phase were concerned merely with changes in the details of a given outline. The most notable was the reinforcement of the position of the party secretary, who henceforth became an ex officio member of some of the principal national committees and could also be summoned to sessions of the cabinet.[38]

It is a strange fact that the establishment of a hierarchy of the party structure, the depriving of power and disciplining of lower organs, are not attributable to a central will to power; on the contrary, the most emphatic demands on the part of the opposition during the Matteotti crisis had contributed so greatly to this process, namely, the demand for a normalization of conditions in the country, for an end to chaotic conditions in many provinces and to the arbitrary rule of the *alti commissari* and *fiduciari politici* of the party. In this context belongs Mussolini's famous circular to the prefects,[39] which has constantly been cited to attest to the priority of the state over the party in Italy. But although the establishment of *Gauleiter* rule was in the main prevented, it must not be forgotten that a considerable and steadily growing number of the prefects were party men themselves and thus did not represent the "state" at all in the traditional sense. It was not "state authority" which was being reinforced, but, in the final analysis, the position of the supreme state and party leader. On him alone depended which side of his dual nature would gain the upper hand in the future.

Chances were on the side of the party. The inherited rational nature of the state prohibited it from carrying on a boundless leadership cult. The party recognized no such handicap. And although during the Matteotti crisis Mussolini still made statements evincing an aloof and ironic attitude toward flattery, after January 3 he offered no further resistance to the currents of unashamed panegyrics which transformed him into a latter-day Midas at whose touch everything turned in retrospect to gold. Here too F. T. Marinetti had anticipated the future with clairvoyant instinct, and as early as the summer of 1925 had addressed Mussolini as *grande, invincibile Duce*.[40] It was not long before praise of the incomparable savior who "is always right" rang out from the ministries to the factories, from university rostrum to elementary school books,[41] covering with a stifling layer of pinchbeck what had once been the alert and critical awareness of the Italian people. Wherever Mussolini went, he was engulfed in the *ritmo cadenzato* of well-rehearsed choruses: "Duce, Duce, Duce!"; and it soon became impossible to imagine that this Caesar-like hero had once in prehistoric moderation been called, even while he was prime minister, simply *l'on. Mussolini* (Deputy Mussolini).

The party stage-managed the people at all ceremonial demonstrations, and the great memorial days of the movement—March 23 and October 28—had long since put the national victory celebration day of November 4 in the shade. By solemnly handing membership cards and rifles to its young members at the *Leva fascista*,[42] the party made a reality of that ceremonial and public swearing of allegiance by young recruits in which during the World War Mussolini had in a flash of insight glimpsed the design of a great future.[43] At official functions the party provided its symbols, the *gagliardetti*, with an escort of its own armed force, the militia: indeed, it even managed to ensure military salutes on the part of the national army for some of the most important among them.

Mussolini was well aware of the value of the party to him. He openly ridiculed the suggestions of the most moderate group among the Fascists that the party had fulfilled its tasks and hence could now be dissolved in the unified nation, and he praised the party as the *organizzazione capillare del regime* which penetrated everywhere and whose significance was fundamental.[44]

In actual fact, a state apparatus can be a willing and respectful servant to an outstanding leader—only a party such as the Fascist party and its leader can reciprocally confirm and spur each other on in irrational oscillation. And since the party had no will of its own vis-à-vis Mussolini, one might say that it was the stimulant with which Mussolini helped certain sides of his nature to overcome the others.

The Starace Era (1931–1939)

This situation became quite obvious in the Starace era (beginning in October, 1931). Whereas the previous party secretaries (Giunta, Farinacci, Augusto Turati, Giurati) had managed to maintain themselves up to a certain point as separate personalities as distinct from Mussolini, Achille Starace[45] was merely the servant of his master. As a reward he was permitted to be the undisputed master of the party, from which he succeeded in driving out the last vestiges of independent activity and initiative. It was probably for this very reason that matters progressed so smoothly along preconceived lines: the Starace era signified the peak of the party's expansion and influence, the consummation of the fascist style, the greatest efficiency of the impulse given by Mussolini.

Soon after Starace took office the party barrier was lifted, and many hundreds of thousands of new members streamed into the organization. From then on it almost ceased to be a distinction to belong to the party, while not to belong was a very palpable disadvantage. Party membership was made a requirement for the civil service, practically speaking even for all types of public and lucrative activity. (The small nucleus of party veterans managed, however, to create a number of special privileges for themselves, as a compensation, and these privileges were laid down in the best bureaucratic tradition in an *ordine di preferenza*.) Also, in line with the law of expansion, in 1937 all youth organizations were merged into a single state youth group, the *Gioventù Italiana del Littorio* (GIL), and within a short time membership was made obligatory by the *Carta della Scuola*.[46]

However, expansion did not take place solely in a quantitative sense; it showed itself just as much in an intensification of the demands made on the individual. As early as September, 1934, a law was enacted concerning pre-military training. This applied even to eight-year-old children[47] and later found expression in the "supreme commands" and "chiefs of staff" of the GIL. Increasing importance was also attached to the military and political training of adults; to this end the *Sabato fascista* was created and a record of performance kept in a *libretto personale di valutazione dello stato fisico e della preparazione del cittadino.*

In the militia, too, expansion was closely linked with intensification. Through the growth of *battaglioni d'assalto* into divisions, it was impossible to maintain either their former character of part-time activity or the old idea of the (individual) absorption of the militia by the army in case of mobilization. The "large militia units" thus became regular troops which fought in the army as separate groups. But during the Abyssinian war the ties already began to loosen, and it was possible to foresee that this unit would become an independent party instrument potentially aimed at the army. The famous *Colonna Celere* under the personal command of party secretary Starace carried out a remarkable action (the capture of Gondar) entirely under its own name and command. The Spanish war greatly enhanced this trend, the Blackshirts having to bear the brunt of this intervention. But although the militia had certain noteworthy privileges from the outset, such as the Roman salute (even to army officers), it still did not succeed in becoming a body of elite troops as important as the *Waffen-SS.* The reasons for this are complex and cannot be gone into here. Nevertheless, it can be said that as late as 1938 Italy was ahead of Germany in the development of a party army.

This is not true of the secret police. The former *polizia segreta fascista,* probably on account of its local limitations, had not really flourished. The name of the OVRA[48] was much more party-oriented than that of the Gestapo, yet it was headed by a government official (Bocchini), and it never became the personal instrument of a top party leader. Basically, however, an ideological distinction was expressed in the differences in police organization: since Italy was not a despotism of destruction the principal instrument of such a despotism could not develop.

To deduce from this that totalitarian pressure on the population was a lesser one, would be premature. What was important was the regimentation of intellectual life. The *Ufficio propaganda* was one of the oldest departments in the party secretariat; yet before it became, by way of a series of stages, the notorious Minculpop (*Ministero per la Cultura popolare*), Mussolini's initial hesitation to apply the same yardstick to art and philosophy as to political life had to give way to a will, untrammeled by scruples, to total *inquadramento.* The *Istituto fascista di cultura,* the overall organization of intellectuals in the broadest sense, had close to one hundred thousand members; and the characteristic fact that as late as March, 1943, Mussolini found it "scandalous" for a university newspaper to express itself favorably concerning Benedetto

Croce, speaks for the thoroughness of the work of the *Istituto* as effectively as a thousand details.[49]

What was lacking was certain institutions for the elite, such as party universities or political training schools, unless we wish to include Vito Mussolini's *scuola di mistica fascista*. Their place was taken by gymnastics and endurance tests for the "hierarchs," the value of which, if any, more often than not consisted of presenting a picturesque spectacle.

Expansion and intensification of party influence were just as evident at top government levels as among the people. The fact that the party secretary was given the status and rank of minister may be regarded as incidental. It was of much greater consequence that the Fascist Grand Council became more and more the supreme state organ, and had no inhibitions about issuing "directives" to the cabinet that were tantamount to orders. Although this shift in power was devoid of practical significance because of Mussolini's overriding position in both councils, it was nevertheless more than a mere fiction inasmuch as it was evidence of the steadily growing importance of the party element in Mussolini's own person. Exactly the same applies to the transformation of parliament into the *Camera dei Fasci e delle Corporazioni*, whereby the provincial secretaries of the party combined with the ministers and undersecretaries to form a new kind of party assembly. In foreign policy this priority of the party found an expression of world-historical importance when *Fascist* Italy allied itself with *National Socialist* Germany in the "steel pact": in other words, the regime with the regime.[50]

The consummation of party priority corresponded to the consummation of the fascist style. Three examples should suffice to demonstrate this.

The start of the Abyssinian war was not announced by the head of state via a note, but by the leader of people and party via a speech addressed to the gigantic *Adunata delle forze del regime*. This rally had been prepared by weeks of ceaseless propaganda, and no Italian could be in doubt as to its purpose. On the evening of October 2 the ringing of church bells at last proclaimed the great event. The wailing of sirens mingled stirringly with the venerable sounds, and in every town in Italy "Giovinezza" and the "Marcia Reale" resounded from countless public loud-speakers. The overall command was in the hands of Starace operating from the Palazzo Vidoni. *Fiumane di popolo* surged along the streets to the prearranged assembly points. In Rome the masses formed as if by magic into columns singing old wartime songs, wave upon wave of tumultuous cheering roared from the untold multitudes toward the Palazzo Venezia; when the Duce appeared it was like the *scatenarsi di una tempesta* ("unleashing of a tempest"). In clipped, ringing words, Mussolini announced his decision; twenty million people heard him, gathered in the squares of their towns, all over Italy; twenty million people thrilled (so it was claimed) to a sense of their spiritual oneness with this unique man; in the *quartieri popolari* especially there were, according to reliable reports, overwhelming demonstrations. This was

Europe's last romantic outbreak of war and truly a masterpiece of fascism, whose fundamental faith was that of the infinitely unifying power of war.[51]

Nothing shows more clearly or more horribly the fascist skill in exploiting the uniting force of tradition, while simultaneously destroying it from within, than a report on the inaugural Mass at *Campo Dux* in 1938, a camp consisting of youth battalions organized regularly each year before the gates of Rome and devoted to military and athletic pursuits. The Mass started off with the singing of "Giovinezza," followed by a prayer for Mussolini as the *fondatore dell' Impero*. The party secretary himself assisted the priest at the altar: fascist Italy is Catholic. At the raising of the Host, fifteen thousand bayonets were pointed as one sharply toward the sky; Catholic Italy is *sopratutto* fascist and honors its God with the point of sword.[52]

But not only tradition: nature, too, was not exempt from the wiles of its friends and saviors. On June 20, 1937, Mussolini addressed sixty thousand fascist women as follows: "You must be the custodians of the hearth [the crowd: Yes, yes!], with your vigilant attention, with your tireless love, you must give the first imprint to the offspring whom we wish to be numerous and brave [the crowd: Yes, yes!]."[53] Can one imagine a more repellent and unnatural scene than these sixty thousand marching women consenting in unison to the numerous children expected of them by state and party? Surely no clearer proof can ever have been given of the truth of the philosophical remark that certain virtues and things must not be striven for *as* such, since otherwise they sink into unreality or even turn into their opposite.

No doubt the Italians at that time, with a few exceptions, did not think that far ahead. Everyone was aware of certain measures with which Mussolini intended to change his people's way of life and which Starace managed to accentuate and aggravate. And yet actually these measures were extremely consistent. They made the old dreams of fascist extremists come true and aspired to "de-Europeanize" the Italians, to wean them away from Paris and London. The fact that the orientation remained and that all that occurred was a change in direction, may not have been clear to Mussolini at first; but his people knew better than he did that the newly introduced *passo romano* was nothing but an imitation of the Prussian goosestep. "Cries of devotion and love" at times still punctuated Mussolini's speeches at every sentence; but even before the outbreak of war he was obliged to deal publicly with a criticism which he attempted to dismiss and denounce as "bourgeois" but which ultimately expressed that elemental mood of the people which did not desire war alongside the old enemy and against former allies.[54] Hence this mood was directed only superficially against Starace, of whom even top party leaders said that he was forcing the country "under the leaden weight of his personal sectarian tyranny."[55] The fact is that it was not the party secretary who was the chief cause, and Mussolini did not solve the problem when he dismissed

Starace at the end of 1939. He did, however, end an era and thereby, as it turned out, the last epoch to bear the stamp of the party.

Epilogue

Not that all of a sudden the influence of the party collapsed altogether. That is no more true than the assumption that Mussolini's leadership now encountered the unanimous opposition of the entire population. If at times the wish not to be left behind was a fairly widespread feeling in Italy,[56] if failures were later repeatedly offset by successes and Mussolini's popularity showed itself more often than not equal to the acid test, at least the evolution of the fascist organization[57] seemed to continue on a straight course for some time to come.

Never did the party have so many members as during the war: in June, 1943, there were almost five million. No further appointments of public interest could be made without prior consultation with the party; no draft legislation even remotely affecting its interests could be introduced otherwise than jointly with the party secretary. Never had it been entrusted with tasks of such magnitude: its job was to carry out civil mobilization, and by this time there was not one single Italian who did not, even in day-to-day reality, come up against the party in its promotional and guiding capacity. Never had Mussolini emphasized and acclaimed its role more strongly: "You know me for a eulogist of the party. The party is in truth the soul, the motor of the nation."[58] And was it possible for the party to be elevated more unequivocally above the state than by the astonishing definition which concluded the two decades of evolution: "The party will make politics on a big scale, the state will represent the police on a big scale"?[59]

And yet all this may be compared to the uncanny and paradoxical growth of the hair and nails of a corpse. For essential to it was that fatal undermining of belief in Mussolini's greatness at the outbreak of war, the war which he had not managed to prevent or to exploit for his own purposes or to deny in Italy's behalf. The profound insecurity of Mussolini's leadership was already apparent in his choice of the new party secretary and in his attempts—which, after the first mistake, became increasingly frantic and unsuccessful—to find the right man for this important post. Muti, Serena, Vidussoni, Scorza vied with each other only in failures, and this was not to be wondered at. Two of them were heroes of the Blackshirts, "gold medalists," with plenty of determination and not much brain; the third was a veteran squad leader and the most outstanding deed in his books was the assault upon Giovanni Amendola which resulted in Amendola's death; the fourth one lacked even this distinction. Mussolini reaped the fruits of fascist training, whose praises he had so often sung and of which from the very first it was possible to say with certainty that it would not be capable of begetting a Giolitti, let alone a Mussolini.

But who could suppose these young men would be equal to their task, seeing that their master himself stood the test of war so badly? The diaries of his son-in-law give a comprehensive and dismaying idea of the impulsiveness and lack of discipline of Mussolini's emotions and way of thinking. One of his hasty decisions, and one of the most disastrous for the party, was that of January, 1941, to dispatch to the front all hierarchs, including the ministers, who were in any way fit for service. Once again he allowed personal ethics to supersede statesmanship. Due to the interweaving of party, state, and the life of the citizenry, this precipitate measure could not fail to lead to a disorganization of major proportions and, what was more, it created a large number of *malumori* directly affecting the ethos of the nation and ultimately contributing in no small measure to the events of July 25, 1943. It is, of course, a paradox that a wartime measure should be the very thing to contribute so largely to the dissolution of martial fascism; but in its context this can be as readily understood as the fact that what had once been a surge of renewal had petered out into an involved system of cliques, favoritism, and corruption.[60]

The great test of the war, but also the law of its own evolution, led the Fascist party back again to its basic components: to the small group of runaway revolutionaries or radical ideologists and the great mass of that citizens' militia which had clothed in revolutionary speeches its will *not* to abdicate. They were Antaeus and Earth to each other; only together did they have the strength which the world had so long admired. But when the war placed one group in a position to jeopardize the interests of the other by exploiting a universally detested situation,[61] the whole gigantic organizational edifice was bound to topple because it no longer wished to support itself; from then on the style became insipid and feeble because it was no longer founded on even the *appearance* of the whole; from then on a few clumsy turns of speech on the part of the man who had once been such an object of worship sufficed to make him a target of ridicule and mockery in South and North, among Fascists and anti-Fascists.[62]

Mussolini had lost sight of the basic form of fascist practice and hence the practical essence of fascism: an excessive, self-glorifying reaction to the action of the weaker adversary. At first, therefore, fascism really was that which has so frequently been offered as a definition: a citizens' militia, given to deeds of violence, in a West European country of ancient middle-class tradition but of only moderate industrial development, against the proletariat's attempt at the impossible revolution. But the point is that it was an excessive reaction and hence not limited to this situation. It could fix on another opponent and even produce the provocative action of that opponent artificially,[63] it could release its violence from its brachial limitation, widen its radius (to "punitive expeditions beyond the border," for instance), elaborate its style. This formal nature renders impossible that definition of content which appears natural in the case of Maurras and Hitler.

But there was one thing which fascism by nature could not and must not do: fight at the side of the stronger ally against the stronger opponent. It was inevitable that at this point fascism should begin to tire internally, and that Fascists should go different ways: the national fascist bourgeois became national bourgeois again and were no longer Fascists, the national fascist revolutionaries went over to the stronger power and became merely more revolutionary and no longer national.[64] In speaking of the "betrayal" by members of the Grand Council, Mussolini based his political evaluation, as he so often did, on a maxim of purely private ethics. At this moment in time, the Duce of fascism could no longer be betrayed because he had himself destroyed Italian national fascism.

National Socialism

CHAPTER ONE

National Socialism and Fascism

If the relationship between Italian fascism and the Action Française was hard to define, no comparable problem exists with regard to National Socialism and fascism. The similarity is at once apparent, nor is it merely a matter of parallel phenomena. In the early days, when Hitler was being tried by the Munich People's Court, he was already citing Mussolini as a precedent. Ideological conceptions as to the nature of fascism were contributing factors to the most arbitrary and unpopular political decision of his time of struggle—the renunciation of South Tirol. In his study in the Brown House stood a large bust of Mussolini.[1] In 1935 Hitler wrote a preface to the German translation of an Italian book on fascism[2] in which he stated that the intimate relationship between the new Italian and German concepts of state was indisputable. That same year Joseph Goebbels published a pamphlet entitled *Der Faschismus und seine praktischen Ergebnisse*; in it he openly acknowledged that fascism was the first movement to force Marxism to its knees from social rather than reactionary motives, and he was clearly impressed by the totalitarian will of fascism, which placed youth training and mass leisure, the film industry and architecture, so firmly at the service of its new unity of party and state that it was ten years ahead of Germany.[3] The speed with which Germany caught up with this head start, the extent to which, between 1937 and 1943, National Socialism and Italian fascism became each other's nemesis, is well known. As late as 1941 Hitler indicated that, without the victory of fascism, young National Socialism would probably not have been able to survive;[4] and even when, in his final conversations early in 1945, he condemned Italy and thus his own Italian policy, he specifically excluded the Duce from his condemnation and acknowledged him to be his only "peer" among all living men.[5]

Nevertheless, there can be no question of imitation. The origins of the two movements were simultaneous and entirely independent; the separate elements show almost as many differences as similarities. Both parties, for example, stressed the extreme principle of leadership, but the leader derived in one case from the ex-socialist source of the movement, in the other from the radical-conservative. However, all individual differences do not cancel out the similarity of both phenomena in their totality; hence there need be no hesitation in beginning this study by emphasizing these differences. This will show that in more subtle matters National Socialism was closer to the Action Française than to Italian fascism, and that in certain respects it may be regarded as a synthesis of the two older trends.

CHAPTER TWO

The Background: The Race Doctrine

An initial analogy of this kind may already be seen in the fact that certain fixed and clearly defined ideological assumptions form the basis for National Socialism—and hence primarily for Hitler—to a much greater extent than for Italian fascism. It is, of course, truer to speak of background than of forerunners in the sense which was valid for Maurras and the Action Française. There is no certainty that Hitler ever read even Gobineau and H. S. Chamberlain thoroughly. Presumably he developed the basic outlines of his *Weltanschauung* in Vienna more under the influence of pamphlets, newspapers, and conversation than by plowing through bulky volumes.[1] Even when he was the world-renowned leader of a large party he did not read—or read only a small portion of—the book of the party theoretician, although it was obviously of prime importance for the official intellectual position; the reason he gave was that it was written "in a much too abstract style."[2] It is certain that his only thorough knowledge was of anti-Semitic literature. Since about 1890 this literature had been defined and controlled entirely by that branch of European thought which has become known as "race doctrine," or the anthropological view of history. Hitler did not creatively expand Gobineau's and Chamberlain's doctrines as Maurras expanded the doctrines of his predecessors; it is even possible that he was only superficially acquainted with them. Nevertheless Gobineau and Chamberlain were his masters, and never at any time did he retreat from the foundations they laid or the atmosphere they created.

Yet it is not necessary, in order to give a clear picture of this atmosphere, to go back to that long line of thinkers who founded German nationalism: Fichte, Arndt, Lagarde, Treitschke, and many others. True, they make the climate in which Hitler could operate more readily understandable; but the totality of the *objective* preconditions cannot be given for any historical phenomenon, and without this totality the phenomenon cannot be properly understood. Nowhere, however, is there more justification for considering only the *subjective* preconditions than in the case of the various types of fascism, for which the only things that can be relevant are those which the spirit of the leader has acknowledged and endorsed. There is little likelihood that Fichte or Treitschke were anything more than names to Hitler.[3]

This is not the place to write a history of race doctrine. It can be exemplified by a brief study of three men: Gobineau, Vacher de Lapouge,[4] and Chamberlain.

It may be assumed that the doctrine of Count Gobineau is generally known: the doctrine of the inequality of the human races which, in fact, means incommensurability since the monopoly of creative strength is originally attributable to the blood of the white race, and all existing inequalities derive merely from the varying extent to which the white race, the basis of all history, unites with lesser races to produce culture.

Even if one knew nothing of the Count's early conservative political activities, of the deep sympathy for the newly secured feudal conditions in Germany which he displayed during his diplomatic participation in the Frankfurt Diet soon after the 1848 revolution, it would hardly be possible to overlook the fact that, in spite of the size of the book and its claims to a scientific basis, what it actually amounts to is a depiction of a grandiose class struggle on two fronts. The dedication to George V, King of Hanover, quite clearly states that the development of a kind of historical chemistry is intended to make it impossible for the theoreticians of revolution to continue to pile up their storm clouds and turn their fabricated illusions of unreal human beings into political reality.[5] Later he says that a theory is to be presented against which "the viper's tooth of demagogic doctrines" is powerless.[6] In fact: if class equals race, if nobility, middle class, and lower class are chiefly distinguished by their proportion of Aryan blood, then the priority of birth is unshakably fixed, then the historical development of recent centuries, although it cannot be denied, can be branded as disintegration and decay and regarded across an unbridgeable gulf in contrast to the truly creative heroic eras.

But demagogues are not the only enemy: there is also absolutism, which deprived the feudal aristocracy of power and independence and led to war against the remains of Teutonism in France. For Gobineau, Teutonism is characterized by its proud individualism and its aversion to the Roman's and Slav's "communal sense." Since the tendency toward despotism is attributable to Semitic blood, that is, to race chaos, this enemy also does not escape moral devastation.

There can seldom have been a doctrine so frank in the exposure of its reactionary motivation. All Gobineau did was to revert to that self-image—already unmistakably oriented toward class warfare—of the French aristocracy which Boulainvilliers had formulated a hundred years earlier and which was the chief target of the revolutionary concept of the "nation." And yet for some decades after Gobineau's death, this theory was regarded as one of the most modern and was incorporated in the strongest and most effective nationalist movement of the twentieth century as a powerful, albeit ambivalent, element. It is one of the most striking examples of the way the course of history in the most general sense follows a straight line but in the multiplicity of reality constantly resembles a vortex.

Some of the reasons are not hard to understand. There were larger and more vital groups than the French aristocracy which could adopt this theory as their sword and buckler. To base a view of history on an analogy with the natural sciences was a premise resulting from autonomously defined tendencies of science. To approach history with radical evaluations has been one of the constant tendencies of the human heart since the telling of the story of Cain and Abel. When these three elements fused in a new form it was possible to predict the explosive and far-reaching impact of Gobineau's doctrine, so totally feudal-reactionary and so totally French in origin. This explosive force would, of course, also be directed against the doctrine itself, for some of its elements and implications were not capable of development, while others were merely waiting to be brought into prominence.

Scarcely capable of development and yet hardly entirely eradicable, is the gloomy, grandiose pessimism which envelops the whole doctrine and which is the most unmistakable indication of its provenance. The problem of the "death origin" of human societies is the starting point: inexorable, irremovable, the primordial factor of history itself is for Gobineau the mixing of races and to that extent the creation of equality, and this problem causes him to feel with a deep shudder "that the rapacious hand of fate is already upon us," of that fate which will allow the "human herds" of future humanity to vegetate "insensibly in their nothingness."[7]

But even if this paralyzing pessimism can be eliminated, there is still that underlying fear which sees the individuality of "our" culture hovering in constant peril at the brink of an abyss: the abyss of the race confusion of large cities, of the tendency of degenerate slaves toward revolt and revolution, of the stagnant swamp of the racially inferior masses of one's own people.

Also hard to eliminate is the potential hostility toward history on the part of this eulogist of heroic events, for whom the pristine intactness of Aryan blood lies in inaccessible darkness *prior to* all history, just like the *liberté originelle* of his principal enemy, Rousseau. Thus real history consists mainly in degeneration.

Of lasting duration must be the contradiction which causes the spokesman of culture to look askance at the highest reality of culture: Athens in its anarchy as well as the Roman writers who were a product of the Semiticized masses.

The ascribing to modern Germanic civilization of the need "to eradicate completely and on all sides everything which was not in accordance with its way of thinking" takes on a positive note when expressed by Gobineau. Our civilization, he says, is the only one to have possessed "this power of murdering."[8] It does not occur to Gobineau to ascribe this particular quality exclusively to the Jews. His book shows only rudimentary traces of anti-Semitism. But in this area a number of developments appear likely.

Developments concerning his relationship to Christianity can be predicted with certainty. For Gobineau himself sounds neither convincing nor convinced when he excludes the church fathers and their "supernal flame" from his condemnation of the race chaos of late antiquity,[9] or when he extols Christianity because, unlike the heathen religions, it does not presuppose outright surrender to the race instinct.

His German imitators (except for the most radical among them, such as Hitler) were bound to reject Gobineau's statement that the bulk of the German people was un-Germanic, however desirable they found his contempt for the Slavs as an unwarlike people. Gobineau preferred the Anglo-Saxons and the Scandinavians. Actually he was of no more use to German nationalism than to French. But Hitler was at the same time both less and more of a nationalist than Maurras.

Gobineau's work on race is not a book in which his pen was guided by unprejudiced reasoning and cool logic. It has its place among those brilliant outlines which by means of scientific insights, insofar as they uncritically adopt the new categories, can only be narrowed and limited, but which dilettantes, taking them as indispensable starting points for the uninhibited urge toward constructs, are even less able to expand and adjust to reality.

Vacher de Lapouge's work on the Aryan[10] was written twenty-five years later than the *Essai sur l'inégalité des races humaines*, and it bears the unmistakable stamp of the late nineteenth century which was so much more naturalistic than liberal, although the connection had not yet been quite dissolved. Here the faith in immortality is no longer, as with Gobineau, a permanent characteristic of the Aryan: the author notes with approval that monism and social hygiene are on the way toward eradicating the idea of religion and morals. Here the results of skull measurements are tabulated and comparisons made on the basis of these figures. Gone is all mention of the divine spark, which for Gobineau existed in every cannibal. Man is firmly thrust back into the great kingdom of the animal world and made subject to its sole law, the law of violence: "Every man is related to all men and all living creatures. Therefore there are no human rights, any more than there are ... rights of the armadillo. As soon as man loses his right to be a separate entity in the image of God, he no longer has any more right than any other mammal. The idea of justice is in itself an illusion. Nothing exists but violence."[11]

Similarly there can be no question of any kind of autonomy of the individual vis-à-vis his group, of that controlling of the race instinct which Gobineau had at least declared to be possible: "One enters neither a family nor a nation through a decision. The blood which one has in one's veins at birth one keeps all one's life. The individual is stifled by his race and is nothing. The race, the nation, is all."[12]

What immediately strikes one as strange is that Lapouge himself is nowhere near identifying himself with his nation. For he does not refrain from either praise and blame or from an absolute criterion. The *rocher de bronze*, on which he firmly plants himself, is the blood of the "long skull," of Aryan(!), blood which, apart from being more potent, is also more noble. The superiority of the Aryan is everywhere apparent. He is the motive force of modern civilization; in art, industry, trade, and science he represents the element of energy, he pours into the towns, and the higher the level of a social stratum the more often he appears in it. Once upon a time he even founded the greatness of France, but through the revolution the "short skulls" came into power and thus damaged France's position of power, with the result that France was overtaken not only by England and America but also Russia and Germany. For Lapouge no hostile separation existed between martial aristocracy and industrial middle class. He admired both equally. But his version of the race doctrine was already just as destructive for the nation then, as at any time later. How, he asks, is one to admire this French nation of his if it is itself to blame[13] for possessing the lowest number of racially pure specimens of *Homo europaeus* among all the great powers, fewer even than Austria? What is one to think of Germany's national coherence when the proportion of "long skulls" in the North German population corresponds to the English proportion but is seven times as high as that of South Germany? Even in its bourgeois scientific form, this race doctrine cannot deny its origin in the antinational sense of the superiority of the prerevolutionary aristocracy.

However, the liberal character displayed by Germanophiles in Latin countries does not entirely disappear in Lapouge. That the Aryans are a "master race" is shown in the trend toward civic liberties: toward personal freedom, freedom of speech and the press, freedom of assembly and association.[14] Only Protestant peoples, he says, have these qualities today, for the Reformation is to be regarded as an attempt to adapt Christianity to the hereditary characteristics of the Aryan race.[15]

His optimism regarding civilization, the result of his partiality for Protestantism and the Anglo-Saxons, speaks louder than his despair over his own country. But it is seriously jeopardized by a law of natural science—the law of the growth of skull coefficients, that is, the steady increase in the number of roundheads since prehistoric times. Lapouge attributes this to their being more tractable and better suited to a civilization based more and more on the subordination of the individual. Thus out of statistics and conclusions the pessimism so typical of Gobineau once again appears.

Optimism and pessimism are strangely mingled in Lapouge's thoughts on the future domination of the earth and the significance of living space in the battle for supremacy. France and Germany have no chance at all in his eyes, their living space being completely settled with no possibility of an increased population being able to feed itself. America and Russia are another matter. There can be no question as to the future unity of the world: the only question is which of these two powers is to be its originator and master. In any event it will be the victory of a state with an excellent race constitution since—leaving aside America—at least the population of Siberia is purer and nobler as to race than any European people. But because the law of the growth of skull coefficients remains valid under all circumstances, Lapouge cannot regard the inexorable fate of unity without secret apprehension.

For him as for Gobineau, this trend is the outcome of a world law and in no way attributable to the conduct of a small group of people. In other words, he does not hold the Jews responsible for it, although anti-Semitism is more pronounced with him than with Gobineau. Anti-Semitism is in Lapouge's case still a kind of personal whim, similar to that which allows him to find round-heads to be especially prevalent among students of the classical disciplines. In this he resembles all those natural scientists, headed by Taine, who plunge like Achilles in impenetrable armor into the fray of political and historical issues but who, instead of having their vulnerable spots concealed, like Achilles, on their heels, carry them exposed in the middle of their foreheads—visible to all but themselves.

Nevertheless, Lapouge's importance can scarcely be overestimated. He transformed Gobineau's work and rescued it for science; long before Ratzel, let alone the geopoliticians, he established a theory of living space and combined it with a notion of race-struggle;[16] he worked out a method which matched the favorite ideas of his age by creating a place in the interpretation of history for compasses and ruler. And he points far beyond himself when he attacks Christian mercy, which inhibits the natural process of extermination of the unfit, and makes proposals as to how "systematic selection" can be effected by means of certain injections.[17]

Houston Stewart Chamberlain is not a direct descendant of this lineage. With his *Grundlagen des XIX. Jahrhunderts*, published in 1898, he placed the race doctrine in Germany for the first time on an effective footing; he was the first writer anywhere who attempted to open all the doors of history with the new key—that is, who undertook an interpretation of history, down to the last detail, on the basis of the race doctrine. In his political convictions, however, he was solid middle-class and a liberal, who bitterly attacked the absolutism of monarchs and the despotism of the church. He raised the banner of individual liberty and national individuality against the dark Middle Ages and the race-destroying universalism of the Roman Church; he defended empirical science against dogmatism and superstition. All this—on the threshold of the twentieth century—would not be particularly interesting or even symptomatic were it not for the fact that it acquired new aspects in the context of the race doctrine. For it turned out that it was considerably more difficult to defend liberalism against its new ally than against church and Jesuits.

Chamberlain's aversion to absolutism was indeed so great that he did not subscribe to the usual interpretation of the French revolution as an uprising of racially inferior "Celtic" groups. On the contrary, he claimed that in this revolution the population rose up "with the proverbial rage of the long-suffering Germanic people";[18] it signified not a milestone in history but a much delayed catching-up with the Reformation. He was close enough to German idealism to formulate the idea of the "completely humanized Jew"[19] and to find something sensible to say concerning the "positively ridiculous tendency to make the Jew the general scapegoat for all the vices of our time."[20] Finally, it often looks as if he wanted to detach the idea of race from its natural and mysterious source in such a way as to make the nation the precondition of race rather than its consequence.

Taken to its logical conclusion, this should lead to a doctrine of cultures and nations for which the idea of "race" would possess at most the significance of a hypothetical marginal value. But there is reason to believe that Chamberlain's polemic against Gobineau's unmistakable "thing in itself" of primordial races merely represents an attempt to introduce the optimism of his time into the race doctrine which, due to its origin, is so deeply pessimistic. The fact that the concepts of breeding and race cultivation can thus be easily substantiated links him with Lapouge. The extent to which objective needs forced him to transcend even his own favorite opinions is clearly shown by his attitude toward the question of the origin of Jesus. "In the face of a phenomenon of this kind," racial characteristics seemed to him to shrink to nothing—and yet a few pages further on he declared the question of racial origin to be unavoidable, since only during the night of the Middle Ages could anyone believe that the soul had its seat outside the body.[21] Continuing on this assumption, he then tried to prove that Jesus was not a Jew. The same vacillation is evident when on the one hand he tried to cling to the Kantian doctrine of two worlds—indeed, made it the basis for the whole contrast between the Germanic type and the raceless universal church (the Germanic type is outwardly limited but inwardly limit-less; the universal church is outwardly limitless but inwardly limited)—while on the other hand he tried to categorize man "unreservedly" as part of nature.[22] That the second tendency is the stronger seems likely when Chamberlain writes such sentences as: the population contains a large number of half-, quarter-, and eighth-Germanic types, who consequently represent half-, quarter-, or eighth- (or even anti-) Germanic ideas. Arithmetic becomes as powerful here as with Lapouge, and there is no longer any question of a liberal doctrine of culture. For Chamberlain "everything" depends on the proportion of Germanic blood; it is clear that the peoples of Europe have made this principle their lodestar from the very beginning, for "only men of Germanic race occupy the thrones of Europe."[23] That a nation never fails to nationalize its king, as

Maurras continually stressed, is something with which Chamberlain obviously does not credit the unique individualities of his nations.

It must be assumed that his "completely humanized Jew" is merely a display Jew, for the anti-Semitic note evident in his writings is much more pronounced than with Gobineau and Lapouge. When Chamberlain calls the Jewish revolution a "direct criminal attack on all the peoples of the earth,"[24] when he declares that the Jew's accursed fixed ideas made every Jew (even the broad-minded) the enemy of mankind, it is not hard to decide whether the spiritual nature of the subject or the uncouthness of the predicate is more important. There can really be no doubt that it is not the remains of liberalism but the beginnings of antiliberalism which gain the upper hand even with Chamberlain, and that for his successors they are of cardinal importance.

Chamberlain probably exerted even greater influence through his method of attaching a "race" label to every historical manifestation. Since it is possible to define the capitalist but not the Germanic type (which is said to be the sole possessor of all great and positive traits), since all idea of a guiding principle of progressive human development has been abandoned, the racial view of history consists in enumerating positive and negative qualities according to the social standing and personal preference of the observer, and in claiming objectivity for this procedure by always reverting to the primary fact of race. Chamberlain's position is that of the bourgeois semiliberal of the end of the century, who loves the national state of the Hohenzollerns with a love intensified by special circumstances but whose mental outlook is still that of the period of German idealism. That is why he rejects the German princes, almost all of whom he regarded as criminals; he denounces intolerance as being a Jewish racial trait, grants a Germanic trait only to the mechanical world concept of Democritus, despises the Emperor of Austria as the ruler of a "formless mass of human beings,"[25] yet displays a striking preference for St. Paul (who was perhaps not a Jew by race at all) and that free metaphysical speculation with which the dogmatic narrow-mindedness and gloom of all Christian churches can be countered. His arbitrariness often assumes absurd forms: Louis XIV was simultaneously Germanic—he opposed Rome—and anti-Germanic—he instituted absolutism.[26] And finally Chamberlain's dilettantism highlighted these antics in strange ways: for instance, Lucian's contempt for Phidias as a mere artisan was due to his own mixed racial background.

Although Chamberlain is discussed here solely because of the influences he exerted and not for his personal significance,[27] it would be doing him an injustice to omit mention of that anxiety, that suspicion, which set and kept this whole business of historical interpretation in motion like the steam in a steam engine. His anxiety was for the nation, that familiar phenomenon, which was being imperiled by a universal trend and a political party. A "war to the knife" against personality, the element of the national-liberal state, was being waged equally by socialism and by the economic trend toward anonymity and mass production.[28] However, Chamberlain never actually attacked "capitalism": he still took the Germanic nature of modern civilization too much for granted, his pride in that civilization was still too strong. His only real target was the socialist enemy. This is the root of Chamberlain's anti-Semitism, for at the heart of the revolutionary threat he finds the Jews and "their gift for planning impossible socialist and economic Messianic kingdoms, with no thought as to whether in doing so they would destroy our whole laboriously won civilization and culture."[29] And although, in the midst of Wilhelminian hopes for a new harmonious Germanic culture, this anxiety did not assume panic proportions, it was obviously the principle guiding the pen of the cultured and humane author when he regretted that the Germanic race had not "exterminated more thoroughly" at the time of the migration of peoples, and when he maintained that the Germanic peoples had laid the firmest foundations for the loftiest and most moral principles wherever they slaughtered whole peoples and tribes (in territories of the Teutonic Knights, in America) or, by means of general demoralization, slowly killed them off in order to make room for themselves.[30]

This look at the three authors, brief as it is, is sufficient to underline some of the chief characteristics of the race doctrine. First and foremost, it is the instrument of defense of a threatened leading class which, although possibly no longer powerful, is still influential and confident. Its primary intention is to deny not the factualness but the value of historical development and to provide its self-confidence with an unassailable basis. Its weakness consists in the necessity of interpreting history as inescapable degeneration, so that inactivity becomes the price of an assured self-confidence.

Yet to call it a mere defense ideology is not enough, for it satisfies one of the liveliest desires of the age of natural science: to stress the natural elements in historical life in order to glimpse reality.[31] This means that it can benefit science in many different ways. But science can benefit it even more. For if its well-nigh ineradicable lust for evaluation unites with science's desire for activity, it can overcome the burdensome legacy of pessimism and expand into an activist "race cultivation." But it also has the ability to combine with another emotion of the time, one with quite a different source: the nostalgia for vanishing individuality, the most general form of which is the individuality of the nation or the cultural group. Race would seem to provide man with one last individuality—indestructible and impregnable. Race consciousness thus becomes the manifestation of a national feeling that is no longer certain of itself. Whether the rock to which this feeling clings is reliable is, of course, debatable.

Finally, then, race doctrine, hostile to history though it clearly is, can from another aspect approach the historicism which criticizes universal concepts and works out the relativity of human reality.

However, in order to understand the functions and significance of the race doctrine it is also necessary to bear in mind the existence of historical material-ism. In Marx's doctrine the "productive forces" and "classes" appear as the moving elements of the historical process. But are they not merely "things"? Is not man himself, in Marx's own words, "the basis of his material production, as of any other which he carries out"?[32] Marx had said himself that racial characteristics could modify the historical process.[33] Did not *Das Kapital* describe processes which were limited exclusively to a narrow geographical and ethnic area? If the race doctrine was for some decades the best-known adversary of historical materialism, one reason for this was that it seemed to fill a place which, because of lack of clarification of the term "productive force," had remained vacant in Marxism: the place of subjectivity, of "man himself" in his differences and his unity. Had it expanded in this direction the race doctrine would have been bound to come up against Marxism and philo-sophical anthropology, not as a successful thesis but as an ever-deepening problem.

But this was not the direction the political race doctrine took; at most it profited by the inkling of this relationship. What it developed more than anything else was the element of arbitrariness, an integral part of itself; fear replaced anxiety as a dominant emotion; a narrow conception of nature was countered with that of antinature which—most fateful step of all—was identified with a particular human group.

Gobineau, Lapouge, and Chamberlain were a long way from such conclu-sions. Yet even in the form they gave to it, the race doctrine was already an extreme manifestation which, despite some points of contact, stood outside the highly differentiated main strand of European thinking. And this extreme doctrine was waiting for the extremist who would be able to pursue it to its most acute and radical form and, armed with this weapon, to intervene in reality.

CHAPTER THREE

History

Adolf Hitler

No one is likely to query the statement that Hitler was even more essential to National Socialism than Maurras was to the Action Française or Mussolini to Italian fascism. He also did not create his movement from nothing, of course, and objective factors of great significance combined with a thousand favorable circumstances to work to his advantage; nevertheless, it is very much easier to imagine fascism without Mussolini than National Socialism without Hitler.

The fact that right from the start Hitler was a more extreme figure than Mussolini or Maurras is accounted for only in small part by the circumstances and events of his youth. Indeed, there are as many analogies here as deviations.

In common with Maurras and Mussolini, Hitler came from the provincial lower middle class of a Catholic country, although he alone lived under the shadow of the dreaded unknown factor in his family history.[1] He too had a nonbelieving father and a pious and beloved mother. At fourteen he also was a "freethinker," but, unlike Mussolini, he was not offered a coherent system of political faith as a substitute.

As a young man he went to the distant capital to devote himself to an artistic profession; in helpless rage he looked upon the strangeness around him, typified for him—as for Maurras—by the Jew. He became acquainted with poverty and even, like Mussolini, tried begging. But his ideas did not develop, as Maurras' did, under the critical eye of a literary public; he lectured on his *Weltanschauung* to the inmates of men's hostels and shelters for the destitute; he did not, as did Mussolini, receive any vocational training. He left school early and lived for two years in his mother's house without a job; then, until he was twenty-five, he wandered around Vienna and Munich, eking out a meager living by painting postcards. The Dreyfus affair made a politician out of Maurras—a not entirely unknown writer who enjoyed the esteem of friends who were celebrities; World War I confronted Mussolini, a party leader of considerable standing, with the most important decision of his career; the war was a cataclysmic experience for Hitler too, but even though it brought him for the first time face to face with an overwhelming reality to which he enthusiastically responded, it merely cast him from the nothingness of bourgeois existence into the nothingness of the obscure common soldier, and when in 1918 he decided to enter politics the material foundation of his life was still nothingness.

The differences in the circumstances surrounding their lives were therefore not so much objective facts as the products of differing reactions. Maurras and Mussolini came to terms with the intellectual premises and random happenings of their lives with a similar prompt and clear-cut decisiveness. There were some things to which Hitler did not react at all—hence his inertia, his aimless drifting, his inconsistency—as against others which provoked an extremely sharp reaction. A psychological description of Maurras and Mussolini was superfluous; references to the outstanding intelligence and literary bent of the one, and the "impressionability" of the other, merely served to indicate normal characteristics intensified to a supranormal degree.

Hitler was different. In his case certain dominant traits came to the fore which, although they cannot immediately be dubbed "abnormal," did approach the abnormal and are best described in psychopathological terms. In view of the unchanging nature of character and convictions which Hitler shared with Maurras, it is permissible to cite examples side by side from all periods of his life.

The fact that, according to August Kubizek, the friend of his youth, Hitler's favorite stories were legends of German heroes, that he steeped himself in the world of those ancient times and identified himself with their heroes, was no doubt something he had in common with innumerable boys of his age.[2] The fact that he designed a magnificent house in the Renaissance style for the woman he silently adored from afar merely put him on a level with a smaller group of young men.[3] But that he should plan, down to the last detail, a luxurious apartment for himself and his friend in the firm hope of winning a lottery, that he should mentally engage an "exceptionally refined elderly lady" as receptionist and tutor for the two art students, that after the disillusionment of the lottery drawing he should passionately and in all seriousness inveigh against the lottery in particular and the world in general[4]—this must have removed him some considerable distance from the majority of even the most fanciful of his age group.

Moreover, this extraordinary capacity for wishful thinking, this mingling of reality and dream, did not diminish with time. Scarcely had one of his companions in a Vienna men's hostel described certain technical plans, of direct concern to him as a future engineer, than Hitler already saw himself part owner of the firm "Greiner & Hitler, Airplane Construction."[5] In *Hitler's Table Talk* (published in America as *Hitler's Secret Conversations*), Hitler speaks of the poverty of that period of his life. "But in my imagination I dwelled in palaces."[6] It was during that time, he said, that he drew up the first plans for the remodeling of Berlin.

There are many witnesses to the fact that during his time of struggle he was already living in the Third Reich, untouched by doubts of any kind, impervious to counsels of moderation, devoid of any desire for sober assessment and calculation. Hermann Rauschning's *Gespräche mit Hitler* provide what is probably the most vivid picture of the utter lack of restraint of this inordinate imagination.[7]

When he was in the throes of remodeling Berlin and Linz, his plans were far from exhausted. The new Reich Chancellery had to be so vast that all would recognize it immediately as the seat of the "master of the world," and by comparison St. Peter's would seem a mere toy.[8] No turn of events in the war could shake the power of this desire, this vision, nor was its force of conviction affected by the fact that this dream was just as divorced from reality as it had been during his youth.

In January, 1945, the *Gauleiter* of Danzig came to Hitler, disheartened and full of defiant resolve to confront Hitler with the whole truth about the desperate situation of his city. He left the room, according to the secretary, a changed man, miraculously cheered and encouraged: the Führer had promised him relief.[9] There was no relief anywhere in sight, but Hitler saw it in his mind's eye and was able to convince a man with perfect vision that he was blind.

As late as March, 1945, his secretary saw him standing interminably in front of the wooden model of the future city of Linz.[10] He was still dreaming the dreams of his youth.

The dominant trait in Hitler's personality was infantilism. It explains the most prominent as well as the strangest of his characteristics and actions. The frequently awesome consistency of his thoughts and behavior must be seen in conjunction with the stupendous force of his rage,[11] which reduced field marshals to trembling nonentities. If at the age of fifty he built the Danube bridge in Linz down to the last detail exactly as he had designed it at the age of fifteen before the eyes of his astonished boyhood friend,[12] this was not a mark of consistency in a mature man, one who has learned and pondered, criticized and been criticized, but the stubbornness of the child who is aware of nothing except himself and his mental image and to whom time means nothing because childishness has not been broken and forced into the sober give-and-take of the adult world. Hitler's rage was the uncontrollable fury of the child who bangs the chair because the chair refuses to do as it is told; his dreaded harshness, which nonchalantly sent millions of people to their death, was much closer to the rambling imaginings of a boy than to the iron grasp of a man, and is therefore intimately and typically related to his profound aversion to the cruelty of hunting, vivisection, and the consumption of meat generally.

And how close to the sinister is the grotesque! The first thing Hitler did after being released from the Landsberg prison was to buy a Mercedes for twenty-six thousand marks—the car he had been dreaming of while serving his sentence.[13] Until 1933 he insisted on passing every car on the road.[14] In Vienna alone he had heard *Tristan and Isolde* between thirty and forty times,[15] and had time as chancellor to see six performances of *The Merry Widow* in as many months.[16] Nor was this all. According to Otto Dietrich he reread all Karl May's boys' adventure books during 1933 and 1934,[17] and this is perfectly credible since in *Hitler's Table Talk* he bestowed high praise on this author and credited him with no less than opening his eyes to the world.[18] It is in the conversations related in *Hitler's Table Talk* that he treated his listeners to such frequent and vindictive schoolboy reminiscences that it seems as if this man never emerged from his boyhood and completely lacked the experience of time and its broadening, reconciling powers.

The monomaniacal element in Hitler's nature is obviously closely related to his infantilism. It is based largely on his elemental urge toward tangibility, intelligibility, simplicity. In *Mein Kampf* he expressed the maxim that the masses should never be shown more than *one* enemy. He was himself the most loyal exponent of this precept, and not from motives of tactical calculation alone. He never allowed himself to face more than one enemy at a time; on this enemy he concentrated all the hatred of which he was so inordinately capable, and it was this that enabled him during this period to show the other enemies a reassuring and "subjectively" sincere face. During the crisis in Czechoslovakia he even forgot the Jews over Beneš. His enemy was always concrete and personal, never merely the expression but also the cause of an obscure or complex event. The Weimar system was caused by the "November criminals," the predicament of the Germans in Austria by the Hapsburgs, capitalism and bolshevism equally by the Jews.

A good example of the emergence and function of the clearly defined hate figure, which took the place of the causal connection he really had in mind, is to be found in *Mein Kampf*. Here Hitler draws a vivid picture of the miseries of proletarian existence as he came to know it in Vienna—deserted, frustrated, devoid of hope.[19] This description seems to lead inevitably to an obvious conclusion: that these people, if they were not wholly insensible, were bound to be led with compelling logic to the socialist doctrine, to their "lack of patriotism," their hatred of religion, their merciless indictment of the ruling class. It should, however, have also led to a self-critical insight: that the only reason he remained so aloof from the collective emotions of these masses was because he had enjoyed a different upbringing, middle-class and provincial, because despite his poverty he never really worked, and because he was not married. Nothing of the kind! When he was watching spellbound one day as the long column of demonstrating workers wound its way through the streets, his first query was about the "wirepullers."[20] His voracity for reading, his allegedly thorough study of Marxist theories, did not spur him on to cast his gaze beyond the frontier and realize that such demonstrations were taking place in every city in Europe, or to take note of the "rabble-rousing" articles of a certain Mussolini, which he would doubtless have regarded as "spiritual vitriol" like those in the *Arbeiterzeitung*.

What Hitler discovered was the many Jewish names among the leaders of Austrian Marxism, and now the scales fell from his eyes—at last he saw who it was who, beside the Hapsburgs, wanted to wipe out the German element in Austria. Now he began to preach his conclusions to his first audiences; now he was no longer speaking, as until recently he had spoken to Kubizek, to hear the sound of his own voice: he wanted to convince. But he did not have much success. The management of the men's hostel looked on him as an insufferable politicizer, and for most of his fellow inmates he was a "reactionary swine."[21] He got beaten up by workers, and in conversations with Jews and Social Democrats he was evidently often the loser, being no match for their diabolical glibness and dialectic. This made the image of the archenemy appear all the more vivid to him, all the more firmly entrenched. Thirty years later the most experienced statesmen took him for a confidence-inspiring statesman after meeting him personally; hard-bitten soldiers found he was a man they could talk to; educated supporters saw in him the people's social leader. Hitler himself, however, made the following observations in the presence of the generals and party leaders around his table: though Dietrich Eckart had considered that from many aspects Streicher was a fool, it was impossible to conquer the masses without such people, ... though Streicher was criticized for his paper, *Der Stürmer*; in actual fact Streicher idealized the Jew. The Jew was far more ignoble, unruly, and diabolical than Streicher had depicted him.[22]

Hitler rose from the gutter to be the master of Europe. There is no doubt that he learned an enormous amount. In the flexible outer layer of his personality he could be all things to all men: a statesman to the statesmen, a commander to the generals, a charmer to women, a father to the people. But in the hard monomaniacal core of his being he did not change one iota from Vienna to Rastenburg.

Yet if his people had found that he intended after the war to prohibit smoking[23] and make the world of the future vegetarian[24] it is probable that even the SS would have rebelled. There are thousands of monomaniacal and infantile types in every large community, but they seldom play a role other than among their own kind. These two traits do not explain how Hitler was able to rise to power.

August Kubizek tells a strange story which there is little reason to doubt[25] and which sheds as much light on the moment when Hitler decided to enter politics as on the basis and prospects of that decision. After a performance of *Rienzi* in Linz, Kubizek relates, Hitler had taken him up to a nearby hill and talked to him with shining eyes and trembling voice of the mandate he would one day receive from his people to lead them out of servitude to the heights of liberty. It seemed as if another self were speaking from Hitler's lips, as if he himself were looking on at what was happening in numb astonishment. Here the infantile basis is once again unmistakable. The identification with the hero of the dramatic opera bore him aloft, erupted from him like a separate being. There were many subsequent occasions testifying to this very process. When Hitler chatted, his manner of talking was often unbearably flat; when he described something, it was dull; when he theorized, it was stilted; when he started up a hymn of hate, repulsive. But time and again his speeches contained passages of irresistible force and compelling conviction, such as no other speaker of his time was capable of producing. These are always the places where his "faith" finds expression, and it was obviously this faith which induced that emotion among the masses to which even the most hostile observer testified. But at no time do these passages reveal anything new, never do they make the listener reflect or exert his critical faculty: all they ever do is conjure up magically before his eyes that which already existed in him as vague feeling, inarticulate longing. What else did he express but the secret desires of his judges when he declared before the People's Court: "The army we have trained is growing day by day, faster by the hour. It is in these very days that I have the proud hope that the hour will come when these unruly bands become battalions, the battalions regiments, the regiments divisions, when the old cockade is raised from the dust, when the old flags flutter again on high, when at last reconciliation takes place before the eternal Last Judgment, which we are prepared to face."[26]

His behavior at a rally has often been described: how, uncertain at first, he would rely on the trivial, then get the feel of the atmosphere for several minutes, slowly establish contact, score a bull's-eye with the right phrase, gather momentum with the applause, finally burst out with words which seemed positively to erupt through him, and at the end, in the midst of thunderous cheering, shout a vow to heaven or, amid breathless silence, bring forth a solemn Amen. And after the speech he was as wet as if he had taken a steambath and had lost as much weight as if he had been through a week's strict training.

He told every rally what it wanted to hear—yet what he voiced was not the trivial interests and desires of the day but the great universal, obvious hopes: that Germany should once again become what it had been, that the economy should function, that the farmer should get his rights, likewise the townsman, the worker, and the employer, that they should forget their differences and become one in the most important thing of all—their love for Germany. He never embarked on discussion, he permitted no heckling, he never dealt with any of the day-to-day problems of politics. When he knew that a rally was in a critical mood and wanted information instead of *Weltanschauung*, he was capable of calling off his speech at the last moment.

There should be no doubt as to the mediumistic trait in Hitler.[27] He was the medium who communicated to the masses their own, deeply buried spirit. It was because of this, not because of his monomaniacal obsession, that a third of his people loved him long before he became chancellor, long before he was their victorious supreme commander. But mediumistic popular idols are usually simpletons fit for ecstasy rather than fulfillment. In the turmoil of postwar Germany it would have been *impossible* to love Hitler had not monomaniacal obsession driven the man on and infantile wishful thinking carried him beyond the workaday world with its problems and conflicts. Singly, any one of these three characteristics would have made Hitler a freak and a fool; combined, they raised him for a brief time to be lord and master of his troubled era.

A psychological portrait of Hitler such as this must, however, give rise to doubts in more ways than one. Does the portrait not approach that over-polemical and oversimplified talk of the "madman" or the "criminal"? There is no intention of claiming that this represents a clinical diagnosis. It is not even the purpose of this analysis to define and categorize Hitler as an "infantile mediumistic monomaniac." What has been discussed is merely the existence of infantile, mediumistic, and monomaniacal traits. They are not intended to exhaust the nature of the man Hitler, nor do they of themselves belong to the field of the medically abnormal. Rather do they represent individually an indispensable ingredient of the exceptional. There can be few artists without a streak of infantilism, few ideological politicians without a monomaniacal element in their make-up. It is not so much the potency of each element singly as the combination of all three which gives Hitler his unique face. Whether this combination is pathological in the clinical sense is very doubtful, but there can be no doubt that it excludes historical greatness in the traditional sense.

A second objection is that the psychological description prevents the socio-logical typification which from the point of view of history is so much more productive. Many attempts have been made to understand Hitler as typical of the angry petit bourgeois. The snag in this interpretation is that it cannot stand without a psychologizing adjective and almost always suggests a goal which is obviously psychological as well as polemical. What this theory tries to express is that Hitler was "actually only a petit bourgeois," in other words, something puny and contemptible. But it is precisely from the psychological standpoint that the petit bourgeois can best be defined as the normal image of the "adult": Hitler was exactly the reverse. What is correct, however, is that, from the sociological standpoint, bourgeois elements may be present in an entirely nonbourgeois psychological form. It remains to be shown how very petit bourgeois was Hitler's immediate reaction to Marxism. However, it was only by means of that "form" which cannot be deduced by sociological methods that his first reaction underwent its momentous transformation.

The third objection is the most serious. The historical phenomenon of National Socialism might be considered overparticularized if it is based solely on the unusual, not to say abnormal, personality of one man. Does not this interpretation in the final analysis even approach that all too transparent apologia which tries to see in Hitler, and only in him, the "*causa efficiens* of the whole sequence of events"?[28] But this is not necessarily logical. It is only from one aspect that the infantile person is more remote from the world than other people; from another aspect he is much closer to it. For he does not dredge up the stuff of his dreams and longings out of nothing; on the contrary, he compresses the world of his more normal fellow men, sometimes by intensifying, sometimes by contrasting. From the complexity of life, monomaniacal natures often wrest an abstruse characteristic, quite frequently a comical aspect, but at times a really essential element. However, the mediumistic trait guarantees that nothing peripheral is compressed, nothing trivial monomaniacally grasped. It is not that a nature of this kind particularizes the historical, but that this nature is itself brought into focus by the historical. Although far from being a true mirror of the times—indeed, it is more of a monstrous distortion—nothing goes into it that is pure invention; and what does go into it arises from certain traits of its own. Hitler sometimes compared himself to a magnet which attracted all that was brave and heroic; it would probably be more accurate to say that certain extreme characteristics of the era attracted this nature like magnets, to become in that personality even more extreme and visible. Hence from now on there will be little mention of Hitler's psyche, but all the more of the conditions, forces, and trends of his environment to which he stood in some relationship. For whether he merely interpreted these conditions or intervened in them, whether he placed himself on the side of these forces or opposed them, whether he let himself be borne along by these trends or fought them: something of this force or this trend never failed to emerge in extreme form. In this sense Hitler's nature may be called a historical substance.

The first situation with which he had to cope differed considerably from that in which Maurras and Mussolini were placed: he was aware of belonging to two great European states speaking the same language but having entirely different structures.

Austria: The Progressive Feudal State

In calling Austria[29] a progressive feudal state, a closer definition is required. Feudal state does not, in this case, imply the true feudal state of the Middle Ages, based on purely personal loyalty and obedience. This state, like all those in Europe, had passed through its period of absolutism, which meant that it possessed its own bureaucracy and a highly developed state-oriented outlook. Nevertheless, in a wider sense it could be called feudal. The lead was taken by the aristocracy, socially as well as politically, factually as well as juristically; and, as in medieval times, its way of life was based on rank and splendor, far removed from the ascetic, production-minded bourgeois world of the present day. To a large extent it even set its stamp on the middle classes, a fact which inevitably placed the rising proletariat in an even more alien and hostile position.

The conditions contributing to such an atmosphere are just as important from the standpoint of a state as, say, the question of suffrage, for around 1900 universal suffrage, equal and secret, was nonexistent not only in Austria but in Italy, Prussia, and England as well. Above all, Austria had preserved a fundamental characteristic of the feudal state: the priority of the dynasty over nationality. It was a state of nationalities, with the result that all European liberals and socialists regarded it as a relic that must disappear as soon as possible. The fact was overlooked, however, that for the most part it had been fortuitous circumstance that had allowed the formation of large national homogeneous states in England, France, Italy, and Germany, and that it had never occurred to Prussia, for instance, to renounce its Polish possessions, which had come down to it from feudal times, for the sake of the homogeneous national state. The crucial question for Austria was whether fortuitous dynastic circumstances had been the *only* reason for the political unity of the Danube area, and whether if necessary this unity could be divested of its dynastic-feudal basis and provided with a new one. Had Francis Ferdinand ascended the throne, with Karl Lueger as prime minister, this is probably the direction that would have been taken. It is impossible to say now whether or not it would have been successful. But it is just as impossible to prove that the likelihood did not exist. One thing is certain: if it had been successful Austria would have represented one of the most modern and promising state principles. It is in this sense that it was a *progressive* feudal state.

But this state was progressive, full of the seeds of the future, in yet another and more tangible respect. Under its unique conditions, parties developed which, because of their programs and methods, numbered among the most momentous phenomena of the Europe of that time, some of them marching at the very head of developments.

This applies to the Social Democratic party of Austria. Although it was not founded until 1888–89, at the Hainfeld party congress, long after the German party, and although it did not possess anything like the autochthonous tradition of the French socialist parties, it was the only party (aside from the Russian) to preserve on an everyday basis that most remarkable of all the movement's characteristics, its internationalism. It was the only one whose flanks were exposed at a very early stage to the highly tangible competition of a nationalist party, the Czech National Socialists, who were joined soon afterward by the German Workers' party (DAP). The proposals of Karl Renner and Otto Bauer for the solution of the nationality problem are among the most important theoretical works of socialist literature.

Of greater originality, however, was Karl Lueger's Christian Social People's party. While Italy's Catholics were still silent, while France's clerical movement made hesitating and sporadic attempts to achieve a breakthrough to the masses, while Germany's Center party remained a religious minority's defense party composed of dignitaries, the son of the humblest Viennese lower class succeeded in creating a mass political expression for the anticapitalist feelings of the petite bourgeoisie, which neither could nor wanted to unite with Social Democracy. Vienna's liberal press called him an Austrian Boulanger, but he was infinitely more successful than the French general. He was the only man in prewar Europe who managed to create a durable synthesis of old and new, that synthesis which Stoecker and Drumont, Romolo Murri and Marc Sangnier, in their rivalry with the socialists' radical revolutionary program, tried in vain to achieve. Those elements of social doctrine which de La Tour du Pin attempted to introduce into France's nationalist movement he had learned from Baron Vogelsang, and Vogelsang became the friend and mentor of Lueger. Lueger was the first to create the classless popular party, which leaves the classes as such intact, although it renders changes in their emphasis unavoidable. This explains why, although the press had just denounced him as the leader of the rabble and the emperor had refused three times to ratify his appointment as mayor of Vienna, he was able to appear immediately as the pillar of order. Convinced that the principle of Austria was as right as it was viable, he had no reason to fear either universal suffrage or the emancipation of nationalities which it would entail. Furthermore, there were no signs of any serious conflict with the allied conservative power. For the principles were common to both,[30] and the necessary concessions of the senior partner were assured by the existence of the Social Democratic party. Lueger's premature death was hardly less fatal for Austria's future than Francis Ferdinand's assassination four years later.

More radical than any other European party of that time—at least from certain aspects—were Georg von Schönerer's Pan-Germans.[31] For they attacked not only certain institutions but the state as such. All over Europe the socialists' theoretical hostility to the state was combining more and more with the acceptance in practice of whatever state was in power: the Action Française's hostility to the state was aimed at a certain form of state, the Young Czechs in their strivings for independence inscribed the struggle for an oppressed people on their banners. But the Germans in Austria were without any doubt the leading people in the monarchy; to claim that they were in danger of being "slaughtered," as Schönerer was fond of maintaining, was obviously a mania born of fear. It was true, of course, that, within the framework of the Austrian state, the past form of sovereign rule had to be steered toward a new form of co-operation, and the fact that Czech nationalists did not on the whole behave very sensibly did not make this any easier. But in Austria there was nothing new about a "compromise" of this kind, and as far as could be seen they had to allow German hegemony to continue to exist in proportion to the actual extent of German pre-eminence in cultural and technical matters.

It is remarkable how much more calmly the aristocracy was able to accept inevitable losses in power than the middle classes which had only just achieved political awareness. For Schönerer had started out as a liberal, and no other than Viktor Adler, subsequently leader of the Social Democrats, had collaborated in the Linz program of 1882: this was how close the early days still were, when bourgeois and socialist democracy were not yet divided. The Pan-Germans never quite lost the character of a bourgeois-democratic movement. Nevertheless, it was they who made fear the cornerstone of politics, and rage, denunciation, and universal hostility its elements. In conciliatory Austria they developed a racial anti-Semitism entailing the most radical ideological consequences; they initiated the "Away From Rome Movement," which was bound to isolate them hopelessly. Schönerer's own disagreeable personality and the alliance with the German Reich also played their part; by and large the Pan-Germans remained without influence, but they demonstrated a new discovery for the future—that the threat to a national supremacy arouses no less emotion than the undermining of a social pre-eminence and the jeopardizing of a cultural position, and that it tends equally to the creation of bogies. Hitherto every struggle for nationality had gone hand in hand with antifeudal strivings and been supported by strongly optimistic feelings of class progress. Only in France, the oldest national state of Continental Europe, was there a similar sense of threat to nationality and fear of exclusion. But in that case it was transmitted much more strongly by historical memory.

The most interesting of the Austrian parties from the standpoint of the fascist problem was the DAP (German Workers' party)[32] founded in 1904 in Trautenau—the very party Hitler did not mention in *Mein Kampf*, and the only one which could later boast of a direct and even organizational connection with the NSDAP.[33] It was the first National Socialist German Workers' party,[34] and it had far more right to call itself by that name than its gigantic offspring. The species of socialism which it represented had been derided by Marx fifty years earlier as "petit-bourgeois socialism," but there is no doubt that the DAP is genuinely entitled to be included in the variegated cosmos of socialist trends. The young party criticized the injustice of capitalist production methods, demanded full yield of their labor for the workers, encouraged a return to the "Germanic co-operative idea" of guilds and to the Germanic agrarian rights of the Middle Ages.[35] It owed its existence to the experience of that great fundamental fact which Marxists, at least in their ceremonial robes, had overlooked and which was soon to force them to undertake such a profound alteration in their theory: the fact that "the" proletariat was neither homogeneous nor on an equal level everywhere. The party was born of a new class struggle within the proletariat—the resistance of the Sudeten German workers to the infiltration of cheap Czech labor. This class struggle made reconciliation possible with the larger "organic" unity of the nation in which it hoped to find protection, thereby spontaneously leading the way to fulfilling one of the principal bourgeois desiderata: the incorporation of the workers in the common national destiny. But did not *this* kind of class reconciliation, in order to be durable, presuppose the perpetuation of a state of emergency against another people?

In *Mein Kampf* Hitler dealt at length with all these parties (except the DAP). He had already become a young German nationalist and supporter of Schönerer in Linz, not least because of the influence of his history teacher. But the impetus which gave consistency and determination to his political inclinations was obviously his encounter with Social Democratic views, with the Marxism which from then on was the object of his everlasting hatred. In this encounter Hitler displayed such a marked, indeed penetrating bourgeois reaction that the frank depiction of it in *Mein Kampf* cannot fail to astonish.[36] In reply he proposed a synthesis of Schönerer and Lueger, of German nationalist truth and the mass desire of the threatened petite bourgeoisie. To judge by appearances,[37] Hitler was already dreaming in his Vienna days of putting the sword arm of a mass social movement at the disposal of the unpopular nationalistic efforts. Thus he criticized Schönerer for his inability to appeal to the masses and his unwise challenge to the church, Lueger for his desire to rescue the Hapsburg state. It is clear that, while his conviction drew him to the Pan-Germans, his admiration was for the "greatest German mayor of all time." However, in the case of the former, he seized upon the core while with the latter he grasped only the shell.

A description of Hitler's experiences in Austria would be incomplete without mention of a man of whom he spoke as little as of the DAP but to whom in all likelihood he was somewhat indebted. This man was Adolf Lanz, who was probably the author of the pamphlets which Hitler described as the first anti-Semitic reading of his life.[38] He was also, although in a very dubious sense, one of Austria's progressive figures, for he pursued the race doctrine to a well-nigh unparalleled pitch of absurdity. It is true that his expressions were far newer than his ideas, but the work of this renegade monk with an assumed title of nobility is nevertheless one of the most striking examples not only of the fascination the aristocratic conception of the significance of blood had at one time for certain sections of the middle classes, but also of the social background of the anthropological view of history.[39] Hitler's ideas can be rendered completely intelligible without Lanz; but in his Austrian background this Austrian is entitled to a place.

The German Reich: The Feudal Industrial State

All parties and movements in Austria were basically agreed upon the necessity of drastic change. Even Francis Ferdinand and Lueger were at heart revolutionaries, for the transformation they envisaged went far beyond the mere introduction of new institutions, even that of universal suffrage.

In the German Reich the only revolutionary movement was the Social Democratic movement, but for increasingly large sections of the party it was now simply a matter of completing the "bourgeois revolution," that is, of a process which might even take place legally. "Conditions in Germany" had long ceased to be the pre-1848 conditions which had caused the whole middle class and the rudiments of the proletariat to form a united opposition. The old demand that Germany finally become united and modern had in any case been fulfilled. At the turn of the century Germany was Europe's leading industrial state—not only on the basis of production figures but also in its way of thinking and general outlook. One was inclined to forget that it still bore a number of feudal traits and differed considerably from Western Europe in its actual constitution. In the same way that universal Reichstag suffrage was drawn like a mask over the census system of the ruling federal state, so the enthusiasm for the Reich on the part of the national-liberal middle class scarcely hid the fact that in essence this state was neither a Reich nor even a true national state—which is created by its citizens, its capital, and its dominant intellectual and spiritual traditions[40]—but rather one particular feudal state expanded out of all proportion: Greater Prussia. The reason the difference was less obvious than might have been thought was that the Prussian aristocracy represented, not a seignorial class with an outlook diametrically opposed to that of the middle class, but a group of hard-working civil servants and officers of the king who had turned the Prussian army into an instrument of the highest rational perfection, so that in many ways it could be regarded as the very paragon of an industrial organization. The problem facing Germany was whether the contradiction in its existence should be decided in favor of one or the other of the two extremes—whether the feudal characteristics would be slowly dissolved along the lines of the Western states in favor of parliament and parties, or whether middle-class life would be organized on the pattern of the army. In the long run, however, the state of conflict was untenable.[41]

Each of the two possibilities was backed by a party which was far greater and stronger than any mere political organization. The Social Democrats were not alone in criticizing German "militarism." Criticism of the feudal and Prussian nature of the state penetrated far into the liberal middle classes. Even before World War I the critics included a man of the stature of Max Weber, by background a national liberal.

But the monarchistic forces were composed not only of officers and landowners from east of the Elbe. They were joined by the majority of German intellectuals, although from diverse motives: in most cases because they wanted to outdo the West in imperialism, but not infrequently because they wanted to defend German profundity against the increasing shallowness threatened by the spirit of modern Europe. But above all it was possible to exploit fear of the revolutionary Social Democrats and thereby to deal incessant debilitating blows to the enemy. And finally they had at their disposal the only national organization, apart from that of the Social Democrats, rich in tradition and conviction: the army. The German people was not sufficiently illiterate to have a cudgeled and apathetic peasants' army like the Russian; but it was not sufficiently accustomed to criticism and independence to desire and control a citizens' army. Thus, despite all Social Democratic antimilitarism, the German people was the last people in Europe to pay homage to Mars, and the hour could come when critics of the army might be reviled not merely as enemies of the Reich but as blasphemers.

But this people of Mars was nevertheless a peaceful people. Although from time to time the Kaiser overdid his role of supreme commander and alarmed the neighbors by his saber-rattling, German policy during the age of imperialism was on the whole more moderate than that of most of the great powers. Parliamentary England waged war on the Boers; the France of the victorious Dreyfusards attacked Morocco; Italy, regarded by all as harmless, declared war on the Sultan; but the people of Mars pursued a peaceful policy, although it was not without its empty gestures and ill-considered provocations.

Peace favored the parliamentary party, but it also delayed its progress. It can be taken as symptomatic that the vanguard of its opponents, the Pan-Germans, was only a small, albeit very influential group, while its own avant-garde, the Social Democratic party—ambiguous though it was and in its utterances ever more radical and revolutionary—represented the first mass party on German soil.

In the long run, however, conflict became intolerable. Conservatives, who only wished to preserve the *status quo*, put forward the most impossible of all proposals. Parliamentary monarchy was perhaps the most obvious solution, the one which was closest to a synthesis and which did not entirely deprive the vanquished party of its right to exist. But one third of the voters appeared to want a republic and the social revolution. And on the other side the leader of the Pan-Germans had worked out a program in 1912 aimed at a new form of monarchistic absolutism and hence an industrial feudalism, involving the wholesale elimination of the internal enemy and the solution of the social problem by the conquest of new living space.[42]

However, these domestic political problems were only one aspect of the situation in Germany before the outbreak of the war, and are to be explained by a wider context which warrants at least a brief glance.

The specific situation of the German people in Europe and the world is best understood when the basic fact of European expansion is taken as the point of departure, for it was only through this expansion that world history came into being. In simplest terms, three main forms of this expansion are distinguishable: first, the expansion at various points overseas of the Venetians, Spaniards, Dutch, and English; second, the extensive settlement of the Americans and Russians; third, the German colonization in Eastern Europe.[43] The first one plunged the peoples of four continents into the vortex of European civilization and led to the planting of new states, which yielded no tangible or lasting political profit to the parent state. Americans and Russians penetrated into vast areas which were either sparsely inhabited or populated by tribes of a low cultural level, thus creating for themselves the foundations of a unique position of power. But at considerable cost: what has been called American or Russian lack of culture is the outcome of this undertaking, which devoured—and still devours—the energies of whole generations. In its first stage German colonization in Eastern Europe could also be said to have involved conquest and the opening up of whole territories, but, as soon as it encountered "Christian" peoples, this colonization took place in scattered areas, upon request or invitation, often for the sake of providing aid and progress, but always as the prototype of a higher form of life. Although in the West, Germany lost some ground to the encroaching French national state, this was offset by the far greater influence exerted by Germans all over Eastern Europe. If European expansion is regarded not as a national effort but as a universal process in the course of which the obvious forms of early domination were being replaced more and more by complicated adjustments and even "partnerships," then the German colonization in Eastern Europe represented the utmost paradigm of that expansion.[44]

The process might have been declared complete for Germany, so that it could have become a normal national state. True, there might then have been despair at the vagaries of German history, but perhaps it would have been possible to make a fresh start on a new basis. That was what Schönerer might have envisaged. But he came either too early or too late. In that case Germany would have become the first power voluntarily to relinquish its political spheres of influence, its "colonies," in order to look to its domestic power of production as its sole basis from then on. The time was obviously not yet ripe for this. But from another aspect it was already too late. The revolution of 1848 had been strong enough to cause the Germans to demand the right of self-determination; it was too weak to fulfill it. It could have created a state which included all Austria and thus formed the basis for a federated Central Europe determined by Germans but not controlled by them. It could have carved Austria up into its ethnic sections and created the Pan-German state which would thus have become a "normal" Western European bourgeois national state. Finally, it could have let Prussia be absorbed by a northern, liberal *Kleindeutschland*. It foundered on powerful resistances: the feudal bastions within the individual states, fear of the radical democratic and proletarian revolution from below, lack of willingness on the part of Austria to separate from its non-German territories. But it did not fail because of intervention from outside, like the Italian uprising of 1848. It seemed to be history's revenge that in 1871 German liberalism could not, like Italian liberalism, appear beside the victorious monarch as the second and vital apex of the national revolution of unification: all it could do was march as a stirrup-holder in the arms-bristling triumphal procession of the three victorious wars. Bismarck's empire was bought at a high price: by the power of arms, Austria was banished from the Reich; a state whose very core had always developed in conflict with the Reich and some of the strongest German traditions could not rely on anyone except the Junkers and Protestant National Liberals. Nevertheless, this state made extraordinary progress, and Maurras based his whole doctrine on the conviction that the Prussian monarchy was the *cause* of just this industrial expansion.

How Hitler felt at the time about the problems of German politics is described in *Mein Kampf* in the chapter on Munich. This attitude was very much less concrete and thorough than his opinion on the Austrian situation; it is impossible to tell with certainty to what extent it reflected his actual thoughts. However, the fact that he started with the rejection of the German policy of alliances would seem to indicate that it did, and in its basic outlines it would seem to correspond to the Hitler of 1913 and 1914.

According to Hitler's view, Germany's alliance with the Hapsburg monarchy not only delivered up the Germans in Austria to "extermination,"[45] it united against Germany all those states which wanted to profit from the legacy of the declining Danubian monarchy, and above all it prevented a policy of armed conquest.[46] For conquest, bluntly and without reservation, was the focal idea in Hitler's policy, and it was Hitler himself who traced its origin to his own shrouded distant past. Conquest was essential in order to acquire territory, so as to adjust the geographical area of the state to the increasing population. Birth control, domestic colonization, economic expansion, were all unsuitable means of doing justice to the prime needs of the struggle for life. Only through newly acquired land and soil could the "overflowing" population be accommodated and the peasant class continue to be maintained as the foundation of the nation, so that industry and trade would retreat from their unhealthy position of leadership and take their place "in the general framework of a national economy based on needs and fulfillment."[47] Moreover, this was the only way to prevent the deterioration of the nation's military and political situation. It was, of course, essential not to succumb to the idea of acquiring colonial possessions—that is, acquisitions which could not be militarily secured. In Europe, land and soil could be obtained "by and large only at the expense of Russia";[48] Germany should have followed in the footsteps of the German knights of old and allied itself with England, instead of chaining itself to the corpse of the Danube monarchy and nursing cowardly dreams of a peaceful economic conquest of the world. The primary condition for this would have been the utter destruction of Marxism, which, as "poison" and "world plague," was the chief stumbling block in the way of a policy guided by the "humanity of nature" (the philosophy of which Hitler developed in this context).

To today's observer, of course, these views of Hitler on German policy seem like the ravings of a madman, especially when seen in conjunction with the fourteenth chapter of Part II of *Mein Kampf* on "Eastern Orientation or Eastern Policy." Here Hitler formulates the program of a predatory war of extermination by Germany against its eastern neighbors so decisively, and places it in a position of such central importance, that any kind of denial, attenuation, or alteration is absurd. If it is permissible to regard the German people of the pre-1933 period as politically mature and fully responsible, these would represent a much more convincing proof of the theory of collective guilt than the many isolated or obscured events which were later cited to substantiate it.

However, the historian must not be content with the perspective of the years after 1945. Ravings are of no interest to him as such, and he will therefore have the following observations to make in regard to Hitler's theses:

1. They are in direct contradiction to the possible main lines of German policy deduced above from German tradition and the realities of Western European history. They do not stand in isolation in Germany but are a continuation of Pan-German thinking.[49]

2. They are to be found during this period in many places. Not long before, Cecil Rhodes had designed a program of conquest of even greater dimensions; Corradini had extolled war and its ability to solve social problems even more enthusiastically; Maurras dreamed of Germany being plunged back into the chaos of the time following on the Peace of Westphalia (1648). If we could imagine these programs being crystallized by as vital a late-comer as Germany, the result would no doubt approach Hitler's theories.

3. They replace the outline of a specifically German expansion with that of the American and Russian expansion over sparsely populated continents, thereby revealing a contempt for history and historical facts which make one wonder how a love for "Germany"—that is, for something possessed of concrete historical existence—can be substantiated in this nationalism. Nevertheless, Hitler's conception was undoubtedly supported by the earliest aspects of German eastern colonization. And it was to be assumed that, in the post-World War I period, an appeal of this primitive warlike type to the defeated yet unconquered people of Mars was bound to exert a fatal fascination.

4. Hitler's hatred of "Marxism," which was reconfirmed in Munich, originally had nothing to do with the Bolshevik revolution and not much with social-revolutionary elements. Hitler's antagonism was directed at Social Democracy as Schönerer's chief adversary and the enemy of German influence in Austria, as the stronghold of the trends blocking German "*Lebensraum* policy." Presumably he would have hated it no less if even before the war it had been a revisionist and out-and-out parliamentary party.

It may be said on the whole that Hitler's ideas—if indeed they do go back basically to his first Munich period—at that time already possessed the innate force of a radical alternative solution, a solution toward which tended many wiser and more moderate Germans who in peaceful times would have strenuously denied having anything in common with the extremism of the street-corner politician.

War, Revolution, and Peace Treaty

War, revolution, and the peace treaty inevitably provided him with a unique opportunity, although he was submerged in the nameless millions as a completely unknown personality. It is true, of course, that one reason this war was welcomed in Germany with a sense of relief was because it put an end to the daily political squabbles and with one magic stroke created that exhilarating unity which had been so sadly missing in time of peace. The most popular remark the Kaiser ever made was that he no longer recognized the existence of parties, only of Germans, and even firmly entrenched Marxist convictions could not resist the rapture of those August days (especially as they could hide behind the fig leaf of the "war of liberation" against Tsarist despotism). But all too soon new trends emerged, often cutting clear across these reconciled groups, and that old, deep-rooted dissension reared its head again.

It is a remarkable fact that the group which first made this dissension visible was the very one that had most rejoiced over the previous harmony. Long before the leftist radicals began to make themselves noticeable, an influential group demanded war goals which were completely incompatible with that other, equally famous remark of the Kaiser's: "We are not motivated by a lust for conquest."[50] From Belgium to the Baltic, from the ores of Lorraine to the wheat of the Ukraine, stretched the span of Pan-German desires, and the expropriation of industry or the expulsion of the local population in favor of German settlers frequently became items in a new kind of program of total conquest. The German people may have been subjectively and sincerely convinced that they were not to blame for the war, but they did not sufficiently take into account that the other side also had a clear conscience and had waxed just as indignant over the German invasion of Belgium as the Germans had once been over England's attack on the Boers. Was it any wonder that in the eyes of the world a state whose spokesmen tried to turn an alleged act of defense into a profitable business or even an act of historical necessity was a cold-blooded and well-prepared aggressor?

This agitation, which became increasingly widespread and had already gained a foothold in the Supreme Command, did not receive an unequivocal and official reply until the Reichstag adopted its peace resolution in July, 1917. But what had been accepted in August, 1914, as the imperial expression of a people secure in their sense of unity and right, was now made to look like the beginning of the end and the voicing of defeatist feelings. Mussolini did not regard this resolution at all as the Pan-Germans did; he passionately denounced it as the insidious attempt of the Germans to stabilize a momentarily favorable war situation and thus at the last minute make a victory out of what in the long run was an inevitable defeat, by making it look like a draw.[51]

Presumably he saw things more clearly than those Germans who favored a victorious peace, a *Siegfrieden*. However, they resisted the peace resolution not only for reasons of foreign policy but also—and mainly—because it was an action of the Reichstag, that is, of its leftist majority. For in matters of internal policy they had taken just as firm a stand as in foreign policy, and here they were even more frank in making conservative party interests their guiding principle. The phrase that parties no longer existed was interpreted by them to mean that from an institutional standpoint nothing must be changed and that above all the Prussian three-class suffrage must not disappear. Yet it was obvious—and a man like Max Weber repeatedly emphasized this[52]—that the war was a democratizing force of unique effectiveness, and that the returning soldiers could not possibly be refused the right to full participation in the shaping of political conditions. Had not the war even destroyed the exclusiveness of the officers' corps and raised the lower middle class to what had once been jealously guarded positions?

But perhaps it was precisely at this point that the internal political situation merged with the foreign political viewpoint, to give the arguments of the supporters of the *Siegfrieden* fresh and unexpected strength. Is it not the language of absolute determination that has the greatest appeal to the masses in wartime? Was it a foregone conclusion that "the warriors" should lay the weight of their newly won political influence on the scales of those parties which wanted to turn them into bourgeois citizens again? Was it perhaps merely the defeatist influence of Social Democrats which was responsible for the fact that the masses obviously did not think as the bulk of those new "democratic" officers appeared to do? Did not the mistake lie ultimately in the fact that the excessive and illegal power of the Supreme Command, about which even the Reich Chancellor complained, was still not extensive enough?

It is impossible to determine which arguments were the stronger. But it is easy to see on which horizon they moved. Ludendorff's horizon was that of total war on an unprecedented scale and with incalculable possibilities. The Reichstag was thinking along the lines of a postwar order which by and large would leave the *status quo* intact. This conception was certainly not one which could match Ludendorff's in sweep. The exigencies of logic alone compelled the creation of a second position forcing the Reichstag conception into the middle and in turn attacking it with its own artillery. For this second position the war was not a deplorable calamity and still less a heroically welcomed human destiny: it was a crime, one which could be precisely localized and fought, and which had emerged from the swamp of the *status quo* and must of necessity move toward the potential military totalitarianism of Ludendorff. This was the position of the radicals of Zimmerwald and Kiental, of Karl Liebknecht and Rosa Luxemburg. But before the war was over this position, too, had lost its limpid clear-cut simplicity. A Pan-German might wonder in a dark hour whether his agitation might not bring ruin on his country more than on anything else; a parliamentarian might be tortured by misgivings as to whether it was his activity that deprived parliament of its popular basis; Lenin had to admit to himself that his own actions had supplied German imperialism with the greatest of all triumphs and had forced even him onto a path which soon bore more resemblance to the banal conditions existing in other states than to the ideas set out in his work *State and Revolution*. None of the basic answers had been refuted when the war came to an end, but they had all been placed in a position of profound ambiguity.

The first answer, in order to maintain itself, had been forced into a lie. For the German army *had* been conquered in battle, albeit after heroic resistance, and with crushing defeats. In Mussolini's articles the developments of the final summer can be followed with convincing clarity: the fear, barely concealed, as the great German offensives were launched, but from August on the feeling of confidence, a definite premonition, of victory at hand. That decisive German defeats were soon to be expected was as apparent to Ludendorff as to Mussolini; to avoid them, he pressed at the end of September with such sudden and determined vigor for an immediate armistice that even his Pan-German friends lost confidence in him. But never at any time did the general contradict the lie which was then propagated and destined to become a potent reality in German postwar developments: namely, that the revolution of November 9 had brought about the collapse of the unconquered German army by a *Dolchstoss* (stab in the back).

In actual fact, not even the milder version holds water—that the revolution weakened the German bargaining position and rendered a possible resumption of a final resistance impossible. For an essential preliminary to the revolution were conditions and measures which bore all too clearly the imprint of hopelessness or of actions born of despair. The German revolution was simply the manifestation of collapse. The reason it was not crowned with the wreath of a national uprising, like the French revolution of 1870, was because it came at a relatively different point in time; the Pan-Germans were the very ones least entitled to blame the German people for their respect for authority. It could, of course, be maintained that the German people should have been much more obedient and followed their Kaiser if necessary to the death. In thought and word the "downfall" of the German people had been used so thoroughly and unmercifully as an argument[53] that this was not illogical. And in this way the lie could ultimately be turned into a truth—everything which was looked on as weakness, every remnant of civil liberty, every plaintive cry in the letters of half-starved women to their husbands at the front, and certainly every wage dispute and every agitation on the part of leftist Social Democrats, could be interpreted as signs of a deep-seated breakdown, indeed a stab in the back insofar as the home front in any way lagged behind the self-sacrifice and fighting spirit of the battle front. And what army has ever been inclined to do otherwise than blame its defeat on obscure processes? Moreover, the German army was convinced that it was the best army in the world, and the war had confirmed its reputation. It was precisely in its most primitive form that the legend of the stab in the back was the one with the greatest appeal to the masses. It was thus possible to predict a great future for Pan-German agitation when in February, 1919—before the Treaty of Versailles, before the Munich Soviet Republic—the Pan-Germans declared war on the November Republic and in a sweeping gesture made the bankruptcy receivers responsible for the bankruptcy.[54]

Those occupying the middle position had no need to lie, but they were the victims of a terrible self-delusion and thus, contrary to their intentions, played into the hands of their enemies. For they believed that the German republic would be granted a good peace. And indeed enemy propaganda had constantly asserted that the war was being fought not against the German people but against the outworn feudal and autocratic system. But had not the German people identified themselves with this system for more than four years of war? Had the republicans ever displayed the energy and courage which would have made them worthy of confidence? Was it *they* who had forced the acceptance of Wilson's Fourteen Points, or had it not rather been the Supreme Command which very tardily discovered Wilson's program to be a providential gift of the gods with the aid of which it could remove the armistice petition from the authority of the enemy military leaders? But no revolution has ever been made without hope. The hopes this revolution aroused dug the grave of the republic as surely as did the lie of the *Dolchstoss*.

The most intact and hitherto justified faith was that of Karl Liebknecht and Rosa Luxemburg. The victims of the Russian revolution still hardly counted when compared with the hecatombs of the war; the conviction still held good that the capitalist system as such was the cause of wars, and that only its elimination could secure peace forever. But Liebknecht and Luxemburg were defeated—before they were assassinated. Even at the elections on the occasion of the first congress of *Arbeiter- und Soldatenräte* (Workers' and Soldiers' Councils) they remained hopelessly in the minority. The "revisionist" inclinations of the workers became apparent just as early as the bourgeois nature of the state and society. It is not wholly impossible that the confusion in December and January might have led to a seizure of power in Berlin by the Spartacus League. But in any case the revolutionary forces would have had no permanent prospects; Allied intervention would have destroyed them and, what is more, probably met with the support of nine tenths of the German population. Even Rosa Luxemburg could not hide her misgivings over the Bolshevik methods. If the socialist revolution along Soviet lines had proved impossible in Italy, in Germany it would have had even less of a chance, and only the turmoil of the first postwar months, part and parcel of the defeat as it was, could make it appear otherwise.

That Germany was thereby either saved from ruin or salvaged for Western culture is something it would be hard to maintain in the light of subsequent events; but one thing is certain—that Germany was assured of a specific place in one particular development of European history.

This development, far from being continuous, was marked by deep and violent cleavages; one of its elements was revolution. And this revolution did not, as it did almost everywhere in Asia, mean merely the drastic substitution of one ruling class by another, with the bulk of the population remaining more or less untouched in the stability of their daily lives: it was a "social" process which was profound in its roots and profound in its consequences. The French revolution really was a bourgeois revolution in that it brought a new class of the population to power and made of it a reservoir of directional energy. But the French revolution was *not* simply a matter of replacing one class with another. Aristocrats had taken part in preparing this revolution, aristocrats played a leading role in it, the rule of the radicals under Robespierre and Saint-Just collapsed after a short time; if Napoleon may be regarded as having continued and completed the revolution, he simultaneously combined it to a surprising degree with the forms and categories of the old Europe; under the Restoration, legitimist and Napoleonic nobility stood side by side, and the peasants had their ownership of ecclesiastical land confirmed. The revolution was therefore a cleft in the development and yet not actually a barrier; the new triumphed by learning from the old and uniting with it; the old passed on its forms of life and thought to the profoundly altered future in a process which admittedly bore no resemblance to plant growth, since it took place with bloody battles, mutual misunderstanding, and bitter hatred.

If the Spartacist revolution had succeeded, it would have resulted in the wholesale elimination of what was until then the ruling class. Whether such an elimination would have been merited is not relevant here. Whether it would have been possible must remain a matter for historical theorizing. But there is no doubt that in Germany it would have meant a hitherto unknown method of discharging and replacing the wielders of power. To regret that the revolution did not completely unseat the monarchistically-minded civil servants and officers, is to stand on Spartacist ground. It was in accordance with the genre of European revolution for two heterogeneous elements to combine, form a new class, and develop a new entity which was their joint product. For if the deciding factor in the German revolution was that the majority of the workers denied their allegiance to the Spartacist variety of radicalism, its most striking characteristic was that the indispensable order was created by the future Reichswehr. And when one considers the possibility of this amalgamation, one should perhaps think less about the sometimes questionable behavior of Seeckt or the antirepublican utterances of high-ranking civil servants, than about the fierce hatred displayed in the ranks of the irregular *Freikorps* and nationalist-radical associations toward the Reichswehr generals and their policy. In France the republic needed seven years after 1870 to become more or less consolidated; if the German republic was supposed to have to go through a critical period lasting three times as long, there was still no need to despair of its fate.

It is very much open to doubt whether the men of the republic such as Ebert, Scheidemann, and Erzberger, Reinhardt, Seeckt, and Lossow, were the more impressive and admirable figures. Ludendorff and Helfferich were more at one with themselves, and they had colossal achievements to their credit; Liebknecht and Luxemburg were richer in ideas and had close associations with a universal movement of world-historical significance. But the men of the Weimar Republic had their place in the line of European history. What Mussolini was in those days only postulating for Italy—the creation of a new ruling class by incorporating the representatives of hitherto absent (internally more than externally) sections of the population—seemed almost to fall into their laps. Yet they were not particularly conscious of this. Perhaps the soldiers among them could have foreseen that what was being offered was not a return to the past but merely the choice between this ally and another—one who if they were obstinate would treat them in a manner very different from that of Ebert, the former harness-maker from Bremen.

It may be objected that it was not lack of insight that led the leaders of the republic onto the path of destruction but the immense factor of the peace treaty, which burdened the young state with a mortgage of such dimensions that it was bound to collapse under it. This is not the place to embark on a thorough analysis of that copious treaty, to examine whether a remorseless will to destruction wished to deprive a conquered people of the basis of life and every possibility for the future. A world which in 1939 listened to Hitler boasting of spending ninety billion Reichsmarks on armaments, and which has since become aware of the peace terms of World War II, has in any case become skeptical toward such ideas and is inclined to accuse the Versailles peace if of anything, of its halfheartedness. In this context the only considerations which are of interest are those which derive either from generally known facts or from specific questions arising out of analysis. Such considerations must lead to the following:

1. If the Frankfurt Peace of 1871 and the more important peace terms of World War II are taken as points of comparison, it is found that the Treaty of Versailles, as far as Germany was concerned, was in every sense a peace of the nineteenth century. France's war contribution of five billion francs was, for the standards of the times and in relation to the damage and costs, not much less vast than the sum of 132 billion Reichsmarks demanded from Germany; by comparison, the amount actually paid in the end was even smaller. Bismarck's demand for the surrender of two rich provinces which, although not French-speaking, were undeniably French in outlook, was no less terrible than the territorial surrender demanded of Germany by the Treaty of Versailles. And finally the social struggles triggered by the war and the peace were much bloodier and grimmer in France. A comparison with the peace treaties of Bucharest and Brest Litovsk, as well as with the Pan-German conceptions of a victorious peace, also puts the Treaty of Versailles in a favorable light.

2. Germany's implacable opponents in the enemy countries were far from satisfied.

Maurras especially waged a furious battle against the *mauvais traité* and blamed the
ideological prejudices of the socialists and democrats for the fact that German unity
was respected. And certainly the treaty was based to a large extent on negotiation and
compromise: on negotiation not, it is true, with the enemy, but nevertheless among
the Allies; on compromise between the demands of power and the postulates of
principles. It was this indecisive character that was responsible for the treaty's weakness and that gave rise to some of its most wounding severities. That the Germans in
Austria were not granted self-determination seemed illogical and outrageous in the
face of the majesty of the principles which had been formulated as timeless truths;
the issue would have looked entirely different had it been borne in mind that the right
to self-determination also has its day and its hour, and that Austria had twice been
excluded from Germany, and excluded itself from Germany, in free self-determination.
And it ought really to have been obvious that France's severity, the object of so much
recrimination, sprang from the justifiable anxiety of being left alone, without Anglo-
American guarantees, with an enemy which had been neither critically weakened nor
essentially altered.

3. The fatal effect of the peace treaty in Germany arose just as much from Ger-
many's preoccupation with its own problems as from objective circumstances. Who in
Germany gave a thought to the lunar landscapes of Belgium and Northern France?
Who even noticed that similar confusion and distress were afflicting victorious Italy?
Who realized that the hatred of the enemies was not grounded in mystical and
mysterious ulterior motives, but was an entirely natural phenomenon?

Obviously the opportunities and advantages offered by the treaty and circumstances in general were not as easy to grasp and convert into indignation as the
surrender of the fleet or the continuation of the blockade. But that did not
make them any the less real. That the gap as against Western constitutional
reality had been eliminated was looked on as an injury; that national unity
had been preserved was taken for granted. That the loss of colonies could mean
an enormous advantage was something even the most perspicacious minds
could not grasp. But the reparations clearly implied that by the consent of all
concerned Germany was to become once again the greatest industrial power on
the Continent, while the bolshevization of Russia signified even more clearly
that Germany would derive no less advantage from the fate of its neighbor in
peace than it had just done in war. In the long run Lenin's revolution could not
fail to bring the small European states, under certain conditions, onto the side
of Germany, and above all it was bound to make Germany the object of Anglo-
American friendship. It immensely enhanced Germany's value as an ally, since
Germany's freedom of choice was never for a moment seriously affected from
the outside. Although the dream of some nationalist revolutionaries to disrupt
the capitalist world in alliance with the Soviet Union can hardly be considered
as having progressed beyond the blueprint stage, there is little doubt that
Germany had the choice of participating in the great world conflict to come
either in mindless panic or with constructive concepts answering the needs of
the unique hour. In either case its role was bound to be, although not unique,
a significant one. For uniqueness meant universal hostility, and the war should
have taught the German people at least one lesson of cardinal importance: that

universal hostility was henceforward out of the question because it must destroy national existence in the event of defeat, or the historical individuality of the people in the unlikely event of a victory over the whole world. Seen objectively, the price paid for this insight—the price of a few years of crisis, unrest, and disappointing negotiations—was not too high.

If the objective judgment of the German[55] reaction to the Treaty of Versailles is bound to be somewhat harsh, it can only constitute the first half of this study, that is, within the framework of the examination of fascism. For:

1. The Franco-Prussian war of 1870–71 was a profound shock to French feeling and thought. If it was capable of changing the outlook and attitude of men like Renan and Taine, namely, in a direction which may justifiably be called fascistoid, is it any wonder that after 1918 the one anxiety of the German intelligentsia was how to restore the old Germany or transform it to match the times, and thus nullify the consequences of the war?

2. If Italy's relatively minor and artificial disillusionment over the Treaty of Versailles resulted in many thousands of former officers and soldiers flocking to D'Annunzio in Fiume, if for a whole year the Comandante was allowed with impunity to oppose his own government and make a mockery of the Supreme Allied Council in Paris, is it surprising that Germany was full of *Freikorps*, of agitated students and disillusioned former officers?

Germany's political dilemma had not after all been really solved by war, revolution, and the peace treaty; it had merely been shifted onto another level. The parliamentary party had, it is true, been successful—more than its desire and will had called for. It had been immensely reinforced by the Social Democrats going firmly over onto its side. But it had triumphed not of its own strength but as an outcome of the defeat. The path it proposed to tread was hard and unglamorous; its goal was the incorporation of Germany into a larger system, a system in which Germany would play a significant but not a dominant role. This path had little in common with some of the most powerful Prussian and German traditions.

Instead of the great mass of prewar Social Democrats, the parliamentary party had to its left the small Communist party, which was shaken by internal crises and had been crippled as much as reinforced by the existence of the Soviet Union, whose policy depended on Germany. However, this Communist party undoubtedly exerted considerable influence on some supporters of the Social Democrats, and the more the position of the working class appeared threatened by "reaction," the stronger this influence became. Its strength was thus in direct proportion to the strength of the rightists.

But the strength and character of the Right also depended primarily on the real or imagined strength of the Communists. Hence the two poles were bound always to gain in strength with and through each other, at the cost of the parliamentary center, which lost its leftist and rightist peripheral groups. Each could only hope to win if its own breakthrough went much deeper than that of its adversary. The Communists had a certain advantage in that they knew how to handle the masses. But they had to contend with the growing handicap of being an offshoot of the Soviet development. The old feudal Right, insofar as it did not join the parliamentary camp to complete that threatened and crucial alliance, had essentially maintained its social positions of power, but it had lost enormously in political influence. On the other hand, the war, the revolution, and Versailles represented as many potential expansions. The immense advantage of the Right consisted in the fact that the peripheral groups it could reach were larger and—more easily frightened. For the Right everything depended on establishing contact with the masses and creating that fear which alone could bring "the people" onto its side. But this contingency was foreign to it and its consequences were unpredictable.

The main requirement for the self-preservation of the parliamentary center was that it recognize its own homogeneity and render its own path, if not attractive, at least intelligible to the thinking segment of the population. In 1919 its point of departure had not been unfavorable, but until a few years earlier its strongest component had been a social-revolutionary party and it had thus remained exposed to self-seeking and fatal identification with the Communists.

Thus the configuration of German politics after the first consolidation resembled that of all the large European states with the exception of the Soviet Union, although it was modified by the specific conditions existing in Germany after its defeat. The man who was fated to become the central figure in German politics, the helmsman of Germany's destiny, was the one who was capable of shattering the fragile equilibrium of the hostile elements on the most sustained basis and thus of finally blocking that much jeopardized trend toward republicanism.

Hitler's Political Beginnings

The future revealed this man to be no other than Adolf Hitler. However, this was due much less to the man himself than to the profound change in conditions which followed in the wake of the war. *His* convictions had been established in outline before the war, but no one listened to the fears and idiosyncrasies of the self-exiled vagabond.[56] The war converted them into widespread phenomena, but to Hitler it also gave something personally decisive, a firmly appointed place among his fellow men: the army (in which he performed very creditably), and the determination to oppose the threat, now manifest to all, with the same single-mindedness that the war had taught him.

Thousands of others must have had similar aspirations, but Hitler's earliest experiences showed he had a unique gift of appealing to "the people," because what he now exemplified was the most radical expression of the longings, hopes, and fears of that people. What kind of a "people" was it to whom he appealed?

It was not the "Marxist-infested" masses whom Hitler the orator had the power to "nationalize," to infuse with patriotism. Until his seizure of power the percentage of "Marxist" votes remained more or less constant. Nor was it the Catholic bourgeoisie of Munich and later of Germany who became his followers, although for a time they followed his career with a certain amount of sympathy. Even the nationalistic Right went over to him only in its peripheral sections; it had its own organizational forms and preserved them until 1933. The cadres of the liberal parties remained for the most part intact.

Two remarks of Hitler's made during the war provide an important indication, especially when they are supplemented by a local event of far-reaching importance which took place in Munich in 1918.

In 1915, in one of the very few of his letters from the front still extant, Hitler expressed the desire "that our internal internationalism also collapse. That would be worth more than any territorial gain."[57]

Looking back in 1924 he reproduced his thoughts on the parliamentary issue of the summer of 1918 as follows: "What concern of ours was universal suffrage? Was it for that we fought for four years? ... It was not with the cry of 'Long live universal secret suffrage' that the young regiments went to their death in Flanders, but with the shout of 'Germany above all else in the world.' "[58]

On March 7, 1918, the Free Workers' Committee for a Good Peace was founded by Anton Drexler, a toolmaker employed by the state railway in Munich. The committee had some forty members, chiefly colleagues of Drexler's. This group was a kind of popular edition of the Independent Committee for a German Peace, headed by Dietrich Schäfer, to which the Pan-German League was godparent.

To begin with, Hitler's comment on suffrage: that it was a matter of lack of *equality* within the Prussian electoral system apparently never entered Hitler's mind; still less did he seem to be conscious of the profound and intolerable humiliation the soldier must have felt at the fact that equality in the face of death was not matched by equality in political rights. This violent disparity between external and internal political viewpoints is the hallmark of either an aristocratic ruling class or of that nonpolitical—perhaps more appropriately called semipolitical—class which under moderate rule does not protest because it derives its self-awareness either from sources other than political ones or from a proud sense of the power of the state as a whole, of which it is after all a part and by no means a negligible part. This class was first stirred up by the war, and the violence with which it was roused to action was all the greater because of its previous quiescence. The war had threatened the powerful whole, perhaps even through the impalpable influences of an "internal internationalism" but the effect of the revolution on this class was just as drastic, for the revolution jeopardized its modest but acknowledged place within society, and long before the appearance of Hitler these often touching and personally highly respectable people sought each other out and sometimes—as in Drexler's group—found each other.[59] It was not to the petite bourgeoisie as such that Hitler appealed, but to those sections of it which politically speaking were still virgin, which had not participated in the fight for the emancipation of the middle classes or were not familiar with their traditions. In close proximity to them were the younger officers and soldiers whose world had been the war, and that "most German of all" group among the intellectuals for whom Thomas Mann had recently emerged as spokesman. In some aspects Hitler belonged to all three groups. Judged by the standards of the prewar years, he belonged to the proletarian dregs of the semipolitical petite bourgeoisie. The war made him place the army ahead of all else as an institution. That he would have much preferred to wander through Italy as an "unknown painter" and only embarked on a political course—a course that was actually foreign to him—because of the threat to the "German race," was something he continued to assert, and with a good deal of conviction, right up to the latter part of his life.[60]

All three groups bore the mark of their dual relationship to bourgeois society. Although from one standpoint they had nothing in common with it and so were forever dreaming of "conquering" it, still where the proletarian attempt at revolution was concerned, they proved to be its last reserve. Therefore they did not lack support from influential circles, while the crisis in Marxism enabled them to make some inroads into socialist ranks. Thus it was possible for an apparently classless popular party to arise, a party of a new, that is, fascist, type, which before the war would generally speaking have been impossible: a mass party[61] characterized by the juxtaposition of formerly nonpolitical petit bourgeois and soldiers, radical-conservative intellectuals, and former social-ists,[62] dominated by a leader, supported by conservative forces, hostile to the Marxist revolution and capitalist society, although not to both in the same degree.

Despite fundamental similarities in structure, it is possible to imagine a number of differences between various parties and a wealth of possibilities for development within one party: the relative importance of the three main groups can vary or shift, the principle of leadership may express itself with less or more emphasis, at an earlier or a later date, the relationship to established powers can be, or become, less or more tense, and so on. Here one of the chief differences between Italian fascism and National Socialism already becomes very apparent: Italian fascism was first and foremost a militant bourgeois resistance to the acute and incalculable threat of socialist revolution, a resis-tance which gained substance in the paradoxical confluence with the group of former Marxist and syndicalist revolutionaries surrounding Mussolini. National Socialism was primarily a reaction to the lost war; the preponderance of soldiers in it was thus stronger from the very beginning, while the socialist elements were all petit bourgeois and reformist in origin. But the vital difference lies in the fact that National Socialism had by artificial means to maintain, and as much as possible intensify, the social agitation which in Italian fascism was the result of circumstances and was taken for granted.

As has been shown, Mussolini fought for years to win over the Social

Democrats because he knew from experience that, from the standpoint of the organic expansion of capitalist production, the autonomous re-entry of the socialist working class into the state was a prime requirement. Hitler was incapable of such insight. It would have been the very thing to impede the growth of his party. For Germany was ahead of Italy inasmuch as by far the greater part of the socialist movement had of its own accord taken the step which Turati never dared to take: the step toward a modifying collaboration with the bourgeois state. It was precisely this essential requirement that Hitler had to forget and to render forgotten, in order to have "Marxism" as such for his opponent. To this end he could make use of anti-Semitism which, except in a rudimentary fashion, Italian fascism had been able to dispense with. What Hitler hated in Marxism was not so much its proletarian as its bourgeois nature, which in his view was crippling Germany's driving force and military preparedness. This alone enabled him to describe Marxism in *Mein Kampf* as "the essence of the present-day *Weltanschauung*."[63] To give up all idea of collaborating with the forces of a socialist movement which was spontaneously moving toward revisionism was something that had been forced on Mussolini by the Matteotti crisis; for Hitler it had always been a matter of course, basic to his very existence, in fact. Consideration of the Italian example makes it plain that, although National Socialism was based on an amalgamation, it was *not* the amalgamation of nationalism and socialism, and that, although it bridged a gulf, it was not National Socialism that caused the gulf between bourgeoisie and proletariat to disappear. For every synthesis must disclose the nature and tradition of *both* elements.

Hitler was presumably just as little aware of these things as of the fact that he personified the classic amalgamation of the chief components of his movement. But it is reasonably safe to say that neither a soldier like Röhm nor a bourgeois like Frick nor an intellectual like Rosenberg, let alone a socialist like Otto Strasser, could have succeeded in combining the multifarious groups into the one great party, and that it was no accident that, in intensity and totality, Hitler's anti-Semitism went far beyond the hatred of the Jews as felt by even such a man as Streicher.[64]

The processes and events of this early period have recently been so extensively clarified by a number of publications, including that of documents,[65] that Hitler's statements in *Mein Kampf* have become well-nigh superfluous as source material, and they will only be sketched here in outline.

Hitler did not, like Röhm, Eckart, or Feder, emerge at once from the obscurity of the immediate postwar period in the time of the Workers' and Soldiers' Councils; it has never been quite established whether or to what extent he participated in the crushing of this isolated Soviet German interlude. It certainly made a deep impression on him, as did the days of the November revolution; and as a soldier in the reserve forces he took an active, although at first subordinate, part in an "enlightenment project" aimed at raising and reinforcing the morale of the troops which had become somewhat shaky. He was subordinate to a man who might be called the first minister of propaganda of Germany's counterrevolutionary and antirepublican Right, Captain Mayr of the General Staff, head of the Press and Propaganda Division of the Reichswehr Group Command No. 4 in Munich. Hitler made his first appearance as a political figure on July 22, 1919, when, together with some twenty others from the ranks, he was ordered to take part in an "enlightenment project" at Camp Lechfeld.[66] This was plainly a case of "the people" enlightening fellow Germans who had gone astray: bombardiers, riflemen, lance corporals, perhaps a corporal. According to unanimous opinion, Hitler's "temperamental" and "readily understandable" talks were so outstanding that he outshone the leader of the detachment and soon won the high esteem of his superiors. Captain Mayr, for example, entrusted him with the task of replying to a letter which is a typical example of the first inept emergence of political questions in what was patently a hitherto nonpolitical person. The letter dealt with—what else could it have been?—the Jewish problem. Hitler replied to Adolf Gemlich on September 16, 1919, in a long and detailed letter—the first original document from his political career.[67] And in this letter the Hitler of later years was strikingly recognizable even down to the style itself.

Hitler sought to replace anti-Semitism of the emotions with an "anti-Semitism of reason." According to him, this went beyond haphazard antipathies, which found their extreme expression in "Progromen" [sic]—pogroms. Rather was it based on the clear acknowledgment "of the consciously or unconsciously systematic corruptive influence of the Jews as a whole on our nation." For him there could be no question but that Jewry meant race and not a religious community. This "anti-Semitism of reason" defined the essential nature of the Jews as their materialist outlook, the "dance around the golden calf," the "concentration on and striving for money, for power to protect this money." The Jew effortlessly and ceaselessly increased his power in the form of interest and forced the most dangerous of all yokes upon the people. "Everything which makes men strive for higher things, whether it be religion, socialism, or democracy, is for him [the Jew] merely a means to an end, to satisfy his lust for money and power. His influence will result in national race tuberculosis." Anti-Semitism of reason must begin by treating Jews legally as aliens. "But its final goal must unshakably be the total elimination of the Jews." As a "government of national impotence," the "Republick" [sic] [68]could not and would not face this danger: on the contrary, it depended on the Jews and saw its main task in "preventing the struggle of the betrayed people against its betrayers,"[69] in the suppression of the anti-Semitic movement.

In this earliest political document from Hitler's pen, the infantile trait in his character—the attribution of well-known and generally deplored characteristics of modern civilization to a visible agent—becomes clearly apparent, as does the monomaniacal trait calling for "elimination." The strange immutability of his nature and convictions is revealed by nothing so clearly as the fact that at the end of his life there stands a document of which one section links up as smoothly with this letter as a peg fits into a joint.[70]

Four days before this letter, on September 12, 1919, Hitler was instructed to attend a meeting of the newly formed party, the *Deutsche Arbeitspartei* (German Workers' party), into which Anton Drexler had expanded his committee in January, 1919. This was one of the countless little nationalistic groups, closely allied in origin to the Thule Society (one of the first racial-nationalist organizations in Munich after the war) but, since it claimed to be a workers' party, with its own format. On the nationalistic right wing it was an undisputed postulate that the worker must "be made to become national again": hence the little group soon attracted the attention of Dietrich Eckart and Gottfried Feder, while Ernst Röhm became one of its earliest members, since he considered the German Nationalists "too exclusive."[71] It was a sound instinct, therefore, that led Hitler to read Drexler's booklet *Mein politisches Erwachen* with great interest and not to resist the pressure exerted on him to join the party and its executive (as its seventh member).[72] Here those workers and soldiers could meet and unite to form a new force—the very men for whom the Workers' and Soldiers' Councils of the revolution had been the object of intense hatred.

The little group's success in attracting public attention was due solely to Hitler's tireless energy, and at a mass meeting on February 24, 1920, the party program of twenty-five points was announced. Although Hitler had collaborated in its formulation, Drexler must be considered the real originator, he in turn being influenced by Feder. This program certainly contained more of the general ideas of the racial-nationalist movement than typical ideas of Hitler; nevertheless, it is entitled to some attention as being the first public document of Hitler's political existence.

Points 1 and 2 demanded the right of self-determination for all Germans, and equal rights for the German nation by the "abrogation" of the peace treaty.

Point 3 demanded "land and soil [colonies] for the support of our people and the settlement of our excess population."

Point 4 tied civil rights to German blood and specifically excluded Jews from these rights. This demand was elaborated in points 5 to 8, 18, and 23.

Point 11 set forth in bold type the "breaking of the capital-interest yoke" as a central postulate and demanded the abolition of unearned and effortless income. This category also includes points 12, 13, 14, 16, 17, and 19 (confiscation of all war profits, communalization of department stores, agrarian reform, and so forth).

The remaining demands are more general in nature and do not merit much interest, apart from the "moral principles and moral sense of the Germanic race" with which the recognition of positive Christianity is associated (point 24).

Today it is no longer necessary to demonstrate that the "socialist" demands were purely demagogic. While it is not permissible to doubt the subjective sincerity of Drexler and Feder, there is every reason to doubt Hitler's. It is obvious that for him the first four points were all-important; what they actually meant is equally obvious.

Germany's task during the nineteenth century was the achievement of the right to self-determination, and no external power had thwarted it. Whoever made it the cardinal point on a political program at a moment when Russia had linked its national destiny to revolutionary universal perspectives had to be prepared to plunge Germany and Europe into an anachronistic war and, without meaning to do so, put the leading Continental industrial power on a level with an underdeveloped colonial people.

If the first demand (points 1 and 2) belonged to the mid-nineteenth century, the second belonged to the beginning of the twentieth. But it obviously lacked conviction, for after the experiences of the war, there could be no desire in Germany to establish settlement colonies in Africa or Asia. Hitler simply manifested the innermost meaning of this program point when he soon substituted the acquisition of territory in Eastern Europe for that of colonies.

Finally, the third postulate could not fail to set Germany apart from the social evolution of all civilized peoples. It could, of course, acquire a universal meaning, in direct opposition to the Bolshevik program, if it promised to cure the world of its ills by the elimination of the Jews. In this sense, then, it was the only program point which was truly "timely." Hitler's letter to Gemlich contained this interpretation even *ante festum*.

This early program is neither as innocent nor as ridiculous as is often believed. It contains with sufficient clarity the three basic trends of subsequent National Socialist rule: national restitution, conquest of living space, and world salvation. In it the essential homogeneity, which had been present from the very beginning, is manifest. It is highly instructive to compare this program with the early Italian fascist one, in which, in addition to socialist demands, which occupy the most space, there is only the demand for the protection of national unity that had finally been achieved in World War I.

However, it was not this program as such which opened up the way for the NSDAP: it was the unique manner in which Hitler propagated it. By the spring of 1920 he was no longer an entirely unknown personality. At out-of-town rallies of the League for German National Defense (*Deutschvölkischer Schutz- und Trutzbund*) he was announced as a "brilliant speaker." The NSDAP (for "National Socialist" had by now been added to the original party title) now advertised its meetings in Munich's nationalist organ, the *Völkischer Beobachter*, and the first references to it appeared in the opposition press. The NSDAP was slowly beginning to emerge as a clearly defined entity from its nationalistic soil. The *Deutschsozialistische Partei* was destroyed in bitter family feuds: only its Nuremberg *Ortsgruppe* (local branch) under Julius Streicher placed itself *in corpore* under Hitler. Pogrom songs and pounding propaganda, shock troops and raiding parties, introduced a new style into Munich's political life. In December, 1920,[73] with the aid of Reichswehr funds obtained by Dietrich Eckart, it became possible to buy the *Völkischer Beobachter*. Although for the time being it did not appear as a daily newspaper, a decisive step had been taken. Hitler's party became a power in the capital city of Bavaria. By January, 1921, the party felt so strong that Hitler could utter the threat that the National Socialist movement would prevent—by force if necessary—all events and lectures capable of "having a demoralizing effect on our already sick fellow Germans."[74] In February, 1921, the first giant rally took place in the Krone Circus building, and in July Hitler acquired dictatorial power in the party by means of a determined maneuver.

During the summer of 1922 National Socialists could risk breaking up a meeting at which Prime Minister Count Lerchenfeld was speaking; in October, on the occasion of "German Day" in Coburg, they managed, "with resounding music and fluttering flags,"[75] to sweep aside the agreement reached with the unions by the celebration committee, and they were no less successful against the "Red terror" which broke out after the rupture of the agreement. Shortly afterward, the National Socialists received great impetus from the March on Rome, and rousing applause greeted Hermann Esser's announcement that what was possible in Italy was not impossible in Bavaria: the name of the German Mussolini, he said, was Adolf Hitler.[76] The designation *Der Führer* was already in widespread use, and popularly he was known as the "King of Munich." In conflicts with the government, the Reichswehr came to the aid of its now independent offspring, and the Bavarian People's party disliked the Social Democrats far too much for it entirely to drop its somewhat unruly ally. In 1920 Hitler had had to extricate himself from the embraces of the "nationalist strolling scholars" from Thule, the *Reichshammerbund*, the Germanic Orders, and other associations. By 1923, however, he found himself in even more confined and confining contact with the Fatherland Leagues born of fear of revolution and of the socialist councils and reinforced by the disbanding of the home guards which was officially decreed in 1921: Pittinger's *Bavaria and Reich*, Captain Heiss' *Reichsflagge*, the *Oberland* league, and so on. When Röhm succeeded in forming the *Arbeitsgemeinschaft der vaterländischen Kampfverbände* from the most reliable of these groups, an organization which was much more concerned with paramilitary preparation for the threatening and hoped-for war with France than with the political struggle against Marxism, Hitler again found himself trapped and being used for ends only partially his own. The surge of national enthusiasm on "German Day" in Nuremberg benefited Ludendorff far more than Hitler, and the founding of the *Deutscher Kampfbund* with its wholly military orientation seemed to thrust him still more into the background. However, in an irresistible speech made at the end of September before its assembled leaders, Hitler managed to push his way to the top and gain political control of the *Kampfbund*, a power with which it was possible to risk making the great bid for Germany, something he could not have done with only the NSDAP which, by itself, was still too weak an instrument. He was now at the head of the German *fascio di combattimento*; Lieutenant Colonel Kriebel was his Balbo, Munich his Milan, and his version of the March on Rome should have taken him, with the support of Bavarian conservatives surrounding Kahr and Lossow, to Berlin.

But at the head of this state there was no Victor Emmanuel, and Hitler had prepared his march far less thoroughly than Mussolini. It was not he who decided the timing, but the impatience of his troops on the one hand[77] and the preparations of the conservatives in power and their friends for *their* treason on the other. And if even Luigi Federzoni had felt a vague impulse to resistance when he found himself outstripped by the relentless energy of his ally, it is scarcely to be wondered at that Kahr and Lossow in the end resisted their satellite role since, although subject to brutal pressure, they were at the same time so much more powerful than the Italian monarchist friends of the fascist *Putsch*. And so the depressing sense of having been forsaken by authority, coupled with two salvos from the police, sufficed to bring this march on Berlin to an inglorious end before it ever left the Feldherrnhalle on November 9, 1923. Ludendorff alone marched upright and undaunted through the shooting, Hitler and his men fled, although the population was on their side and an efficiently led popular uprising could perhaps have turned the tide.[78]

It is idle to ask who prevented whose *Putsch*. The participants were too close to one another to regard themselves all along as opponents, but they were not close enough to strike jointly. Each was sufficiently strong to allot a subordinate role to his ally, but too weak to manage without him. In consequence they were doomed to wreck one another. However, the lesson of Hitler's *Putsch* is not to be found in the unraveling of these two allies' mutual relations: it lies rather in the clarification of the relationship between fascism and state authority in general. In Munich essentially the same thing happened as two years previously in Sarzana:[79] the illustrious, ever-victorious party composed of brave soldiers fled in panic when the rifles of hitherto co-operative authority were turned on them instead of on the common enemy. Presumably the same thing would have happened if a single battalion of Carabinieri had fired on the advancing columns of Blackshirts on October 28, 1922. Fascist movements are easily quelled if the state is seriously determined on such a course. But to summon up this determination is one of the most difficult things for the state to do (and even in Munich chance played a bigger part than determination), for if it feels strong and not in danger it will contain no fascist movement worth considering. To recognize potential hostility to the state on the part of a helpful ally, when the overt hostility of the declared adversary is attracting all eyes, is considerably less simple than to apportion blame *ex eventu*. Once again the example of Italy shows that this task, too, has varying degrees of difficulty, and that the government of Bavaria, that prime example of order, had a good deal less reason to tremble for its position and to fear the socialist revolution than had the ruler of a kingdom which was shaken to its foundations.

The years 1919 to 1923 in the evolution of National Socialism can be most readily compared with its corresponding period in Italian fascism. For the period 1924 to 1932 there is no counterpart in the history of fascism. After 1933 there was a considerable amount of reciprocal influence and a marked advance of first one and then the other. From 1919 to 1922 (or 1923), however, developments ran largely parallel both in time and actual events: the same modest beginnings, the same sensational upsurge, the same early and violent reach for power. Even the circumstances display startling analogies.[80] Yet at the same time the limits of similarity become apparent.

The attempt has often been made to explain the initial successes of National Socialism by the extraordinary idealism and spirit of self-sacrifice of its supporters.[81] However, there is no evidence that the supporters of the other nationalist trends were any less "idealistic." Only Hitler could form the nucleus around which the imperative and unco-ordinated spirit of sacrifice could crystallize but which this spirit could not of itself produce. At the outset Hitler's monomaniacal obsession, irreducible and wholly individual, stood at the very center of National Socialism in a far more active and comprehensive sense than that in which Mussolini's personality constituted one of the requirements of fascism. But even extreme fanaticism cannot have any lasting effect unless it stands at a crossroads of history. Hitler had a legitimate claim to feel that he was accomplishing something unprecedented and historic. His relationship to the soil of nationalism was very similar to that of Marx and Engels to the many different socialist currents of their time: while adopting its ideas in principle, by means of constricting and hardening he created something new for the practice of politics and imbued it with the will to power and ruthlessness. But he did this with his eyes turned toward the socialist enemy, whom he both imitated and surpassed. Thus he accomplished pragmatically the same thing that the young Mussolini had begun to anticipate mentally: the liberation of the realistic and militant elements of Marxism.

The Marxists had often disturbed or scattered bourgeois meetings by noise or the massing of their supporters; the National Socialists protected their own assemblies and broke up those of their opponents by an organized terror aimed at the physical elimination of every single adversary. The Marxists went out onto the streets; the National Socialists marched in the streets and turned to their advantage anything that had a mental or physical appeal in the way of military discipline and martial sound effects. The Marxists had introduced emotion and the language of violence into politics; the National Socialists let politics be engulfed by an ocean of passion and a tidal wave of abuse. The nationalists dreamed of the elimination of parties, in the paramilitary organizations (*Wehrverbände*) soldierly virtues were being practiced as a preparation for war; only the soldiers of the NSDAP deliberately carried wartime lessons into ordinary life and made politics a continuation of war by using the same methods. That was exactly what Balbo's and Grandi's Fascists had done in Ferrara and Bologna. If it was true that World War I was the gateway to an age of war, then these methods were bound to succeed, for they were completely up-to-date, and tailored precisely to the age.

However, in spite of their modernity they could never even have existed had they not been welcomed by widespread sections of the population. In Bavaria as in Italy, the middle classes had been shocked and frightened by the "Bolshevik" attempt at revolution in 1919. This is the prosaic fundamental fact without which fascism and National Socialism are inconceivable, the indispensable preparation of the soil for the new seed. One may ridicule the middle-class fear of revolution, but to do so shows little understanding of the fact that by its own declared intention the Communist revolution aimed at being a total one, and that therefore if it miscarried it was bound to rouse the most deeply rooted emotions against itself. Yet anyone who regards the "Red terror" as sufficient justification for all that followed forgets that of the ten murdered hostages seven were members of a very active counter-revolutionary organization[82] who had been arrested in the normal way and, according to all the laws pertaining to civil war, were liable to execution, and that the *Freikorps* in turn not only were responsible for a bloodbath among their enemies but also inadvertently shot twenty-one members of a Catholic trade guild.[83] But the Communist leaders Leviné and Lewien, Toller and Eglhofer, must have known that Karl Marx had spoken of the "ripeness" of capitalist conditions as the prerequisite for the proletarian revolution; if they regarded this ripeness as present in Munich, or believed that after all the atrocious events of the war a new atrocious attempt was necessary and justified, success was the *only* thing that could prove the correctness of their view or the reasonableness of their will. Into what layers of the lower middle class and upper working class an agitated reaction penetrated, how powerful it was and how filled with provincial indignation over the "foreign" revolutionaries—all of this cannot be judged on moral grounds, but constitutes an integral part of the very nature of the phenomenon. This was the case in Munich as much as Bologna. It is, of course, quite another question whether this "bourgeoisie" (which actually, as this event proved, extended deep into the ranks of the Social Democrats) correctly understood the historical perspectives, or whether it even acted in its own interests when influential sections of it displayed such marked sympathies for the most extreme form of posthumous reaction.

Moods are indeed part of history's most important material, but they do not make history. Neither Hitler's obsession nor the sympathy of the middle classes would have made such a swift and sharp rise possible for the National Socialist movement had not powerful friends in principal government offices carefully shielded it and consistently befriended it. The Reichswehr's aid, Dietrich Eckart's connections, and the backing of Pöhner, chief of police, scarcely less than Hitler's passion and oratorical gifts, made the NSDAP what it was in 1923. All these men were impelled by the desire to renationalize the "international" masses, because only thus could Germany become strong and sovereign again—that is, capable of waging war. If, as was said by the historian Veit Valentin, the story of Hitler is the story of his underestimation, this shrewd remark must be supplemented by the realization that there might have been no story of Hitler at all had not outstanding men and forces estimated him highly for their own purposes. The collaboration of the state and leading circles of society became just as important for the development of National Socialism as for that of Italian fascism. Indeed, in Bavaria the parasitical nature of fascist movements, their upward growth *after* the elimination of the threat to society, was even more apparent than in Italy. There are plenty of examples of this. According to Frick's testimony,[84] the NSDAP could easily have been suppressed in 1919–20; but how could the necessary desire be expected of a chief of police who, according to Ernst Röhm, replied to an apprehensive informant who told him there were political murder-organizations: "Yes, but not enough"?[85] To all appearances, the number of powerful financial backers extended far into the ranks of foreign capitalists.[86] When in January, 1923, von Knilling's government banned Hitler from holding any demonstrations out-of-doors at the first Reich party congress and finally decreed a state of emergency, Röhm, Epp, and Lossow intervened,[87] with the result that Hitler was saved from a serious defeat and the government lost face. Hitler held his party congress exactly as he had intended to do: Social Democratic mass rallies were banned, however, because of the state of emergency, which thus underwent a transformation of purpose as strange as it was symptomatic.[88]

For National Socialism as for fascism, war and the affirmation of war was the essential background, an attempted socialist revolution its immediate genesis, protection by the state and established conservative forces the atmosphere necessary to its growth, the towering personality of the leader an irreducible element. Historical observation confirms and supplements the sociological analysis, although it emphasizes even more strongly the elements they had in common.[89] And the analogies in events are particularly useful where it is a case not of comparing facts but of considering possibilities. Thus November 9, 1923, for example, makes it appear possible that Italian fascism could also have been defeated. However, the interim period up to 1933 admits of the possibility that Italian fascism might also have overcome such a defeat.

Teachers and Forces Surrounding the Early Hitler

The most thorough analysis of background and events would severely limit the study of the five years 1918–1923, would be less than conclusive, if no attempt were made to deal with the character and ideas of those men who were vitally important to Hitler during his early political activity. It is true that Hitler's

Weltanschauung was already firmly fixed in its contours. But its genesis and formation can only be followed on the strength of his own reports from a later period. It is only after 1919 that we have tangible evidence of the influence of his contacts. He himself testified[90] to the fact that, within the framework of the given pattern, he was capable of being molded. A number of events of crucial importance had indeed expanded the horizon of his Vienna years: the defeat, the Bolshevik revolution, the Bavarian Soviet Republic. He no longer experienced these things as an isolated Austrian Pan-German; these were experiences occupying the minds of the whole German nation. Although unaffected by contradiction and doubt, he gained many new insights which confirmed his own views. And for the first time he came together with men of stature. It was also the last time that he respected and even revered men from his own environment as his equals. After 1923 he was the *Führer* who was surrounded only by followers and for whom the distant star of Mussolini was the sole object of admiration. Some of these men also represented powerful social or intellectual forces; he did not merely exploit them, and they in turn saw in him the man who proclaimed or fulfilled their intentions and ideas. These are the men who may be called his teachers and masters. In rising order of importance for him they are: Gottfried Feder, Erich Ludendorff, Ernst Röhm, and Dietrich Eckart.

Gottfried Feder was the most immediate cause of Hitler's concrete decision to enter politics. He was the principal speaker that evening of September 12, 1919; but Hitler had heard Feder lecture before, and on the very first occasion the idea "darted" through his mind that he had now found one of the chief essentials for the founding of a new party.[91] For Feder opened his eyes to the "speculative as well as the political-economic [*sic*] nature of the stock market and loan capital" and its "eternal precondition of interest."[92] Evidently he now felt for the first time intellectually capable of meeting Marxism on the theoretical level.

Gottfried Feder's name is closely linked with the catchword, the "breaking of the interest yoke." Immediately after the war Feder began writing about his proposals for financial and credit reform in pamphlets and journals;[93] in 1923 as an acknowledged programmatician of the National Socialist party he published a semiofficial book which Hitler describes as the "catechism of the movement": *Der deutsche Staat auf nationaler und sozialer Grundlage. Neue Wege in Staat, Finanz und Wirtschaft.*[94] His basic ideas were briefly as follows:

To supply needs, not to make profits, is the function of national economy. The profit principle, introduced by the Jews, means a fatal separation of capital from labor, hence ultimately the making anonymous of the economy and the emancipation of money, which, instead of being a servant of the economy, becomes its master. Through the interest system it exploits all manifestations of life for the benefit of supranational financial powers, and exacts a vast tribute from productive labor. Release can only come through the refusal to pay interest, especially to foreign countries, and at the same time by abandoning the foolish policy of obtaining credit by way of loans. The obtaining of credit must be a function of the state through the issuing of interest-free treasury notes or building certificates which are fully covered by the newly created values. This means that the individual as well as the state will be released from the bonds of interest obligations, the nation will become truly sovereign, and Jewish world domination will be broken, because the financial power of world Jewry will be destroyed. However, this method does not presuppose the nationalization of property: on the contrary, it means the safeguarding of as many independent existences as possible, including large personal fortunes (as of Krupp). In this way, creative industrial capital will be liberated from greedy loan capital, the body politic will recover from its grave illness, patriarchal benevolence will determine relations between employer and employee, and the state will guarantee every family its own home and garden.

One is tempted to ask whether Feder really represented a social, that is, intellectual force, or whether he should not be regarded as a sectarian who ceased, not merely fortuitously, to play any role at all after 1933, and who died in 1941 in total obscurity. However, it is not the details of his proposals but the contours of his trend of thought which are important. It is not hard to define them: Feder was the embodiment of that narrow-gauge socialism which wanted to rap society over the knuckles without injuring it, which had all the antagonism of Marxism and yet left industrial conditions on the whole untouched, which had no conception whatever of the realistic necessities of modern economy (for instance, which took the process of concentration for a sickness), and hoped to achieve drastic changes by applying half-measures. In all individual matters Hitler was wise enough to move away from him very soon; but did not the subsequent control of international payments through a central government foreign-exchange body correspond to one of Feder's early proposals?[95] Was rearmament with its totally irresponsible expansion of credit volume anything but the state's commitment to cover its obligations by war booty? This, anyway, is the interpretation given it by Hitler in *Table Talk*.[96] It could hardly have been what Feder had in mind, but it was in keeping with his proposals.[97]

General Erich Ludendorff was the first man of world renown to honor Hitler with his esteem. They met in 1920, in Berlin, together with Dietrich Eckart;[98] shortly afterward Ludendorff went to live in Munich and rapidly became the revered mentor of all rightist groups. Although at the end of the war he had fled to Sweden in disguise, he soon returned and participated in various ways in the struggle over the questions of responsibility. In 1923 he published his book on *Kriegführung und Politik*,[99] which presented in a comprehensive approach, with none of his later sectarian obsession,[100] his interpretation of events and his recommendations for the future.

In Ludendorff's eyes the ultimate cause of the loss of the war lay in the discrepancy between the conduct of war and politics—indeed, in the final analysis in their differentness. Before the war, politicians had neglected to make full use of the German military potential and to turn the schools into "incubators of strong patriotic and German feeling";[101] during the war politicians had been incapable of "bringing together all levels of the population to produce the necessary united front."[102] Above all, politicians proved incapable of realizing and adjusting to the principle of destruction underlying all conduct of war. Ludendorff saw this feebleness on the part of German politicians as being mainly attributable to the existence of democratic parties; even Bismarck had overcome these parties by violating the constitution, to the great benefit of the country. Thus during the war the democratic and Social Democratic press, with their polemics against militarism, Junkers, and dynasties, aided and abetted the enemy propaganda. The idea of a peace by consent was the most disastrous abortion to issue from the minds of the Reichstag majority, for it was the direct antithesis to the essence of "national war," of "true war," which was a total one and whose objective must be the destruction of the enemy. Social Democrats and their accomplices were therefore responsible for the loss of the war, because in the end the Supreme Command had no longer been able to withstand the "international-pacifist-defeatist-thinking sector of the people."[103] This political feebleness led to this sector becoming the outright ally of powers whose aim was the destruction of Germany and which included, in addition to England and France, the "leaders of the Jewish people."[104] None of the final and promising measures of the Supreme Command was given a chance to take effect: neither the intention of drawing on the powerful economic reserves of the Ukraine, nor the attempt to raise troops in Finland, the Ukraine, and Georgia. Equally lacking in acceptance were its war aims, whose objective was the securing of Germany's continuing existence as an independent major power after the war by the acquisition of land and raw materials, since a mere *status quo* was bound to prove harmful. Thus for strategic reasons the annexation of a broad strip of Polish territory was absolutely essential, and any disadvantages that might arise could be easily overcome by an energetic policy of settlement and population exchange.[105] On one occasion only did the military command and the politicians collaborate: the sending of Lenin to Russia fulfilled the hopes that had been placed in it.[106] Generally speaking, the enemy nations displayed a much better unanimity between military command and politics: the population was better educated politically, the working class proved to be as nationalist as the ruling classes.

But war remains a link in the divine world order, and "the age of war, which began with the World War, will generate new wars."[107] To survive, the state will in future not be able to bypass the truths which German politicians so wantonly violated during the war: that there is no justification for the distinction between either war and politics or general and statesman.

It is not necessary to show the extent to which Ludendorff's book is a classic document of introversion. It is obvious why he could not help admiring Hitler, the man of the people. The only thing that is hard to see is in what points Hitler did *not* implement Ludendorff's often merely diagrammatic program step by step. But no doubt the general could not imagine what social soil, what methods and what men, would be necessary for his postulates to be realized.

All he should have needed was a glance at Ernst Röhm, at that specimen of the young generation of officers, who was so like him and yet in many respects so different. The younger man was also from a middle-class background and the enthusiastic heir to feudal and monarchist traditions; for him, too, the war had been a divine destiny: "A fountain of youth, hope and fulfillment, all at once";[108] but how much more bitter was his disillusionment after the war, when on his arrival at the railway station in Munich he had actually been obliged to remove the venerable cockade and then even swear an oath of allegiance to the republic. He realized that a soldier has to be political if ultimately "others are not to determine not only the professional but also the private and personal fate of the regular soldier."[109] He doubtless suffered no pangs of conscience when he established the Munich home guard, which was aimed at overthrowing the new constitution, and backed the rightist political groups, very soon showing his preference for the NSDAP. But what an obscure and furtive occupation for a young officer: the clandestine disposal of concealed war material, the hiding of demobilized soldiers, the association with political assassins. And what a frank aversion to the old generals and excellencies, what a strange sympathy for the Communists at times, what a highly suspect but actually very obvious polemic in his book against bourgeois prudery toward giving free rein to "deeply personal urges."[110] Röhm exemplified a younger generation of soldiers which rid itself of every prejudice to cling all the more passionately to the ultimate deity: "Europe, the whole world, may go down in flames, what do we care? Germany must live and be free."[111] And so in the end he shared Ludendorff's basic conception, the idea of the "armed state," a state which solves its social problems like a battalion at the front and directs all its energies outward.[112] From 1919 to 1923 he was in no sense a subordinate of Hitler but, according to well-informed opinion, the "maker" of the National Socialist movement, or at least its "quartermaster."[113] Early in 1934 Reich Chancellor Hitler distinguished his chief of staff of the SA and Reich Minister Röhm by addressing him, and only him of all the veteran fighters of the movement, by using the intimate *Du*. When six months later he had him shot without trial or sentence, Goebbels, unmindful of the proverb about glass houses, reviled the memory of the dead man by referring to the "sons of chaos"; but it is very doubtful whether Hitler ever had any other positive conception than that of Ludendorff's and Röhm's "armed state."

Hitler was, of course, subject to other motivations. Neither Ludendorff nor Röhm experienced the fear which drove him or the perspective which drew him on. Neither their soldierly uprightness nor Feder's didactic dogmatism would ever have produced that unmistakable tone of voice in which anxiety and faith, single-mindedness of purpose and clairvoyant confidence, delusion and logic, harmonized so perfectly that it could cast a spell over a vast population. Next to his psychological make-up and his experiences in Austria, it is his association with Dietrich Eckart which provides a clue to this mystery.

Dietrich Eckart had made a name for himself in Berlin as a metaphysical poet who wrote of the soul's involvement with and detachment from the world; he, too, was drawn toward politics first by the war and then, even more so, by the revolution. During the period of the Bavarian Soviet Republic, he concocted, not without some personal danger, an appeal "to all workers" which he scattered among the crowds from his car; this appeal, in keeping with Feder's principles, contrasted productive industrial capital with greedy loan capital. The roots of world war, he said, were to be found in the power of the Gold International; the real culprits were the Rothschilds and the Mendelssohns, the Bleichroeders and the Kahns, not the agrarians and the industrialists. The necessary revolution was the one against the interest yoke, and this revolution was the only genuine one.[114] Within a short time he founded the *Deutsche Bürgergesellschaft*, which may be regarded as a forerunner of Hitler's party just as much as Drexler's and Harrer's association, especially since Eckart's organ *Auf gut deutsch* was later officially called the first publication of the movement[115] and in its pages Alfred Rosenberg[116] was introduced to the public for the first time, on February 21, 1919. The appeal issued by this society on its founding demanded *true* socialism and denounced the use of the "catchwords" bourgeoisie and proletariat: "We have been goaded long enough. Let only those of *pure German* blood have influence."[117] The sharp anti-Semitism of this journal is quite consistent with this line. Recurrent delight in strong words and tangible threats stands side by side with the curiously evolved metaphysic according to which the Jew had now become the embodiment of this-worldly thinking and a secular outlook, while the Aryan peoples had been destined to preserve otherworldly thinking and to negate the secular outlook. When the two converge, the generally dominating subtleties disappear (the Jewish spirit, says Eckart, exists in every individual, and so it must; it is only harmful in excess), and a sentence such as the following can occur: "No people in the world, not even Attila's race of murderers, would allow him [the Jew] to remain alive if it could suddenly see through to what he *is*, what he *desires*; shrieking with horror it would strangle him the very next instant."[118] Opinions on events in world politics are all couched in metaphysical-eschatological terms: the Bolshevik revolution is "the ritual slaughtering of Christians by the dictatorship of the Jewish world salvation of Lenin and his Elijah, Trotsky-Bronstein";[119] and in the successful series *Aus Ungarns Schreckenstagen*, satanic gargoyle faces, drawn by Otto von Kursell, grin at the reader, each accompanied by a venomous verse by Dietrich Eckart.[120]

Dietrich Eckart met Hitler very early on; in 1920 during the Kapp *Putsch* they both flew to Berlin, and at the end of the year Eckart made the major contribution toward the purchase of the *Völkischer Beobachter* and himself took over the editorship for two years. He spoke with Hitler at rallies and stood at his side during party parades; he put his innumerable connections at Hitler's disposal and took him to the region of the future Berghof. There they spent several weeks together during the summer of 1923 when Eckart was in hiding from the police, and it was there that Eckart died in the last days of December of the same year. He had already been seriously ill before the *Putsch*; he was arrested after it and only released shortly before his death.

Hitler did not forget him. Volume II of *Mein Kampf* ends with his name in bold type. In 1933 the Reich Chancellor publicly acknowledged himself to be the "pupil" of his "fatherly friend."[121] According to a reliable witness, whenever he spoke of Dietrich Eckart his eyes misted over.[122] In *Hitler's Table Talk* there is no figure of comparable stature whom he mentions so often and with such a sincere note of esteeem. Dietrich Eckart and he began the struggle in Bavaria;[123] his deep aversion to lawyers stemmed from Eckart;[124] he looked up to Eckart as to the North Star;[125] the services rendered by Eckart were unsurpassable.[126]

Is it necessary to submit lengthy proof that every utterance of such a man has a claim on our closest attention, more than the books of men like Feder, Ludendorff, or Rosenberg, who were so much more remote from Hitler? And what tremendous interest must be aroused by a publication purporting not only to set out the author's own thoughts, but also to recount conversations with Hitler. Such a publication exists, but strangely enough it has received scarcely any attention.[127] Friends of the movement declared it to be "free invention," but from motives which were all too transparent; enemies of the movement were evidently not convinced of the authenticity of a pamphlet which in level and style is several degrees below *Mein Kampf*. However, there is good reason to assume that this pamphlet contains the most authentic and revealing of all conversations with Hitler.[128]

The publication in question is Dietrich Eckart's last, uncompleted writing. It appeared as a pamphlet a few months after his death, in 1924, published by the Hoheneichenverlag in Munich. It is called: *Der Bolschewismus von Moses bis Lenin. Zwiegespräch zwischen Adolf Hitler und mir.*

The partners in the dialogue are "He" and "I." Hitler's name does not occur in the text, but he is easily recognizable from the temperamental manner of talking: he "cries out," "emits a bitter laugh," "waves aside," "thunders," "stretches up with a laugh," "ridicules," "is angry at," "clenches his teeth," "scorns," and "is disgusted"; Eckart on the other hand "interjects," "emphasizes," "confirms," "amplifies," "quotes," "affirms." In outlining the basic ideas of the dialogue, all utterances can be taken from Hitler's part.

First of all, there is an etiology of history of extreme simplification. The point of departure is the parallel between history and nature, something which the science of history has failed to grasp. Astronomy explains irregularities of the stellar system by an as yet undiscovered force, while history tries to deduce them from the visible and the known. But in history there exists a hidden force which causes its irregularities. This force is "the Jew."

At first, therefore, Hitler simply starts off in the great stream of counter-revolutionary thought which tried to wrest from the Enlightenment its invocation of "nature" (as understood by natural science) and to anchor its own social position in the inviolability of a "natural order." But even de Bonald's *physique sociale* could not get along without the idea of "antiphysics." Even for him the enemy was not so much antidivine as antinatural.

The "irregularity" of which Hitler is thinking appears to be the phenomenon of the death of a race in the sense of internal dissolution and disintegration—for him the very essence of the "antinatural," since races are actually "what is and what remains."[129] This mysterious "element of death" was what Gobineau believed he discovered in racial interbreeding.

The two main currents of French counterrevolutionary thought—the Christian and spiritual trend of de Maistre and de Bonald, and the anti-Christian and naturalistic trend of Gobineau and Lapouge—had always remained apart in their native country. The one was battling, with some optimism, a temporary disturbance of the divine order; the other recognized, in a mood of resignation, a trend in the historical process itself which could not but lead to a diminution in the original value of the race.

In spite of the primitive level of thinking, Hitler (the Hitler of the conversation) takes a firm hold of both trends right at the outset and renders them incomparably more effective by replacing the enigmatic impalpability of "antiphysics" with the intelligible picture of a tangible branch of the human race, thus transforming the fatalistic pessimism of Gobineau into an aggressive optimism. This means that he can blend the substantialism of the race doctrine with an extreme decisionism, and can offset the innate immutability of the eternal machinator by a new will to salvation.

The first step, however, is the unveiling of history, the unmasking of the originator of decadence within it: a rudimentary historical philosophy which is nevertheless more detailed and coherent than anything to be found elsewhere on this topic in Hitler's writings.

Hitler presents an emphatic interpretation of the Exodus from Egypt which he claims is entirely original. By quoting from Isaiah 19:2 and 3, and Exodus 12:38, he explains this mass migration as the result of a revolutionary and murderous assault of the Jews on the ruling class of Egypt. "Just as among us," the Jews were able to win over the lower classes (the "rabble") by dint of humanitarian phrases and the slogan "Proletarians of the world, unite"; the slaying of the first-born was supposed to be the signal for the beginning of the revolution, but at the last moment the revolution was prevented by those Egyptians who had remained "nationalist," and it had then been finally thwarted by the expulsion of the Jews and the "rabble." Consequently Moses was the first leader of bolshevism.

The explosive political effect of this identification of Jewry with bolshevism is obvious. That capitalism was Jewish was an old and worn-out theme; but the experience of the Bolshevik revolution among the middle classes in Germany was so immediate, so close to home, and so disquieting, and statistics seemed to prove the overwhelming participation of Jewish ringleaders so irrefutably, that this thesis of identification found credulous listeners even in liberal circles. Not, of course, that it was Hitler's invention; it was the common property of a whole literature from Henry Ford to Otto Hauser—one might be tempted to say that Hitler was *its* invention. In any event, this interpretation—product of Eckart's brain though it may have been—emphasizes the peculiar relationship between a world-historical thesis and *its* man, and the second principal thesis of this work, the claim that Lenin was also a Jew, proceeds from it out of sheer organic necessity.[130]

The claim that Christianity was a form of bolshevism was something not even Hitler at the height of his power ever dared to express in so many words. Nevertheless, it is the central thesis of *Hitler's Table Talk*. And it is something that even in those early days he took for granted. Christ Himself—as was usually the case—was relegated to a "totally different" world. The responsibility fell, in contrast to Houston Stewart Chamberlain's subtle distinctions, entirely on St. Paul: "He goes to the Greeks, to the Romans. And he takes them *his* 'Christianity.' Something which can unhinge the Roman Empire. All men are equal! Fraternity! Pacifism! No more dignity! And the Jew triumphed."

His opinion of the Catholic form of Christianity was remarkably positive and unreligious. The reason for the praise he extended to a number of popes was always the same: they fought the pernicious principle of equality for the Jews. Here as elsewhere in this pamphlet the sole standard by which he judged historical personages was their attitude toward Jewry.

The Reformation, on the other hand, like the humanism of Reuchlin and Hutten, was rejected as being a Judeophile enterprise. But since the anti-Semitism of Luther's later years must, of course, be accorded highest praise, the Reformation as such had to be termed, grotesquely enough, *Lutherersatztum* ("substitute Lutherism"). "By their fruits ye shall know them, Puritans, Anabaptists, Jehovah's Witnesses, those are the juiciest ones. In each of them sits the Jewish maggot."

Sharp attacks on the German monarchs (including Frederick the Great) and Zionism led to the final significant phenomenon: bolshevism.

This, then, was no longer an isolated and unprecedented phenomenon. It had revealed itself as the most recent form of the ancient conspiracy. To those in the know, the thirty million victims of its carnage did not represent a new and undreamed-of horror, as they were aware of the true *aitía*, the hidden instigator, and its long history, and could thus prepare all the more vigorously for the great conflict which gave the present age greatness and crucial importance for thousands of years to come. For only an overwhelming victory could finally safeguard the will of nature, the existence of races, from the assault of pernicious, ambivalent form, whose body consisted of inferior masses and whose head was the Jewish mind. After this victory the properly led "elite races of the world" would "respect and protect" each other, now that the cause of all antinatural dissolution had been eliminated, the Jew, to whom "each and every social injustice of significance," "as well as every upheaval," could be traced, and whose nature could be described not in ordinary terms but at best by an image: "A parasitic growth over the whole earth, sometimes creeping, sometimes leaping. Everywhere it sucks and sucks. At first the bursting abundance, finally the withered sap."

After this diagnosis there can be no doubt as to the therapy. When Eckart mentioned Luther's demand that the synagogues and Jewish schools be burned down, Hitler waved this aside with a "Hopeless!": "Burning them down would do us precious little good. That's the trouble! Even if there had never been a synagogue, or a Jewish school, or the Old Testament, the Jewish spirit would still exist and exert its influence. It has been there from the beginning, and there is no Jew, not a single one, who does not personify it."

What is the meaning of these somewhat obscure words, from which the conversation then quickly moves away again? Is it perhaps that the struggle was not to be carried on by brutal methods, that it could only be settled on a spiritual level, that each person must first fight the Jewish spirit within himself? A continuation along these lines would have corresponded to Eckart's spiritualism. For the extreme consequence of the race doctrine in its Manichaean and activist form, such as is represented by Hitler's thoughts and deeds, these words mean exactly the opposite. If spirit is racial character, and if a harmful spirit exists at all times, it can only be eliminated by the destruction of its "substance of flesh and blood"[131] which for Hitler is the primary reality.

If there is such a thing as a secret of Adolf Hitler, perhaps it is here that it stands first and most clearly disclosed. But, far from being the personal, hidden whim of a dreamer, it marks with the utmost precision the precise spot at which a powerful trend in modern intellectual development was pointed.

To call this pamphlet "anti-Semitic" is not only insufficient: from an intellectual standpoint it is also quite inadequate.[132] For it must not be forgotten that every significant ideology of the nineteenth century had its own brand of anti-Semitism. Liberal anti-Semitism accused the Jews of antihistorical rigidity, intolerance, and "national separateness." In socialist thought, the Jews often stood for the chief exemplifiers of the capitalist spirit and its "mammonism." What conservatives disliked most about the Jews was their spirit of unrest, their tendency toward revolution. The existence of these accusations, mutually exclusive and yet not entirely baseless as they were, is of itself sufficient proof of what in any event is probably the case: that the historical movement of the nineteenth century had a peculiarly destructive and challenging effect on the Jewish group.

Racial anti-Semitism gathered up all these accusations at once and led them back to the inalterable fact of race. But racial anti-Semitism could also assume the guise of liberal, socialist, or conservative criticism, however much it denied their basis.

Chamberlain's anti-Semitism had liberal features: for him the Jews were essentially the fathers of Roman narrow-mindedness and intolerance. Here, in an entirely conventional way, early Christianity was contrasted positively with Catholicism. Chamberlain did not subscribe to the central theme of fascist ideology—that Catholicism with its hierarchy and discipline represented the overcoming of Christian-revolutionary anarchy. And Rosenberg's attitude toward Catholic compulsion of conscience and dogmatism was also motivated just as much by liberal hatred as by the Pan-German arrogance of the Aryan *Herrenmensch*. The attitude of both these men clearly reveals the difficulty of developing a fascism in Germanic-Protestant countries with their Bible tradition and their religious individualism.

For Hitler this difficulty did not exist. His anti-Semitism belonged outright to the radical-conservative wing which regarded Jewry primarily as a revolutionary force and early Christianity and the Reformation as its pernicious heirs, as against Rome, the bulwark of the will to rule. As an ideological thinker Hitler is closer to Maurras than to Rosenberg; this is a conclusion of the utmost importance, which Eckart's pamphlet confirms but does not originate.[133]

There is another, equally important deduction to be drawn from a study of Hitler's teachers as a group. In the case of Feder, the connection between the battle against the interest yoke and the ideas of a petit-bourgeois "narrow-gauge socialism" is obvious. Ludendorff's and Röhm's will to a new, more skillfully conducted war proceeds organically and naturally from their position as officers. Eckart's anti-Semitism is closely associated with a certain German intellectual tradition to which by background and career he belongs. But Hitler stood apart from each of these worlds and traditions. He was, in Barrès' words, a *détaché*. And perhaps this is why he was able to avail himself of their most extreme formulations and their consequences—just because he did not share their roots and hence their indwelling limitations.

The Fresh Start (1925–1930)

The *Putsch* of November 9, 1923, marks the end of the first period of Hitler's political activity. This period is by far the most important for his development and until recently by far the least familiar. During this time foundations were laid and his course was set. After that he learned from superficial levels of experience only; for tactical reasons he would temporarily emphasize or underplay this or that idea, this or that trait, but even *Mein Kampf* was no more than a comprehensive selection from the bulk of ideas and experiences of those years. Hölderlin's words—that the strongest factor is birth and the beam of light that plays on the newborn—apply to National Socialism more than to the Action Française, and much more than to Italian fascism.

According to all the laws of probability, the *Putsch* should have meant the end of Hitler's political career. In any normal state, an act of armed treason forever excludes the chief perpetrator from ordinary life and even more so from political life; even under the weak Germanic Confederation, the leaders of the Baden-Palatinate uprising all died abroad or in prison. Moreover, Hitler was a foreigner, and his behavior at the Feldherrnhalle had been far from courageous or even honorable.

But Bavaria was not a normal state: it was a self-confident regional state, whose leaders were deeply involved in the treasonable enterprise and whose highest ecclesiastical prince had recently called the revolution of 1918 "perjury and treason."[134] Thus Hitler could speak from the heart as a "revolutionary against the revolution" as much to his judges as to the public. For the first time he was given a platform from which the whole world could hear his denunciation.

The short and honorable detention in the fortress of Landsberg provided him with the leisure to dictate the first volume of his principal work and thus to take the second big step away from the provincial limitations of Bavaria. His absence from politics demonstrated to the nationalists how very necessary he was to them. At the same time it led to his separation from Ludendorff and—temporarily—from Röhm. Thus in a certain sense it was a new party which he founded in January, 1925. Circumstances were altered hardly less profoundly: the postwar confusion had been overcome, the Weimar Republic was consolidated.

Hitler pursued the change in the party to its extreme, an extreme which after all was merely the reality of an existing trend: his position as Führer was finally determined by statute, from then on he had only followers.

He disregarded the change in conditions. If he had been *only* a monomaniac he would have continued merely to talk and write against the November criminals and the "Jewish" republic. But he was aware that one essential thing had to be done, while the other indispensable thing must not be left undone. He reassured the Bavarian prime minister and the church—some nationalist groups began to suspect his "opportunism." But he also had the courage to proceed specifically against the favorite ideas of the nationalists. He obstinately defended the thesis that South Tirol must not be allowed to stand in the way of the alliance between Germany and Italy; it would be wrong to feed the inhabitants of South Tirol with false hopes: instead, the country should be regarded as a bridge between the two states.[135] This policy of renunciation on *his* part did him a lot of harm, although actually only among the "protest patriots" and "nationalist leagues" whom he so heartily despised. For, in terms of his assumptions, his thought processes were of compelling logic: it would be mistaken to launch a frontal attack on emotional grounds against all the victorious powers; rather, it was necessary to break off a few individual states from what had formerly been the enemy coalition and to form a new group with common interests and new goals.[136] Only in this way could one hope to set oneself the war aim which would be worth the effort and the sacrifice of blood—land to secure the threatened existence of the nation. What Stresemann (apparently) carried on for the sake of peace, a policy aimed at liquidating war,[137] Hitler wanted to embark on for the sake of better war. It was easy enough to realize that the reconciliation with the Bavarian People's party and the Catholic Church served no other purpose than this, and that the "system" was to be ruthlessly destroyed after being skillfully deprived of potential support.

But this path did not lead him upward as rapidly as the first. Hindenburg's election as Reich president was in no way comparable with the taking over of the Bavarian government by von Kahr in 1919; although it might attest to the power of monarchistic traditions among the German people, it was from other aspects a virtual victory for the republic, and during the ensuing years the rightist national element more than once bade a despairing farewell to its former hero. Hitler respected only on certain conditions, while he always hated without reservation; he respected von Kahr because they both hated Berlin, that "sink of iniquity," but Hindenburg had now become a part of the "system." And this system meant progress, Communist uprisings were something that could only occur in the nightmares of alarmists, and Germany had once again become a factor in European politics. This was no longer Hitler's hour. For a time he seemed—as Maurras always and Mussolini intermittently had seemed—to have no position of power other than his newspaper, and the resurrected SA, which served mainly to distribute the party newspaper[138]— exactly like the *Camelots du Roi*. There was yet a third and more important analogy. Just as Grandi and Balbo had worked for and against Mussolini in Emilia, so others now worked simultaneously for and against Hitler all over North Germany. These others represented a second form of socialism within the "National Socialist" party, and they were not all, like Gottfried Feder, to be fobbed off with words of praise. This time Hitler had to fight for the effectiveness of the party in German society and thus for its fascist character.

This struggle is linked with the name of Gregor Strasser, and even more with that of his brother Otto, but the two brothers from Landshut were probably not so much the cause as the agents of this struggle. They carried the NSDAP into North Germany and particularly into the Ruhr, but much of what had been loudly applauded in Munich sounded alien. When in 1925 the North and West German *Gauleiter* founded their own *Arbeitsgemeinschaft* in Hanover under the aegis of Strasser, this *Fronde* group included a good portion of North German Protestant individualists who were unwilling to take orders from the "pope" in Munich. And in the Ruhr it was impossible to denounce Marxism as being simply an invention of the Jews. In this area anticapitalist feeling sprang directly from living conditions, it permeated the atmosphere so thoroughly that a "revolutionary" party was forced to be socialist far more sincerely than in Munich. This new socialism first found an outlet in the *Nationalsozialistische Briefe* which Strasser began publishing at the end of 1925 and which were edited by the young Paul Joseph Goebbels.

Here class warfare was acclaimed, profit participation was discussed, the alliance with the Soviet Union and all oppressed peoples was proclaimed, along the same lines that some radical nationalist revolutionaries had followed.[139] Rosenberg tried in the *Völkischer Beobachter*, without much success, to set the confused minds straight and reinstate the formula "Soviet Russia = Soviet Judea." Hitler never for a moment deviated from his "Western orientation" (which, due to the unaltered hostility toward France, had admittedly become weaker and hence unconvincing); nor did he swerve in his high regard for the "individual" and his rights to personal property, and in the matter of the indemnification of deposed ruling houses, he inflicted a severe defeat on Strasser's socialism, which took the side of the leftist parties. At the Bamberg Leaders' Congress of February, 1926, which Hitler had prepared with great skill, Strasser found himself isolated; his "young man" Goebbels went over into Hitler's camp and very soon became the protagonist of a Führer-cult, which many of the North Germans, among whom Rosenberg must also be numbered, for a long time found highly distasteful.[140] But this did not decide the battle. The Strasser brothers founded the Kampf publishing house in Berlin and for a while controlled the capital's National Socialist press. Even the language which Goebbels, as Hitler's newly appointed *Gauleiter* of Berlin, spoke in those early years is proof of the strength of the socialist trends. He contrasted the decadent spirit of liberalism with the "socialist formative power of that fourth estate, the workers." The proletariat, he claimed, was international because of the tragic realization that until now it had not been shown a national way to solve its problems. His instructions were to show "Brownshirts, German proletarians ... enveloped by the fluttering Red storm flag"[141] on posters. It was only with the passing of time that all this became a completely unbelievable cliché.

Otto Strasser's socialism was much more durable and much more carefully thought out. No doubt Marx would have called him a petit-bourgeois socialist. In his best-known publication on his program[142] he spoke of a Reich corporative chamber and the guilds, of hereditary fiefs and the reagrarianization of Germany. Strasser called for autarky and domestic currency, the war of revolution against Versailles, and a military aristocracy. But there was more than mere demagogy in his demands for splitting up of large estates, for profit participation, for a people's state of Germanic democracy. On the whole it was a genuinely socialist program, at least to the extent to which it was imbued with the emotional appeal of the expansion and attainment of freedom.

With a program of this kind, however, there was little likelihood of gaining allies, and certainly not the ones who were now the most desirable. For with the Young Plan and the first signs of economic crisis, German industry's sympathies for the republic began to wane. Hugenberg became the leader of the German Nationals, and that meant that the integration of the political Right with the republic, which had already begun, now came to a halt or was even revoked. His "Reich Committee for the German Plebiscite against the Young Plan and the War-Guilt Lie" was the first form of that coalition to which three years later the republic was to succumb. By joining this coalition Hitler's party again became what it had once been in Bavaria: the acknowledged vociferous partner of powerful groups which were too weak to govern the whole country by themselves. How could Hitler continue to tolerate an Otto Strasser at that stage? In a final discussion lasting many hours, the quarrel—the outcome of which was already decided—was brought out into the open.[143] If one is to believe the report of one participant, Hitler opposed Strasser's National Socialism with his own doctrine of the supremacy of the Greco-Nordic race in the sharpest possible way, and one which was as little national as it was socialist. Not long afterward, Otto Strasser left the party and his paper appeared with the headline: "The Socialists Leave The Party." In actual fact it was not an important event, but in the realm of ideas it was of considerable significance. From then on there were "anti-Fascists" on the Right too.[144] From then on even the most suspicious capitalist no longer needed to regard the NSDAP as a party of the Left.

Appeal to the Masses and Rise to Power (1930–1931)

However, there could be no greater error than to regard the support of Hugenberg and some industrialists[145] as the *cause* of the meteoric rise of the NSDAP. It was only one contributing factor, and not the only one. The German Nationals received much greater financial support and yet remained weak. The economic crisis, now being felt in Germany as well, was no longer merely one factor but the very foundation. Throughout Germany it gave rise to a "deeply disturbed population," just as the Soviet Republic had done earlier in Bavaria. But the crisis was equally favorable to the Communists, and even they never became powerful. The real cause lies in the specific logic of the situation which, in a deeply disturbed bourgeois society, appeared to strengthen rightist radicalism in proportion to leftist radicalism's loss of its mass base—provided the rightist radicals could give the impression of existing *above* the warring parties. There is no doubt that the awareness of this position accounted in large part for that extraordinary activity which had no parallel even among the Communists. But this still does not indicate the kind of fighting method and simplification to be chosen by this, so to speak, malleable activist radicalism of the Right. It would have existed even without Hitler and presumably would also have become powerful under Gregor Strasser; but Hitler alone shaped its face, because of all the *simplificateurs terribles* of the era he was the most simple and the most natural. This is how he begins his appeal to the people on the occasion of the Reichstag election of September 14, 1930:

> What did the old parties promise, which promises did they keep?
> Now the end has come!
> A period of the greatest political promises and equally great hopes ends in general political, moral, and economic bankruptcy.
> The sovereign people can thank its leaders today. For they are responsible for its fate.[146]

The infantile trait of the masses which always places responsibility on people as causes and agents had found its great interpreter. The most anonymous, stratified, and obscure process carried to the top that man who offered the simplest and most intelligible explanation for this process.

At this Reichstag election, parliamentary representation of the NSDAP rose from twelve to one hundred and seven deputies. The Weimar Republic's struggle for existence now entered upon its final phase.

This struggle had some new distinguishing features, although it could be compared to events in Italy before the March on Rome. Here, as in Italy, there was an ill-timed (or at least miscalculated) dissolution of parliament two years before the expiration of the legislative term—the immediate cause of Hitler's, and Mussolini's, new positions of power. In Italy, however, the Fascists remained limited to three dozen deputies, those who had won the election for them in May, 1921. It is true that a year later they were the best-organized party in the country with the largest membership, but the suspicion persisted that the methods of the "squadrist" minority had obtained many not entirely voluntary supporters for fascism. In Germany no one was compelled to join the National Socialists. And yet the wave continued to swell, irresistibly, so it seemed, with propaganda being expended on a giant scale like war matériel in battle. On its second poll the presidential election in April, 1932, brought Hitler over thirteen million votes, and the Reichstag election in the summer swept two hundred and thirty National Socialist deputies into parliament. This meant that the NSDAP was by far the largest party. Although it was still a long way from having an absolute majority, and the election of November 6 represented a serious rebuff, the fact remained that an antigovernment party sought to seize power by legal means—a totally new phenomenon, with little relation to the fascist example and even less to the Bolshevik one.

That it was an anticonstitutional party was beyond doubt: there were innumerable utterances of unmistakable meaning, and the famous legality oath which Hitler swore during the trial of the Ulm Reichswehr officers was merely the specific confirmation of a new tactical method and in no sense an acceptance of the meaning of the constitution.

It must be remembered that the emergence of the antigovernment mass party was well calculated to produce confusion, alarm and perplexity. Everything depended on whether and how those concerned could remain aware of the anticonstitutional nature of the party. As long as they managed to do this, the struggle was by no means hopeless, for the comparison with Italy shows that not all conditions in Germany were less favorable.

In Germany there was never an actual "time of struggle." This was confirmed by Hitler himself, when he placed the civil war achievements of the Fascists far above those of his own party.[147] At no time could any one in the German Reich dare to attack even the local headquarters of the enemy and set them on fire. At no time could the chief of staff of the SA dream of conquering even a single town in the Italian fascist style. In January, 1932, Reichswehr Minister Groener said in unmistakably Prussian tones at a private conference: "There will be no civil war. Anyone who rears his head will be crushed with the utmost brutality, no matter who he is."[148] Within a few months he decreed a ban on uniforms for the SA and the SS which was obeyed without demur. In a similar situation a threat of Mussolini's had forced the Italian government to back down hastily. Even such events as the "Bloody Sunday of Altona" had been merely clashes, albeit very bloody ones, and not civil-war-type actions; and during that famous war maneuver, apparently the cause of Schleicher's resignation, the flattering but paradoxical conclusion was arrived at that Reichswehr and police could not guarantee order and safety in the event of a simultaneous attack by National Socialists, Communists, and Poles (!).[149] In other words, the Prussian-German state was and continued to be (objectively speaking, that is, in comparison to Italy) a strong state.

This is enough to show that a "Communist danger" did not exist.[150] The Communists knew this better than anyone else. Why, otherwise, would they have looked forward hopefully to Hitler's seizure of power, since they regarded this as their only chance of restoring the "united proletarian front"?[151] Their illusion would have been understandable if the Italian Communists had not expressed exactly the same hopes ten years earlier.[152]

However, the greatest difference as against Italy could have been the securest pledge for a potential successful resistance. In Germany there were no Maximalists: on the contrary, the Social Democrats were a pillar of the bourgeois state. This may have been regretted or welcomed; although it betokened a diminution of faith and heroism, it was also a sign that Germany was one of the most highly developed industrial nations. The three and a half million members of the republican *Reichsbanner* did not regard bourgeois democracy simply as a lie which was as bad as fascism, and the "Iron Republican Front for Defense against Fascism" was not composed mainly—as was the *Alleanza del Lavoro*—of people who wanted to "weave the shroud" of bourgeois society. The common danger could have strengthened the alliance on which the republic depended. But the end of the great coalition in March, 1930, was already a fatal indication. Admittedly the coalition partners were justified in arguing about the distribution of the social burdens, which had been aggravated by crisis, but the fact that there were more vital interests than the size of unemployment insurance contributions was something that neither side could grasp.[153] Was Brüning's presidentially appointed cabinet the beginning of the end? Not necessarily, and Hindenburg's election through a kind of extended Weimar coalition offered a last and by no means negligible chance. But the conservatives, with typically German self-preoccupation, which precluded an understanding of the specific nature of the German situation, were so deluded that they felt closer to Hitler than to the Prussian socialist leader Otto Braun. They were right insofar as Hitler was closer than Braun to their principles. But they were mistaken when they believed that they would benefit more by encouraging the extremes of their own position than by uniting former opposites. When within a few years they had been trampled in the dust of humiliation,[154] shot or hanged, it was too late.

On February 25, 1932, Hindenburg sent a letter to the former chairman of the German League of Aristocrats, Friedrich von Berg (Markienen), in which he justified his acceptance of the presidential candidacy.[155] He assured him he was not a "candidate of the Left" or of the "black-and-red-coalition" and was not campaigning against "national Germany." He would resist a purely National Socialist party dictatorship, but not a rightist government. He served Germany without self-interest on the strength of his former views and his past, in order that the country might be spared civil war and ineffectualness in foreign policy. The *Stahlhelm* had only his protection to thank for not having been dissolved long ago, and this made him all the more bitter toward that body's present attitude.

At the end of the same year Hitler wrote to Colonel von Reichenau, chief of staff of the army command in Königsberg.[156] In this letter he said among other things that the German people now consisted of two ideological groups of which one was more or less pacifist or even antiself-defense; the threat by the Communist *Weltanschauung*, which had already seized Russia as a bastion, could only be met by Germany through an "internal, spiritual rearming," which in turn could only be accomplished by a *Weltanschauung* whose steadfast purpose was the eradication of Marxism.

These two letters are enough to explain why Hindenburg did not fulfill the hopes which may have accompanied his re-election, and how inevitable it was that the officers corps had no desire to resist Hitler.

The primary aim of the conservatives was not to defend the constitution but to obtain Germany's "freedom to defend itself," that is, rearmament. Internally this presupposed and assured a stable rule, while externally the goal was the "restitution" of the nation (usually understood to mean the restoration of the 1914 frontiers or the achievement of self-determination). Hitler wanted this too, only on a wider and more purposeful basis. In times of unrest, however, it is generally the more extreme version of the same idea which achieves priority.

It can certainly be assumed that Papen and Schleicher had no sympathy for Hitler and preferred to see their own pre-eminence rather than his. But it did not occur to them to obtain Hindenburg's consent to use the power of their dictatorship against Hitler as vigorously as against the Communist leader Thälmann. Was opposition to the strongest party anticonstitutional and impossible? As if they would not have fought to the last drop of blood for their possessions and traditions, even if two thirds of all votes had gone to the Communists! And it was much more likely that the inflated National Socialist party would not stand up to a new election fight and the overt hostility of the government than that it would obtain fifty per cent of the votes. The plain truth was that, to them, peace outside and freedom inside the country were not worth a struggle.

They wanted to channel the National Socialist movement and tame it, to fence Hitler in and tame him. That is exactly what Luigi Facta had had in mind ten years earlier. But the Italian could take as an excuse the fact that he was the first to come up against fascism and that Mussolini had never said anything about a new war of conquest or the unconditional rule of a new ideology directly at variance with the constitution. Perhaps it is useless to reproach a section of the German people which was willing to entrust its fate unconditionally to a man whose book or program it had obviously either not read or not taken seriously. A knowledge of recent history and familiarity with Hitler's writings were to be expected from the political leaders, but these men displayed neither.

However, it is not true that the intriguing of a small clique opened up Hitler's way to power. All that this intriguing accomplished was to destroy the lukewarm idea of resistance, which had taken shape too hesitatingly among too small a group. In November Hindenburg had seen to it that Hitler's dictatorship was rejected unequivocally,[157] and to the very end it was resisted by the greater part of the German people. In the hour of decision there was no one to honor the president's word or protect the majority of the people.

Farce followed hard on the heels of tragedy. Shortly before Hitler was sworn in, the "contained" chancellor of the cabinet of national concentration demanded no less from his conservative colleagues than the dissolution of the Reichstag and a new election. It was a revolutionary demand: the avoidance of a fresh appeal to the people, and hence of disturbances with unpredictable consequences, had after all been the whole purpose of conservative efforts. Hugenberg put up a spirited resistance, but, since State Secretary Meissner was urging that the Reich president could not be kept waiting, the leader of the German Nationals yielded in return for certain assurances of patent insincerity, and with his own hands dug a grave for himself and his party. The Field Marshal President's time was more important than the responsibility of the politician and the fate of the state. As late as 1932 Germany could still, like England, have achieved the European synthesis: free of the burdens of the colonial age, and above all of the Soviet Union's agonizing efforts to catch up, Germany was destined to become Europe's strongest point of attraction. Instead, on January 30 the wantonness of its leaders brought about the uniting of the traditionalist and revolutionary aspects of the old Germany, a union which, unless it achieved its goal by opposing the whole world, was bound to drag state and people down into the abyss.

Single-Minded Seizure of Power (1933)

At first this union seemed to act like a magic spell dissolving all distress, doubts, and fears, and leading the people back to the unity of one great family. Had Germany ever known such an outburst of thrilling excitement, happiness, and triumph as the mammoth torchlight procession which wound for hours through nighttime Berlin to glorify the aged general of World War I and the young "People's Chancellor"? Did not similar processions form all over Germany, usually quite spontaneously? Did not strangers embrace, sobbing with emotion and beside themselves with joy? The appeal of the Reich government, broadcast to every home on February 1, expressed the feelings of millions, and it combined a historic picture of compelling simplicity with the invocation of all valuable traditions and irresistible optimism: "More than fourteen years have gone by since the unhappy day when, blinded by promises from within and without, the German people forgot the greatest possessions of our past, of the Reich, of its honor and its freedom, and thereby lost everything. Since those days of betrayal, the Almighty has withdrawn His blessing from our people. ... Beginning with the family, transcending all conceptions of honor and loyalty, people and fatherland, culture and economics, to the very foundations of our morality and faith, nothing was spared by this all-negating, all-destroying idea. Fourteen years of Marxism have ruined Germany. ... [The national government] will preserve and defend the foundations on which rests the strength of our nation. It will steadfastly protect Christianity as the basis of our whole morality, and the family as the germ cell of our people and our body politic. ... Loyal to the command of our Field Marshal, we will begin. May our work find favor in the eyes of Almighty God, may He shape our will, bless our understanding, and make us happy with the trust of our people. For we will fight not for ourselves, but for Germany."[158]

In every hamlet the swastika flags waved side by side with the black-white-and-red of the old Reich; no administration, no region, no class remained unaffected. Forces which hitherto had been only barely held in check broke out overnight. The SA marched through the streets, and every official position was taken over or controlled by a National Socialist. The most famous philosopher, the most brilliant professor of law, the best-known poet, stood up in front of their students, their colleagues, the nation, and interpreted the national revolution to their audiences. Many a pastor saw his dreams come true and fervently implored God's blessing; in a mood of deep emotion, countless teachers told their pupils of the new course upon which Germany's destiny had embarked. And when in the venerable old garrison church in Potsdam, before a background of brilliant uniforms, the simple corporal bowed to the wartime field marshal, it seemed as if an act of unique symbolic strength had put the crowning touch to a unique revolution, and Goebbels wrote in his diary: "A historic moment. The shield of German honor has been washed clean again. The standards with our eagles rise on high. ... On the streetcars and buses, men, women, and children stand cheering and singing. A fantastic sight, unique in history."[159]

It *was* a unique revolution. In St. Petersburg in 1917, starving crowds had stormed the government palace, a group of gray-faced men, barely returned from exile and imprisonment, had embarked in silence on an apparently hopeless task; in Rome in 1922 the Blackshirts entering the city (but behind schedule) and a few bands of citizens had cheered the king and Mussolini, but generally speaking the population had adopted a wait-and-see attitude. In Germany a revolution took place without any revolutionary breach of legality, yet without any regard for it either;[160] above all, it was a revolution against the revolution. From now on there would be no more revolutions in Germany—this promise and this trust were presumably what caused this order-loving people to burst the bonds of all order.

To arrive at a correct assessment of the political processes of those months, this popular agitation must be neither denied nor overlooked. It exerted pressure on the Center party during the negotiations over the Enabling Act, it forced Hugenberg to fall into line, its unprecedented nature broke the resistance of the Social Democratic Reichstag faction (insofar as its members had remained in Germany).[161] But by the same token the validity of this rejoicing is open to question. A people may rejoice when it wins a war, perhaps even when it embarks on a war. But here one half of the people were rejoicing over the defeat of the other half. For innumerable eyes had looked on those torchlight processions in horror, and millions were wondering in bewilderment: How are those people going to make use of power who are so frantically celebrating their victory and yet obtained fewer votes than the opposing party group had obtained nearly fifteen years earlier? Such sentiments of pastors and poets, thinkers and teachers, met with the ridicule or contempt of a scarcely less important group which included a considerable number of the most honored names in the German intellectual world. Flags waved above wholesale arrests and wholesale flight. It was in truth a very much reduced "German soul" which, according to Rosenberg's later interpretation, was "never so at one with itself" as in those days.[162]

Nor was there any clear definition of the basis for this "oneness." Did the government have anything new or concrete to say politically? Did it not protest its love of peace and its loyalty to traditional commitments just as preceding governments had done? Had not the annulment of reparations, the recognition in essence of German equality, already been achieved? One might speak of a collective compensation for all the accumulated dissatisfactions of the past fifteen years among broad sections of the population; but it is more likely that, in the face of the raised banners, the marching columns, the blaring of trumpets, the god who had been pushed aside gripped the hearts of his errant people again and offered them an enticing vision of that unity which had once lifted battalions above and beyond all the tribulations and discord of civilian existence. No matter how many waves of illusion and false awareness might ruffle the ocean of the primitive, no matter how many millions might suppress the urge to ask about the purpose of *this* unity: the sole relevant question was whether a determined will could form and stabilize the elemental impetus, and how far (not in what direction) this will could lead it. When in the spring of 1933 one half of the German people triumphed over the other half which, powerless and crippled, was almost incapable of resistance, one basic potential of German politics, in a new guise to match the new age, gained ascendancy over the other. Even in 1933 it was absurd to maintain that this new form was merely an improved imitation of the previous one, however often Hitler might stress this. In those days he was the last to accord himself the honor to which he was entitled: that of being a radical pioneer of a powerful principle. Thus it was in a complete absence of awareness that the cheering crowds joined in what they took to be a new beginning but which was actually the beginning of something new.

Domestic political developments, on the other hand, presented quite a different picture, and it was no accident that Hitler had often declared internal politics to be the basis for external politics.[163] Again the Italian parallel offers an outstanding example of the hitherto unknown phenomenon: the single-minded total seizure of power.[164]

Single-mindedness precludes neither detailed planning nor hesitation and uncertainty at some moments. Hitler may have been agitated and alarmed by the Reichstag fire,[165] but it would be quite wrong to suppose that, like Mussolini, he was led mainly by circumstances and the actions of the opponent to achieve totalitarian fulfillment. Instead, he was skillful enough to utilize every opportunity to urge matters on in the same direction, and very often he created the opportunity himself.

Thus on February 1, 1933, Hindenburg dissolved the Reichstag on the grounds that the formation of a working majority had proved impossible. But Hitler had only pretended to negotiate with the Center, and he never approached the Bavarian People's party at all.[166] On February 4, the Reich president's decree for the protection of the German people gave the National

Socialist party most of the advantages which the Fascist party in Italy had gained from the 1924 elections. This makes it all the more remarkable that, unlike Mussolini, Hitler still failed to gain an absolute majority in the election.

The Reichstag fire, blamed on the Communist party in defiance of all reason and probability,[167] provided, with the ensuing emergency regulations of the decree "For the Protection of People and State," the legal basis for twelve years of National Socialist rule. A comparable law, but far more limited in terms of capital punishment, was not passed in Italy until after the fourth attempt on Mussolini's life, at the end of October, 1926.

From many points of view, the Enabling Act was among the more harmless measures of the seizure of power. It contained certain safeguards (all of which were very soon broken) and had precedents in the Weimar Republic. Mussolini was provided with a similar act very early, and when it expired he waived its renewal. However, in the meantime he had a fascist majority in the parliament.

The law for the restoration of the civil service postulated, after two months, that submissiveness on the part of civil servants which in Italy had not been enjoined on bureaucracy until the coming of Alfredo Rocco's *Leggi fascistissime*.

The laws integrating the *Länder* in Germany into the Reich were perhaps matched in centralized Italy by the replacement of the elected mayor with the government-appointed *podestà*. A far more direct comparison can be made between laws covering the "organization" of cultural affairs and the press; the initial stages of state control of labor relations also bear some similarity.

The abolition of parties and its legal ratification was achieved in Germany barely six months after take-over. In Italy it required the Matteotti crisis and several attempts on Mussolini's life. Mussolini had also deprived his nationalist allies of their independence shortly after his seizure of power, but the terms and conditions were much more honorable than those which Hugenberg, the powerful and confident Hitler-tamer of a short while before, was obliged to accept.[168] In both cases the initial coalition government lasted only a few months.

On October 14 the cautious jockeying for position within a complex external political situation culminated in a first strident note. Germany resigned from the League of Nations. The reason given was the snail's pace of disarmament negotiations. In a similar way, shortly after assuming the reins of government, Mussolini had loudly asserted Italy's self-confidence by bombarding Corfu. But that was a local event, soon settled. In Germany the people were called to the polls, and for the first time the Chancellor's policy was confirmed with a "totalitarian" majority.

The developments which are comparable with those that took place in Italy are rounded off with the "Law for the Safeguarding of the Unity of Party and State," passed on December 1, 1933. In this law the NSDAP was called the "embodiment of the German idea of state" and was formally brought into indissoluble union with the state. A separate party and SA jurisdiction was recognized by the state. The Führer's deputy and the SA chief of staff became ex officio members of the Reich government. In Italy it was 1929 before the party secretary was admitted to sessions of the council of ministers. (There was no parallel in Germany for the Fascist Grand Council.)

This is not the place to examine the possible degree and extent of direct or indirect influences. The vital point is that the process of unrestricted political seizure of power, which took seven years in Italy, was accomplished in Germany in ten months. Goebbels underestimated when he noted in his diary on April 17, 1933: "Within a year all Germany will be in our hands."[169]

At the end of 1933 one could have believed that all these measures served that "instruction" of the people which in the early years in Italy had been essential to the drama of rehabilitation and the surmounting of the economic crisis. But in the first place this thesis is a doubtful one even in its relation to Italy, and in the second place conditions in Germany were quite different. It is true that with the creation of employment and the building of the new super-highways there was a "Let's get down to work" upsurge similar to that in Italy, but Germany was not an undeveloped country. Here it was not a question of creating new possibilities of life and employment, but of getting an already existing, gigantic production apparatus under way again. Yet if Germany did not want to wait for the end of the world depression, where was its surplus production to go?

This problem did not exist in Italy. How Hitler proposed to solve it did not remain concealed, at least not from the Reichswehr generals. On February 3, 1933, when he had been Reich Chancellor for less than a week, he addressed the highest-ranking officers of the army and navy somewhat as follows: the aim of policy as a whole is the reconquest of political power and hence the total destruction of every attitude and activity opposed to rearmament. How political power is to be used after it has been obtained is not yet told. "Perhaps to win new export outlets, perhaps—and probably better—to conquer new *Lebensraum* in the East [of Europe] and to Germanize that *Lebensraum* ruthlessly."[170]

Hitler was much more perceptive than all those who believed one must divest a modern people of every manifestation of inner antagonism: one must put them in uniform and play a march in order for them to learn to work. However, it might be assumed that this radicalism would learn moderation, and that the steam it generated would turn the wheels of national restitution. That must have been what the generals thought. But within a few weeks a large-scale boycott against Jewish businesses was staged under the direction of Julius Streicher, as a reaction to the "Jewish atrocity stories in the world." There was obviously no change whatever in the trend to make a group of people "racially"—that is, without the slightest individual, sociological, or ideological distinction— responsible for a highly complicated state of affairs. Although at no time did Hitler seem further removed from *Mein Kampf* than during 1933, even that year demonstrates sufficient essential continuity, at least to retrospective eyes.

War in Peacetime (1934–1939)

If the period of the seizure of power shows a striking number of analogies with the course of Italian fascism, in the years that followed the differences emerge more strongly. Yet it is precisely in these structural distinctions that we find the first interlocking of the regimes in the sphere of the causal. For ten years, and in spite of many an imperialistic speech and trend on the part of Mussolini, Italy had been a factor in European stability. In the second and third years of his rule Hitler already plainly showed a different face; relatively much sooner than Mussolini, in point of time simultaneously, for it was in 1935 that the Duce decided to conquer an empire on African soil.

In Germany, however, again internal politics constitutes the beginning; here for the first time Hitler solved a problem in such a way that it is permissible to speak of warlike action in peacetime.

The issue as such was the same in Italy and Germany: the fate of the armed party army. During the first years of fascist rule in Italy, no demand was made more often or more emphatically in the most diverse quarters than that Mussolini should dissolve his MVSN and thus restore conditions of constitutional order. It was the Matteotti crisis which cut the knot: it forced Mussolini to a compromise, to have the militia swear allegiance to the king, and at the same time released him from a potentially dangerous rival, because Balbo had to resign as Generalissimus due to accusations raised against him.

In Germany a different situation existed.[171] In the first place, the position of the SA as against the party was much more independent than that of the MVSN, and in the second place Röhm, its leader, was the last of the friends and teachers from Hitler's early days who was still in a position of authority. Finally, the SA was numerically much stronger than the Reichswehr, and it had been cheated of its revolution. It is not surprising that there was a good deal of dissatisfaction in its ranks and talk of the coming "second revolution." It was the third wave of socialism, which became visible within the National Socialist movement—a kind of plebeian soldiers' socialism which sought no theoretical definition. For Röhm it was closely linked with his dream of replacing the Reichswehr and its reactionary officers' corps by the National Socialist people's army—under his leadership, of course. That such ideas were equally alarming to Wehrmacht and industry alike goes without saying. Tensions increased visibly during the summer of 1934; Göring and Himmler went over to the side of Röhm's enemies.

It is hardly likely that Hitler was seriously undecided, but he probably did hesitate for quite a while. He may have believed in the danger of a *Putsch*, but it is highly improbable that he believed the revolt to be imminent. For the SA was on furlough, and its high command was meeting for a congress in Bad Wiessee in which he had apparently consented to participate. All the more shocking was the brutality[172] with which he struck. He had the SA leaders dragged from their beds and shot without trial or sentence;[173] in Berlin Göring and Himmler chose the victims for the firing squads. Here the SS won top honors—the prize was its independence—in a shooting match in which their former comrades and commanding officers were the targets, but at the same time it settled a number of political accounts from days long past. Generals Schleicher and Bredow paid the penalty for their former obstinacy, Gregor Strasser died for his "treason," Papen's colleagues paid with their lives for the vice-chancellor's speech in Marburg,[174] Gustav von Kahr met the revenge for his behavior at the Munich *Putsch*, the fate of Father Bernhard Stempfle was perhaps sealed by his corrections to the original draft of *Mein Kampf*. It was a mass murder for which there is absolutely no parallel in a civilized country. But the government summarily declared all the events of June 30, July 1, and July 2 to have been self-defense of the state and hence "justifiable"; Germany's best-known professor of law sung their praises under the title *Der Führer schützt das Recht*. Unquestionably a feeling of relief rather than indignation ran through the German people. The unsurpassed shamelessness with which details of the murdered men's sexual lives were exposed, details familiar for years to the informed and especially to the Führer, may have contributed to this. Press and radio were sufficiently co-ordinated to prevent the whole truth coming to light. Nevertheless, a comparison with events after the murder of Matteotti is not entirely out of the question, and it is scarcely favorable to Germany and the Germans.

The only way to endow events with coherence and intelligibility is to regard them as an application of martial law. In time of peace, men who have been arrested and thus rendered harmless may not under any circumstances be executed without trial; in time of war, mutineers are shot on the spot, especially when they imperil the attainment of important objectives. The strategic objective which Röhm and his men imperiled was the fastest possible build-up of the Wehrmacht from the cadres of the Reichswehr. If Hitler wished to be ready for action *soon*, he had to be on good terms with the Reichswehr. And it is known that he was firmly convinced he had very little time. Whoever stood in the way of this understanding must fall, just as the man who refuses to obey a command must die. In the past Hitler had achieved his first successes in Munich by carrying the methods of war onto the street and into civilian life. Now his great strategy as chancellor of the Reich only becomes lucid and compelling if it is defined as war in peacetime.

It is only as a wartime oath of allegiance to the supreme *Condottiere* that we can understand that formula which, after Hindenburg's death, the Wehrmacht was obliged to accept as a price of its victory and in which "unconditional obedience" was sworn to the person of the supreme commander with no other safeguards whatever.

The National Socialist uprising in Vienna, which cost Federal Chancellor

Dollfuss his life, was an act of war. No matter how Berlin denied the connection and singled out its minister as the scapegoat, the memorial tablet which was affixed years later to the Vienna Federal Chancellery building spoke a different and truer language.[175]

The march into the demilitarized Rhineland, which constituted a breach of the Locarno Pact, was an extremely bold commando enterprise jeopardizing all the gains of two years with a daring which by external political standards could be neither justified nor comprehended.

The context and objective of all political and economic measures were disclosed in the memorandum on the purpose of the Four Year Plan which in the summer of 1936 Hitler made available as a top-secret document[176] to the country's key government leaders only. As the "final solution" of the German struggle for existence it named the "expansion of living space, that is, of the raw material and food basis of our people," demanded that war be prepared in peacetime, and closed with the words: "I hereby set the following task: I. The German army must be ready for action in four years. II. The German economy must be ready for war in four years."

In the autumn of 1936 the German-Italian rapprochement began. It has been shown via which stages and with what inherent logic it led to the "Pact of Steel"—that is, to the unconditional military alliance of the two regimes.

A vitally important date which became known more or less by chance is November 5, 1937. On that day Hitler informed the ministers of war and foreign affairs, together with the three supreme commanders of the Wehrmacht branches, in the presence of the Wehrmacht Adjutant Colonel Hossbach (who made a written record a few days later), of his ideas on strategy and his military plans.[177] The heart of the matter was once again Germany's lack of living space. Hitler declared it his "unalterable determination" to solve the *Lebensraum* problem at latest between 1943 and 1945. As for the immediate future, he was considering "attacks on Czechoslovakia and Austria." This undertaking was also regarded solely from the standpoint of "acquiring foodstuffs," and a forced emigration of two million people from Czechoslovakia and one million from Austria formed part of his calculation.

As far as the Wehrmacht was concerned, this discussion doubtless meant that, after the conclusion of the initial armament phase, the army was to bow to Hitler's will. This (perhaps not entirely uninfluenced by Mussolini's visit)[178] was after three years to close the strange gap consisting of the fact that as head of state and supreme commander Hitler was far ahead of the Duce while in actual influence on the country's armed forces he lagged behind him. None of his audience could be in any doubt as to the objective of this revision of the basic pact with the principal conservative force: to those listeners at least, he revealed the author of *Mein Kampf* to be the quintessence of the Führer and Reich Chancellor.

Nevertheless, it is doubtful whether the generals were aware of the full implications of these statements. It is certainly a fact that General von Fritsch in particular was very noncommittal in his reaction to the immediate war plans. Once again, with consummate histrionic art and a lordly contempt for all moral precepts, Hitler utilized an opportunity which chance offered to get rid of this inconvenient man.[179] With the taking over of the Supreme Command and the reorganizing of the top leadership in the Wehrmacht, the statesman became a general—quite consistent with Ludendorff's conception, although not in its direction. If for four years Hitler had hardly ever seen the Chief of General Staff of the Army, General Beck, the new men, Keitel and Jodl, became his daily colleagues.

The first foreign statesman to realize that the lava of an unbridled emotionalism could erupt from the summit figure of the general-statesman on occasions other than in speeches aimed at the masses, was the Austrian Federal Chancellor von Schuschnigg. Foreign policy is as full of threats and compulsion as domestic policy; but the difference had always been that these objective conditions were not apparent in the relations between its representatives. Hitler, however, stormed and raved against Schuschnigg personally, and called for Keitel in that threatening tone of voice with which a tribal chieftain might have summoned the leader of his bodyguard so as to frighten the visitor with his war paint.[180]

The *Anschluss* with Austria occurred in much the same way. The telephone conversations during the night of March 11, 1938,[181] were more reminiscent of cheap melodrama than of the traditional image of even the most severe diplomatic pressure. Not even where Seyss-Inquart was concerned did they lose their aspect of an out-and-out act of violence. After a few hours, of course, a mass rejoicing, on a scale which apparently surprised even Hitler, reduced all this to insignificance.

Six months later, together with the Duce of fascist Italy, the Führer of Greater Germany forced on the Western European powers, by threatening war, an agreement which would "normally" have been attainable only through a large-scale war.

Less than six months later, by breaking solemn promises and by a blackmailing double-dealing of extreme brutality, he deprived Czechoslovakia of its scant independence and gave it a status compared with which its situation in the Hapsburg monarchy had been a paradise of liberty and self-determination.

Now for the first time he ran into the determined opposition of England. The most reasonable of all his demands—invalidated, it is true, by the preceding events—fell on deaf ears in Warsaw. He then isolated the enemy by his most staggering *volte face*—the treaty with the Soviet Union. This ensured victory before military operations had even begun. Hitler despised the English and the French—since Munich, anyway—so thoroughly[182] that he was convinced the conflict could be localized.

On August 22, 1939, before high-ranking officers on the Obersalzberg he made a speech which now revealed more openly the Adolf Hitler of the early Munich years as the true personality hiding behind the People's Chancellor of the peace speeches of 1933 and the victor of the self-determination rights of 1938.[183] He announced his war aim and summarized his convictions with the words: "We must close and harden our hearts. He who has pondered on the order of this world realizes that its meaning lies in the warlike survival of the fittest. But the German people are among the fittest people on earth. Providence has made us the leaders of this people, thus it is our task to provide the German people, crowded together with a hundred and forty inhabitants to the square kilometer, with necessary living space. In carrying out this task, the greatest severity can be the greatest kindness." This could have been written word for word in *Mein Kampf*. And it only confirmed what was in fact obvious to all: it removed the accidental nature from the incipient war and stamped it with the mark of timely decision. Not long afterward he made the connection clear when he said, looking back: "Basically I did not set up the Wehrmacht in order not to strike. The decision to strike was always in me."[184]

It was the most compelling and at the same time the most crucial decision Hitler ever made. In a broader sense he had already struck many times, but always under such circumstances that his enemies did not strike back with the same means. War presupposes an equality of means. Now they met on an equal level, and the only issue was how far the superiority carried over from the war-in-peace period would suffice and how long Hitler would be able to keep apart those whom he had always declared to be his enemies.

But let us pause here for a moment. The question as to how Hitler could rise with such dizzying speed to the position of absolute master of the most powerful military state on earth has been answered: alone among his contemporaries he systematically and single-mindedly carried on war in peacetime. It remains to be asked why so few obstacles were put in the way of this rise, and what the implications of this rise actually were.

It must be borne in mind that in the beginning he rode along, as it were, on the back of a necessary and legitimate process. Germany's return to the community of European powers as a member of equal standing had been prepared by the Weimar Republic with dogged persistence and in its essentials was already a *fait accompli*. Hitler's determination completed the final stages of national restitution more swiftly and spectacularly than had been expected, but he did not create them out of nothing. His enemies were paralyzed by the feeling that they were up against an elemental, long-predictable process. It was thus that the uniting of Austria with the German Reich came about: completion and summit of a national policy of restitution whose aims had scarcely an opponent in Germany (although, of course, this was not *all* it was).

However, this does not sufficiently explain why a policy of war in the midst of peace—a policy which, after all, was also clearly visible in the field of internal affairs—did not lead to a collective resistance on the part of those who were threatened. A contributing fact was, no doubt, the natural conflicts of interest, especially between France and England, which after 1918 had often been of such assistance to Germany and which explain, for example, why England double-crossed its French ally with the separate naval agreement of June 18, 1935, and rendered the Versailles system untenable. But what was much more crucial was the existence of the Soviet Union. In the same way that Hitler had the Bavarian Soviet Republic and Thälmann to thank for his rise inside Germany, so his successes in the area of foreign politics are inconceivable without Stalin. England's appeasement policy must be regarded essentially as a countermove to that trend of France which, in keeping with Litvinov's intentions, was bringing the Soviet Union into Europe. From the standpoint of national states, the Munich agreement is a matchless example of the betrayal of two great powers for their commitments of alliance and friendship; from the standpoint of world politics, it represents rather the successful pact of conservative powers with the younger and more dynamic partners in the alliance. In a similar way—also in Munich—Gustav von Kahr had, fifteen years earlier, placed his hand in that of Adolf Hitler: under compulsion, true, but not reluctantly, since the object was to march against the common enemy. But not even Daladier, prime minister of the most profoundly humbled great power not to mention Neville Chamberlain), came to a decision as von Kahr had done; on the eve of the conference he publicly vented his anger on the "warmongers" of the Left in his own country. His words corresponded exactly to the ruthless campaign of Maurras (and the entire Right).[185] Far more than a victory of a national state fighting for self-determination, Munich was the historic triumph of the fascist powers which received the tacit recognition of Western Europe's conservative governments as the champions of antibolshevism, while the United States persisted in its self-chosen isolation and was apparently not involved. There was a good deal to indicate that Munich was another united nationalist front, aimed this time at crushing communism once and for all in its power position as a state.

There are few things more enlightening than the realization that the achievement of self-determination by the German people in the midst of the twentieth century was only possible in conjunction with another and broader aim. Presumably the only reason Hitler achieved the first objective was that deep down he was impelled by quite different motives.

Whether these motives could ever have been consistent with the Western powers' interests and traditions, prepared as these were to make concessions, was something that Chamberlain could have found out for himself—before, and still more after, Munich—by examining the course of political events inside Germany. Had not the Nuremberg laws put into effect that fourth point in the party program which was completely incompatible with Western liberal tradition, since in principle it placed "blood" above "decision"? Did not the increasingly overt hostility toward the churches make it plain that Germany was no longer willing to recognize that "basis" of common European existence which the appeal of the government of February 1, 1933, had so strongly emphasized? Did not the burnings and murders of the organized giant pogrom of November, 1938, serve to show with agonizing clarity that in the heart of Europe something had become reality which had been regarded as a far-off nightmare from the Tsarist Russia of the terrorist "Black Hundred"? Did not the grim prophecy of the destruction of Jewry, as given in Hitler's Reichstag speech of January 30, 1939,[186] reveal to all who had eyes to see the appalling cleft in the soul of this powerful man, who, as even an amateur student of history, *must* have known that his policy had engendered more tensions than any event before any war during the past hundred years?[187]

But Chamberlain did not change his mind until after the annihilation of Czechoslovakia, and even then only halfheartedly, so that the whole profound perplexity of the dweller in the happy isles, when faced by the mysterious phenomena of bolshevism and fascism, stood revealed in all its paralyzing reality. It is hardly correct to make the inner affinity or reciprocal sympathy of the two totalitarian systems responsible for the conclusion of the non-aggression pact; the appalling lack of decision and dilatoriness of Western diplomacy and the readily understandable fears of the arrogant ruling class in Poland were reason enough.

For all that, however, it is not unjustified to ask whether, if Hitler had died shortly after the Munich triumph, he would not have gone down in history as one of the greatest of all Germans. The creation of the Greater German Reich satisfied a profound and centuries-old desire, and it was of itself (apart from the complication presented by the timing) not one jot less legitimate than the creation of the French or Italian national states. Is it not reasonable to assume that the spectacular success of Germany's national restoration would have proved the essential element, while the remainder—the dreams of "living-space policy," the totalitarianism, the policy toward the Jews—would have been regarded simply as passing whims or temporary expedients which the more moderate successors would have skillfully brushed aside after the attainment of the real objective?

A clear-cut answer to this question is no more possible than to any other historical hypothesis. However, an affirmative answer would assume that Hitler was not outstanding enough to imbue his movement and his successor with something of his own spirit; it would also ignore the force of objective circumstances. In the deliberations of the Weimar period, the problem of East Prussia—that is, relations with Poland—had often seemed to suggest a military solution, and the Polish Corridor must indeed have seemed a thorn in the flesh to a Germany that possessed Vienna and Carlsbad. The only question was whether Poland should perhaps be offered sufficiently large and convincing compensation (at the cost of the Soviet Union, of course). Whichever way the problem was regarded, after Munich everything pointed toward war. Even

Göring would have found it virtually impossible to bring the thundering express to a halt at the last moment.

Another question, and one which can be answered with greater certainty although less universal validity, is whether, under the most favorable circumstances possible, the gains would have been worth the sacrifices. In 1939, even a Germany without Hitler would have remained under the control of narrow minds and fanatical temperaments. What had once been the richest intellectual soil in the world would have continued to resemble a mown field, only that the glorification of the living Führer would have been replaced by the cult of the dead one. That concept of Germany's task and policy, which acquired its most powerful and radical-fascist form through Hitler, could not, even in its more harmless manifestations, escape its innate law. Whatever happened, it had to make Austria a province and all Germany a barracks. It could rule Greater Germany, but only as a spiritual desert. Those who were not aware of the desert could regard German history as having reached its summit; but these sentiments were not even shared by all those who had bestowed their confidence and aid on Hitler as the champion of national restoration. Before war had broken out, that "battle of the gods"[188] had begun among the once rightist bourgeoisie, a battle which was to bring about so many realignments.

Levels of War and Degrees of Resistance

There can be no doubt that Hitler wanted war, but hardly *that* war at *that* time.[189] Ample evidence exists of his deep dismay, and that of his colleagues, at England's and France's declarations of war. Obviously he believed and hoped he would be able to force the Western powers once again to yield;[190] but not for a moment was he prepared to abandon his attack on Poland. All his efforts at peace were based on the contemptuous belief that the "little worms" whom he had met at Munich knew only calculation and no honor.

Thus began World War II, and to the surprise of its originator the local clash immediately spread to a European conflict. It did not acquire its continental and ideological character until almost two years later with the attack on the Soviet Union; the final world configuration resulted in December, 1941, with the Japanese attack[191] on Pearl Harbor and the German-Italian declaration of war on the United States.

It seems more enlightening, however, to replace this sequence in time with a sequence in implication.

The war against Poland started out as a typical war of national restitution, just like the war on which Mussolini had embarked in 1915. The war against France and England appeared to be its complement—a normal European war designed to safeguard and confirm the shift in the balance of power. It was on a similar basis that Italy had been obliged to take on Germany in 1916.

It followed that to millions of people this struggle appeared at first to be merely a resumption of World War I in a smaller and more skillfully chosen framework, whereas in actual fact it displayed from the very beginning a totally different character.

From an objective standpoint, the campaign in Poland proved that an agrarian people is virtually helpless when confronted by an attack from a highly armed industrial nation. Subjectively, the treatment Hitler meted out to the conquered people could not be judged by any standard of European history. It is true that—again objectively—this was the fourth time Poland was partitioned between Russia and Germany, but this time even the social vestiges of national independence disappeared. For the first time in history the world saw a nation thrust back into a state of slavery, without rights and even without educational facilities.[192] In a memorandum of May, 1940, Himmler postulated the following: "For the non-German population of the East [of Europe] there is to be no higher school than the four-grade elementary school. The sole aim of this elementary school shall be: simple arithmetic up to five hundred and no further, writing of one's name, and instruction that it is a divine law to obey the Germans and be honest, hard-working, and well-behaved. I do not regard reading as necessary."[193] Similarly, the annexation of vast areas going far beyond what had formerly been Prussian territory, and the open intention— quickly put into effect—of expelling the Polish and Jewish population in favor of new German settlers, made the nature of the policy being pursued here quite plain: the policy of "ruthless Germanization" together with the enslavement and biological "debilitation" of the rest of the indigenous population.

But the second and next step of the new policy is also to be found in this laboratory of horror: the policy of annihilation. In this, its first appearance, it was directed not against Jews and not against Bolsheviks, but against the Polish intelligentsia. On May 30, 1940, at a session of the police, Governor-General Frank announced the following maxim as being the Führer's personal instructions: "Whatever leading class in Poland we have discovered to exist is to be liquidated, whatever grows up to take its place is to be isolated by us and eliminated as soon as practicable."[194]

It is not surprising that from then on Mussolini could be neither model nor even partner. Munich was a triumph for both fascist powers and leaders; Mussolini's attempt at conciliation on September 2, 1939, was merely the feeble beginning of *Nonbelligeranza* in contravention of the treaty, and the so-called joint victory over France only served to stress that Mussolini had become a satellite. Hitler was now the sole master of Europe, and every fascist movement on the Continent looked to him for direction—from Szálasi to Doriot, from Quisling to Ante Pavelić. However, it was not simply Italy's much smaller war potential that caused Mussolini to sink so rapidly. Although he had conducted a large-scale colonial war of conquest against Ethiopia, pursued a policy of the strictest race segregation, and crushed rebellions with extreme brutality, and although he was still to have the opportunity of carrying on a policy of partition against a neighbouring country: the creation of a regime of enslavement and physical annihilation in the heart of Europe was beyond the powers of Mussolini and *his* fascism. In the field of concrete social evolution and internal political style, he was still the teacher and model; when the national element and the mythicizing of social processes—both so much more marked in Germany—really came into their own with the outbreak of war, the hour of radical fascism was at hand, and the star of normal fascism was on the wane. Mussolini even attempted to interpose a word on Poland's behalf,[195] but he could hardly have been surprised that it was completely ignored.

However, while in Eastern Europe the SS was pursuing a "Germanization" policy and rehearsing radical-fascist annihilation methods, in the West the German Wehrmacht was conducting a triumphant war of national restitution. Within six weeks a technically perfect co-ordination of all arms brought to its knees the great power whose army had only a few years earlier been considered the strongest in the world. When German troops entered Paris on June 14, when a few days later the German conditions were handed to the French intermediary in the forest of Compiègne, the site of the 1918 armistice, the hearts of the entire German nation beat faster at the restitution of rights which had finally been achieved, and hundreds of thousands must have suppressed any doubts they may have had and welcomed the destiny which made them contemporaries of Adolf Hitler.

This war, too, was a living demonstration. It demonstrated that France was much too weak for the position of hegemony to which it laid claim in Europe. It revealed that the principal power of continental European democracy had lost faith in itself, that Maurras' and Déat's defeatism had also prepared the soil internally for the regime of Marshal Pétain with which, whatever else might be thought of it, France finally lost its avant-garde position in world politics. But the war also proved that Hitler really was a military strategist,[196] that his most original creation—the application of war methods to political life—could be reapplied to war, and that here too the uncompromising nature of the will to annihilation[197] and the bold concentration of forces resulted in the most extraordinary successes.

Nevertheless, the war against France, both in the way it was fought and in the temporary peace settlement, was a normal European war; and even the occupation of Denmark and Norway, Belgium and Holland, still remained within the framework of the familiar and the traditional in spite of the infringe-ment of neutrality. Admittedly the Pan-German desires and dreams found a belated and excessive satisfaction, but no one thought of evacuating French provinces for purposes of German settlement, let alone of wiping out the French intelligentsia. Indeed, the war in the air over Britain and the battles of the Africa Corps were fought on a highly chivalrous level. Apparently Hitler never ceased to be aware of the fact that he had not really wanted the war in the West—not at that particular time, at least. His peace overtures to England were no doubt sincere, although in the utmost degree naïve. He would clearly have been happy to return to his former position and, with English backing, be the pioneer in the fight against bolshevism. But in the meantime it had become only too evident that this seemingly idealistic position was identical with his materialist policy of living-space conquest, so that for England to yield would have meant moral capitulation.

Thus Hitler had to learn that the first mistake which he made from his standpoint could not be undone: he had broken with his conservative allies before defeating the revolutionary enemy. To compensate for this he made his second and much more serious mistake.[198]

It is not quite clear at what moment Hitler decided to attack the Soviet Union, but there is good reason to suppose that the idea already matured in his mind during the Western campaign.[199] When early on the morning of June 22, 1941, in spite of Stalin's desperate protestations of friendship, the German armies crossed the frontier with no declaration of war and with vastly superior forces, there began a war which quickly made the Polish example pale by comparison. From the first moment on, it was proclaimed as the struggle between two *Weltanschauungen* and systems, and a ruthlessness was postulated which then proceeded to create its own preconditions. One of Hitler's first preparatory orders was that all Bolshevik commissars were to be shot. In the well-known edicts of Marshals von Reichenau and von Manstein there is indeed something reminiscent of the officers' dread of the unfamiliar phenomenon of the 1918 revolution. Nevertheless, the talk about the struggle between the ideologies was never anything but a lie, for it tried without justification to imply the usual meaning of the term *Weltanschauung*. On the basis of National Socialism's own race-doctrine assumptions, however, the aim could never be anything but the annihilation of the "Jewish-Bolshevik head"[200] and hence the return of the Slavic masses to their natural state of slavery, so that the superior race could find space to ensure its existence, and subjects over which to exert its claim to hegemony. Even Alfred Rosenberg, who later on as a weak and uninfluential Minister of the East sometimes displayed the liberal and scholarly side of his nature, expressed himself before the start of the campaign in no uncertain terms as follows: "The 'crusade' we are carrying on today against bolshevism is not solely for the purpose of saving the 'poor Russians' from bolshevism for all time: it is in pursuance of Germany's world policy to safeguard the existence of the German Reich."[201] Before long, Hitler himself with matchless cynicism exposed the innate untruthfulness of all the talk of "liberation of the Eastern European peoples," and of "Europe's war against bolshevism" (of which a "shameless Vichy newspaper" had spoken) when he said: "Basically it is a matter of cutting up the giant cake in manageable pieces so that we can first control it, second administer it, and third exploit it."[202]

In Hitler's eyes, apparently, the "Jewish-Bolshevik head" was the only thing endangering the attainment of such a predestined goal.

Under these auspices began the most atrocious war of conquest, enslavement, and annihilation known to modern history. While at the front technical perfection, patriotic sense of duty, and at times no doubt anti-Bolshevik indignation as well, inflicted one Cannae after another, behind the front the commandos of the occupation forces were exterminating the Jewish population by the tens of thousand, sparing neither children nor old people. While the troops were usually able to sabotage the implementing of the "Commissar Order," Gestapo officials were combing the prisoner-of-war camps in the Reich and having all dangerous elements executed: not only Jews, but officers, intellectuals, fanatical Communists, and the incurably ill.[203] And from 1942 the annihilation was planned on a grand scale but at the same time also departmentalized and industrialized.[204] The allegedly Jewish commissars in Moscow and the allegedly Jewish bankers in New York, who were carrying on the war, were out of reach; so their alleged biological origin must be attacked, and in train after train the wretched Jewish proletariat of the East and what was left of the Jews in Europe were trundled off to the gigantic factories of swift and hygienic extermination. What this cold-blooded madness of rational destruction of a "race" ultimately meant—this is not yet the place to ask such a question; but of one thing we can be certain, that it will be counted for all time among mankind's most extreme experiences of horror.

Compared with the implementing of the program of annihilation, the policy of conquest and enslavement in the Soviet Union scarcely went beyond the planning stage.[205] *Hitler's Table Talk*, however, makes it plain what the population of Eastern Europe had in store for them in the event of his victory.[206] Moreover, it shows that in the case of the Soviet Union the relatively accidental cause also lay well within the scope of lifelong plans: to talk as he did one must have dreamed for decades of ruling over vast areas and subject peoples. And a document such as *Generalplan Ost*, which foresaw many millions of people being resettled, "transplanted," or eliminated, was not some unreal private work of fantasy but a logical and far from isolated emanation of the "new" thinking and race-biological planning.[207] It is not necessary to prove that this thinking is much more remote than the Marxist theory from the traditions of European thought. Even the most conservative-minded must have felt that this cure was worse than the disease. In the end inimical worlds joined forces to oppose it, and that was anything but accidental.

The three levels of the war were at all times linked but never identical. For Colonel Helmut Stieff, his first stay in newly occupied Poland was enough to deprive him in one swift blow of all professional army sympathy for Hitler.[208] On the other hand, even during the final phase of the war the favorite country of German Irredentism, South Tirol, returned to the Reich, and Hitler trod ever more vigorously in the footsteps of the Hapsburgs, with the result that he finally wanted to annex even Trieste and Venice. At the focal point of all the combined energies (which went to make up the levels) stood the solitary figure of Hitler, and in him alone they encouraged each other to display that strength and single-mindedness which none would ever have been able to produce individually. Even his closest collaborators may have only been entirely at home on one of these levels. Only one of the three planes was exposed to the full light of day and propaganda at any one time. The Nuremberg trials have shown that the principle of secrecy and strict division of labor[209] probably deprived even the highest functionaries of the Reich Security Department of the possibility of an overall view and precise knowledge.

On the other hand, one cannot accept the theory that only personal criminal tendencies of Hitler and some of the "archvillains" around him were responsible for those more hidden "levels." It would be more accurate to say that Hitler was the only one bold enough to take the full consequences, that there were more men in Germany who were only partially prepared to do so than later appeared to be the case. Auschwitz was as firmly embedded in the principles of the National Socialist race doctrine as the fruit in the seed, and many a man who found the fruit too bitter was fertilizing the soil. For even the most withdrawn person a chance event—and these were not so rare—could have lifted the veil for an instant from the work of destruction. In other words, no one *had* to know the three levels, but there was scarcely anyone who was *unable* to know them, at least vaguely or by implication.

The complex nature of the Hitler war meant that resistance to it also took place on various levels and should not be indiscriminately lumped together.[210] The most obvious distinction is that between a patriotic "Resistance" in the occupied countries and a resistance inside Germany which fed on other sources. However, this distinction oversimplifies and fails to recognize the nature of a fascist war which manages to find convinced collaborators and diffused sympathy in every country. Of greater importance is the difference in ideology and parties which is subject to variation according to the situation of the country in question.

It was only in Germany and Italy, of course, that there was that violent protest resulting from exhaustion and weakness which always starts to show itself at a certain point in time, even in purely national wars, and which as a lowest stage can hardly be called resistance.

Religious objection to war as such is something else again, but its lack of association with specific situations links it with the first stage.

Communist resistance, while not something existing apart from specific situations, was virtually changeless. It was the Communists whom Hitler had opposed the most bitterly, it was they who had first denounced him. They remained what they were—aside from that short interlude of the Hitler-Stalin pact, the details and general implications of which they later viewed with reluctance.

The position of convinced Christians and Social Democrats was comparable. For the most part they had merely to work out their attitude afresh, and they all desired a mutual alliance more sincerely than before they were confronted with fascism.

There was an underlying change, although of a tactical nature, to the resistance of all those conservatives who were becoming more and more disillusioned with Hitler and who were trying at the last moment to snatch at the wheels of the runaway coach in order to save the Fatherland—that is, mainly to prevent the threatened bolshevization of Germany.

Resistance transcending any political calculation was the outcome of the change undergone by those who as young men had once stood behind Hitler and who had arrived at that "No" through the experience of those unlit levels, who were undaunted by the prospect of uniting with the Communists and possibly that of the heavy burden of treason.[211] For a man to seek to save his country from the threat of ruin is honorable; for him to remain loyal to the traditional *esprit de corps* and code of honor, in defiance of all assaults upon them, is understandable; but for civilians and officers to come to deny Hitler's aspirations and nature so drastically that they would rather join forces with the Communist adversary than with their mortal enemy who had emerged from their own ranks: this was a process of the utmost historical significance, for it meant the end of an era. New struggles were bound to arise from this union, but on a new level, one on which the bourgeois extreme of traditional social opposition was capable after bitter experience of overcoming the effects of fascist seduction and thus of giving the enemy the opportunity to change also.[212]

It is hard to determine the extent to which resistance in all its forms contributed to Hitler's defeat. It is certainly foolish to ascribe this defeat to "betrayal." It might be said that, if Hitler wanted to carry on a war without resistance determined by situation, all he had to do was wage a genuine war of national restitution. But this statement is superficial. For Germany, a mere war of national restitution was at that time and in that situation already an anachronism. That is why it had to assume the form of a fascist war—one which was waged from more than purely national aspects. The only war Germany could wage without resistance was a national war of defense. Hitler gave Stalin the unique opportunity for such a war. The resistance evoked by his own war was a precise indication on the one hand of the remoteness of that war from a national war of defense, and on the other of the degree to which the German people were not mere obedience machines and cold-blooded race fanatics.

Universal Hostility and End

By December 11, 1941, the day Hitler declared war on the United States, the war had taken on its essential aspect, but was still a particularized war. The entry of the United States turned it into a world war. To the very end, the center of gravity continued to be in the war in Eastern Europe, and it was here alone that the multiple significance of this war unfolded to its final logical conclusion, whereas the conflict with the United States remained consistently within the terms of a normal European war;[213] but events showed what the simplest calculation could have demonstrated earlier—that the weight of the participating elements had undergone a decisive change.

For obvious reasons Hitler had not wanted this extension of the war and had done much to prevent it. The "nonbelligerence" which Mussolini had invented and which represented a hitherto unknown condition on the far side of neutrality, now worked to England's advantage as a result of President Roosevelt's attitude, and for the first time in his life, because of such things as Roosevelt's "order to shoot," Hitler could regard himself as the object of unwarranted attack. Nevertheless, it was his third and last great mistake when, in keeping with the sense but not the letter of the Three Power Pact, he let himself be drawn into the conflict between America and Japan.

For the random way it began was no indication that it was random by nature, and this war, which to Germany may have seemed incidental at first, had to be fought with all the ruthlessness of a critical ideological battle. And so, not long after this war was declared, Hitler spoke in a message to the veteran party members of the "final confrontation and settlement with that conspiracy which [pursued] the same goal from the banking houses of the plutocratic world to the vaults of the Kremlin": "The extermination of Aryan races and people."[214] Now at last he could ignore diplomatic discretion and give vent on a worldwide scale to that deep-seated universal hostility which had governed him and his men from the very beginning and which he, unlike Ludendorff, had known how to disguise at times for the sake of skillfully chosen alliances. Now he could try and derive comfort and confidence from the analogy which appeared complete. What took place during his period of struggle as a struggle among the parties within Germany, was now taking place—so he said at his headquarters on July 22, 1942—as a struggle among the nations in the outside world. Now, he went on, the USSR was the battering-ram as the German Communist party had been during the time of struggle, while the capitalist states, like the bourgeois parties of old, were merely making their debut on the outer edge.[215]

However, the comparison had more than one flaw, and the discrepancy was a vital one. This time Hitler no longer had a powerful section of the "bourgeois" world on his side. Now he had no further resources to which his enemies could not reply. Now the whole world was talking to him in the language of which he had believed himself to be the sole master: the language of war. It followed that his defeat was only a matter of time.

For more than two years he had been the one with far superior strength who had wiped the floor with the weaker and less prepared opponent virtually as he pleased. For a year the balance was even, and in a triumphant and desperate race with destiny the German armies reached the furthest limits of their advance in the Caucasus and Egypt. Then the pendulum swung back, and the siege of Stalingrad and the Anglo-American landing in North Africa initiated two years of unbroken defeat representing a symmetry which implied not adjustment and reconciliation, but total ruin.

The Soviet armies adopted the tactics of pincer-movement and breakthrough, and for the first time in its history the Prussian-German army knew the meaning of headlong flight and the capitulation of entire armies; the Anglo-Americans were able to make Hitler's allies defect and to inaugurate aerial warfare of extraordinary brutality; in the ranks of Germany's own army, resistance became increasingly palpable. In three major new efforts[216] Hitler tried to win back his lost initiative.

To an ever-increasing extent he placed his greatest hopes on new secret weapons. He appeared to regard them as the new creation which was to give him superiority in his desperate plight, as the novel style of rally and fighting had once done in Munich. But he could not invent these weapons himself. The technical inventiveness of German research was certainly equal to the task, and with its V-missiles and fighter-jets it contributed no less to the expansion of military technology than the British with their invention of radar. But it is characteristic and hardly accidental that what was truly new and revolutionary —the development of the atom bomb—took place in America, although here too the basis had once been laid in Germany.[217]

The second attempt meant entering on a course which in some ways[218] could be regarded as a vindication of Röhm. Since the war began, the *Waffen-SS* had grown from small beginnings to gigantic size and strength. This was to produce an army of fanatical ideological fighters, the highly personal weapon of the National Socialist state, in contrast to the Wehrmacht, which had always remained essentially unpolitical and was stamped with pernicious traditions. But while Hitler could raise one SS division after another, while after Stauffenberg's attempted coup he could decimate the General Staff and have field marshals hanged or removed, while he could force the Wehrmacht to give the Hitler salute and to accept National Socialist "indoctrination officers," the creation of an absolutely dependable armed force was not within his power. Generally speaking, up to the very end his war was waged chiefly by men who wanted nothing beyond national restitution, and who therefore in the inferno of this complex war had nothing to fall back on but a sense of duty which was often deeply undermined and at best purely formal. It was to create and safeguard Germany that this army had once crossed into foreign lands; when five years later it was thrown back into its own country, it could no longer believe wholeheartedly in Germany.

The third and apparently most obvious course was taken by Hitler with reluctance and typically enough he left the execution of it largely to others. This was the turning of the concept of "Europe" and "idealistic" antibolshevism into reality.[219] The curve of this course was in direct proportion to that of the German defeats. Although the race doctrine certainly contained a "European" element, the nationalist components always gained the upper hand. Even in the SS, which pursued such a zealous policy of Greater Germanism[220] that it finally even organized Moslem divisions, no non-German ever attained an important position of leadership. Indeed, Hitler's antibolshevism *was* nothing but the will to annihilate the Jews and to weaken the Slavs biologically so as to eliminate forever all danger to the German-Germanic Reich; in his eyes a national Russian military power under Vlassov was no less a threat—because of its biological potential—than Stalin's Bolshevik Russia. And Rosenberg's aversion to the general was virtually as great: his affection for the Ukrainians pursued a similar goal to Hitler's but with milder methods. So, although a great deal of idealism flowed from East and West into the units of the foreign volunteers, if ever there was a deluded and probably also self-deluding idealism, this was it.

But the greatest obstacle to Hitler proved to be Hitler himself. He had been an outstanding general for as long as he had been able to attack; now that he was attacked himself, all he could think of was to persist in clinging to the same position like an obstinate child.[221] His monomaniacal concentration on one thing and one enemy no longer produced success, for there were too many enemies, and what he promised everyone was lacking everywhere. The only sense in which he continued to be a medium was that he still knew how to persuade himself and others of what was sweet to hear but a fatal self-deception to believe. When in its final phase the war took on the form of a national war of defense, there no longer existed a nation which could have risen up against the enemy with a clear conscience and the sense of a just cause. Radical fascism had consumed the energies of the people in that which was peculiar to itself: attack. For the defense of native soil there was little energy and courage left. Within a few weeks Germany collapsed, as Poland had done at the beginning of the war; but it had less hope of resurrection than its neighbor had been justified in nursing at that time. Hitler was right in one thing: there was no revolution like the one in 1918. But in many places it was felt—clearly or obscurely—that a people cannot be worse off than if it is unable to rise in revolution at any time.

Hitler had driven one potential of German politics to its uttermost limits— once to the heights, now to the depths. It was gone forever. But he had also inflicted terrible injury on the other potential, and that presumably had been his intention.

While the Soviet Russian armies were gathering in the bridgehead of Baranov, still far inside Poland, for the most pulverizing of their thrusts, Hitler ordered the last and best German forces to launch the offensive in the Ardennes. This, together with the local party authorities' blind lust for prestige, sealed the dreadful fate of the population of East Germany.

When in March all possibility of halting the enemy advances in East and West was past, Hitler decided on a scorched-earth policy for Germany too. In reply to Speer's remonstrances, he stated that it was not necessary to consider the German people's livelihood, the good ones were dead, the future now belonged exclusively to the stronger people of Eastern Europe.[222] Thus apocalyptic reality appeared to have smashed at least one of Hitler's basic concepts. But this was an illusion.

On April 28 in the bunker of the Reich Chancellery, Hitler received the news of Mussolini's death. Once again the Duce seemed to have become his model, if only in a negative sense. He even avoided *that* contact with reality which Mussolini had evinced in his last days on earth and in his death. Thirteen years earlier Hitler had threatened during the hours of the Strasser crisis that, if the party should crumble, he would end his life with a pistol within three minutes.[225] Now the Reich lay in ruins and all hope had vanished: now his own pistol really pointed to the lonely way out. The lie that he fell fighting bolshevism with his last breath was a legend with feet of clay—a legend which pretended one last time that he was something which he was not.

What he was is to be seen from the political testament he dictated shortly before he committed suicide. It closed with the words: "Above all, I demand of the nation's leaders and followers scrupulous adherence to the race laws and to ruthless resistance against the world poisoners of all peoples, international Jewry."[224]

The implication of that sentence could have been contained in that first document of his political activity, the letter to Gemlich. A quarter of a century had gone by, filled with appalling happenings of which one of the most recent bore the name of Auschwitz: Adolf Hitler never changed. Evidently he only spoke of the "stronger people of Eastern Europe" so as not to have to admit that *he* was the cause of the lost war and that "the Jew" was the victor of this colossal struggle.

Hitler was not a socialist—no proof of this is necessary. But he was also not a nationalist. This is shown, if by nothing else, by those final words apropos the German people. He was a man on the border line of sickness, driven by pathological fears, originated, it seemed to him in his infantile-identifying capacity, by "the Jew." But his fear as such was the fear of a people, a culture, an era. This moves him away from Mussolini and toward Maurras.

CHAPTER FOUR

Practice as Fulfillment

1919–1923

In calling the National Socialist practice "fulfillment," what is meant, of course, is the fulfillment of Hitler's "doctrine," for without this practice the doctrine would indeed never have been anything but the distortion of a diagram which had long since been implemented by superior thinkers and not least by Maurras. At the same time it is not advisable, any more than it was with the Action Française, to describe the practice *after* analyzing the doctrine, for here too it is intimately linked with its history. And again, this history could not be told without outlining the doctrine. At this point, therefore, the meaning of "fulfillment" has been established in a preliminary sense, yet sufficiently.

Unlike Italian fascism but like the Action Française, National Socialism seeks from the very beginning to preach a doctrine. But its practice, as against that of the Action Française, is not a mode or action proceeding logically from a carefully developed conviction. In its specific nature it is rather an integral part of the proclamation of the *Weltanschauung*, of ideology, itself, and it is the practice which gives this ideology its real effectiveness. In *Mein Kampf* Hitler with good reason placed the power of the spoken word far above that of the written word. It is unlikely that his book won him many supporters for National Socialism, whereas his speeches fascinated the masses over and over again. But on every occasion a Hitler speech was staged and protected. The staging and protecting of these speeches was the very heart of early National Socialist practice; that is why Hitler could say of propaganda that it attempted to *force* a doctrine on the entire population.[1] Since indoctrination is achieved by force, it is permissible to call the practice fulfillment even in the early days; after the seizure of power it amounted primarily to implementation, without ever quite losing the first meaning.

But this definition requires the study of two essential conditions without which National Socialism could never have been born and which distinguish it considerably from Italian fascism.

Anyone trying in the Red Bologna of 1920 to preach the National Socialist ideology, or force it onto his audience, would hardly have escaped from the city alive. National Socialism and fascism developed on two totally different types of soil. Even when Mussolini was already the most powerful party leader in Italy, in the summer of 1922, the city administration of Milan was still in socialist hands. In Ferrara, in Bologna, in Mantua—everywhere the Fascists had risen up in bitter fighting in the midst of revolutionary-minded masses. In Munich, on the other hand, the Reichswehr and the Home Guard were in control after the downfall of the Soviet Republic; the other voices in the political concert were provided by the Bavarian People's party and the German National People's party. After the terrible bloodletting and vengeance of May, 1919, there were virtually no more Communists,[2] and the Social Democrats of the majority were more bourgeois than anywhere else in Germany. In this city Röhm and his friends "nationalized" the masses by having the café orchestras play patriotic songs and beating up anyone who did not immediately rise to his feet.[3] Here many organizations of the radical Right had continued to operate even under the Soviet Republic. And the popular mood was just as much against the Jews in Bavaria as against the "Bolsheviks" in Berlin—even if not always from the same motives. In other words, in the Munich of 1919 onward, there could be absolutely no question of that threat of "bolshevism" which in Italy was a reality. And it was this that enabled the proponents of a most intense anti-Marxist *Weltanschauung* to set about forcing their outlook on the predisposed masses.

However, young National Socialism would presumably never have emerged from the many other similar groups had it not—unlike fascism—been motived by a *Führungsimpuls*, a leadership urge, which nothing could withstand. It is true that for nearly two years Hitler was only the director of propaganda for the party and took orders from the party executive, of which Anton Drexler was chairman. But there is no reason to doubt his assertion that he never brooked interference in his own field, and what was the youthful NSDAP without its propaganda? In July, 1921, Hitler managed to terminate the first party crisis by becoming first chairman with dictatorial powers and being only *pro forma* responsible to a remains of democratic control by members and leading executive bodies. Mussolini could not possibly have served as a model here, for it was just at this time that he was entering upon his bitterest conflicts with the new Fascists outside Milan, and not even before the March on Rome could he be called the "dictator" of his party. In terms of both relative and absolute time, the leadership principle became paramount earlier in National Socialism than in Italian fascism.

At first Hitler's leadership urge was directed solely toward increasing the size and frequency of rallies and the care with which he organized them. In the very earliest days, his restless drive for publicity and proselytizing constituted a real revolution for Drexler's and Harrer's publicity-shy group. It began with a few dozen listeners in smoke-filled back rooms in obscure taverns; the program rally already took place in the Hofbräuhaus, and in February, 1921, Hitler could risk hiring the huge hall of the Krone Circus. Yet although he managed to attract bigger and bigger crowds and to bring them under his spell, it was hardly the novelty or perceptiveness of his *Weltanschauung* which were responsible for these triumphs. More than any of the other similar personalities of his kind in Munich, he had the gift of *communicating an emotion.*

But this communication had to be protected from disruptive influences. Hence the important thing was, from the very beginning, to turn his listeners from an audience into a community. The system of guarding the hall and maintaining an *Ordnertruppe* is attributable to this basic requirement no less than to the alleged terrorist fighting methods of the Marxist foes. For the ordinary citizen was at that time still accustomed to heckle and argue during political meetings. And the "Marxists" were only more brutal inasmuch as they had developed habit into a method and sometimes tried to "blow up" hostile meetings by noise and catcalls. But hecklers were thrown out of Hitler rallies long before the "Gymnastic and Athletic Division of the NSDAP" was officially founded in August, 1921. A paragraph from one of those naïve reports the Reichswehr group command had drawn up illustrates this; it was dated August 14, 1920: "Then Herr Hitler spoke about this subject, but he became enraged and shouted so loud that at the back it was impossible to understand much. When Herr Hitler spoke, a fellow always shouted 'Pfui,' while the others always backed him up with 'quite right.' But this fellow was soon taken care of. He was thrown right across the hall, on the steps he was immediately protected by a policeman, otherwise perhaps he would not have got home in one piece."[4] In *Hitler's Table Talk* Hitler himself described the re-markably rough methods he used to silence women who attempted to embark on arguments and whom he could not very well have thrown out by the hall guards.[5] There is little reason to take for granted those sections of his report on the early days which were anxious to give the impression that Munich was a city ruled by the Red mob. A more likely reason for the loving care Hitler expended on the organization of the *Ordnertruppe* was his endeavor to safeguard the communicating of emotion from *any* kind of interference.

This is not to imply that organized attempts at interference did not take place. It was here that the typical difference in fighting methods became apparent. Wilhelm Hoegner reported that Social Democratic workers tried to disrupt the meeting of February 24, 1920, but that armed National Socialists made mince-meat of them with life preservers, rubber truncheons, and riding whips.[6] If even in Italy the difference between red and white terror could hardly be ignored, in the Munich of the years following the Soviet *Putsch* this difference reached proportions of complete incommensurability.[7]

It was also present in the famous brawl in the Hofbräuhaus of November, 1921, which Hitler described in such glowing terms and which was the immediate cause of the *Ordnertruppe* being given the honorable title of *Sturmabteilung* (SA). For it is clear from his description that the Marxist majority which had infiltrated into the hall intended to break up the meeting merely by making a lot of noise or at most hurling beer mugs around, according to local custom. Even superhuman bravery would not have enabled the weak *Ordnertruppe* to stand up to a crowd twenty times as strong if only some of the other side had had real weapons and the intention to attack. However, that was so patently not the case that the speaker was able to remain calmly in his place. From then on, according to Hitler, there were no more organized attempts at disturbance—although even before that they were few and far between[8]—and so the unrestricted monopoly which the National Socialists had always claimed for their assemblies was maintained, and the dissemination of the new ideology never failed to find an audience in the proper frame of mind.

Thus Hitler had learned from his enemies and to a certain extent outdone them by creating a qualitatively new style of assembly. This also applied to the propagandist preparation of the rallies. Who had ever heard of a "bourgeois" party having its posters printed in bright red, of having a red flag carried at the head of its parades? Who else but the proletariat had till then (although no longer precisely in Munich) ridden on red-draped trucks through the streets? But these posters were covered with short, inflammatory words which were much more intelligible to the man in the street than Marxist expressions; the men who waved from these trucks were no longer the shabby proletarian figures of past days, but young soldiers whose shouts met with a warm response on the part of the people in the streets. Although the flag was blood-red, that alarming expanse of a single color was now embellished by a symbol (albeit strange) of salvation and hope in the middle. Moreover, this group worked harder than any other party. Armies of men pasting up posters were at work at all hours, either armed themselves or guarded by escorts with rubber truncheons, steel rods, and pistols. Great swastikas appeared on house walls and bridges everywhere. It was not long before as many as six or even twelve assemblies were arranged for one evening, and at each one of them *der Führer* held forth. This growth in the direction of the gigantic was bound to alter the functions of the SA. The propaganda troops were no longer limited to staging and protecting speeches: they acquired an importance of their own as a demonstration of will and energy. The protection of the Führer became the special duty of the *Stosstruppe Hitler*, from which later grew the SS; the SA as a whole soon split up into units of a hundred men and assumed more and more the character of a private army.[9] But Hitler wanted it to remain a party army and a body of propaganda troops whose job it was to rule the streets and with giant parades wage the "war of annihilation against Marxism." "What we needed and still need," he said in *Mein Kampf*, "was not and is not a hundred or two hundred bold conspirators, but hundreds and hundreds of thousands of fanatical fighters for our ideology."[10]

The concealed polemic of these words was aimed at a third characteristic that the SA was increasingly assuming under Röhm's influence and which could not fail to remove it from the area of the ideological battlefield: the character of a volunteer unit (*Wehrverband*). Although as a volunteer unit it received arms and support from the Reichswehr, it was also removed from the absolute control of the party leader; it became absorbed by secret military training and took its place among other volunteer units. In this matter, however, Hitler had to yield in 1922–23, and thus his own most personal creation, the SA, acquired for him something of the aspect of the moon, which always only turns one side toward the earth. There are many instances in *Mein Kampf* of this first serious intraparty bone of contention.

At the heart of its practice, therefore, early National Socialism was quite distinct from early Italian fascism. Fascism at first had nothing to do with the preaching of an ideology, it did not fight its battles in meetings, its fighting troops were not a body *beside* the party, and no one tried to detach them from it. Common to both were basic intention and basic character, both fought a war of annihilation against Marxism by adopting and typically transforming Marxist methods. The "fascist minimum" certainly did not exclude deeply rooted differences.

In those points where the organization was determined directly by the stronger leadership urge and the requirements of ideological propagation, the differences are obvious. They unfold in two main directions. From the leadership principle proceeds the postulate that the entire effort first be concentrated in one single place and that *Ortsgruppen* be formed only when the authority of the headquarters in Munich could be considered unquestioningly acknowledged.[11] Hence National Socialism never had anything like fascism's *Ras*;[12] on the other hand, until the November *Putsch* it remained a local phenomenon limited to Bavaria and in fact to Munich. Its revelatory character gave rise to an extremely sharp distinction between "members" and "followers," between activist nucleus and merely listening, sympathizing crowds. The extent to which Hitler regarded his people as an object, while the masters and potential occupants of the "nerve centers of the state" were to remain a small number of members, is to be seen with matchless clarity from some pages of his book printed in bold type.[13] If the SA was separated more strictly from the NSDAP than the militia from the Fascist party, this applied even more to the associated organizations of which some—communications corps, youth league, motorized detachment, for instance—had been founded in the early days.[14]

The most obvious points in which the two parties agree were probably those of *style*. It is easy to see why: both parties could be regarded as the expression of those military divisions which had never been spiritually demobilized. Hence their appearance in public was always determined by a paramilitary style—

parades bands, flags, escorts—although this style, taken by itself, was not enough to typify fascism as such, since it is also common to nonpartisan veterans' associations and other volunteer groups. Fascism was distinguished by the ability to transform this style typically and to make it the hallmark of the whole party and, ultimately, of the population. At first both these elements were present in both parties in rudimentary form only. Gabriele D'Annunzio's theatrical genius set an example which for the time being both Italian fascism and National Socialism could only approach. The National Socialist storm troops of 1923 were essentially mere groups of civilians shouldering rifles, with only a hint of uniform in their armbands and windbreakers. In the great parades of patriotic associations they were hardly distinguishable from the other formations. However, at the mammoth demonstration in August, 1922, against the "Law for the Defense of the Republic" the SA was the only group to carry banners and for this reason was applauded at the Königsplatz with special warmth. But Hitler spoke as one among many, and at no time during this period did the NSDAP control a joint rally with the monopoly and pre-eminence of the Fascist party at the rallies of Trieste and Bologna. At German Day in Nuremberg Hitler, wearing a raincoat, stood among a fairly large group and took the salute at ground level. Whenever the SA adopted a decidedly military note and drove up on motorcycles with the "swastika on their steel helmets," it did so in its capacity of volunteer unit. Nowhere was the "fascist salute"[15] yet in evidence, nor was the brown shirt.

What was genuinely new and typically transformed was the party flag. The swastika did not, like the lictor's bundle, recall a remote but nevertheless still tangible historical era: as an ancient and prehistoric symbol of salvation it was supposed to proclaim the future victory of "Aryan man." Just as Mussolini's oratorical style, even in its worst outbursts, seemed controlled and moderate when compared to Hitler's, so the recalling by the Fascists of the Roman imperial tradition seemed, despite its dubious aspect from a national stand-point, concrete and historically valid when compared with this appeal to the prehistoric and the archaic. Not only in ideas: in sight and sound, too, the extreme nature of the young movement, although its fighting methods were much less bloody, is easily recognizable in comparison with fascism.

1925–1932

After Hitler's return from Landsberg there was a far-reaching change in certain elements of National Socialist practice, particularly in their mutual relationship. For a considerable time Hitler was banned from public speaking, and this affected the very heart of past practice. Dissemination of the ideology was transferred to the newspaper and, more specifically, to the propaganda activities of the principal men under Hitler. His book did not attract much attention to begin with. The successes in North Germany of Strasser and later Goebbels made it clear that Hitler and National Socialism were by no means identical, and that a pan-nationalist movement had a considerable future quite apart from his personality. Although the question of whether a nonfascist National Socialism could have developed under Strasser's leadership is not an idle one, it cannot be discussed in this context. Similarly, what went on during the political struggle between the Strasser and Hitler wings is of no interest here. The only fact to be emphasized at this point is that Hitler succeeded in establishing his position of power in the newly founded party on a statutory basis and in further developing the organization to a highly remarkable degree. While all the other elements in the practice evolved normally—although quantitatively rather than qualitatively—Hitler (with the considerable assistance of Strasser) gave the party an organization which was no longer even remotely comparable to the rudimentary beginnings of the early Munich days.

The refounding of the party in February, 1925, was sufficient testimony to Hitler's unbroken authority, and after the satisfactory termination of the leaders' conference in Bamberg new statutes were laid down at a general assembly on May 22, 1926. They declared the cornerstone of the party to be the National Socialist German Workers' Union in Munich, the leaders of which were *eo ipso* identical with the leaders of the party as a whole. This body consisted of a collective organ—made up of the executive, the chairmen of the committees, and the chief administrator—but the first chairman was not subject to majority decisions, and this gave him dictatorial powers, especially as it was he who appointed the chairmen of the subcommittees—that is, for propaganda, organization, athletics and gymnastics (SA), and investigation and arbitration (*Uschla*)—and the two other members of the executive (secretary and treasurer) were in any case appointments of no political influence. The sole safeguard against arbitrary action was the provision of a right of control on the part of the members of the general assembly over the first chairman; since, however, these consisted by statute entirely of members of the Munich *Ortsgruppe*, the whole of the rest of the Reich party found itself in the position of a completely dependent province. Thus it was quite consistent with the spirit of these statutes that the *Gauleiter* were also to be appointed by Munich.[16]

It is here that the difference is to be found as against the comparable Fascist party statute.[17] There the regional deputies, who were not appointed from above, corresponded to the Munich committee chairmen. In Germany there had never been room for more than a minute degree of local spontaneity: the election of the *Ortsgruppen* leaders by the members. But by 1929 even this had been abolished.[18]

From the committees there very soon developed the central offices of the Reich administration, and by 1928 their most remarkable characteristic was already established, for in fact there were two organizational divisions, the "attack department" under Gregor Strasser, and the "development department" under Konstantin Hierl. The first had subsections for foreign countries, press, and organization; the second for agriculture, race and culture, internal affairs, and so forth. The first took care of the day-to-day tasks of the organization and hence wielded more practical influence, while the second—in the midst of the Weimar period—planned the National Socialist state and for this reason was by far the more interesting. It had no counterpart in the Fascist party before the March on Rome, whereas Strasser's department can very well be compared with the fascist general secretariat, and the SA under Pfeffer von Salomon with the militia under Balbo. The men of the "development departments," like Hitler himself, were already living in the Third Reich. It was here, for instance, after his appointment in 1930, that Walter Darré,[19] who was in charge of agrarian-political affairs, planned those laws which were to give a large section of the German farmers the unique position which could be described as "serf-aristocracy."

These offices were continually being augmented by new bureaus and sub-departments, so that by 1932 a bureaucracy of considerable dimensions had been created which stood ready to occupy the nerve centers of the state—to use Hitler's expression in *Mein Kampf*. It will be enough to name some of the bureaus of the five chief sections: internal affairs, juridical affairs, national health and race, national education, military and foreign affairs, civil servants, NSBO (trade-unions organization), press, federations of doctors, lawyers, teachers and students, areas of currency, finance, and production, horticulture, stock market, the Eastern territories, settlement, poultry-farming. Even if in 1933 the immediate occupation of all the corresponding government offices by this parastate party administration was not feasible, the NSDAP had nevertheless prepared itself for its seizure of power much more thoroughly than was within the power or intention of any other totalitarian party.

Moreover, it was essential that it should do so, seeing that the terms and conditions for its struggle had radically altered. After 1925 it was no longer the sheltered, cherished ally of the governments. What else could Hitler do but adopt a tactic of legality—in other words, avoid getting into an altogether hostile relationship with the state? Yet had he really ever pursued a tactic of illegality and revolt? In 1923 the whole of Bavaria had wanted to march on Berlin, and all Hitler had wanted was to take the lead. In the early Munich days he had had to fight more against his anonymity first, and later his own partisans, than against actual political adversaries. It is significant that before November 9, 1923, the movement did not have a single death to its name.

After 1925 all this changed. The attitude of the ruling party in Bavaria toward the traitor released from prison was surprisingly generous, although by no means cordial. Throughout Prussia and in Berlin a hard fight had to be fought. The Reichswehr had dissociated itself from the National Socialists. Until the plebiscite against the Young Plan, the party received almost no support. It managed to keep going essentially on the strength of its own efforts, thereby refuting the argument that a fascist party can *only* thrive on the support of powerful financial and political circles. The fact that after 1930 it could become the largest mass party in German history was something it had chiefly itself to thank for—that is, Hitler's power as an orator and his will to leadership, an organization already geared to an assault, the untiring energies of some tens of thousands of activist supporters, the susceptibility of the German people to its style, and not least the absence of a program in the social field which allowed it to be all things to all people. The world economic crisis was merely the wave which lifted up the superbly prepared swimmer. Nevertheless, it was important to meet with plenty of sympathy from leading social circles without encountering any determined antagonism on the part of the state. The connection between these two phenomena is revealed in a number of utterances made by the Reichswehr command, which was not nearly as favorably inclined as the Italian army in 1921–22 or the Bavarian Reichswehr of 1921–23.[20] The manifest result was that Goebbels, for example, could afford to behave in his speeches with an insolence toward the Weimar "system" in "Red" Berlin which today seems incredible and yet which became one of the hallmarks of reconstituted National Socialism.[21]

On the whole the style developed consistently and with continuity, enriched by the essential element of honoring the dead and the "blood banner." At the Weimar party conference in the summer of 1926, the SA columns marching past Hitler already wore their brown shirts and held their right arms outstretched, while Hitler took the salute standing in a large open car, his arm extended unwearyingly in salute. During the years that followed, the marching brown detachments became an ever more familiar picture in Germany, with new additions to their uniforms and insignia showing elaborate gradations of rank, occasionally involved in street-fighting, but usually parading in a peacefully threatening manner, never resorting to open battle, like the Italian Fascists, against the institutions of the enemy. Even in 1931–32 there was certainly no civil war in Germany, and yet under altered circumstances and on a larger scale there was a repetition of the picture of 1918 and 1919: the columns of Communists, in which thousands of ill-dressed civilians, shouting "Hunger" and raising their fists, marched behind a vanguard in shabby uniforms and at most a primitive brass band, were matched by the parades of the National Socialists, and here behind banners and flags, to the accompaniment of shouted commands and military music, company after company of jack-booted men marched in strict discipline and perfect step. Fifteen years earlier, the crowds of poorly armed Spartacists had likewise faced the detachments of the uniformed *Freikorps* as deadly enemies. The configuration was now radically altered: the state had long ceased to fear the Communists in their isolation, but the victors of those days had multiplied their ranks much more swiftly and showed a more determined face.

Hitler evidently judged the German people of his era more correctly than Rosa Luxemburg had done when he said in 1927: "We have a third value: the sense of battle. It is there, merely buried under a jumble of foreign theories and doctrines. A powerful great party tries to prove the opposite, until suddenly a quite ordinary military band comes along and plays, then sometimes the hanger-on wakes up from his dreamlike state, all of a sudden he begins to feel himself one with the marching people, and he falls in step. That is how it is today. Our people have only to be shown this better thing—and you see, we are already on the march."[22] It seemed as if the people of Mars had merely rediscovered and renewed their old style when, under Brüning's government, the SA military columns, stretching away as far as the eye could see, marched past the party leader Hitler in front of the Brunswick Palace just as the guards and fusiliers had once marched past their Kaiser.

But how great the difference actually was could be seen from every rally at which this Führer spoke. As early as 1927, when the speaking ban was lifted even in Prussia, this was where the heart of National Socialist practice lay. By 1932 the dimensions had expanded enormously: Hitler spoke to tens and hundreds of thousands, he was the first German politician to make frequent use of the airplane, he knew how to maintain tactical silence on many subjects, and he had long since cast off his previous awkward manner with people. But the essential element remained quite unchanged. He still, to use the words of the reporter of those early days, "flew into a rage," he still communicated an unbridled emotionalism to the expectant crowds and received in return wave upon wave of delirious rapture. Indeed, if the appeal to soldierly traditions and the magic of the military style decided this political battle, they were implemented by a man who could not have been further removed from the traditional nature and ethos of the soldier. This paradoxical synthesis, however, was vital to victory.

1933–1939

It must not be imagined that with the seizure of power the practice of National Socialism immediately and uniformly became the practice of state and society, but in every direction the process of integration or totalization began without delay. In the field of propaganda, a new National Socialist creation replaced the institutions of the old state which had been but barely developed—whereas the Catholic Church could maintain and even legally reinforce its independent position, although at the cost of severe sacrifices and considerable loss of prestige. The party's agricultural section provided the existing ministry with its head and principal functionaries, while the foreign affairs bureau did not manage to make the leap into the foreign office, and it remained comparatively without influence. The SA tried in vain to obtain control over the Wehrmacht; the SS, on the other hand, after a few attempts took over the police. According to their differing personalities, the *Gauleiter* gained varying degrees of influence over the administration of their regions, while a number of National Socialist ministers were captured, as it were, by the large established apparatuses of the central sections with the aid of some concessions. In some spheres of life, the introduction of the leadership principle met with what was often a felt need, in others it led to absurd results. Some measures, the book-burning, for example, produced cries of horror all over the world; others, such as the vigorous steps taken against the Communists, met with considerable approval—overt or tacit—in many foreign circles.

The task of presenting the whole process in its stratified unity and its *specific* efforts toward totality is one which, despite some significant initial attempts, cannot be considered complete.[23] In this context it cannot even be a matter of outlining certain points of view or observation methods. The first limitation derives from the comparison with fascist Italy. A second consists in the fact that events which in a narrower sense may be called political must be excluded here. But even then the task would be much too extensive. For instance, it would be highly interesting to examine the relationship between the "corporative state structure" in Italy and the "regulation of national labor" laid down in Germany by the law of January 20, 1934, and especially how the institution of the German Labor Front which, of course, comprised employees *and* employers, is to be evaluated when compared with Italy. But a precise answer requires a relatively too extensive examination, while no research is necessary to grasp that it was a system of party-state definition of the relationship between capital and labor which in the practical field greatly favored the employers but which was not without danger to them. Of no less interest would be a comparison of the educational system of both parties, in which the German system with its Adolf Hitler schools and *Ordensburgen* (training institutes) was undeniably ahead. It would also be valuable to examine the various degrees of undermining and impoverishment in the various sciences and their institutions.

The only possible method is by selection. It may seem arbitrary because in each case one must neglect or overlook some essential item. In making this selection it would not be right to try and counterbalance the twelve years of extravagantly staged lighting effects by illuminating only the cellar regions of the building where the spotlights never fell, or by letting so-called justice attempt to balance the "positive" and the "negative" fairly and symmetrically. It is much more important to realize that, in the specific practice of National Socialism as well as in its history and ideology, the so-called positive and the so-called negative constitute a closely knit whole deriving from uniform roots.

Since historical description must to a large extent depend on documents which did not come to light until later, the only examples selected will be those manifestations which were generally known during their own time. In each of these the elements of National Socialist practice must be so recognizably combined that a detailed analysis is superfluous; each must be comparable, although to a varying degree, with an Italian counterpart. The following will therefore be briefly discussed: (1) A Reich party conference; (2) Legislation on race and hereditary health; and (3) Evolution and self-evaluation of the SS. As the 1937 party congress, occurring as it does immediately before the start of the big changes in foreign policy, seems to be the most suitable for this study, points 1 and 2 will be reversed.

The National Socialist race policy was developed during the peace years in three principal legislative thrusts, with considerable intervals between them, in order evidently to stabilize what had been achieved and accustom the population to the new laws. The turbulent beginnings in 1933 were followed by a year and a half of comparative quiet, until the Nuremberg laws pitched developments another substantial step forward. Then for two and a half years nothing much happened, but early in 1938 one new measure followed rapidly on the heels of another, and only for their climax in November, 1938, was the crime of Herschel Grynszpan taken as a pretext. At the same time the geographical expansion of the race legislation began. This expansion had always been aimed at Jewish property and even before the outbreak of war it constituted a wartime measure.

The beginnings of the anti-Semitic policy were disguised as a reaction to the "atrocity stories" of the Jewish emigrants. A committee headed by Julius Streicher appealed to the public for a boycott of Jewish shops and businesses, and on April 1, 1933, members of the SA spent the day on sentry duty in every town and village in Germany, holding placards and challenging the citizens, with more or less threatening looks, not to patronize the businesses of this particular group of their fellow citizens. It was a pseudorevolutionary action—a feast for the cameras of all the foreign journalists and offensive also to the order-loving German people who, with all their enthusiasm for the national revolution, must at that moment have experienced their first inkling of things to come. The action was hurriedly called off, and Julius Streicher never again took the spotlight in such a significant and obvious capacity. But the thinking of the new men was disclosed by the most recently appointed Reich minister, Dr. Goebbels, more effectively than whole weeks of boycott could ever have done, for in his broadcast speech of April 1 he had the following to say about the German Jews: "If they maintain today that they cannot help it if their racial brothers in England and America drag Germany's national regime down into the mire, then we cannot help it if the German people take it out on them." And he threatened that the boycott would be resumed in such a way "that German Jewry will be annihilated."[24]

This was the kind of sophistry that till then the Germans had delighted in dubbing "Jewish," and anyone who, on the strength of the reports of some emigrants (or, worse still, of the universal reaction of world opinion), used this argument to declare as hostages hundreds of thousands of human beings because of their "blood," could not be surprised if he was held capable of the most dire deeds and intentions.

From now on the "elimination of Jews from the body of the German nation" was undertaken not by way of mass demonstrations and revelatory speeches, but by legal measures. The *Gesetz zur Wiederherstellung des Berufsbeamtentums* (law for the restoration of the civil service) of April 7, 1933, laid the foundation; this was the first law to contain the "Aryan paragraph" and thus to pension off all civil servants of non-Aryan descent, with the exception of veterans and their dependents.[25] This paragraph was very soon extended to include first lawyers and doctors under the municipal health schemes, and soon afterward writers and artists, university and high-school students; it was not long before "proof of Aryan descent" became a matter of vital concern for most Germans.

On June 28, 1933, Reich Minister for the Interior Frick made a speech[26] before the newly appointed "Advisory Council of Experts for Population and Race Policy." In it the concepts of the National Socialist policy of racial health for the nation were officially presented, and distributed in pamphlet form. The minister began by pointing out the impending racial death of the nation as a result of the decline in the birth figures, and calculated that the "reproductive output" of German women was some thirty per cent below what was required merely to ensure maintenance of the population figure. But increase must be the objective. To achieve this, particularly strenuous efforts were needed since by no means *every* German child was welcome. In cautious and yet scarcely mistakable phraseology, the minister mentioned that, according to some authors, twenty per cent of the German population must be considered biologically impaired from a hereditary standpoint, and that propagation on the part of these people was therefore not desirable. Liberalism and industrialization had, he said, brought about a sharp deterioration of the family, and that was all the more dangerous since the neighbors to the East and the inferior layers among Germany's own population showed a very high birth rate. Miscegenation was contributing toward further debasement of the race. Above all it was necessary, apart from the elimination of the Jews, drastically to reduce expenditure on asocial and mentally unfit members of the community; the state must use its resources for the healthy and valuable members, the continuance and racial improvement of the people were its objectives. Tax adjustments would favor large families, economic measures would return working wives to their families, instruction in race hygiene must be assured of a place in schools. One must once again have the courage to classify the body of the nation according to its hereditary values.

The first legal measure to be forecast by the speech was implemented on July 14, 1933: the *Gesetz zur Verhütung erbkranken Nachwuchses* (law for the prevention of progeny suffering from hereditary disease). The hereditary diseases named varied greatly in character and diagnostability (that is, schizophrenia and manic-depressive madness appeared side by side with hereditary blindness and deafness), but its crucial and novel feature was that, instead of the wishes of the patient or his legal representative being the yardstick, the official doctor or director of the institution could apply for sterilization of the patient, and such applications were decided on by a "tribunal for hereditary health."[27]

The same day saw the announcement of the *Gesetz über den Widerruf von Einbürgerungen und die Aberkennung der deutschen Staatsangehörigkeit*[28] (law concerning the revocation of naturalization and the annulment of German nationality). This made it possible for "undesirable" naturalizations between 1918 and 1933 to be revoked, thus fulfilling an old postulate of the party, but in principle it also abolished the continuity of the state. A state which deprives a section of its citizens of citizenship, through no fault of their own, in fact abrogates all other contracts and commitments from the past. Practically speaking, the depriving of emigrants of their citizenship identified state and regime, yet it is much less novel than the first part of the law. It punished the deed, and that links it to the ancient traditions of European justice.

Here was where the Nuremberg laws differed.[29] They punished "a state of existence," thereby constituting a fundamental break in the course of German justice. From the narrow juristical standpoint, they could, it is true, be regarded as a codification and hence improvement of an arbitrary practice, and it can be taken for fact that the experts involved saw to it that the draft most favorable to the Jews was adopted.[30] But as long as principles differ qualitatively from mere customs and circumstances, September 15, 1935, will remain a date of cardinal importance. It can be objected, of course, that it was after all only a discrimination, not a punishment, and that many analogies can be cited: the United States "race legislation" has been repeatedly put forward as an example. In actual fact, however, this argument merely proves a lack of understanding of historical fact and the distinction between "implementation" and "cancellation." It might also be said that the Soviet Union deprived whole strata of the population of their political rights and, as a logical conclusion of certain measures, condemned them to death. But there is a great difference between social and biological existence, between a "law" and a "wholesale procedure." It is impossible to avoid the conclusion that the Nuremberg laws represented an entirely new departure in history.

The *Reichsbürgergesetz* (Reich citizenship law) distinguished between the ordinary citizen and the Reich citizen, the sole beneficiary of full political rights, and thus implemented the fourth point of the party program.

The *Gesetz zum Schutze des deutschen Blutes und der deutschen Ehre* (law for the protection of German blood and German honor) rendered sexual intercourse between adults of mixed "blood" a criminal offense—it even prohibited a mere presumed *proxima occasio*. Incidentally, the restriction of the threat of punishment to the man alone was an indication of the new-old evaluation of the sexes.

Of the utmost practical importance were the regulations governing the execution of these laws. These regulations facilitated the tightening of laws in some cases and the removal of certain restrictions in others. The tendency to equate Jewish veterans with the rest of the Jews followed logically from the intention of these laws. On the whole, however, this thrust forward was followed by a long period of quiet; and it was a proof, not, indeed, of a humane attitude, but of the shrewdness of National Socialist policy, that Jews could participate in the economy, although impeded in many ways, for another two years or more.

However, even during 1936 and 1937 these matters were not lost sight of, as events in Upper Silesia showed. There the Jews had invoked the regulations for the protection of minorities contained in the agreement on Upper Silesia inaugurated by the League of Nations, and the Reich government had been forced to recognize this interpretation. But when the regulations expired in 1937 the race laws were immediately introduced.[31]

1938 saw the vigorous resumption of the policy of "the recovery of racial health." New regulations governing the implementation of the *Reichsbürgergesetz* revoked the licenses of Jewish doctors and removed the exceptions still existing for lawyers and patent attorneys. This was followed by a "purging" of the country's entire medical system. In 1938 even the laws governing taxes underwent a "racial" extension: for instance, tax exemptions for the children of Jews were discontinued. A decree of Göring's concerning the reporting of Jewish property gave a hint of the future course of events. In July the practice of certain trades was prohibited. In October the passports of all Jews were ordered to be stamped with a "J". The law of January 5, 1938, dealing with the changing of family and first names had already had the same end in view. Like naturalization, the assimilation of names was now also revoked. In August a regulation made the addition of one Jewish first name (Sara or Israel) mandatory.[32]

Following the assassination of the German legation secretary vom Rath in Paris, the line of "direct action" which had been so hurriedly abandoned in 1933 was resumed. Organized giant pogroms and special taxes amounting to a billion marks can only be comprehended if they are regarded as the acts of primitive tribal warfare; likewise all the legal measures which, instead of being merely the revocation of political emancipation, now forced the Jews back into the pariah existence they had led during the Middle Ages—the only difference, and a far from negligible one, being that now even their financial resources had been taken from them. The Jews' affection for Germany must have been immense if *such* measures were necessary to compel them to emigrate. In actual fact the explanation was much more commonplace. It is impossible to exert strenuous efforts to rearm and at the same time finance an extensive emigration with foreign currency.[33] With idle talk about emigrating to Madagascar (which was French, after all), people tried to hide the fundamental fact that through its own policy Germany had been turned into a prison for the larger, less prosperous section of the German Jews and those among them with few connections abroad. It is fair to ask, however, whether the intelligence of the leaders must not be assessed somewhat higher. Rosenberg, at least, stated on February 7, 1939, that Jewish emigration was an *international* problem of the most far-reaching significance, thus complicating still further what was already an extremely difficult situation. And *could* Hitler in his notorious threat to the Jewish warmongers really not fail to see that *his* war had begun long ago and had dispossessed the enemy to an extent far beyond anything that any war in the history of Europe had ever so much as contemplated? In the summer of 1939 Jews were no longer permitted to take part in German cultural events, or to show themselves at certain hours and in certain places, or to drive any motorized vehicle. With the swiftly mounting danger of war, virtually only two possibilities remained open. The first was for Germany to acquire living space for them by force of arms.[34] The second was death. Even before the war broke out, only a thin wall stood between them and death. A system such as National Socialism made the most extraordinary things possible; but it was incapable of what appeared to be the simplest of all: to come to a halt and go no further.

Once again, it is very helpful to look at Mussolini's Italy to discover the particular features of the National Socialist population and race policy. Frick's speech offers a good starting point. There is no doubt that it cited a number of measures which were acknowledged in every country as more or less correct and desirable. What gave the speech its fascist flavor was that he overemphasized the intentions in question, made them the elements of a secular process of salvation, and linked them undeniably and pre-eminently with the military potential. All this comes through just as clearly in Mussolini's speeches and decrees on the population policy; indeed, some of his ordinances are even sharper than their German counterparts. For example, in Italy in 1938 marriage was made compulsory for the obtaining of high administrative posts.[35] What was entirely absent in Mussolini, however, was the tendency to classify the body of the nation according to its hereditary biological values, and to declare the progeny of considerable sections of the population to be undesirable. Actually this tendency never materialized to any great extent in Germany, but its potential existence is in itself sufficient to warrant its being regarded as the radical-fascist element in the German population policy.

In regard to the race laws, as has been shown, a comparison is also not entirely out of the question.[36] But on the whole it is not particularly helpful, the National Socialist race policy being too much *sui generis* for it not to be subjected to an isolated scrutiny.

The insights which it forces on the observer are bitter in either direction: bitter for the Jews, more bitter still for the Germans—even if, and especially if, moral judgments on individuals are avoided and its further expansion during the war is not considered.

For to suppose that Hitler could have provided the Germans with victims in the form of Jehovah's Witnesses or alcoholics instead of Jews as a substitute for the forbidden class warfare is incorrect. It is true that Germany with its Jewish population of one per cent knew no such sociological Jewish problem as Rumania or Poland, but the fact remained that in some professions and occupations a proportion of Jews had been reached which could not be maintained indefinitely. Anti-Semitism is by no means a relic of the Middle Ages or the expression of petit-bourgeois social envy; in an age of the growing awareness of national and social differences it is under certain conditions an element of national consciousness itself. Even liberals, far from being philo-Semitic, were hostile to the idea of "Jewish national self-segregation," although, of course, they were also against segregation counter to the will of those concerned as carried out by the proponents of racial anti-Semitism. However, the consciousness that the Jews were not merely a religious community but a people had been roused just as much by Zionism[37] as by anti-Semitism. It may sound hard, but it remains a fact that German Jewry, as a group which, though not without its own differentiations, was on the whole readily distinguishable, faced an inexorable decline after the deceptive upsurge of the first years of its complete emancipation; it could not escape being crushed between the two extremes which it had itself generated—complete assimilation and Zionism. Even with the most terrible of his deeds Hitler did not simply fly in the face of history: here, too, he rode its trends which he then manipulated so that they could operate in reverse. In this way he transformed the inevitable restoration of Germany into a war of aggression, the expansion of German influence in the world into the conquest of living space, the spiritual self-dissolution of German Jewry into physical annihilation.

However, this last transformation, even in its early phase before the war, was no less fatal to Germany than to the Jews, however little public evidence of this catastrophe there was.

In its most universal sense, the legislation dealing with the Jews meant the revoking of emancipation. It follows that Germany thereby denied the advantages which it had itself derived from emancipation. When in the name of Germany, Hitler even excluded Jewish veterans from the German "national body," he clearly denied nationhood itself which above all else means "common destiny," and in this way rendered Germany's legal claim to nationality problematical.

Because Hitler did not even grant the Jews the rights of a national minority (as was demonstrated by the affair in Upper Silesia), he virtually rendered the German minorities in Eastern Europe defenseless also, and threw away one of the trump cards which Germany had obtained from the Versailles Treaty.[38]

By making hundreds of thousands of Jews answerable for the deed of one man, the leaders of the state were preparing the soil for the day when millions of Germans were to be made responsible for the deeds of one man.

There was nothing clandestine about any of the laws, measures, and speeches

which have been cited; that they grew out of one central impulse toward
leadership was explicitly announced by Hitler in his proclamation at the Reich
party congress of 1937: "Germany has experienced the greatest revolution,
however, in the national and racial hygiene which was undertaken for the first
time on an organized basis in this country. The consequences of this German
race policy will be more decisive for the future of our people than the effects
of any other law. For they are creating the new man."[39]

Nevertheless, they did not appear in the full illumination of open publicity.
Inasmuch as this is part of the National Socialist style, it would seem appropriate to give a brief description of this Reich party congress in 1937. In doing
so, we shall try not to minimize the spell which, according to many witnesses,
was cast by these events, and the description will therefore closely follow
official reports.

The ninth party congress of the NSDAP, designated the Reich Party Congress
of Labor, lasted from Monday, September 6, to Monday, September 13, and
took place in Nuremberg as it had done ever since 1927.

Adolf Hitler arrived in Nuremberg late on the Monday afternoon and began
by inspecting his personal bodyguard, which received him in perfect formation,
with fixed bayonets and wearing full-dress uniforms. To the ringing of church
bells he drove through the sea of flags in the gaily decorated city to the town
hall; there, standing in the enormous open car, his arm raised constantly in
salute, he greeted the cheering populace which lined the streets and waved
from every window. With a fanfare of trumpets he entered the great hall, on the
façade of which the swastika banners framed the shrine of the Reich insignia,
and there, ready to receive him, stood the entire leadership corps of party,
state, and Wehrmacht, all in uniform. He was welcomed by the mayor, who
praised the great progress made in laying out the Reich party congress grounds.
In his reply Hitler also spoke of the realization of his gigantic plans for the
grounds. On his way back he was again greeted by the cheers of the multitude.
The official report states: "like a storm it breaks over everyone. The Führer
is here, now the city is truly alive."[40]

On Tuesday morning the Reich party congress was ceremonially opened in
the Congress Hall. Wave upon wave of marching columns and hurrying people
filled the city from early morning. The vast hall was crowded with delegates
from every party organization and many guests of honor, among them a
delegation from the Fascist party of Italy. Once again to a fanfare of trumpets
Hitler entered the hall with the opening notes of the "Badenweiler March."
The "blood banner" (the swastika flag that had been carried in the Munich
Putsch) was borne into the hall, reverently saluted by all present, and placed
immediately behind the speaker's rostrum. Behind it, the standards of every
corner of Germany formed serried ranks. The overture to *Tannhäuser* began,
followed by the old Netherlands hymn of thanksgiving.

Rudolf Hess proceeded to pay homage to the dead, and in his speech he sounded the keynote of the congress—the contrast between National Socialism and its will to rebuild and its joy in work, and communism with its decay, forced labor, and hopelessness. The Führer's proclamation, read by a *Gauleiter*, dealt with the same theme; it contrasted Bolshevik chaos and will to destroy with National Socialism's staggering achievements in reconstruction, as a result of which unemployment had been completely eliminated. Under the impact of this message the tens of thousands of listeners broke into prolonged and rapturous cheering.

That evening the cultural session took place at the opera house, where for the first time the newly created "national prize for art and science" was awarded. The session signified "the proclamation of German sovereignty in cultural achievements and art," and in a highly meaningful sense, for Hitler had banned the acceptance of the Nobel Prize by Germans for all time.[41] The first prize winner was Alfred Rosenberg. The Führer himself gave a long address attacking modern art as well as the literary clique which had resulted from this disgraceful "retrogressive trend." By contrast, National Socialism made the cultural achievements of the past accessible to the broad masses and was itself creating buildings which were among the greatest and noblest architectural achievements in German history.

Wednesday morning saw the parade of the Reich Labor Force on the Zeppelin Field, and its morning service at which the massed voices of tens of thousands uttered songs, speeches, and vows: "A service in the cathedral of the German countryside."[42]

In the evening the congress was continued; the most outstanding speaker was Alfred Rosenberg, who gave an interpretation of the times and history from the standpoint of the eternal struggle between creation and destruction, a struggle which aligned National Socialism against bolshevism in the same way that Rome had once confronted the Syrian plague spot of Carthage. Reports on the achievements of the *Winterhilfe* program and health policy brought the evening to a close.

On Thursday, "in a solemn act of thrilling beauty,"[43] the Führer laid the cornerstone of the giant German Stadium, at the same time opening the National Socialist Athletic Contest, at which the main emphasis was on team and military sports. In the evening Goebbels violently attacked Spanish bolshevism; it was destroying the churches, he said, and yet being defended by Western intellectuals and churchmen, who were devoid of sound instincts. Hans Frank gave a report on "Law and Justice in the National Socialist Reich." He stressed the fact that during the previous year the last stipulations of the Versailles Treaty to restrict the sovereignty of the Reich had been removed, so that the "restoration of Reich sovereignty" was now a *fait accompli*. Otto Dietrich, head of the Reich press, unmasked the innate falsity of the liberal "freedom of the press."

Friday morning was given over to the police and the demonstration of its unity with the SS. The Führer dedicated its new flags by touching them with the "blood banner," and interpreted this act as the integration of the police "with that great unified marching column of the German *Volksgemeinschaft*."[44]

Impressive figures were contributed to the congress in the reports of Darré, Amann, and Todt. No one could accuse Dr. Todt of lying when he said that a few years previously the progress made in building the *Autobahnen* would have been beyond the dreams of the boldest civil engineer, and that these achievements had only been possible as a whole through the impulse of a powerful will unhampered by parliamentary institutions.

In the afternoon "the women [marched into the hall] in long columns."[45] They listened to a report given by the Reich Leader of Women on the many ways of safeguarding the German family. The Führer himself explained to them the ultimate goal of all National Socialist efforts: the German child. Brought up as a hardy race, in future the men would provide the women with a "true and genuine protection and shield."[46] "Seemingly endless applause" followed his address.

Perhaps the most impressive event of the congress was the roll call of the one hundred and ten thousand political leaders Friday evening on the Zeppelin Field. With military precision the thirty-two *Gau* (district) columns marched toward the field from all sides and met exactly on time for their entry. Shortly before ten o'clock the Führer arrived. Standing stiffly at attention Dr. Ley reported all present. "At that moment the surrounding darkness is suddenly flooded with white light. The beams of the hundred and fifty giant searchlights shoot up like meteors into the obscurity of the black night sky. High up the columns of light join on the cloud ceiling to form a flaming square wreath. It is an overpowering sight: moved by the gentle breeze, the flags on the stands all around the field wave slowly back and forth in the shining light. ... The northern side is closed off by the main reviewing stand. The huge structure is bathed in brilliance, crowned by the golden rays of the swastika in the wreath of oak leaves. On the end pillars to the left and right, flames leap up from great bowls. ... The crowd stands waiting in awestruck silence."[47] With a fanfare of trumpets the Führer strode to the main rostrum.

Then came the banners: thirty-two thousand of them. The banner song of the men of the Vogelsang *Ordensburg* rang out through the air: "What took a thousand years to come, the Führer forced into existence. With flags and banners flying, it rolls on roaring to eternity." Then the Führer spoke of the sufferings of the time of struggle and of the happiness of the present, now that a people imbued with faith had found its place in the "united battle front of the nation," which would never let go of and never abandon its people from the *Jungvolk* via the *Hitlerjugend, Arbeitsdienst,* and Wehrmacht through to the party and its organizations. The old guard of the National Socialist revolution had brought this miracle to pass, and to the accompaniment of protracted demonstrations of enthusiasm and emotion he formulated the innermost secret of this miracle as follows: "That you have found *me* and that you have believed in me, this is what has given your life a new meaning, a new task. That I have found *you*, this is what has made my life and my struggle possible."[48] He closed with a *Heil!* for Germany, and from a hundred thousand throats the "Song of the Germans" surged forth "like organ music." Then the Führer left the rostrum, passing through the lane formed by his bodyguard, accompanied by shouts of *Heil!* But for a long time the shining searchlight wreath remained in the night sky "like a cathedral."

On Saturday morning there was the solemn ceremony of one hundred and fifteen thousand eighteen-year-olds swearing their oath of allegiance to the Führer. Confronted by his young people the prophetic spirit came over Adolf Hitler once more: "Just as you stand before me today, so year after year for centuries the young generation will stand before future Führers and will continue to bear witness to their devotion to the Germany that we have fought for and won today."[49]

This was followed shortly afterward by the annual conference of the German Labor Front. Robert Ley deployed his principles for the solution of the social problem: "Same step, same pack, same march: then there is nothing to tell me outwardly whether the man is an employer or a worker."[50] The concept of "soldier of labor," he went on, will finally overcome class distinction. In the evening a long report stressed the achievements of the *Deutsche Arbeitsfront*, with special reference to the social services of the National Socialist community "Strength through Joy" and the organizations "Leisure Time" and "Beauty of Work."

Sunday morning was devoted to the parade of the political fighting units of the party for the great roll call in the presence of the Führer. To the more than one hundred thousand men in their brown and black uniforms, Adolf Hitler spoke of the discords of the past and the people's new sense of ethnic unity (*Volksgemeinschaft*)—achieved by such fanatical struggles—which now followed one command, one order, as a single bloc. Massed around their symbol of triumph, the symbol of their blood, he said, the people, certain of victory, turned their eyes toward the banner of the old foe, who "confounds the nations." After the dedication of the new flags and banners, Dietrich Eckart's song, "Germany Awake," brought the parade to an end, and shortly afterward "the army of one hundred and twenty thousand" marched for five hours past their Führer. A particularly powerful impression was left by the parade of the black cadres of the "*Schutzkorps* of the Movement," among whom the units of the special duty detachment and the bodyguard were the most striking.

Monday was Wehrmacht day. There were military maneuvers of extreme precision on the field, while many hundreds of planes of the fighting squadrons roared across the sky. The "unique method" of presentation was so perfect that the onlookers obtained "a co-ordinated and thrilling picture of the course of a modern infantry battle."[51] The "unity and power" of the parade which followed whipped the audience to one storm of applause after another.

In the evening the great final address of the Führer brought the ninth Reich party congress to a close, after the standards of the movement, to the strains of Wagner's "March of the Nibelungs," had been carried into the hall. Adolf Hitler spoke of the ineradicable impression made by "a new generation's confession of faith founded on a national ideology,"[52] he explained his historical philosophy from the creative race nuclei to his description of the dictatorship of the proletariat as a "dictatorship of Jewish intellectualism,"[53] and he declared in impassioned language that the National Socialist state would tolerate no shift in the balance of power in favor of bolshevism in Europe, beginning with Spain, and that, in the case of a threat, it "would stand up and fight for its existence with a fanaticism different from that of the bourgeois Reich of old."[54] Many hundreds of thousands, he said, had marched in Nuremberg, "in uniform ranks like the grenadiers of the best regiments," borne up by an inward harmony of soul and yet still merely the vanguard of the great people's army of Germany, just as the soldiers, whose maneuvers had been admired, were after all only "the point of a sword" which protected their native land.[55] He closed with the words: "The German nation has indeed obtained its Germanic Reich." Thunderous applause surged toward the creator of this Reich, and the songs of the nation, accompanied on the organ, mounted solemnly to the sky. At midnight the congress came to its traditional close with the tattoo and taps of the Wehrmacht.

Indeed, after all this what could strike one more forcibly than the thought that no boyhood dream ever attained a more complete, more brilliant fulfillment? Had it not become a reality, "the Reich" of which Hitler had so often spoken to Kubizek? Had it not been created, this united body of the nation of which he used to preach: impervious to Jewish intellectualism, fixed in its own purposes, proceeding along the paths of nature? Had not the abyss of the past actually swallowed up all that had once posed as political reality—conservatism, liberalism, and socialism, Center and Social Democrats alike? A dispassionate opponent would presumably have answered by saying that all Hitler had done was transform the old Prussian-German barracks state into one single state barracks, and that this was the basis of all his successes. But it was precisely in this transformation that the problem lay. For it was not a matter of "backward" but of "forward," of modernization. Hitler had succeeded in imparting mass-effectiveness and mass-accessibility to those things which had formerly been the preserve of small sections of the population. To this end he had made use of the most modern means offered by technology.[56] And his actions were based on certain premises the truth of which was not acceptable to many of his opponents. Even if a hundred thousand people in Nuremberg stayed home or clenched their fists in their pockets: a rejoicing of this kind is quite impossible among a people which was and is really imbued with an irreducible class enmity. National Socialism was as good a proof as Social Democratic revisionism of Lenin's thesis concerning the workers' aristocracy. All the elements of this style were already present in the style of fascist Italy; however, the difference in quantity and relative timing is of qualitative significance here.

Nevertheless, the objection has an obvious merit, although perhaps it should be formulated less tritely and less polemically: the old god had blessed his people again when, after straying briefly from the path, it found its way back to him. But was everyone aware of the sacrifice necessary to make this blessing a lasting one? Hitler knew it: two months after his Reich party congress he summoned the chiefs of staff to the Hossbach conference.

For today's observer, the picture of all that rejoicing and marching, all those uniforms, raises one paramount question: How could it happen that such an overwhelming display of total mobilization inside and outside Germany—a display that could have only one implication—was not universally taken for what it plainly was, a declaration of war? And if this picture of a people which in peacetime had turned itself into a single shining well-equipped army was not enough: How could the meaning of "Germanic Reich" and "safeguarding existence" as interpreted by *Mein Kampf* have been overlooked? How could the people themselves—once known as the nation of thinkers—seriously suppose that their Führer was a wizard who, alone among all earth-dwellers, knew how to create employment and economic recovery out of nothing while producing quantities of unproductive weapons?[57] There are probably three main factors capable of offering some explanation of the inexplicable:

1. Paralysis in the face of the unheard-of and the unprecedented. When the German imperial army slightly increased its peacetime strength, France introduced three-year conscription. When Hitler increased Germany's military potential tenfold, a hundredfold, France was as petrified as the proverbial rabbit confronted by a snake.

2. The hope of a lightning conductor, that is, the expectation that, in view of the anti-Bolshevik attitude of the regime, the Soviet Union would have to foot the bill.

3. The unique position of the German people in process of "secularization." This people had never become reconciled on its intellectual levels with the process underlying its rise to the position of foremost economic power in continental Europe. It still hankered after metaphysics, unity, and profundity, and National Socialism meant the translation of these things into politics, however much—and with good reason—it would sooner or later repel the best representatives of this nostalgia. Under the dome of light on the Zeppelin Field, in the thunder of mass cheering, a German was justified in believing that this unity was for its own sake alone.

However, the study of this party congress or of any other similar rally can also convey valuable insights into the nature of totalitarianism.

Under the immediate impact of war there has been an excessive tendency to identify totalitarianism with "terror" and "horror." But "totality" is in the nature of all great achievements which challenge and embrace individuals and groups. In them enthusiasm precedes terror—which is merely the obverse of enthusiasm, directed at hostility and resistance. The question is, what generates such enthusiasm and when; what are its characteristics and those of the terror that may result from it? Experience and reflection seem to show equally well that keeping up with industrial developments under unfavorable conditions is the only great social task which must today be tackled with enthusiasm and hence in a totalitarian manner. In other words: under certain circumstances that often concealed and yet all-dominating technological and economic revolution (which until 1918 was a seemingly isolated phenomenon and took place everywhere in more or less liberal guise) must assume political shape and force everything into total subjection. It was the Bolshevik revolution of 1917 which marked this crucial point in world history. It founded a system which carries out that development in a completely different, that is, totalitarian, form, and which has proved itself equal to the task with terrible concomitant manifestations and in the face of enormous resistance. Those who regarded a lead in development as an eternal birthright were bound to feel threatened. What complicated matters still further was that the revolutionary power rested on a theory of revolution based on entirely different premises, namely a non-totalitarian revolution to emancipate the individual in the most advanced countries. The disparity between ideology and reality could not but enhance the sense of being threatened, especially in the neighboring countries. Yet, it was anti-Bolshevik propaganda, with its polemic against the starvation and misery in the Soviet Union, the "Bolshevik chaos," that proved how it could not possibly be a manifestation of military aggressiveness. The Soviet Union was not imperialistic before the Hitler-Stalin pact, and, even after it, only in the sense of desiring a glacis fortification in the face of threatened attack—not for reasons of virtue, but because it had to catch up, laboriously and under the most adverse conditions, with a development of several decades. It *had* to be totalitarian, and thus did not need to look to war as its final stage. An industrial power, on the other hand, which had its place in the front ranks of development, could not in Hitler's era want anything but war if it embarked on a totalitarian effort.

Seen thus, fascism appears to lack inherent necessity: a totalitarianism with no *raison d'être*. But that does not mean there was no motive for it. According to motive and character, it shows various levels. Italian fascism, born of bourgeois resistance to the attempted Communist revolution, did not deny the Soviet Union its right to exist and its own kind of historical necessity; with this as an example, it would be possible to discuss the important question of whether a fascism can, legitimately and permanently, be a "development dictatorship." German National Socialism, the offspring of defeat in war and a temporary economic depression, saw itself as the implacable enemy of a "world danger." However, for National Socialism the Soviet Union represented a "world danger" not merely in its capacity of imaginary "plague spot" and center of the Jewish conspiracy, but also in a more real sense, because an industrialized Eastern Europe meant *eo ipso* the negation of total, that is, primarily military and geographical, German sovereignty. Hence the specific totalitarian nature of the German form of fascism *had* to be military, with the whole colossal striking power aimed principally at its great neighbor to the East and its "necessary" totalitarianism.

The similarity between certain manifestations ought not to allow one to forget the fundamental differences. It would, of course, have been possible—for theoretical hindsight, at least—to combat bolshevism solely on account of its bloody excesses and world-revolutionary ideology, in order then to provide the peoples of Eastern Europe with another and no less effective form of confrontation with their basic problem. In this way it might have been possible to demonstrate that bolshevism was *not* a necessary totalitarianism but that, even without it, Russia could have kept up with the headlong development in Europe and the U.S.A. But in that case would totalitarianism—with the premises of the race doctrine—have been worth the effort? That would have meant an affirmation in principle of this course, the acknowledgment of it as a universal necessity, whereas it was not even possible to affirm it with a clear conscience as a racial privilege! Hitler was always fully aware of these relationships, and Rosenberg wanted to ensure that the peoples of Eastern Europe were as agrarian peoples protected from the assault of centralizing bolshevism.[58] A fascist Germany was incapable of doing otherwise than carrying on its war in Eastern Europe in order to achieve unqualified sovereignty; and it could only hope to safeguard itself finally against what it felt was the threatened development of the peoples of Eastern Europe if it could discover and eliminate the agent of these processes.

This law of existence for National Socialism can be deduced from a study of the Reich party congress no less clearly than from an analysis of Hitler's ideas. But for the totality of his political intentions, all the cheering and enthusiasm, all the military precision and discipline of the Reich party congress, are not enough. The Wehrmacht stood ready to ward off the assault of an enemy; there was no problem in winning over the masses who were members of the National Socialist armed units for an attack on bolshevism; but for the true ends of the totalitarian war of National Socialist Germany, neither of these two factors sufficed. Hitler needed a body of men who stood unconditionally at his disposal for all his political intentions, because they knew what was at stake and because they desired it. All the signposts of the 1937 demonstration of power pointed toward the SS.

The place occupied by the SS in the system can therefore be deduced. At this point it is enough to trace the historical development in outline[59] and then (without for the time being resorting to documents which remained secret for many years) to allow the group to present its own image of itself, as formulated with the greatest authority by Heinrich Himmler.

Hitler had always striven for a politically oriented body of men which would be at his exclusive disposal. When in 1923 Röhm and Kriebel turned the SA more and more into a military unit, the *Stosstrupp Hitler* (Hitler shock troop) was organized, the principal function of which was the personal protection of the Führer. The setting up of a personal *Stabswache* (staff guard) under Julius Schreck in March, 1925, had a similar objective; it was a countermove to Röhm's *Frontbann* plans. During the late summer of 1925, the *Stabswache* became the *Schutzstaffel* (guard detachment), which was extended beyond Munich and at the party congress in Weimar was accorded a significant privilege: Hitler handed over the "blood banner" to it for safekeeping. With the reorganization of the SA it lost in importance; yet in its small number (as compared to the mass movement of the SA) was contained the potential of its elite character and, in its specific bodyguard function, the direct link with the Führer.

The man who perceived its innate possibilities and vigorously followed them up was Heinrich Himmler, son of a Bavarian schoolteacher; he had gone through the period of the Bavarian Soviet Republic as a very young officer's candidate and had later been Gregor Strasser's secretary for many years. When he took over the SS in January, 1929, it had less than three hundred members. He insisted on having photographs of new recruits submitted to him and inspecting them for racial traits, and he only accepted men over five feet seven inches in height. The reasons for this were at first as pragmatic as they were typical. He indicated them in a later speech as follows:[60] the "Soldiers' Soviets types" of 1918 and 1919 had all had "something funny" about their appearance, and that must be attributable to an admixture of foreign blood.[61] "To have good blood" meant for Himmler: to be soldierly and unconditionally counterrevolutionary. Before long he was bound to hit on the idea that a body of men of good blood contained that "racial nucleus" of which Hitler had so often spoken. However, this racial nucleus could only be permanently dominant if it had a clear awareness of race and the determination to preserve it. Himmler therefore singled out the SS from all other formations by the "Betrothal and Marriage Order of the Reich SS-Führer" of December 31, 1931. This made marriage for SS men dependent on the Reich SS-Führer's consent—that is, stipulated a racial inspection of the fiancée and her genealogy by a race department established expressly for this purpose. The SS was to be more than a mere association of men: it was to be a community of genealogically high-grade families. Since Himmler was an *Artamane*[62] and an agriculturist by profession, it is not surprising that the office of inspection soon turned into a department for race and settlement under the direction of the Minister of

Agriculture and Chief of the Reich Peasants, SS-*Obergruppenführer* R. Walter Darré. The SS distinguished itself in 1931 by helping to suppress the SA uprising of Captain Stennes; on that occasion Hitler gave it the motto: "SS man, your honor is called loyalty." And finally, also in 1931, there began the organization of its own intelligence service under the onetime naval lieutenant Reinhard Heydrich. When Hitler seized power, the SS was still, with its fifty thousand members, a small organization and under the authority of the chief of staff of the SA, but the seeds of its future significance were already present.

In March, 1933, Hitler created from its ranks a new *Stabswache* under Joseph Dietrich; this later became the *Leibstandarte Adolf Hitler* (Adolf Hitler's personal bodyguard), while armed special units of the SS in other cities became the matrix of the subsequent special duty SS. This secured for Hitler an armed force of his own stamp permanently at his disposal: it was "part of neither the Wehrmacht nor the police,"[63] and bound to him by a more personal and less specific oath than that which attached the soldiers to the Wehrmacht. The full implication of the SS oath became apparent for the first time on June 30, 1934. No firing squad of the Wehrmacht would have been permitted to kill the SA leaders without process of law: for the SS there already existed only the will of the Führer as sole law above and beyond all regulations and principles. There was little reason to believe that this formation would ever refuse to carry out *any* order of their Führer.

In March, 1933, with the appointment of Himmler as provisional chief of police in Munich, the SS began its penetration of the police. Within a year Himmler was given control of every regional police force in Germany, and in June, 1936, he was appointed chief of the German police. Since the Röhm crisis he had been head of an independent branch of the party: now both offices were combined in a single institution, the "Reich Führer of the SS and Chief of the German Police" was accorded a position unique in the constitution, one which a formal subordination to the Reich minister for the interior did not weaken but reinforced. For through this steady coalescing of SS and police, a sphere was created which, while protected by the state, was at the same time removed from the control of the state, a field which was becoming less and less subject to the control of regular state administration, and this was what made it so useful for the carrying out of the Führer's own revolutionary decisions. The unity of state and nonstate elements was henceforward to be the, at times, opaque characteristic of the principal institutions of the SS.[64] Special obligations entail special rights: thus every member of the SS was given a privilege which singled him out from his fellow citizens—the right to defend his honor with arms.

In his speech of January, 1937,[65] on "The Nature and Functions of the SS and the Police," Himmler named five "pillars" of the SS. The *Allgemeine SS* (general SS) consisted, apart from its top leaders, of men earning their living in civilian life. Its regional organization corresponded to that of the Wehrmacht; it passed on its young candidates to the army and received them back again, to maintain their health and hardihood through sports and athletic contests, in the process of which it also formed a counterbalance to the dangers of urban living and misuse of alcohol.

The *Verfügungstruppe* (special duty unit) was to fight in the field but was also, by way of constant exchange, involved in the activities of the police; for in the coming war the police was by hook or by crook to keep the home front (the "fourth war theater, inside Germany") "healthy," since bolshevism as a sub-human organization would try to stir up the dregs of this home front and incite it to a new stab in the back.

The third pillar was the *Totenkopfverbände* (death's head units), formed from the guards of the concentration camps. Their function was also the immediate safeguarding of the internal security of the Reich. They had custody of the "dregs of the criminal world, a mass of racially inferior trash," including many professional criminals kept in preventive and usually permanent confinement.

In fourth place Himmler named the *Sicherheitsdienst* (security service), "the great ideological intelligence service of the party and ultimately of the state." The fifth pillar was the *Rasse- und Siedlungshauptamt* (department of race and settlement), whose functions were of a positive nature: processing of marriage applications and genealogical histories submitted (as far back as 1750), problems of settlement and ideological instruction, as well as the furthering of science insofar as it was of political value.

Thus each of the five pillars in its own way served a single objective: the *Gesundung* (restoring to health) and safeguarding of "blood," threatened as it was in such multifarious ways. The SS was therefore simply the most complete organizational concretization of Hitler's doctrine. The concluding words of Himmler's address show that an analogy to Hitler's fear was not unknown to the SS leader: coming decades would represent "the war of destruction of all the subhuman enemies in the world against Germany" as the leading nation of white humanity, a war which, so Himmler apparently believed, could only be survived because a fortunate circumstance had allowed it to occur in a time "in which once in two thousand years an Adolf Hitler is born."

Himmler gave this address to officers of the Wehrmacht, and it was printed "for official purposes only." But two years earlier, in 1935, the Reich SS-Führer had already conveyed his ideas about the SS to the public at large on the occasion of the *Reichsbauerntag* (Reich Peasants Congress) in Goslar, and under the title of "The SS as an Anti-Bolshevik Combat Organization"[66] these ideas had been widely disseminated.

The most typical feature of this speech is that it starts off by depicting the eternal and universal nature of the Jewish-Bolshevik mortal enemy with a forcefulness and naïveté that remind one instantly of Dietrich Eckart's *Zwiege-spräch*: the Bolshevik spirit had at one time led the Jews to exterminate the best Aryans from among the Persian people, in Verdun the eternal enemy had brandished the executioner's sword of Charles the Frank over thousands of Saxon chieftains, by means of the Inquisition (!)[67] it had dealt Spain a mortal blow, in the French revolution it had slaughtered the fair-haired and the blue-eyed, and finally in Russia, with the aid of the Jew Kerenski, it had opened up the way for the Jewish GPU to its work of destruction. For centuries the Jew had been hurling poison and murderous weapons at the Aryan peoples, he had allowed whole tribes which were not desirable to the Jews to starve to death, in this secular strife there were only victors or vanquished, and in this case to be vanquished meant the death of a people.

It is in this perspective that Himmler deliberately placed the character of the SS. Through a process of constant selection it filtered a stream of the best German blood. The positive side of its will permitted the SS to understand the value and sacredness of the soil, to perceive its goal in settlement, and to stand beside the German farmer as his most faithful friend: it was no mere accident, Himmler pointed out, that as the Reich SS-Führer he himself was a farmer. But the negative side of its will enabled the SS to be "a ruthless executioner's sword" toward all forces of the Jewish-Bolshevik subhuman revolution at the slightest attempt at revolt. The concluding sentences of the speech were frequently quoted in National Socialist literature: "So we have assembled, and according to immutable laws we march as a National Socialist, soldierly order of Nordic men and as a sworn community of their clans on the road to a distant future, and we desire and believe that we may be not only the grandsons, who fought it out better, but beyond that the ancestors of later generations necessary for the eternal life of the German Germanic people."

If one bears in mind *what*, according to Hitler and Himmler, was to be "fought out," what an "eternal life" of the German people presupposed in the eyes of these men, one sees that it was possible even in 1935 to describe the SS with accuracy: an unconditionally obedient *tool* in the hands of the Führer for the implementation of the true aims of his policy—the safeguarding of an eternal sovereign life of the Germanic-German Reich by settlement-conquest on the one hand, by annihilation of the mortal enemy on the other; but at the same time also the highest *goal* of this policy, as that racial nucleus of the best— that is, soldier-peasant—blood destined to be the ruling class of the Reich.

One might say that in Italy the development of the party army followed a more fortunate course. The *Moschettieri di Mussolini* never amounted to anything more than an insignificant prestige unit, because they were not required to shoot the commanders of the militia. Moreover, before the war this militia had been a larger and more renowned army than the *Waffen-SS*, having victoriously fought a full-scale war in Spain. There had, of course, been problems with the national army, but these had been overcome. Could not the SA with a little more luck have evolved in this direction? Yet this comparison shows how vitally necessary the SS was to the National Socialist regime. For, in keeping with its origin and structure, the SA was primarily the mass auxiliary formation of the Wehrmacht for purposes of national restitution. The doctrine which had now become the state itself—that of the creative race nucleus, its laws of existence and the deadly threats to it—needed just such an incomparable elite formation for the attainment of its real objectives. In spite of the many random happenings and incongruities in the historical development (for example, even up to the end of the war there was never complete identity between police and SS), there is no doubt either of the indispensability of the SS to the regime or of its inner solidarity.[68]

1939–1945

National Socialist practice, as distinct from fascist practice, underwent considerable changes during the war. When, for instance, the wavering German front was stabilized during the winter of 1941–42, Hitler displayed a hitherto unsuspected leadership drive. It was undoubtedly an innovation in style when, after the victory over France, field-marshal generals were appointed en masse at the Reichstag session of July 19, 1940.[69] The war organization as such, in its penetration of the spheres of state, party, Wehrmacht, and SS, is a subject meriting thorough exploration. But even in such a remarkable phenomenon as the *Einsatzstab Rosenberg* (Rosenberg operational staff), typical traits came to light which had to remain hidden in peacetime.

However, among all the institutions of the National Socialist state, the SS was the most powerful in its evolution and its consequences. It is true that there was nothing exactly new in this evolution, but its extraordinary logicality makes it a fascinating object of study. Here, too, however, it is not really possible to obtain a detailed view of the whole. For example, the increase of the *Waffen-SS* from barely thirty thousand men to a gigantic army of nearly one million did not begin until after the outbreak of war; only then were the legal foundations actually laid and the authoritative statements made.[70] It was at this juncture that the elite corps saw itself exposed to all manner of influences, and it became a heavily stratified and not readily definable structure.

Once again the selection of three manifestations, taken this time from a single area,[71] will serve to throw light on some of the most typical aspects of National Socialist practice. This area is the activity of the SS in three fields of primary importance. These fields cannot be completely separated, although essentially they can be allocated to certain subdivisions of the organization: the consolidation of the German people, the ferreting out and disarming of all adversaries, and the destruction of the chief enemy.

The first task was allotted to the Reich SS-Führer as the Reich Commissar for the Consolidating of the German People (RKF), by a secret decree of Hitler dated October 7, 1939.[72] It was broken down into three separate measures: return of Reich ethnic Germans (*Volksdeutsche*) from foreign countries; elimination of the harmful influence of foreign elements among the population; and establishment of new settlement areas by resettlement. This was a program made to order for the SS; here negative and positive measures were to balance each other with pristine clarity. But in addition an energy and loyalty to principles were demanded which could not be expected of ministerial departments and which could only be displayed by a "political" organization, that is to say, one which was not bound by traditional standards.[73] Hence Himmler as RKF "made use of" these government authorities but demoted them to the position of mere tools, without right of veto or control. After certain initial difficulties, especially with its own Department for Race and Settlement, the bureau of the RKF achieved considerable power and was given a place in the circle of twelve chief SS departments.

The legal basis for the negative aspect of Himmler's activity as RKF was the decree concerning Polish property of September 17, 1940, which in the incorporated Eastern European territories—the vast area of West Poland with over eight million Poles—officially abolished Polish private property, although in practice its existence had already been completely ignored. Himmler defined the implementation of this decree as follows: "The prerequisite for potential confiscation according to Section 2, Paragraph 2a, is present objectively when, for example, it is a case of land belonging to a Pole. For all Polish landed property is required without exception for the consolidation of the German people."[74]

Thus by very simple means the department in charge of land distribution created the *Lebensraum* for those German groups brought back from all over Eastern Europe which had played such an invaluable role in German *ethnic* influence but which were now being taken back by the RKF's resettlement commission to reinforce German *state* power. But in July, 1942, Himmler as RKF was also responsible within the *Generalgouvernement* for a brutal action of expulsion and resettlement designed to make the city of Lublin and its surrounding territory the first German settlement bulwark in the Polish heartland.[75] Yet all this was a mere trifle compared to what was planned for the postwar period. At the conference of group leaders in Poznań, Himmler disclosed some of these measures: "If the SS together with the farmers, and we together with our friend Backe, then pursue the settlement in the East, without restraint, without ever concerning ourselves with what is traditional, with *élan* and revolutionary zeal, then in twenty years we shall have thrust back the ethnic boundaries five hundred kilometers further to the East."[76]

The identity of the "negative" and "positive" intentions is obvious here. In 1939 and 1940 a number of portentous measures were already aimed at serving this identity. A valuable insight into Himmler's positive ideas is provided by the instructions for the agricultural development of the new Eastern European territories which he promulgated in his capacity of RKF on November 26, 1940.[77] It is particularly revealing that, although the creation of medium-sized hereditary farms was regarded as the basis of German ethnic (*Volkstum*) policy, social gradations were carefully specified; the lowest level of the hierarchy was to be occupied by German farm laborers, but on the higher levels the farms were to encourage the "stabilization and creation of a new class of indigenous leaders." Layout and architectural style of the villages and farmhouses were prescribed in detail. Dwellings of Polish farm laborers had to be located at a distance from the German settlement. Special attention was to be given the planting of trees and shrubs, since this would set the stamp on the German settlement of Eastern Europe. The inherited love of Germans for trees, shrubs, and flowers had to be preserved: hence the village oak and the village linden tree were to be present everywhere. Each village had to contain a party building, each town a hall for functions. The individual farmhouses were "to be the visible expression of a new German peasant culture." Old architectural styles and harmonious integration with the landscape were to be combined with the demands of modern hygiene and technology.

A third function of the RKF was likewise positive, but here he had to watch his step. It concerned the retrieving of dispersed Germanic blood. A regulation dating from 1940 reveals the principles by which Himmler was guided and the objectives he pursued: "Necessary though it is for a lasting purification of the German Eastern territories that the foreign elements living there should not be permanent or allowed to become permanent, it is equally essential that the German blood present in those areas be retrieved for the German nation in cases where the person of this blood has become Polish in his religion and language. It was these very people of German blood who provided the former Polish state with those leaders who—whether from blindness or in conscious or unconscious failure to recognize their blood relationship—adopted the most intensely hostile attitude toward their own German ethnic origin."[78] Soon the "prevention of any further increase in the Polish intellectual class" and the "increase of the racially desirable population growth for the German people" were announced as immediate objectives. Accordingly many Poles were scrutinized by experts as to their "Germanness" and where necessary transferred to a German environment for "renationalization," in the process of which there was in principle nothing to prevent children being taken from their homes and being taught, against the will of their parents, to hearken to the true "voice of blood." So the old theoretical destruction of the concept of nation by the nonhistorical race doctrine was implemented a thousandfold in practice. But one can hardly fail to recognize the underlying fear in Himmler's words with their false ring of truculence: "Either we obtain the good blood which we can make use of, and integrate it with our nation, or, gentlemen—you may call it cruel, but nature is cruel—we destroy that blood."[79] Never again, he said, was the enemy to obtain capable leaders and commanders; any false pity at the present time would imperil the existence of the German people in the future.

For the German people was surrounded by enemies, indeed they were to be found everywhere in its very midst. Himmler cited as enemies: all Communists, all Freemasons, all democrats, all convinced Christians, all nationalists even.[80] If one adds Himmler's not entirely unfounded doubts as to the political reliability of the Wehrmacht officers' corps, it could be supposed that the SS alone was the true German people and that its enemies were as legion as the sands on the seashore. How was it to defend itself against these enemies now, as well as to safeguard its pre-eminence for all time?

The institution established by the SS specifically for investigating and combating all enemies was the *Reichssicherheitshauptamt* (Reich Security Department), a veritable model of the blending of "state" and "party" authorities and interests. It came into being in September, 1939, by combining various police and SS bureaus and was placed under the command of Reinhard Heydrich as Chief of Security Police and the SD (Security Department). A glance at the organization chart (of October 1, 1943) shows its functions.[81]

Of the seven bureaus, the most interesting in this context is Bureau IV, the office for the "Investigating and Combating of Enemies." It was identical with the former Gestapo and was headed by the Gestapo chief, SS-Group Leader Müller.[82] In common with all the other bureaus, it was divided into groups and subsections. Group IV–A concerned itself with "enemies, sabotage, and security"; the various subsections dealt among other things with Communists, Marxists, and affiliated organizations, reactionaries, the opposition, legitimists, liberals, also with the products of ideological opposition such as sabotage, illegal propaganda, or political counterfeiting.

Group IV-B dealt with political Catholicism, political Protestantism, sects, other churches, and Freemasons. In charge of Jewish affairs, among other things, was Subsection IV-B4, "Political Church, Sects, and Jews," headed by SS-*Obersturmbannführer* Eichmann.

The chief function of Group IV-C concerned protective custody; Group IV-D dealt with foreign workers, enemy aliens, and emigrants. The remaining groups were concerned with the regular duties of the political police such as security and passports.

Bureau VII, "Ideological Investigation and Evaluation," was directly concerned with the specific enemies of National Socialism. This was the scientific counterpart to Bureau IV, with its own subsections for Freemasons, Jews, political churches, Marxists, liberals, political emigration, separatists, pacifists, and reactionaries.

Other bureaus too, in particular the Foreign Intelligence Service (VI) under SS-*Oberführer* Schellenberg, were concerned in many different ways with the enemies not only of the German state but also of the National Socialist ideology. "Positive" work was also undertaken in the Reich Security Department, especially in Bureau III, "Spheres of German Life" under SS-*Brigade-*

führer Ohlendorff, which included groups for ethnic affairs and culture with subsections for (among other things) "Racial and National Health," "Science," and "Education and Religious Life."[83]

Thus Hitler's doctrine of the enemies had grown into a gigantic organization whose significance increased from year to year. It is noteworthy that the concentration camps—to the outside world the best-known consequence of National Socialism's systematic combating of enemies—developed from relatively small beginnings. In 1937, after the initial phase of uncontrolled terror, conducted mainly by the SA in improvised camps against its enemies, there were only three camps left, under the "Leader of the Death's Head Units and Concentration Camps." These camps contained a few thousand inmates, not all of whom were political prisoners. It was no mere chance that National Socialism had achieved victory by riding the wave of its alliance with the nationalist revolution, and if it did not immediately deal severely with all its enemies, this was partly because it had not yet revealed to all the scope and intrinsic nature of its opposition. But 1938 already saw a marked increase in the number of inmates, especially in the wake of the pogrom of November, 1938. From then on, "protective custody," which the Gestapo was empowered to decree, took the place, both in extent and severity, more and more of the regular punishments of the law, and during the war the German concentration camps soon became in size and importance the institutions the world later came to know. Nevertheless, this was not due *solely* to a striving for power on the part of the Reich Security Department, any more than was the increasing take-over of the functions of the courts, which found notorious expression, for example, in the agreement between Himmler and Thierack.[84] Rather, one must take into consideration the fact that as the years went by, the enormous and implacable opposition which National Socialism had created for itself emerged with growing clarity and self-confidence, and that the center of the attack on this opposition, the SS and the Reich Security Department, had to increase the severity of its measures to match the increasing resistance which this severity called forth.

And so the transition is made to the final and most terrible chapter of all. This is not to imply that the *will to destruction* emerged only during one stage of the ever-intensifying battle. On the contrary, it is highly typical that this will was palpable in the very first days of the war, that it exerted its influence in many areas, that it pursued its course with the participation of the most varied departments: in other words, it formed part of the original severity. However, this does not preclude the fact that it became more intense as time went on till it finally could give the impression of being impelled.

September 1, 1939, is the date of a decree of Hitler's which became the basis for the Third Reich's program of euthanasia. Soon after the defeat of Poland, Hitler ordered Frank to eliminate the Polish intelligentsia. The decree relating to the commissars ordered the wholesale elimination of the political commissars of the Red Army.

Nevertheless, for Hitler and Himmler as well as for posterity, the emphasis was entirely on the annihilation of the Jews. This process differed essentially from all other extermination actions, both as to scope and to intention. It is impossible here to go deeply into its organization, just as its history could not be depicted earlier in this study. A few indications should be enough to show what these events meant in the light of practice.

A secret decree of Hitler's in the summer of 1941 apparently gave the signal to begin this gigantic task.[85] It was directed by a small subsection of the Reich Security Department headed by a man with the rank of *Oberregierungsrat* (chief privy councilor). There is reason to believe the statement of one of the participants that scarcely more than a hundred persons were directly involved in this undertaking.

The extermination camps themselves were planned and administered by a section of the Economic and Administration Department of the SS, the existence of which was probably hardly known to most of the members of this enormous apparatus (who were chiefly concerned with the arming of the *Waffen-SS*). The selections and the extermination process itself were handled by only an infinitesimal number of SS men, since the actual burden was shifted onto Jewish prisoners.

Even those men who were principally concerned with the execution of the plan were not criminals by nature and had no criminal tendencies in the legal sense. The commandant of Auschwitz, Rudolf Höss, had had a strict Catholic upbringing and had volunteered during World War I as an enthusiastic sixteen-year-old. Admittedly he had been found guilty of political assassination and sent to the penitentiary (Martin Bormann had also been involved in the same incident), but while there his aversion to common criminals increased, and as an *Artamane* he dreamed of sunlight and new settlements until he finally ended up in the "death's head unit" and under the strict discipline of Theodor Eicke, who taught him that an SS man must be able to destroy even the members of his immediate family circle if they transgressed against the state or Adolf Hitler's ideas.[86] On the whole he was probably less of a criminal in the conventional sense than a sentimentalist.

Himmler's ideas are well illustrated by a letter he wrote to the commandant of a concentration camp he visited.[87] He was indignant that a young girl of racially good appearance should be employed in the camp bordello. Only old, completely degenerate prostitutes were to be used for such purposes; he never wanted to have to reproach himself for forsaking a young member of the *Volksgemeinschaft* without cause, and abandoning her once and for all to crime; the SS must not place itself on a level with the law, in whose prisons young people were corrupted for the rest of their lives.

There is a third noteworthy aspect. The transportation of Jews robbed the

Wehrmacht of precious freight space, the number of armament workers was reduced in defiance of all economic reason; the closer the Russian armies approached, the more fanatically did Eichmann endeavor to see that the Hungarian Jews were also carried off to their fate.

All this leads to the following conclusions:

This procedure, kept secret though it was, nevertheless corresponded to the central intention of National Socialism. In his Poznań speech Himmler said: "We had the moral right, we had the obligation toward our people, to kill this people which wanted to kill us."[88] A bacillus had been exterminated; now the important thing was to survive the operation without suffering injury to the soul, to the character. National Socialism had been talking for twenty-five years about this bacillus and the world sickness it caused. Alfred Rosenberg may have all his life considered the talk of "extermination" and "elimination" to be metaphorical,[89] but Hitler and Himmler at any rate were more logically consistent.

Not only were they more consistent: in terms of their own thinking they were also right. One cannot make implacable enemies of Communists and democrats, reactionaries and Christians, Russians and Anglo-Saxons, and still believe in a lasting victory without assuming that all this opposition aroused by one's own demands is attributable to an identifiable "instigator."

In Hitler's extermination of the Jews it was not a case of criminals committing criminal deeds, but of a uniquely monstrous action in which principles ran riot in a frenzy of self-destruction.

The fact that National Socialism had to execute the very essence of its doctrine as a clandestine process, but that it also was unable and unwilling to keep it sufficiently secret for it not to be suspected gradually by the uninitiated, had a curious and very characteristic result. When Hitler's retinue of leaders were on trial at Nuremberg, there was not one who had not been inspired by moderate and sensible views. Sabotage of Hitler's extreme commands had—it now became apparent—begun with the next man in line in the government[90] and was effectively carried out down to the lowest levels in the chain of command. Even the chief of the Security Police and Security Service, SS-*Obergruppenführer* Kaltenbrunner had, according to his testimony, endeavored to apply the brakes and improve the situation wherever he could, and in the end whatever he did was done out of regard for the future of his native land Austria.[91] After the Führer's death the core of leadership of the National Socialist state snapped back, like a steel spring wound up too long, to its original position and became a body of well-meaning and cultured Central Europeans.

The astonishment of many prosecutors, who had naïvely imagined a fascist dictatorship to be a conspiracy of bandits, was no doubt considerable. Not a single one of the accused made any attempt whatever to justify the extermination measures. Not one testified defiantly to the necessity of the war for the conquest of living space and its unprecedented methods. These men had been better people than most of the world had assumed.[92] But they had been weaker in spirit than one might have supposed. They wanted German sovereignty, but they did not, like Hitler, take into account what sovereignty means today. They wanted a war-efficient state, but they did not, like Hitler, consider what a modern and autonomously waged war implies; they vigorously defended the social order in the traditional German sense, but they did not realize the sole means by which it could be finally secured. They combated the Jews, but they failed to recognize that even a complete emigration, according to the intrinsic meaning of the National Socialist doctrine, could not accomplish any genuinely essential changes. No wonder they became the prey of the more logically consistent mind.

But what is the meaning of a consistency which no one is prepared to profess any more? Even after a total defeat of the Western democracies, countless people would have clung to the conviction which is the very cornerstone of liberal and democratic belief—that personal inviolability and dignity must be the boundary and objective of all politics. Even after a destruction of the Soviet Union, countless people the world over would have defended the doctrine which is the heart of communism—that only socialization of the means of production can open up the path to a better world. The core of National Socialism, the doctrine of world salvation through the elimination of the disease-spreading Jews, was forsaken after the defeat even by the innermost circles among the leaders. All that remained was a few trivialities and shallow claims. It was not the documents of the prosecution but the documents of the defense that set the final seal on Adolf Hitler's death. And this death meant, if not the end of fascism, certainly the end of its era.

CHAPTER FIVE

The Doctrine in Context

Fear and Its Intentions

The statement that fear was Hitler's basic emotion may come as a surprise. Did he not frequently brag about his toughness, did he not glorify health and struggle? And yet all this will not assume proper perspective if the dominant underlying factor is overlooked. True though it is that there is even less of a theoretically elaborated thought system with Hitler than with Maurras, it is equally true that a similar foundation gave rise to a similar thought context.[1]

Hitler's fear is not for the fragility of all that is beautiful. It is the Austrian Pan-German's naked fear for existence which Georg von Schönerer passed on to his pupil as a continuing heritage. In the eyes of the young Hitler, the Hapsburgs are about to "exterminate" and "extinguish" the German race;[2] their policy means the "slow destruction" and the "end" of the German people in Austria,[3] the rising tide of a medley of peoples "is corroding" the old cultural center of Vienna.[4] In 1914 the entire German people lacked the proper awareness of "threatening nonexistence."[5] Not even after the revolution did the German people sufficiently realize the "state of threatening extermination,"[6] in spite of being surrounded by a "pack of rapacious enemies" whose final triumph must mean the "death" of the German people.[7] The revolution within, the implacable enemy, France, without, represent frightful dangers which threaten to "destroy" Germany.[8] Except by the acquisition of land there is no way for the constantly expanding population to exist, it is threatened with "extinction."[9] In another hundred years Germany will be flanked by giant states some of which will have grown up out of its own blood.[10] Heedless optimists should learn from history that many peoples and states have become extinct.[11] Although other peoples are not free of grave symptoms, the process of destruction is advancing more swiftly in Germany.[12] It need not necessarily be a physical destruction: the German people as a whole might become a "rootless metropolitan element."[13] The fate of insecurity and dependence this entails is proved to the Hitler of 1928 by the fact that American automobiles are swamping the German market "to an alarming degree."[14] To the Hitler of the Eastern campaign, the Russian birth rate[15] seems alarming, or the vast Asiatic human reservoir.[16] The German location is territorially "wretched" and, from a military-geographical standpoint, "terrible."[17] The much-vaunted German economy is an unsettling factor in the world and will not cease to call down a thousand perils on Germany's head.[18] The vision of physical extinction is always close at hand; if the Jew triumphs, the planet will travel its course void of human life as it did millions of years ago.[19] This powerful man's fear extended to the banal and the physical: no one was ever permitted to smoke in Hitler's presence, for smoke and warmth provide a favorable climate for the cold virus—"The microbes pounce on me."[20]

The *subject* of Hitler's fear can be easily determined, and yet it is not easy to define. It is Germany, the nation, the Fatherland—the "dearest thing given to us in this world,"[21] and apparently the only thing with a claim to unconditional love—"We National Socialists want to love our Fatherland and learn to love it and it alone, and to tolerate no other idols beside it. We know only *one* interest, and that is the interest of our people."[22] Exactly as in the case of Maurras, nation and humanity are explicitly dissociated; the young Hitler is prepared to laugh at the curses of the whole world if these curses can bring about the freedom of the German race.[23] Maurras' well-known formula is reflected almost word for word in the basic postulate: "The Fatherland alone, first and last!"[24]

What this Germany was, is much less clear. For Hitler there was no distinct period of history, as there was for Maurras, to provide him with an orientation and a constant object of fresh eulogy. In his early days he frequently extolled the Bismarck Reich and its "wonderful energy and strength,"[25] but what he praised was usually individual institutions, such as the army and civil service; the era as a whole was the object of his sharp criticism, which did not spare the person of the monarch and still less the monarch's "servile" entourage. And the older he became, the more he looked toward non-German manifestations, the more Germany became *his* Third Reich—a Reich which was yet to be created.

The *object* of Hitler's fear, and hence of his hate, emerges far more often and more clearly than its subject. It is typical of Hitler that his fear was instantly transformed into hate. Otherwise he could not have hoped or believed, for: "How can a condition be altered for which there is no immediate culprit?"[26] The universal culprit was known to be the Jew. But first those manifestations must be enumerated (with no special emphasis on causal relationship) which Hitler regarded as signs of decay and which therefore filled him with fear.

The innate strength of the seemingly powerful prewar Germany was weakened—according to the analysis in *Mein Kampf*[27]—mainly by an "industrialization which was as unbridled as it was harmful," and which entailed a dangerous regression of the farming class. The aristocracy of the sword gave way to the aristocracy of finance, but equally disastrous was the diminution of personal property rights in the economy and the handing over of property to anonymous limited companies. This signified an alienation of property as against the employee, and the internationalism of the economy. This mammonization led at the same time to the Hebraization of spiritual life and to the decline of the mating urge; this latter furthered the incidence of syphilis and hence of the greatest sin of all, that which was "contrary to blood and race." On the spiritual level there was the similar threat of the plague of art-bolshevism which substituted cubist distortions for beauty, thereby tending to destroy the foundations of culture. Alongside this, the liberal press, with its championing of tolerance and democracy and its mendacious attack on "militarism," was digging the German people's grave. Jewish influence in thought led to contempt for manual labor, thus wrenching open that cleavage among the people which had been responsible for the lost war and the successful revolution.

Many different utterances in speeches and conversations augment this picture. The idea that the depersonalization of the economy was tantamount to the triumph of Jewish influence remained fixed; now and again his accusations were aimed directly at the middle classes as such. It was a great historical offense that the bourgeoisie had shown no concern whatever for the newly emerging Fourth Estate.[28] But it was even worse that with the middle classes the wrong section of the people had assumed leadership, a section which lacked the "heroic and epic qualities."[29] One section of the middle classes which in Hitler's eyes was particularly close to the Jews was that of the intellectuals. They had a gift for complicating everything and for bringing confusion into the simplest things. Science, which they had produced, caused the greatest harm,[30] since it "renders incompetent" and encourages weakness. If the world were given over to German professors, they would change mankind into cretins with huge heads.

Jewish intellectualism invented the "emancipation of women," which sought to mix those spheres which God had separated; it even undertook something as insane as the emancipation of negroes, the education of semiapes. The carping criticism of the intellectuals had no useful social function; its object and intention was to demoralize. The art-Bolsheviks had even worse in mind, the way they painted fields blue, the sky green, clouds sulphurous yellow,[31] and allowed free rein to their dirty imagination—they wanted to kill the people's soul.[32] They were in no wise different from those Jews who organized night life and turned all normal morals upside down.[33]

But there were also more remote phenomena which he identified as symptoms of decadence. With their robbers' motto of "free trade," the Jews destroyed the centuries-old stability of the price of bread in Venice,[34] and it was merely the logical extension of this principle that land had become the object of speculation.[35]

Only on rare occasions did he allude to cultural conditions in a more general way, without direct political reference and accusation, for instance: Germany was slowly becoming an object of views and prospects,[36] or: "Nothing is anchored any more, nothing is rooted in our spiritual life any more. Everything is superficial, flees past us. Restlessness and haste mark the thinking of our people. The whole of life is being torn completely apart, and today the ordinary man no longer understands the intelligentsia of the German nation."[37]

It is obvious that Hitler aimed his criticism, like Maurras, at the emancipatory process as a whole. Needless to say, this all contained many familiar clichés of conservative cultural criticism in its anti-Semitic form, and one cannot even look for literary originality in them. But it is legitimate to ask whether any practical politician of stature has ever expressed convictions of this kind as frequently and as emphatically. Hitler is certainly original in the utterly monomaniacal obstinacy with which he seeks the "instigator" of all these alarming processes and finds him every time and without exception in the Jew.

The attributing of highly complicated and essential processes to one single and visible instigator or agent always means an obvious simplification and usually an immense overestimation of the "instigator." Apropos of the Jew in the economy, for example, he says: "He is, of course, destroying with increasing thoroughness the foundations of an economy of genuine benefit to the nation. By the devious method of share issues, he injects himself into the mainstream of national production, turns this into a commercial, or rather, marketable bargaining object, and thus deprives manufacturing concerns of the basis of personal ownership. This is where employer and employee enter upon that spiritual estrangement which later leads to political class cleavage."[38] Or Hitler asks in an early speech: "Who is the real champion of birth control and the idea of emigration? International Jewry."[39]

Hence the monstrous thesis that the Jew was "the wirepuller of the destinies of mankind"[40] can no longer astonish, although it does disclose what was meant by "the Jew": namely, the historical process itself. And those early conversations with Dietrich Eckart had always moved within the horizon of this identity.[41]

Hitler's theories therefore have nothing of the subtlety and differentiation to be found in Maurras' doctrine of the enemy. After all, he had discovered long ago that the Jews were the leaders of Social Democracy. Only the Jew could praise parliament, an institution which "is as dirty and untruthful as he is himself."[42] Whatever of catastrophic elements in the world is conducive to harming Germany is always traced back to the same roots: because both are Jewish, it is possible for Marxism to be the spearhead of international finance.[43] Although Maurras awarded the Jew a certain priority among the host of enemies, it was Hitler who perfected the image[44] while at the same time placing him on the lowest possible level. Hitler's excursions on Jewish sexuality in *Mein*

Kampf are reminiscent of Lanz zu Liebenfels and give a hint of what was to come in Streicher's infamous *Der Stürmer*.

Hitler always succumbed to an ungovernable passion on the subject of bolshevism.[45] He regarded it as the most radical form of Jewish genocide ever known—all his meager, pallid historical constructs culminate in this. Important though the Vienna period certainly was for Hitler, it nevertheless remains doubtful whether, without the experience of the Bolshevik revolution and without Dietrich Eckart (whose interpretation of it obviously impressed him more than any other), he would have become the man as whom he has imprinted himself on history. The conclusion of those constructs in *Mein Kampf* probably expresses more directly than anything else the initial thesis of his political activity: "Now begins the last great revolution. By wresting political power for himself, the Jew casts off the few remaining shreds of disguise he still wears. The democratic plebeian Jew turns into the blood Jew and the tyrant of peoples. In a few years he will try to exterminate the national pillars of intelligence and, by robbing the peoples of their natural spiritual leadership, will make them ripe for the slavish lot of a permanent subjugation. The most terrible example of this is Russia. ... But the end is not merely the end of the liberty of the peoples suppressed by the Jew: it is also the end of this parasite of the peoples himself. After the death of the victim, sooner or later the vampire dies too."[46]

However, according to Eckart's book Hitler had specified another bolshevism ahead of Lenin's as an origin—that of Moses! History was placed between these two bolshevisms and interpreted as a struggle between two principles, in such a way that the individual historical phenomena were each arranged and evaluated according to their relationship to these principles. This pursuit of the enemy throughout history, which occupies such a large place in Maurras' writings, is not much in evidence in those works of Hitler's which were for public consumption. And indeed how could he have displayed, in Protestant Germany, that conception of the Reformation which Eckart ascribes to him? Moreover, until 1945 Germany remained too Christian for even the most powerful man in all Germany's history to have dared publicly to call the Apostle Paul a Bolshevik. He had merely been able to indicate more than once that he considered bolshevism—as the revolt (led by Jews) of inferior strata against their masters—to be a timeless phenomenon, and that many parallels could be drawn between the present day and the era of declining Rome. But the fact that for him Apostle Paul really did remain, as in Eckart's book, a central figure of Jewish bolshevism (as he had been for Maurras) was finally proved with the publication of *Hitler's Table Talk*.

Paul, so he stated here, had taken the idea of the Aryan Christ as a crystallization point for slaves of all kinds against their masters and authority. The religion of Paul of Tarsus, later known as Christianity, was simply the communism of today.[47] This Christianity was the severest blow mankind had ever suffered. It had destroyed the Roman Empire, and the result had been centuries of darkness.[48] Christianity was an early form of bolshevism, bolshevism an offspring of Christianity—and both were inventions of the Jew for the purpose of disrupting society. Christianity had destroyed the serene, limpid world of antiquity, bolshevism was getting ready to destroy the pre-eminence of the white race in the world.[49] Yesterday's agitator was called Sha'ul, today's was called Mordecai.[50]

Of course these ideas, as theories, are anything but original, and they remain within the framework of the "whole anti-Semitic literature" which Hitler had always boasted of knowing.[51] But it is precisely from this aspect that they reveal a striking and characteristic feature—his hatred for Christianity was in direct proportion to his high opinion of the Roman Catholic Church as a form of dominion.[52] Hitler therefore presented a doctrine of the historical manifestations of the terrifying and odious enemy which exactly corresponds to Maurras' doctrine, although it is much more naïve.

Unconditional Sovereignty

If the Jewish objective was "indisputably the expansion of an invisible Jewish state as a supreme tyranny over the whole world,"[53] then the attack was aimed primarily at the sovereignty of states and peoples. Hence the defense and preservation of sovereignty was the noblest duty of a race-conscious body of national leaders.

For Hitler, however, sovereignty was not a legal concept but actual independence, predicated on two essentials. First, a sovereign people must be capable of living entirely off the yield of its own soil. Second, its territory must offer military-geographical protection.

If either of these conditions was absent, independence was already forfeited, however solemnly the possession of sovereignty might be pledged; for it was obvious "that, in an age when the fate of the world depends on huge countries, on states of eleven to seventeen million square kilometers, an age in which countries with a hundred million inhabitants determine the fate of the world, it is no longer possible to talk in terms of the sovereignty of small states."[54]

The German nation was in a situation in which both requirements were rapidly disappearing and was thus threatened with a decline to the level of a small state. It had long ceased to be able to feed its population and had therefore been obliged to turn to an industrialization which was "harmful" above all from the point of view of sovereignty. Moreover, as a result of technical developments its territory was no longer a power factor, "for with the airplane our German territory is crossed in barely four hours. It is no longer an area of innate protection, such as Russia, whose geographical expanse is a power in itself, a safety coefficient."[55]

The only escape from this dilemma is shown by nature. For throughout the ages it was the living who multiplied; that which nourished, however, space, never changed.[56] From this Malthusian premise Hitler proceeded to consequences which might be called a particular and biological form of Marxism. Life, which is seen primarily as the quantity of the (nation's) "flesh and blood substance," is continually growing beyond the area at its disposal, just as Marxists always regard production power as being stronger than the conditions of production. Hitler's counterpart to the Marxist revolution which breaks a trail for the new is war which adjusts living space to the population figure. War can, of course, only be waged when the "spiritual value" of the people guarantees the successful embarking on its "struggle for life." This premise explains much of Hitler's fear and of his race theory. For he more than once regarded the German people with severity and lack of affection,[57] and his faith was only restored by the belief "that a people which over the centuries has offered countless examples of the highest spiritual value cannot overnight have suddenly lost this innate traditional value."[58] Hence it must have been a very real alternative for him when he said: "We shall perish if we no longer possess the strength to acquire for ourselves the land and soil we need."[59] To perish means in this case: to lose complete autonomy and total independence. This is what he meant when he wrote in *Mein Kampf*: "The only thing which will ensure a people its freedom of existence is sufficient space on this earth."[60]

Hitler's doctrine of *Lebensraum* must not be regarded simply as a theory which he picked up from Ratzel, Haushofer, or even Mackinder. If one takes the categories of the peasant's and the soldier's way of thinking, combines them with the German distrust of the non-German world, and places them in an age of actually diminishing state sovereignty, one cannot fail to arrive at the concept of *Lebensraum* and territorial acquisition as an elementary necessity of life itself. It is true, of course, that Hitler was neither a peasant nor a soldier; but that does not mean he did not think in peasant-soldier categories. First and foremost he was a German, and all he knew and all he cared to know was Germany; and in some of its most significant traditions this Germany closely approached Hitler's thinking. For example, in "the most advanced" industrial nation in Europe it was possible for ideas to be revived which appeared to stem from the time of the migration of peoples: "Geopolitical nations have always been peasant and soldier peoples. The sword protects the plow, and the plow feeds the sword."[61]

When less than twenty years after writing *Mein Kampf* Hitler seemed to have implemented his program and conquered half of Russia, he could at last look with confidence into the future: Germany was going to become the most autarkic state in the world, in every respect, there would even be a surplus of cotton. And he sang the praises of the peasant who, just as he should, plowed back all his confidence into the soil.[62]

But the problem of autarky in foodstuffs is only one aspect of the National

Socialist *Lebensraum* policy; the other, and perhaps more important, is the safeguarding of military self-sufficiency and defensibility. It is this aspect which accounts for some of the apparent paradoxes of this policy during the war, for it very soon became obvious that more territory had been conquered than it was possible to settle. Now suddenly the population figure had to be adjusted to the area—in other words, increased as much as possible, as rapidly as possible. The old measures formerly used to bolster the population policy were now woefully inadequate: attempts were made to settle people from Holland and Scandinavia in Eastern Europe, Himmler turned his attention to the conquest of "good blood" and robbed the vanquished not only of their land but their children, serious thought was given to turning Germany into a great breeding stable with the most efficient exploitation of the sexual powers of each man and woman.[63]

All this seems grotesque and unbelievable if looked at merely as an attempt to implement strange theories; it becomes coherent and logical if regarded as stages in the desperate race toward the goal of total, completely secure sovereignty.

Eternal War

The relationship of war to sovereignty is not simply that of a means to an end. It is sovereignty's supreme act and true fulfillment, for it always bursts the confines of space which threaten to spell doom to sovereignty. Wars were for Hitler the revolutions of healthy peoples. That is why he called war "the most powerful and classic expression of life."[64] And he regarded it as especially characteristic of the era that "the horoscope of the age [indicates] not peace but war."[65]

Hitler had always taken the endorsement of war for granted; it was not something he had had to learn, like Mussolini. Even as a boy, so he tells in *Mein Kampf,* he had cursed the fate which had allowed him to be born in an era of peace with its "casual mutual cheating," and the Boer War had seemed like a flickering light on the horizon.[66] There may be more than a hint of self-dramatization in these reminiscences,[67] but certainly Hitler was only peripherally affected, if at all, by the pacifist mood of the prewar period. However, he was not the type, as Röhm was, to glorify war romantically. If one did not take his remarks about territorial acquisition seriously, his theses in *Mein Kampf* on war and peace were no different from the convictions of many of his contemporaries. That mankind must perish in eternal peace had been Corradini's and Maurras' belief too; and the postulate that the "sole preparation for a coming passage of arms" must be undertaken by other than parliamentary forces[68] is to be found *sub rosa* among historical analyses.

Hitler's cause was not so much to talk about war as to prepare the nation practically for it. Hitler's *Table Talk* exposes in the most startling manner the determination with which he always wanted war and the lack of scruples with which he financed war in full anticipation of the booty it would yield.[69] Although his statements may have been inaccurate in detail,[70] they reveal with the utmost clarity the spirit dominating even the "peace years" of 1933 to 1939. Every thorough analysis of Hitler's thinking must confirm that he was not merely diverted from an original idea of being "social leader of the people"; on the contrary, his statements on war display the remarkable and essentially unchanging coherence of his nature. Thus in the midst of war he was capable of uttering the axiom that a peace lasting longer than twenty-five years was harmful to a nation.[71] The prospect of a constant state of war on the Eastern border filled him with satisfaction: it would, he said, help build a strong race and prevent Germany from sinking back into European decadence.[72] Himmler filled in the picture down to the last detail.[73] Hence Hitler's idea of "world domination" is not to be understood as a permanent state of peace, but as a constant state of war with the assurance of German pre-eminence: with a number of small armies it would be possible to dominate a large number of peoples permanently.[74] How far Hitler was from envisaging any real alteration in the relationship between nations is to be seen from his remark that, if the Duce's reforestation program was carried out, it might be necessary in a hundred years to wage war on Italy.[75]

Hitler's war is quite inadequately described if it is called a war of aggression. It was a war of pillage and annihilation, and this made it, in Hitler's opinion, the highest form of life which transformed the youth into a man and the people into a "race." Hitler was right when he said war had rediscovered its pristine form.[76] Indeed, it was not a religion setting off to disseminate its faith;[77] it was not a nation rising to achieve unity: a totemistic tribe headed by its all powerful war chief was on the march to wrest and verify its own life through the death of others. Yet it is part of the mysterious totality of the phenomenon that this struggle was also, in an even more precise sense, a war of defense.

Absolute Supremacy

The question remains: *Who* wages this war for absolute sovereignty, that is, what is the social structure of this people on the march?

At first sight there seems much to be said for the theory that National Socialism was a popular mass movement with its leader, Hitler, acclaimed by plebiscite. All mass movements of this kind are permeated with sharp resentment toward prevailing social distinctions, and as a rule their leaders come to power against the will of the leading classes.

Comradeship, unity, national solidarity, appeared to be the chief catchwords of young National Socialism, and millions joined the movement under this impression. Hitler voiced a distillation of a plebeian mass emotion when he fulminated against Papen's government in 1932: "these high and mighty gentlemen who form part of an entirely different humanity by reason of their birth."[78] And right after his victory he confirmed the ubiquitous sense of unity by saying, for example, that this movement meant the recognition by millions of people that they were brothers and sisters.[79] This was obviously also the implication of the much-used term *Volkwerdung* (becoming a people); and it pointed in the same direction when Hitler at a very early stage repudiated class distinction, saying that all Germans were of the same blood and their common race must be stronger than any economic differences.[80] Hitler was always finding phrases for an almost mystical communion with the masses, and this rapport showed up his contrast with German nationalists: "The struggle which alone can make Germany free will be fought with the forces welling up from the broad masses. Without the German worker they will never achieve a German Reich! It is not in our political salons that the strength of the nation lies, but in the fists, the brow, and the will of the broad masses. As always: liberation will not come from the top down but will leap out from below."[81] Later on conservative critics often took such pronouncements to support their theory that Hitler had been a plebeian mass leader who had actually carried on the French revolution's work of melting down the aristocracy and who was therefore to be placed among Rousseau's successors.[82]

As against such an interpretation, however, there are—side by side with the polemic against the "racial mishmash of the uniform people"[83]—those numerous statements in *Mein Kampf* which display a frank and lordly contempt for the masses and depict their inertia and feminine nature with a cynical eye. Even more significant are his remarks concerning the nature and emergence of states, remarks which reveal themselves—and not in *Mein Kampf* only—as a focal point of Hitler's political ideas:[84] the doctrine of the creative race nuclei and of the state as a racial order of authority. These are merely a paraphrase of Gobineau's theory, although Hitler developed it in one particular point, that is, related it to a phenomenon of his own time.

As bringers of light and sole conveyors of a "culturally creative primeval force,"[85] Aryan racial nuclei have from time immemorial penetrated the masses of inferior men and women and, supported by the labors of subjugated peoples, deployed all their creative qualities. They perish when they succumb to original sin and mingle their blood with that of their slaves.[86]

This "prenational" doctrine was a natural basis for the self-image of the French aristocracy. The reason Hitler adopted it was obviously not only because, since Drumont, it had become a highly esteemed basis of attack on the parasitic Jew in anti-Semitic literature, but also because it gave him the chance of a deeper insight into communism. For it enables one to attribute the inferiority of the opponent's ideology, as well as the superiority of one's own, to an alleged fact of nature. Communism is merely the attempted revolt of the racially inferior population strata which had once been subjugated, strata which are related all over Europe and hence susceptible to an international appeal. Only a superficial understanding of Hitler's race theory can advance the opinion that he regarded the nation as a community of common origin: in actual fact he saw it as a structure of authority made up of races of differing values. Moreover, this doctrine (to which there is only a rudimentary similarity in Italian fascism's concept of the elite), which destroys the unity of the nation and really establishes the Marxist class theory in what amounts to a counter-world of Platonic stability, was not merely expounded by Hitler before small groups: it is to be found as clear as day in that famous address to West German industrialists which, with remarkable contempt for his fellow men, was disseminated in tens of thousands of copies:

> However, if this ideology encroaches upon us too, we must not forget that our people is also composed of the most varied elements, that we must therefore see much more in the slogan "Proletarians of the world, unite!" than a mere political battle cry. In reality it is the expression of the will of men who by nature actually possess a certain affinity with analogous peoples of a lower cultural level. Our people and our state were also at one time built up simply through the exercise of the absolute authority and ruling spirit of so-called Nordic men, of the Aryan race components which to this day we still possess in our people.[87]

If one considers that the genocidal appeal to the racially inferior layer—that is, the appeal which destroys the structure of authority by breaking down racial barriers—is that of the Jewish intellect, and that the peoples of Eastern Europe represent the most powerful massing of inferior human beings, then it becomes obvious that Hitler's social mythology (which is the interpretation of a familiar and easily explicable fact)[88] forms the focal point of his political thoughts and emotions; and, moreover, that it can determine what seems at first to be the much more potent national motive. This leader of the masses succumbs in effect to the most radical form of the conservative anti-"masses" defense ideology—and this is precisely the outstanding feature of radical fascism.

There is, of course, an important modification that must not be overlooked. Hitler rightly called the recognition of the inequality of persons the "final logical conclusion" of the race doctrine. The fact that he himself was the person of the highest value and hence destined to be the Führer, that is, the ruler, was something Hitler at first tacitly assumed but later explicitly stressed. But the primary and most outstanding of his leadership qualities was that like a magnet he extracted the valuable elements from the people and collected them around him.[89] It followed that the NSDAP was simply that reincarnated Aryan race nucleus in the German people which was ordained by nature to rule. Between the NSDAP and the Führer there existed a relationship of mysterious identity which nevertheless did not preclude the strict order of authority. In 1938 Hitler told a hundred and fifty thousand assembled functionaries in Nuremberg that they *were* the German people.[90] In this way he disarmed the aristocracy of their principle and even turned it against them by enabling the humblest street cleaner to regard himself as a member of what was racially the best section of the population and to look down on the degenerate aristocrats, some of whom even had Jewish blood, as long as he listened only to the Führer's race-revealing challenge. It is true, of course, that in this Hitler merely adopted the most despicable trait of a certain kind of bourgeois literature which, while admiring the principles of aristocracy with fawning servility, provided plebeian resentment with a convenient safety valve by making sly digs at the allegedly inadequate reality of the aristocracy.[91]

Seen politically, however, the whims and fancies of plebeian aristocratism proved an excellent *modus operandi*. One did not make an irrevocable enemy of either side; in bad times one could feel secretly superior to both, while in good times one could actually gain the upper hand. The emphasis on the "aristocratic principle of nature"[92] pleased the aristocrats, the defense of the principle of leading personalities attracted the industrialists (who showed much sympathy for the vital connection between political and economic leadership), and the doctrine of the inevitable triumph of the stronger represented a blank check in favor of the most rabid elements of the masses. However, it was not simply a case of a shrewdly conceived method: the point was that Hitler, in his person and in his thinking, was the embodiment of that "third force" between the ruling class and the populace which, during a certain period of bourgeois history and under certain conditions, can represent the most successful—that is, fascist—synthesis. In its most radical form it created the "race state" right in the twentieth century: above the broad layer of racially inferior and politically disfranchised average citizens, whose former leaders had been either wiped out, banished, or imprisoned, but which was disciplined and kept contented by a firm hand, the ruling elite of the Nordic race nucleus rose up in varying degrees, while this elite was in turn ruled absolutely by the Führer, whose "will is the constitution."[93]

At this point a paradox makes its appearance—namely, that heredity, in defiance of the most primitive assumptions of the race doctrine, is to play no part, and the solid middle-class principle of achievement is to be the sole governing factor; and also that up to the very end the Führer made a number of statements placing German citizens above foreign nations of like racial origin.

However, all ambiguity vanishes the moment the race state directs its authority outward. For by comparison with the subjugated inhabitants of Eastern Europe, the Germans as a whole appear as the racially superior masters. It is here that the principle of race rule is displayed with the greatest clarity.

In *Hitler's Table Talk* Hitler drew a picture of the future of the Eastern European territories which was not without significance, although it never became a reality. Today it numbers among the most incredible and yet best-authenticated of his life's visions and is so typical of his ideas that it must not be passed over.

Underlying everything is the total disfranchisement of the subjugated. They have no claims of any kind, except an early death. They are forbidden to learn to read and write; to concern themselves with history or politics is a crime worthy of death. Any communication whatever going beyond the confines of the village is strictly prohibited. They are regarded by their masters "as redskins" and do not even merit warning signs on the *Autobahnen*: Why should they not be run over since there are too many of them anyway? In order to sell them contraceptive devices, Hitler jokes, one ought perhaps even to employ the Jews. They are to live in their filthy hovels without hygiene or inoculation, while the German settlers, strictly segregated, own splendid villages and spacious fortress-farms. From time to time a troop of Kirghizes will be conducted through Germany's capital, "Germania," so that, full of awed astonishment, they can report in their distant homeland on the monumental cultural achievements of the Germans and spread belief in the godlike nature of the master race.[94]

Infantile imaginings? Of course. But in Poland they had become a reality in many vital initial points. And structures of authority of this kind really have existed in the past. Hitler might have said with as much justification as he did apropos of his war that here social order and structure of authority had reverted to their pristine form. But, in contrast to his prophecy of eternal war, there is in his constructs on absolute authority an unmistakable note of anxiety: "If we ever give one of the conquered provinces the right to build up its own army or air force, it will mean the end of our authority," or: "The path to self-administration leads to independence."[95]

Distant Models

The models which Hitler emulated underwent a certain change; moreover, they are to be found on different levels. On the whole it can be said less of him than of Maurras that he was "seduced by history," for he was far less inclined to be guided by specific periods of Germany's history.

Inasmuch as he was at all, it was mostly in *Mein Kampf* and during his early period. There he extolled not only the army and civil service of Bismarck's Germany; he wanted to restore Germany to "what it had once been,"[96] to pick up "the old cockade out of the dirt."[97] It was clear that his criticism of democracy and the parliamentary system was the result of looking back on this better Germany, but even during his period of struggle it was a long way from being that which the age of Louis XIV had meant for Maurras. After the seizure of power he stressed the unique nature of his own enterprise, and in *Hitler's Table Talk* he expressed his thanks to the Social Democrats for having got rid of the monarchs.[98] The only period in German history which now found favor in his eyes was the medieval imperial age, "the greatest epic" since the downfall of the Roman Empire.[99] But even that he regarded less from the aspect of what it was than from the vision of what it might have been.

What never changed was his devotion to the Roman Empire. It is highly probable that in his mind he never compared himself with the old Germanic hero Arminius but that he did place himself on a level with the great Roman emperors. His great respect for the Catholic Church (on account of its dogmatism, discipline, and stability), which was so often repugnant to his North German Protestant followers, can probably be regarded simply as a variant of this devotion.

Even more revealing is his lifelong admiration of Sparta: in a speech given in 1929 he called it the "purest race state in history."[100] The fact that six thousand masters managed to lord it over three hundred and forty-five thousand slaves appears in *Hitler's Table Talk* as a direct model for future German hegemony in Eastern Europe.[101]

He felt closer to the example of the British, and frequently reiterated that Eastern Europe must become for Germany what India was for England. A new human type must be created there: viceroys.[102] Only wide open spaces could produce self-confidence and the overcoming of petit-bourgeois narrow-mindedness; the Germans would at last be on an equal footing with the British. British arrogance and insolence were to be admired and copied. England's national unity was an impressive example to follow.

To the American people—before the disappointment caused by Roosevelt— he ascribed a far higher value than to any of the European peoples (because it had been the best Europeans who had emigrated). He declared the immigration policy of the United States to be a paradigm of clear-cut race consciousness.

The present-day reality which Hitler took as his departure point was the domination of the world by the white race (among which he evidently did not number the Jews and the Slavs). His numerous offers to guarantee the British Empire are well known; the regret he expressed during the war, that he could not wage war on bolshevism with the British air force and navy as his partners, was absolutely sincere.[103]

His actual partners were the Japanese, and there were many occasions when he had to defend himself—in his own eyes too—against the reproach of betraying his own race principles. But the pragmatic reasons he gave from time to time did not tell the essential truth: he really did sincerely admire the land in the Far East. Untouched as it was by Christianity, inaccessible to Jews, internally united and dedicated to hero-worship, Japan was for him a land of natural fascism, pointing the way for his own endeavors.[104]

Finally, among Hitler's models the Jews must not be forgotten. Their racial unity had always aroused his envy and fear. To what extent his bitterest struggle was based on an apparently highly overestimated evaluation of the enemy, but also to what extent all the Madagascar plans seemed to him to be mere palliatives, is revealed by a casual remark in *Hitler's Table Talk*: if five thousand

Jews were to be transferred to Sweden, within a short time they would have acquired all the leading positions.[105]

What is common to all these models is that they are quite remote from concrete German reality and history. It is an extraordinary fact that Germany's bitterest struggle to maintain itself was bound up with a spiritual capitulation which spared nothing. What did he mean by "Germany" anyway, now that his most burning desire was to become like the Anglo-Americans, the Japanese, and the Spartans? But here too a universal attribute of fascism emerges: its (at least potential) hostility to history despite its traditionalist beginnings.[106] At the same time one must not overlook that already mentioned personal "detachment" of Hitler as a reinforcing element.

Global Struggle for "Recovery"

The objectives which the National Socialist movement sought in referring to these models were the acquisition and maintenance of total sovereignty for the Germanic race state in eternal war. Yet this does not sufficiently describe the nature of this struggle as it appeared to Hitler.

Its most general characteristic is that of the struggle for recovery. As was always the case with Hitler, the negative emerges more strongly than the positive, disease more strongly than good health.

Hitler never tired of emphasizing that the many manifestations of decay all pointed to *one* great process of disease. That this disease must have an agent was a premise underlying all his thinking and convictions. This was a case of tuberculosis, of poisoning, of plague. All the nostrums in the world were of no avail as long as the tubercles continued their work of destruction.[107] World War I was lost because the "parasites" were not attacked on the home front, because Germany hesitated to expose "twelve or fifteen thousand of these Hebrew corrupters of the people to poison gas," which was what hundreds of thousands had to endure at the front.[108] But how could people have combated the poison who carried it around in themselves,[109] infected as they were with humanitarian and democratic ideas? Were they not bound to recoil from the idea of exterminating the "international poisoners" of the masses?[110] On a par with Hitler's all-permeating fear of the "extermination," "extinction," and "annihilation" of the German people was his tireless appeal for the "extermination," "removal," and "elimination" of that agent of the deadly disease. At the end of February, 1942—that is, after the Wannsee conference, which organized the "final solution"—he said to the guests around his table: "The discovery of the Jewish virus is one of the greatest revolutions that has ever taken place. The fight we are carrying on is of the same nature as that waged by Pasteur and Koch during the last century. How many diseases have their origin in the Jewish virus! ... We shall only regain our health when we eliminate the Jew."[111] And in his final monologues he laid claim to the gratitude of the world for having "lanced the Jewish abscess."[112]

The fact that Hitler resorted to biological and medical categories to interpret his struggle placed his war on that third level, the level of annihilation. Hitler was certainly not the only one to talk in this way, but he alone had the courage to take the consequences.[113] However, the destruction of the Jewish bacillus was not the sole function of the negative policy of recovery. An essential requirement was the elimination of those who did not fight the poison with determination because they carried it within themselves—that is, the bourgeois and conservative parties. But equally essential was the removal of the biologically weak and inferior. Long before the laws pertaining to hereditary health and the measures for killing off of the incurably ill, it was possible to hear the following calculation in an early speech of Hitler's: "If a million children were born annually in Germany and seven to eight hundred thousand of the weak eliminated, the end result would perhaps even be an increased strength."[114]

Measures relating to the positive policy of recovery formed part of the practice of the regime and are not relevant here. What was of paramount importance for Hitler in this field was shown by the way he extolled the racially beneficial activities of the SS divisions in the Berchtesgaden area and elsewhere, or the remark that he would have no peace of mind until he had succeeded in providing a future generation of Nordic blood wherever the population required a regeneration.[115]

For Hitler, the struggle for the regaining of Germany's health had never been a provincial concern only. Since this struggle was to ward off the attack of a world-wide sickness and its cause, it was universal in *scope* and could not cease until the force of the disease was broken on all sides. Hence it was a matter of world salvation. Even early in his political career Hitler had shown no reluctance to compare himself with Christ and his "fight against the Jewish poison." In September, 1923, he said: "What is now getting under way will be greater than the war! It will be fought out on German soil for the whole world. There are only two possibilities: we shall be either the sacrificial lamb or the victor."[116]

The *spirit* of such a struggle cannot be provided only by the political shrewdness involved in mere protection of interests. If the nation is to come out of it victoriously, it must be saturated with the conviction that this is a life-and-death struggle.[117] Hence the statement that it is not the economy or science that can move mountains, but faith—always and only faith.[118] The faith of followers in the Führer, of the Führer in the movement, must be blind and fanatical. The new ideology demanded "complete and utter recognition."[119] Only thus could it produce the required ruthlessness in battle. Humane considerations were thus "absolutely" eliminated,[120] as already laid down in *Mein Kampf*. In *Hitler's Table Talk* Hitler envisaged the following measures for the hypothetical possibility that a mutiny might break out somewhere in the Reich: all leaders of opposing trends, even of political Catholicism, were to be executed; all inmates of concentration camps were to be shot; all criminal elements were to be eliminated: a total of some hundreds of thousands of people—the potential leaders and followers of a revolution.[121]

It might well be asked what would be beyond the powers of a man who thought along lines of such absolutely unparalleled brutality. The answer is: the eating of meat, for instance, and hunting. This is also an indication of the extraordinary nature of a *Weltanschauung* which arose from the postulate that the ideology of the enemy is to be opposed by an ideology of a different kind.

What was the *objective* of this global struggle which was unleashed by a man who wished to make "the exclusive recognition of the rights of [his] own nation"[122] the supreme educational principle? Insofar as the objective coincides with the goal, it has already been named. But it is typical of this objective that it cannot be separated from that which one is instinctively inclined to call the means. The new Reich, so Hitler says in *Hitler's Table Talk*, will be the strongest ethnic community in the world; nothing will be able to impair its crystalline hardness. The affection of every member of this natural community will be restricted to the other members.[123] This Reich will absorb all good blood from everywhere and thus become impregnable. No longer will the far too mobile intellect of the former upper class take the lead: the elite, trained in strict discipline to unquestioning bravery, will guarantee the inviolate inner stability of the Reich. No longer will a decadent "nation of poets and thinkers" be extolled by the rest of the world with interested indulgence: its very own delegate, its party, will bare its teeth to the world as the "most voracious beast of prey the world has ever seen."[124] Courage is more important than the wisdom of understanding, and it alone can restore "order" to a disintegrated people—that "living, enduring, essential thing," the content of the state—"Then the armed state will arise which I see in my dreams. An 'armed state' not only because every man will bear arms from youth to old age, but because he is also armed spiritually and prepared, when necessary, to use his weapon."[125] There will be no more cracks, no more gulfs, dividing the "flesh and blood substance," and the people as a whole will become strong and healthy at last, comparable to that individual "who is outwardly and inwardly completely in harmony, who is rooted in his soil"—the peasant.[126]

Indeed, nothing could be further from the truth than to regard National Socialism as a doctrine of world salvation in the sense that all men were to be freed from want, danger, or debt for their own sake. The world was to be cured *of* the Jewish-Christian-Marxist doctrine of world redemption and converted *to* that absolute sovereignty which was to bind the slaves forever to their slave fate. National Socialism can only be understood as the expression of a particularity which sees itself threatened as such, and hence, by casting off its *historical* individuality, emphasizes the natural primitive traits of its existence and endeavors to preserve them forever.

Nature and Antinature

Once again, before proceeding to the final definition it is as well to pause for a moment. Attention should first be turned to those instances in which Hitler's thinking attains a level of marked generality, such as where he speaks of "nature."

The main features of his doctrine are well known: life is a struggle in which the stronger prevails and thus does nature's bidding, for nature has given life to her creatures for the purpose of eternal struggle to ensure a rising evolution rather than a general putrefaction.

These are banalities; the point is to discover what meaningful conceptions might be hidden in them. It must therefore be asked: *Who* is struggling, *what* kind of a struggle is it, *why* must it be emphasized?

First of all, what Hitler quite obviously always has in mind is a struggle of human beings against other human beings. Every example he cites from nature has but one purpose: to illustrate the essence of this struggle. The exemplification, however, is highly revealing. Every animal mates with one of its own kind, he says at the beginning of the chapter on "People and Race" in *Mein Kampf*. Titmouse pairs off with titmouse, finch with finch, stork with stork; the species are strictly separated, and there is no such thing as a fox with humane impulses toward geese, or a cat with friendly feelings toward mice.[127] Hitler's intention is obvious: he equates (human) race with (animal) species, thus attempting on the one hand to create unbridgeable gulfs between people, and on the other to force the individual human being inextricably into his race, which thereby becomes the supreme and sole motivation for his actions. Hitler is very fond of comparing human beings with animals or objects. A German is under no compulsion to let himself be devoured by Jews, just as a tiger cannot help eating people.[128] Apes trample individualists in their herds to death for being antisocial—the same rule should apply to human beings.[129] "Tough as leather, swift as a greyhound, hard as Krupp steel"—that is what the man of the coming Reich will be like.[130] This leads to apparently quite serious theses of sectarian fanaticism; comparison with the life phases of dogs shows that man eats the wrong kind of food, his normal life span should be a hundred and forty to a hundred and eighty years;[131] or: apes are vegetarians and point to the right way for mankind.[132] Hence the subjects of the struggle are closely knit races or racial power-structures (nations). This is what Hitler meant when he said: "God created peoples but not classes."[133]

The distinguishing mark of this struggle is war. Hitler obviously meant this when he said: "One creature drinks the blood of another. The death of one nourishes the other. One should not drivel about humane feelings. ... The struggle goes on."[134] Its result will decide who shall be master and who shall be slave. For Hitler, no other sociological categories existed. That is why for him there are "only conquerors and serfs,"[135] that is why a people of fifteen million cannot hope to be anything but the "slaves ... of others."[136]

Hitler usually defined his purpose as the preservation of the species, frequently also as the selective breeding and improvement of mankind. Emphasis is entirely on the first definition; where it is not a case of a pseudoliberal residue, the second must be understood as proceeding from the first.[137]

This is Hitler's world of eternal struggle in which all who live must fight; war to decide hegemony or slavery between the races as the ultimate and supreme eternal fact of life. And this is the heart of his religious message, to which he wanted to devote all his time after the victory:[138] "Unconditional submission to the divine law of existence,"[139] devout regard for the "fundamental necessity of the rule of nature."[140]

But why preach what is self-evident? Does "nature" perhaps have an enemy, that one must go to her defense? Indeed! There is for Hitler also something which "detaches [mankind] from the instinct of nature."[141] Sometimes he calls it semieducation, sometimes materialist science; cause and agent in his eyes is always the Jew. Man might think that he can "correct nature," that he is something more than a bacillus on the planet.[142] "Pathological ideas of cowardly know-alls and critics of nature"[143] can cause man to regard himself as the "lord of creation," that is, exempt from its fundamental laws.[144] Then a people can lose its sound instinct that it must acquire land by force of arms.[145] Then the Jew can open the "breach" within the people itself and invent a social problem to disrupt the people's unity. Then the intellectuals come to the fore with their uncertain instincts and their vacillation. Then the Jewish-Christian work of antinature is complete. Then the nation stands on the brink of annihilation. For it seems there is an innate peril in man himself, a root of disease, a sword of antinature: "Man alone, of all living creatures, attempts to transgress the laws of nature."[146]

The Führer and the movement snatch the race back from the brink, and force it once more onto nature's path. As the vanguard of the "cruel queen of all wisdom,"[147] at the eleventh hour they take up the battle against antinature, whose tool is the Jewish people, for "the German people is the typical land-rooted people, the Jewish is the typical landless people."[148] Primordial principles themselves confront each other here; the only alternative is victory or extinction—and this decides the fate of the world.

No further quotations are needed to make it clear what is meant by saying that the power of "antinature" fills Hitler with dread: it is this "going beyond" in human nature which is capable of transforming the essence of human order and relations—transcendence. What Hitler—and not only Hitler—feels to be threatened are certain basic structures of social existence. He too—like

Maurras—is afraid *of* man *for* man. But he did not only think, he acted. And in his actions he carried his principle to its final and utmost logical conclusion and at the same time to its irrevocable end. Hence it is possible to define Hitler's radical fascism, which called itself "National Socialism," as follows: NATIONAL SOCIALISM WAS THE DEATH THROES OF THE SOVEREIGN, MARTIAL, IN-WARDLY ANTAGONISTIC GROUP. IT WAS THE PRACTICAL AND VIOLENT RESISTANCE TO TRANSCENDENCE.

The parallelism of Hitler's and Maurras' thinking is remarkable, even—and especially—in those points where Hitler crudely simplifies Maurras' subtlety or clearly exposes his contradictions. The light each throws on the other substantiates whatever appears to be speculative in this definition. That Maurras' whole thought represents a resistance to transcendence and uncondi-tional defense of the autarkic-sovereign, martial, aristocratic state of the *ancien régime* as a paradigm for France for all time, can hardly be doubted. It has been shown that Maurras was not really a man of the *ancien régime*, and that it was perhaps only from his perspective that he could so clearly emphasize those traits. Nevertheless, he was infinitely closer to his paradigmatic epoch than Hitler was to his and had a far more concrete conception of it. Hitler thought in peasant-soldier categories—yet between him and the peasant-soldier nature[150] there yawned an unbridgeable gulf. He mythicized the fear of bolshevism of the ruling classes—yet he felt nothing but hatred and contempt for those classes. He correctly perceived the relationship between science and "antinature"—yet again and again he displayed the crassest features of a scientific and enlightened age.[151] He was so far removed spiritually from all the phenomena he cham-pioned that it has frequently and justifiably been suspected that he was driven by nothing but the pure will to power.[152] One has only to look at the changeless basic traits of his thoughts and emotions to see the error of this view; but this much of it remains correct: that it was precisely his curious and uncanny detachment that enabled Hitler to uncover the naked basic structures of each phenomenon.

Sovereign is any group which in practice lives independently of others. Through the ages, lack of communication alone has permitted innumerable groups to exist in a state of only nominally restricted sovereignty and quite a few in a state of actually unrestricted sovereignty.

Martial is what every such group must be that is subject to threat from outside. The variety of circumstances produces numerous levels in history ranging from an out-and-out warrior-state to a peaceful insular existence. But the second possibility is an imperfect manifestation of the first and unfailingly attributable to especially favorable conditions.

Inwardly antagonistic is any group which in circumstances of essential shortages is stratified according to occupation or class, with the result that certain members of society are excluded from full participation in the material and spiritual benefits of the community, either in principle or in fact. Apart from the hypothetical communist primordial society, this was more or less the case with all hitherto existing groups, while here too the more radical manifestation of a strictly hierarchically organized society has claim to priority.

The first two characteristics proceed logically from the concept of the particular society. The third can be derived from the concept of differentiation and can in any case be demonstrated everywhere in the field of historical experience.

Sovereignty, endorsement of active war, and internal antagonism may therefore be considered basic characteristics of *all* hitherto existing human societies. However, it is an insight of the most crucial importance that people *never* derived their self-image exclusively or even principally from this reality of their existence, at least since the emergence of the great redemptive religions.

No matter how independent a Christian state may have been, it always ascribed ultimate sovereignty to God alone. No matter how belligerent a Moslem warrior may have been, he always related his deeds to a transcendental realm of peace. Although in Buddhist states social differences may have been crasser than elsewhere, the servants of the prevailing religion relegated them by example and doctrine to a transitory level.

In all great societies throughout history, a universal doctrine and a particular reality have always lived in a precarious symbiosis. From a certain level of consciousness on, nothing could be more convincing than to call this symbiosis a lie, and to declare the doctrine to be an ideological transfiguration of the imperfect and odious reality.

With the growth of bourgeois society and the emergence of the liberal philosophies, a conception arose in Europe which regarded the elimination of the particular reality as well as of the ideological "superstructure" as possible. It sought to replace them with a universal society which would dispense certainly with war and if possible with internal antagonism.

It is now all-important to recognize that National Socialism is not an ideology for the very reason that it aims ruthlessly at opposing the liberal and Marxist doctrine of the realization of the universal nature of man. Hence its *Weltanschauung* consists essentially in accusing all ideologies in the traditional sense of demoralizing tendencies because they introduce a germ of disintegration into the blood-rooted unity of the race and infect the original healthy state with a virus. In its positive sense, therefore, the National Socialist doctrine is not at all that—possibly mendacious—invocation of a superior good, a universal purpose: it is in a very primitive way a mere "legend" which seeks, by alluding to better blood, not so much to legitimize as to establish the rule of the rulers in the eyes of the subjugated.

Consequently, fascism is the first phenomenon after the long epoch of ideological history in which the particular reality seeks itself and only itself (although with varying degrees of clarity in the different manifestations of fascism). Now for the first time its fundamental structures attain a definite self-awareness. But they only become aware of that which is no longer self-evident. Where the real desires itself for its own sake, it is about to elude itself and thus plunges into its *death throes*.

Moreover, it is not only a deduction of this kind but the reality of history since 1945 which justifies the term "death throes." Hitler's death did not in any sense mean that the world had seen the last of sovereignty and the claim to it; but even the two great powers of our day do not seek it as such and for all time. The thesis that the war of aggression of one of the powers would entail its own destruction is equivalent to the realization that unconditional particular sovereignty is today neither possible nor desirable.

This is certainly not to imply that war has ceased to be an ever-present threat. But now no one dares extol it for its own sake: not because man is better, but because war has become more potent, too potent for man. There are still soldiers, and they are indispensable, but for the first time in history it is not permissible for them to desire the active execution of their occupation.

Nor does it mean that societies have ceased to be differentiated and stratified. But nowhere does a ruling class derive its self-image from its opposition to the ruled; nowhere, except in insignificant pockets, is hegemony still a manifest matter of principle. Life has become too complex, the distribution of labor too universal, for the simple pattern of master and slave to lay any claim to validity. It is not the proofs of philosophers or the speeches of moralists that have brought about this world change; the power of the hitherto sovereign groups is too great, the violence of war too powerful, social distinctions too comprehensive, for sovereignty, war, and hegemony to continue to exist, although it may be assumed that it will be less a matter of simple elimination than of a change in the forms of these principles. There is no world power left today that could offer fundamental resistance to these changes.

This fundamental resistance was the very essence of fascist doctrines and powers. And this explains the sense in which one can speak of Hitler's epochal significance.

He seized upon the war, which in 1914 broke almost accidentally over a virtually pacifist world, with a passion and affirmation which were to have momentous consequences. It was no mere chance that he was the one to demarcate and thus to a certain extent create the *era of world wars*, for without him World War II would not have broken out, or at least not at that particular moment; without him the Soviet Union and the United States would in all likelihood have remained outside European history for decades to come. In this context, the era of world wars implies that period in which the means of warfare and communications were powerful enough to involve the whole earth in the struggle, but still weak enough to be accepted by a large number, particularly of leading men, and to be applied as a means of politics. Hitler can rightly be regarded as the central figure of this and *only* this era, while Lenin and Wilson transcend it in their significance.[153]

At the same time it becomes apparent to what degree he has to share this prestige with others. He would have been a nationalist only, had the supra-national social motive—the struggle against Marxism—not been a powerful and even decisive element in his actions. But this element had been developed by Mussolini in a manner far more significant because it was more authentic and less mythicizing. And Mussolini in turn certainly did not lack an analogous and perhaps even more interesting relationship to war. If fascism is regarded as a phenomenon belonging *only* to the era of the world wars, it is merely the accident of inferior means of power and a consequent lesser effectiveness that puts Mussolini in second place behind Hitler.

However, only of Hitler can it be said that he ended a far greater era because he brought its real fundamentals one by one to light and totally rejected its "ideological" nature. In this sense Hitler was a radical fascist and left Mussolini far behind.

Nevertheless, the earliest fascistoid thought trends emanated not from anxiety over war or the class structure of society, but from fear for the existing "culture." And obviously everything that had been called culture was produced by sovereign, martial, and self-antagonistic societies. It was a highly sympto-matic event when one of the fathers of European socialism, Pierre Joseph Proudhon, acknowledged the cardinal and positive significance of war through-out history without insisting on its necessity for the future.[154] Nietzsche's entire thinking is to be explained by this premise. His fundamental insight and anxiety was that "culture," as it had been created through the ages by privileged leisured classes, would no longer be able to exist in the basic change in the structure of society planned by liberals and socialists. He did not know yet that it can also have no abode in a fascist society, because its second and more vital root has been removed. Maurras' thinking is determined primarily by this anxiety for "culture," and this is why one can apply the term "early fascism" to his party.

This anxiety is present as an element in Hitler as well. He was no doubt sincere when he said that he was waging the war for the sake of a higher purpose—culture.[155] But in comparison with Maurras one realizes how little weight and intrinsic value this element contains in Hitler's case, and the parallel with Mussolini has in turn shown that the development of the social motive was much less genuine with Hitler than with the Italian. It needs the combination of Maurras, Mussolini, and Hitler to show the complete, layered structure of the phenomenon; although the structure as a whole is present in each of them individually, it is not complete.

If this interpretation is correct, it should wipe out the impression that Hitler was a rather incomprehensible accident in the history of Germany and Europe. It becomes clear that he was possessed by "something," and that this "some-thing" was in no sense casual or trivial. He no longer appears as an epochal figure but as the termination of an age.

The last thing this is meant to imply is that Hitler was a hero. Instead, it accords to the millions of his victims the highest of all honors: it implies that those who were exterminated as bacilli did not die as the unfortunate objects of a repulsive crime but as deputies in the most desperate assault ever made upon the human being and the transcendence within him.

PART FIVE

Fascism as a Metapolitical Phenomenon

The Concept of Transcendence

Fascism has been defined on three levels. On the first level it was examined as an internal political phenomenon and described as "anti-Marxism" seeking to destroy the enemy by the development of a radically opposed yet related ideology and the application of nearly identical, although typically transformed methods; always, however, within the unyielding framework of national self-assertation and autonomy. This definition is valid for all forms of fascism.[1]

The second definition, which describes fascism as the "life-and-death struggle of the sovereign, martial, inwardly antagonistic group," no longer looks at it as a manifestation within politics, but sees in it the natural foundation of politics itself brought to light and to self-consciousness. This definition could only be unequivocally demonstrated by the radical-fascist form and could be adequately illustrated within the context of this derivation.

On the third level—the least accessible and the most fundamental—fascism was termed "resistance to transcendence." This definition could be derived from fascism's oldest as well as its most recent forms: it describes fascism as a metapolitical phenomenon. It can be neither illustrated by historical details nor demonstrated by simple considerations. It requires a new departure in thought if it is not to remain a mere suggestion in the semiobscurity of approximate insight.

The historical section of this analysis was completed with the definition of fascism on internal and external political levels; the third level has hardly been touched, let alone demarcated. To grasp the phenomenon in its entirety, a final step must be taken and the nature of fascism explored in purely philosophical terms, even if only in outline and despite the danger that the object may seem to disappear for a time and that the striving for abstraction may mean sacrificing the support of demonstrable evidence. Nevertheless, this abstraction is no airy speculation. It is the means of probing to the hidden foundations of the structure. For in these foundations are situated all the complexity, all the tensions, of the edifice. It is not a featureless, uniform basis: on the contrary, it has its own characteristic measurements and proportions, and it is these which this method of abstraction seeks to uncover.

It becomes clear that this third approach is not simply an appendage which could just as well be left out when it is realized that the three definitions are something more than unconnected links in a random pile of associations. From certain aspects the first definition already contains the second, and a concept as central as that of ideology in turn requires the context of the second definition in order to achieve final clarification. The second definition for its part is irresistibly propelled toward the third, since politics itself is not a political fact and can only be manifested as such when set off against a foil whose nature differs from its own.

However, we are not setting foot on this third level for the first time. It was disclosed long ago as an element of the phenomenon itself. The most central of Maurras' ideas have been seen to penetrate to this level. By "monotheism" and "antinature" he did not imply a political process: he related these terms to the tradition of Western philosophy and religion, and left no doubt that for him they were adjuncts not only of Rousseau's notion of liberty but also of the Christian Gospels and Parmenides' concept of being.[2] It is equally obvious that he regarded the unity of world economics, technology, science, and emancipation merely as another and more recent form of this "antinature." It was not difficult to find a place for Hitler's ideas as a cruder and more recent expression of this schema. Maurras' and Hitler's real enemy was seen to be "freedom toward the infinite" which, intrinsic in the individual and a reality in evolution, threatens to destroy the familiar and the beloved. From all this it begins to be apparent what is meant by "transcendence."

Finally, there is little reason to doubt the legitimacy, indeed the inevitability, of the question. All historical probing must ultimately encounter something elemental and primordial; sometimes this is called "man," sometimes "history," occasionally "God," even at a time when man is exploring himself in greater perplexity than ever before. Since Hegel's death, philosophy and history have been going separate ways. But since this separation has left behind an unstanchable wound, the so-called peripheral questions are often discussed in works which, instead of being oriented by either strict philosophical exposition or thorough historical research, deal freely with "man" and "the image of man," with "nihilism" and "the decay of culture."

The term "transcendence" has been chosen here to demonstrate the scientific intention behind the relating of philosophical and historical thematic material. Moreover, it seems more appropriate than any other to denote that uniform and yet intrinsically differing fundamental process of which such terms as "faith" or "emancipation" merely reveal certain aspects.

It is true, of course, that no philosophical agreement exists as to the interpretation of this term. "Transcendence" is sometimes used to denote "God" or "ultimate reality," and is thus placed in opposition to man even when it embraces him along with everything else and is to that extent not merely an object; the opposite of this transcendence is immanence, the sphere of the within-worldly and the nondivine—a sphere to which man is in thrall as long as he is unable to raise himself to transcendence by thought, prayer, or faith.

But it is from this theological interpretation of transcendence that we can derive that neutral structural concept which is to be the foundation of what follows. For if in the welter of questions and answers a common element exists on which all thinkers from Parmenides to Hegel agree, it is the distinction between those things which are partial and dependent on time and place and the "One" ("existence," "nature," "God"), which contains none of the negative characteristics of finite being and which therefore alone completely fulfills the absolute meaning of existence: in other words, the distinction between a *finite* and an *eternal* existence. It is on this distinction that the whole emphasis rests. But there is an analogous distinction in man who with his highest capacity— that of thought—can reach out to eternal existence, although as a being among beings he is shackled to his finite environment. For thought alone can form the concept of the whole as distinct from all that exists and all that is individual.[3]

It can be debated whether this "whole" is matter or spirit, cosmos or chaos, God or Devil; it is not inconceivable that, on its course toward the whole, thought must needs go astray: these are all metaphysical problems, and the contrasting of transcendence with immanence constitutes a metaphysical concept. But indisputable and basic to all truth is the fact of differentiation itself, and this structure of existence may more properly be called transcendence.[4] Regardless of the results achieved by the philosophical process, its very existence proves the truth of its thesis, that man belongs as much to an unspecified whole as to his familiar environment, and that he is therefore not a complete unit but, from one aspect, more than himself. For by what yardstick is the disengagement which the philosophical process entails to be measured and possibly proved nonexistent? A line of thought which takes transcendence as follows: transcendence, looking back on what has been and forward to clearly characterized by transcendence). Its central idea can be formulated as follows: Transcendence, looking back on what has been and forward to what is coming, reaches out toward the whole.[5]

It might be called "human nature" if the adjective "human" did not give the misleading impression that transcendence was the property of man. It would be more accurate to call man a "transcendental creature" and the property of transcendence.

But what has this most general of definitions to do with political thinking, let alone with the practical politics of the most recent past? How can man exert "resistance to transcendence" if he himself is a transcendental creature? Is there such a thing as man's resistance to himself?

The question is easily answered if we realize what the philosophical process implies and what are the elements in it which account for its unmistakable form.

Philosophy implies a unique and immense alienation, or disengagement, from the "world" (as the embodiment of all existing and familiar things), although it is obviously not the originator of this process but merely its most radical manifestation. For even mythology, romanticized today as the well-being of inviolable intimacy with the world, was presumably, during the earlier magical and fetishistic age, a stage of that alienation process. However, this process must not necessarily and always be regarded as release and distinguishing mark—from a particular moment onward it can also be felt as burden, torture, and curse.

Only a creature that with the aid of the philosophical process manages to reach out beyond that which exists can perceive something "better" and hence exert a critique on that which is. The common historical origin of philosophy and criticism is well known. But it is equally true that the only creature which can love existing things is one which can encounter them as such. Criticism and love meet head-on, and both are rooted in transcendence. They are not elements of equal validity, and criticism is more powerful than love. However, their contest knows no end and is the primordial pain.

This contest finds its most particular expression in the rivalry between revolution and conservation. Only a transcendental creature can be revolutionary, but only for such a creature is conservation essential to existence. Revolutionary in this sense does not imply an arbitrary uprising; we must also discard the widest interpretation, in which the philosophical process per se may be called a revolution. Revolution can only be termed a political and at the same time transcendental phenomenon when it emanates from the experience of a process which is not solely political and yet not exclusively intellectual, and when it sets itself goals going beyond a mere change in the political firmament. In this sense a revolution is only conceivable when in the sphere of practical politics transcendence becomes perceptible. This is the case as soon as philosophy and religion are no longer taken for granted as offering the sole possibilities of relating to the whole. Essential to this concept of revolution is practical transcendence.

The concept of practical transcendence is not justifiable in terms of the metaphysical contrast between transcendence and immanence. For even if man extends the scope of his power over the entire globe and reaches deep into outer space, even if the fate of every individual is determined more and more by the sum total of social conditions instead of by natural conditions: man still remains rooted in immanence and becomes ever more desperately enmeshed in it.

Here we may hark back to Kant. The outcome of his critique of reason is this: that not even the mind can manage to grasp the whole and find peace in it, but that this whole, the "world," must be understood only as a directional point co-ordinating and animating the movement of scientific research. For Kant it is not the "subreptions" of theoretical reason in which the transcendence of man is truly realized, but rather the moral actions through which—as seen from the most general law of reason—self-determination evinces a practical ability transcending all nature. If we bear in mind that for Kant even moral action in "pathologically affected" man can never be an indisputable possession, but rather a mere direction of the will, and further that it is a matter not merely of personal and private morality but of demands being made which rebel against existing immoral reality,[6] then it becomes evident that for Kant theoretical and practical transcendence are homologous basic processes constituting not a departure from the sphere of immanence but the penetration and shaping of this sphere.

However, the point of orientation of these processes lies beyond any "immanence." Maurras knew what he was about when he countered Kant's single duty with "duties." And it is no accident that the phenomenon of bourgeois society achieves philosophical dignity for the first time with Kant. True, he makes bourgeois society's "concept of law" the premise for the concept of "eternal peace," and it cannot be said that his thinking establishes the link between philosophy and "economics" which was so totally foreign to antiquity[7] and which is the hallmark of a universal theory of bourgeois society: this link makes its first appearance with Marx. But the fact that bourgeois society is that form of society in which practical transcendence first becomes perceptible is already demonstrated by Kant, and it is even possible to find the claim of its most radical protagonists anticipated—namely, that on its higher levels practical transcendence will take the place of theoretical transcendence. In any case, Kant laid the foundations for that line of thought which binds theoretical and practical transcendence together as one uniform occurrence: dialectic as doctrine of "realization," of the self-dissipating yet self-enriching inflow of transcendence into reality.[8]

In summing up the following definitions may be given:

Theoretical transcendence may be taken to mean the reaching out of the mind beyond what exists and what can exist toward an absolute whole; in a broader sense this may be applied to all that goes beyond, that releases man from the confines of the everyday world and which, as an "awareness of the horizon," makes it possible for him to experience the world as a whole.

Practical transcendence can be taken to mean the social process, even its early stages, which continually widens human relationships, thereby rendering them in general more subtle and more abstract—the process which disengages the individual from traditional ties and increases the power of the group until it finally assails even the primordial forces of nature and history. However, since it is only possible to experience it as transcendence when it reaches its universal stage, the concept is usually limited to this stage. As a synonym the term "abstraction of life" can be used, as against "abstraction of thought" for theoretical transcendence.

A phenomenon will be called transcendental in which transcendence achieves dominant form, or which adopts a specific relationship to it. But (with an ambivalence already present in Kant) a method of observation will also be called transcendental when it seeks to uncover the transcendental nature of an object which in the case of a political phenomenon may be called "metapolitical."

The discussion seems to have moved a long way from fascism into the undemonstrable realm of philosophical terminology. But the point of furthest removal also represents the turning toward evidence of a connection. For the attempt at a transcendental definition of fascism will not rest on solid ground until its relationship to an existing thought process has been established. Fascism per se has never been subjected to a continuous transcendental approach. Hence the concepts evolved in the foregoing serve also to illuminate the work of three great thinkers and to crystallize their mutual relationships by offering the proposition that their work constitutes a transcendental definition of bourgeois society. Since there can be no doubt as to a connection between fascism and bourgeois society, we may expect to find a vital portion of the way at least opened up. These three writers are Marx, Nietzsche, and Max Weber.

Marx: Philosophical Discovery and Critique of Bourgeois Society

If ever there was a junction in the history of ideas, it was the point at which Marx stood. After the new philosophical departures of Kant, Fichte, and Hegel, and the evolution of the classic concept of political economy by Smith, Malthus, and Ricardo which was relevant at best to popular philosophy, the time was ripe for the discovery of the total process of practical transcendence taking place in bourgeois society. In one single vast schema (which, however, for methodological reasons may be split up into its components), Marx discovers the revolution of bourgeois society, criticizes it from the standpoint of the individual human being and his universal nature, and postulates a second revolution which will eliminate the destructive schism.

1. Never has any work of political economy extolled bourgeois society and its leading class to such an extent as the *Communist Manifesto*. It sweeps away all the scruples and inhibitions which prevented Kant and Hegel from proclaiming bourgeois society as the dominant reality of the age.

The bourgeoisie was the first to prove what human activity is capable of: its achievements outshine the Pyramids of Egypt and the Gothic cathedrals. It constantly revolutionizes tools of production and thus all social conditions. It agglomerates the population, centralizes means of production, and concentrates property. It thereby draws all nations, even the most barbaric, into civilization:

"The old local and national self-sufficiency and seclusion is being replaced by communication in every direction, by an all-round interdependence of nations."[9] Thus a world market is established and a world literature made possible. At the same time, all that is "indigenous" is being increasingly dissolved; if the workers have "no fatherland"[10] this means that, like the upper bourgeoisie, they will be dependent no longer on the next-to-last form of historical development, but solely on the most recent and all-embracing form of this development.

By dissolving all indigenous and "narrow-minded" relationships and achieving a genuine unification of mankind, bourgeois society is merely acting in accordance with the law of human nature. For in his early works Marx never tires of stressing that man is a universally producing and hence free creature that relates to himself and simultaneously annexes all of nature as an inorganic part of his body. Nature as a whole becomes his creation in that he "re-creates himself not only intellectually and consciously but also actually and actively, and hence sees himself in a world which he has created."[11] And this is just what the bourgeoisie does: "It creates a world after its own image."[12]

The way has now become open for the discovery and definition of that of which philosophy has never so much as been aware: "We see now the history of industry, and what has become the objective existence of industry is the open book of natural human forces, the physically present human psychology, which until now was never regarded in its relation to the *nature* of man but always only in an external utilitarian relationship, because we could only grasp—operating within the state of alienation—the general existence of man, religion, or history in their abstract and universal aspect, in the form of politics, art, literature, and so forth, as the reality of human natural forces and as human generic acts."[13]

First of all, then, Marx's work signifies the philosophical discovery of the economic and industrial universality of bourgeois society and hence the development of a more general concept of practical transcendence in its homology with theoretical transcendence, the only hitherto known form.

2. In Marx's earliest period the premise of his critique of bourgeois society is that bourgeois society is incapable of providing the individual with a congruent universality. He adopts Hegel's concept that the state is the sphere of universal reason whereas bourgeois society is the realm of *bellum omnium contra omnes*, in which "man behaves as a private individual, regards others as means, debases himself to being a means, and is at the mercy of foreign forces."[14] But while Hegel perceives in this difference the reasonably and organically articulated concept, for Marx it is always the mark of untruth and unreason. For man is a universal creature: he is only truly a man when participation in the whole is the stamp of his individuality. As long as he can only fulfill this nature of his within the state, his existence is "abstract." He lives as a "common creature" in the "heaven" of the political world, while in the earthly existence of society he is a

self-seeking, narrow-minded atom. The materialism of bourgeois society stands in sharp contrast to the nonmaterialism of the state.

Marx's problem during this early period may be summarized as follows: How can the now divided individual return, on the new level of practical universality created by bourgeois society, to that harmony with his world which existed in ancient and medieval times? For the Marx of that time the key is the realization of philosophy. He takes a momentous step by discovering in the proletariat a class of human beings which is the special product of bourgeois society while yet no longer part of that society because, due to its universal suffering, it possesses a universal character also in the subjective sense: "Philosophy cannot be realized without the elimination of the proletariat, the proletariat cannot be eliminated without the realization of philosophy."[15] But Marx only hit on the proletariat because he was looking for it. Marxism does not spring from the contemplation of reality or a sense of outrage: it is a philosophical construct seeking to fuse the newly discovered sphere of the universal but unaware bourgeois society with the reality of the individual and the philosophical concept of man as a universal being.

What bourgeois society does to the individual emerges in a new light during Marx's second period, exemplified by his first sojourn in Paris, his study of political economy, and the composing of *Die ökonomisch-philosophischen Manuskripte*. Now the concept of "alienation" moves into the spotlight; not only does bourgeois society fail to elevate the individual to genuine universality: it also deprives and "denatures" him.

This is the situation of the worker in such a society: "The more the worker exhausts himself, the more powerful becomes the alien objective world which he creates, the poorer he and his inner world become, the less belongs to him. ... Hence the greater the activity, the more objectless the worker."[16] True, he receives the subsistence he requires to maintain physical existence; but this is just where the worst of all perversions lies, for he is a man, that is to say, a living being, capable of producing universally. If all his efforts are directed toward maintaining bodily existence, he turns his essence into a mere means of existence: hence he must do to himself with his own hands what Kant had forbidden man to do to his fellow man. However, what Marx sees is not the injuries men do to each other but the inhumanity of a system in which "the devaluation of the human world" increases in direct proportion "to the exploitation of the material world."[17] Bourgeois society is the living contradiction. It creates a world of commodities, but only because the creators in this world have become commodities themselves; it makes leisure possible, but only because all leisure is withheld from its lower stratum; it is universal, but only because the majority of its members have been deprived of human universality.

The more the concept of "division of labor" becomes central for Marx—*The German Ideology* marks this stage in his progress—the more strongly does a third indictment of bourgeois society emerge: it disfranchises the individual.

This accusation, of course, reaches back far beyond bourgeois society: division of labor has been a primary factor throughout history, and indeed he puts all history on trial. For prior to all known history there existed the condition in which man's relationship to things was "in order." In that state the only thing which belonged to an individual was what he had produced himself. Here the product of labor remained unmistakably something which had its appointed subordinate place in man's life process. This relationship could be called the closed production cycle. In it the subject dominated the object, the producer the product, in keeping with his true nature. But this production cycle is isolated and hence "narrow." Not until man alienates himself from his product and hands it over to someone else does he emerge from his isolation. But the forfeiting of barriers means the forfeiting of possessions. It means that the conditions in which man lives become opaque. It means a limitation to activity, and human dependence on material relationships. What had been the subject is now the object. The production cycle of a collective has no subject which is its equal or its superior. The rulers consume, the ruled produce: both are dehumanized, made subservient to the product and its laws. As the universal production cycle, bourgeois society is the clearest manifestation of this cleavage. *All* individuals stand powerless and helpless in the face of the uncontrolled and senseless movement of the world of commodities. But this disfranchisement began in the earliest historical times. Consequently he says in *The German Ideology*: "For as soon as work begins to be divided, each person has one particular circle of activity imposed upon him from which he cannot escape. ... This immobilizing of social activity, this consolidation of our own product into an impartial force over us, which grows away from our control, cuts across our expectations, nullifies our calculations, is one of the chief elements in all historical development to date."[18]

There is no denying the radical-reactionary trait in Marx's critique of bourgeois society.[19] It emerges very soon in Marx's high estimation of ancient and medieval times (in which the life of people and state were identical, albeit restricted), it appears again in Engels' latter-day predilection for the prehistoric tribal constitution.[20] But it is the philosophical concept of subjectivity which seems to substantiate this feeling, and it is the Hegelian concept of dialectic which reconciles this feeling with history.

It is a mistake to believe that with *Das Kapital* Marx's critique of bourgeois society changed its character and became scientific rather than philosophical. True, terms such as "generic nature" and "true reality" give way to highly specialized analyses of profit rates and land rents, accumulation and crisis. It is also true that many critical descriptions go no further than what had already been observed by other socialist writers and some time later was to become the commonplace of every critique of culture: that the manufacturing system imposes a crippling abnormality on the worker by a hothouse forcing of specialized skills and by turning him into the automatic mechanism for producing a single part.[21] But despite its scientific garb, the underlying philosophical conception keeps cropping up.

For what is "capital" but the alienated reality of human universality which has become master of its own origin? Capital would not exist if "surplus value" were not continually draining into it: surplus labor, contributed by the worker, in excess of his own value as a commodity and without pay. His ability to create in excess of the mere value of his productive power (the production and reproduction costs of his physical existence) is what stamps him as a human being. "Surplus value" is not primarily an economic category: it is the worker's objectivized "surplus existence," that is, "human existence." Only because generations of workers have had to renounce the realization, within and for their own lives, of their creative power that exceeds mere physical existence, are their grandsons faced with the alien and opaque world of means of production, a world to which they are admitted only on certain conditions and for limited periods. Only because the unlived lives of countless human beings are absorbed by capital has *it* now become the real life on which all existing things depend. It only *appears* to bring profit and pleasure to its owners, the capitalists, who can in fact only survive in a pitiless struggle against each other if they become mere exponents of the productive forces. What counts now everywhere is not the human being but an inhuman being which, although dead, "comes to life like a vampire by sucking in living labor,"[22] and which is actually an object although it is the dominant subject of the age.

When this perversion becomes the absurd mumbo jumbo of the "paper world" of the credit system, it has its origin in the "fetishism" of the simplest commodity which causes human beings to view "the social characteristics of their own labor as the objective characteristics of the products of labor themselves."[23] Hence for human beings today "their own social action takes the form of the action of objects, which rule the producers instead of being ruled by them."[24] It is doubtlessly true that today man is living for the first time in one world; but this world is perverted in its roots because man is divided and alienated from himself and the world has become something of which he is deprived rather than, as it should be, something of which he is possessed.

How can we doubt that the powerful breath of this critique is philosophical and not scientific? It is of incalculable significance that the philosophical discoverer of bourgeois society was at the same time its most passionate critic. But the sole *telos* of this critique is the individual, whom Marx regards, in contrast to Hegel, as a reality; in contrast to Adam Smith, as universal; and in contrast to Kant, as self-alienated in history.

3. What, then, would a society have to be like in which the real human being per se was universal and at the same time had regained the primordial obviousness of his relationship with his products?

He would have to live in a universal society and no longer be subjected to division of labor. He would have to feel the sum total of social production to be his own work in which he joyfully participated in various capacities and which in any case he could see in its entirety. He should not require either the compulsions, consolations, or illusions of the old society.

In fact Marx's critique of bourgeois society suddenly becomes the blueprint of the no-longer-bourgeois, the classless, society, a blueprint which had implicitly always underlain his critique. In the various periods of his life he gave it various formulations in which the inherent unity of the idea keeps reappearing, not always with equal clarity but always recognizable.

In his earliest period he deals with "human emancipation" and describes it thus: "Only when the real individual human being takes back the abstract citizen in himself and as an individual human being has become a generic creature in his empirical life, his personal work, and his personal relationships, when man recognizes his *forces propres* as social forces and has organized them and hence ceases to separate social force from himself in the form of political force, only then has human emancipation been achieved."[25]

In *Die ökonomisch-philosophischen Manuskripte* he speaks of communism as the "reintegration" of man and defines it as follows: "This communism is as perfect naturalism=humanism, as perfect humanism=naturalism, it is the *genuine* resolving of the struggle between existence and being, between objectivization and confirmation of self, between freedom and necessity, between the individual and the species. It is the answer to the riddle of history, and is aware of itself as this answer."[26]

In its sweeping claim this definition proves the following: if Kant saw the priority of practical transcendence in the interminable striving of a "nonsocial-social" creature of irreducible finiteness, if for Hegel the schema of the dialectic of fulfillment could only be carried to completion in theoretical transcendence, then Marx brings the poles together and comes up with the proposition of an achievable practical transcendence. This is defined in such a way that those extremes which are the universal prerequisites for the very existence of history are conceived of as one. Scholasticism defined the nature of the angel as the union of individual and species; Marx uses theological methods to construct the communist man of the near future.

There is no comparable boldness in *Das Kapital*. There are only sporadic instances of dealing with future education, for example, or "absolute availability for changing labor demands"[27] which the future worker will have to possess. Only once does Marx deal with a concrete problem of future society, and that is the controlling of investments, which in capitalist society is mechanically conducted by market automatism based on the profit principle. The problem is reduced, according to Marx, "simply" to the fact that "society" must calculate in advance how much labor and means of production it can apply to long-range projects without suffering impairment.[28] This would be a superficial answer even if offered by someone who merely suggested that the economy should be controlled by a wise bureaucracy instead of the unconscious market; but coming from a thinker who desires to abolish division of labor, it is positively irresponsible. Who, after all, constitutes the "society" which calculates? How is the calculation carried out? How does the individual participate in it? Is not the projected absence of domination already in its theoretical roots turning into a new domination of man over man?

A discussion of the concept of the classless society would be incomplete without considering its underlying principles and its ultimate significance.

According to the schema of the dialectic, the underlying principle is that the existence of the proletariat is "alienation which hastens toward completion and hence its own elimination."[29] It is the compulsion of his speculative basis that leads Marx to his "theory of progressive pauperization," to that part of his doctrine which was the first to be visibly exploded with the most far-reaching consequences.[30]

The ultimate significance of the classless society lies in the fact that it is called upon to replace theoretical transcendence. For Marx is far from declaring, as was often done during the Enlightenment, that religion and philosophy are a delusion and a fraud perpetrated by priests. The much-quoted words about religion being the opiate of the masses do not in any way stress the poisonous nature of opium. True, religion is merely the "realization in fantasy of human nature," but it is nevertheless man's sole legitimate existence as long as this existence possesses no genuine, that is, earthly, reality: "Poverty in religion is simultaneously the expression of real poverty and the protest against real poverty. Religion is the sigh of the oppressed creature, it is feeling in a heartless world, just as it is the spirit of nonspiritual conditions."[31] It is not of utilitarian world-reformers and clever technicians that Marx inquires as to the nature of man, but of theologians and philosophers. And it is precisely for this reason that the classless society can be *essentially* atheistic, because, instead of combating and supplanting religion, it makes religion's legitimate intention a reality, thereby rendering it superfluous.

With the aid of these concepts, the philosophical content of Marxism can be summarized as follows: from bourgeois society's "abstraction of life" (which is merely unconscious and collective practical transcendence), the individual, who after the proletarian revolution has attained genuine universality, regains his original sovereignty and home in a self-sufficient production cycle, with the result that the various types of theoretical transcendence in which the individual had hitherto to confirm his existence are doomed to extinction.[32]

This philosophical content represents the core of Marxism. Here for the first time the secular problem of the age, man's relationship to his new world, to "industry," is profoundly and passionately explored. That it did not proceed by observation and empiricism goes without saying.

Of course, this is not the whole of Marxism. As is usually the case, the significant concept met with more response even in daily life than the pallid understanding of the workaday world. Its transcending nature formed the historic link with the most recent social phenomenon, the still oppressed but already emerging proletariat, thus enabling it to become Europe's most recent faith. At the same time Marx managed to weld into his doctrine scientific theories which had existed long before him.[33] It was this apparently monolithic unity which engendered that widespread fear and hatred without which fascism could never have arisen, for in its negation fascism took this unity with desperate seriousness, although it was the obvious flaws in this unity that contributed to the triumph of fascism.

Nietzsche: The Prebourgeois Soil of "Culture"

However, it was not so much the structure of this unity as the philosophical core which, long before Maurras and Hitler, made of Nietzsche the most significant and radical adversary of Marxism.

This proposition may come as a surprise, for the younger man never knew the older one other than indirectly,[34] neither does the thematic material of their work seem to display much similarity. From first to last, Nietzsche was concerned with "culture," and for him this was no less than man's communion with himself in philosophy, art, and religion—in short, theoretical transcendence. The discovery of the Dionysian background of tragedy, the defense of genius against the masses, the insistence on the necessity of slavery, serve no other purpose than to explicate the elements of genuine culture: its background, reality, and basis. They are developed along with the indictment of the enemies of culture: science and its logical (Socratic) optimism, mass emancipation and its shallow utilitarian outlook, revolution and its pernicious effects. But although almost all his ideas foreshadow the future (especially his attack on Parmenides and the latter's overwhelming abstraction of thought), on the whole the young Nietzsche discovers the incompatibility of "culture" with "industry," of theoretical with practical transcendence, so naïvely and undialectically that he cannot be regarded as a true opponent of Marx. After all, Marx was anything but a complacent extoller of modern achievements like David Friedrich Strauss, who was torn to shreds by the young Nietzsche in a brilliant and high-spirited attack.

There is little that anticipates the outline of future developments as markedly as the fact that Nietzsche could only arrive at Marx's level after allowing his oldest enemy to reign in his own heart for a time, leaving traces which never quite disappeared. During his so-called period of enlightenment, the son of the pastor and royal tutor[35] caught up with a whole century's history of ideas in one swift and violent development. With a determined gesture he sacrifices religion and art to science, genius to the competent average, antiquity's state of freemen and slaves to modern democracy. The despiser of the modern became the spokesman of a scientifically emancipatory mass culture, which he evidently interpreted as practical transcendence. But as a steady accompaniment to all this, a note of dissension becomes audible, attesting to the continuing influence of his early days. Nietzsche's late philosophy was born the moment this influence finally gained the upper hand, and the short period of enlightenment together with the new perspectives of ecumenical breadth and modern austerity became the basis for the triumphant resurrection of his youthful problems and attempts at solution. However, what had then been rudimentary and sketchy had now become a coherent system of thought which rejected or transformed most of what the young Nietzsche had esteemed and loved. And it is this which places him and even the most subtle concepts of his philosophy in such diametric opposition to Marx that probably no two thinkers have ever stood in such close yet opposite proximity, like mask and face, negative and print.

Nietzsche had now grasped that the abstraction of life dominating European existence and manifesting itself as science, industry, mass democracy, socialism, constitutes a single phenomenon and *as such* is inimical to culture. In its trend toward a closed cycle of production and knowledge, it cuts the ground from under the feet of creative genius, the ground of "reality," in which all "life" is rooted. That which for Hegel was "progress in the consciousness of freedom," for Marx alienation but at the same time realization, becomes for Nietzsche an *Attentat*, a crime, the origin of which goes back to earliest times.

He now develops more firmly the idea that abstraction of life ultimately springs from abstraction of thought, the earliest schema of Western metaphysics, which contrasted "being" with "becoming" and believed it had thereby achieved a standpoint outside reality and hence had arrived at an attitude of judgment toward life. This metaphysical approach has been carried on in Christianity; socialism, which believes itself capable of altering the very essence of reality, is merely its most radical consequence. The nature of European "horizon-consciousness" leads to the autonomy of the universal cycle of knowledge and production which levels all men, absorbs them as parts of itself, and hence destroys culture. This life-negating synthesis of theoretical and practical transcendence Nietzsche calls "morality." In so doing he regains a context which Hegel took for granted but which Marx had in his turn pushed back into the darkness. At the same time, however, he sets himself the task of developing an entirely new form of "horizon-consciousness." For if "everything which has hitherto been known as truth" is recognized as the most harmful and insidious form of lie, as the "ruse for sucking out life itself and making it anemic," if "morality" appears as "vampirism,"[36] then a new truth and a new philosophy are required. Its content is the doctrine of the "eternal recurrence," its reality is the "superman," its soil is created by the "lords of the earth."[37]

But it also requires the unrelenting struggle against destruction and the *Attentat*. And since Nietzsche seeks to interpret life-inimical morality more and more as a deficient and inferior form of life itself, *his* concept of life becomes, contrary to its original meaning, more and more biological. Thus he is forced to offset *décadence* with the completely sound and healthy life: the concept of the "blond beast" is not a freak—it is the logical result of Nietzsche's thought.

It might be said that Nietzsche continually aims his big guns, from every side and every distance, at one single target: Marx's "Theses on Feuerbach"—that the important thing was to change the world. For this does not merely envisage a political revolution or even a superficial dynamism: it postulates a change of "reality," of the essential structure of the world. The possibility of denying and refuting such a change, of detesting and unmasking its champions, is the passionate and compelling need controlling all Nietzsche's thought. Such a change would destroy culture, while to the very end culture remains for him "the most important thing."[38]

The glorification of *this* reality, with all its terrors, wars, exploitation, and affirmation of the here and now, is the meaning of his doctrine of the eternal recurrence. Only when all things, and within them man, eternally recur exactly as they are now, will it cease to be possible to transcend them toward a goal, toward a "beyond"; at last a new metaphysic encounters *this* life with powerful emphasis, in the "great noontide" of life, every apparent, that is, criticizable, world fades away with the "true" world. And that is what will deprive those who are unable to endure this present, real life—the underprivileged and the pariahs—of their worlds of consolation and their supports, of their yearning gaze into an ultimate realm either here or beyond. The beloved name of the god Dionysus rises to Nietzsche's lips once more when he describes the condition "in which man feels himself in every way to be a deified form and justification of nature."[39]

But the price Nietzsche has to pay for his metaphysics of the glorification of life is a high one. It implies the immortalization of the contradiction *in* the world and thus of the possibility of culture. However, since it excludes the contradiction *with* the world, all transcendence in man becomes petrified in the total affirmation of the world as it is, and this doctrine becomes *nolens volens* the exact counterpart of the concept of the perfect classless society: and culture in Nietzsche's original sense is as impossible in one as in the other.

Properly interpreted, the "superman" is not a biological species but the creator in the new culture. "To create" means for Nietzsche primarily to give "meaning" and define values. The superman not only provides peoples and times with their tables and values: he creates "meaning" for the earth as a whole and for all aeons to come. "He who defines values and controls the will of millennia by controlling the most superior natures, is the supreme man."[40]

The most superior natures are the "lords of the earth," the tools of the superman. Hence his rule is superior to any rule hitherto: it is neither common and direct, like that of statesmen in the past, nor indirect and disguised, like that of philosophers in the past. Consequently he can set the supreme goal for his creation; he no longer works in matter or pure spirit: he is able to "shape man himself as an artist."

Such shaping is fulfillment, and yet again merely a precondition of his creating. For the ruthlessness with which he destroys failures permits, after thousands of years of mediocritization, the re-creation of that ancient and terrible soil out of which supreme creation alone can find fulfillment. For Nietzsche this is the meaning of tragedy: "That new party of life which undertakes the greatest of all tasks, the improvement of mankind, including the ruthless destruction of all that is degenerate and parasitical, will make possible again that excess of life on earth from which the Dionysian condition must once more grow. I promise a tragic age: the supreme art in the affirmation of life, tragedy, will be born again. ..."[41]

That is Nietzsche's testament as presented in *Ecce homo*, a few months before his collapse: a gloomy and clairvoyant prophecy which errs only where it loves. Here it becomes quite plain what he means by the superman—he is the man who can even create the soil of life, that soil hitherto provided by nature only: the terrors of existence as the underlying basis of culture.

It is already clear to what extent the concept of destruction[42] must inevitably become the center of Nietzsche's late philosophy. For if history amounts to nothing more than the petty and sterile calculation of the last "squinting" men, who neither obey nor rule and desire to be neither poor nor rich, then the most mighty effort is required to force them back into the state of slavery which is their rightful place. The unmasking of their origin is the first essential.

Consequently, all Nietzsche's late work is dominated by a shrill, frenzied voice, the voice of one seeking to pass judgment on and negate, not "life" as it is imagined but history as it really is.

Everything in the European tradition which is not classical Greek or Roman antiquity is interpreted as morality's revolt of the slaves, beginning with the Jews, "the sacerdotal people of *ressentiment par excellence*,"[43] and continuing via Christianity, the "wholesale revolt of all the downtrodden, the poverty-stricken, the failures, the underprivileged,"[44] to their "daughter and continuer," the French revolution. Today, however, the democratic movement has become the legacy of the Christian movement: everything is imbued with "the pessimism of indignation," with the "instinct against caste, against the well-bred, against the last-remaining privileges,"[45] and together with the democratic movement the "emancipation of women," anarchy, and socialism are part and parcel of the phenomenon of the "total decadence of mankind."[46]

Nietzsche's real enemy is obviously the concept of realization; it is at this that he aims such terms as *ressentiment*, *décadence*, and "total decadence." From a philosophical standpoint there is clearly only one unassailable counterconcept: that of the wholly nondecadent man, the "beast of prey, the magnificent roaming blond beast lusting for booty and victory,"[47] the magnificent animality of "the pack of blond beasts of prey."[48]

In practice, however, Nietzsche allies himself with certain phenomena of his day, and these bear little resemblance to the bourgeois society of Smith or

Kant: "The maintenance of the military state is the ultimate means of resuming or preserving the great tradition of the supreme human type, the strong type. And as a result all concepts which prolong the state of hostility and distinction of rank between states appear to be sanctioned (for example, nationalism, protective tariffs)."[49]

The fantastic alliance of philosophy and proletariat under the banner of the reintegrating "changing of the world" is confronted by the desperate comradeship in arms of the martial society and the culture proceeding from it with its battle cry of "salvation" and "annihilation."

Not the "decayed ruling classes,"[50] but the future lords of the earth as the "spiritual and physical aristocracy,"[51] as the "ruling caste with the most spacious souls,"[52] know how they have to change the world that it may remain as it is.

"The Biblical commandment, 'Thou shalt not kill,' is naïve compared to the seriousness of the life commandment to the *décadents*: 'Thou shalt not reproduce!' "[53] "The weak and the failures shall be destroyed: first lesson of *our* love for our fellow man. And we must help them on their way."[54]

"... If his strength rank still higher in the hierarchy ... , it is not sufficient for him to be capable of cruelty merely at the *sight* of much suffering, perishing, and destruction: such a man must be capable of himself creating pain and suffering and experiencing pleasure in so doing, he must be cruel in hand and deed (and not merely with the eyes of the spirit)."[55]

In fact, Nietzsche's whole thought represents the very antithesis of the Marxist conception, and the idea of destruction is the negative aspect of its core. For if history is not realization but an *Attentat* thousands of years old, then only the destruction of the perpetrator of this crime can restore things to their true balance. Nietzsche is not in any obvious sense the spiritual father of fascism;[56] but he was the first to give voice to that spiritual focal point toward which all fascism must gravitate: the assault on practical *and* theoretical transcendence, for the sake of a "more beautiful" form of "life." Nietzsche was not concerned with magnificent animality for its own sake,[57] nor was destruction per se Hitler's goal. Their ultimate aim was a "supreme culture" of the future. Yet it was inevitable that the positive concept of both men, in its fantastic abstractness (for what is "culture" without the acknowledgment of real history?), was completely outweighed by the concrete aspect of their negative will. Many decades in advance, Nietzsche provided the political radical anti-Marxism of fascism with its original spiritual image, an image of which even Hitler never quite showed himself the equal.[58]

However, although this most radical of all antitheses takes place on the soil of bourgeois society, it is not the appropriate expression of opposites immanent in it. Marxism is not the spontaneous self-consciousness of the proletariat: it is above all a doctrine, by means of which a powerful mind grounded in classical German philosophy desired to utilize bourgeois society's most recent product for his boundless hopes for a reintegration of mankind. Nietzsche's thought is not an ideology of the bourgeoisie: on the one hand it is a deeply disturbed protest of the artistic temperament against the general world trend, on the other it is the violent reaction of the feudal element in bourgeois society at being threatened. So although both doctrines could establish a close relation with basic social phenomena and the movements arising out of them, and to some extent accurately voice these trends, essentially they extended far beyond them and were both revealed as the products of that unrestrained intellectual stratum which, in the interplay of its unauthoritative and hence particularly daring schemata, represents the self-consciousness of bourgeois society. What distinguished these two doctrines from all others was their ability to push the society which was their soil to the outermost limits of its existence: to the eschatologically envisaged reality of the universal community of labor and exchange toward which it was heading—to the nontranscendental self-assertion of the sovereign, martial, and inwardly antagonistic group of which it was the offspring.

Max Weber: The Theoretician of Bourgeois Society before Fascism

What stronger evidence in favor of this thesis could there be than the fact that Max Weber, in defiance of every probability of a hypothetical development, is much less close than Nietzsche to fascism? Yet this son of an upper-class family was very much part of the imperialist Germany of the turn of the century, and he was certainly no stranger to all the trends and characteristics of the age pointing back to Nietzsche and on to Hitler. Indeed, his inaugural speech at Freiburg University in 1895 abounds in phrases which, in meaning and some-times even formulation, could have appeared in *Mein Kampf*. Nevertheless, this same speech contains the starting point of a distinction which, when further developed, makes it possible to see him as representing the basic anti-Hitler potential of German politics.[59] For our purposes only one element need be singled out: his attitude toward Marx and Marxism and thus indirectly his relationship to Nietzsche and the spiritual core of fascism. It happens to be a highly important element; moreover, it throws light on his position toward and within bourgeois society.

Max Weber knew nothing of the fear of the socialist movement which is the wellspring of fascism. He had only contempt for the cowardice of the bourgeoisie when confronted by Social Democracy, but he also despised the potential obverse of this cowardice—rank brutality. He sees socialism as a manifestation of bourgeois society which has to find a place within this society. He formed the concept of the "workers' aristocracy" long before Lenin.[60] Hence in 1907 it was natural for him to ask why the Social Democrats should *not* rule the communes. As for himself, he says, he is convinced that the attempt would be more dangerous for the ideologists among them than for bourgeois society.[61] It is the "discovery of the reality of the proletariat" which gave him this confidence, the discovery which was then being made in many places and which opened the first cracks in Marx's speculative thesis of the homogeneity of the world proletariat (without eliminating it, for its continued existence was still a *sine qua non* of fascism).[62]

Max Weber does not stop at a substantiated assumption. He seeks to prove empirically what Marx had established by philosophical premises: As a result of technical innovations, will qualified workers be replaced by people of lesser or higher qualifications? Is the working class moving toward qualitative and economic differentiation or toward uniformity? What is the relationship between the upper working class and the petite bourgeoisie? Not only does this provide him with evidence for his view that, broadly speaking, the West European working class is a section of the bourgeoisie (a view, incidentally, which Engels had anticipated by half a century);[63] he also makes it possible for himself to divide the scientific elements in Marx's work from the nonscientific. In this way he contributes to the dissolution of the synthesis of mass appeal, science, and philosophical concept which had constituted the real effectiveness of Marxism and yet had been an all too vulnerable element of it.

More important, however, is Max Weber's attitude to the core of Marx's thought. For Weber's real subject is identical with Marx's: practical transcendence.

He seeks to trace "the unfolding of an efficient economy from its beginnings as an instinctive reactive search for food,"[64] that "process of rationalization and socialization whose progressive reaching out into all communal activity must be pursued in every field as the essential motivating force of evolution."[65] If the disintegration of original family communism and the increasing trend toward calculativeness are merely two aspects of the same thing, then today, in "universal market integration," the production process has largely detached itself from its dependence on the individual and the terms of organic existence, and has created social conditions of extreme impersonality, complexity, and differentiation. Hence the West is characterized merely by one particular most advanced stage of a universal process of which the rudiments are to be found everywhere, and which Max Weber paraphrases by such terms as "systematization," "sublimation," "rationalization," "intellectualization." Thus Max Weber is concerned with bourgeois society within the framework of the world-historical process, exactly like Kant, Hegel, and Marx. But he discards some dogmatic premises which are typically Marxist.

He does not accept the later thesis of Marx that at no time have religious forces played an important role in this process. On the contrary, his most significant analyses serve to clarify the connections between theoretical and practical transcendence, so that actually he restores a link which Kant, Hegel, and Nietzsche took for granted and which figured also in the work of the young Marx, and even in later intimations,[66] although these were not elaborated.

He does not adopt the unclarified Marxist concept of productive force. The term "development of the productive force" merely poses a problem without offering any solution to it. Max Weber's answer is to be found in the concept of "charisma" which, although the most polyvalent word in all his writings, in essence means the underivable power of "invention."

He does not share Marx's belief that only total alienation would produce a sudden total restoration of human nature. He was not without sympathy for Marx's concept of the "history of alienation," but because he augments it— separation of the producer from the means of production took place also in armies and was now taking place in universities—he sees it as an irreversible process which can never achieve a "higher unity" with the individual. It is not based on the private ownership of the means of production; a socialist economy would not reverse the expropriation of the workers—it would only augment it by the dispossession of the owners. Because in a socialist economy a struggle for "positions of advantage"[67] would inevitably begin and real power of disposal would only rest with a few, that "iron shell"[68] which modern times have built around the individual is bound to become even more solid and unbreakable. The trend toward "minimization"[69] of rule, displayed by some forms of democracy and particularly by socialism, was something Weber never quite believed in; essential to his own struggle for the parliamentary system and internal political freedom was the conviction that the power of bureaucracy would become ever more firmly rooted and impossible to dislodge, and that one could merely strive to ensure a minimum of control and individual freedom of movement. History, he says, inexorably gives birth to new aristocracies; neither the fear nor the hope (according to one's outlook) existed that there would ever be too much freedom in the world. Weber shares with Marx his evaluation of the present trend and also his fear of the "parceling" of man; but where Marx had seen a recovery, Weber sees a deterioration, because he recognizes that "socialization" is bureaucratization and regards the notion of universal, reintegrated man who is no longer subjected to division of labor as nonsensical wishful thinking.

Thus Max Weber corrects that "irresponsibility" with which Marx allows "the" society of the future to carry out its plans, and with the concept of the dialectic of perfection tears the very heart out of Marxist faith. We can only shake our heads sadly over the question of whether he or Marx gauged bureaucracy more accurately. Max Weber had not been dead ten years when Trotsky, the most important surviving leader of the Russian revolution, began to indict the bureaucratic degeneration of the state, and Weber's posthumous star witness was no other than Stalin when the latter evolved his theory of a "revolution from above," for which there is absolutely no foundation in Marx's thought. The only possible objection is that the concept of bureaucracy is an equivocal one, and that Weber based his ideas too much on the Prussian-German form. But the interesting question here is not whether, where, and to what extent Max Weber was right as opposed to Marx. The heart of the matter is something quite different.

The very fact that Max Weber turns a penetrating and rational gaze on the inconsistencies of Marx's theories is what divides him by an abyss from the radicalness of Nietzsche's antithesis and even more so from Hitler's mythicizing search for "agents." He has no intention of "destroying" Marx intellectually, or even of replacing the materialistic view of history with a nonmaterialistic doctrine of the priority of religious attitudes in history. To interpret his works on religious sociology in this way is to misinterpret them. They are far more of an augmentation than a refutation. For Max Weber, Marx always remains the great fellow thinker, and there exists a broad range of insights and evaluations common to both.

For Weber, too, class struggle is a fundamental reality of the age, capitalism means the dispossession of the producer, and the cleavage of society into bourgeoisie and proletariat is the chief hallmark of modern times. His description of industrial conditions often recalls those of Marx. However, this congruity, far from being imitative, brings to light the simple fact, yet one which is often overlooked, that only a small part of "Marxism" stems genuinely from Marx: the theory of class struggle, the economic view of history, the analysis of capitalism—all these had been developed before and side by side with Marx by "bourgeois" theoreticians, and Weber simply took back what belonged to the theory of bourgeois society.

Hence he does not show even a trace of that sweeping "doctrine of the enemy" and its cogency, which is as central for Maurras and Hitler as for Nietzsche. He acknowledged having political enemies, of course, and he fought them with intensity and determination. But when he discloses their historical origin they become more understandable instead of more alarming; they never appear in a line of descent more or less identical with European history.

Max Weber is thus not tempted to repudiate his own assumptions and to conceive a "history of decay." He leaves no doubt that he regards himself as the heir to those Puritans whose ethical rigorism and world-conquering faith gave birth to modern capitalism; no human type provided him with as much guidance and support as the Jewish prophets, with whom that antimagical and rationalistic reshaping of the world began which is the fundamental trait of the history of the West. As a result he expresses himself quite favorably concerning the great Western revolutions, including the French.

It is equally true, of course, that Max Weber repeatedly shows a strange vacillation toward just those principal phenomena to which he gave his closest attention. In his eyes, rationalization is not merely typical of the West: it is also the root of his torturing anxiety as to whether man has even the strength to withstand the fearful rupturing effects of the irrevocable perversion of all natural conditions within the "apparatus" of the modern world. The concept of "progress" entirely loses its traditional positive accent; its use is frankly stated to be "inopportune." Most revealing of all, perhaps, is the use of the term "disenchantment," which in the total context of his work has a quite positive meaning and yet in one of Weber's best-known utterances is imbued with the melancholy sound of Stefan George's laments.[70]

This vacillation of such a man as Weber is possibly more indicative of the profound change in the intellectual climate favoring fascism than all the books written by Bergson or Klages. But at the same time it makes it clear that there is more to this change than a purely sociological "escape into irrationalism."

And finally, a simplified interpretation does not exhaust what the Weber doctrine contains of the fateful and inconclusive battle of the various "gods," that is, scales of value, and thus in the last resort of the various manifestations of theoretical transcendence. For the thesis that fate, rather than science, holds sway over these gods and their battles[71] sounds very curious coming from a man whose lifework culminated in the insight that there is no more fateful power today than science and the rationalization associated with it. This proposition can only be understood against the background of that uncertainty vis-à-vis his own central concept, an uncertainty which, although it notes the reality of "progress," has begun to doubt the desirability of progress. However, can it really be taken for granted that other scales of value—"gods"—present themselves as alternatives, which the specific social movement has not created but which are left behind and endowed with an extremely intensive self-awareness? Is this perhaps the strangest characteristic of bourgeois society in its relation to the forms of theoretical transcendence?

Outline of a Transcendental Sociology of this Period

A "transcendental definition of bourgeois society" is now no longer a strange-sounding postulate: it has been contained, although sometimes only by implication, in the thinking of Marx, Nietzsche, and Max Weber. All that remains is to summarize, with the aid of the concepts previously developed, avoiding the specific definitions of each thought system, and then to apply this to the new phenomena of bolshevism and fascism, which at this point can only be seen in unity although not *as* a unity. Fascism, although it is still the theme, requires but a few sentences; for if in the main historical section the era was only to be interpreted by examining fascism, in the same way the metapolitical method of observing fascism only becomes definable within a context far transcending fascism.

Typical of the transcendental nature of bourgeois society is that within it practical transcendence has developed to an undreamed-of efficacy, without supplanting the traditional forms of theoretical transcendence. The politico-sociological aspect (which is superficial when isolated) may be formulated as follows:

Bourgeois society is that form of society in which the leading class performs its task of establishing the technical and economic unity of the world, and emancipating all men for participation in this undertaking, in ever new political and intellectual compromises with the hitherto ruling powers: it is the society of synthesis. Hence in bourgeois society the historically new and specific—that unprecedented expansion of the practical scope of mankind and the revolutionary change in the status of the individual and all groups within society as a whole which is summarily known as "industrialization"—is proceeding almost clandestinely and without the consent of considerable sections of its own intellectual stratum, whose spiritual home is after all theoretical transcendence, however arbitrarily and undogmatically they may interpret it.

The thesis that when threatened this stratum ultimately aligns itself with bourgeois society and *its* class and that its thinking is therefore dependent on its environment, is, although generally speaking correct, nevertheless remarkably naïve. For its relative (and in some cases absolute) disengagement is precisely what is so astonishing, so singular, and so much in need of explanation. Bourgeois society gave birth to practical transcendence, at the same time endowing it with a guilty conscience. Its self-consciousness is only precariously derived from the contest of a plethora of modes of thought of which the most extreme are a utopian reaching into the future, or a glorifying emphasis on certain typical features of the past. This character of bourgeois society is without doubt associated with the fact that within the state private entrepreneurs have initiated the movement of this society and kept it going: but presumably it could also be "socialistically" organized, without sacrificing its transcendental nature, provided the starting point was abundance and not want, and that power did not fall into the hands of dogmatists. For bourgeois society did not remain unchanged in its structure; within its own framework it produced that new class, the "technical intelligentsia" which Marx had completely ignored and which combined on various levels with the older classes, turning out to be the most productive and expansive group within this structure. It is advisable, therefore, to abandon the narrow term "bourgeois society" and to speak instead of "liberal society."

Liberal society is a society of abundance—all forms of theoretical transcendence can develop independently, although not without being affected externally; a self-critical society—the attainment of practical transcendence remains subject to criticism; an uncertain society—it is continually subject to self-doubts.

Kant's and Hegel's ideas show how unquestionably the early self-image of this society is rooted in philosophy; Marx and Nietzsche mark the extremes of this self-doubting—which is, of course, a product of their philosophical detachment. For the obvious possibility of a nontranscendental yet advantageous subordination of individuals in the social process—the basic supposition of classical political economy—is rejected by both with equal fervor. Their antithetical solutions were adopted by social structures which are transcendentally distinct from liberal society. But Max Weber's work demonstrates that this society need not necessarily be driven in directions where it will retain mere fragments of its uncurtailed self.

Bolshevism achieved power in Russia in defiance of the acknowledged premises of the Marxist doctrine, and it modeled itself on the master's more esoteric expectations for a short time only. Nevertheless, it is to some extent entitled to invoke Marx as its authority.

Lenin found it difficult to forsake the orthodox assumption that what was really on the agenda was the revolution of the Western European proletariat, and that his own enterprise was historically premature. At first he was still convinced that the functions of power-wielding were by that time so simplified that they were open "to every nonilliterate,"[72] and that the age of nonrule was hence rapidly approaching: "Under socialism *all* will rule in turn and quickly get used to the fact that no one rules."[73]

But it was not long before the Marxist postulates were replaced, both in practical measures and a number of theoretical utterances, by a complete mobilization, directed by a single will, of the cluster of races that is Russia in a grim struggle for existence. He realized it was not a matter of setting mankind an example of a higher and better way of life—the crossroad at which the country now stood was more commonplace, more ruthless: "Go under, or forge full steam ahead. That is the question put by history."[74] It was a matter of "catching up," of struggling up out of backwardness, lack of culture, want, and poverty in the midst of a hostile world. In their overwhelming simplicity and conviction, a great number of utterances from his latest period leave no doubt whatever that this more modest interpretation represents Lenin's final insight rather than this or that bombastic pronouncement about the victory of socialism over capitalism.[75]

Thus the "day-to-day problems of the economy" became "the most important affairs of state."[76] It is easier to grasp the nature of bolshevism from any front page of any Soviet daily newspaper than from the most shocking reports of famine and barbarism. Famine and barbarism have always existed; but never since the existence of a bourgeois society and of newspapers had the headlines dealt with production records, reports on working methods, and appeals for increased productivity. Bolshevism signifies the dominating emergence of the element that had remained half-hidden in bourgeois society: it is the most unequivocal affirmation of material production and at the same time of practical transcendence. Society[77] thereby loses its spiritual wealth and the spur of self-criticism, and acquires an unshakable complacency and a hitherto unknown enthusiasm in its sense of historical necessity.

But in this case all that remains, if anything, of Marx's own special and personal concepts, which in his eyes alone justify the unique quality of practical transcendence, is a propagandistic semblance. As a result, bolshevism's battle with the orthodox Marxists in its own ranks is among the most tragic and moving chapters of the history of our time. And yet the Soviet Union has conformed to Marxist thought insofar as it has always regarded the emancipation of its own peoples (that is, their adaptation to the exigencies of industrial society) in terms of a higher world process. True, the concept of "world revolution" has led more than any other to the defeats of bolshevism in its confrontation with developed bourgeois society; at the same time, it constitutes a hallmark of world-historical distinction, since it is evidence of a relationship not only to a selfishly interpreted "industrial production" but also to the total process of practical transcendence. For this very reason the term "development dictatorship" is inadequate as applied to the Soviet Union and, despite all structural similarities, the difference as against fascism is fundamental. The fact that, alone among non-Western powers, the Soviet Union could complete its industrialization[78] on the strength of its own initiative and to a large extent under its own steam; that, in spite of the known harshness of its methods of government, it enjoys what often seems a mysterious prestige among the underdeveloped nations; that it was the first state to succeed in penetrating outer space—these are all closely related facts which become intelligible when seen against a background of transcendental definition.

It has now become evident what fascism actually is. It is not that resistance to practical transcendence which is more or less common to all conservative movements. It was only when theoretical transcendence, from which that resistance originally emanated, was likewise denied that fascism made its appearance. Thus fascism is at the same time resistance to practical transcendence and struggle against theoretical transcendence. But this struggle must needs be concealed, since the original motivations can never be entirely dispensed with. And insofar as practical transcendence from its most superficial aspect is nothing but the possibility of concentration of power, fascism pursues its resistance to transcendence from within that transcendence and at times in the clear consciousness of a struggle for world hegemony. That is the transcendental expression of the sociological fact that fascism has at its command forces which are born of the emancipation process and then turn against their own origin. If it may be called the despair of the[79] feudal section of bourgeois society for its traditions, and the bourgeois element's betrayal of its revolution, now it is clear what this tradition and this revolution actually are. Fascism represents the second and gravest crisis of liberal society, since it achieves power on its own soil, and in its radical form is the most complete and effective denial of that society.

It is precisely in this broadest of all perspectives that the observer cannot withhold from fascism that "sympathy" of which we have spoken. This sympathy is directed not toward persons or deeds, but toward the perplexity underlying the colossal attempt to overcome that perplexity, which is the most universal characteristic of an era whose end cannot be foreseen. For transcendence, when properly understood, is infinitely remote from the harmlessness of safe "cultural progress"; it is not the couch of the finite human being, but in some mysterious unity his throne and his cross.

Nevertheless, fascism as a metapolitical phenomenon still serves as a means of understanding the world today: only when liberal society, after steadfast and serious reflection, accepts practical transcendence as its own although no longer exclusive product; when theoretical transcendence escapes from its ancient political entanglements into genuine freedom; when Communist society looks at itself and its past with realistic but not cynical eyes and ceases to evade either one; when the love of individuality and barriers no longer assumes political form, and thought has become a friend of man—only then can man be said to have finally crossed the border into a postfascist era.

Appendix A

At this point it is relevant to reply to some preliminary questions.

The legitimacy of the term "fascism" has been questioned from time to time on account of the remarkable diversity of the movements under review. But when we look more closely we see that there are equally striking differences among the various parliamentary systems or species of liberalism. That the transition from radical conservatism to fascism is smoother than that from leftist liberalism to socialism is a characteristic of fascism, but it does not disprove its existence. In the case of a great many manifestations, it may be doubtful whether they should be counted as belonging to fascism; yet it is absurd to deny the unity of a phenomenon so deeply rooted in the basic elements of the era *as* a unit and, as a unit, so passionately disputed.

In actual fact the proposal to limit the term "fascism" to Mussolini's party never succeeded. There is evidently an imperative need for a term for those political systems (and their corresponding strivings) which differ as much from the democratic-parliamentary type as from the Communist, and yet which are not merely military dictatorships or conservative regimes. Not even the Communist tendency to apply the term as a weapon against all opponents has prevented it from being used by a very large number of Western authors, although they usually do so by implication rather than overtly.[1]

However, the fascist movements themselves had above all a strong sense of kinship covering various aspects of mutual support, influence, and dependence. Hitler's admiration for Mussolini is well known, nor was it on a purely personal level. He revered the Italian as the first destroyer of Marxism, and if Hitler had died in 1930 a historian would hardly hesitate to call the man, whose study contained a bust of the Duce, a disciple and imitator of Mussolini. Close ties also bound him to Oswald Mosley, and during the war he looked back regretfully on Codreanu as having been the "man predestined" to lead Rumania.[2]

The primary reason for Mussolini's rapprochement with Germany after 1935 was not political but ideological: admiration for the successes of the Third Reich's population policy. During the early years after World War I, Julius Gömbös was closely associated with Röhm's circles in Munich; in 1922 Codreanu rejoiced in Berlin over Mussolini's triumph "as if it were a victory of my own country";[3] Oswald Mosley experienced his long-awaited Damascus in Rome; Hitler and Mussolini helped Franco to power; and at the fronts of Falangist Spain fell not only Italian militiamen and German volunteers but Codreanu's friends and collaborators, Ion Motza and Vasile Marin. Very often a sense of fellow-feeling helped surmount the barriers of material differences; without it, Hitler would not have found convinced and fanatical collaborators all over Europe, from Quisling to Mussert, from Szálasi to Doriot. And side by side with the somewhat nebulous common interests in the negative sense there were in fact a whole series of positive areas of agreement which could not be overlooked: the "principle of leadership" and the desire for a "new world," the love of power and the dramatic appeal of youth, elite-consciousness and mass influence, revolutionary ardor and veneration of tradition. It was no mere chance that the paradoxical efforts toward a fascist international began in the very early days.[4] It is true that they did not get very far (nor was that by chance either), yet this trend speaks as strongly for the kinship among the systems as does the prevailing opinion of observers.

This *consensus auctorum et rerum* confirms the existence in fact of an object whose reality historical analysis has suggested is possible in essence and whose effect on the world is placed beyond doubt by looking at its opponents.

Admittedly this does not answer the question of whether an attitude of scientific objectivity toward this phenomenon is as yet feasible. The possible tangential reasons for this are well known; there is no need to list the obvious here. But if fascism is only to be presented in its era, this limitation requires that fascism should have set its stamp on only *one* era and that today it be dead—if not in all manifestations, certainly as a phenomenon of world significance. And scholarship must be allowed to have its say about the dead, however great the individual difficulties may be. But perhaps there is no more favorable moment for historical objectivity than that at which something regarded as being alive ceases to be alive, and, once this premise is acknowledged, the metamorphosis into another merely spiritual, albeit shadowy, life, becomes possible. This objectivity, however, represents neither an Olympian impartiality nor a timid cataloguing of "good" and "bad" traits. It is an attempt at understanding: hence the emergence of common traits as differences are uncovered. It must be based on the will and the ability to let the thing itself and all its leading opponents "have their say" in broad terms, and refrain from indiscriminately adopting the point of view of one side. Thus the inadequacies of the individual attempt stem merely from the personal weaknesses of its author but are no argument against an objectivity which, beside being scientific, must of necessity remain a human and finite one.

Finally, totalitarianism as such is not the main object of this study. If totalitarianism is taken to mean the opposite of a nontotalitarian—that is, liberal—form of constitution, then it existed in the remote past and continues to exist today as a widespread political manifestation. It should not be restricted to a particular era. Moreover, this manifestation has many modifications. The modification is not understood if it is subsumed in the general concept. The principles of modification are, among others, differences in situation, in definition of purpose, and in the respective substrata (peoples, classes). It is these differences which go to make up the content of the single manifestation, rather than the general manifestation at any given place or time. Indeed, discussion of the issue of totalitarianism would not have acquired the overwhelming significance it has had for the past ten years were it not based on the conviction that there is a specifically modern form of totalitarianism, and that within this form National Socialism and bolshevism are essentially identical. But when two manifestations show considerable similarities which neither derived from the same situation nor dispose over a comparable substratum, nor profess similar goals, then either this similarity is merely one of form, or one manifestation has come to approximate the other. Possibly bolshevism at a certain stage should be called fascist, and fascism in its entirety Bolshevik: the only way to decide this is first to examine the conceptual meaning of fascism and bolshevism from the point of view of the particular nature of each, rather than to start off by subsuming them under the formal concept of "totalitarianism."

The question can, of course, be placed on a more subtle level, and it then merges with the most difficult and obscure aspect of the problem of objectivity. For if the declared aim of totalitarianism is totalitarianism itself, the concept is no longer one of form. The attack on the freedom and dignity of the individual then turns out to be a material component, and all definitions of purpose (liberation of the people or of the class, elimination of influences inimical to culture, keeping abreast of world developments, etc.) stand revealed as mere pretexts. Totalitarianism interpreted in this way has no claim on that "sympathy" which, according to the teachings of the classic historians, is an unalterable prerequisite to objectivity because it enables the observer to acknowledge the endless variety and homogeneity of the human scene. For the enemy is in fact not the will of a few people but the inexorable compulsion of an inhuman system. But if we are not to dispute the sincerity and effectiveness of fascism's definition of purpose, one of the principal elements of its distinctive nature, is not that sympathy then bound to return?

Yet fascism *as* fascism in its most extreme form has committed that crime which is beyond comparison with anything the world has ever seen—even including Stalin's reign of terror against his own people and his own party—because it was at one and the same time rational to the point of perfection and irrational to the point of excess, and regarded its victims no longer as human beings but either as creatures of the devil or tools without rights. For even if only one man bears the legal responsibility for this crime, the foundations for it had been laid long ago in a powerful and undeniably international trend of thought and feeling. It was not an inhuman system from which human beings could dissociate themselves that paved the way for this crime, but, on the contrary, all too human troubles and fears. No limitation of the theme, no desire for scientific objectivity, can absolve us from trying to answer the most urgent question of our time; but only if we have sufficient patience to hold fast to it throughout a long and painstaking study will we have a chance of bringing forth something other than angry accusation or whitewashing apologia.

Appendix B

If there can be a "History of European Communism," it should perhaps be possible to write a "History of Fascism." Historiography, it is true, is always in danger of trying in vain to cover up, by resorting to great preoccupation with detail, one consuming deficiency: the adoption of a certain concept without sufficient substantiation. But this need not be so, and all significant historiography transcends a mere narration of events which reviews sources but not itself.

The difficulties precluding this method for fascism are of another kind. The unity of fascism is not to be compared to that of communism. It was formed neither by a central authority nor by an acknowledged doctrine; rather it was founded on the analogy of circumstances, common emotions, and the comparable nature of a trend. It might be possible to write a "History of the Fascist Movements," but such a book would have either to take for granted the concept of fascism or develop it by some other method. Moreover, it would have to go so deeply into the circumstances of the various countries in which fascism, as a form of nationalism, remains much more firmly embedded than communism, that it would end up by being a "History of Europe in the Era of Fascism." But the time for such a history seems far from ripe; of the essential components only one has so far been submitted: *La Storia d'Italia nel periodo fascista*, by Salvatorelli and Mira.[1]

More promising and appropriate is the evolvement of a typology. This is, of course, primarily a thought construct, but it offers empirical material unlimited scope for verification.

Between two opposite poles seen from one point of view (for instance, authoritarianism and totalitarianism as forms of exertion of power), certain distinctive, that is, typical, positions are occupied by particular forms of fascism.

The first pole is represented by a manifestation which obviously does not yet meet the requirements of the concept and so can supply the starting point and dividing line, while the second represents a point of orientation which is only reached in an extreme form, or which only exists ideally. In other words, there would be four typological positions: the not-yet-fascist of the lower pole, which might be called the prefascist; the first point of the inner area, which should be called early fascist if chronological circumstances so permit (it can function in abbreviated form as pole, that is, inner pole); the normal fascist central position; and the radical fascist upper pole. The assumption that a reality exists not only this side of fascism but also beyond it, and that fascism reaches out toward it, would probably only be valid in a specific and very limited sense.[2] Within this scale, in any case, all types of fascism could find their proper place. Typology lays the foundations for a topology.

Since there are a considerable number of important points of view, the order can hardly remain constant, hence the various concepts can receive their due without eclecticism. We might think of it as a circle of mirrors formed by a variety of sequences in which each link can throw light on all the others. Only an overall view will decide whether it is legitimate to use terms such as early fascism, normal fascism, and radical fascism, and whether a precise allocation of these terms can be made. For the invention of an ideal type in the sense of an imaginary radical fascism composed of the most extreme traits of all types of fascism does not seem a very fruitful endeavor. On the other hand, this thought process enables the concept which starts out as a vague hypothesis to advance progressively toward clarity and precision.

The poles of authoritarianism and totalitarianism bracket a span ranging from Pilsudski's regime, via the political totalitarianism of Falangist Spain, to the all-encompassing totalitarianism of Mussolini and Hitler.

The most marked characteristic of any fascism—and fascism always remained "national fascism" in its era[3]—is the combination of a nationalistic and a socialist motif. The socialistic motif always recedes further into the background, not only typologically but at each progressive stage of development. Hence early Italian fascism would have to be placed on the lower (inner) pole, just like the early Falange, both of which were driven over the years to a more central position, while German National Socialism started out from this central position and before long allowed the socialistic motif to give way entirely to the nationalistic.

Officially speaking, anti-Semitism did not exist in Italian fascism until well into the thirties. But there is evidence of its potential existence much earlier, even with Mussolini, and it is present in every brand of fascism. The "normal position" is occupied by countries in which, as in Rumania, a Jewish question really constituted a social problem. No one went further than Hitler: it was left to him to attribute to the Jews "all" the class struggles and all the "antinatural" disputes the world has ever known.

A remarkable intertwining of particular and universal tendencies is to be found in every fascist movement. Furthermore, in the movement toward extreme fascism it is not the progressive overcoming of one or the other tendency which we note, but rather the increasing paradox inherent in the relationship. Thus Codreanu's eyes are generally fixed only on Rumania, but for the combating of international Jewry he maintains the necessity of an international plan. Universal tendencies were inherent in Mussolini's fascism from the very beginning, and this undoubtedly attests to the continuing latent influence of the internationalistic convictions of his youth. But when he was finally able, during the war, to bring his friend Ante Pavelić to power in Agram, there was little sign of international fascist solidarity in the settling of frontier disputes. In the case of National Socialism the paradox was already apparent in the race doctrine. For what is "race" but a people which has achieved a nonhistorical pseudouniversality by means of the most radical particularization? Hitler could never escape the pincer grasp of the paradox that on the one hand he set National Socialism the task of solving the world's problems, and on the other regarded it as a kind of private German magic which must be carefully withheld from other peoples.

The test of fascist universalism is in its relationship to other forms of fascism. For its fellow-feeling toward those of like conviction in other countries could never do away with the fact that these friends, being representatives of an antagonistic nationalism, were at the same time bitter enemies. Hence Mussolini's first comments on Hitler's seizure of power revealed a curious mixture of ideological pride and *Realpolitik* anxiety; and during the war, as can be seen from Ciano's diaries, he felt just as often united with his people against the "barbarians" as united with the Nordic *Herrenvolk* against his own people. And Hitler, even at the very moment when he came to believe that one of the chief causes of Germany's defeat lay in the alliance with Italy, could hardly overlook the fact that the main reason behind this alliance had been his—Adolf Hitler's—National Socialist admiration for the Duce of fascism, the first man in Europe "to crush Marxism." However, the extreme of either pole is represented neither by Hitler nor Mussolini, but on the one hand by the quisling governments, which pledged themselves to their ideological allies *against* their national interests, and on the other by Austro-fascism, whose *raison d'être* since 1933 had been resistance to National Socialist aggression.

Yet it is not only toward their friends but toward their enemies that fascist movements show a deeply ambivalent relationship. A man like Codreanu is the furthest from exhibiting the features of the enemy in his own face, while Hitler's *Weltanschauung* is in certain aspects nothing but a mirror-image of the Jewish conception as he imagined it to be. Before World War I Mussolini had been one of the outstanding figures of European socialism: the aftereffects of fifteen years of Marxism can be demonstrated every step of the way, and his quarrel with Lenin, which was one of jealousy rather than bitterness, runs through his whole fascist life.

Extensive statistical studies would be required for a scale by which the substratum of each form of fascism—that is, a division into classes—would be the criterion. It is generally known that all fascist movements, apart from the awkward problem of Peronism, were movements of the middle classes. Useful though detailed examinations and demarcations would doubtless be, they are liable to ignore the fact that the "fascist character" does not derive primarily from an aggregate of supporters, who vary considerably according to time and place, but from the relatively classless phenomenon of the leading stratum and its self-image which is nourished everywhere by similar political and historical sources.

The most important scale of all is that in which the aim becomes the determining point of view. This is precisely the one, however, which presupposes conceptual discussions and distinctions which cannot be entered into here. In referring briefly to these[4] it can be said at this point that this scale ranges from Kemalism at the outer pole as a national defense and development dictatorship, via Italian fascism, which was a development dictatorship and finally a despotism of territorial conquest, to National Socialism, which stands simultaneously for the dictatorship of national restitution and the despotism of territorial conquest and world salvation.

Thus the typological method enables us to correlate vast quantities of material and a number of important points of view (which our examples by no means exhaust), so that reality is always permeated by the idea, and the idea substantiated by reality.

However, its shortcomings and weaknesses must not be overlooked. Typology does not render the object sufficiently alive, nor does it go far enough into distinguishing detail. It speaks of "Marxism," but as if it were a stamp of universally recognized value. It characterizes Hitler, but out of tens of thousands of utterances it cites at best a dozen. On the other hand, it draws directly on a limitless fund of items which no one can sufficiently master. In order to do complete justice to Ferenc Szálasi and his Arrow Cross units, for example, it would be necessary to be familiar with his copious diary. But even among the few people who understand Hungarian there will be very few researchers with access to the manuscript. Hence typology cannot rely primarily on the study of sources. Even if it is a synthesis of empiricism and construction, it is again far too much at the mercy of each of the two elements.

There is another factor. Because typology looks at many things, it compares chiefly those things which frequently stand out. Now the relationship to war is without doubt basic to fascism as such, and it is certain that Szálasi's Hungarianist program, for example, could never have been implemented without war. But how could a philosophy of war become of paramount importance in a country like Hungary which could never have started a war on its own? How could a certain kind of subtle culture critique have become a vital political factor in Rumania, at the edge of Europe? It is not fascism itself, but the clear development of certain essential characteristics, which is dependent on the size of a country and the significance of its spiritual traditions.

Notes

For Part One and Part Five, respectively, the notes have been numbered in sequence throughout the part; otherwise, notes have been numbered consecutively within each chapter. Notes to the appendices follow the notes to the text.

All references are to editions, page numbers, and the like used by the author in the original German edition, even in those cases where he has used a German translation of a non-German work (e.g., Ciano's diaries) or where different editions of the same work are available (e.g., *Hitler's Table Talk* [London, 1953], published in New York as *Hitler's Secret Conversations*).

The following abbreviations have been used in the notes:

O.O.   *Opera Omnia di Benito Mussolini.* The complete works of Benito Mussolini, published in Florence, 1951 ff.

HKG   Karl Marx and Friedrich Engels, *Historisch-kritische Gesamtausgabe.* The historical-critical edition of the complete works of Marx and of Engels, published in Frankfurt a.M., Berlin, and Moscow, 1927 ff.

IMG   *Der Prozess gegen die Hauptkriegsverbrecher vor dem Internationalen Militärgerichtshof.* The trial of the major war criminals before the International Military Tribunal, published in Nuremberg, 1947 ff.

Preface

1. The oldest national account of fascism is Luigi Salvatorelli's and Giovanni Mira's *Storia del fascismo*, 1st ed. (Rome, 1952). Giampiero Carocci gives a short and reliable description in *Storia del fascismo* (Milan, 1959). Giacomo Perticone's *L'Italia contemporanea* (Milan, 1962), is a detailed and profusely illustrated history of Italy up to 1948.

   The most recent and to date the only comprehensive work to have appeared in Germany is Friedrich Glum's *Der Nationalsozialismus* (Munich, 1962). As part of the history of Germany, National Socialism is dealt with by Karl Dietrich Erdmann in Bruno Gebhardt's *Handbuch der deutschen Geschichte*, Vol. IV (Stuttgart, 1959).

   The Action Française is alone in having received a scholarly scrutiny, the results of which may well be regarded as definitive for years to come: Eugen Weber, *Action française: Royalism and Reaction in Twentieth-Century France* (Stanford, Cal., 1962). A small book by Henri Lemaître, *Les fascimes dans l'histoire* (Paris, 1959), is a clever attempt to grapple with the problem of fascism as a whole.

2. Michel Mourre, *Charles Maurras* (Paris: Editions Universitaires, 1958); Federico

Chabod, *L'Italia contemporanea* (Turin: Piccola Biblioteca Einaudi, 1961); and Hermann Glaser, *Das Dritte Reich—Anspruch und Wirklichkeit*, Vol. XCII (Freiburg: Herder-Bücherei, 1961).

PART ONE

Fascism and the Era of World Wars

1. Otto Ernst Schüddekopf, *Linke Leute von rechts* (Stuttgart, 1960), p. 340.
2. Cf. Wilhelm Pieck, Georgi Dimitroff, Palmiro Togliatti, *Die Offensive des Faschismus und die Aufgaben der Kommunisten im Kampf für die Volksfront gegen Krieg und Faschismus*, Reports made at the 7th Congress of the Communist International, 1935 (Berlin, 1957).
3. E.g., Ludwig Dehio, "Deutschland und die Epoche der Weltkriege," in *Deutschland und die Weltpolitik im 20. Jahrhundert* (Munich, 1955).
4. E.g., Waldemar Besson, "Periodisierung, Zeitgeschichte," in Fischer-Lexikon, Vol. XXIV, *Geschichte* (Frankfurt a.M., 1961).
5. E.g., Hans Herzfeld, *Die moderne Welt*, Vol. II (Braunschweig, 1960).
6. Hans Rothfels, "Sinn und Aufgabe der Zeitgeschichte," in *Zeitgeschichtliche Betrachtungen* (Göttingen, 1959).
7. *Opera Omnia di Benito Mussolini* (Florence, 1951), XXVI, 45. [*Opera Omnia*, hereafter referred to as *O.O.*]
8. *Ibid.*, XXIX, 2.
9. Thomas Mann, *Gesammelte Werke*, 12 vols. (Frankfurt a.M., 1960), XII, 831 f.
10. *Ibid.*, p. 930.
11. *Ibid.*, IX, 702.
12. Georg Lukács, *Die Zerstörung der Vernunft* (Berlin, 1954), p. 5.
13. Hitler objected to Rosenberg contrasting the myth of the twentieth century with the scientific nineteenth century, and maintained that the myth of the nineteenth century should be contrasted with National Socialism as the scientific truth of the twentieth century (*Hitler's Table Talk, 1941–1944* [London, 1953], Para. 190). In his short essay "Bruder Hitler," Thomas Mann discovers to his shocked amazement a deep relationship between the peculiar existence of Hitler and his own basic conception of the artistic nature (Mann, *Werke*, Vol. XII).

    In a letter to Marx dated August 15, 1870, Friedrich Engels states that it is absurd "to try, à la Liebknecht, to make all history since 1866 null and void," i.e., to find no further positive significance in it (Marx-Engels, *Historisch-kritische Gesamtausgabe* [hereafter referred to as *HKG*], Part III, Vol. IV, [Berlin, 1931]). Lukács involuntarily approaches the "rejection en bloc" of entire historical eras which is usually regarded as characteristic of fascism.
14. A typical example is the most active and original group in Italian antifascism, Carlo Rosselli's *Giustizia e Libertà*, whose program, even including the style, reveals many striking similarities with some of Mussolini's utterances made during the years 1919–1921. See *Quaderni di Giustizia e Libertà*, I (1932), 4 f.
15. Cf. Susanne Leonhard, *Gestohlenes Leben* (Stuttgart, 1959); esp. pp. 9, 36, 67, 681; Leonard Schapiro, *Die Geschichte der Kommunistischen Partei der Sowjetunion* (Frankfurt a.M., 1961); esp. pp. 210, 259, 296, 390.

16. Franz Borkenau, *Der europäische Kommunismus* (Munich, n.d.), p. 64.

17. John Gunther, *Roosevelt in Retrospect* (New York, 1950), pp. 281, 313.

18. Franklin D. Roosevelt, *Links von der Mitte* (Frankfurt a.M., 1951), p. 226.

19. *Ibid.*, pp. 153 f.

20. There seems to be no doubt that, without the existence of Hitler, Roosevelt would not have agreed to stand for re-election in 1940. See Gunther, *op. cit.*, p. 275.

21. Alfred Rosenberg, *Letzte Aufzeichnungen* (Göttingen, 1955), pp. 77 f.

22. On Hungary generally, cf. Carlile A. Macartney, *October Fifteenth—A History of Modern Hungary 1929–1945*, Vols. I and II (Edinburgh, 1956).

23. Gasi Mustafa Kemal Pasha, *Der Weg zur Freiheit 1919–1920* (Leipzig, 1928).

24. Ernstgert Kalbe, "Über die faschistische Diktatur der 20er Jahre in Bulgarien und die deutschen Hilfsaktionen für die bulgarischen Arbeiter und Bauern," *Zeitschrift für Geschichtswissenschaft*, V (1957), 754.

25. For an early example of the use of the term by liberals, see the collective volume *Internationaler Faschismus*, edited by Karl Landauer and Hans Honegger (Karlsruhe, 1928), with a summary by Moritz Julius Bonn.

26. The Falange is an outstanding example of this intertwining. A strong feeling for the underdeveloped state of the country—a feeling which was quite unknown in Germany—was accompanied by a sharply defined and (subjectively) sincere desire for social revolution. At the same time the leaders were filled with a great and uncritical admiration for Mussolini, and even for Hitler. Early in 1933 José Antonio Primo de Rivera wanted to found a newspaper called *El Fascio*, Onesimo Redondo published the first translations from *Mein Kampf*, and even Ramiro Ledesma Ramos was completely Germany-oriented. Cf. Emmet J. Hughes, *Report from Spain* (New York, 1947), pp. 20–48; esp. pp. 24–30.

27. Arns K. Chesterton, *Mosley-Geschichte und Programm des britischen Faschismus* (Leipzig, 1937).

28. Werner Haas, *Europa will leben—Die nationalen Erneuerungsbewegungen in Wort und Bild* (Berlin, 1936), p. 130.

29. Cf. Martin Broszat, "Die Eiserne Garde und das Dritte Reich," *Politische Studien*, IX (1958), 628–636; Ion Gheorghe, *Rumäniens Weg zum Satellitenstaat* (Heidelberg, 1952).

30. Macartney, *op. cit.*, p. 29.

31. Oliveira Salazar, *Le Portugal et la crise européenne* (Paris, 1940).

32. Claude Martin, *Franco—Soldat et Chef d'État* (Paris, 1959), pp. 203 f.; cf. Hughes, *op. cit.* and the much more positive presentation of Richard Pattee and Anton M. Rothbauer, *Spanien—Mythos und Wirklichkeit* (Graz, n.d.), pp. 313 f., which plays down the fascist traits.

33. The official Communist definition of fascism is as follows: Fascism is the unconcealed terrorist dictatorship of the most reactionary, chauvinistic, and imperialistic elements of financial capital (13th Plenary Session of the Executive Committee of the Communist International, December, 1933). Examples of this interpretation are to be found today particularly in *Zeitschrift für Geschichtswissenschaft*.

34. E.g., Angelo Tasca, *Nascita e avvento del fascismo—L'Italia dal 1918 al 1922* (Florence, 1950); esp. pp. lxii–lxxvii and 513–567. Examples of the socialist

conception in German literature are: Franz Neumann, *Behemoth*, 2nd ed. (New York, 1944), and Ernst Niekisch, *Das Reich der niederen Dämonen* (Hamburg, 1953).

35. Giuseppe Antonio Borgese, *Golia—Marcia del fascismo* (Milan, 1946), pp. 383 f.
36. Carl J. Friedrich, *Totalitäre Diktatur* (Stuttgart, 1957).
37. *Der Prozess gegen die Hauptkriegsverbrecher vor dem Internationalen Militär-gerichtshof* (Nuremberg, 1947 ff). [Hereafter referred to as *IMG*.]
38. E.g., Hannah Arendt, *Elemente und Ursprünge totaler Herrschaft* (Frankfurt, a.M., 1958).
39. A convincing example is Don Luigi Sturzo's description of fascism as rightist bolshevism in *Italy and Fascismo* (London, 1926).
40. *Du hast mich heimgesucht bei Nacht*, edited by Helmut Gollwitzer, Käthe Kuhn, and Reinhold Schneider (Munich, 1954).
41. Walter Künneth, *Der grosse Abfall* (Hamburg, 1947), pp. 180 f.
42. E.g., James Strachey Barnes, *The Universal Aspects of Fascism* (London, 1928).
43. See the brief but very revealing documentation, "Ein NS-Funktionär zum Niemöllerprozess," *Vierteljahrshefte für Zeitgeschichte*, IV (1956), 307–315; esp. p. 315.
44. Hermann Rauschning, *The Revolution of Nihilism* (New York, 1939).
45. E.g., Erik v. Kuehnelt-Leddihn, *Freiheit oder Gleichheit* (Salzburg, 1953).
46. Hermann Rauschning, *Masken und Metamorphosen des Nihilismus* (Vienna, 1954), pp. 161–176.
47. A very early and typical example is an article by Leopold Schwarzschild in No. 3 of *Neues Tagebuch* (Paris; July, 1933), which sharply contrasts National Social-ism as a retrogression to anthropophagy with all other political systems, including fascism. Hannah Arendt, *op. cit.*, regards Stalinism as a continuation of the Trotskyist world conspiracy.
48. E.g., Ignazio Silone, *The School for Dictators* (New York, 1938).
49. Talcott Parsons, "Some Sociological Aspects of the Fascist Movement," *Essays in Sociological Theory* (Glencoe, 1954).
50. In its isolated form the definition lays no claim to originality. The basic paradox is already contained in the term "conservative revolution." Gustav Adolf Rein, in *Bonapartismus und Faschismus* (Göttingen, 1960), describes fascism as counter-revolution on the soil of revolution. The definition comes to life only within the framework of the study as a whole.
51. There is in existence an authoritative although indirect and unintentional evaluation of the (objective) relationship between the Action Française and National Socialism. In February, 1926, Alfred Rosenberg wrote an article in the *Völkischer Beobachter* entitled "Nationsozialistische Bestrebungen in Frank-reich?" (reprinted in *Kampf um die Macht*, published in Munich in 1937, pp. 391–395). He refers to Georges Valois' *Nouveau Siècle*, finds "astonishing resemblances" concerning criticism of Marxism and capitalism, and voices his satisfaction at the fact that ideas were now being put forward in France too which National Socialism had been preaching in Germany for the previous five years. A decided shortcoming, however, so he goes on, is that not a word is said about Jews and Freemasons, and hence it is impossible to talk seriously of National Socialist efforts in France. Rosenberg did not know that he was

criticizing that very characteristic which distinguishes Valois from the Action Française. Certain conclusions immediately spring to mind.

PART TWO

The Action Française

1 The Disparate Roots

1. The "objective" prehistory of National Socialism is dealt with in some wartime writings by Anglo-Saxon authors, and understandably enough these tend to make National Socialism the inevitable result of German history as a whole. A most recent and well-known example of this trend is William Shirer's *The Rise and Fall of the Third Reich* (New York, 1959). As yet there is no scholarly monograph on conservative and nationalist thought in Germany; for the time being the best substitute is Franz Schnabel's *Deutsche Geschichte im Neunzehnten Jahrhundert*, 4 vols. (Freiburg, 1947 ff.), as far as the first half of the century is concerned. Jean Neurohr in his *Der Mythos vom Dritten Reich* (Stuttgart, 1957) deals solely with the precursors of National Socialism. The intellectual atmosphere in which National Socialism developed has been described by Klemens von Klemperer and Kurt Sontheimer in *Konservative Bewegungen zwischen Kaiserreich und Nationalsozialismus* (Munich, 1962), and *Antidemokratisches Denken in der Weimarer Republik* (Munich, 1962). Armin Mohler's *Die französische Rechte* (Munich, 1958) contains a bibliography on the French rightist movement.

A strange state of affairs exists in Italy, where during the nineteenth century counterrevolutionary thought was virtually identical with the sphere of influence of the Catholic Church, and this sphere was thrust into a kind of ghetto by the national unification movement (see pp. 145 f.). An outline of the prehistory of Italian fascism and of National Socialism is to be presented by the author in two collective works soon to be published. Italian history from 1870 to 1960 is the subject of his contribution to *Handbuch der europäischen Geschichte*, edited by Theodor Schieder (Stuttgart: Union Verlag), and the development of the German rightist movement is described by him in *The European Right*, edited by Eugen Weber and Hans Rogger (Berkeley: University of California Press).

2. The doctrine of the Action Française achieved its original, clearest, and most comprehensive expression in Charles Maurras. They cannot be separated, despite the fact that the Action Française is more than Maurras alone. Cf. Léon Daudet, *Charles Maurras et son temps* (Paris, 1930), pp. 91 f.: "La doctrine de l'Action française [c'est-à-dire de Maurras] ..."

3. The name of Sainte-Beuve should also be added, although his influence was chiefly of a formal nature. Louis Veuillot should also be mentioned, from whom Maurras took one of his most memorable formulas ("Le roi, chef des républiques françaises"). The contemporary whom Maurras quotes the most often is Anatole France, and always the same passage: the conversation between the Abbé Lantaigne and Professor Bergeret in *L'Orme du Mail* (Paris, n.d.), p. 219 ("La république n'est pas destructible, elle est la destruction. Elle est la disper-

sion, elle est la discontinuité, elle est la diversité, elle est le mal"). Others politically significant to him were Paul Bourget and Jules Lemaître.

4. Cf. Albert Schinz, *La pensée de Jean-Jacques Rousseau* (Paris, 1929), pp. 174 ff.

5. *Oeuvres choisies de Jean-Jacques Rousseau* (Paris, n.d.), "Classiques Garnier," p. 35: "car ce n'est pas une légère entreprise, de démêler ce qu'il y a d'originaire et d'artificiel dans la nature actuelle de l'homme, et de bien connaître un état qui n'existe plus, qui n'a peut-être point existé, qui probablement n'existera jamais, et dont il est pourtant nécessaire d'avoir des notions justes, pour bien juger de notre état présent."

6. "Trouver une forme d'association ... par laquelle chacun, s'unissant à tous, n'obéisse pourtant qu'à lui-même, et reste aussi libre qu'auparavant" (*Contrat social*, in *Oeuvres choisies*, p. 243).

7. Joseph de Maistre, *Considérations sur la France* (Geneva, Paris, and Montreal, n.d.), Chapts. IV and V.

8. Joseph de Maistre, *Les soirées de Saint-Petersbourg*, 7e entretien, in E. M. Cioran (ed.), *Joseph de Maistre, Textes choisis et présentés par E. M. Cioran* (Monaco-Ville, n.d.).

9. *Ibid.*, 1er entretien.

10. de Maistre, *Considérations sur la France*, Chapt. VIII.

11. de Maistre, *Les soirées de Saint-Petersbourg*, 8e entretien.

12. Joseph de Maistre, *Réflexions sur le protestantisme dans ses rapports avec la souveraineté*, in Cioran, *op. cit.*, p. 113.

13. Joseph de Maistre, *Du Pape*, Livre III, Chapt. 2, 2nd ed. (Lyon, 1821).

14. de Maistre, *Les soirées de Saint-Petersbourg*, 2e entretien.

15. *Ibid.*, 7e entretien.

16. de Maistre, *Considérations sur la France*, Chapt. VIII.

17. "... son berceau doit être environné de dogmes," in *Étude sur la souveraineté*, Cioran, *op. cit.*, p. 152; "la plante humaine," in *Examen de la philosophie de Bacon, ibid.*, p. 253.

18. "Quant à celui qui parle ou écrit pour ôter un dogme national au peuple, il doit être pendu comme voleur domestique," in de Maistre, *Les soirées de Saint-Petersbourg*, 8e entretien.
Jean-Jacques Rousseau: "Que si quelqu'un, après avoir reconnu publiquement ces mêmes dogmes, se conduit comme ne les croyant pas, qu'il soit puni de mort; il a commis le plus grand des crimes; il a menti devant les lois," in *Du contrat social*, Livre IV, Chapt. VIII, *Oeuvres choisies*, p. 335.

19. Joseph de Maistre, *Essai sur le principe générateur des constitutions politiques*, in Cioran, *op. cit.*, p. 175.

20. de Maistre, *Les soirées de Saint-Petersbourg*, 6e entretien.

21. *Ibid.*

22. Charles Maurras, *Anthinéa* (Paris, 1901). Cf. Léon S. Roudiez, *Maurras jusqu'à l'Action française* (Paris, 1957), p. 101.

23. de Maistre, *Considérations sur la France*, Chapt. V.

24. Joseph de Maistre, *A Mme. de St. Réal 1806*, in Cioran, *op. cit.*, p. 218; *Au chevalier de Rossi, 1805*, in Cioran, p. 275.

25. Rousseau, *op. cit.*, p. 330.

26. Louis de Bonald, *Essai analytique sur les lois naturelles de l'ordre social ou du Pouvoir, du Ministre et du Sujet dans la société,* 2nd ed. (Paris, 1817), pp. 10 f.
27. *Ibid.,* p. 72.
28. *Ibid.,* p. 195.
29. *Ibid.,* p. 169.
30. *Ibid.,* p. 232.
31. *Ibid.,* p. 30.
32. *Ibid.,* p. 48.
33. *Ibid.,* p. 109.
34. *Ibid.,* pp. 101 f.
35. Auguste Comte, *Abhandlung über den Geist des Positivismus* (Leipzig, 1915), Chapt. III.
36. Auguste Comte, *Die Soziologie* (Leipzig: Kröners Taschenausgabe), CVII, 15.
37. Frédéric Le Play, *La Réforme Sociale en France,* IV (Paris, 1878), 136.
38. *Ibid.,* p. 127.
39. *Ibid.,* I, 276.
40. *Ibid.,* p. 28.
41. *Ibid.,* II, 148.
42. *Ibid.,* IV, 109.
43. *Ibid.,* II, 211.
44. *Ibid.,* p. 311.
45. *Ibid.,* IV, 190 f.
46. *Ibid.,* I, 106.
47. *Ibid.,* III, 22 f.
48. *Ibid.,* I, 238 f.; II, 406 f.
49. *Ibid.,* III, 158 f.
50. *Ibid.,* IV, 73 f.
51. Ernest Renan, *Oeuvres Complètes* (Paris, n.d.), I, 65.
52. *Ibid.,* p. 240.
53. *Ibid.,* p. 69.
54. *Ibid.,* p. 169.
55. *Ibid.,* p. 433.
56. *Ibid.,* p. 349.
57. *Ibid.,* p. 349.
58. *Ibid.,* p. 399.
59. *Ibid.,* p. 360.
60. *Ibid.,* p. 401.
61. However, it was all too often overlooked by Maurras and his school that Renan causes the most extreme theses of this treatise to be uttered by a fictitious person, that is, that he only expresses them with reservations, although there is no doubt that this is where his sympathies lie, rather than with the likewise hypothetically expressed liberal-democratic counterthesis.
62. Renan, *op. cit.,* p. 597.
63. *Ibid.,* pp. 921 f.
64. Renan, *Oeuvres,* II, 1067–1086.
65. Hippolyte Taine, "Introduction," *Histoire de la littérature anglaise,* 18th ed. (Paris, n.d.).

66. H. Taine, *Die Entstehung des modernen Frankreich*, 3 vols. (Leipzig, n.d.). Vol. I, *Das vorrevolutionäre Frankreich*; Vol. II, *Das revolutionäre Frankreich*; Vol. III, *Das nachrevolutionäre Frankreich*. English edition: *The French Revolution (The Origins of Contemporary France)*, 5 vols. (New York, 1892).

67. *Ibid.*, I, 36.

68. *Ibid.*, I, 126.

69. While at first the advocate merely "translates" the feelings of the peasants to him (*Ibid.*, I, 410), shortly afterward the peasant appears to be "guided" by the envious advocate (*Ibid.*, I, 432).

70. *Ibid.*, Vol. II, Part I, p. 102.

71. *Ibid.*, Vol. II, Part III, p. 65.

72. Fustel de Coulanges, "Introduction," *La Cité antique*, 1st ed. (Paris, 1864).

73. Fustel de Coulanges, "De la manière d'écrire l'histoire en France et en Allemagne depuis 50 ans"; "La politique d'envahissement: Louvois et M. de Bismarck"; "L'Alsace est-elle allemande ou française?" and "Réponse à M. Mommsen"; in *Questions contemporaines* (Paris, 1916).

74. René de La Tour du Pin La Charce, *Vers un ordre social chrétien (Jalons de Route 1882–1907)* (Paris, n.d.), p. vii.

75. *Ibid.*, p. 92.

76. *Ibid.*, pp. 350 f.

77. *Ibid.*, p. 348.

78. Cf. Robert Byrnes, *Antisemitism in Modern France* (New Brunswick, 1950).

79. Édouard Drumont, *Mon vieux Paris* (Paris, 1878).

80. Édouard Drumont, *Le testament d'un antisémite* (Paris, 1891), p. viii.

81. *Ibid.*, p. 409.

82. *Ibid.*, p. 15.

83. There is, of course, no single beginning to modern anti-Semitism. Germany (Paul W. Massing, *Rehearsal for Destruction* [New York, 1949]) and Austria were in advance of Drumont—he invokes Stoecker as well as Lueger—but did not produce any relevant literature of note. However, as early as 1845 Alphonse Toussenel (who was a pupil of Fourier and had chiefly the Saint-Simonists in mind) published his *Les Juifs rois de l'époque*. As for the "reality content" of the various forms of anti-Semitism, compare Bismarck's statement that in Germany the rich Jews exerted no undue influence—in Paris it might be otherwise (Massing, *Rehearsal for Destruction*, p. 39).

84. Édouard Drumont, *La France juive*, II (Paris, 1886), 208 f.

85. Édouard Drumont, *La fin d'un monde* (Paris, 1889), pp. 2 f.

86. *Ibid.*, p. 139.

87. *Ibid.*, p. 44.

88. Drumont, *Le testament d'un antisémite*, p. 201.

89. Maurice Barrès, *Scènes et doctrines du nationalisme*, I (Paris, 1902), 153.

90. *Ibid.*, p. 8.

91. Maurice Barrès, *Mes Cahiers* (Paris, 1929–1957), IX, 370.

92. *Ibid.*, XIV, 96.

93. Barrès, *Scènes et doctrines du nationalisme*, I, 40.

94. *Ibid.*, p. 46.

95. *Ibid.*, p. 211.

2 History

1. Cf. Georges Sorel, *La Révolution Dreyfusienne* (Paris, 1909).
2. It should be noted that Millerand became minister only with the consent of his party comrades but not *as* their representative, hence his participation in the government was only unofficial.
3. The only reason that the bible of revisionism, Eduard Bernstein's *Die Voraussetzungen des Sozialismus und die Aufgabe der Sozialdemokratie*, caused such a commotion among the revolutionaries was no doubt because it happened to appear in 1899 and, due to the behavior of the French socialists, was removed so conspicuously from the sphere of pure theory.
4. Theodor Herzl spent the years 1891 to 1895 in Paris; it was the experience of anti-Semitism as set in motion by the Dreyfus affair that made him a Zionist. See Adolf Böhm, *Die zionistische Bewegung bis zum Ende des Weltkrieges*, I (Tel Aviv, 1935), 157.
5. In the 5th edition of his *Die Judenfrage als Frage des Rassencharakters und seiner Schädlichkeiten für Völkerexistenz, Sitte und Kultur* (Nowawes, 1901), Eugen Dühring, referring specifically to the Dreyfus affair, the "trial of trials and scandal of scandals," dissociates himself from the "casual half-measures" which he had recommended in earlier editions, frankly demanding instead "that the whole dubious type be made to disappear" (p. 113).
6. Cf. Hannah Arendt, *Elemente und Ursprünge totaler Herrschaft*, p. 160.
7. See Siegfried Thalheimer, *Macht und Gerechtigkeit—Ein Beitrag zur Geschichte des Falles Dreyfus* (Munich, 1958). Also Joseph Reinach, *Histoire de l'affaire Dreyfus*, 7 vols. (Paris, 1901–1911); Henri Dutrait-Crozon (pseudonym, Action Française), *Précis de l'affaire Dreyfus* (Paris, 1909); further references in Thalheimer and in Arendt, *op. cit.*
8. A convenient summary of works by and on Maurras is contained in Michel Mourre, *Charles Maurras* (Paris, 1958). For more thorough detail, see Roger Joseph-Jean Forges, *Biblio-iconographie générale de Charles Maurras*, 2 vols. (Paris, 1953). For works in general on Maurras, see Albert Thibaudet, *Les idées de Charles Maurras* (Paris, 1920); Henri Massis, *Maurras et notre temps*, 2 vols. (Paris, 1951); Michael Curtis, *Three Against the Third Republic—Sorel, Barrès and Maurras* (Princeton, 1959).
9. Charles Maurras, *Au signe de Flore*, 2nd ed. (Paris, 1933), p. 81.
10. Maurras clung to the version that Henry's forgery had merely been intended to take the place of a document that was too secret to be shown; in diplomacy, for instance, he maintained, such action was quite common and legitimate.
11. Title of a book by Drumont.
12. Maurras, *Au signe de Flore*, p. 82.
13. Maurice Barrès, *Mes Cahiers*, II (Paris, 1929), 177.
14. Robert Havard de la Montagne, *Histoire de l'Action française* (Paris, 1950), p. 50; Charles Maurras, *La contre-révolution spontanée* (Lyons, 1943), p. 261.
15. *Le procès de Charles Maurras* (Paris, 1946), p. 371.
16. Cf. Charles Maurras, *Au signe de Flore; Pour un jeune Français* (Paris, 1949), and

Enfances, in *Oeuvres Capitales*, IV (Paris, 1954), 7 f.; also Roudiez, *Maurras jusqu'à l'Action française*.

17. Charles Maurras, *Pour un jeune Français*, p. 19.
18. Maurras' concept of romanticism includes also the poets of Parnassus and the symbolists.
19. Charles Maurras, *Quand les Français ne s'aimaient pas*, 2nd ed. (Paris, 1926), p. xiii.
20. Charles Maurras, *L'Action française et la religion catholique* (Paris, 1921), p. 462.
21. Maurras, *Au signe de Flore*, p. 31.
22. *Ibid.*, pp. 31 f.
23. Friedrich Nietzsche, *Die Unschuld des Werdens*, II (Leipzig, 1931), 372.
24. Roudiez, *op. cit.*, p. 229.
25. Charles Maurras, *Vers l'Espagne de Franco* (Paris, 1943), p. 114.
26. *Ibid.*
27. Maurras, *Pour un jeune Français*, p. 27.
28. Quoted from *Anthinéa* (Paris, 1901). Later suppressed; cf. Roudiez, *op. cit.*, p. 101.
29. Charles Maurras, *Le Chemin de Paradis*, in *Oeuvres Capitales*, I, 155.
30. *Ibid.*, p. 29.
31. Friedrich Nietzsche, *Ecce homo*, in *Nietzsches Werke*, XI (Leipzig: Taschen-ausgabe, n.d.), 325 f.
32. Cf. Claude Digeon, *La crise allemande de la pensée française* (Paris, 1959); on Maurras: pp. 434 f.
33. Maurras, *Pour un jeune Français*, p. 94.
34. *Ibid.*
35. Charles Maurras, *Gaulois, Germains, Latins* (Paris, 1926), p. 25.
36. Maurras, *Au signe de Flore*, p. 71.
37. Maurras, *Oeuvres Capitales*, I, 267.
38. Havard de la Montagne, *op. cit.*, p. 13; Maurras, *Au signe de Flore*, pp. 90 f.
39. Charles Maurras, *Tombeaux* (Paris, 1921), p. 153: "Il a eu des collaborateurs, des compagnons d'armes. L'initiateur, ce fut lui."
40. Maurras, *Au signe de Flore*, p. 130: "Mon désir serait de raviver, en les mettant en présence, ces deux vérités pures, celle du passé et celle de l'avenir, celle du parti réactionnaire et celle du parti socialiste, de faire voir leur égale noblesse. ..."
41. Jacques Bainville, born 1879, met Maurras after his first journey to Germany, and willingly accepted the solutions of the older man for the alarming problem of Germany's superior power. After that, Germany never let him go. (In contrast to Maurras, he was acquainted with Germany by thorough observation and wide knowledge of its literature.) Narrower than Maurras intellectually but broader in understanding, he went beyond the "sectlike character" of the Action Française without ever abandoning it, for, in his own lofty words, he owed Maurras "tout, sauf le jour." However, the renown of his clear and apparently moderate spirit outshone that of the master's; he died in 1936, just after being appointed to Poincaré's chair in the Académie Française.
42. Léon Daudet came from republican beginnings via Drumont's *Libre Parole* to the Action Française. A powerful orator and a mediocre novelist, he was blunt

in his ideas—see *Le stupide XIXe siècle* (Paris, 1922)—but he was a first-rate portrayer of people and situations—see *Souvenirs des milieux littéraires, politiques, artistiques et médicaux* (Paris, 1920).

43. Louis Dimier, at first the sole practicing Catholic among the leading members of the group, by inclination and background an art historian, played an important part in establishing contacts with Rome. Fairly familiar with German conditions and problems, during the war he submitted a detailed plan for the partition of Germany: *Les tronçons du serpent* (Paris, 1915). After the war he broke with his former friends as a result of tactical and personal differences. His book *Vingt ans d'Action française et autres souvenirs* (Paris, 1926), is the principal source of information for the internal conditions of the Action Française, and presents a highly acute, "hate-love" characterization of Maurras: "il portait sur un nihilisme absolu ... il n'avait d'estime que pour lui ... l'orgueil le plus aveugle, le plus déchainé que j'aie jamais vu ... Maurras était la dispersion, l'ajournement, le retard et l'oubli" (pp. 330 f.).

44. Pierre Lasserre, whose book *Le romantisme français* (Paris, 1907), enjoyed a stupendous success and in spite of everything remained a standard work of literary criticism, also split off later from the Action Française.

45. Reprinted in shortened form in Maurras, *Au signe de Flore*, pp. 157 f.

46. Cf. René Rémond, *La Droite en France de 1815 à nos jours* (Paris, 1954), pp. 199 f. The standard work on the development of French nationalism during the decade before the outbreak of the war is Eugen Weber, *The Nationalist Revival in France, 1905–1914* (Berkeley and Los Angeles, 1959).

47. The point at issue was the disputed interpretation of Paragraph 445 of the "Code d'Instruction Criminelle." The court of appeal quashed the sentence without referring the case back to the military tribunal for a new trial.

48. Cf. Waldemar Gurian, *Die sozialen und politischen Ideen des französischen Katholizismus 1789–1914* (Mönchen-Gladbach, 1929), p. 205.

49. Defense of the Syllabus: *La politique religieuse*, 3rd ed. (Paris, 1914), pp. 141 f.

50. Chiefly the Curia Cardinal Billot and the Archbishop of Montpellier, Cardinal de Cabrières.

51. Charles Maurras, *Le bienheureux Pie X., sauveur de la France* (Paris, 1953), p. 52.

52. *Ibid.*, p. 71.

53. In 1908 the Action Française defended striking workers against Clemenceau's harsh measures; on the other hand, some syndicalists had indignantly hung the bust of the "Republic" out of the window of the Bourse du Travail in Paris. See Maurras, *Pour un jeune Français*, p. 127.

54. Georges Valois (Alfred Georges Gressent) is the only one among the Action Française leaders whose background and education permit him to be compared with Mussolini. His primitive "philosophy of authority" with which he made his debut at the age of twenty-five (*L'homme qui vient*) is a strange mixture of Nietzsche, Maurras, Sorel, and Christianity. After the war he broke with Maurras, founded the first political group in France which imitated Mussolini (*Le Faisceau*, 1925), and finally became a democrat. Of some importance are his memoirs, *D'un siècle à l'autre* (Paris, 1924) and *L'homme contre l'argent* (Paris, 1928).

55. Maurras, *L'Action française et la religion catholique*, p. 485.

56. Cf. Michael Freund, *Georges Sorel—Der revolutionäre Konservativismus* (Frankfurt, 1932), p. 231.

57. Léon Daudet, *L'Avant-Guerre—Études et documents sur l'espionnage juif-allemand en France depuis l'affaire Dreyfus* (Paris, 1913).

58. However, Maurras had no part whatever in the highly successful policy of alliance pursued by France, since his concept of France was on principle not that of an "ally" but solely of a sovereign master in the manipulation of temporary situations. On this basis he could even contemplate an alliance with Germany.

59. Title of a book by Etienne Rey, *Le réveil de l'orgueil français*.

60. Cf. Romain Rolland, *Péguy* (Tübingen-Stuttgart, n.d.), p. 318.

61. Maurras, *Le bienheureux Pie X.*, p. 204.

62. Cf. Charles Maurras, "Discours préliminaire," *Enquête sur la monarchie*, 1st ed. (Paris, 1900), pp. xlvi f.

63. "Lettre à Schrameck," in *Dictionnaire politique et critique* (Paris, 1931–1934), IV, 55 f. The *Dictionnaire* is a compilation of statements by Maurras edited by one of his followers under the pseudonym of Pierre Chardon.

64. Charles Maurras, *Le mauvais traité—De la victoire à Locarno, chronique d'une décadence* (Paris, 1928).

65. *Ibid.*, I, 55.

66. *Ibid.*, II, 107.

67. Cf. Adrien Dansette, "L'Action française et le Vatican," *Esprit*, XIX (1951), 275–299; 446–458.

68. *Ibid.*, p. 293.

69. Havard de la Montagne, *op. cit.*, p. 123.

70. Dansette, *op. cit.*, p. 447.

71. Cf. Note 50. Cardinal Billot was obliged to doff the purple.

72. If one wished to write a history of the renegades of the radical Left, France would offer the most varied and interesting material. A continuous movement of secession goes from Millerand, Briand, and Laval through to Doriot, Déat, and Marion. In Italy everything is concentrated around one towering personality, Mussolini, who is perhaps the only one to possess a reason for his change-over of more than empirical nature. Cf. Ernst Nolte, "Marx und Nietzsche im Sozialismus des jungen Mussolini," in *Historische Zeitschrift*, Vol. CXCI, 2 (October, 1960), pp. 249–335.

    Before Mussolini some lesser figures took the opportunity of the Libyan war to swing to the "national" line, and in his wake followed such a man as Nicola Bombacci, but these men were all of minor importance. In Germany there was nothing comparable; the renegades of the extreme Left all stayed "left." There are few facts which throw such a revealing light on the differences in the political climate of the three countries. Cf. Margret Boveri, *Der Verrat im XX. Jahrhundert* (Hamburg, 1956–57); on Maurras, see II, 150.

73. Cf. Rémond, *op. cit.*, pp. 199 f.

74. *Ibid.*, p. 206.

75. Jacques Bainville, *Journal*, II (Paris, 1949), 172, 174.

76. *Dictionnaire politique et critique*, III, 126.

77. For this he was sentenced to a term of imprisonment and spent the greater part of

1937 in the Santé. Here Maurras wrote among other things the important preface to *Mes idées politiques* (Paris, 1937).

78. Rémond, *op. cit.*, pp. 292 f.

79. Charles Maurras, *Vers L'Espagne de Franco* (Paris, 1943).

80. Preface to Renée de Dreux-Brézé, *Deux mois chez les Nazis d'Autriche* (Paris, 1936), p. 11; but in 1918 he had already called Germanism the "Islam des terres sans soleil," in Charles Maurras, *Décernez-moi le prix Nobel de la Paix* (Paris, 1931), p. 41.

81. Charles Maurras, *Devant l'Allemagne Éternelle* (Paris, 1937), p. viii: "Un statut nouveau de l'humanité se prépare, un droit particulier est élaboré: un code de nouveaux devoirs, auprès desquels les pauvres petites corvées et translations pangermanistes de 1918 feront l'effet de jeux d'enfants."

82. It was Maurras' double "betrayal"—of France's honor and of the socialist trend of his own early days—that made of Georges Bernanos his most powerful enemy, both in speech and feeling. Bernanos had been a *Camelot du Roi* since 1909 and, full of enthusiasm and hope for a new age, he had sung "Henri IV" and the "International" alternately while in prison with some young syndicalists. The *Cercle Proudhon* corresponded most to his hopes: it was not for nothing that he was profoundly influenced by Édouard Drumont, to whom as late as 1931 he dedicated an important but confused book, *La grande peur des bien-pensants— Edouard Drumont* (Paris, 1931). Although his ties with Maurras became looser soon after the war, he sided with the Action Française even after its condemnation by Rome. His relationship to Maurras was mysterious and profound, as in *Nous autres Français*, 27th ed. (Paris, 1950), p. 66: "il nous tient de près, il nous tient à l'âme ... l'homme pour qui nous nous sommes vus privés de sacrements, menacés d'une agonie sans prêtre." For this very reason he condemns him transcendentally in *Scandale de la vérité* (Paris, 1939), p. 28: "Son destin extraordinaire ... ressemble à l'une des formes les plus cruelles de la damnation en ce monde." But just as the disordered reflections of this unruly soul have their political origin—the experience of the anti-Christian white terror in Spain— so political utterances are to be found in their torrent of melodrama which are of extraordinary insight and effectiveness: for example, his characterization of Hitler: "Il réalisait un rêve d'enfant. C'est une chose terrible que la solitude de l'enfant parmi les hommes et quand un être a rompu cette solitude, il voit accourir les foules, son destin éclate comme la foudre" (*Nous autres Français*, p. 128); or his description of Hitlerian thoughts concerning France: "non seulement ces négroides renient leur parole, mais ils s'en vantent" (*Ibid.*, p. 57).

83. Concerning this whole section: Robert Aron, *Histoire de Vichy 1940–1944* (Paris, 1955).

84. By contrast, Maurras' personal and direct influence on Pétain was and continued to be small.

85. Charles Maurras, *La seule France* (Lyons, 1941), p. 188.

86. Charles Maurras, *De la colère à la justice* (Geneva, 1942), pp. 85 f.

87. Maurras, *La seule France*, p. 289: "Mais que pensez-vous du parti adopté?— Rien du tout. Pas d'opinion. Aucune ... Je n'assistais pas aux délibérations, je n'ai pas vu ce dossier: je ne pense rien."

88. Waldemar Gurian, *Der integrale Nationalismus in Frankreich—Charles Maurras und die Action française* (Frankfurt a.M., 1931), p. 92.

89. Maurras, *La seule France*, p. 178.

90. Robert Brasillach had looked after the literary side of the *Action Française* before he became editor-in-chief of the collaborationist and fascist journal *Je suis partout* after the armistice, and for Maurras this made him a traitor. A literary critic of the highest rank, despite his youth, and profoundly influenced by that atmosphere of fresh youthful vitality which he called "fascist," he was shot in 1945 as a collaborator; the opposite of Bernanos, he represented that other radical pole of potential development of a Maurras disciple. Cf. Raoul Girardet, "Notes sur l'esprit d'un fascisme français 1934–1939," *Revue française de science politique*, V (1955), 529–546.

91. Maurras, *La seule France*, p. 196.

92. Charles Maurras, *Pour réveiller le Grand Juge* (Paris, 1951), p. 168.

93. *Ibid.*, p. 164, and *Le procès de Charles Maurras*, stenographic minutes in "Collections des grands procès contemporains," published under the editorship of Maurice Garçon (Paris: Editions Albin Michel, 1946), p. 155.

94. Cf. Aron, *op. cit.*, p. 459.

95. *Ibid.*, p. 576.

96. Charles Maurras, *Lettres de prison* (Paris, 1958), p. 114.

97. Charles Maurras, *Barbarie et poésie*, in *L'Oeuvre de Charles Maurras*, VI (Paris, 1925), 144.

98. Cf. *Le procès de Charles Maurras*.

99. Maurras, *Pour réveiller le Grand Juge*, p. 30.

100. A typical example: Charles Maurras, *Votre bel Aujourd'hui—Dernière lettre à M. Vincent Auriol* (Paris, 1953), p. 487.

101. Marius Plateau, leader of the *Camelots du Roi*, had been murdered in January, 1923. Maurras declared the murder to be a (successful!) German assault on Poincaré's policy. See *Enquête sur la Monarchie*, in Charles Maurras, *Oeuvres*, I (Paris, 1928), cxxxviii. It was in keeping with this outlook when Maurras attributed Hitler's great election victory of 1930 not to the world economic crisis but to the withdrawal of French troops from Mainz. See his trial, *Le procès de Charles Maurras*, p. 74.

102. Maurras, *Pour réveiller le Grand Juge*, p. 44.

103. Maurras, *Le bienheureux Pie X.*, pp. 178 f.

104. Maurras, *Pour un jeune Français*, p. 205.

105. *Ibid.*, p. 96.

106. *Ibid.*

107. *Le procès de Charles Maurras*, p. 76.

108. Charles Maurras, *La contre-révolution spontanée* (Lyons, 1943), p. 65.

109. Maurras, *Vers l'Espagne de Franco*, p. 113.

110. *Ibid.*, p. 13.

111. Aristide Cormier, *Mes entretiens de prêtre avec Charles Maurras* (Paris, 1953).

112. Maurras, *Oeuvres Capitales*, IV, 462 f.

113. An immediate successor to the *Action Française* is the weekly journal *Aspects de la France*. Cf. Raoul Girardet, "L'héritage de l'Action française," *Revue*

française de science politique, VII (1957), 765–792 (de Gaulle's relationship to Maurras would merit a thorough examination).

3 Practice as Consequence

1. Alphonse Lugan, *La fin d'une mystification—L'Action française, son histoire, sa doctrine, sa politique* (Paris, 1928), p. 229.
2. Louis Dimier, *Vingt ans d'Action française* (Paris, 1926), p. 98.
3. *Ibid.*, p. 100.
4. The most important work on the *Camelots du Roi* is Maurice Pujo, *Les Camelots du Roi* (Paris, 1933).
5. Maurras, *Tombeaux*, p. 267.
6. Charlotte Montard, *Quatre ans à l'Action française* (Neuilly sur Seine, 1931), p. 103.
7. Pujo, *op. cit.*, p. 210.
8. There are no detailed studies of the class structure of the Action Française and its various organizations. It is certain that the *Camelots du Roi* were not *merely* a student association; it is highly unlikely that a *considerable* number of members were workers. Essentially the Action Française was neither feudal nor upper middle class in character; rather it was the product of a group of that social level which was supported by powerful forces in the officers' corps, the aristocracy, and the church. The matter of who supplied the financial support is less interesting than might appear. The part played by the industrialist François Coty is well known, but Maurras' statement that he showed Coty the door the moment he attempted to interfere with the newspaper's independence (*La contre-révolution spontanée*) is entirely believable. A paper as doctrinaire as the *Action Française* is not to be bought; at best it will accept financial aid. Moreover, the members of the league and the other organizations regarded it as their highest duty to stand by the paper in its financial difficulties: in this way large sums of money were received. On the other hand, according to Dimier, *op. cit.*, p. 233, the financial administration was a strange one; of all the leaders of the Action Française, only Georges Valois was associated with finance or industry.
9. Pujo, *op. cit.*, p. 25.
10. Dimier, *op. cit.*, p. 127.
11. *O.O.*, IV, 46.
12. The songs are in Pujo, *op. cit.*, pp. 49 f., 151 f.

13. Vivent les Camelots du Roi, ma mère,
    Vivent les Camelots du Roi!
    Ce sont des gens qui se fichent des lois,
    Vivent les Camelots du Roi!

14. Et vive le Roi, à bas la République
    et vive le Roi, la Gueuse on la pendra.

15. Briand nag'ra comme il a la manière
    Et Jaurès boira

son ventre s'emplira.
Et les députés
S'en aller comme des chiens crevés.

16.   Charles Maurras, *Le nouveau Kiel et Tanger* (Paris, 1921), p. 243.

17.   Le Juif ayant tout pris
Tout raflé dans Paris,
Dit à la France:
Tu n'appartiens qu'à nous:
Obéissance
Tout le monde à genoux!

> *Refrain:*
> Non, non, la France bouge
> Et voit rouge,
> Non, non!
> Assez de trahison.

Juif insolent, tais-toi!
Voici venir le Roi!
Et notre race
Court au-devant de lui:
Juif, à ta place!
Notre roi nous conduit.

> *Refrain:*
> Un, deux, la France bouge
> et voit rouge,
> Un, deux
> Les Français sont chez eux.

Demain, sur nos tombeaux
Les blés seront plus beaux.
Formons nos lignes!
Nous avons cet été
Du vin aux vignes,
Avec la royauté.

> *Refrain:*
> Un, deux, la France bouge
> et voit rouge,
> Un, deux
> Les Français sont chez eux.

18.   Georges Valois, *Contre le mensonge et la calomnie* (Paris, 1926).
19.   Pujo, *op. cit.*, p. 208.
20.   Dimier, *op. cit.*, p. 235.

21. *Ibid.*, p. 224.
22. Daudet, *Charles Maurras et son temps*, pp. 97 f.
23. "Lettre à Schrameck," in *Dictionnaire politique et critique*.
24. Valois, *op. cit.*, pp. ix f.
25. Francisque Gay, *Non, l'Action française n'a bien servi ni l'Église ni la France* (Paris, n.d., but after 1926), p. 153.
26. Valois, *op. cit.*, p. 165.
27. Gay, *op. cit.*, p. 105.
28. *Ibid.*, p. 110.
29. *Ibid.*, p. 160.
30. *Ibid.*, p. 169; J. Maritain *et al.*, *Clairvoyance de Rome* (Paris, 1929), p. 209.
31. Dimier, *op. cit.*, p. 121.
32. In detail: Montard, *op. cit.*, pp. 193 f.
33. Maurras, *La contre-révolution spontanée*, p. 99.
34. Henry Bordeaux *et al.* (eds.), *Charles Maurras Témoignages* (Paris, 1953).

4 The Doctrine

1. Concerning method, the following is to be noted: until 1914 the Action Française was unique: a radical-conservative doctrine, an organization and action in a parliamentary republican state which had arisen out of the defeat of conservative forces. This study is based mainly on the years 1899–1914, not on clandestine utterances but on the leading articles and books effective in their day. However, since Maurras' thought reveals no gaps or surprising developments after 1914 it has been considered permissible to draw from time to time on later utterances. In most cases the publication dates of the books for these years are irrelevant, having regard to Maurras' method of composition and to the fact that it has not always been possible to make use of first editions.
2. Charles Maurras, *L'Étang de Marthe*, in *Oeuvres Capitales*, I (Paris, 1954), p. 383.
3. Maurras, *Anthinéa*, in *Oeuvres Capitales*, I, 195.
4. Maurras, *Quand les Français ne s'aimaient pas*, p. 134.
5. Charles Maurras, *Kiel et Tanger* (Paris, 1910), pp. 200 f.
6. Maurras, *Barbarie et poésie*, in *L'Oeuvre de Charles Maurras*, VI, 128.
7. Charles Maurras, *Enquête sur la Monarchie*, 6th ed. (Paris, 1914), p. 213; 1st ed. (1900).
8. Maurras, *Anthinéa*, *op. cit.*, p. 256.
9. Maurras, *Enquête sur la Monarchie*, p. 189.
10. Maurras, *Quand les Français ne s'aimaient pas*, pp. 181 f.
11. *Ibid.*, p. 134.
12. Charles Maurras, *Gaulois, Germains, Latins* (Paris, 1926), p. 25.
13. Charles Maurras, *Romantisme et révolution*, in *L'Oeuvre de Charles Maurras*, III, 211.
14. *Ibid.*, p. 151.
15. Maurras, *Le bienheureux Pie X.*, p. 35.
16. Maurras, *Enquête sur la Monarchie*, p. 474.
17. Maurras, *Quand les Français ne s'aimaient pas*, p. 293.

18. Maurras, *Vingt-cinq ans de monarchisme*, in *Oeuvres Capitales*, II, 511.
19. Maurras, "Discours préliminaire," *Enquête sur la Monarchie*, p. cxvi.
20. Charles Maurras, *L'avenir de l'Intelligence*, in *Oeuvres Capitales*, II, 110.
21. Charles Maurras, *Trois idées politiques*, in *Oeuvres Capitales*, II, 64.
22. Charles Maurras, *Le dilemme de Marc Sangnier* (Paris, 1921), pp. 92 f; 1st ed. (1906).
23. Maurras, *Enquête sur la Monarchie*, p. 226.
24. Leon Trotsky, *Über Lenin* (Berlin, 1924), p. 14.
25. Maurras, *Kiel et Tanger*, p. 235.
26. Maurras, *Enquête sur la Monarchie*, p. 494.
27. Vivent les Camelots du Roi,
    ce sont des gens qui se fichent des lois.
    (Maurras, *La contre-révolution spontanée*, p. 125.)
28. Maurras did not speak German, nor did he have any personal knowledge of Germany. A "course rapide" which he undertook through Southern Germany and Bohemia in 1910, and which did not even engender but merely confirmed a "mélange d'envie et de mépris," cannot be regarded as knowledge.
    In Jacques Bainville, however, he had a first-rate expert on Germany at his side. But he gave the younger man concepts and categories instead of receiving them from him as the better-informed. Indeed, it appears that Maurras' fateful hostility toward Germany was due solely to an overwhelming impression received in his childhood, one which conditioned the thinking of this otherwise virile man until the end of his days. In 1943 at the sight of German soldiers he said: "Voilà réalisé le cauchemar de mon existence. J'ai toujours redouté qu'ils ne vinssent en Provence jusqu'à Martigues" (Massis, *Maurras et notre temps*, II, 212). And as a young man he had stated that William II was looking greedily at Provence, formerly a part of the Holy Roman Empire (*Kiel et Tanger*, p. 109).
29. Maurras, *Kiel et Tanger*, pp. 78 f.
30. *Ibid.*, p. 72.
31. Maurras, *Devant l'Allemagne Éternelle* (Paris, 1937), p. 18.
32. Maurras, *Le dilemme de Marc Sangnier*, p. 118.
33. *Maurras, Quand les Français ne s'aimaient pas*, p. 267.
34. Maurras, *Au signe de Flore*, 2nd ed. (Paris, 1933), p. 118.
35. Maurras, *Le mauvais traité*, II (Paris, 1928), 54.
36. Maurras, *Enquête sur la Monarchie*, p. 203.
37. Maurras, *Le nouveau Kiel et Tanger* (Paris, 1921), p. 240.
38. Maurras, "Une Campagne royaliste au Figaro," in *Enquête sur la Monarchie*, p. 500.
39. Maurras, *De la colère à la justice* (Geneva, 1942), p. 155.
40. S'ils s'obstiennent ces cannibales
    de faire de nous des héros,
    ils sauront bientôt que nos balles
    sont pour nos propres généraux.
    (Maurras, *Quand les Français ne s'aimaient pas*, p. 216.)
41. Maurras, *Le nouveau Kiel et Tanger*, p. 226.
42. *Ibid.*, p. 213.
43. *Ibid.*, p. 208.

44. Maurras, *Kiel et Tanger* (Preface to the definitive edition), p. 23.

45. Maurras, *Enquête sur la Monarchie*, p. 313.

46. Maurras, *Kiel et Tanger*, p. 128.

47. Maurras, *Le dilemme de Marc Sangnier*, p. 126.

48. Maurras, *Enquête sur la Monarchie*, p. 119.

49. Rousseau, *op. cit.*, p. 281.

50. Marx-Engels, *Ausgewählte Schriften*, II (Berlin, 1955), p. 26.

51. The end of this chapter possibly marks the point of the most surprising rapprochement between Rousseau and Nietzsche: "Quoi, la liberté ne se maintient qu'à l'appui de la servitude? Peut-être. Les deux excès se touchent. ... Il y a telles positions malheureuses où l'on ne peut conserver sa liberté qu'aux dépens d'autrui. ... Telle était la position de Sparte. Pour vous, peuples modernes, vous n'avez point d'esclaves, mais vous l'êtes" (Rousseau, *op. cit.*, p. 303).

52. Maurras, "Une campagne royaliste au Figaro," in *Enquête sur la Monarchie*, p. 510.

53. Maurras, *Vingt-cinq ans de monarchisme*, p. 407.

54. Maurras, "Une campagne royaliste au Figaro," p. 511.

55. Maurras, *Kiel et Tanger*, p. 207.

56. Maurras, *Le mauvais traité*, II, 350.

57. Maurras, *Kiel et Tanger*, p. 218.

58. Maurras, "Discours préliminaire," *Enquête sur la Monarchie*, p. xlix.

59. Maurras, *Kiel et Tanger*, p. 198.

60. Maurras, *Gaulois, Germains, Latins*, p. 99.

61. Maurras, *Le mauvais traité*, I, 296–310.

62. Charles Maurras, *La politique religieuse* (Paris, 1914), p. 360.

63. Maurras, *Le dilemme de Marc Sangnier*, p. 108.

64. Maurras, *Kiel et Tanger*, p. 95.

65. Maurras, *Quand les Français ne s'aimaient pas*, p. 226.

66. Maurras, *Décernez-moi le prix Nobel de la Paix* (Paris, 1931), p. 29.

67. *Ibid.*, p. 28.

68. Rousseau's and Marx's attitude to war cannot be defined in a few words, yet it is hardly deniable that Rousseau praises martial virtues more highly than almost any others. On the other hand, there are many utterances reflecting the gentle spirit of the Enlightenment. For Marx as for all socialists, the end of class society also means the end of war; but more than any other socialist he stresses the warlike character of class warfare. As for national wars, he displays no pacifist indignation whatever: on the contrary, he quite realistically accords them their own necessary place in his "system."

69. Maurras, *Décernez-moi le prix Nobel de la Paix*, pp. 17, 25.

70. *Ibid.*, p. 94.

71. *Ibid.*, pp. 85 f.

72. Maurras, *Quand les Français ne s'aimaient pas*, p. 273.

73. *Ibid.*, p. 270.

74. Maurras, *Le dilemme de Marc Sangnier*, p. 60.

75. Maurras, *Tombeaux*, pp. 315 f.

76. Maurras, *Trois idée politiques*, in *Oeuvres Capitales*, II, 97

77. Maurras, *La politique religieuse*, p. 362.
78. *Ibid.*, p. 251.
79. *Ibid.*, p. 369.
80. Maurras, *Le dilemme de Marc Sangnier*, p. 128.
81. *Ibid.*, pp. 72 f.
82. Maurras, *Enquête sur la Monarchie*, p. 303.
83. *Ibid.*, p. 506.
84. Maurras, *La politique religieuse*, p. xix.
85. *Ibid.*, p. 123.
86. Charles Maurras, *Le Chemin de Paradis*, in *Oeuvres Capitales*, I, 28.
87. *Ibid.*, p. 27.
88. Maurras, *L'Étang de Marthe*, in *Oeuvres Capitales*, I, 374.
89. Maurras, *Enquête sur la Monarchie*, p. 228.
90. Maurras, "Introduction," *Ibid.*, p. lxxxviii.
91. *Ibid.*, p. 370.
92. *Quand les Français ne s'aimaient pas*, p. 328.
93. Maurras, *Le mauvais traité*, II, 138.
94. *Ibid.*, p. 143.
95. It is significant that he opposes Jaurès far more vehemently than Guesde, and that he does not deny recognition and a certain sympathy to the Marxist in order to play him off against the humanitarian pacifist.
96. Maurras, *La seule France*, Lyons 1941, p. 221.
97. "Une campagne royaliste au Figaro," *Enquête sur la Monarchie*, p. 517.
98. *Ibid.*, p. 515.
99. Maurras, *Le nouveau Kiel et Tanger*, p. 247.
100. Maurras, *La contre-révolution spontanée*, p. 121.
101. Maurice Paléologue, *Tagebuch der Affäre Dreyfus* (Stuttgart, 1957), p. 86.
102. Maurras, *Le mauvais traité*, II, 22.
103. Maurras, *L'avenir de l'intelligence*, in *Oeuvres Capitales*, II, p. 147.
104. Cf. pp. 106 f.
105. Maurras, *Réflexions préalables sur la critique et sur l'action*, in *Oeuvres Capitales*, III, 217.
106. Maurras, *Barbarie et Poésie*, in *L'Oeuvre de Charles Maurras*, VI, p. 199.
107. Maurras, "Preface," *Romantisme et révolution*, in *Oeuvres Capitales*, II, 34 f.
108. Charles Maurras, *Victor Hugo*, in *Oeuvres Capitales*, III, 343.
109. "Preface," *Romantisme et révolution*, in *Oeuvres Capitales*, II, 33.
110. *Ibid.*
111. Maurras, *Trois idées politiques*, p. 90.
112. Maurras, *Le Chemin de Paradis*, p. 29. (Omitted here, only in the first edition of 1895.)
113. Maurras, *Anthinéa*, pp. 370–387.
114. "Unprecedented" not in the sense of a personal invention. Drumont had anticipated Maurras with such images, and in the German Reichstag Ahlwardt had called the Jews "cholera bacilli" (Massing, *Rehearsal for Destruction*, p. 302). The images are "unprecedented" in a suprapersonal and general sense.
115. Maurras, *Kiel et Tanger*, p. 99.
116. Maurras, *La politique religieuse*, p. xxv.

117. Maurras, *Le mauvais traité*, I, 66.

118. *Ibid.*, pp. 166 f.

119. *Ibid.*, p. 193.

120. Maurras was undoubtedly the very first to demand that Berlin be made a free city (April 7, 1915). See *Gaulois, Germains, Latins*, p. 98.

121. Maurras, *La seule France*, p. 263: "Ne subordonnons pas l'esprit classique aux lieux et temps. Il est l'esprit de l'Eternel et de l'Universel." His comments on archaic Greek art and the "sauvageries de Mycènes" are fantastically radical. See *Anthinéa*, p. 199.

122. In one of his best-known passages, Maurras, in opposition to Clemenceau, emphatically declares himself to be a Roman: "Je suis Romain ... " (*La politique religieuse*, p. 395).

123. In the *Enquête*, Maurras defines his position vis-à-vis fashionable irrationalism as follows: "Ils savent que toute force est inconsciente, mais ils n'ignorent pas que, dans l'ordre humain, la direction de ces forces appartient à la pensée et à la raison ... " (pp. 286 f.). However, the mood of Maurras' life was not so far removed from the irrational climate of the era as might be supposed. After Maurras' death one of his former colleagues wrote: "Il vivait devant nous, au milieu de nous ... dans un perpétuel état d'alerte, d'enthousiasme, de foi, de passion ..." (Bordeaux *et al.* (eds.), *Charles Maurras Témoignages*, p. 190). But Maurras never stooped to making an argument out of his "faith." Even Dimier's highly unfavorable assessment of Maurras' character does not necessarily contradict this image.

124. Maurras, *Enquête sur la Monarchie*, p. 240.

125. *Ibid.*, p. 421.

126. *Ibid.*, p. 495.

127. "Une campagne royaliste au Figaro," in *ibid.*, p. 512.

128. *Ibid.*, p. liii.

129. *Ibid.*, p. xlix.

130. Maurras, *Mes idées politiques*, p. 210.

131. Maurras, *Tombeaux*, p. 299.

132. Maurras, *Vingt-cinq ans de monarchisme*, p. 405.

133. It is as well to keep all the narrowness of Maurras' provincialism clearly in mind and to regard it as the paradigm of a wider phenomenon: of the strange relationship between dynamic (pre-) fascist nationalism and desperate regionalism. A phrase in an autobiographical review of his past, written after his arrest in 1944, is indicative: "Je ne me connais aucun descendant qui soit né hors de Provence ni même au nord d'Orange ou de Gréoulx." See Maurras, *Pour réveiller le Grand Juge* (Paris, 1951), p. 142.

134. Maurras, *La politique religieuse*, p. 30.

135. Maurras, *Le dilemme de Marc Sangnier*, p. 62.

136. Maurras, *Kiel et Tanger*, p. 335.

137. Maurras, *Trois idées politiques*, p. 81.

138. Maurras, *Quand les Français ne s'aimaient pas*, p. 62.

139. *Ibid.*, p. 27.

140. Maurras, *Gaulois, Germains, Latins*, p. 87.

141. Maurras, *Devant l'Allemagne Éternelle*, p. 279.

142. Maurras, *Gaulois, Germains, Latins*, p. 85.
143. Charles Maurras, *Dictateur et Roi*, in *Oeuvres Capitales*, II, 394.
144. Maurras, *Le dilemme de Marc Sangnier*, p. 84.
145. Maurras, *Le nouveau Kiel et Tanger*, p. 249.
146. Maurras, *Kiel et Tanger*, p. 321.
147. Even Lyautey, a man for whom Maurras was otherwise full of praise, is the target of a story Maurras tells to illustrate Lyautey's behavior during the Dreyfus affair, and this anecdote could not shed a more unfavorable light on the loyalty and intelligence of the marshal. See Maurras, *La contre-révolution spontanée*, p. 184.
148. *Ibid.*, p. 274.
149. *Ibid.*, pp. 82 f.
150. Maurras, *Le mauvais traité*, I, 241.
151. Maurras, *Décernez-moi le prix Nobel de la Paix*, p. 50.
152. Maurras, *Gaulois, Germains, Latins*, p. 100.
153. Maurras, *Au signe de Flore*, p. 184.
154. Maurras, *La politique religieuse*, p. 393.
155. Maurras' concept of "juif bien né" indicates the barrier between this concept and the "racist" one. *Tombeaux* contains an article entitled "Pierre David, un héros juif d'Action française." Maurras states categorically here: "La nationalité se crée par l'hérédité, par la naissance: le mot le dit. Elle peut s'enquérir par de bons services rendus" (p. 285). But the scope allowed here to freedom should not be overestimated; it hardly counts when weighed against "hérédité" and "naissance." Yet it is important that he does not deny the possibility of it in principle. Maurras' position as regards race doctrine is determined by Gobineau's "Germanism." He cannot counter it with "Francism" since the facts seem to point to France's inferiority, which a race doctrine would merely "substantiate." Hence the struggle against race doctrine is among the primary conditions of Maurras' doctrine: "se demander, quelle cause précise dissout une société dont les membres ne sont nullement dissolus mais, au contraire, se sentent pleins de rigueur et débordent de vie. Il sera toujours temps de mettre en cause le pays. Avant de l'accuser, il convient au moins d'examiner son gouvernement." See Maurras, "Introduction," *Enquête sur la Monarchie*, p. xi. But even the most radical race doctrine cannot avoid the search for a destructive cause. And, vice versa, the emphasis on what is "natural" in society and nation, and its manifestation in heredity, leads Maurras back repeatedly toward a race doctrine. This applies even more strongly to his fear of the centrifugal trends of the originally "racial" components of France: Gauls, Romans, Germans. Hence his relationship to Gobineau is after all not so unequivocal and negative as he makes it out to be during the latter part of his life. Granted that he calls the Count a "Rousseau gentillâtre" and a "visionnaire," he nevertheless admires (1905) the "vérités de détail ou d'ensemble que l'on peut rencontrer dans l'Essai sur l'inégalité des races." See Maurras, *Gaulois, Germains, Latins*, p. 30.
156. Charles Maurras, *L'Action française et la religion catholique* (Paris, 1921), p.4 71.
157. Maurras, *Enquête sur la Monarchie*, pp. 406 f.

158. *Ibid.*, p. 139.
159. *Ibid.*, p. 491.
160. "Si le coup de force est possible," in *ibid.*, p. 593.
161. *Ibid.*, p. 469.
162. Maurras, *Kiel et Tanger*, p. 98.
163. Maurras, *Gaulois, Germains, Latins*, p. 69.
164. Maurras, *Enquête sur la Monarchie*, p. 500.
165. *Ibid.*, p. 509.
166. "Si le coup de force est possible," in *ibid.*, p. 563.
167. *Ibid.*, p. 556.
168. "Une campagne royaliste au Figaro," in *ibid.*, p. 484.
169. "Si le coup de force est possible," in *ibid.*, p. 556.
170. *Ibid.*, p. 549.
171. *Ibid.*
172. *Ibid.*, p. 546.
173. *Ibid.*, p. 550.
174. Maurras, *Kiel et Tanger*, p. 217.
175. *Ibid.*, p. 13.
176. Maurras 1925: "Il n'y aura pas à discuter avec les politiques républicains, Caillaux, Herriot ou tous autres qui auront ramené sur la France les conditions de la guerre de 1914. Mais il faudra les fusiller." See *Le mauvais traité*, II, 333.
177. Maurras 1924: "Mussolini a su agir, demander, menacer. C'est que, même aux plus mauvais jours, l'Italie dispose d'un gouvernement national, qui savait manier l'esprit public de la nation" ("Introduction," *Enquête sur la Monarchie*, p. lxix). But in *Kiel et Tanger* he already demanded the establishment of an "office public" to keep alive the idea of revenge (p. 36).
178. Maurras, "Une campagne royaliste au Figaro," in *Enquête sur la Monarchie*, p. 486.
179. Maurras, "Discours préliminaire," *Enquête sur la Monarchie*, p. xiv.
180. Maurras, "Postface," *Le Chemin de Paradis*, p. 160.
181. Maurras, *Le Nouveau Kiel et Tanger*, p. 255.
182. Maurras, *Enquête sur la Monarchie*, p. 373.
183. Maurras, *Au signe de Flore*, p. 194.
184. Maurras, *Le dilemme de Marc Sangnier*, p. 74. It might seem surprising that such an apparently fundamental principle of Maurras' work as the struggle against the doctrine of social contract and of the presocial state of nature does not receive more emphasis in the text. In the first place, these doctrines are among the oldest and most obvious components of the conservative doctrine; in the second place, they are directed against a misunderstood (or, as is admitted, self-misunderstanding) Rousseau; and in the third place they misunderstand themselves. For Rousseau, too, "man" and "society" are inseparable concepts: likewise and even more markedly for Marx. The evidence that man is "by nature" a social animal is much too common to be of service to any political doctrine or party. The contract theory can only polemically mean a description of a historical event. In actual fact it is, from a political point of view, the potential justification for a definite fact, for revolution; or (usually simultaneously) the precedence given to contractual over instinctive and purely

historical ties; seen philosophically, it signifies a distant reminder of "transcendental" freedom, going beyond the existing state and only to be experienced in the individual. It *can* turn against *this* society and always limits the dimension of any society. Neither thesis must be jeopardized by Christian-conservative thought, otherwise Christianity, as the new age and the heart of its gospel, would become incomprehensible or alien to this thought. Although this step is foreseeable in de Maistre and de Bonald, it needed Maurras to complete it. In this sense he is a genuine opponent of the contract theory, both as to letter and universal meaning. However, in this opposition he concurs completely with Rousseau and Marx; consequently the opposition as such has no relevance. In his case, as with most conservatives, its political significance is to be found in μετάβασις εις αλλο γένος, the confusion between "society" and "this society": "que la société ne naît point d'une convention, mais qu'elle est naturelle ... qu'enfin il est contradictoire de juger 'absurde' ou 'criminelle' ou 'abominable' cette société sans laquelle il n'y aurait même point lieu de porter un seul jugement rationnel ou moral." See Maurras, *Quand les Français ne s'aimaient pas*, p. 138.

185. *Ibid.*, p. 347.
186. Maurras, *Enquête sur la Monarchie*, p. 391.
187. Maurras, "Postface," *Le Chemin de Paradis*, p. 161.
188. Maurras, *Enquête sur la Monarchie*, p. 391.
189. Maurras, *Barbarie et Poésie*, in *L'Oeuvre de Charles Maurras*, VI, 144 f.
190. Maurras, *Le nouveau Kiel et Tanger*, p. 220.
191. Maurras, *Trois idées politiques*, p. 88 (see below, pp. 432 ff.).
192. Maurras, *Barbarie et Poésie*, in *L'Oeuvre de Charles Maurras*, VI, 301.
193. *Ibid.*, p. 127.
194. Maurras, "Une campagne royaliste au Figaro," in *Enquête sur la Monarchie*, p. 506. Dimier reports a remark of Maurras' which is entirely credible and which dispenses with the usual cautious limitation to a heretical and anti-Roman Christianity: "Avec votre religion, me dit-il un jour, il faut que l'on vous dise que depuis dix-huit cent ans, vous avez étrangement sali le monde." See Dimier, *op. cit.*, p. 30.
195. Maurras, *Quand les Français ne s'aimaient pas*, p. 246. Closely linked with the critique of transcendental idealism is Maurras' criticism of "Hitlerism," which he regards as nothing but a renaissance of Fichteanism—nor will he allow it to be anything else! "... *Mein Kampf* peut être comparé à une édition populaire et rajeunie des anciennes doctrines de Fichte" (*La seule France*, p. 27). Although this thesis agrees with the famous prophecies of Heine, there is no doubt that it is inadequate and erroneous. But it is significant proof of the fact that two phenomena which first, and even after closer observation, appear obviously similar (in this case Action Française and National Socialism) can, with the aid of a few skillfully chosen categories, be shown to be mutually opposed.
196. Maurras, *Romantisme et révolution*, in *L'Oeuvre de Charles Maurras*, III, 194.
197. Maurras, *Trois idées politiques*, p. 81.
198. Charles Maurras, *La Montagne provençale*, in *Oeuvres Capitales*, IV, 133.
199. Maurras, *Barbarie et Poésie*, in *L'Oeuvre de Charles Maurras*, VI, 364.

200. *Ibid.*
201. For the concept of "transcendence," cf. pp. 429 ff.
202. Nietzsche, "ce sarmate ingénieux et passionné" (see Maurras' *Quand les Français ne s'aimaient pas*, p. 114), was for Maurras "notre condisciple" (*Enquête sur la Monarchie*, p. 257), and the accuracy of this description can hardly be doubted, however extravagant the hope that Maurras voices in the same passage: that the young men of France had already surpassed him and would soon relegate him to oblivion.
203. That Maurras knew more about it than he generally showed becomes quite clear in an article which he wrote on the occasion of the first crossing of the Mediterranean by the aviator Garros, entitled "La mort du temps" (*Action Française*, Sept. 24, 1913). He takes as his premise that it will now become technically possible to be in different places at the same time. But essential to all dignified human existence are, according to Alfred de Vigny, "la marche et le repos." "La marche et le repos seront pratiquement abolis: que sera la vie? La solution commune de tant de questions si diverses est invariable: discipline et discipline. Si, moralement, intellectuellement, socialement, les principes de l'ordre ne sont pas renforcés, l'homme ne pourra que rouler tout entier aux dissolutions." (It is interesting to compare the infinitely more naïve, credulous utterances of the young Mussolini, made at about the same time, in respect of a very similar subject. *O.O.*, II, 194.)
204. Maurras, *Pour un jeune Français*, p. 95.
205. "Le genre humain c'est notre France": see the article "Civilisation," in *Dictionnaire politique et critique*.
206. Maurras, *La politique religieuse*, p. 11.

PART THREE

Italian Fascism

1 History

1. Two very revealing utterances of Mussolini on this subject are reported by Yvon De Begnac, *Palazzo Venezia—Storia di un regime* (Rome, 1950), pp. 185, 647. According to this, Mussolini had replied to Georges Valois' claim that "l'Action Française è stato il nido del fascismo" by saying: "Sì, ma, nella culla, il bébé ce l'ho messo io." An analysis dating from 1939 is more serious in tone: "… Dietro ogni patriottismo, resta l'urgenza storica ed economica che lo alimenta. Il romanticismo e la retorica dei Lemaître ed dei Barrès non concludono nulla in argomento. Diverso, molto diverso, Maurras. Egli proviniva dal proibito campo sociale. Il suo patriottismo monarchico nulla ha da invidiare al patriottismo repubblicano dei Déroulède et dei Drumont, in quanto ad intensità di ispirazioni e di pensieri. Giunse a tanto da incapsulare nelle proprie spire persino quell'orso selvatico che fu Georges Sorel …" Almost thirty years earlier he had written: "La parabola di Giorgio Sorel à altamente significativa. Quest'uomo è passato—quasi impunemente—dalla teoria del sindacato a quella dei … camelots du roi …" (*O.O.*, IV, 46). There can be no doubt, there-

fore, that the Action Française occupied Mussolini's political thinking long and deeply.

2. Giuseppe Mazzini, "Ai Giovani d'Italia," in *Le più belle pagine di Giuseppe Mazzini—Scelte da Carlo Sforza* (Milan, 1923), p. 63.
3. Giuseppe Mazzini, "La Pace," *ibid.*, p. 69.
4. It is significant that the report on the party conference by Ettore Ciccotti in *La Voce* did not mention Mussolini by name. See *La cultura italiana del' 900 attraverso le riviste, Vol. II: La Voce* (Turin, 1960), pp. 470 f.
5. Alfredo Oriani, *Rivolta Ideale* (Bologna, 1943), p. 268.
6. Giosuè Carducci, *Odi barbare—Alle fonti del Clitumno.*
7. Gabriele D'Annunzio, "Il Trionfo della Morte," *Prose di Romanzi*, I (Milan, 1954), 958.
8. *La cultura italiana del' 900 attraverso le riviste, Vol. I: Leonardo, Hermes; Vol. II: La Voce* (cf. p. 313: "Bisogna fare qualcosa d'importante").
9. To be quite accurate, one should also mention the futurists led by Filippo Tommaso as well as the revolutionary syndicalists, whose chief representative was Filippo Corridoni, who was killed in the war and later made a fascist martyr. But Marinetti's role in fascism was hardly more than a picturesque one (in 1921 he demanded in the Fascist Central Committee that the pope be banished to Avignon), although it is true that the futurists' prewar postulates ("svecchiare, pacificare, innovare et velocizzare l'Italia") contributed to the forming of the fascist spirit. The most outstanding fascist personality to emerge from the ranks of the futurists was Giuseppe Bottai, still a very young man when the war ended, who was for a time on the staff of *Roma futurista* (cf. also Giorgio Alberto Chiurco, *Storia della rivoluzione fascista*, I, 21 f. [see Note 173]). In Italy the "syndicalists" were not always readily distinguishable from the Marxists: Edmondo Rossoni, for example, whose development was similar in many ways to Mussolini's before he became organizer and leader of the fascist syndicates. The actual anarcho-syndicalists on the whole played a peripheral or temporary role in fascism: e.g., Alceste De Ambris, one of the motivators of D'Annunzio's *Carta del Carnaro*, and Massimo Rocca (Libero Tancredi), leader of the first *gruppi di competenza*, which were a germ cell of corporatism. Both these men later emigrated. A veteran anarchist was Leandro Arpinati, *Ras* of Bologna and from 1929 to 1933 secretary of state for the ministry of the interior. During the internal struggle for power, he was sidelined by Starace and forced into exile (cf. De Begnac, *op. cit.*, pp. 557 f.).
10. E.g., G. A. Borgese, *Golia—Marcia del fascismo*, pp. 189, 206.
11. He insists, for instance, that Plato's sophistic principle in *The State*, "to do good to one's friends, evil to one's enemies," is a Socratic maxim (e.g., *O.O.*, XXI, 310); and he attributes the *homo mensura* sentence to Anaxagoras (*O.O.*, XXXI, 188).
12. Cf. Ernst Nolte, "Marx und Nietzsche im Sozialismus des jungen Mussolini," *Historische Zeitschrift*, Vol. CXCI, 2. Note Mussolini's remarks (quoted by De Begnac, *op. cit.*, p. 359) in a letter to Nicola Bombacci, who had been sentenced to several months' imprisonment: "Quanto ai libri, io credo che tu possa farti mandare la nuova edizione delle opere di Marx, Engels, Lassalle ... e ne avrai abbastanza per 4 mesi."

13. Torquato Nanni, Mussolini's first biographer and, during the socialist epoch, probably his closest personal friend, says cautiously that Mussolini had never been a "complete" Marxist and had given a Blanquist interpretation to the concept of power; in *Bolscevismo e fascismo nel lume della critica marxista— Benito Mussolini* (Bologna, 1924), p. 154. Mussolini himself attached much importance in his first chamber speech to this former "Blanquism" of his, thereby determining the direction of the later interpretation. See *O.O.*, XVI, 440.

14. Among more recent publications: Paolo Alatri, *Le origini del fascismo* (Rome, 1956), p. 323; Paolo Monelli, *Mussolini piccolo borghese* (Milan, 1950).

15. For the early history of Italian socialism, cf. Ernesto Ragionieri, *Socialdemocrazia tedesca e socialisti italiani 1875–1895* (Milan, 1961).

16. Particularly in Mussolini's *La mia vita* [written 1911–12], 1st ed. (Rome, 1947), pp. 25, 32; now also in *O.O.*, Vol. XXXIII.

17. Cf. *O.O.*, I, 251.

18. (Erotic) brutality and self-centeredness emerge with astonishing frankness in *La mia vita*. But it should not be forgotten that this first and most reliable autobiography was the product of imprisonment.

19. E.g. Yvon De Begnac, *Vita di Benito Mussolini*, 3 vols. (Milan, 1936 ff.); Margherita Sarfatti, *Dux* (Milan, 1926). Cf. Nolte, *op. cit.*, p. 250; pp. 292 f.

20. *O.O.*, IV, 155.

21. *O.O.*, II, 32.

22. E.g., *O.O.*, III, 308.

23. *O.O.*, II, 431.

24. *O.O.*, I, 44; and II, 235.

25. *O.O.*, III, 83.

26. *O.O.*, I, 51.

27. Cf. Gaudens Megaro, *Mussolini in the Making* (London, 1938), p. 81; not in *O.O.*

28. *O.O.*, I, 102.

29. *O.O.*, II, 126.

30. *O.O.*, III, 271.

31. *O.O.*, IV, 153.

32. *O.O.*, VI, 179.

33. *O.O.*, V, 249.

34. *O.O.*, IV, 142.

35. The marked extent to which all Italian socialism bore bourgeois and humanitarian characteristics is shown by Roberto Michels, *Storia critica del movimento socialista italiano* (Florence, 1926).

36. *O.O.*, III, 355.

37. *O.O.*, XVI, 440: "Conosco i comunisti. Li conosco perchè parte di loro sono i miei figli ... intendiamoci ... spirituali ... e riconosco con una sincerità che può parere cinica, che io per primo ho infettato codesta gente, quando ho introdutto nella circolazione del socialismo italiano un po' di Bergson mescolato a molto Blanqui."

38. The first was probably Claudio Treves at the party conference at Ancona (*O.O.*, VI, 478).

39. *O.O.*, VI, 7.

40. *O.O.*, IV, 156.

41. *O.O.*, V, 176.
42. *O.O.*, VI, 173.
43. "The whole thing in Germany wird abhängen von der Möglichkeit, to back the Proletarian revolution by some second edition of the Peasants' war." See Marx-Engels, *Ausgewählte Schriften*, II (Berlin, 1955), 426.
44. *O.O.*, V, 138.
45. *O.O.*, VI, 81.
46. *O.O.*, V, 69.
47. "Noi, marxisti e catastrofici," *O.O.*, I, 116.
48. Lenin, *Ausgewählte Werke*, I (Berlin, 1955), 508: "Revolutions are the feast days of the exploited and the oppressed."
49. *O.O.*, V, 346.
50. *Ibid.*, p. 121.
51. *HKG*, II, 340, Engels to Marx, Oct. 7, 1858: "so that this most bourgeois of all nations apparently wants to end up by possessing a bourgeois aristocracy and a bourgeois proletariat *as well as* the bourgeoisie."
52. "In Germany the Communist party, whenever the bourgeoisie behaves in a revolutionary manner, fights side by side with the bourgeoisie against absolute monarchy, feudal ownership of land, and the petite bourgeoisie." See *Kommunistisches Manifest*, in Marx-Engels, *Ausgewählte Schriften*, I, p. 53.
53. Lenin, *op. cit.*, I, 63.
54. *O.O.*, III, 313.
55. *Ibid.*, p. 47.
56. *O.O.*, VI, 51.
57. *Ibid.*, p. 50.
58. *O.O.*, V, 126.
59. *O.O.*, II, 75.
60. *O.O.*, V, 114: "Colla rapidità del fulmine la selezione tra i forti e i deboli, tra gli apostoli e i mestieranti, tra i coraggiosi e i villi."
61. *Ibid.*, pp. 268, 271.
62. *O.O.*, IV, 156.
63. Cf. *O.O.*, Vol. I, p. 128.
64. Marx-Engels, *Ausgewählte Schriften*, II, 322.
65. *Ibid.*, p. 328.
66. Lenin, *op. cit.*, I, 879.
67. *O.O.*, IV, 154.
68. *O.O.*, III, 206.
69. *O.O.*, V, 67.
70. E.g., *O.O.*, II, 53.
71. *O.O.*, VI, 248.
72. *O.O.*, V, 24.
73. *Ibid.*, p. 134.
74. *O.O.*, VI, 80.
75. *O.O.*, III, 5.
76. *O.O.*, V, 314.
77. *O.O.*, I, 138.
78. *O.O.*, III, 312.

79. *O.O.*, II, 187.
80. *Ibid.*, pp. 194 f.
81. *O.O.*, VI, 82.
82. *O.O.*, II, 240.
83. *O.O.*, III, 19.
84. *O.O.*, V, 211.
85. *O.O.*, III, 254.
86. *O.O.*, IV, 191 f. Mussolini spoke frequently to De Begnac of his profound nostalgia for the young Mussolini: "Sì, il dissidio tra i due Mussolini c'è. Ed è, tal volta, profondo, terrible ..." (November, 1938). In talking to the young man he attributed the conflict to the tautology that in those days he had been (young and) free and now was (old and) burdened with many ties. Quotations such as the foregoing throw quite a different light on this utterance. See De Begnac, *op. cit.*, p. 567.
87. *O.O.*, VI, 85.
88. *O.O.*, IV, 174.
89. *O.O.*, V, 122.
90. *O.O.*, VI, 75.
91. *O.O.*, II, 169.
92. *O.O.*, III, 280.
93. *O.O.*, II, 206.
94. *O.O.*, I, 120.
95. *O.O.*, IV, 53.
96. *Ibid.*, p. 155.
97. *Ibid.*
98. *O.O.*, III, 137.
99. *O.O.*, IV, 199.
100. *Ibid.*, p. 235.
101. Cf. Note 19.
102. *O.O.*, I, 24.
103. *Ibid.*, p. 132.
104. *O.O.*, III, 137.
105. *O.O.*, IV, 130.
106. *O.O.*, V, 180.
107. *O.O.*, I, 120.
108. Franz Mehring (ed.), *Aus dem literarischen Nachlass von Karl Marx, Friedrich Engels und Ferdinand Lassalle*, 3 vols. (Stuttgart, 1913).
109. Marx-Engels, *Ausgewählte Schriften*, I, 319.
110. In detail, Nolte, *op. cit.*
111. Marx-Engels, *Ausgewählte Schriften*, II, 425.
112. In Vol. XVIII of the German edition of Lenin, Mussolini is described in this way.
113. This is one of the theses by which Angelica Balabanov disqualifies her book, *Wesen und Werdegang des italienischen Faschismus* (Vienna and Leipzig, 1931), p. 197.
114. Lenin, *op. cit.*, I, 884.
115. *Ibid.*

116. *O.O.*, VI, 311.
117. *Ibid.*, p. 290.
118. *O.O.*, V, 351.
119. *O.O.*, VI, 402 f.
120. *Ibid.*, p. 382.
121. *Ibid.*, p. 318.
122. He was later to become one of the principal leaders of Italian communism.
123. *O.O.*, VI, 331 f.
124. *Ibid.*, pp. 339 f.
125. *La cultura Italiana del' 900 attraverso le riviste, Vol. II: La Voce*, p. 716.
126. When Mussolini said much later (in 1943), in order to justify Italy's entry into World War II, that at the time only three men had wanted the war: Corridoni, D'Annunzio, and himself (*O.O.*, XXXI, 161), this is only correct when taken with several grains of salt.
127. *O.O.*, VI, 391.
128. The fact that Mussolini was able to write such a decisive article without having to ask for anyone's consent, clearly shows the strength of his position within the party.
129. *O.O.*, VI, 410.
130. *Ibid.*, p. 443.
131. Cf. Gaetano Salvemini, "Mussolini e l'oro francese," in the appendix to his book, *Mussolini diplomatico* (Bari, 1952), pp. 419–431.
132. *O.O.*, VII, 441.
133. Michele Bianchi later played an important role as secretary general of the party and quadrumvir of the March on Rome. After the victory, however, Mussolini gave him positions of only second and third rank. Cesare Rossi remained one of Mussolini's closest collaborators, until they were divided by the Matteotti murder. Rossi's revelations almost caused Mussolini's downfall; he did not escape the powerful man's wrath, was brought back from Switzerland and sentenced to long imprisonment by the "special political tribunal." After the war he wrote: *Mussolini com'era* (Rome, 1947); *Il Tribunale Speciale* (Milan, 1952).
134. *O.O.*, VII, 70.
135. *Ibid.*, p. 81.
136. *Ibid.*, p. 99.
137. *Ibid.*, p. 153.
138. Although Mussolini's behavior during the war was not heroic, it does not warrant the accusations of cowardice and timidity often leveled against him by his enemies (e.g., Balabanov, *op. cit.*).
139. Cf. the memoirs of Erzberger and Fürst Bülow, neither of whom mentions Mussolini.
140. *O.O.*, VII, 386.
141. *O.O.*, VIII, 11.
142. *Ibid.*, p. 13.
143. *O.O.*, IX, 5.
144. *O.O.*, XI, 343.
145. *O.O.*, VIII, 157.
146. *O.O.*, X, 136.

147. *Ibid.*, p. 158.
148. *O.O.*, XI, 446.
149. *Ibid.*, p. 249.
150. As late as Aug. 26, 1914, he contemptuously dismissed the nationalists: "è assai ridicolo pretendere d'ingannare il prossimo col portare sulle spalle l'ermellino di Grande Potenza quando—come diceva Bismarck dei nobili polacchi—non si ha la camicia sotto ..." (*O.O.*, VI, 341). Five months later he said: "Insomnia, bisogna decidersi: o la guerra o se no finiamola con la commedia della Grande Potenza. Facciamo delle bische, degli alberghi, dei postriboli e ingraniamo" (*O.O.*, VII, 147).
151. *O.O.*, IX, 21 f.
152. *O.O.*, X, 415 f.
153. Cf. Note 150.
154. *O.O.*, XI, 175.
155. Apparently Lenin also knew and esteemed Mussolini; he is said to have reproached the Italian party for having lost him (cf. De Begnac, *op. cit.*, p. 360: "Già nel novembre 1914 egli rimproverava al Partito Socialista di avermi perduto. Lessi di lui quel poco che mi capitava sottomano tradotto in francese od in tedesco. Subivi il fascino della sua interpretazione catastrofico-marxista della storia"). Trotsky is reported to have made a similar statement (*Ibid.*, p. 644). However, Lenin's name appears nowhere in the writings of the Marxist Mussolini.
156. *O.O.*, IX, 74.
157. *O.O.*, VIII, 286.
158. *O.O.*, IX, 75.
159. *Ibid.*, p. 176.
160. *Ibid.*, p. 286.
161. *O.O.*, X, 41. The name "Zederbaum" apparently arose from a confusion with Martow (cedar tree). Apfelbaum, Rosenfeld, and Bronstein are the original names of Sinoviev, Kamenev, and Trotsky.
162. Cf. "The Action Française," p. 124 f. That which remained for Mussolini a momentary impulse, became for Hitler the basis of his whole political thought and emotion (cf. Ernst Nolte, "Eine frühe Quelle zu Hitlers Antisemitimus," *Historische Zeitschrift*, Vol. CXCIII, 3, pp. 584 f.). During this early period Mussolini shows practically no indications of incipient anti-Semitism.
163. *O.O.*, X, 393.
164. *O.O.*, XI, 231.
165. *Ibid.*, p. 341.
166. *Ibid.*, p. 191.
167. In August, 1918, he dropped the subtitle "Socialist Newspaper" and replaced it with "giornale dei combattenti e dei produttori" (*Ibid.*, p. 241). Soon afterward he gave an explanation for this in keeping with the spirit of his "life-philosophy": "Sono socialista? Primo di rispondere: non, ho dovuto colla fredda ragione soffocare i richiami nostalgici del sentimento, oscurare il 'chiaro di luna' dei ricordi della famiglia e della giovinezza, passare oltre gli scogli che sembravano insuperabili, nel mare di tante memorie, spezzare definitivamente un' abitudine mentale. Mi sono persuaso che, per me, la

parola 'socialista' era vuota di significato. Un uomo intelligente non può essere una cosa sola. ... Lo spirito è sopratutto 'mobilità' " (*Ibid.*, p. 271).

168. *O.O.*, X, 435.
169. Cf. *O.O.*, VII, 156.
170. *O.O.*, XI, 461.
171. There is no better demonstration of the true situation in Fiume than the fact that, after D'Annunzio's flight, free elections resulted in the victory of the "autonomists" under Zanella whom Mussolini liked to call "Croats." It required a fascist *Putsch* to restore Fiume to "Italian" hands. The final solution, negotiated by Mussolini as prime minister, brought more or less the same result as could have been achieved with no difficulty before D'Annunzio's march: renunciation of Dalmatia except for Zara, Fiume Italian except for the port of Baross. The "Dalmatians" among Mussolini's followers did not at all approve of his attitude; right in the fascist parliament a significant altercation took place between Mussolini and Giunta (*O.O.*, XII, 350 f.).
172. The Treaty of Rapallo between Italy and Yugoslavia (1920) made Fiume a "free city."
173. They have been described in varying degrees of detail in all histories of fascism. Because of the involved nature of the subject, the only reports of interest to us today are those which are fully documented. On the fascist side, the following may be mentioned: Giorgio Alberto Chiurco, *Storia della rivoluzione fascista*, 5 vols. (Florence, 1929 ff.), a chronicle of the events in the separate provinces, without survey or continuity, highly partisan in presentation but constituting a vast collection of material (the appendix contains a detailed bibliography on the postwar situation, Fiume, nationalism, etc.). The work of an anti-Fascist (no longer Communist), one of the former directors of *L'Ordine Nuovo* of Turin (with Antonio Gramsci, Umberto Terracini, and Palmiro Togliatti), Angelo Tasca's *Nascita e avvento del fascismo* (Florence, 1950), is far more ambitious and significant. Unfortunately, Tasca's understandable prejudice against Mussolini causes him at times to quote misleadingly (cf. Tasca, p. 40, with *O.O.*, XII, 180 f.). It was first published in Paris in 1935 under the author's pseudonym A. Rossi as *La naissance du fascisme*.
174. Much later on the Duce Mussolini ascribed this role to the Piave battle of June, 1918 (*O.O.*, XXV, 214). The contemporary Mussolini saw things much more matter-of-factly (*O.O.*, XI, 148 f.).
175. Cf. Note 171.
176. Don Sturzo's Popular Party (PPI) might be called its Right and Catholic wing; it continued to be the only one that figured publicly.
177. *O.O.*, XII, 255.
178. *O.O.*, XIII, 58.
179. It is very strange that A. Tasca, *op. cit.*, was often obliged to admit that Mussolini was right as against himself (the Tasca of 1919–1922).
180. Among those present were many Fascists whose names later became very familiar, such as Italo Bresciani, Roberto Farinacci, Filippo Tommaso Marinetti, Giovanni Marinelli, Mario Giampaoli, Umberto Pasella.
181. *O.O.*, VIII, 220.
182. *Ibid.*, p. 18.

183. *O.O.*, XII, 338.
184. President of the *Confederazione Generale del Lavoro*, the largest trade-union organization in the country. Existing side by side with it were the *Unione Sindacale Italiana*, run by the anarchists, and the *Unione Nazionale del Lavoro*, from which came most of the fascist syndicalists, including Edmondo Rossoni.
185. President of the metal workers' union.
186. *O.O.*, XII, 71.
187. *O.O.*, XIV, 9.
188. *O.O.*, XIII, 170. Here are even to be found the rudiments of a political race doctrine: the revolution of Fiume, he says, resulted in two races and two mentalities being brought face to face; all those who took part in war were essentially different from those who stayed at home (*O.O.*, XIV, 21); the socialist deputies were in many cases anthropological idiots (*O.O.*, XIII, 199).
189. Concerning the Arditi, cf. Manlio Cancogni, *Storia dello squadrismo* (Milan, 1959), pp. 13 f.
190. In 1912 Mussolini had had Bissolati expelled from the Socialist party; during the war (much of which Bissolati, then close to sixty, spent in the trenches as a volunteer), Mussolini regarded him as a representative of the leftist interventionists in the cabinet; when after the war Bissolati wanted to make the spirit of the Risorgimento the guiding line instead of mere decoration, Mussolini quickly dubbed him "leader [*sic*] dei tedeschi" (*O.O.*, XII, 143), and again a year later he wrote a glowing obituary about him (*O.O.*, XIV, 437). Cf. also p. 148 above.
191. This episode, as well as the fact that the socialists did not attempt any revenge on the *Popolo d'Italia*, is a clear indication that from the very beginning they were inferior in the sphere of organized violence. The reply consisted of the workers raising an extremely large sum of money for their newspaper, funds which far exceeded the losses. But it was not the last fire at *Avanti!*.
192. *O.O.*, XII, 233.
193. Born 1867 in Samminiatello near Montelupo (in the province of Florence) of small-farmer parents, Corradini was for many years a professor in Florence; as a dramatist and novelist he was influenced by D'Annunzio and, although not very successful before 1900, he was for some time editor of the important journal *Marzocco*. After the establishing of *Il Regno* he was active as a politician only, and made a political work of his most successful novel, *La patria lontana*, which dealt with Italian emigrants in South America. Later he was among the principal champions of the merging of nationalism and fascism, and in 1923 he became a senator under Mussolini and in 1928 a minister of state (rank only). The most convenient selection from his works is *La Rinascita nazionale*, edited by Goffredo Bellonci (Florence, 1929). Concerning Italian nationalism cf. Paolo Alatri, "L'ideologia del nazionalismo e l'esperienza fascista," in: *Le origini del fascismo*.
194. *La cultura italiana del' 900 attraverso le riviste, Vol. II: La Voce*, p. 441.
195. *Ibid.*, p. 452.
196. *Ibid.*, pp. 532 f.
197. Enrico Corradini, *Il Volere d'Italia* (Naples, 1911), p. 205.
198. Francesco Coppola, born 1878 in Naples, in 1918 (together with Alfredo Rocco)

founded *Politica*, the largest Italian journal for international politics (concerning the relationship with the Action Française and Italian nationalism, cf. Maurras, *Dictionnaire politique et critique*, III, 125).

199. Francesco Coppola, Introduction to *La crisi italiana* (Rome, 1916).

200. *Ibid.*, p. 165.

201. Alfredo Rocco, born in 1875, outstanding professor of law at the universities of Padua and Rome, rendered Mussolini (especially during 1925–26) invaluable services by preparing the *leggi fascistissime* (cf. p. 218 below). Rocco's works, *Scritti e discorsi politici*, 3 vols. (Milan, 1938), contains in Vol. III the first attempt at a "doctrine of fascism": *La dottrina politica del fascismo*; in Vol. II a revealing essay: "Il fascismo verso [*sic*] il nazionalismo," with the confident opinion concerning the "originarie scorie pseudorivoluzionarie e pseudo-democratiche" of fascism (pp. 696 f.).

202. Enrico Corradini, *Il Nazionalismo italiano* (Milan, 1914), p. 126: "Come la terra di atmosfera, così la cosiddetta rivoluzione italiana è fasciata di tutto lo spirito della rivoluzione francese. ... Ne conseguí una debolezza nel costituirsi del popolo italiano a nazione, non tanto perchè quel sostituirsi avveniva sotto l'influsso di idee straniere, quanto perchè queste idee formarano il codice morale per una rivoluzione sociale e non per una emancipazione nationale."

203. Enrico Corradini, *L'Ombra della vita* (Naples, 1908), pp. 170–173.

204. In 1914 it became a daily paper. Its editorial staff consisted of: Roberto Forges-Davanzati, Francesco Coppola, Enrico Corradini, Luigi Federzoni, Maurizio Maraviglia.

205. Luigi Federzoni, born in 1878, originally a writer and journalist, was the most outstanding parliamentarian of the small nationalist faction. In 1921–22 he was a kind of teacher of Mussolini's on the floor of Montecitorio; after the Matteotti murder he played an important role as minister for the interior; pushed to one side by opponents in the party (he was considered a confidant of king and court) to less influential posts—president of the Senate, president of the Italian academy—he was a member of the Grand Council as late as 1943, and voted with the majority against Mussolini.

206. For a contemporary point of view on the part of a foreigner, cf. J. N. Macdonald, *A Political Escapade: The Story of Fiume and d'Annunzio* (London, 1921). D'Annunzio's political writings from the war and postwar period are now assembled in his collected works published by Mondadori, Milan: *Prose di recerca, di lotta, di comanda, di conquista, di tormento, d'indovinamento, di rinnovamento, di celebrazione, di rivendicazione, di liberazione, di favole, di giochi, di baleni*, Vol. I (Milan, 1954). The quotations in the text are from contemporary editions.

207. Shortly before the elections, D'Annunzio placed Fiume under martial law and threatened death to "chiunque professi sentimenti ostili alla causa di Fiume" (!). See Tasca, *op. cit.*, p. 75.

208. Gabriele D'Annunzio, *Italia e Vita* (Rome, 1920), p. 83.

209. Cf. Anthony Rhodes, *The Poet as Superman—A Life of Gabriele D'Annunzio* (London, 1959), p. 196.

210. D'Annunzio, *Italia e Vita*, pp. 51, 58.

211. *Ibid.*, p. 32.

212. *Ibid.*, p. 42.
213. Gabriele D'Annunzio, *La Reggenza italiana del Carnaro—Disegno di un nuovo ordinamento dello Stato libero di Fiume* (Novara, 1925). Also in *Prose di recerca* ... , I, 107–134.
214. Malatesta was one of the last survivors from Bakunin's alliance and, according to the opinion of well-informed persons, the sole serious revolutionary in the Italy of that time. Cf. Tasca, *op. cit.*, p. 78.
215. Doubtless it was not ordinary cowardice that led him to do this; more likely it was an aversion to the logical but not esthetic consequence.
216. The official who was looking after and guarding D'Annunzio announced the poet's death to Mussolini with a very revealing *lapsus linguae*: "I have the pleasure to inform you of some bad news." See Galeazzo Ciano, *Tagebücher 1937–1938* (Hamburg, 1949), p. 116.
217. *O.O.*, XIV, 16.
218. *O.O.*, XV, 196.
219. *Ibid.*, p. 313.
220. *O.O.*, XIV, 60.
221. *O.O.*, XV, 194. Torquato Nanni, *op. cit.*, p. 162, relates that, side by side with Schopenhauer and Nietzsche, Stirner was also always to be found on the young Mussolini's desk.
222. *O.O.*, XIV, 398.
223. *Ibid.*, p. 193. However, Marx's significance for the later Mussolini should not be judged only by the number of polemical quotations. Marxist phrases, altered to a greater or lesser degree in word and meaning, frequently flow from his pen, apparently unconsciously: e.g., the liberation of the working class must be the work of the working class itself; or, "C'è uno spettro in Italia ... lo spettro del fascismo," *O.O.*, XVI, 198.
224. *O.O.*, XIV, 232.
225. *Ibid.*, p. 341.
226. *Ibid.*, p. 80.
227. *Ibid.*, p. 445.
228. *Ibid.*, p. 350.
229. *Ibid.*, p. 176.
230. *O.O.*, XV, 93. Cf. the all too revealing concluding words of an interview given to the *Echo de Paris* in October, 1933: "Intendo sperimentare come stanno facendo Roosevelt e Stalin." In the Italian version this sentence was omitted. See Gaetano Salvemini, *Sotto la scure del fascismo* (Turin, 1948 [first edition, New York, 1936]), p. 128. Strangely enough it also does not occur in *Opera Omnia*.
231. *O.O.*, XV, 19.
232. *O.O.*, XVI, 7.
233. *O.O.*, XIV, 480.
234. *Ibid.*, p. 316.
235. *O.O.*, XV, 151.
236. *Ibid.*, p. 231: "Quella che si è svolta in Italia, in questo settembre che muore, è stata una rivoluzione, o, se si vuole essere più esatti, una fase della rivoluzione, cominciata, da noi, nel maggio 1915. ... Un rapporto giuridico plurisecolare

è stato spezzato. Il rapporto giuridico di ieri era questo: merce-lavoro da parte dell' operaio, salario da parte del datore di lavoro. ... Da ieri questo rapporto è stato alterato. L'operaio, nella sua qualità di produttore, entra nel recesso che gli era conteso, e conquista il diritto di controllare tutta l'attività economica, nella quale egli ha parte."

237. *Ibid.*, pp. 226 f.

238. *Ibid.*, p. 273.

239. Chiurco, *op. cit.*, III, 25.

240. Spokesmen for maximalism were, among others, Count Antonio Graziadei and Professor Adelchi Baratono, who gave a quotation from Horace as the title of an article in *Avanti!*, thus incurring Mussolini's ridicule. See *O.O.*, XVIII, 400.

241. Alatri, *op. cit.*, p. 248.

242. It is hard to believe that a socialist attempt at revolution, even if an outstanding leader had been present, could have been successful at any time. It is inconceivable that socialism could have attained a point of departure such as had been won by the Fascists in October, 1922, thanks to the complicity of the state and the goodwill of the army. However, had there been a single determined division under firm command, the fascist attempt would in all probability have failed. A simultaneous outbreak of popular rising could not be expected considering the highly differentiated conditions throughout Italy.

243. Tasca, *op. cit.*, p. 21.

244. Cf. Antonio Gramsci, *L'Ordine Nuovo* (Turin, 1955). Mussolini on Gramsci: "mostruoso e deforme nel corpo e nell' anima..." (*O.O.*, XVI, 225), "un sardo gobbo ... un cervello indubbiamente potente" (*O.O.*, XVII, 291). Gramsci on Mussolini: "il tipo concentrato del piccolo borghese italiano rabbioso, feroce, impasto di tutti i detriti lasciati sul suolo nazionale dai vari secoli di dominazione degli stranieri e dei preti." Quoted by Tasca, *op. cit.*, p. xxix.

245. Chiurco, *op. cit.*, II, 49.

246. Cf. the comment of a landed property owner, as reported by Tasca: "Non abbiamo mica paura di Bombacci, è Baldini che ci fa paura perchè, colla sua Federazione delle Cooperative, ci fa sostituire dappertutto." See Tasca, *op. cit.*, p. 151.

247. De Begnac, *op. cit.*, p. 492.

248. Tasca, *op. cit.*, p. 119.

249. *O.O.*, XII, 314.

250. The earliest report on events was given in Germany by Robert Michels in *Archiv für Sozialwissenschaft*. Also in *Sozialismus und Faschismus in Italien*, II (Munich, 1925), pp. 201 f.

251. Tasca, *op. cit.*, p. 78.

252. E.g., "Non è il fascismo che ha vinto la rivoluzione, è l'inconsistenza della rivoluzione che provoca il sorgere del fascismo." Tasca, *op. cit.*, p. 123.

253. Salvatorelli-Mira, *Storia del fascismo*, p. 108.

254. Dino Grandi, born in 1895 near Imola, a lawyer, together with Balbo and Bottai probably the most independent and outstanding personality among the fascist politicians; 1926–1929, secretary of state in the foreign ministry, 1929–1932, foreign minister, 1932–1939, ambassador to London, chief spokesman for Italy's

Western orientation. His draft resolution for the Grand Council session of July 25, 1943, contributed in large degree to the fall of Mussolini.

255. Chiurco, *op. cit.*, II, 214.

256. Giacinto Menotti Serrati, close friend of the young Mussolini, in 1914 his successor as editor of *Avanti!*, after the war the chief spokesman of maximalism in Italy.

257. Cancogni, *op. cit.*, pp. 59 f.

258. To be accurate it should be added that here the resistance of the *Arditi del popolo* and the population of the Old City had found the support of the troops. The defender of Parma, Guido Picelli, fell fifteen years later in Madrid. See Tasca, *op. cit.*, pp. 335 f.; 369.

259. Socialist versions completely ignore the deeds of the *teppa*: cannibalistic acts of horrifying cruelty (cf. Chiurco, *op. cit.*, II, 78; 168). Fascist historians always attempt to depict fascist actions as reprisals. But even an extremist like Roberto Farinacci admits in his book on the fascist revolution that in the fascist punitive expeditions the bounds of moderation were often exceeded. See Roberto Farinacci, *Die faschistische Revolution* (Munich, 1939), II, 246. Similarly he does not deny the class-war nature of the struggle, or the fact that police and officers were often on the side of the Fascists.

260. *O.O.*, XV, 267.

261. E.g., Chiurco, *op. cit.*, III, 41, 113.

262. Cf. Alatri, *op. cit.*, p. 82.

263. Generally speaking, Mussolini is far from concrete when it comes to naming fascist measures, but the above-mentioned facts can be documented in his writing. See *O.O.*, XVI, 357.

264. The Fascists of Florence, city of art and literature, were known to be the most fanatical of all. Their leader was the (militarily demoted) Marchese Dino Perrone Compagni; other important personalities were Dumini (who later murdered Matteotti) and Tamburini (a schoolteacher who had been dismissed from office and who finally became chief of police of the *Repubblica di Salò*. For details see Cancogni, *op. cit.*

265. The immediate cause was no doubt the hunger strike undertaken by Errico Malatesta and certain other anarchists in prison in Milan. Cf. the report of a survivor: Armando Borghi, "L'attentato del Diana," in *Il Ponte* (1954), pp. 725–735.

266. Tasca, *op. cit.*, p. 160.

267. Cancogni, *op. cit.*, pp. 106 f.

268. *Ibid.*, p. 124.

269. *Giornale d'Italia*, January 23, 1921; Chiurco, *op. cit.*, III, 32.

270. This view was also expressed by the parliamentary commission which examined the events in Bologna: antisocialist reaction, it stated, had been evinced by various parties, the Fascists had merely voiced it more prominently than any other; it was only after the disaster of the Palazzo d'Accursio that fascism had exerted a special attraction, particularly on young people and students. See Chiurco, *op. cit.*, III, 48.

271. Italo Balbo, born 1896 near Ferrara, a republican, Freemason, editor of *Voce Mazziniana*, an officer of the *Alpini*, after the war he obtained his degree with a

thesis on Mazzini's social thought; generalissimo of the militia, quadrumvir, later minister of aviation, air marshal, and governor of Libya, the only Fascist who, despite Mussolini's jealousy and suspicion, managed to preserve his unmistakable individuality, due in large part to his squadron flights over the Atlantic. Although Hitler thought very highly of him and saw in him a "Renaissance man" and a worthy successor to the Duce (*Hitler's Table Talk*, p. 613), Balbo was sharply opposed to the Germanophile course and was almost the only member of the Grand Council to take the part of the Jews. He fell in the summer of 1940, shot down by his own antiaircraft over Sollum.

272. Cesare Maria de Vecchi (later Conte di Val Cismon), born 1884 near Turin, a lawyer, convinced monarchist, the representative of big landowners.

273. Emilio De Bono, born 1866, officer, in 1920 transferred at his own request as a general to a "posizione ausiliaria speciale" in order to devote his energies to fascism; quadrumvir, later marshal of Italy, shot in Verona on January 11, 1944.

274. Costanzo Ciano, naval officer, commandant of the *Beffa di Buccari* made famous by D'Annunzio's participation, closely linked to the plutocracy of Leghorn, important mediator between Mussolini and industry, later admiral and chamber president.

275. Special mention must be made here of the use of castor oil, which forces the human being to surrender to nature in the most degrading manner possible; also the use of the strangely shaped cudgel (*manganello*), which has been described as the special symbol of fascist culture. Cf. Pietro Calamandrei, "Santo Manganello," in *Il Ponte* (1952), pp. 1444 f. Also extraordinarily symbolic was the *tessera speciale* of the *Squadra Celibano* in Ferrara: a piece of hide bearing the name on the front and decorated with animals on the back (Cancogni, *op. cit.*, p. 82; illustration in Chiurco).

276. Chiurco, *op. cit.*, III, 256.

277. Renato Ricci, 1919–20 a legionary of D'Annunzio, then squad leader in Carrara, later leader of the *Balilla*, minister of corporations, commandant of the militia in the *Repubblica di Salò*.

278. Chiurco, *op. cit.*, III, 459 f.

279. The hostility shown by the population of Rome to the Fascist National Congress of November, 1921, was largely attributable to the fact that various fascist divisions had used threats and violence to try and obtain respect.

280. *O.O.*, XVI, 31.

281. *O.O.*, XI, 344.

282. *O.O.*, XVI, 44.

283. *Ibid.*, p. 276.

284. *Ibid.*, p. 182.

285. *Ibid.*, p. 288.

286. *Ibid.*, p. 241.

287. *Ibid.*, p. 287.

288. *Ibid.*, p. 347.

289. *Ibid.*, p. 124.

290. *Ibid.*, p. 127.

291. *Ibid.*, p. 212.

292. *O.O.*, XVII, 51 f.
293. *O.O.*, XVI, 239. Although Mussolini acknowledged race warfare to be the actual reality of the fascist-socialist confrontation in Trieste and went on, "la razza è un fatto, duro come il granito" (*ibid.*, p. 138), this must not be taken as the beginning of a political race doctrine. In this case *razza* corresponds to the German *Volkstum* (nationality, race).
294. *Ibid.*, p. 335.
295. "Li spazzeremo" (re: the South Tiroleans), "vi romperemo fascisticamente le ossa" (re: the socialists), *ibid.*, p. 301.
296. *Ibid.*, p. 157. Moreover, the battle with Lenin found itself united on one point, that of analysis and prophecy: the revolution in Russia was not socialistic, but agrarian, of the democratic petit-bourgeois type (*ibid.*, p. 152); Lenin's historical merit consisted in having prepared the soil for Stinnes, one day Russia would be one of the most powerful productive forces in the world (*ibid.*, p. 121).
297. *Ibid.*, pp. 359 f.
298. These consisted chiefly in the fact that Mussolini voiced his doubts about the idea of the "controllo sindacale" (*ibid.*, p. 360).
299. *Ibid.*, p. 363.
300. *Ibid.*, p. 367.
301. *Ibid.*, p. 372.
302. *Ibid.*, p. 383.
303. *Ibid.*, p. 431.
304. Cf. a remark from the year 1939: "... Altri consiglieri di Leandro Arpinati si salvarono, allora. I migliori, i più sinceri, mossero diretti verso il confino. Erano tutti vecchi repubblicani o socialisti" (De Begnac, *op. cit.*, p. 112).
305. *O.O.*, XVII, 21.
306. *Ibid.*, p. 66.
307. *Ibid.*, p. 75.
308. *Ibid.*, pp. 72, 101.
309. Concerning the meeting at Todi, see a short and unclear version in Chiurco, *op. cit.*, III, 510.
310. *O.O.*, XVII, 80.
311. *Ibid.*, p. 91.
312. *Ibid.*, p. 105.
313. Cf. his remark made in July 1921 to Turati: "Voi mi avete tacciato di Maddaleno pentito. Pessima frase. Infelicissima ... accetto il fascimo in blocco" (*ibid.*, p. 64).
314. That he could previously only be called thus in an unreal sense is shown among other things by a remark of his quoted by De Begnac, *op. cit.*, p. 299, "Il 'Movimento' avveva un comitato centrale, di cui io facevo parte, senza particolar predominio sugli altri membri."
315. Shortly before the congress, Mussolini studied in detail Adriano Tilgher's book, *Relativisti contemporanei*, and stated: "... noi siamo veramente i relativisti per eccellenza e la nostra azione si richiama direttamente ai più attuali movimenti dello spirito europeo." The context shows that this is said primarily in connection with Marx's self-liberation. The way he goes on is indicative: "... si, come Wahinger [Vaihinger] afferma, il relativismo si riannoda a

Nietzsche e al suo Willen zur Macht, il fascismo italiano è stato ed è la più formidabile creazione di una 'volontà di potenza' individuale e nazionale." See *O.O.*, XVII, 269.

316. *O.O.*, XVII, 268.
317. *O.O.*, XVIII, 453.
318. *Ibid.*, p. 277.
319. *Ibid.*, p. 282.
320. *O.O.*, XVII, 99.
321. Cf. the detailed study by Paolo Alatri, "Il secondo ministero Facta e la marcia su Roma," in *Le origini del fascismo*.
322. Tasca, *op. cit.*, p. 276.
323. *O.O.*, XVIII, 331.
324. *Ibid.*, p. 340.
325. *Ibid.*, p. 358.
326. Cf. Italo Balbo, *Diario 1922* (Milan, 1932), entries for July 28, 29, and 30; Tasca, *op. cit.*, pp. 315 f., Chiurco, *op. cit.*, IV, 166–191.
327. The expression was first used by the reformist paper *La Giustizia*, edited by Claudio Treves.
328. Benedetto Croce was also among the guests.
329. D'Annunzio seemed to be assuming more and more the role of protector of a new and nation-reconciling labor party. He evinced particular goodwill toward the *Federazione Italiana dei Lavoratori del Mare* (led by Captain Giulietti), which had rendered very effective support to the Fiume enterprise but which was now seriously threatened by the growth of the fascist counter-syndicate. To the horror of his syndicalists, Mussolini surrendered the fascist organizations in a formal agreement, thus obtaining D'Annunzio's shortsighted goodwill. See *O.O.*, XVIII, 565 f.
330. Chiurco, *op. cit.*, V, 208.
331. *O.O.*, XVIII, 419.
332. *Ibid.*, p. 416.
333. *Ibid.*, p. 581.
334. Cancogni, *op. cit.*, p. 164.
335. Chiurco, *op. cit.*, V, 122.
336. *Ibid.*, p. 159.
337. During Mussolini's triumphal journey to Rome, there were always two Blueshirts in his entourage.
338. "All barracks in Siena occupied by Fascists. Field-gray and Blackshirts fraternizing." See Chiurco, *op. cit.*, V, 141.
339. Ulisse Igliori had been D'Annunzio's adjutant in Fiume.
340. Cf. the General's report in: *Il Ponte* (1952), pp. 123–126; Emanuele Pugliese, "L'esercito e la marcia su Roma."
341. Among these they unhesitatingly numbered several leftist-bourgeois newspapers such as *Secolo* and *Epoca*.
342. Apparently Mussolini originally considered including representatives of the CGL, but at the last moment he abandoned the idea, probably as the result of certain pressures. See Tasca, *op. cit.*, p. 459.
343. The principal secretary of state position of the interior was given to Aldo Finzi,

a Jew and former member of D'Annunzio's most famous air squadron. Mussolini praised him as having been chiefly responsible for the growth of the militia (*O.O.*, XIX, 351), but during the Matteotti crisis he dropped him as he did Cesare Rossi. In 1944 Finzi was shot by the Germans as the leader of an antifascist group of partisans.

344. This merely accentuated and accelerated a natural process which was taking place in every country. However, until 1925 there were still some "fascist" strikes.

345. *O.O.*, XIX, 187.

346. *O.O.*, XX, 167.

347. *O.O.*, XIX, 17.

348. Mussolini, "Forza e consenso," in *Gerarchia* (March, 1923). This article contains the famous and infamous remark: "Si sappia dunque, una volta per tutte, che il fascismo non conosce idoli, non adora feticci e, se sarà necessario, tornerà ancora tranquillamente a passare sul corpo più o meno decomposto della Dea Libertà." See *O.O.*, XIX, 196.

349. Cf. Gaetano Salvemini, *La terreur fasciste 1922–1926* (Paris, 1938).

350. "Se cioè questi residui di cui parlavo poco fa intendessero occupare ancora un po' la scena politica, essi sanno, e tutti gli italiani debbono sapere, che io chiamerei le camicie nere, molte delle quali mordono il freno e sono impazienti" (*O.O.*, XIX, 274). "Ditemi dunque, o camicie nere di Toscana e di Firenze, se è necessario di recominciare, ricominceremo?" ("Sì, sì, bene" Applausi scroscianti) (*ibid.*, p. 277).

351. To the members of the central committee of the nationalists after the agreed fusion, March 5, 1923: "Io, sinceramente, vi dico che voi ci dovete dare dei quadri, degli uomini, dei valori. Ma con questo non si deve credere che il fascismo sia stato senza teorie ..." (*ibid.*, pp. 161 f.). Cf. also Mussolini's memorial speech in honor of Enrico Corradini (December 11, 1931), which calls the founder of nationalism a Fascist "of the very first hour," namely of 1896. See *O.O.*, XXV, 71.

352. On freedom (cf. Note 348): "Lo Stato cos'è? È il carabiniere" (*O.O.*, XIX, 316). Cf. further Mussolini, "Preludio al Machiavelli," first appeared in *Gerarchia*, (April, 1924), in *O.O.*, XX, 251–254.

353. E.g., *O.O.*, XX, p. 127.

354. Cf. Giacomo Matteotti, *Reliquie* (Milan, 1924). Also contains the last speech with all interruptions (pp. 263–282). The most complete description of the crime and what led up to it is to be found in Gaetano Salvemini, *La terreur fasciste, 1922–1926* (Paris, 1930).

355. *O.O.*, XX, 318, 324.

356. *Ibid.*, p. 329.

357. *O.O.*, XXI, 70, 206.

358. Cf. Monelli, *op. cit.*, p. 161.

359. *O.O.*, XXI, 235 f.: "... Se il fascismo è stato una associazione a delinquere, io sono il capo di questa associazione a delinquere ... la spedizione dell' Aventino ha sfonda repubblicano." The timing of the speech was no doubt determined by the publication of the *Memoriale Rossi* on December 27, 1924, in which his former colleague mercilessly exposed the practices of fascism.

360. The young man alleged to be responsible was lynched by the crowd under suspicious circumstances. Mussolini's own comments indicated that the perpetrator was unknown. The rumor has never died that it was an assassination carried out on orders, or the work of Fascist extremists. Cf. Gaetano Salvemini, "Mussolini storico di se stesso," in *Il Ponte*, V (1949), 707 f.

361. Cf. below pp. 221 ff.

362. *O.O.*, XXI, 266.

363. Concerning the murders in Florence, see Gaetano Salvemini, *La terreur fasciste*, pp. 27 f.; Cancogni, *op. cit.*, p. 186.

364. Roberto Farinacci, *Un periodo aureo del partito nazionale fascista* (Foligno, 1927), pp. 147, 231, 273, 339.

365. A comprehensive survey of the constitutional and legal situation is contained in Helmut Vollweiler, *Der Staats- und Wirtschaftsaufbau im faschistischen Italien* (Würzburg, 1939).

366. *O.O.*, XXI, 362.

367. *O.O.*, XXII, 379.

368. "Legge sulle società segrete, Legge suoi fuorusciti, Legge sulla burocrazia, Legge sulla difesa dello Stato."

369. "Legge sulla facoltà del potere esecutivo di emanare norme giuridiche, Legge sulle attribuzioni e prerogative del capo del governo primo ministro segretario di Stato, Riforma della rappresentanza politica, Ordinamento e attribuzioni del Gran Consiglio del fascismo."

370. "Legge sulla disciplina giuridica dei rapporti collettivi del lavoro, Costituzione e funzioni delle corporazioni."

371. *O.O.*, XXII, 109. The sentence describes the relations extremely vaguely; not only has "controllare" a different meaning in each of the three cases: it even combines completely different circumstances in one single utterance. The organizations of the employers were not "controlled" in the same manner as those of the employees.

372. *Ibid.*, p. 91.

373. Cf. Vollweiler, *op. cit.*, p. 73.

374. *O.O.*, XXIV, 101.

375. Cf. this work, p. 261.

376. *O.O.*, XXIV, 89.

377. Cf. Luigi Salvatorelli, "La chiesa e il fascismo," in *Il Ponte*, VI (1950), 594–605.

378. Emigration among the political general staffs of the antifascist parties was as wholesale as it was in Germany (among the emigrants were Turati, Treves, Amendola, Don Sturzo, Nitti, Buozzi, Nenni, Tasca, Togliatti). The new political beginnings, which in Germany managed to develop within the country, could only arise among the Italians who had left the country (e.g., Carlo Rosselli and the group *Giustizia e Libertà*). A considerable portion of the intellectual elite emigrated even without racial persecution: Salvemini, G. A. Borgese, De Bosis, Silone, Gobetti.

379. *O.O.*, XXII, 246.

380. E.g., Gaetano Salvemini, *Sotto la scure del fascismo*, p. 309. A very unpleasant feature that resulted was pointed out by Salvemini: "In Italia, è impossibile

costruire nel più piccolo villaggio un lavatoio pubblico senza che i giornali ne parlino come di un inaudito avvenimento" (p. 315).

381. *O.O.*, XXIII, 216.
382. Salvatorelli-Mira, *op. cit.*, p. 675.
383. *O.O.*, XXV, 185.
384. *Ibid.*, p. 49.
385. *O.O.*, XXIV, 224.
386. His tendency to brag becomes very evident when he claims to have taken an interest in two million affairs of citizens in the course of a few years.
387. Emil Ludwig, *Gespräche mit Mussolini* (Leipzig, 1932). Mussolini's words in his chamber speech on "Conciliazione" are very significant (although meant as a threat): "Nessuno creda che l'ultimo fogliuocolo che esca dall' ultima parocchia non sia conosciuto da Mussolini." See *O.O.*, XXIV, 89.
388. E.g., in his speech of February 6, 1926 (*O.O.*, XXII). Side by side with the government's avowed will to destruction, it was the unofficial violence of local party organs (corresponding nevertheless to official intentions) which made the nationality struggle in South Tirol and the Venezia Giulia stand out from the "normal" European picture. The fact that the fate of the South Tiroleans caused feeling to run high in Germany was not due solely to romantic affection for the southernmost German region. It stands to reason that a politician of the Right like Hitler could only approve of Mussolini's policy without losing his own self-respect if he was planning something infinitely "greater" for Germany than the defense of an existing and ethnic reality. For details of the persecution, cf., for example, F. K. Hennersdorf [Felix Krauss], *Südtirol unter italienischer Herrschaft* (Charlottenburg, 1926). Conditions in the Venezia Giulia are reported from the Yugoslavian point of view in *Italian Genocide Policy against the Slovenes and Croats*, published by the Institute for International Politics and Economy (Belgrade, 1954).
389. *O.O.*, XXIII, 142.
390. *O.O.*, XXV, 147 f.
391. *O.O.*, XXVI, 84.
392. *O.O.*, XXII, 197.
393. *O.O.*, XXVI, 259; cf. *O.O.*, XXI, 444.
394. *O.O.*, XXIV, 236.
395. *O.O.*, XXVI, 308.
396. *O.O.*, XXVII, 17.
397. *O.O.*, XXIII, 74.
398. *O.O.*, XXVI, 233.
399. *Ibid.*, p. 310. The most famous utterance on this subject is that from the Bari speech of September 6, 1934: "Trenta secoli di storia ci permettono di guardare con sovrana pietà talune dottrine di oltr' Alpe, sostenute dalla progenie di gente che ignorava la scrittura, con la quale tramandare i documenti della propria vita, nel tempo in cui Roma aveva Cesare, Virgilio e Augusto" (*ibid.*, p. 319).
400. Cf. the reports of his journey to Germany early in 1922, *O.O.*, XVIII, 93 f. Words which in their context sound quite harmless today attract our special attention, fixing as they do Mussolini's first encounter with the swastika:

"L'unico distintivo che si vede qua e là è la croce uncinata, che sarebbe come chi dicesses il distintivo degli antisemiti" (*ibid.*, p. 97).

401. That Mussolini was not without such thoughts as late as 1938 is shown by his remark to Ciano that he would eventually lead the whole world united against Germanism and crush Germany for at least two hundred years. See Ciano, *Tagebücher 1937–1938*, p. 153.

402. *O.O.*, XXVI, 45.

403. *O.O.*, XXVII, 36.

404. Galeazzo Ciano claims that in May, 1935, Flandin advised him how best to initiate the conflict. See Ciano, *Tagebücher 1937–1938*, p. 301.

405. Mussolini ordered Badoglio to use gas and flame throwers extensively (*O.O.*, XXVII, 306), wished to see *all* war measures in use (p. 310), ordered summary executions when Addis Ababa was occupied (p. 320), insisted on "a systematic policy of terror and extermination" against rebels and the accomplices among the population. See *O.O.*, XXVIII, 266.

406. *O.O.*, XXVII, 269.

407. *Ibid.*, p. 394.

408. Cf. letter to D'Annunzio, *ibid.*, p. 302.

409. *O.O.*, XXVIII, 267.

410. When he first used the word it did not have the "steely" character of later times: it was meant to signify the opposite of a "diaframma" (*ibid.*, p. 70, November 1, 1936).

411. *Ibid.*, p. 197.

412. Cf. Hitler's description of Mussolini as reported by Ciano (October, 1936): "... the leading statesman in the world, to whom none may even remotely compare himself." See *Ciano's Diplomatic Papers* (London, 1948), p. 56.

413. *O.O.*, XXVIII, 252. The texts of the speeches and toasts of Hitler and Mussolini are also contained in *Weltgeschichte der Gegenwart in Dokumenten*, edited by Michael Freund, 2nd ed. (Essen, 1942), V, 333 f.

414. The term "imperialism" is totally inadequate to describe Hitler's intentions. Even liberal and nonliberal colonial policy should not be covered by one term.

415. Cf. Galeazzo Ciano, *Tagebücher 1939–1943* (Bern, 1947), pp. 123, 128.

416. Cf. below, pp. 329 ff.

417. In the summer of 1938, Mussolini told Ciano he wanted to turn Migurtinia into a Jewish settlement. Matters would be facilitated by notable natural resources, among them shark-hunting, "very favorably, because at first many Jews would be devoured in this way" (Ciano, *Tagebücher 1937–1938*, p. 214). On the subject of Mussolini's "humanity" toward political opponents, cf. the remark reported by De Begnac, *op. cit.*, p. 377: "Preferisco primo umiliare e, poi, perdonnare. Preferisco obbligare gli altri a fare quello che io, vinto, mai mi sentirei disposto a compiere. ..."

418. E.g., *O.O.*, I, 177: "La morale degli schiavi finisce per avvelenare la gioia del tramonto alle vecchie caste—e i deboli trionfano sui forti e i pallidi giudei sfasciano Roma."

419. E.g., "nuovi miti semitico-orientali" (*O.O.*, XIV, 135), "gli irati numi dell'olimpo semitico che dirige il bolscevismo" (*O.O.*, XVII, 35). Cf. also above p. 176. However, in "Ebrei, bolscevismo e sionismo italiano," *O.O.*, XV, 269 f.,

he explicitly denies the identification, yet issues a serious warning to the Italian Jews not to support Zionism; only on these terms, he says, would there be no anti-Semitism in Italy.

420. This dispute evidently originated in a misunderstanding of the journal's use of the term "race" in a spiritual sense and deduced from it a justification for an anti-Jewish racism. See *O.O.*, XXVIII, 202 f. For the subject as a whole, cf. Antonio Spinosa, "Le persecuzioni razziali in Italia," in *Il Ponte*, VIII (1952), 964–978, 1078–1096, 1604–1622, and IX (1953), 950–968; Meir Michaelis, "On the Jewish Question in Fascist Italy," in *Yad Washem Studies*, IV (1960), and the series of articles entitled "Gli ebrei italiani sotto il regime fascista," in *La Rassegna mensile di Israel* (Rome, 1962 ff.). Comprehensive and disputed: Renzo De Felice, *Storia degli ebrei italiani sotto il fascismo* (Turin, 1962).

421. The best-known anti-Semite (even before 1914) was Giovanni Preziosi; his journal: *La Vita Italiana*.

422. Even during the campaign he displayed genuine indignation over a report that Italian soldiers were engaging in friendly card-games with natives in Massaua. A strict ban was immediately decreed. See *O.O.*, XXVII, 321.

423. *O.O.*, XXIX, 126.

424. *Ibid.*, p. 146.

425. *Ibid.*, pp. 168 f.

426. Ciano, *Tagebücher 1937–1938*, p. 218.

427. The background to the signing of the "steel pact," which was to result in so much tragedy, seems like a bad farce. See Ciano, *Tagebücher 1939–1943*, p. 14. For a critical view, see Ferdinand Siebert, *Italiens Weg in den Zweiten Weltkrieg* (Frankfurt a.M. and Bonn, 1962), pp. 171 f.

428. Fascists and National Socialists vied with each other in contemptuous and indignant opinions concerning the royal court; but the fact that the *existence* of the monarchy still set definite bounds to fascist power is shown by Ciano in *Tagebücher 1937–1938*, p. 288.

429. *O.O.*, XXIX, 143.

430. Cf. *O.O.*, XI, 82.

431. Typical of how the state had become a completely private affair is Ciano's report (*Tagebücher 1937–1938*, p. 122): "Actually one works solely in order to see him satisfied: when one is successful, that is the supreme reward." Galeazzo Ciano, born 1903, the son of one of the highest dignitaries of the regime and husband of Mussolini's daughter, may be regarded as the *princeps* of fascist youth. For him war was a sport, life an adventure, revolution a word, and social position a very serious reality (cf. p. 514, Note 61). Only his own and Italy's declining fortunes gave him seriousness of purpose and finally a courageous death (January 11, 1944, in Verona).

432. On August 4, 1922, Michele Bianchi sent the following telegram to D'Annunzio: "Il Partito Nazionale Fascista raccoglie il vostro altissimo monito e ricambia il grido di viva il fascismo!" The poet replied: "Vi è un solo grido da scambiare oggi fra italiani: Viva l'Italia! È il mio. ... Credo che debba essere anche il vostro. ..." See *O.O.*, XVIII, 535 f. Some time previously Mussolini had

spoken specifically of a "duplice amore": "la nazione e il fascismo." See *O.O.*, XVII, 264.

433. However, if Hitler later tried to regard this as one of the determining factors for the loss of the war, he was not always of this opinion. Mussolini reported quite convincingly that in the spring of 1942 Hitler regarded the Duce's actions in Greece as one of Providence's most fortunate dispensations, since without them "the Balkan plague-spot" would not have been cauterized. See *O.O.*, XXXI, 56.

434. *O.O.*, XII, 226: "... si può tranquillamente intonare il De profundis alla Jugoslavia. La poverina è morta. Prima ancora di essere nata, è morta."

435. *O.O.*, XXIX, 366.

436. "Noi siamo alleati d'una grande, potentissima nazione militare. E la nostra non-belligeranza è data dal fatto che questa grande nazione ancora non ha avuto bisogno de noi, non ci ha chiesto nulla ..." (*ibid.*, p. 375).

437. *Ibid.*, p. 395.

438. *O.O.*, XXX, 113.

439. Ciano, *Tagebücher 1939–1943*, pp. 300 f.

440. *O.O.*, XXX, 150.

441. *O.O.*, XXXI, 138.

442. Cf. Benito Mussolini, *Storia di un anno*, in *O.O.*, Vol. XXXIV; G. Bottai, *Vent'anni e un giorno, 24. Luglio 1943* (Milan, 1949); Dino Grandi, *Dino Grandi racconta* (Venice, 1945).

443. *O.O.*, XXXI, 223.

444. *O.O.*, XXXII, 1–5.

445. The most important were: Alessandro Pavolini, the new party secretary, Fernando Mezzasoma, minister of popular culture, Renato Ricci, supreme commander of the militia, Roberto Farinacci.

446. Those sentenced at the Verona trial and summarily executed included: Ciano, Marinelli, and De Bono. The remaining members of the Grand Council who had voted against Mussolini were sentenced to death *in contumaciam*.

447. In May, 1944, the monument to Nazario Sauro in Capodistria was destroyed, in August the war memorial in Gorizia was blown up. See Salvatorelli-Mira, *op. cit.*, p. 976. For events in and around Trieste, cf. Martino Pescatore, "Venti mesi di alleanza nazi-fascista nella Venezia Giulia," in *Il Ponte*, X (1954), 14–28.

448. The Verona manifest and much other documentary material on the *Repubblica di Salò* is to be found in G. Perticone, *La politica italiana nell'ultimo trentennio*, Vol. III: *La repubblica di Salò* (Rome, 1947), pp. 157–161. The history of the RSI has been written by Edmondo Cione. The report of Mussolini's last private secretary, Giovanni Dolfin, *Con Mussolini nella tragedia* (Milan, 1949), is very revealing.

449. *O.O.*, XXXII, 7.

450. *Ibid.*, p. 434.

451. *Ibid.*, p. 61.

452. The only attempt to grapple with one of the great social problems of the country which had been on the agenda since 1918 was made by Mussolini just before the outbreak of the war "per la liquidazione del latifondo siciliano." The measures provided for were far from sweeping; but due to the war even

these could not achieve any real effectiveness. The descriptions given by Mussolini in this context concerning living conditions in Sicily are among the very few examples from the fascist period where the curtains of rhetoric are drawn back and the interior of the edifice is revealed. See *O.O.*, XXIX, 306; and XXXI, 1 f. As far as the effects of fascist rule on the standard of living of the population as a whole are concerned, one is justified, despite all uncertain factors, in giving credence to Salvemini's statement that in 1934 Italian workers could buy less than two-thirds of the goods with their wages than they had been able to buy before the March on Rome (*Sotto la scure del fascismo*, p. 272).

453. As late as 1925 fascism suffered heavy defeats at all works' council elections (cf. Mussolini's speech in the Senate of December 5, 1924, in *O.O.*, XXI, 201).

454. Cf. *O.O.*, XXXII, 294.

455. *Ibid.*, p. 20.

456. This was the "Raggruppamento nazionale repubblicano socialista" under Edmondo Cione, whose chief supporter was Concetto Pettinato (director of *La Stampa*), the last survivor of the host of former nationalists who was still loyal to Mussolini. See Perticone, *op. cit.*, III, 291 f.

457. *O.O.*, XXXII, 92.

458. *Ibid.*, p. 91.

459. "Dialogo quasi socratico," in *ibid.*, pp. 92 f.

460. *O.O.*, XXXI, 165.

461. In the introduction to his early work (1911), "Il Trentino veduto da un socialista," in *O.O.*, XXXIII, 153 f.

462. *O.O.*, XXXI, 250.

463. E.g., *O.O.*, XXXII, 115.

464. Mussolini, *Storia di un anno—Il tempo del bastone e della carota* (first published in Milan, 1944), now in *O.O.*, Vol. XXXIV.

465. *O.O.*, XXXII, 138.

466. *Ibid.*, p. 132.

467. *Ibid.*, p. 201.

468. "I tedeschi sono responsabili di tutto" (*ibid.*, p. 190).

469. *Ibid.*, p. 189.

470. *Ibid.*, p. 197.

471. Most condensed in a letter dated October 18, 1944: "Chi non ha fatto la guerra, non è un uomo" (*ibid.*, p. 211).

472. *Ibid.*, p. 202.

473. Among them, and shot, were: Alessandro Pavolini, Fernando Mezzasoma, Goffredo Coppola, Nicola Bombacci (who in 1920 as a Communist leader had been the terror of the bourgeoisie). Among those executed by partisans in other places on the same days were Farinacci, Starace, Arpinati, Dino Grandi, De Vecchi, and others escaped to South America.

474. Monelli, *op. cit.*, p. 347.

475. Cf. Note 304.

2 The Fixed Doctrine

1. "Fascismo," in *Enciclopedia Italiana*, Vol. XIV. The three-volume work of Antonio Canepa, *Sistema di dottrina fascismo* (Rome, 1937), represents a unique

attempt at scholarly systematization; it deals with all the literature published up to that time but, significantly enough, does not go beyond the preliminaries. Mussolini had little gratitude for such undertakings. Cf. *O.O.*, XXVI, 284.

2. "Non era proprio necessario che, allora, tutti conoscessero il mio passato di iconoclasta." See De Begnac, *op. cit.*, p. 112.

3. Sergio Panunzio, *Allgemeine Theorie des faschistischen Staates* (Berlin and Leipzig, 1934), p. 45.

4. Giovanni Gentile, *Grundlagen des Faschismus* (Cologne, 1936), p. 47.

5. *Enciclopedia Italiana*, XIV, 848a.

6. *O.O.*, XXX, 231.

7. *Enciclopedia Italiana*, XIV, 849a.

8. *Ibid.*, p. 850b.

9. *Ibid.*: "è individuo che è nazione e patria, legge morale che stringe insieme individui e generazioni in una tradizione e in una missione."

10. *Ibid.*

11. *Ibid.*

12. *Ibid.*, p. 849b.

13. *Ibid.*

14. *Ibid.*, p. 849a: "la bassa democrazia, che sembra dover condurre all'estinzione di ogni cultura difficile e di ogni più alta disciplina."

3   The Irksome Precursors

1. *O.O.*, XXVI, 284.

2. *O.O.*, XI, 205.

3. *O.O.*, XXI, 366.

4. *O.O.*, XX, 136.

5. *Ibid.*, p. 176.

6. *O.O.*, XXIV, 58.

7. *Ibid.*, p. 283.

8. *O.O.*, XXV, 111.

9. *Ibid.*, p. 261.

10. *O.O.*, XXVI, 27.

11. Cf. *O.O.*, XXI, 365.

12. *O.O.*, XXII, 192.

13. "Antitesi netta, categorica, definitiva," *O.O.*, XXII, p. 109.

14. First on July 27, 1924, in *La Stampa*. See Salvatorelli-Mira, *op. cit.*, p. 378.

15. Curzio Malaparte, *L'Europa vivente* (Florence, 1923). Cf. also Curzio Malaparte, *L'Italia barbara*, 2nd ed. (Rome, 1928). Curzio Malaparte Suckert appears in Chiurco among the first fascist syndicalists; see Chiurco, *op. cit.*, V, 329.

16. During the early fascist period, Asvero Gravelli held a high post in youth work; during the RSI he was deputy chief of staff of the "Guardia Nazionale Repubblicana." Hence he was more than a mere literary figure.

17. Giulio Evola was not politically active; nevertheless he was not a "nonpolitical archaic type": on the contrary, he was an ardent collaborator in the race campaign. His best-known books are *Imperialismo pagano* (Todi and Rome, 1928); *La rivolta contro il mondo moderno* (Milan, 1934).

18. Cf. below p. 512, Note 27.
19. Gentile, *op. cit.*, p. 49.

4 Practice as Premise

1. *O.O.*, XIII, 60.
2. Close ties existed between the Associazione Arditi and the Fascists. As president of the Associazione, Vecchi was at the same time a member of the Fascist Central Committee.
3. Among all the countless photographs, there is one that seems to reflect most clearly this basic manifestation. The subject is the punishment of the hated deserter Misiano (Salvatorelli-Mira, *op. cit.*, p. 125). The Communist deputy, wearing a placard around his neck, is being led through the streets by a great crowd in brutal and exultant triumph. Offended power reacts by humiliating: the expressions on the faces of the victim as well as the conquerors speak clearer than any description could do. Probably the most comprehensive collection of photographs is in Mario Fusti Carofiglio, *Vita di Mussolini e storia del fascismo* (Turin, 1949).
4. *O.O.*, XIV, 44.
5. I nostri bersaglieri con Ceccherini in testa
   Andranno da Cagoia e gli faràn la festa.
6. Quando vorrà il comandante,
   Dove vorrà il comandante!
   Uno per tutti, tutti per uno.
7. Roberto Farinacci had been a revolutionary socialist, then an interventionist, and had taken part in the Fascists' founding ceremony in the Piazza San Sepolcro. He was and continued to be the highest-ranking extremist of the party; Mussolini always excluded him from participation in actual power (until 1925–1926).
8. Trieste had also given Mussolini a magnificent reception in September, although on a smaller scale.
9. *O.O.*, XVI, 468 f.
10. The first directorate included the following names: Mussolini, Grandi, Marsich, Dudan, Sansanelli, Bolzon, Calza-Bini, Bastianini, Rocca, Postiglione, Secretary-General Bianchi. See *O.O.*, XVII, 272.
11. *Ibid.*, pp. 340 f.
12. Chiurco, *op. cit.*, pp. 486 f.
13. *Ibid.*, pp. 490 f.
14. *Ibid.*
15. This is the gist of an alleged circular of Minister of War Bonomi, the existence of which was disputed by Bonomi. The story is also vigorously denied by Luigi Salvatorelli in his review of Tasca's book; cf. *Rivista Storica Italiana*, LXIV (1952), 114. It may be assumed, however, that lower-ranking military authorities expressed themselves in this way. Furthermore, the case of De Bono is sufficiently revealing.
16. Chiurco, *op. cit.*, III, 84 f.
17. The report of Secretary-General Pasella at the congress in Rome, dealing with

the occupational classification of the 300,000 supporters, is very informative. Students, landed property owners, and industrial workers correspond more or less in numbers; agricultural workers form the largest group and are roughly twice as strong as the students. See *ibid.*, pp. 582 f.

18. *O.O.*, XVI, 325.

19. *O.O.*, XVIII, 549: "La cerimonia, brevissima, è stata semplice e solenne. Al primo sparo di petardo, seguito ad uno squillo di tromba, tutte le decine di migliaia di fascisti presenti—e tra essi Mussolini e altri capi—hanno assunto la posizione di 'attenti'; al secondo sparo, i gagliardetti sono stati scoperti al vento, i fascisti hanno fatto il saluto e quindici musiche hanno intonato l'inno fascista; al terzo sparo, tutti i presenti sono tornati in posizione di 'riposo'."

20. *Ibid.*, pp. 546 f.

21. *Ibid.*, p. 438.

22. Balbo, Dudan, Acerbo, Rossi, Torre.

23. The significance of this is revealed in Mussolini's remark: "Giolitti sull'Aventino avrebbe significato la nostra fine." See de Begnac, *op. cit.*, p. 357.

24. Not only that of self-defense. Cf. the following utterance of Mussolini (*O.O.*, XIX, 254): "... non si può in tre mesi prendere dei giovani, che erano stati abituati per due anni ad una ginnastica specialissima e farne dei soldatini di piombo. ..."

25. Collective agreements had not previously been common in Italy.

26. That it was not the industrialists who were urging participation in World War II, is as irrefutably obvious from Ciano's diaries as their fear of Mussolini. See Ciano, *Tagebücher 1937–1938*, pp. 15, 101, 262. It is a well-known fact that, immediately after the seizure of power, the fascist government introduced important measures which were very much in the capitalists' favor (e.g., the reintroduction of bearer shares); to call Mussolini the "candidate" of "big business" on this account has not been sufficiently substantiated, not even by Daniel Guérin in *Fascism and Big Business* (New York, 1939) [Original French title: *Fascisme et Grand Capital*]. It can hardly be doubted that, for the industrialists as for Federzoni, the presidency of Salandra would have been far more acceptable. Furthermore, during the war Mussolini changed the bearer shares back to registered shares.

27. "A nod from me would suffice to unleash all the anticlericalism of our people, which has had the greatest difficulty in swallowing a Jewish God. ... I am a Catholic and anti-Christian" (August, 1938); see Ciano, *Tagebücher 1937–1938*, p. 203.

28. Cf. Dante L. Germino, *The Italian Fascist Party in Power* (Minneapolis, 1959), pp. 65 f. See also Herman Finer, *Mussolini's Italy* (London, 1935), which deals with all organizational matters but with a stronger historical orientation.

29. *O.O.*, XXI, 119.

30. *O.O.*, XX, 42 f.

31. *Ibid.*, p. 42.

32. *O.O.*, XXII, 502–507.

33. *Ibid.*, p. 502.

34. The only ones to retain a certain degree of power were the quadrumvirs, who were lifetime members of the Grand Council.

35. *Ibid.*, p. 506.

36. *O.O.*, XXIV, 386–391.

37. The kind of thing that was possible in Italy is shown by Salvemini's report of an episode which was as absurd as it was horrifying: the Catholic priest Don Razzoli of Reggio Emilia was struck off the register in 1929 because he had advised his readers to save money on account of the impending hard winter (See Salvemini, *Sotto la scure*, p. 98). But it is only horrifying when a man is sentenced to five years' imprisonment for giving 300 lire to support the mother of an emigrant. See Salvatorelli-Mira, *op. cit.*, p. 325.

38. "Commissione suprema del Consiglio superiore dell'Educazione nazionale, Consiglio nazionale delle corporazioni, Comitato Centrale corporative."

39. *O.O.*, XXII, 467 f.

40. *O.O.*, XXI, 481.

41. With a "Storia del costume fascista" cf. the special issue of *Il Ponte* commemorating the thirtieth anniversary of the March on Rome, VIII (1952), 1337–1592; also contains extracts from schoolbooks on pp. 1430 f.

42. After 1929 also the *Dottrina del fascismo*.

43. *O.O.*, XI, 103.

44. *O.O.*, XXIV, 141.

45. Achille Starace, born 1889, Bersaglieri officer, founder of fascist movement in Trento, contributed greatly to the "conquest" of South Tirol by the Fascists; before 1931 for some time one of the vice-secretaries of the party, after October 31, 1939, chief of staff of the militia. After 1941 he withdrew from politics. Because he did not join the RSI he was kept in prison by Mussolini; nevertheless he was executed (*giustiziato*) by partisans on April 28, 1945.

46. The only organization to remain outside the GIL was that of the students (GUF). Cf. Germino, *op. cit.*, pp. 68 f. The text of the "Carta della Scuola" (in German) is contained in Benito Mussolini, *Der Geist des Faschismus*, edited and annotated by Horst Wagenführ (Munich, 1943), pp. 60–75.

47. Shortly before the outbreak of the war, Mussolini publicly voiced his delight over the magnificent exploits of a twelve-year-old *caporalino balilla moschettiere* who had led his troops "like an experienced officer." See *O.O.*, XXIX, 275 f.

48. Since its name contained the idea of "repressione antifascista."

49. *O.O.*, XXXI, 164.

50. For the legally unequivocal implications which were not, however, used by the king and Badoglio, cf. Gaetano Salvemini, "Badoglio nella seconda guerra mondiale," in *Il Ponte*, IX (1952), 1736 f.

51. *O.O.*, XXVII, 351 f.

52. Germino, *op. cit.*, p. 70.

53. *O.O.*, XXVIII, 205.

54. Seldom has an enemy ever spoken more disparagingly about a people than did Mussolini about his own: "From morning to night it must be kept in strict discipline and in uniform, and beaten, beaten, beaten" (see Ciano, *Tagebücher 1939–1943*, p. 194). Certainly no despot has ever dared to express publicly such an idea as that rationing should be permanently retained in order to balance production and consumption. See *O.O.*, XXX, 222.

55. Ciano, *Tagebücher 1937–1938*, p. 263.

56. *Ibid.*, pp. 236 f.
57. Unless one wishes to see a development of the fascist style in the fact that a composer dedicated a "mistica pura esaltazione" entitled *Felix Mater* to Mussolini's mother and that it was performed by the choir of the women's academy of the GIL. (See *O.O.*, XXIX, 373.)
58. *O.O.*, XXXI, 143.
59. *O.O.*, XXX, 154.
60. The continued development of the militia, particularly the "Bataillone Mussolini," ceased to have any independent significance, since it took place entirely under German influence and according to the German pattern.
61. Few things are more revealing than Ciano's entry in his diary (*Tagebücher 1939–1943*, p. 435) after a conversation with party secretary Vidussoni: "One gains the impression of listening to those people talk whom we crushed in 1920 and 1921. ... Nevertheless they should not overdo it, for there are many people who are beginning to be fed up ... we have no intention of giving up anything for the alleged reasons."
62. This was the so-called "Discorso del bagnasciuga" of June 24, 1943. See *O.O.*, XXXI, 188 f.
63. The "incidente" was Mussolini's greatest anxiety before the Abyssinian campaign. See *O.O.*, XXVII, 296. Before the war with Greece, Ciano guaranteed for it. See *O.O.*, XXX, 22.
64. The distinction on p. 209 has no bearing here; no one's decision, it is true, was determined entirely by his past—Giovanni Marinelli, a colleague of Mussolini's even in the *Avanti!* days, was shot in Verona; Dr. Alessandro Pavolini became the most feared man in the republic.

PART FOUR

National Socialism

1 National Socialism and Fascism

1. Hans Frank, *Im Angesicht des Galgens* (Munich, 1953), p. 92.
   Due to the vast quantity of literature extant, it should be pointed out that only verbatim remarks and the more important paraphrases and references have been documented. [E.N.]
2. Vincenzo Meletti, *Wesen, Wollen, Wirken des Faschismus* (Berlin, 1935).
3. Joseph Goebbels, "Der Faschismus und seine praktischen Ergebnisse," in *Schriften der deutschen Hochschule für Politik*, I (Berlin, 1935), 30.
4. *Libres propos sur la guerre et la paix*, Version française de François Genoud (Paris, 1952), p. 10.
5. *Le Testament politique de Hitler* (Paris, 1959), p. 107.

2 The Background: The Race Doctrine

1. Hitler relates that in Vienna he read "an enormous amount and very thoroughly." See *Mein Kampf*, 73rd ed. (1933), p. 21. Joseph Greiner (in many respects an

unreliable source) gives an impressive reading list extending from Sophocles, Aristophanes, and Buddha to Renan. See Joseph Greiner, *Das Ende des Hitler-Mythos* (Zürich, Leipzig and Vienna, 1947), p. 83. The description of his reading methods, together with the fact that of all this erudition virtually nothing was transferred to his conversation, speeches, or books, makes it very doubtful whether one can legitimately speak of "absorbing" this knowledge. However, it is reasonably likely that he read Gobineau, because of certain turns of phrase and indirectly because of a report by August Kubizek, *Hitler mein Jugendfreund* (Graz and Göttingen, 1953), p. 280. Also, Hitler sometimes criticizes Chamberlain's views. See *Hitler's Table Talk 1941–1944*, with an Introductory Essay by Hugh R. Trevor-Roper (London, 1953).

2. *Hitler's Table Talk*, p. 422.

3. He quotes Mommsen's famous remark about the Jews being the ferment of decomposition no differently from the way it is quoted in all anti-Semitic literature: misleadingly. Furthermore, it should hardly be necessary to point out that it is doing a man like Treitschke an injustice to pin him down solely on the basis of the remark, "The Jews are our misfortune."

4. Hitler was probably not familiar with Vacher de Lapouge, but the ideas which Lapouge was one of the first to express were well known to him.

5. Arthur Count Gobineau, *Versuch über die Ungleichheit der Menschenrassen*, I (Stuttgart, 1939), xvi.

6. *Ibid.*, p. 287.

7. *Ibid.*, IV, 312 f. In his basic historical-philosophical conception, therefore, Gobineau is not so far removed from Alexis de Tocqueville, at one time his mentor and superior, as might be supposed. Nor were Tocqueville's ideas by any means absolutely opposed to Gobineau's.

8. *Ibid.*, pp. 280 f.

9. *Ibid.*, III, 418.

10. Georges Vacher de Lapouge, *L'Aryen, son rôle social*, 1st ed. (Paris, 1899). The book is based on a course in political science given at the University of Montpellier in 1889–90. German translation: *Der Arier und seine Bedeutung für die Gemeinschaft* (Frankfurt, 1939).

11. *Ibid.*, p. 340.

12. *Ibid.*

13. The "two great fatal mistakes" of French history are for Lapouge the suspending of the Edict of Nantes and the French revolution (*ibid.*, p. 325).

14. *Ibid.*, p. 244.

15. *Ibid.*, p. 252.

16. He did not invent it, however. A book entitled *Der Rassenkampf* had already appeared in Innsbruck in 1883. The author was Ludwig Gumplowicz, an Austrian and a Jew.

17. Because it can easily be misunderstood, the term "Social Darwinism" should only be used with caution. But cf. the instructive analysis by Hedwig Conrad-Martius, *Utopien der Menschenzüchtung—Der Sozialdarwinismus und seine Folgen* (Munich, 1955).

18. Houston Stewart Chamberlain, *Die Grundlagen des XIX. Jahrhunderts*, 2nd ed. (Munich, 1900), p. 851. How easy it is to use the race doctrine to give opposite

interpretations to the same event is shown by the fact that Ludwig Woltmann (who had once been a Social Democrat) attributes the development of the German Socialist party to the rise of the Germanically oriented upper strata of the working class, while Hitler regards it as the result of the race-destroying appeal of Jewish intellectuals to the racially inferior lower strata. See Ludwig Woltmann, *Politische Anthropologie* (Jena, n.d.), p. 326.

19. Chamberlain, *op. cit.*, p. 457.
20. *Ibid.*, p. 18.
21. *Ibid.*, pp. 127, 210.
22. *Ibid.*, p. 927.
23. *Ibid.*, p. 260.
24. *Ibid.*, p. 448.
25. *Ibid.*, p. 669.
26. *Ibid.*, p. 722.
27. This is not the place to ask or decide whether and in what way Chamberlain was an important figure. But to the question of whether as a political thinker Chamberlain has a similar significance to Maurras' it is enough to recall a passage such as the following (*ibid.*, pp. 221 f.), which is by no means isolated and which typifies the thinker as much as the stylist: "This man [the Aryan] is jolly, zestful, ambitious, reckless, he drinks and gambles, he hunts and smokes; but suddenly he stops short: the great riddle of existence takes hold of him— not, however, as a purely rationalistic problem, ... but as an immediately compelling necessity of life ... and in order to discover this harmony he raises his own voice in song, tries all manner of sounds, practices in all manner of ways, then he listens reverently. His call does not remain unanswered: he is aware of mysterious voices ..." etc., etc.
28. *Ibid.*, p. 682.
29. *Ibid.*, pp. 450 f.
30. *Ibid.*, p. 726.
31. Nowhere is this as clear as in what is probably the most outstanding example of unbridled fanaticism in anti-Semitic literature: Eugen Dühring, *Die Judenfrage als Racen-, Sitten- und Culturfrage* (Karlsruhe, 1881).
32. Karl Marx, *Theorien über den Mehrwert*, edited by Karl Kautsky, Part I (Stuttgart, 1905), p. 389.
33. Karl Marx, *Das Kapital*, Vol. III, Part I (Hamburg, 1904), pp. 324 f.

3 History

1. His father Alois was the illegitimate son of a servant girl and evidently possessed of a remarkably strong sex drive. Hitler was the offspring of his father's third marriage, this time with a much younger cousin. Of all his relatives, the only one to play an important part later in his life was the daughter of his half-sister Angela. Every aspect of his family history and early youth is gone into with what is often excessive thoroughness in Franz Jetzinger, *Hitlers Jugend* (Vienna, 1956). The question of Alois Hitler's origin has still not been cleared up. Until Alois was forty he used his mother's name (Schicklgruber), although his alleged father had married his mother, and he was only posthumously legitimized through an

illegal hoax on the part of his uncle and foster father. Hence it has been suggested that the child's father was the son of Anna Maria Schicklgruber's Graz employer, who may have been a Jew. What Hans Frank has to say on the subject warrants the supposition that from his childhood on Hitler was aware of this possibility (Frank, *op. cit.*, pp. 330 f.). This would naturally be a much more important fact than the evidence, which is difficult to prove, that Hitler was a quarter Jewish.

2. Kubizek *op. cit.*, pp. 75, 99, 226.

3. *Ibid.*, p. 85.

4. *Ibid.*, pp. 129 f.

5. Greiner, *op. cit.*, p. 106. Greiner is an important source of information regarding Hitler's Vienna period. Unfortunately he is too ambitious in his book, with the result that his reports are only interesting when they are corroborated in principle by other evidence.

6. *Libres propos sur la guerre et la paix*, p. 46.

7. However, in these conversations Hitler appears more philosophical and full of ideas than anywhere else. Other testimony offers little reason to suppose that this was *not* due to Rauschning.

8. *Libres propos sur la guerre et la paix*, p. 81.

9. Albert Zoller, *Hitler privat—Erlebnisbericht seiner Geheimsekretärin* (Düsseldorf, 1949), pp. 29 f.

10. *Ibid.*, p. 57.

11. A particularly ridiculous example is described by Otto Dietrich, *Zwölf Jahre mit Hitler* (Munich, 1955), p. 225: when the German press did not give sufficient prominence to the death of an opera singer of whom Hitler thought very highly, the Reich Chancellor gave way to an outburst of rage which rendered him incapable of work for the whole day.

12. Kubizek, *op. cit.*, p. 120.

13. *Libres propos sur la guerre et la paix*, p. 276.

14. Dietrich, *op. cit.*, p. 180.

15. *Libres propos sur la guerre et la paix*, p. 322.

16. Dietrich, *op. cit.*, p. 165.

17. *Ibid.*, p. 164.

18. *Libres propos sur la guerre et la paix*, p. 306.

19. Hitler, *Mein Kampf*, 73rd ed. (1933), pp. 32 f.

20. *Ibid.*, p. 43.

21. Greiner, *op. cit.*, pp. 21 f.

22. *Libres propos sur la guerre et la paix*, p. 151.

23. Zoller, *op. cit.*, pp. 73, 78.

24. *Libres propos sur la guerre et la paix*, p. 123.

25. Kubizek, *op. cit.*, pp. 133 f. Kubizek relates that in 1939 Hitler confirmed, in Winifred Wagner's presence, that his political vocation dated from that moment (*ibid.*, p. 142).

26. Hitler's concluding words before the People's Court in, among other works, *Adolf Hitlers Reden*, edited by Ernst Boepple (Munich, 1933), pp. 111 f.

27. It was frequently noticed and described, very clearly, for instance, by Otto Strasser, *Hitler und ich* (Constance, 1948), pp. 87 f.

28. Frank, *op. cit.*, p. 329.

29. Cf. Hugo Hantsch, *Geschichte Oesterreichs 1648–1818*, 2nd ed. (Graz, Vienna and Cologne, 1953).

30. Lueger's anti-Semitism was far more propagandistic than ideological and did not approach Schönerer's racial anti-Semitism. Cf. Kurt Skalnik's admittedly overextenuating account in *Dr. Karl Lueger—Der Mann zwischen den Zeiten* (Vienna and Munich, 1954).

31. Of excessive dimensions is the six-volume work by Eduard Pichl, *Georg von Schönerer und die Entwicklung des Alldeutschtums in der Ostmark*, 2nd ed. (Oldenburg and Berlin, 1938). Also cf. Paul Molisch, *Geschichte der deutschnationalen Bewegung in Oesterreich* (Jena, 1926).

32. Cf. the recent instructive contribution by Andrew G. Whiteside, "Nationaler Sozialismus in Osterreich vor 1818," *Vierteljahrshefte für Zeitgeschichte*, IX (1961), 333–359.

33. On August 7 and 8, 1920, all National Socialist movements in Austria, the Reich, and Czechoslovakia united at the party conference in Salzburg in the National Socialist party of the German people. However, for all practical purposes this union remained a purely formal one.

34. But the name *Deutsche Arbeiterpartei* (DAP), German Workers' party, was not changed to *Deutsche Nationalsozialistische Arbeiterpartei* (DNSAP) until 1918.

35. The best-known description of its ideology is to be found in Rudolf Jung, *Der nationale Sozialismus*, 2nd ed. (Munich, 1922).

36. Hitler, *Mein Kampf*, pp. 40 f.: "My first encounter with Social Democrats took place ... at the building site. Right from the start it was not very pleasant. My clothes were still fairly decent, my speech careful, and my manner reserved. ... I drank my bottle of milk and ate my sandwich somewhere off to one side and cautiously studied my new surroundings or pondered my miserable fate ..."

37. No doubt a number of later ideas found their way into his description of his early years. On the whole, however, it is confirmed by the Vienna witnesses—Kubizek, Greiner, and Hanisch, who was Konrad Heiden's informant. Greiner, *op. cit.*, p. 81, relates that Hitler hung framed rhymes by Schönerer over his bed, e.g.: "Ohne Juda, ohne Rom wird gebaut Germaniens Dom" (Without Judea, without Rome, Germany will build her own cathedral); or, "Wir schauen frei und offen, wir schauen unverwandt, wir schauen froh hinüber ins deutsche Vaterland! Heil!" (We gaze free and frankly, we gaze steadfastly, we gaze joyfully across to the German Fatherland! Heil!).

38. The credit for this discovery goes to Wilfried Daim, nor is it diminished by the exaggerating title, *Der Mann, der Hitler die Ideen gab* [The Man Who Gave Hitler His Ideas] (Munich, 1958).

39. He called the noble race *Asinge, Heldlinge*, or *Arioheroiker*, those of inferior race *Tschandalen, Waninge, Äfflinge*, he writes his "theozoology" in order "to justify the princely and noble classes," later he prophesied that the "socialist-Bolshevik, primitive human race" would undergo "racial warfare to the castration knife." See Daim, *op. cit.*, pp. 25, 51, 89.

40. Although Italy had been united from an outer bastion, the new ancient capital of Rome soon rendered the beginnings in Piedmont unrecognizable. In France

it required the revolution to develop the single state of the monarchy into a (homogeneous) nation.

41. That this conflict was carried on even in philosophy, without, however, being clearly described or resolved here either, is shown, for example, by Max Scheler's wartime pamphlet, *Die Ursachen des Deutschenhasses* (Leipzig, 1917).

42. Daniel Frymann (i.e., Heinrich Class), *Wenn ich der Kaiser wär* (Leipzig, 1912).

43. These prototypal categories do not, of course, deny the existence of intermediate forms or claim validity for each of the countless individual cases. Cf. also Walter Schlesinger, "Die geschichtliche Stellung der mittelalterlichen deutschen Ostbewegung," *Historische Zeitschrift*, CLXXXIII (1957), 517–542.

44. When from time to time reference is made in the text to a potential of German policy which contrasted with Hitler's solution, the potential existence of what did not take place is taken for granted.

45. Hitler, *Mein Kampf*, p. 142.

46. *Ibid.*, p. 160.

47. *Ibid.*, p. 152.

48. *Ibid.*, p. 154.

49. Cf. Alfred Kruck, *Geschichte des Alldeutschen Verbandes 1890–1939* (Wiesbaden, 1954), e.g., pp. 36, 86.

50. Cf. Klaus Schwabe, "Zur politischen Haltung der deutschen Professoren im Ersten Weltkrieg," *Historische Zeitschrift*, Vol. CXCIII, 3 (1961), pp. 601–634.

51. *O.O.*, IX, 54 f.

52. Max Weber, *Politische Schriften*, 2nd ed. (Tübingen, 1958), esp. "Wahlrecht und Demokratie in Deutschland," pp. 233–279, and "Parlament und Regierung im neugeordneten Deutschland," pp. 294–431.

53. Erich Eyck, *Geschichte der Weimarer Republik* (Erlenbach, Zürich and Stuttgart, 1954–1956), V, 45.

54. Kruck, *op. cit.*, p. 127.

55. Obviously the general term is used merely for brevity and refers to the principal opinion-forming classes of the population.

56. The first years in Munich are the most obscure in Hitler's life. Hence it is not clear what he means when he claims that, in "various circles, some of which are today loyal supporters of the National Socialist movement," he called the problem of the destruction of Marxism the problem of the future of the German nation (*Mein Kampf*, p. 171). At all events, these were addresses of no consequence made to people of no influence.

57. Albert Reich, *Vom 9. November 1918 zum 9. November 1923—Die Entstehung der deutschen Freiheitsbewegung* (Munich, 1933), pp. 40 f.

58. Hitler, *Mein Kampf*, p. 218.

59. A membership list of the NSDAP dating from 1920 shows the following occupations under "H": "manufacturer, manservant, locksmith, directress, cabinetmaker, businessman, doctor, manufacturer, doctor, proprietor of ornamental ironworks, electrician, author [Hitler], soldier, businessman, senior secretary, roofer, businessman, bank filing clerk, proprietress of business school, newspaper representative, deputy sergeant, wife of businessman, pharmacist, businessman, wife of artist, bank official, engineer, clerk, mechanic, medical student, apprentice, doctor's wife" (Reich, *op. cit.*, p. 44).

60. *Libres propos sur la guerre et la paix*, pp. 11, 45.

61. Whether or not a political group is a "mass party" cannot be determined by the size of its membership. By inclination, the Action Française was also a mass party, since it depended on the organizational form of the League; by the same token, the Fascist and National Socialist parties did not shed their aristocratic self-image when their members numbered in the millions.

62. However, the fact that the ranks of the NSDAP included no prominent former socialist—except perhaps Otto Strasser—exemplifies one of the most remarkable differences by comparison with Italian fascism. But there is substantial evidence of a degree of fluctuation between National Socialists and Communists in the lower ranks, and certain socialist trends were so inescapably apparent that for a long time they were a matter for serious concern on the part of industry.

63. Hitler, *Mein Kampf*, p. 420.

64. Cf. Note 22.

65. Chiefly, Ernst Deuerlein, "Hitlers Eintritt in die Politik und die Reichswehr," *Vierteljahrshefte für Zeitgeschichte*, VII (1959), 177–227; Hanns H. Hofmann, *Der Hitlerputsch* (Munich, 1961); Georg Franz-Willing, *Die Hitlerbewegung—I. Der Ursprung 1919–1922* (Hamburg and Berlin, 1962). Ernst Deuerlein's documentation is thorough but limited to a short period; Hanns H. Hofmann presents a carefully authenticated account of the political prehistory and events of the *Putsch* but is inclined to underestimate Hitler's role by somewhat vociferously claiming to destroy the "legends." Georg Franz-Willing has unearthed a quantity of important documents from private ownership and is chiefly concerned with exploring the role and moods of the masses. Unfortunately he limits his investigation to the testimony, and still more the categories, of the "national" side, but in important points his results actually reinforce the opposite interpretation. Of continuing and indispensable value is Konrad Heiden, *Geschichte des Nationalsozialismus* (Berlin, 1932).

66. Deuerlein, *op. cit.*, p. 195.

67. *Ibid.*, pp. 205 f.

68. Thus in the original. In Deuerlein the spelling has been corrected.

69. The text erroneously has "Brüder" (brothers).

70. See Note 224, p. 529.

71. Ernst Röhm, *Die Geschichte eines Hochverräters*, 5th ed. (Munich, 1934), p. 124.

72. Hitler, *Mein Kampf*. pp. 238 f.

73. Official party archives; Hans Volz, *Daten der Geschichte der NSDAP*, 4th ed. (Berlin, 1935).

74. Franz-Willing, *op. cit.*, p. 154.

75. Hitler, *Mein Kampf*, p. 615.

76. Franz-Willing, *op. cit.*, p. 221.

77. According to Röhm, *op. cit.*, p. 228, the temporary volunteer corps was already carrying out maneuvers on the Berlin map.

78. The most detailed recent description, Hofmann, *op. cit.*, pp. 208 f.

79. See section "Italian Fascism," p. 202.

80. Hitler's early relationship to Italy and Mussolini is carefully examined by Walter Werner Pese, "Hitler und Italien 1920–1926," *Vierteljahrshefte für Zeitgeschichte*, III (1955), 113–126.

81. Thus Franz-Willing, *op. cit.*, *passim.*
82. *Ibid.*, pp. 30, 33 f.
83. Wilhelm Hoegner, *Der schwierige Aussenseiter* (Munich, 1959), p. 14.
84. Franz-Willing, *op. cit.*, p. 201.
85. Röhm, *op. cit.*, p. 131.
86. Cf. Franz-Willing, *op. cit.*, pp. 177 f.
87. Röhm, *op. cit.*, p. 164.
88. Franz-Willing, *op. cit.*, p. 234.
89. One of the main differences was the encouragement of National Socialism by Bavarian particularism. Hitler's attacks on the "Berlin Soviet Jews" or the "Asiatics of Berlin" were not alien to the Bavarian mood. See Franz-Willing, *op. cit.*, p. 209; cf. Heinz Gollwitzer, "Bayern 1918–1933," *Vierteljahrshefte für Zeitgeschichte*, III (1955), 363–387.
90. *Libres propos sur la guerre et la paix*, p. 212: "A l'époque, j'étais intellectuellement un enfant au biberon."
91. Hitler, *Mein Kampf*, p. 229.
92. *Ibid.*
93. Particularly: Gottfried Feder, *Das Manifest zur Brechung der Zinsknechtschaft des Geldes* (Diessen, 1919); *Der Staatsbankrott die Rettung* (Diessen, 1919). The best-known summary: *Das Programm der NSDAP und seine weltanschaulichen Grundgedanken* (NS-Bibliothek, No. 1), 1st ed. (Munich, 1927).
94. Gottfried Feder, *Der deutsche Staat auf nationaler und sozialer Grundlage— Neue Wege in Staat, Finanz und Wirtschaft* (Munich, 1923).
95. *Ibid.*, p. 127.
96. *Hitler's Table Talk 1941–1944*, p. 427.
97. In the trend represented by Feder must also be included Rudolf Jung's work, *Der Nationale Sozialismus*, 2nd ed. (Munich, 1922), in which the orientation along the lines of medieval economy emerges even more clearly. The function of this socialism and the distracting nature of its basic anti-Semitic trait are revealed most plainly in Julius Streicher's early essays, *Ruf zur Tat—Aufsätze aus den Kampfjahren 1920–1922* (Nuremberg, 1937).
98. Walter Görlitz and Herbert A. Quint, *Adolf Hitler* (Stuttgart, 1952), p. 143.
99. Erich Ludendorff, *Kriegführung und Politik* (Berlin, 1923).
100. His later opposition to the "suprastate powers" did not shrink from a criticism of Hitler, a criticism which originates "from the Right" and makes it plain that fascism must not be defined simply as the "most extreme Right": at best it may be called the "most effective part" of the extreme Right. Cf. Hans Buchheims, "Gutachten über das Verhältnis des 'Hauses Ludendorff' zum Nationalsozialismus," in *Gutachten des Instituts für Zeitgeschichte* (Munich 1958), pp. 356–370.
101. Ludendorff, *op. cit.*, p. 44.
102. *Ibid.*, p. 331.
103. *Ibid.*, p. 146.
104. *Ibid.*, p. 52.
105. *Ibid.*, p. 286.
106. *Ibid.*, p. 200.
107. *Ibid.*, p. 321.

108. Röhm, *op. cit.*, p. 9.

109. *Ibid.*, p. 113.

110. *Ibid.*, pp. 127, 268 f., 273.

111. *Ibid.*, p. 366.

112. *Ibid.*, p. 173.

113. *Ibid.*, p. 204.

114. Reich, *op. cit.*, pp. 14 f. (photograph).

115. Alfred Rosenberg, *Dietrich Eckart—Ein Vermächtnis*, 3rd ed. (Munich, 1935), p. 52.

116. Alfred Rosenberg was for many years Dietrich Eckart's "young man" whom he vigorously supported until 1923 in the editorial offices of *Auf gut deutsch* and the *Völkischer Beobachter*. The Catholic Bavarian and the Protestant Baltic German did not, of course, always see eye to eye—the manner in which the office of editor-in-chief was transferred from Eckart to Rosenberg left behind on the one side a feeling of disappointment and, on the other, a sense of guilt or, at least, thoughtlessness. See Rosenberg, *Letzte Aufzeichnungen*, p. 106.

117. Reich, *op. cit.*, p. 35.

118. In *Auf gut deutsch* (1920), p. 392.

119. *Ibid.*, p. 402.

120. E.g., to Béla Kun:

> "Nur schauen, schauen!
> Mehr ist hier nicht not
> Uns klarzumachen was auch uns bedroht."

> (Just look, look!
> No more is needed
> To show us what threatens us.)

121. Paul Herrmann Wiedeburg, *Dietrich Eckart*, Dissertation at the University of Erlangen (Hamburg, 1939), p. 5.

122. Zoller, *op. cit.*, p. 119.

123. *Hitler's Table Talk*, p. 377.

124. *Ibid.*

125. *Libres propos sur la guerre et la paix*, p. 212.

126. *Ibid.*, p. 153.

127. Only Konrad Heiden mentions the work, i.e., quotes from it. See *Adolf Hitler*, I (Zürich, 1936), 56 f., 86; and *Geschichte des Nationalsozialismus* (Berlin, 1932), p. 115. In the latter it also appears in the bibliography.

128. For a more detailed description and analysis: Ernst Nolte, "Eine frühe Quelle zu Hitlers Antisemitismus," *Historische Zeitschrift*, Vol. CXCII, 3 (June, 1961), pp. 584–606.

129. "Reichstagsrede vom 30. January 1937," in *Dokumente der deutschen Politik*, edited by Paul Meier-Benneckenstein, V (Berlin, 1938), 32.

130. However, this necessity is, of course, only a compelling one when it refers to the collective Jewish "head" of bolshevism. And Hitler never wavered in this view, except perhaps just before his death, when strangely enough "the more powerful people of the East" appeared to him to be the true winners of the war.

131. Max Domarus, *Hitler-Reden und Proklamationen 1932–1945*, I (Würzburg, 1962), 804.

132. A most valuable advantage which it offers can only be mentioned marginally here: it refers frequently to certain books and sources, thus revealing some of the literature that was discussed in Eckart's and Hitler's conversations or with which acquaintance was assumed. The six most frequently mentioned works are: Otto Hauser, *Geschichte des Judentums* (Weimar, 1921); Werner Sombart, *Die Juden und das Wirtschaftsleben* (Leipzig, 1911); Henry Ford, *Der internationale Jude* (Leipzig, 1921); Gougenot des Mousseaux, *Der Jude, das Judentum und die Verjudung der christlichen Völker*, translated into German by Alfred Rosenberg (Munich, 1921); Theodor Fritsch, *Handbuch der Judenfrage*, 26th ed. (Hamburg, 1907); Friedrich Delitzsch, *Die grosse Täuschung* (Stuttgart and Berlin, 1920–1921). A familiarity with *Die Protokolle der Weisen von Zion* is taken tacitly for granted throughout (an edition of *Die Protokolle*, edited by Gottfried zur Beek, appeared in Munich in 1920).

133. It is hardly a coincidence that Hitler only dipped into Rosenberg's *Mythus*, finding it written in "a far too abstract style" (*Hitler's Table Talk*, p. 422). Presumably Rosenberg's chief importance for Hitler was as an eye-witness to the Bolshevik revolution and as the author of anti-Semitic publications: *Die Protokolle der Weisen von Zion und die jüdische Weltpolitik* (Munich, 1923); *Der staatsfeindliche Zionismus* (Hamburg, 1922); *Die Spur des Juden im Wandel der Zeiten* (Munich, 1920). Rosenberg's liberal-Protestant background is clearly indicated by his description of the shock he felt in 1911 at the sight of the bishops' skeletons in the monastery at Ettal. See *Letzte Aufzeichnungen*, pp. 274 f.

134. Franz-Willing, *op. cit.*, p. 220.

135. Hitler, *Mein Kampf*, Vol. II, Chapt. 13, "Deutsche Bündnispolitik nach dem Kriege," esp. pp. 707 f.; *Hitlers Zweites Buch* (Stuttgart, 1961), pp. 176 f.

136. *Ibid.*, p. 160.

137. Cf. Anneliese Thimme, "Gustav Stresemann—Legende und Wirklichkeit," *Historische Zeitschrift*, CLXXXI, 287–335.

138. Konrad Heiden, *Geschichte des Nationalsozialismus*, p. 20.

139. Cf. Otto-Ernst Schüddekopf, *Linke Leute von rechts—Die nationalrevolutionären Minderheiten und der Kommunismus in der Weimarer Republik* (Stuttgart, 1960), esp. Chapts. 14 and 23.

140. Krebs, the former *Gauleiter* of Hamburg, states that he even dared tell Hitler to his face that he was not a leader in the Germanic sense but an Oriental despot. See Albert Krebs, *Tendenzen und Gestalten der NSDAP* (Stuttgart, 1959), p. 156.

141. Joseph Goebbels, *Wege ins Dritte Reich* (Munich, 1927), pp. 14, 25, 33.

142. Otto Strasser, *Aufbau des deutschen Sozialismus* (Leipzig, 1932).

143. Strasser, *Hitler und ich*, pp. 131–147.

144. In 1932 Otto Strasser planned, in the case of Hitler's joining the government, to summon a great "antifascist congress" to include such organizations as the Jungdo, Tannenbergbund, Tatkreis, Widerstandskreis (resistance group). See Schüddekopf, *op. cit.*, p. 340. The first equations of National Socialism and fascism were, of course, to be found in the local Munich press. Toward the end

of his life even Alfred Rosenberg spoke more or less along these lines in *Letzte Aufzeichnungen*, p. 342.

145. One of the most complicated questions, because so many interests are involved, concerned the extent of financial and moral support rendered Hitler by "big business." On the one hand, an inordinately harmless picture is presented, for example, by Otto Dietrich, *Zwölf Jahre mit Hitler* (Munich, 1955), p. 186, while on the other it is noteworthy that the historians of the German Democratic Republic have not been able to produce any new facts and rely mainly on the familiar sources and researches (Thyssen, Heiden, Hallgarten); cf. Fritz Klein, "Zur Vorbereitung der faschistischen Diktatur durch die deutsche Grossbourgeoisie 1929–1932," *Zeitschrift für Geschichtswissenschaft*, I (1953), 872–904. The most important document still being quoted today is "Die Eingabe deutscher Finanzmagnaten, Monopolisten und Junker an Hindenburg für die Berufung Hitlers zum Reichskanzler," *IMG*, XXXIII, 531; the quotation is the title of an essay by Albert Schreiner in *Zeitschrift für Geschichtswissenschaft*, IV (1956), 366–369. However, this petition (*Eingabe*) does not explain the strength of the National Socialist movement since it actually presupposes it; of interest in this connection are Schacht's remarks concerning industry's "inertia" in a letter to Hitler written during the same period. See *IMG*, XXXVI, 535.

146. *Dokumente der deutschen Politik und Geschichte, 1919–1933*, edited by Johannes Hohlfeld (Berlin, n.d.), III, 340.

147. *Hitler's Table Talk*, p. 437; *Libres propos sur la guerre et la paix*, p. 259.

148. Documentation: Thilo Vogelsang, "Neue Dokumente zur Geschichte der Reichswehr 1930–1933," *Vierteljahrshefte für Zeitgeschichte*, II (1954), 417 f.

149. Karl Dietrich Bracher, *Die Auflösung der Weimarer Republik*, 3rd ed. (Villingen, 1960), pp. 674 f.

150. An entry in Goebbels' diary dated February 16, 1932, is highly indicative, on the one hand of conservative circles' ungovernable fear of the Communists, and on the other of influential National Socialists' thoroughly realistic appraisal of the situation: he states that an important German National deputy had told him he thought Thälmann had a better chance than Hindenburg. "It is terrible, how remote these people are from the true popular feeling." See Joseph Goebbels, *Vom Kaiserhof zur Reichskanzlei*, 19th ed. (Munich, 1937), p. 46.

151. Bracher, *op. cit.*, p. 504.

152. Cf. paragraph on Italian fascism on p. 211.

153. That, in spite of accurate insights, the German Social Democratic party also underestimated Hitler is shown by a memorandum of the Social Democratic party faction quoted by Bracher, *op. cit.*, p. 370: "A Hitler government would aim at a repetition of the example in Italy. That is to say, crushing of all working-class organizations, perpetual martial law, abolition of all press, assembly, and other political liberties, constant danger of civil war at home and war of revenge abroad."

154. No one was more deeply humiliated than the man who was most to blame, the irresponsible Franz von Papen, whose closest collaborators were shot in his

stead on June 30 and yet who remained a valuable subordinate colleague of Hitler's.

155. Documentation: Erich Matthias, "Hindenburg zwischen den Fronten 1932," *Vierteljahrshefte für Zeitgeschichte*, VIII (1960), 78 f.

156. Documentation: Thilo Vogelsang, "Hitlers Brief an Reichenau vom 4. Dezember 1932," *Vierteljahrshefte für Zeitgeschichte*, VII (1950), 429 f.

157. *Dokumente der deutschen Politik und Geschichte*, III, 451.

158. *Ibid.*, IV, 7–11.

159. Goebbels, *Vom Kaiserhof zur Reichskanzlei*, p. 286.

160. Events surrounding the seizing and consolidating of power can be described at best as semilegal. They were accompanied and promoted by illegal circumstances from the very beginning. See Karl Dietrich Bracher, Wolfgang Sauer and Gerhard Schulz, *Die nationalsozialistische Machtergreifung* (Cologne and Opladen, 1960).

161. Erich Matthias' documentation is very instructive: "Der Untergang der Sozialdemokratie 1933," *Vierteljahrshefte für Zeitgeschichte*, IV (1956), 179–226.

162. Rosenberg, *Letzte Aufzeichnungen*, p. 316.

163. E.g., "Thus, in contrast to our official government, I see the means of Germany's revival not primarily in Germany's foreign policy, but primarily in the restoration of a sound, national, and effective German body politic." See *Vortrag Adolf Hitlers vor westdeutschen Wirtschaftlern im Industrie-Klub zu Düsseldorf am 27. Januar 1932* (Munich, n.d.), p. 30.

164. The Bolshevik seizure of power was also not single-minded in this sense. Granted it had clearly defined goals, but these were to a large extent quite different from those which, after a period of severe defeats and withdrawals, the party set about putting into practice.

165. Fritz Tobias, *Der Reichstagsbrand* (Rastatt, 1962), presents convincing evidence of the origin of the antifascist legend.

166. *Dokumente der deutschen Politik und Geschichte*, IV, 3–7.

167. If indeed one does concede to the National Socialist leaders all the fear and alarm which Tobias, *op. cit.*, pp. 133 f., attributes to them, the successful arrests should have been enough completely to allay their fears.

168. Cf. the documentation of Anton Ritthaler, "Zum Rücktritt Hugenbergs 1933," *Vierteljahrshefte für Zeitgeschichte*, VIII (1960), 193–219.

169. Goebbels, *Vom Kaiserhof zur Reichskanzlei*, p. 299.

170. *Neue Dokumente zur Geschichte der Reichswehr 1930–1933*, pp. 434 f.

171. Cf. Hermann Mau's important article, "Die 'Zweite Revolution'—Der 30. Juni 1934," *Vierteljahrshefte für Zeitgeschichte*, I (1953), 119–137. Also Bracher, Sauer and Schulz, *op. cit.*, pp. 829–972; also "Promemoria eines bayerischen Richters zu den Juni-Morden 1934," *Vierteljahrshefte für Zeitgeschichte*, V (1957), 102 f.

172. Mau, *op. cit.*, p. 128.

173. Hans Franks, *op. cit.*, pp. 147 f., gives a vivid eye-witness account of the utter callousness with which Hitler decided the life-or-death fate of his oldest campaigners.

174. This was a paradox in that the speech in question had been entirely in favor of the Reichswehr. For the complete speech, see *IMG*, XL, 543–558.

175. *Dokumente der deutschen Politik und Geschichte*, IV, 173.
176. *Vierteljahrshefte für Zeitgeschichte*, III (1955), 184–210.
177. Apparently General Hossbach did not intend to surrender his knowledge. It
      was only by chance that this document came into Allied hands. It is discussed
      at the end of Friedrich Hossbach, *Zwischen Wehrmacht und Hitler 1934–1938*
      (Wolfenbüttel-Hanover, 1949). The document itself is No. 386-PS in *IMG*,
      XXV, 402–413; extracts in *Dokumente der deutschen Politik und Geschichte*,
      IV, 366–375; Walther Hofer, *Der Nationalsozialismus—Dokumente 1933–1945*
      (Frankfurt, 1957), pp. 193–196. Latterly doubts have been cast on the value
      of the memorandum as evidence, in particular by A. J. P. Taylor, *The Origins
      of the Second World War* (London, 1961), pp. 131 f., and David L. Hoggan,
      Der erzwungene Krieg (Tübingen, 1961), pp. 116 f. It is not that Taylor believes
      the facts to be distorted but that he considers Hossbach's interpretation of them
      mistaken.
178. Cf. Hossbach, *op. cit.*, p. 187.
179. Hitler had known of the document in question for years and had even ordered
      it to be burned. The confrontation of the general with the homosexual black-
      mailer in the library of the Reich Chancellery must be almost without precedent.
      Cf. Hermann Foertsch's book on the Fritsch crisis, *Schuld und Verhängnis*
      (Stuttgart, 1951). Fritsch's strange defenselessness against Hitler becomes
      understandable when one considers the phrase which Hossbach quotes as
      having been made several times by the general: "Hitler is Germany's fate in
      good and evil" (Hossbach, *op. cit.*, p. 107).
180. *Dokumente der deutschen Politik und Geschichte*, IV, 390 f.; esp. 397.
181. *IMG*, XXXI, 354–368.
182. One of the unsigned copies of the address of August 22, 1939, includes the
      sentence: "Our enemies are little worms. I saw them in Munich." See *IMG*,
      XXVI, 343.
183. Many versions of this speech exist, most of them unsigned. The most reliable
      is probably Admiral General Boehm's record, which was submitted to the
      Nuremberg tribunal as a document in defense of Raeder (*IMG*, XLI, 17–25).
      The quotation is taken from this version.
184. In the "Ansprache an die Oberbefehlshaber vom 23. November 1939," *IMG*,
      XXVI, 327 f.
185. Ciano, *Tagebücher 1937–1938*, p. 242.
186. "Today I wish to be a prophet again: If the international finance Jewry inside
      and outside of Europe should succeed in once again plunging the nations into
      a world war, the result would be not the bolshevization of the earth and thus
      the victory of Jewry, but the destruction of the Jewish race in Europe." See
      Dokumente der deutschen Politik und Geschichte, V, 8.
187. He concluded the above-quoted remarks to the generals on February 3, 1933,
      with the statement that the most dangerous period was that of the reconstruc-
      tion of the Wehrmacht. It would become clear whether or not France possessed
      statesmen. If it did, it would not give Germany time but would attack it,
      presumably with Eastern satellites. See *Vierteljahrshefte für Zeitgeschichte*, II
      (1954), 396–436.
188. In his well-known essay, "Vom inneren Beruf zur Wissenschaft," *Gesammelte*

Aufsätze zur Wissenschaftslehre (Tübingen, 1951), pp. 588 f., Max Weber speaks of the "battle of the gods of the various orders and values."

189. If this sentence is correct, it makes the sense and nonsense of a "war guilt discussion" readily understandable.

190. This does not exclude the fact that he nevertheless regarded a clash with the Western powers as inevitable—but at a later date. This is unquestionably the tenor of his speech of August 22, 1939.

191. The attack on Pearl Harbor is still a "surprise attack" even if it was provoked by Roosevelt's intransigence in the negotiations.

192. Cf. Martin Broszat, *Nationalsozialistische Polenpolitik 1939–1945*, in *Schriftenreihe der Vierteljahrshefte für Zeitgeschichte*, No. 2 (Stuttgart, 1961).

193. Documentation: "Denkschrift Himmlers über die Behandlung der Fremdvölkischen im Osten [May, 1940]," *Vierteljahrshefte für Zeitgeschichte*, V (1957), 194–198; quotation: p. 197.

194. *IMG*, XXIX, 444.

195. Letter dated January 3, 1940; *O.O.*, XXIX, 424.

196. The studies undertaken by Franz Halder and Gert Buchheit do not manage to convince one of the opposite, being too much concerned with detail. See Franz Halder, *Hitler als Feldherr* (Munich, 1949); Gert Buchheit, *Hitler der Feldherr* (Rastatt, 1958).

197. The well-known decision to halt the panzer attack before Dunkirk is no contradiction, although it resulted in the British expeditionary force being able to get away—especially as Hitler's motive cannot be ascertained with accuracy (in the *Testament politique* the phrase occurs: "Nous avons évité en effet de les anéantir à Dunkerque," p. 133). Cf. Hans Meier-Welcker, "Der Entschluss zum Anhalten der deutschen Panzertruppen in Flandern 1940," *Vierteljahrshefte für Zeitgeschichte*, II (1954), 274–290.

198. Mussolini had urged him to knock out England in the Mediterranean. However, it is by no means certain that this course would have led to ultimate success, quite apart even from Hitler's ideological premises.

199. Cf. Gerhard L. Weinberg, "Der deutsche Entschluss zum Angriff auf die Sowjetunion," *Vierteljahrshefte für Zeitgeschichte*, I (1953), 301–318. Weinberg ascribes a crucial significance to a conference held on July 31, 1940. The refutation by Hans G. Seraphim and Andreas Hillgruber in *Vierteljahrshefte für Zeitgeschichte*, II (1954), 240–249, defends the idea of political motives and a later timing, but is partially invalidated by a reference to an irrelevant diary entry of Rosenberg. It is interesting to note a remark of Jodl's in a draft speech of November, 1943, to the effect that Hitler had already informed him during the Western campaign of his firm determination to grapple with the Bolshevik menace. See *IMG*, XXXVII, 638.

200. Whether Hitler actually still believed in a "Jewish head" of bolshevism during the period of Stalin's unrestricted hegemony, is a matter of some doubt. Against this theory is a letter written by Hitler to Mussolini dated March 6, 1940, which indicates that Germany had to come to terms with Russia since it was only the (former) Jewish international attitude, and not the (Stalinist) Russian-nationalist state ideology which had led National Socialism into a hostile relationship with communism. However, there is undoubtedly significance in a

statement made on January 20, 1941, that after Stalin's death the Jews, who now only occupied positions of second and third rank, would be able to move up onto the top level. See *IMG*, XXXIV, 469.

201. *IMG*, XXVI, 641.
202. *IMG*, XXXVIII, 88.
203. *Ibid.*, p. 425.
204. A thorough analysis is given by Gerald Reitlinger, *The Final Solution—The Attempt to Exterminate the Jews of Europe* (London, 1953).
205. This "planning stage" is described by Alexander Dallin, *Deutsche Herrschaft in Russland 1941–1945* (Düsseldorf, 1958).
206. Cf. pp. 413 f.
207. Documentation: Helmut Heiber, "Der Generalplan Ost," *Vierteljahrshefte für Zeitgeschichte*, VI (1958), 281–325.
208. Documentation: Hans Rothfels, "Ausgewählte Briefe von Generalmajor Helmuth Stieff," *Vierteljahrshefte für Zeitgeschichte*, II (1954), 291–305.
209. Cf. the concluding words of the "Besprechung vom 23.5.39" in *IMG*, XXXVII, 556.
210. These levels of resistance appear most clearly in *Der lautlose Aufstand—Bericht über die Widerstandsbewegung des deutschen Volkes*, edited by Günther Weisenborn (Hamburg, 1953). A Communist attempt at refutation of the standard work by Hans Rothfels, *Die deutsche Opposition gegen Hitler*, 3rd ed. (Frankfurt, 1958), as well as of Walther Hofer's documentation, is given by Horst Laschitza, "Faschismus und Widerstand—Fälschung und Wirklichkeit. Auseinandersetzung mit Auffassungen der westdeutschen Historiker Hans Rothfels und Walther Hofer," *Zeitschrift für Geschichtswissenschaft*, IX (1961), 1847–1860.
211. "Treason" is a term belonging to the sphere of purely national conflicts and wars. To make this the sole and supreme criterion is to fail to recognize the specific nature of World War II. To deny it all significance, however, is to declare this war erroneously as a *purely* ideological one. The inextricable mingling of two heterogeneous elements was what constituted the tragic cleavage which tormented thousands of conscientious men and women and which did not bring an end to suffering even for those who had made their decision. Cf. Margret Boveri, *Der Verrat im XX. Jahrhundert* (Hamburg, 1956 f.); English translation: *Treason in the Twentieth Century* (London, 1961).
212. The association of these levels with specific names has been deliberately avoided. It can be taken for granted that in life things are less clear-cut than in theory.
213. Neither the "commando order" and the execution of prisoners of war on one side, nor the bombing attacks on the other, is any exception to this, since the phrase "normal war" is not intended to convey the idea of an idyll.
214. *IMG*, XLI, 544.
215. *Hitlers Tischgespräche* (Bonn, 1951), p. 187.
216. Measures such as "*totaler Kriegseinsatz*" (all-out war effort [Sauckel]) or the organizing of the *Volkssturm* (people's militia) were either routine in character or betokened desperation, and need not be mentioned here.
217. The atom bomb might be called—insofar as any ethnological designation is permissible—the end-product of the German-Jewish symbiosis and the first

consequence of its dissolution. It was Jewish emigrants from Germany who started Roosevelt off on the development of the new weapon (Albert Einstein and Leo Szilard), and Otto Hahn's closest collaborator had been Lise Meitner. But the international aspect of fascism was reflected here too in the international character of antifascism: one of the most outstanding scientists engaged in the project was Enrico Fermi, who had left the Italy of Mussolini on account of his Jewish wife.

218. The necessary reservations are to be found on pp. 390 ff.
219. Cf. Paul Kluke, "Nationalsozialistische Europaideologie," *Vierteljahrshefte für Zeitgeschichte*, III (1955), 240–275.
220. Cf. Hans Dietrich Loock, "Zur 'grossgermanischen Politik' des Dritten Reiches," *Vierteljahrshefte für Zeitgeschichte*, VIII (1960), 37–63.
221. Nevertheless it is evidence of the narrow horizon of the mere technician to complain of "lost victories." One cannot seriously expect a demonic will to create an instrument of undreamed-of perfection and then modestly to hand it over to the experts for appropriate use. Whether some high-ranking officers were right or wrong in blaming Hitler for their failures in the Caucasus and on the Volga: without him they would have lacked the most elementary essentials to their successes as well as their failures.
222. *IMG*, XLI, 428.
223. Goebbels, *Vom Kaiserhof zur Reichskanzlei*, p. 220.
224. *Dokumente der deutschen Politik und Geschichte*, V, 529.

4 Practice as Fulfillment

1. Hitler, *Mein Kampf*, 73rd ed. (1933), p. 652.
2. Wilhelm Hoegner, *Die verratene Republik* (Munich, 1958), p. 36, cites 1,100 dead.
3. Röhm, *op. cit.*, p. 126; Konrad Heiden, *Hitler*, I, 78.
4. Deuerlein, *op. cit.*, Document 23.
5. *Hitlers Tischgespräche*, pp. 421 f.
6. Wilhelm Hoegner, *Der schwierige Aussenseiter*, p. 18.
7. Georg Franz-Willing makes indiscriminate use of Hoegner's statements in order to justify his thesis regarding the "Red terror" as a proven fact.
8. Cf. Hitler, *Mein Kampf*, p. 564.
9. In 1923 the SA regiment in Munich under the command of Brückner consisted of thirteen companies, one guard-duty company, and the *Stosstrupp Hitler*, plus a technical detachment, an artillery detachment, and a bicycle detachment. See Franz-Willing, *op. cit.*, p. 144.
10. Hitler, *Mein Kampf*, p. 608.
11. *Ibid.*, pp. 382 f.
12. The fact that later on the German *Gauleiter* were usually much more powerful than the Italian *federali* is due solely to the will of Hitler himself, since for him the existence of "viceroys" represented a similar counterweight to the deadening tendencies of bureaucratic centralization as the *libertés* did for Maurras.
13. Hitler, *Mein Kampf*, pp. 651 f.
14. Franz-Willing, *op. cit.*, p. 175.

15. Walter M. Espe refers specifically to the "fascist salute" in *Das Buch der NSDAP* (Berlin, 1933), text to Illustration 36.
16. In all matters of organization, cf.: Wolfgang Schäfer, *NSDAP, Entwicklung und Struktur der Staatspartei des Dritten Reiches* (Hanover and Frankfurt a.M., 1956).
17. See section "Italian Fascism," pp. 255 f.
18. Schäfer, *op. cit.*, p. 20.
19. Darré's ideas are described in minute detail in his books, particularly *Das Bauerntum als Lebensquell der nordischen Rasse* (Munich, 1933), and *Neuadel aus Blut und Boden*, 1st ed. (Munich, 1930). His close ties with the SS are worthy of note (cf. pp. 390 f.).
20. Cf. e.g., *Neue Dokumente zur Geschichte der Reichswehr*, pp. 405 f.
21. Cf. the collections of Goebbels' articles and speeches from the "time of struggle": e.g., "Der Angriff" (Munich, 1940), "Signale der neuen Zeit" (Munich, 1934); some also in *Revolution der Deutschen* (Oldenburg, 1933). Also interesting from the standpoint of the petit-bourgeois academic-nihilistic branch of National Socialism represented by Goebbels: his early novel, *Michael*, 17th ed. (Munich, 1942) and his diary notes from 1925–26, edited by Helmut Heiber in *Schriftenreihe der Vierteljahrshefte für Zeitgeschichte*, 2nd ed. (Stuttgart, 1961).
22. *Adolf Hitler in Franken: Reden aus der Kampfzeit*, edited by Julius Streicher (Nuremberg, 1939), p. 81.
23. Primarily the great work of Bracher, Sauer and Schulz.
24. *Dokumente der deutschen Politik*, Vol. I, *Die nationalsozialistische Revolution*, p. 168.
25. *Dokumente der deutschen Politik und Geschichte*, IV, p. 54.
26. *Dokumente der deutschen Politik*, I, 169 f.
27. *Dokumente der deutschen Politik und Geschichte*, IV, 84 f.
28. *Ibid.*, pp. 85 f.
29. *Ibid.*, pp. 255 f.
30. The notes and memoranda of Bernhard Lösener, for many years "race expert" in the ministry of the interior, contain enough harrowing material to provoke a more lenient attitude in judging his "collaborators" in the ministry, but, as might be expected, they deal only with the legal-pragmatic aspect. See *Vierteljahrshefte für Zeitgeschichte*, IX (1961), 262–313.
31. *Dokumente der deutschen Politik*, V, 296 f.
32. All laws and regulations referred to are contained in *Dokumente der deutschen Politik*, VI, 2.
33. For matters pertaining to Jewish emigration and certain differences among the various periods, cf. Graml, "Die Auswanderung der Juden aus Deutschland zwischen 1933 und 1939," *Gutachten des Instituts für Zeitgeschichte*, pp. 79–85.
34. Following on the victory over France, the Madagascar plan briefly entered the limelight once more, but without getting beyond the stage of noncommittal discussion. The talk about Eastern European "reserves" for Jews as the objective of this mass transportation was doubtless merely a salve to consciences.
35. *O.O.*, XXIX, 91.
36. See section "Italian Fascism," pp. 230 f.
37. Nothing throws a better light on the nature of National Socialism than Zionism.

Zionism represented a new national- and race-consciousness on the part of what were at first only a few Jews who sharply attacked the "completely de-Judaized" assimilationists and accused them of "degeneration" and "betrayal of their people." An even worse enemy in their eyes was the Marxist doctrine, since they regarded it as stifling all interest in purely Jewish affairs. Here, too, the notion of humanity was termed an abstraction, an empty concept; and with the *ignis fatuus* of universal brotherhood were contrasted the love of one's native soil, the ideal of the healthy, land-rooted peasant. An escape was sought from the "threat of asphyxiation" and impending racial death, and much thought was given to Palestine, although little to its Arab inhabitants. Moses Hess had already said in 1863 that "race" was the primary factor in the historical process; in 1882 Leo Pinsker added that the Jews represented a nonassimilable element. The symptoms of degeneration contained in assimilation were at times depicted in terms not far removed from anti-Semitic ones.

Even if one supports the doubtful thesis that Zionism was nothing but an imitation of European nationalism, there is no justification for blaming National Socialism per se for ideas and concepts which found such wide response among the Jews. The point is, however, that for the Jews everything was reality which for the National Socialists were the imaginings induced by pathological fear: impending racial extinction, lack of national *Lebensraum*, equal hostility from all contending powers. The great differences that nevertheless did exist cannot be gone into here, nor the question of whether it is permissible to speak of a "Jewish fascism" within Zionism. The parallels themselves are enough to demonstrate the absurdity of National Socialism's central thesis. How could a people which suffered so greatly from the results of emancipation, be the cause of that emancipation? Cf. Adolf Böhm's comprehensive work, *Die zionistische Bewegung bis zum Ende des Weltkrieges.*

38. The laws for the protection of minorities contained in the Treaty of Versailles are due in large part to the efforts of Jewish world organizations.
39. *Der Parteitag der Arbeit vom 6. bis 13. September 1937—Offizieller Bericht über den Verlauf des Reichsparteitages mit sämtlichen Kongressreden* (Munich, 1938), p. 40.
40. *Ibid.*, p. 17.
41. This was prompted by the awarding of the Nobel Peace Prize to Carl von Ossietzky.
42. *Der Parteitag der Arbeit*, p. 89.
43. *Ibid.*, p. 128.
44. *Ibid.*, p. 195.
45. *Ibid.*, p. 231.
46. *Ibid.*, p. 243.
47. *Ibid.*, p. 245.
48. *Ibid.*, p. 249.
49. *Ibid.*, p. 260.
50. *Ibid.*, pp. 270 f.
51. *Ibid.*, p. 353.
52. *Ibid.*, p. 358.
53. *Ibid.*, p. 371.

54. *Ibid.*, p. 381.
55. *Ibid.*, p. 383.
56. Cf. Karlheinz Schmeer, *Die Regie des öffentlichen Lebens im Dritten Reich* (Munich, 1956).
57. On only one occasion was there amid all the rejoicing a note of anxiety and doubtfulness, but even this was only indirect. At the annual conference of the DAF (German Workers' Front), Hermann Göring dismissed as "idle talk" the claims that the new prosperity was an "armaments boom." See *Der Parteitag der Arbeit*, p. 282.
58. *IMG*, XLI, 192.
59. Information on the structure of the SS is contained in Ermenhild Neusüss-Hunkel, *Die SS* (Hanover and Frankfurt a.M., 1956) in *Schriftenreihe des Institutes für wissenschaftliche Politik* (Marburg/Lahn). The principal literature is included in the appendix. Gerald Reitlinger's *The SS, Alibi of a Nation, 1922–1945* (London, 1956), is more in the form of a story. A penetrating study is offered by Hans Buchheim in "Die SS in der Verfassung des Dritten Reiches," *Vierteljahrshefte für Zeitgeschichte*, III (1955), 127–157. The works of apologia give the clearest picture of the (limited) stratification of the structure, e.g., various articles in the journals *Nation Europa* and *Wikingruf*; also Paul Hausser's book, *Waffen-SS im Einsatz* (Göttingen, 1953).
60. "Vortrag Himmlers über Wesen und Aufgabe der SS und der Polizei [January, 1937]," *IMG*, XXIX, 208.
61. *Ibid.*, p. 207.
62. Among the groups of the radical Right, the *Artamanen* were distinguished by their efforts to promote the idea of settlement.
63. This particular formulation occurs for the first time in one of Hitler's orders dating from August, 1938. See *IMG*, XXVI, 190 f.
64. Cf. particularly Buchheim, *op. cit.*
65. *IMG*, XXIX, 206 f.
66. *Dokumente der deutschen Politik*, III, 33 f.
67. Among the more grotesque aspects of National Socialist historical thought is the fact that neither Himmler nor Hitler had apparently ever heard of the anti-Semitic side of the Spanish Inquisition. In his conversations, Hitler frequently stresses the Moorish era as the best in Spanish history and indignantly contrasts it with the "funeral pyre" atmosphere of Christian Madrid. See *Libres propos sur la guerre et la paix*, p. 279; *Hitler's Table Talk 1941–1944*, pp. 607, 667.
68. The duties of the SS were formulated as follows by Himmler in an address to the officers' corps of the bodyguard after one year of war (Metz, September 7, 1940): "It is considerably easier in many cases to go into battle with one's company than in any territory to hold down, with a company, a hostile population of low cultural standards, to carry out executions, remove people from the area, take away sobbing, weeping women, and bring fellow Germans across the frontier from Russia and look after them. I would like to say this: We must, even in the combined *Waffen-SS*, recognize the important activity of the combined SS and the police; you must look upon the duties of the man, in the green uniform as being just as valuable as the duties which you perform. You must regard what the man of the SD or the Security Police does as being every

bit as vital a part of our combined activity as the fact that you can march with weapons ... this sentry duty on guard for ideology, this necessity for consistency, in many cases this is much much harder." See *IMG*, XXIX, 104 f.

69. *Der grossdeutsche Freiheitskampf—Reden Adolf Hitlers*, Vols. I and II, 3rd ed. (Munich: Eher, 1943), pp. 231 f.

70. Cf. the statement made by the party chancellery on February 21, 1940: "As a result of their intensive National Socialist training in matters of race and *Volkstum*, the *Waffen-SS* units consisting of National Socialists are better qualified to carry out duties in the occupied Eastern territories than other armed units" (*IMG*, XXXII, 56); also Hitler's statement of August 6, 1940, brought to the official attention of the officers of the Wehrmacht, that the *Waffen-SS* as a *Staatstruppenpolizei* (state police force) represented a unit capable of resisting pernicious influences in times of crisis, one which, "proud of its purity," would "never fraternize with the proletariat and the subversive underworld" (*IMG*, XXXV, 356). However, the value of both these statements is limited, since each was made at the time for a particular purpose.

71. The very fact that at this point a selection has to be made from a selection, tempts one to present the whole picture of National Socialism by means of songs and photographs. The material available is limitless, and yet of striking monotony. Whatever else appears on hundreds of thousands of photos and films, one thing is scarcely ever absent: uniforms in great variety and with the most diverse rank insignia. And whatever may be the burden of the songs, they are all tuned to one basic theme, which is expressed by one famous battle song: "A youthful nation arises, the storm breaks, raise the flags higher, comrades."

However, against the background of the stereotype, three examples may be considered as offering more concrete characteristics. To start with the oldest of all National Socialist songs, the first verse of Dietrich Eckart's "Storm Song" is as follows:

> Storm! Storm! Storm!
> The serpent, the dragon from Hell, has broken loose!
> Stupidities and lies his chains have burst asunder,
> Lust for gold in the dreadful couch,
> Red as with blood are the Heavens in flames,
> The rooftops collapsed, a sight to appal.
> One after another, the chapel goes too!
> Howling with rage, the dragon dashes it to pieces!
> Ring out for the assault now or never!
> Germany awake!

And in the third verse comes the significance of the image of hell: "... Judas appears, bent on winning the Reich."

Expressed here are German seriousness, the German desire for first principles, the German urge for metaphysical profundity, although not in their most convincing form. To deny that they were a powerful element in this phenomenon, from Hitler down to insignificant local party leaders, is to fail to give it its due. If one combines this with the movement's anti-ideological nature, which is also present, one has penetrated almost to the very heart of the movement.

The second song is the fine old socialist one:

> Brothers, toward sunlight, toward freedom,
> Brothers, arise toward the light,
> In radiance out of the dark past,
> The future is dawning bright.

It was annexed by the National Socialists, altered, and given a new verse:

> Hitler is our leader,
> He is not paid in gold
> Which, from Jewish thrones,
> Before his feet is rolled.

This brutal bit of social demagogy sits strangely indeed in this early witness to socialist piety. But the annexation of certain elements of socialism is a necessary feature of the extreme conservative revolution, while the anti-Semitic development is after all merely one of trend.

The final example is the collection of photographs from the repulsive document compiled on the orders of SS-Brigade Leader Jürgen Stroop after the destruction of the Warsaw ghetto, entitled *Es gibt keinen jüdischen Wohnbezirk in Warschau mehr* ("A Jewish residential area no longer exists in Warsaw"). In the behavior of this man in command of an operation which saw itself as the extermination of vermin, we see the age-old arrogance of the wielder of power in its extreme form and one which is quite unknown to the traditional soldierly mentality. In appalling incongruity with the victims and their fate stands the fact that their death was often noted simply as "perished" (*Verenden*). See *IMG*, XXVI, 628–693; this document has also been published at Neuwied (1960), and edited by Andrzei Wirth. Thus these photographs are an example of that self-nullification by excess which is typical of National Socialism generally.

72. Cf. Hans Buchheim, "Rechtsstellung und Organisation des RKF des deutschen Volkstums," *Gutachten des Instituts für Zeitgeschichte*, pp. 239–279. The secret decree is to be found in *IMG*, XXVI, 255 f.

73. Cf. the letter of the RSHA to Heydrich quoted by Buchheim, *op. cit.*, p. 246.

74. *IMG*, XXXVIII, 239.

75. Broszat, *NS Polenpolitik*, p. 185.

76. *IMG*, XXIX, 171.

77. *Dokumente der deutschen Politik*, Vol. VIII, 2, pp. 566 f.

78. *IMG*, XXXI, 283 f.

79. *IMG*, XXXVII, 517.

80. *IMG*, XXIX, 142.

81. *IMG*, XXXVII, 60 f.

82. For a special study of the Gestapo, see Edward Crankshaw, *Gestapo, Instrument of Tyranny* (London, 1956).

83. Cf. Note 68, p. 532.

84. *IMG*, XXVI, 201, and XXXVIII, 98.

85. Cf. Wisliceny's testimony in *IMG*, IV, 397.

86. *Kommandant in Auschwitz—Autobiographische Aufzeichnungen von Rudolf Höss*, with an introduction and commentary by Martin Broszat (Stuttgart, 1958).

87. *IMG*, XXVII, 349 f.
88. *IMG*, XXIX, 146.
89. His *Letzte Aufzeichnungen* express such views; at least one wartime document offers another interpretation. See *IMG*, XXVII, 270.
90. *IMG*, XL, 257.
91. *Ibid.*, pp. 313, 345.
92. As this is not a psychological study, this statement is not intended to efface the difference between figures like Göring on the one hand and Speer on the other.

   Since the war, the literary apologetics of the chief participants have been entirely along these lines—i.e., each man's good intentions or attributes have been emphasized and all political responsibility passed onto Hitler, who had been led astray by certain arch villains (usually the more successful rivals) at significant times (after the loss of influence on the part of the person in question). The more or less scholarly apologia of German (i.e., Hitlerian) policy as such has been handled differently. As a rule it concentrates on the prehistory of the outbreak of war and arrives at its results by strictly isolating various periods of time, related circumstances, and psychological data. Generally speaking, it does less justice to Hitler than do his worst enemies: it makes him out to be a disastrous blend of windbag and fool. It is even doubtful whether it adequately exerts the corrective function which is the legitimate task of heterodox conceptions (cf. Notes 177 and 189, pp. 526, 527).

5 The Doctrine in Context

1. Apart from the studies of Heiden, Bullock, and Görlitz-Quint, which are not always thematic, there are few definitive works. Probably the first to appear after the war was Alan Bullock's contribution to the collective work, *The Third Reich* (London, 1955), pp. 350–378. In a limited area, Hugh R. Trevor-Roper has tried to demonstrate the coherence of Hitler's thinking in "Hitlers Kriegsziele," *Vierteljahrshefte für Zeitgeschichte*, VIII (1960), 121–133. Erwin Faul has discussed "Hitlers Übermachiavellismus," *Vierteljahrshefte für Zeitgeschichte*, II (1954), 344–372. Martin Broszat gives a thoughtful and penetrating opinion of *Hitlers Zweites Buch* in *Vierteljahrshefte für Zeitgeschichte*, IX (1961), 417–429.
2. *Hitlers Zweites Buch* (Stuttgart, 1961), p. 91.
3. Hitler, *Mein Kampf*, p. 111.
4. *Ibid.*, p. 135.
5. *Hitlers Zweites Buch*, p. 104.
6. *Mein Kampf*, p. 711.
7. *Hitlers Zweites Buch*, p. 76.
8. Espe, *op. cit.*, p. 116.
9. Hitler, *Mein Kampf*, p. 741.
10. *Adolf Hitler in Franken—Reden aus der Kampfzeit* (Nuremberg, 1939), p. 50.
11. *Hitlers Zweites Buch*, p. 71.
12. *Adolf Hitler in Franken*, p. 113.
13. *Ibid.*, p. 97.
14. *Hitlers Zweites Buch*, p. 123.
15. *Libres propos sur la guerre et la paix*, p. 203.

16. *Ibid.*, p. 41.
17. *Hitlers Zweites Buch*, p. 169.
18. *Ibid.*, p. 218.
19. Hitler, *Mein Kampf*, p. 70.
20. *Libres propos sur la guerre et la paix*, p. 225.
21. "Rede vom 13. Juli 1934" in Domarus, *op. cit.*, p. 424.
22. *Adolf Hitlers Reden*, edited by Boepple (Munich, 1933), p. 64.
23. *Adolf Hitler—Sein Leben und Seine Reden*, edited by Adolf-Viktor von Koerber (Munich, 1923), p. 73.
24. Boepple, *op. cit.*, p. 39.
25. Hitler, *Mein Kampf*, p. 309.
26. *Vortrag Adolf Hitlers vor westdeutschen Wirtschaftlern im Industrie-Klub zu Düsseldorf am 27.1.1932* (Munich, n.d.), p. 5.
27. Hitler, *Mein Kampf*, pp. 254 f.
28. *Adolf Hitler in Franken*, p. 53.
29. Robert H. Baynes, *Hitler's Speeches*, 2 vols. (London, 1942), I, 474.
30. *Libres propos sur la guerre et la paix*, p. 305.
31. *Völkischer Beobachter*, July 19, 1937.
32. *Ibid.*, September 12, 1935.
33. "Rede vom 13. Aug. 1920," Hauptarchiv der NSDAP, Fa 88, Fasz. 62, p. 20.
34. *Hitler's Table Talk*, p. 560.
35. Baynes, *op. cit.*, p. 770.
36. *Adolf Hitler in Franken*, p. 116.
37. *Ibid.*, pp. 99 f.
38. Hitler, *Mein Kampf*, pp. 344 f. The thesis probably originated with Sombart's *Die Juden und das Wirtschaftsleben*, which in all likelihood was familiar to Hitler. This book sets out to demonstrate the significance of the Jews in the creation of modern capitalism, but does not make them monocausally responsible for it.
39. *Adolf Hitler in Franken*, p. 131.
40. *Ibid.*, p. 152.
41. See pp. 328 ff.
42. *Mein Kampf*, p. 99.
43. *Ibid.*, p. 702.
44. The only enemy who is not reduced to the Jews with entire success in *Mein Kampf* is France, pp. 763 f.
45. His secretary reports that even when dictating his speeches his voice choked when he pronounced the word bolshevism and a violent rush of blood to his head became visible. See Zoller, *op. cit.*, p. 17.
46. Hitler, *Mein Kampf*, p. 358.
47. *Hitler's Table Talk*, p. 722.
48. *Libres propos sur la guerre et la paix*, p. 8.
49. *Ibid.*
50. His predilection for citing specifically chosen Jewish names is one of the most outstanding proofs of the authenticity of Eckart's *Zwiegespräch*.
51. In a short autobiography, which through the good offices of Dietrich Eckart was intended for an unnamed "Herr Doktor." See NSDAP Hauptarchiv, Fa 88, Fasz. 17a.

52. There are quite a number of utterances of this kind made by Hitler. This characteristic appears most prominently in Eckart's *Zwiegespräch*. In *Tischgespräche* one is struck more by a vulgar anticlericalism; that his orientation toward the Catholic Church, however, has not been lost, is shown by his remark that in Himmler he sees the Ignatius Loyola of National Socialism. See *Libres propos sur la guerre et la paix*, p. 164.

53. Koerber, *op. cit.*, p. 109.

54. *Adolf Hitler in Franken*, p. 125.

55. *Ibid.*, p. 79.

56. *Ibid.*, p. 45.

57. Cf. Hitler, *Mein Kampf*, p. 251; Koerber, *op. cit.*, p. 73; *Adolf Hitler in Franken*, pp. 18 f., 81.

58. *Vortrag Adolf Hitlers vor westdeutschen Wirtschaftlern am 27.1.32*, p. 8.

59. *Adolf Hitler in Franken*, p. 40.

60. Hitler, *Mein Kampf*, p. 728.

61. *Adolf Hitler in Franken*, p. 96.

62. *Hitler's Table Talk*, p. 624.

63. Cf. *IMG*, XXXII, 297.

64. *Hitlers Tischgespräche*, p. 227.

65. Hauptarchiv der NSDAP, Fa 88, Fasz. 54.

66. Hitler, *Mein Kampf*, pp. 172 f.

67. Kubizek tells of the young Hitler's rage toward officers and everything military, *op. cit.*, p. 77.

68. Hitler, *Mein Kampf*, p. 690.

69. Cf. e.g. *Hitlers Tischgespräche*, p. 136; concerning the party congresses as war preparation, *Hitler's Table Talk*, p. 565.

70. Cf. Schacht's attitude in the note to pp. 144 f. of *Tischgespräche*.

71. *Hitler's Table Talk*, p. 661.

72. *Libres propos sur la guerre et la paix*, p. 41.

73. *IMG*, XXIX, 171 f.

74. *Hitler's Table Talk*, p. 672.

75. *Hitlers Tischgespräche*, p. 150.

76. *Libres propos sur la guerre et la paix*, p. 51.

77. Concerning the question of whether and in what sense it was a *Weltanschauung*, cf. the chapter, "Global Struggle for Recovery."

78. Hauptarchiv der NSDAP, Fa 88, Fasz. 53.

79. "Rede in Leipzig am 16. Juli 1933," in Baynes, *op. cit.*, I, 484 (not in Domarus).

80. Koerber, *op. cit.*, p. 30.

81. Espe, *op. cit.*, p. 135.

82. E.g., Kuehnelt-Leddihn, *op. cit.*

83. Hitler, *Mein Kampf*, p. 439.

84. Together with Hitler's well-known address to the industrialists in Düsseldorf, special reference should be made to his address to students (February 7, 1934) in the Berlin Philharmonia. See *Völkischer Beobachter*, February 8, 1934; Baynes, *op. cit.*, II, 990 f.; Domarus, I, 363 (very short excerpt).

85. Hitler, *Mein Kampf*, p. 433.

86. *Ibid.*, pp. 319 f.

87. *Vortrag Adolf Hitlers vor westdeutschen Wirtschaftlern am 27.1.32* (Munich, n.d.), p. 21.
88. Cf. Max Weber, *Wirtschaft und Gesellschaft*, I, 4th ed. (Tübingen, 1956), 298 f.; II, 536 f.
89. "Schlussansprache in Nürnberg," September, 1933, in Baynes, *op. cit.*, I, 479.
90. Domarus, *op. cit.*, p. 895.
91. A typical example is Otto Hauser's *Geschichte des Judentums*, with which Hitler was most probably familiar.
92. Hitler, *Mein Kampf*, p. 69.
93. According to a definition by Hans Frank, *Völkischer Beobachter*, May 20, 1936, in Baynes, *op. cit.*, I, 419.
94. Cf. e.g., *Hitler's Table Talk*, pp. 424 f., 588 f.; *Libres propos sur la guerre et la paix*, p. 25; *Hitlers Tischgespräche*, pp. 44, 72 f.
95. *Hitlers Tischgespräche*, pp. 49 f.
96. *Adolf Hitler in Franken*, p. 177.
97. See pp. 291 f.
98. *Libres propos sur la guerre et la paix*, p. 36.
99. *Ibid.*, p. 283.
100. *Adolf Hitler in Franken*, p. 115.
101. *Libres propos sur la guerre et la paix*, p. 115.
102. *Ibid.*, p. 20.
103. *Hitlers Tischgespräche*, p. 63.
104. Cf. *Hitler's Table Talk*, p. 394; *Libres propos sur la guerre et la paix*, p. 156.
105. *Ibid.*, p. 253.
106. It is a strange fact that Hitler always shows great disrespect for his Germanic ancestors, and whenever "culture" is mentioned he displays a striking preference for the people of the Mediterranean and especially Athens. In discussing ancestors one must always mention the Greeks, says the Führer of the Germanic peoples (*ibid.*, p. 219).
107. Hauptarchiv der NSDAP, Fa 88, Fasz. 60, "Rede vom 28.8.1926 vor dem Nationalklub von 1919 in Hamburg."
108. Hitler, *Mein Kampf*, p. 722.
109. *Adolf Hitler in Franken*, p. 106.
110. *Mein Kampf*, p. 372.
111. *Libres propos sur la guerre et la paix*, p. 321.
112. *Le Testament politique de Hitler*, p. 86.
113. As late as the summer of 1940 even Himmler repudiated "the Bolshevik method of physical extermination of a people, from an inner conviction that it was un-Germanic and impossible." See "Himmler zur Behandlung von Fremdvölkern," *Vierteljahrshefte für Zeitgeschichte*, V (1957), 197. As evidence of a "semiconsistent" man, cf. the documentation, "Aus den Akten des Gauleiters Kube," *Vierteljahrshefte für Zeitgeschichte*, IV (1956), 67–92.
114. *Adolf Hitler in Franken*, pp. 114 f.
115. *Hitler's Table Talk*, p. 475. In all sexual matters Hitler displays a gross vulgarity of outlook, whether he is voicing his opinion as to the assumed relations of priests to their housekeepers or the necessity of the sexual act and child-bearing for women's health.

116. Cf. e.g. Koerber, *op. cit.*, pp. 32 f.
117. *Adolf Hitler in Franken*, p. 106.
118. *Ibid.*, p. 191.
119. Hitler, *Mein Kampf*, p. 506.
120. *Ibid.*, p. 687.
121. *Hitlers Tischgespräche*, p. 229.
122. Hitler, *Mein Kampf*, p. 124.
123. *Hitler's Table Talk*, p. 396.
124. *Libres propos sur la guerre et la paix*, p. 93.
125. "Geheimrede Sonthofen," *Hitlers Tischgespräche*, p. 450.
126. *Adolf Hitler in Franken*, p. 141.
127. Hitler, *Mein Kampf*, pp. 311 f.
128. *Adolf Hitler in Franken*, p. 72.
129. In varying versions: *Hitler's Table Talk*, p. 483; *Hitlers Tischgespräche*, p. 283.
130. Hitler, *Mein Kampf*, p. 392.
131. *Libres propos sur la guerre et la paix*, p. 113.
132. *Ibid.*, p. 225.
133. *Adolf Hitler in Franken*, p. 41.
134. *Ibid.*, p. 144.
135. Boepple, *op. cit.*, p. 125.
136. *Adolf Hitler in Franken*, p. 49.
137. At this point perhaps it is permissible to quote a sentence from Herman Rauschning's *Gespräche mit Hitler* (Zürich, 1940), which was deliberately omitted because to all appearances Rauschning attributes too many Nietzschean ideas and phrases to Hitler: "In my *Ordensburgen* the beautiful god-man who obeys his own laws will stand as a cult image and prepare youth for the approaching step of masculine maturity" (p. 237).
138. *Libres propos sur la guerre et la paix*, p. 140.
139. "Rede in Nürnberg am 6. September 1938," in Domarus, *op. cit.*, p. 894.
140. Hitler, *Mein Kampf*, p. 267.
141. *Ibid.*
142. *Adolf Hitler in Franken*, p. 49.
143. Hitler, *Mein Kampf*, p. 328.
144. *Libres propos sur la guerre et la paix*, p. 86.
145. *Adolf Hitler in Franken*, p. 130.
146. *Libres propos sur la guerre et la paix*, p. 149.
147. Hitler, *Mein Kampf*, p. 144.
148. *Adolf Hitler in Franken*, p. 99.
149. Naturally "the" sovereign, martial, inwardly antagonistic group does not exist as a fact. The aim is to find a simplifying expression for the sovereignty, bellicosity, and inward antagonism as basic traits of *all* groups up to now. It should be obvious, however, that characteristic traits can be "personified."
150. It is only necessary to recall his fantastic statement about the resettlement of the South Tiroleans in the Crimea: "All they have to do is to sail down just one German waterway, the Danube, and there they are" (*Hitler's Table Talk*, p. 548).

151. *Ibid.*, pp. 418 f.
152. "I can understand most things, but I shall never understand why, when one has seized power, one does not hold it with all one's might" (*ibid.*, p. 692). Similarly Goebbels: "Once we have power, we will never give it up, unless they carry our dead bodies out of our offices" (*Vom Kaiserhof zur Reichskanzlei*, p. 139).
153. Cf. Theodor Schieder, "Idee und Gestalt des übernationalen Staates seit dem 19. Jahrhundert," *Historische Zeitschrift*, CLXXXIV, 336–366; and Werner Conze, "Deutschlands weltpolitische Sonderstellung in den zwanziger Jahren," *Vierteljahrshefte für Zeitgeschichte*, IX (1961), 166–177.
154. Pierre Joseph Proudhon, *La Guerre et la Paix*, 1st ed. (Brussels, 1861).
155. *Libres propos sur la guerre et la paix*, p. 82.

PART FIVE

Fascism as a Metapolitical Phenomenon

1. For the Action Française, however, only inasmuch as, in opposing the republic, it was combating the socialist revolution which allegedly was bound to arise out of the democratic soil.
2. Cf. p. 138 f.
3. The earliest classical example of this train of thought is Parmenides' poem with its basic idea of: ἔστι γὰρ εἶναι, "For it is [truly only] the [nothingless] being" and, τὸ γὰρ αὐτό εστι νοεῖν τε χαι εἶναι, "For the same [of identical limitless nature] is thought and being." Closely linked with this is the definition of sensuality as "unseeing eye" and "tempestuous hearing," as well as of ordinary men as "twin heads" and "undiscriminating rabble." Parmenides completely ignores any possible connection between truth and opinion, thought and sensuality, and thus also history.
4. "Transcendence" means "rising above," hence etymologically cannot be conceived without finiteness. The medieval concept of "transcendental" denotes definitions of existence the generality of which "rises above" the generic generality (ens, verum, unum, bonum). The theological concept of transcendence derives from this logical origin.
5. Hence philosophical thought, as the most complete explication of this structure, makes itself and the character of existence of things, as part of the whole (existence, world ground, God, thing-in-itself), its "object." But transcendence is also present in the simplest observation which always takes cognizance of the observed *as* something within an accepted horizon and never without awareness of itself. The term "reaching" implies more than a mere (theoretical) "looking ahead." It is also meant to express the "backward link" which is also contained in the word transcendence.

   In an absolute sense, therefore, transcendence can only be contrasted with a hypothetical "pure nature" in man, while relatively it can be contrasted with elements and forms of itself.

   This definition lays no claim whatever to originality. It is most readily deduced from and explained by Kantian thought.

6. It is enough to recall Kant's attitude toward the French revolution, his rejection of hereditary aristocracy, and his sharp condemnation of colonial exploitation.

7. Classical and medieval "economy" is a doctrine of the proper management of material assets; there was no idea of economy itself being a "philosophical" phenomenon, a developing and universal force affecting human activity as a whole. This separation is the appropriate expression of a society in which thought went far beyond social, practical existence, and for this very reason could only faithfully mirror or ideologically elevate whenever it encountered it. The history of the long-drawn-out, hesitating mutual approach of philosophy and economy has not yet been written; it would be chiefly concerned with such names as Hobbes, Locke, Montesquieu, and Adam Smith, and it would not be identical with a genetic presentation of the theories of national economy.

8. The essential difference between Fichte and Hegel is that the former regards dialectic as never-ending progress, while the latter sees it as an achievable self-realization of the world essence in absolute knowledge. Both men carried the theory of bourgeois society beyond Kant for the very reason that, unlike him, they were not mainly concerned with his "concept of law." Nevertheless the decisive turning point in thought may be regarded as occurring in Kant and later in Marx. Cf. the unpubl. diss. (Freiburg, 1952) by Ernst Nolte, "Selbstentfremdung und Dialektik im deutschen Idealismus und bei Marx."

9. Marx-Engels, *Ausgewählte Schriften*, I, 27.

10. Most of the indignant reactions to this, probably the most famous of all Marx's sayings, overlooks the fact that it is immediately followed by the demand that the proletariat first form itself "into a nation." That Marx and Engels did not lack understanding of the problem of nationality is shown by their attitude during the Franco-Prussian War, when they stressed the priority of a war for national existence over the temporary possibilities of the workers' movement. The fact that they even, at least for a time, inclined toward radical German nationalism is documented by their articles in the *Neue Rheinische Zeitung* with what is sometimes startling clarity. Cf. also the extraordinary letter from Engels to Marx of May 23, 1851 ("Wrest from the Poles in the West what one can; ... send them into the fire, eat their land bare ... !"), *HKG*, Part III, Vol. I.

11. Karl Marx, *Nationalökonomie und Philosophie*, edited by Erich Thier (Cologne and Berlin, 1950), p. 150.

12. Marx-Engels, *Ausgewählte Schriften*, I, 27.

13. Marx, *Nationalökonomie und Philosophie*, p. 192.

14. Karl Marx, *Der Historische Materialismus—Die Frühschriften* (Leipzig, 1932), p. 237.

15. *Ibid.*, p. 280.

16. Marx, *Nationalökonomie und Philosophie*, p. 142.

17. *Ibid.*, p. 141.

18. Karl Marx, *Die deutsche Ideologie* (Berlin, 1932), pp. 22 f.

19. No doubt a study of "Marx in socialism" would yield significant results with particular reference to this trait, provided this study refrained from the misleading distinction between "utopian" and "scientific" socialism. Compared to Fourier, Saint-Simon is an outright realist—and Marx is much closer to Fourier than to Saint-Simon. Fourier, this enemy of "commerce," this anti-Semite and

opponent of "morality," who was born in 1772 and who had practically no knowledge of industrial capitalism, is an excellent example of the confusing intertwining of "progressive" and "reactionary" (or more accurately, primitivist) trends from which no form of socialism has remained entirely free.

20. Cf. also Marx, *Das Kapital*, I, 5th ed. (Hamburg, 1903), 54: "Such a condition of mutual separation did not, however, exist for the members of a primitive society."

21. *Ibid.*, p. 325.

22. *Ibid.*, p. 194.

23. *Ibid.*, p. 38.

24. *Ibid.*, p. 41.

25. Marx, *Der Historische Materialismus*, p. 255.

26. Marx, *Nationalökonomie und Philosophie*, p. 181.

27. Marx, *Das Kapital*, I, 453.

28. *Ibid.*, II, 288.

29. *Marx, Nationalökonomie und Philosophie*, p. 215.

30. Although "pauperization" in the strict sense of the theory must be regarded as relative, the word itself speaks a different language, as does the theory of catastrophe. Cf. *Das Kapital*, I, 728.

31. Marx, *Der Historische Materialismus*, p. 263.

32. It must not be overlooked that there is a subsidiary current in Marx's thought which casts doubt on this monumental and fantastic unity of theoretical and practical transcendence.

    In the *Pariser Manuskripte* he places the alienation of work in a comprehensive process of emancipation, within which the human senses also develop from the groping, sniffing crudity of their beginnings to that freedom which allows them to confront a thing for its own sake, e.g., to regard beauty without self-interest. There is no question here of "resurrection," and nature always means "raw nature."

    In the Feuerbach chapter in *Deutsche Ideologie*, in his first fundamental analysis of the production cycle, Marx gives a definition of consciousness which (apparently entirely against his will) makes it clear that the difference between a world- (horizon-) consciousness and an environment-consciousness is a primordial fact, and that the ensuing process of emancipation of a "pure consciousness" (= theoretical transcendence) is the beginning of history and all emancipation.

    In the introduction to *Kritik der politischen Ökonomie*, Marx makes some observations on Greek mythology which specifically recognize the irrevocability and independence of this form of theoretical transcendence (horizon-consciousness).

    And in a famous passage in Volume III of *Das Kapital*, he carries out a separation between the realm of freedom and the realm of necessity which cannot be substantiated by the dialectic ending in perfection. Since socialism appears here merely as organization of the realm of necessity, the next obvious question is that of the nature of "surplus."

    A hint of an answer may, however, be obtained indirectly by visualizing those figures whom Marx esteemed most highly and whom he regarded as the embodiment of the "self-manifestation of human nature." They were without exception outstanding representatives of theoretical transcendence—Aeschylus and Dante, Milton and Leibniz. The unresolved questions in Marx's work are more interesting than the well-known errors. Among them is, for example, the strange fact that Marx seems not to have been quite convinced of the spontaneity of the "productive forces" and in one passage in *Das Kapital* (Vol. III, Part I, p. 56) attributes them to, among other things, "the development of intellectual work."

33. The theory of concentration and exploitation, for instance, had been developed by Sismondi, and the doctrine of the progressive diminution of profit rates goes back to Ricardo. It is well known that the doctrine of the value of labor is a feature of classical national economy as a whole. Cf. Eduard Heimann, *Geschichte der volkswirtschaftlichen Lehrmeinungen* (Frankfurt a.M., 1949).

34. In a letter to his friend von Gersdorff written in 1868, *Historisch-kritische Gesamtausgabe—Briefe*, II (Munich, 1938), 182, the young Nietzsche relates that he had acquired from a little book a good deal of information "on the state of the social-political parties, and that it, too, radiated "the irrational greatness of Lassalle." It would seem impossible to write a book on Lassalle without describing his relationship to the author of the *Communist Manifesto*. The author of the little book (Joseph Edmund Jörg) was able to—so forgotten was Marx the year *Das Kapital* was published. He is mentioned only once in a trivial and misleading context; Nietzsche is not to blame for not following up this reference. Later Nietzsche frequently referred to the works of Eugen Dühring, which he called "a whole trembling world of subterranean revenge" (VIII, 435). Dühring, *Geschichte der Nationalökonomie und des Sozialismus*, which Nietzsche studied attentively, contains a lengthy chapter on Marx, although without any quotations and written in such a dry, pedagogically critical style that Nietzsche apparently found no reason to pursue his efforts. Nevertheless, these points of contact are quite enough to credit Nietzsche with an intuitive knowledge of the basic intentions of Marxism.

35. Nietzsche's father was not only for a time tutor to the princesses at the ducal court in Altenburg: he also gave his son the names Friedrich Wilhelm as a mark of gratitude toward an "exalted benefactor"; and in 1848, on hearing the news of the king of Prussia's humiliation at the hands of the revolution, he spent days in deep despair and complete seclusion.

36. Friedrich Nietzsche, *Ecce homo*, in *Werke* (Leipzig: Taschenausgabe, n.d.), XI, 385.

37. The cosmology which Nietzsche later developed from his concept of the "will to power" (and which undoubtedly contains some important and stimulating ideas) resembles "dialectical materialism" inasmuch as its secondary and derivative character is very evident.

38. Nietzsche, *Götzendämmerung*, in *Werke*, X, 288.

39. Nietzsche, *Wille zur Macht*, in *Werke*, X, 217.

40. *Ibid.*, p. 187.

41. Nietzsche, *Ecce homo*, in *Werke*, XI, 325 f.

42. It might be objected that the idea of destruction is not specific, that it is equally present in Marxism, in which history is seen to destroy the bourgeoisie. It is true that the middle classes saw themselves threatened politically with destruction

by the socialist program. But it is equally true that it was a legacy of Marxism if scarcely anywhere did the socialist parties attempt to bring about such a destruction (even in Russia they did so only hesitantly and in the struggle for their own survival). For Marxists regard "expropriation of the expropriators" rather as the radical removal of an already tottering obstacle than an actual battle, and certainly not as physical extermination. It is precisely Nietzsche's thought which proves that the fascist idea of destruction must not be regarded primarily as a homogeneous reaction.

43. · Nietzsche, *Genealogie der Moral*, in *Werke*, VIII, 335.

44. Nietzsche, *Götzendämmerung*, in *Werke*, X, 282.

45. Nietzsche, *Wille zur Macht*, in *Werke*, IX, 145.

46. Nietzsche, *Jenseits von Gut und Böse*, in *Werke*, VIII, 139.

47. Nietzsche, *Genealogie der Moral*, in *Werke*, VIII, 322.

48. *Ibid.*, p. 382.

49. Nietzsche, *Wille zur Macht*, in *Werke*, X, 8.

50. *Ibid.*, p. 22.

51. Nietzsche, *Modernität*, in *Werke*, XI, 95.

52. Friedrich Nietzsche, *Die Unschuld des Werdens*, edited by Alfred Bäumler (Leipzig, 1931); *op. cit.*, II, 405.

53. Nietzsche, *Wille zur Macht*, in *Werke*, X, 12.

54. Nietzsche, *Ecce homo*, in *Werke*, XI, 360.

55. Nietzsche, *Die Unschuld des Werdens*, in *Werke*, I, 252.

56. There is no direct connection whatever. Nietzsche's only immediate "pupils" were an apolitical musician (Peter Gast), a Jew (Paul Rée), and a Russian woman (Lou Andreas-Salomé). The "irrationalism" and "estheticism" of his work have had almost as strong an impact on representatives of the political Left as on those of the Right. The most interesting example of direct political influence is probably Mussolini's youthful writings, essentially Marxist though these undoubtedly are. Cf. p. 166 and Nolte, "Marx und Nietzsche im Sozialismus des jungen Mussolini," *op. cit.*

57. In this context it has been possible to pick out only one—albeit a fundamental—line from Nietzsche's thought. Consequently this study is far from doing justice to Nietzsche's highly complex philosophy as a whole or even to the man himself. That he was mainly concerned with the "undetermined quality" of man, i.e., with transcendence, is well known. But it has been necessary to omit from this analysis even a point of such importance as the doctrine of consciousness, so closely related to the Marxist one. Nor has it been possible to examine the "esoteric" line in Nietzsche's thought, in which the superman is the "synthetic" man who, in the midst of the inevitable "universal economic administration" of the earth, manages to "create," i.e., to integrate the otherwise unconscious universal social movement with the individual, in process of which the basic assumption for existence is no longer, as formerly, the unfathomableness of natural existence, but the "mechanization of mankind" (*Werke*, X, 114 f.). This is clearly an exact counterpart to the concept of the classless society. It has also been necessary to pass over entirely the extraordinary inner strife (disclosed in the "Wahnsinnsbriefe," particularly those to Jacob Burckhardt) inherent in Nietzsche the man, who set himself the maxim: "Not to associate with anybody who is involved

in the mendacious race fraud" (*Werke*, VIII, 498), although, again, he claimed that miscegenation was responsible for the triumph of democratic ideals (*Werke*, VIII, 245).

58. For Nietzsche had none of that German provincialism which was part and parcel of National Socialism. One has only to recall how Nietzsche always stressed the great future role of Russia—the Russia of the "lower classes" (*Werke*, XI, 11 f.; cf. also *Die Unschuld des Werdens*, in II, 433, 436).

59. Cf. Ernst Nolte, "Max Weber vor dem Faschismus," *Der Staat*, Vol. II, No. 1 (1963), pp. 1–24.

60. In the inaugural address, Max Weber, *Gesammelte Politische Schriften*, 2nd ed. (Tübingen, 1958), p. 23.

61. Max Weber, *Gesammelte Aufsätze zur Soziologie und Sozialpolitik* (Tübingen, 1924), pp. 407 f.

62. "Homogeneity" or the lack of it is a fact and can in principle be empirically ascertained. However, whether the political alternative must necessarily mean the inclusion of the working class in the nationalism of a section of the bourgeoisie is by no means certain. The internationalism of the workers' movement was not necessarily dependent on the correctness or otherwise of the Marxist theory.

63. Cf. the section "Italian Fascism," the chapter "History," Note 51, p. 490.

64. Max Weber, *Wirtschaft und Gesellschaft*, Half-Vol. I, 4th ed. (Tübingen, 1956), p. 35.

65. *Ibid.*, p. 195.

66. In *Das Kapital* there are frequent scornful references to the puritanical nature of English capitalism.

67. Weber, *Wirtschaft und Gesellschaft*, Half-Vol. I, p. 119.

68. Weber, *Gesammelte Politische Schriften*, p. 242.

69. Weber, *Wirtschaft und Gesellschaft*, Half-Vol. I, pp. 169 f.

70. In "Wissenschaft als Beruf," *Gesammelte Aufsätze zur Wissenschaftslehre*, pp. 578 f.

71. *Ibid.*, p. 588.

72. Lenin, "Staat und Revolution," in *op. cit.*, II, 190.

73. *Ibid.*, p. 250.

74. Lenin, "Die drohende Katastrophe und wie man sie bekämpfen soll," *ibid.*, p. 130.

75. E.g., Lenin, "Über die Naturalsteuer," *ibid.*, p. 830: "... it is our task to learn state capitalism from the Germans, to adopt it with all our might, to shrink from no dictatorial methods to hasten this transferring of Western culture to barbaric Russia, without hesitating to use barbaric fighting methods against barbarism."

"But why do we commit stupidities? That is easy to understand. First, we are a backward country; second, education in our country is minimal; third, we receive no assistance. Not a single civilized state assists us. On the contrary, they are all working against us" ("Fünf Jahre russische Revolution," *ibid.*, pp. 973 f.).

"Not even Marx thought of writing a single word about it [the state capitalism which occurs under communism] and he died without leaving behind a single exact quotation or any irrefutable evidence. So now we have to try and help ourselves" ("Politischer Bericht des ZK auf dem XI. Parteitag," *ibid.*, p. 926; cf. also p. 995).

76. Lenin, "Die nächsten Aufgaben der Sowjetmacht," *ibid.*, p. 377.
77. Here "society" means not the totality of its members but the leading group.
78. "Industrialization" is also meant here as a total process and hence distinguished from feudal Japan's purely technical adoption of industrial forms of production.
79. It is no doubt clear from the foregoing that here the definite article is used not collectively but hypothetically.

Appendix A

1. In Germany latterly: Gustav Adolf Rein, *Bonapartismus und Faschismus in der deutschen Geschichte* (Göttingen, 1960). A very informative survey, despite the thematic limitation, of Western literature and its principal trends is Andrew G. Whiteside, "The Nature and Origins of National Socialism," *Journal of Central European Affairs*, XVII (1957–58), 48–73.
2. *IMG*, XXXIV, 471.
3. Corneliu Z. Codreanu, *Eiserne Garde* (Berlin, 1939), p. 57.
4. Cf. Asvero Gravelli, "Verso l'Internazionale fascista," first appeared in *Antieuropa*, Nos. 11 and 12 (1930).

Appendix B

1. Turin, 1957.
2. Hence it is not the intention of this analysis to demonstrate that bolshevism is really a form of fascism. This impression would result from partial viewpoints only. Even where the line seems to point directly to bolshevism, as with authoritarianism—totalitarianism—it must always be borne in mind that, in order to arrive at a suitable formulation of the question, a different departure point would be required.
3. The term was first used by Luigi Salvatorelli in *Nazionalfascismo* (Turin, 1923).
4. See pp. 228, 416 ff.

Selected Reading List

The following is a short listing of related works available in English:

General

ARENDT, HANNAH. *The Origins of Totalitarianism.* New York and Toronto, 1951. Published in London as *Burden of Our Time,* 1951.

COBBAN, ALFRED. *Dictatorship, its History and Theory.* New York, London and Toronto, 1939.

FRIEDRICH, CARL JOACHIM (ed.). *Totalitarianism.* Cambridge, Mass. and London, 1954.

ROGGER, HANS and EUGEN WEBER (eds.). *The European Right: A Historical Profile.* Berkeley and London, 1965.

STERN, FRITZ. *The Politics of Cultural Despair.* Berkeley, Los Angeles and London, 1961.

TALMON, J. L. *The Origins of Totalitarian Democracy.* New York, 1960; London and Toronto, 1961.

Action Française

BROGAN, D. W. *Development of Modern France, 1870–1939.* London, 1940. Published in New York as *France under the Republic, 1870–1939,* 1940.

———. *French Personalities and Problems.* London, 1946; New York, 1947.

BYRNES, ROBERT F. *Anti-Semitism in Modern France.* Vol. I. New Brunswick, 1950; London, 1951.

CURTIS, MICHAEL. *Three against the Third Republic: Sorel, Barres and Maurras.* Princeton, 1959; London, 1960.

EARLE, EDWARD MEADE (ed.). *Modern France.* Princeton, London and Toronto, 1951.

MICAUD, C. A. *The French Right and Nazi Germany, 1933–1939.* Durham, N.C., 1943; London, 1944.

OSGOOD, SAMUEL M. *French Royalism under the Third and Fourth Republics.* The Hague, 1961.

TANNENBAUM, EDWARD R. *The Action Française.* New York and London, 1962.

WEBER, EUGEN. *Action Française: Royalism and Reaction in Twentieth Century France.* Stanford, 1962.

———. *The Nationalist Revival in France, 1905–1914.* Berkeley and Los Angeles, 1959.

Italian Fascism

CIANO, GALEAZZO, *Ciano's Diary, 1937–1938*. London, 1952.

———. *The Ciano Diaries, 1939–1943*. New York and Toronto, 1946; London, 1947.

DEAKIN, F. W. *The Brutal Friendship: Mussolini, Hitler and the Fall of Italian Fascism.* London, New York and Evanston, 1962.

DELZELL, CHARLES F. *Mussolini's Enemies: The Italian Anti-Fascist Resistance.* Princeton and London, 1961.

EBENSTEIN, WILLIAM. *Fascist Italy*. New York, 1939.

FERMI, LAURA. *Mussolini*. Chicago and London, 1961.

FINER, HERMAN. *Mussolini's Italy*. New York, London and Toronto, 1935.

MUSSOLINI, BENITO. *Fascism: Doctrine and Institutions*. Rome, 1935.

WISKEMANN, ELIZABETH. *The Rome-Berlin Axis. A History of the Relations between Hitler and Mussolini*. London, New York and Toronto, 1949.

National Socialism

ABEL, THEODORE F. *Why Hitler came into Power*. New York and Toronto, 1938.

BAYNES, NORMAN H. (ed.). *The Speeches of Adolf Hitler*. 2 vols. London and Toronto, 1942; New York, 1943.

BULLOCK, ALAN. *Hitler: A Study in Tyranny*. London and New York, 1952.

BUTLER, ROHAN D'OLIER. *The Roots of National Socialism*. London and Toronto, 1941; New York, 1942.

HITLER, ADOLF. *Mein Kampf*. New York, London and Toronto, 1939.

MAU, HERMANN and HELMUT KRAUSNICK. *German History 1933–1945*. London and New York, 1963.

NEUMANN, FRANZ. *Behemoth. The Structure and Practice of National Socialism*. 2nd ed. New York, London and Toronto, 1944.

RAUSCHNING, HERMANN. *The Revolution of Nihilism*. New York, Chicago and Toronto, 1939. Published in London and Toronto as *Germany's Revolution of Destruction, 1939*.

ROTHFELS, HANS. *The German Opposition to Hitler, an Appraisal*. Hinsdale, Ill. and Toronto, 1948.

The Third Reich. International Council for Philosophy and Humanistic Studies. New York, London and Toronto, 1955.

TOYNBEE, ARNOLD and VERONICA (eds.). *Hitler's Europe*. London, New York and Toronto, 1955.

TREVOR-ROPER, H. R. (ed.) *Hitler's Table Talk, 1941–1944*. London, 1953. Published in New York as *Hitler's Secret Conversations, 1941–1944*, 1953.

INDEX

Abetz, Otto, 83
Acerbo, Giacomo, 512 n22
Action Française, and Italian fascism, 25–6, 69, 70, 78, 86, 184, 247, 487 n1; and National Socialism, 26, 78, 86, 276, 466 n5; its revolutionary characteristic, 53, 132; its beginning in the Dreyfus affair, 54, 57, 66, 67; its newspaper (*Action Française*), 66, 68–9, 71, 77, 82, 83, 84, 90, 149, 476 n90, 477 n8; early constitution, 66–8, 89–90; founds a college, 68, 90; use of violence, 69–70, 132–3; and religious issues, 70–1, 76–7; and bourgeoisie, 70, 96; and syndicalism, 71, 90, 115, 473 n53; and the war, 72–3, 90; policy, 73, 74–5; condemned by the Vatican, 76–8, 95; growing ineffectiveness, 78; its close, 84; and the importance of doctrine, 89; structure, 89–90, 94, 477 n8; the *Nouvelle Librairie Nationale*, 90, 93–4; nature defined, 479 n1
Adler, Viktor, 297
Ahlwardt, Hermann, 482 n114
Aeschylus, 542 n32
Alatri, Paolo, 489 n14, 495 n193, 502 n321
Albertini, Luigi, and the *Corriere della Sera*, 17
Alexander I (of Yugoslavia), 14
Althusius, Johannes, 31
Amann, Max, 384
Amendola, Giovanni, 150, 170, 269, 504 n378
Anaxagoras, 488 n11
Andreas-Salomé, Lou, 544 n56
Andrieu, Paulin-Pierre, Cardinal, and Action Française, 76
Angst, see Fear
Antifascism (resistance), 3, 8, 196, 359, 362, 464 n14, 499 n258, 504 n378, 528 nn
Antinature, concept of, 37, 286; Maurras and, 136–7, 138, 139, 430; Hitler and, 330, 332, 420; *see also* Nature
Anti-Semitism, 332–3, 381, 470 n83; in Hitler, 10, 19, 50, 60–1, 82–3, 230, 277, 287, 290, 291, 315, 316, 331–2, 333, 358, 363, 364, 380–2, 398–401, 403–7, 416, 420, 460, 493 n162, 515 nn, 521 n89, 522 n130, 523 n132, 526 n186, 527 n200, 528 nn, 530 nn; in Poland, 11; in Hungary, 13; in fascist movements, 19; forms of, 50; in Maurras, 60–1, 82–3, 93, 114, 119, 121, 124, 125, 230, 405, 484 n155; in Mussolini, 181, 229–30, 460, 493 n162, 506 n417, 507 n420; in National Socialism, 376–82, 393, 400
Aosta, Emanuele Filiberto, Duke of, 213

Arendt, Hannah, 466 nn 38, 47; 471 n6
Arias, Gino, 230
Aristophanes, 514 n1
Aristotle, 34, 138
Arminius, 415
Arndt, Ernst Moritz, 24, 277
Aron, Robert, 475 n83
Arpinati, Leandro, 199, 207, 488 n9, 501 n304, 509 n473

Backe, Herbert, 395
Bacon, Francis, 31, 35, 38, 39
Badoglio, Pietro, 235, 237, 506 n405, 513 n50
Bainville, Jacques, 472 n41, 474 n75; and Action Française, 67, 91; and fascism, 78; his death, 82; and Maurras, 472 n41, 480 n28; *Histoire de deux peuples*, 73; *Conséquences politiques de la guerre*, 75; *Bismarck et la France*, 94
Bakunin, Mikhail Aleksandrovich, 151, 497 n214
Balabanov, Angelica, 176, 230, 491 n13
Balbo, Italo, and fascism, 201, 207, 258, 335, 372, 498 n254, 499 n271, 502 n326; his march on Ravenna, 211; and the March on Rome, 213; biography, 499 nn, 502 n326, 512 n22
Baldini, Nullo, 194
Baratono, Adelchi, and maximalism, 498 n240
Barnes, James Strachey, 466 n42
Barrès, Maurice, 149, 150, 470 n89 ff, 471 n13; Maurras and, 30, 48, 52–3, 58, 91; and French nationalism, 52, 67; his idea of race, 53
Barthou, Jean Louis, 72, 92–3
Bastianini, Giuseppe, 511 n10
Baudelaire, Charles, 59, 149
Bauer, Otto, 295
Baynes, Robert H., 536 nn, 538 nn
Bebel, August, 88
Beck, Ludwig, 350
Bellonci, Goffredo, 495 n193
Beneš, Eduard, 290
Benjamin, René, 80
Benn, Gottfried, 25
Berg (Markienen), Friedrich von, 340
Bergson, Henri, 78, 150, 159, 243
Bernanos, Georges, 52, 95; and Maurras, 475 n82; and Action Française, 475 n82
Bernstein, Eduard, 42, 159, 471 n2
Bernstein, Henri, 69
Berth, Edouard, 71, 115
Besson, Waldemar, 464 n4
Bethlen, Stephan, Count, 11, 13

Bianchi, Michele, 172, 251, 252, 255, 259, 511 n10; and the March on Rome, 213, 492 n133; and d'Annunzio, 507 n432
Billot, Louis, Cardinal, 473 n50, 474 n71
Bismarck, Otto von, 106, 309, 470 n83; his empire, 302, 326, 414
Bissolati, Leonida, 148, 154; attacked by Mussolini, 161, 182, 495 n190
Blanqui, Louis Auguste, 132–3, 164, 176
Bleichröder, Gerson, 328
Blériot, Louis, 160
Blomberg, Werner von, 228
Blum, Léon, 78
Bocchini, Arturo, and OVRA, 266
Bodin, Jean, 31
Boehm, Hermann, 526 n183
Boepple, Ernst, 517 n26, 536 n22
Böhm, Adolf, 471 n4; and Zionism, 530 n37
Bolshevism, 132, 452; Hitler (National Socialism) and, 10, 19, 290, 303, 331, 357, 363, 383, 386, 392–3, 404, 406–7, 411, 415, 527 n200, 536 n45; equated with fascism, 19–20, 26; Maurras and, 125; Mussolini and, 154, 175, 206, 215, 228, 230, 240; (duel with Lenin), 176–7, 181, 189–90, 235, 389, 461, 497 n230, 501 nn; Lenin and, 452; seizure of power, 525 n164
Bolzon, Piero, 207, 511 n10
Bombacci, Nicola, 474 n72, 488 n12, 509 n473
Bonald, Louis de, 40, 330, 469 passim; Maurras and, 30; and Christian conservatism, 36–7, 485 n184; and the French Revolution, 48
Bonn, Moritz Julius, 465 n25
Bonomi, Ivanoe, 148, 160, 511 n15
Bordiga, Amedeo, 169, 492 n122
Borgese, Giuseppe Antonio, 17, 150, 466 n35, 488 n10, 504 n378; and Hermes, 149
Borghi, Armando, 499 n265
Borkenau, Franz, 8, 465 n16
Bormann, Martin, and the extermination of the Jews, 399
Bossuet, Jacques Bénigne, 35
Bottai, Giuseppe, 488 n9, 498 n254, 508 n442; and the March on Rome, 213
Boulainvilliers, Henri de, 278
Boulanger, General Georges, 61, 70, 296
Bourgeois society, raised by social revolution, 5; and fascism, 17, 26, 315, 434; schism in, 115–16; and Italian liberalism, 147; class warfare and, 153, 156; and revolution, 157, 191–2, 322; and sovereignty, 422; and transcendence, 434, 450; bolshevism and, 452
Bourget, Paul, 467 n3
Boveri, Margret, 474 n72, 528 n211
Bracher, Karl Dietrich, 524 n149, 525 n160, 530 n23
Brasillach, Robert, 12, 52, 58, 82, 95; and Action Française, 476 n90; and fascism, 476 n90
Braun, Otto, 340
Bredow, Ferdinand von, 348
Bremond, Henri, 64
Bresciani, Italo, 494 n180

Briand, Aristide, 74, 77, 92, 97, 474 n72
Broszat, Martin, 465 n29, 527 n192, 534 n86, 535 n1
Brückner, Wilhelm, and the SA, 529 n9
Brüning, Heinrich, 340, 374
Bucard, Marcel, 12, 95; his Francists, 78
Buchheim, Hans, 521 n100, 532 n59, 534 n72
Bukharin, Nikolai Ivanovich, and Stalin, 8
Bullock, Alan, The Third Reich, 535 n1
Bülow, Bernhard von, 492 n139
Buozzi, Bruno, 181, 495 n185, 504 n378
Burckhardt, Jacob, 544 n57
Burke, Edmund, 30
Byrnes, Robert, 470 n78

Cabrières, François-Marie de, Cardinal, 473 n50
Caillaux, Joseph, 73, 485 n176
Calamandrei, Piero, 500 n275
Calza-Bini, Gino, 207, 511 n10
Camelots du Roi, 69–70, 72, 90, 98, 476 n101, 477 n8; beginnings of, 91–2; their songs, 92–3, 98, 106, 477 nn, 478 nn
Cancogni, Manlio, 495 n189, 499 n257
Canepa, Antonio, 509 n1
Carducci, Giosuè, 149, 163, 488 n6
Carocci, Giampiero, 463
Carofiglio, Mario Fusti, 511 n3
Carosi, Sandro, 201
Cavaignac, Eugène, 55
Cavour, Camillo, 146
Ceccherini, Sante, 253; and the March on Rome, 213
Chabod, Federico, 463–4
Chamberlain, Houston Stewart, Hitler and, 277; his race doctrine, 282–5, 286, 331, 333, 513 n18, 516 nn
Chamberlain, Neville, 514 n1; and the Munich agreement, 352–3
Chateaubriand, François René de, Maurras and, 123
Chénier, André, 103
Chiurco, Giorgio Alberto, and fascism, 197, 198, 253, 257, 488 n9, 494 n173
Christianity, and fascism, 18; de Maistre and, 34, 35–6; Maurras and, 62, 63, 124, 126, 138, 430; Mussolini and, 175, 189, 261, 268, 512 n27; Hitler and, 331, 360, 406–7; see also Church (Catholic)
Church (Catholic): attitude toward fascism in general, 18, 262; attitude toward Action Française, 57, 70–1, 76–8, 95, 477 n8; attitude toward Italian fascism, 18, 146, 205, 217, 219, 220; attitude toward National Socialism, 18; Maurras and the, 63, 70, 71, 77, 81, 87, 90, 95, 114, 121, 123, 126–7, 138, 141; Mussolini and the, 163, 212, 220, 261–2, 268, 512 n27, 513 n37; Hitler and the, 331, 335, 407, 415, 537 n52, See also Christianity
Ciano, Costanzo, 500 n274
Ciano, Galeazzo, 23, 506 n404; and fascism, 201, 507 n43; his diaries, 229, 231, 270, 461, 463, 497 n216, 506 nn, 507 nn, 511 n61; his death, 508 n446

Ciccotti, Ettore, 488 n4
Cione, Edmondo, 508 n448, 509 n456
Cioran, E. Michel, 468 nn 8, 17
Cipriani, Amilcare, 170
Claudel, Paul, 85
Clausen, Fritz, 12
Clemenceau, Georges, 55, 65, 67, 97, 121, 473 n53, 483 n122; as prime minister, 66, 72, 73, 118; Mussolini and, 175
Codreanu, Coreliu Zelea-, 11, 18, 26, 455, 460, 546 n3
Cohen, Hermann, 124
Comte, Auguste, 40, 78, 112, 469 nn 35, 36; Maurras and, 30, 60, 91, 113, 123–4; his law of three stages, 37, 166; his form of positivism, 38; and the French revolution, 38, 126; his counter-revolutionary tendencies, 38–9
Conservatism, 5, 9, 18; Christian, 33, 35–6, 39, 63; radical, 48–53, 63, 116, 117, 121, 249; Maurras and, 87, 128; concept of, 53; trends of, 53, 132; and National Socialism, 340, 341, 533 n71
Conze, Werner, 540 n153
Coppola, Francesco, 175, 184, 495 n198, 496 nn, 509 n473
Cormier, Aristide, 476 n111
Corporatism, 49, 244, 261
Corradini, Enrico, 147, 150, 162, 303, 409; and Il Regno, 149, 150, 183, 185, 495 n193; Mussolini and, 175, 181; and Italian nationalism, 182, 495 n193, 496 nn; biography, 495 n193
Corridoni, Filippo, 172, 488 n9
Costa, Andrea, 151–2
Coty, François, and Action Française, 477 n8
Coubertin, Pierre, Baron de, 64
Crankshaw, Edward, 534 n82
Crispi, Francesco, 147
Croce, Benedetto, 150; and Mussolini, 214, 266–7, 502 n328
Curtis, Michael, 471 n8

Daim, Wilfried, 518 n38
Daladier, Édouard, 352
Dallin, Alexander, 528 n205
D'Annunzio, Gabriele, 173, 182, 212, 488 n7; and early fascism, 11, 150, 370; his influence on Italy's intellectual youth, 149, 252–3; and Fiume, 185–8, 233, 252, 311, 494 n171, 496 n207; his Parta del Carnaro, 187; and Mussolini, 502 n329
Dansette, Adrien, 474 n67
Dante Alighieri, 542 n32
D'Aragona, Lodovico, 181, 495 n185
Darré, Walter, 372, 384; Minister of Agriculture, 390–1; his ideas, 530 n19
Daudet, Léon, and Action Française, 67, 68–9, 72, 74, 96, 472 n42; his death, 82; his style, 97–8; his arrest and escape, 98; Maurras et son temps, 95, 467 n2, 479 n22; L'Avant-Guerre, 474 n57
De Ambris, Alceste, 187, 488 n9

Déat, Marcel, 12, 78, 80, 81, 356, 474 n72
De Begnac, Yvon, 487 n1, 488 nn 9, 19; 506 n417
De Bono, Emilio, 26; and fascism, 201, 500 n273; and the March on Rome, 213; his death, 508 n446
De Bosis, Lauro, 504 n378
Decay, History of, 430; concept of in Italian nationalism, 184; concept of in Hitler, 403, 404, 416; concept of in Nietzsche, 443, 444; concept of in Weber, 449
Degrelle, Léon, 12
Dehio, Ludwig, 464 n3
Delcassé, Théophile, 97
Delitzsch, Friedrich, 523 n132
Deloncle, Eugène, 95
Democritus, 284
Demosthenes, 109
Denais, Joseph, 97
Descartes, René, 39
Destruction, idea of, 21, 61, 102–3, 139, 220, 398–401, 444–5, 434, 543 n42
Deuerlein, Ernst, 520 nn, 529 n4
De Vecchi, Cesare Maria, and fascism, 201, 248, 500 n272, 511 n2; and the March on Rome, 213; death, 509 n473
Diaz, Armando, 214
Dietrich, Joseph, and the SS, 391
Dietrich, Otto, 290, 383, 517 n11, 524 n145
Digeon, Claude, 472 n32
Dilthey, Wilhelm, 7
Dimier, Louis, and the French revolution, 30; and Action Française, 67, 91, 92, 95, 473 n43, 477 nn; and Maurras, 483 n123, 486 n194; Les Maîtres de la contre-révolution au xixme siècle, 30, 67, 91
Dimitrov, Georgi, 464 n2
Dolfin, Giovanni, 508 n448
Dollfuss, Engelbert, 15, 348–9
Domarus, Max, 523 n131
Domination, concept of, 118, 407, 410, 411; see also Race doctrine
Doriot, Jacques, 12, 13, 80, 81; and the Parti Populaire, 78; and fascism, 96, 355, 456, 474 n72
Dreux-Brézé, Renée de, 475 n80
Drexler, Anton: his Free Workers' Committee, 313; his German Workers' party, 317–18, 328, 366, 367
Dreyfus, Alfred, 25; anti-Semitism and, 50, 51, 52, 54, 417 n5; new patterns of thought initiated by the affair, 54; and Action Française, 54, 69; nature of the "affair", 54–7, 65–6, 67, 471 n5, 473 n47; his trial compared with Maurras', 84, 85
Drieu la Rochelle, Pierre, 12, 82, 95
Drumont, Édouard, and anti-Semitism, 48, 50–1, 118, 470 nn, 482 n114; dislike of the bourgeoisie, 51; his radical conservatism, 51–2, 296; and Bernanos, 475 n82; La France Juive, 50–1, 61
Dudan, Alessandro, 511 n10, 512 n22
Dühring, Eugen, 471 n5, 516 n31, 543 n34
Dumini, Amerigo, 499 n264
Dutrait-Crozon, Henri (pseud.), 471 n7

Ebert, Friedrich, 309
Eckart, Dietrich, x, 24, 291, 315, 385; and the German Workers' party, 317; and the *Völkischer Beobachter*, 319, 328–9, 522 n116; and National Socialism, 322; his influence on Hitler, 324, 325, 328–9, 406; his history, 328–9; his *Zwiegesprach* with Hitler, 329, 392, 405, 406, 536 n50, 537 n52; "Storm Song", 533 n71
Eglhofer, Karl, 322
Eichmann, Karl Adolf, and the Security Department, 397; and the transportation of Jews, 400
Eicke, Theodor, and the SS, 399
Einstein, Albert, 528 n217
Eisner, Kurt, 10; fascism and, 181
Emancipation, 31, 46, 116, 118, 430, 453; Maurras and, 125, 129, 405; anti-Semitism and, 381; Hitler and, 404–5; Marx and, 439; *see also* Transcendence
Enemy, doctrine of the, 36–7; in Maurras, 63, 101, 106, 114, 120 ff, 139, 405, 406, 407, 449; in Hitler, 290, 363, 393, 398, 434, 405, 407, 418, 430, 449; *see also* Anti-Semitism, Bolshevism, Marxism
Engels, Friedrich, 99, 120, 321, 437; and idealism, 155; and the bourgeoisie, 157, 447, 490 n51; and the oppressed, 158; protagonist of Marxism, 165; Mussolini and, 174; and the rejection of history, 464 n13; and nationality, 541 n10
Enlightenment, 31, 34, 35, 37, 330, 440, 481 n68
Epp, Franz Xaver von, 323
Era, concept of, 3, 22; of fascism, 3, 6–9; of world wars, 4–6, 9; of the Counter-Reformation, 6
Erdmann, Karl Dietrich, 463
Erzberger, Matthias, 98, 309, 492 n139
Espe, Walter M., 530 n15, 537 n81
Esser, Hermann, 319
Evola, Giulio, and pagan imperialism, 249; and race doctrine, 510 n17
Eyck, Erich, 519 n53

Facta, Luigi, 210, 212, 213, 341
Farinacci, Roberto, 17, 22, 207, 265, 494 n180, 508 n445; and "squadrism", 217–218, 254, 499 n259, 511 n7; his death, 509 n473
Fascism (in general): use of the word, 3–4, 6, 9, 455, 460, 465 n25, 540 n1; its epochal nature, 3, 6–9, 456; fascist movements, 10–16, 78, 89, 199, 455–6, 465 n26; and anti-Semitism, 11, 13, 230; and conservatism, 15, 19, 245–6, 249; interpretations of, 16–20, 89, 204, 243; concept of, 16,20,71,75,203–4,422–3,459–60; church and, 18; nature defined, 20–1, 78, 243–4, 333, 416, 424, 429, 453, 466 n50; political forerunners, 25–6, 172; a form of anti-Marxism, 29, 429, 441, 445; and the unity of doctrine and practice, 89; early characteristics, 95; relation to Action Française, 145; its appeal to the young,

201, 499 n270; in Germany, 314; philosophical exploration of, 419 ff; sense of kinship in, 455–6; regarded historically, 459 ff; typology and, 459–62; communist definition of, 465 n33
Fascism (Italian), 15, 74, 149, 455; an expression of Mussolini's ideas, 24, 89, 150–151, 172, 188, 203, 243; and Action Française, 25, 70, 79, 252; its earliest forms, 89, 150,1 72, 199, 202, 251; foundation of, 180–1, 251; and National Socialism, 181, 267; first great successes in Trieste, etc., 190–1, 196, 198–9, 254–5, 258; and bourgeoisie, 197, 250, 314; and Italy's revolutionary movement, 196 ff; its numbers, 196, 252, 262, 269; defeat of socialism, 196–202; use of violence, 197, 198–202, 209, 220–1; and nationalism, 198–9, 209, 215, 232, 233; first punitive expeditions, 198–202, 204; and state, 202, 215, 218, 245, 263, 264, 320; nature defined, 203, 221, 243–6, 270, 314; interpretations of, 204, 243–6; and "squadrism", 209–10, 211, 215, 216, 217, 253–4; becomes totalitarian, 217 ff, 259; and World War II, 232–5, 270; and its precursors, 247–9; its organization, 251–2, 255–9, 262; its military sector, 256–7; and syndicalism, 257–8, 261; its style, 254–5, 258–9, 264–5; its expansion in the Starace era, 265 ff; and intellectual life, 266–7; its waning influence, 269–71
Faul, Erwin, 535 n1
Fear, as a basic emotion, 101–3, 135, 139–140, 229, 246, 286, 297, 402
Feder, Gottfried, 315, 521 nn; and the German Workers' party, 317–18; influences Hitler, 324–5; and National Socialism, 324–5, 333
Federzoni, Luigi, 185, 320, 496 n204; biography, 496 n205, 512 n26
Fermi, Enrico, 528 n217
Fichte, Johann Gottlieb, 24, 39, 434; Maurras and *Reden an die Deutsche Nation*, 63, 486 n195; and German socialism, 277; compared with Hegel, 541 n8
Finer, Herman, 512 n28
Finzi, Aldo, 502 n343
Flandin, Pierre-Etienne, 506 n404
Foertsch, Hermann, 526 n179
Ford, Henry, 331, 523 n132
Forges, Jean, 471 n8
Forges-Davanzati, Roberto, 185, 496 n204
Fourier, Charles, 16, 160, 166, 470 n83; and socialism, 541 n19
France, Anatole, 467 n3
Francis Ferdinand, Archduke, 295, 296
Franco, Francisco, 456; forms the Falange, 15, 465 n26; Maurras and, 79
Frank, Hans, 228, 355, 383, 398, 514 n1, 516 n1, 525 n173, 538 n93
Franz Joseph, Emperor, 284
Franz-Willing, Georg, 520 nn, 521 nn, 529 nn

Friedrich II (of Prussia), 331
Freund, Michael, 474 n56, 506 n413
Frick, Wilhelm, 315, 323; and race policy, 377, 380
Friedrich, Carl J., 466 n36
Fritsch, Theodor, 523 n132
Fritsch, Werner von, 350, 526 n179
Frymann, Daniel (Heinrich Class), 519 n42
Führerprinzip, see Principle of Leadership
Fustel de Coulanges, Numa Denis, 470 n73; Maurras and, 30, 47; a counterrevolutionary, 47; *La Cité Antique*, 47, 470 n72

Galilei, Galileo, 39
Garibaldi, Anita, 248
Garibaldi, Giuseppe, 146, 149; Mussolini and, 248, 249
Garros, Roland, 487 n203
Gast, Peter, 544 n56
Gaulle, General Charles de, 83
Gaultier, Jules de, *Le Bovarysme*, 139
Gay, Francisque, 479 nn 25, 27 etc.
Gemlich, Adolf, 316, 364
Genoud, François, 514 n4
Gentile, Giovanni, 22, 150, 237, 259, 510 n4; definition of fascism, 244, 249; and school reform, 261
George, Stefan, 450
Gerlach, Leopold and Ernst Ludwig von, 29
Germany, Maurras and, 61, 63, 64, 72, 75, 76, 77, 79–80, 104, 106, 118–19, 120, 121, 122, 124–5, 129, 130–1, 302, 303, 310, 480 n28; Action Française and, 72, 73, 79; Mussolini and, 169, 174, 176, 177, 225–6
Germino, Dante L., 512 n28
Gersdorff, Carl von, 543 n34
Giampaoli, Mario, 251, 494 n180
Gide, André, 64, 78
Gioberti, Vincenzo, 146, 147
Giolitti, Giovanni, 17, 148, 150, 154, 168, 173, 205, 210, 259; and D'Annunzio, 188; and the occupation of the factories, 195; Mussolini and, 212, 214
Giordani, Giulio, shooting of, 199
Girardet, Raoul, 476 n90, 476 n113
Giulietti, Giuseppe, 502 n329
Giunta, Francesco, 253, 265, 494 n171
Giurati, Giovanni, 261–2, 265
Giusti, Giuseppe, 164
Glaser, Hermann, 464
Glum, Friedrich, 463
Gobetti, Piero, 504 n378
Gobineau, Joseph Arthur de, 43, 47; Hitler and, 277, 514 n1, 515 nn; his race doctrine, 278–80, 283, 284, 286, 330, 411; Maurras and, 484 n155
Goebbels, Joseph Paul, 22, 228, 371; and fascism, 275; and Röhm, 327; joins Hitler, 336; *gauleiter* of Berlin, 336; his speeches, writings, etc., 346, 373, 383, 514 n3, 523 n141, 530 nn; and anti-Semitism, 376; and Communists, 524 n150
Gollwitzer, Heinz, 521 n89

Gollwitzer, Helmut, 466 n40
Gömbös, Julius, and "National Socialism", 10–11, 13–14, 455
Göring, Hermann, 228, 347, 354, 532 n57; and the SA, 348; and anti-Semitism, 379
Görlitz, Walter, 521 n98, 535 n1
Gougenot des Mousseaux, Roger, 523 n132
Goyau, Georges, 97
Graml, Hermann, 530 n33
Gramsci, Antonio, 166; and *Ordine Nuovo*, 193, 494 n173, 498 n244; and Mussolini, 498 n244
Grandi, Dino, 22; and the socialists, 196; and fascism, 201, 207, 208, 235, 255, 335; biography, 498 n254, 509 n473, 511 n10
Gravelli, Asvero, and *Anti-Europa*, 249, 546 n4; and early fascism, 510 n16
Graziadei, Antonio, and maximalism, 498 n240
Greiner, Joseph, 514 n1; and Hitler, 517 n5, 518 n37
Groener, Wilhelm, 339
Guérin, Daniel, 512 n26
Guesde, Jules, 132, 165, 482 n95
Gumplowicz, Ludwig, 515 n16
Gunther, John, 465 n17
Gurian, Waldemar, 81, 473 n48, 476 n88
Guyau, Jean Marie, 159

Haas, Werner, 465 n28
Hahn, Otto, 528 n217
Halder, Franz, 527 n196
Halévy, Daniel, 87
Hallgarten, George W. F., 524 n145
Hanisch, Reinhold, 518 n37
Hantsch, Hugo, 518 n29
Harrer, Hans, 328, 367
Hauser, Otto, 331, 523 n132, 538 n91
Haushofer, Karl, 408
Hausser, Paul, 532 n59
Havard de la Montagne, Robert, 471 n14, 472 n38, 474 n69
Hegel, Georg Wilhelm Friedrich, 7, 30, 39, 166, 430, 434, 438; doctrine of dialectical progress, 116, 159, 437, 442, 541 n8; Marx and, 127, 129, 435; and liberty, 140; Mussolini and, 244, 245; and transcendence, 431; concept of the state, 435; and bourgeois society, 451, 541 n8; compared with Fichte, 541 n8
Heiber, Helmut, 528 n207, 530 n21
Heidegger, Martin, 7
Heiden, Konrad, 518 n37, 520 n65, 522 n127, 523 n138, 524 n145, 529 n3, 535 n1
Heimann, Eduard, 543 n33
Heine, Heinrich, 486 n195
Heiss, Adolf, 319
Helfferich, Karl, 309
Hennersdorf, F. K. (Felix Kraus), 505 n388
Henry, Colonel Hubert, and Dreyfus, 55–6, 471 n10
Herriot, Édouard, 485 n176
Hervé, Gustave, 104, 137, 165; and World War I, 167

Herzfeld, Hans, 463 n5
Herzl, Theodor, 471 n4
Hess, Moses, 530 n37
Hess, Rudolf, and the Nuremberg rally, 383
Heydrich, Reinhard, and the SS, 391, 397
Hierl, Konstantin, 372
Hillgruber, Andreas, 527 n199
Himmler, Heinrich, 22, 228, 347, 348; and Poland, 355, 395–6; and the SS, 390, 391–393, 394–7, 532 n68; as RKF, 394–7, 409; and the annihilation of the Jews, 399; and bolshevism, 538 n113
Hindenburg, Paul von, 13, 14, 176; and Hitler, 219, 341–2; as President, 335, 340–341; dissolves the Reichstag, 344
Hitler, Adolf, 3, 75, 176; equates bolshevism with Jewry, 10, 330–1; overthrows the Bavarian government, 11, 319, 334; the church and, 18; documentation of, 22–3; presentation of his ideas, 23, 29; Maurras and, 79, 80, 287–8; his *Weltanschauung*, 89, 232, 277, 287, 292, 315, 324, 340, 357, 367, 418, 461; a man of the people, 96, 312; relations with Mussolini, 228, 229, 231–2, 236, 244–5, 246, 265, 364, 455, 461, 506 nn; and *Lebensraum*, 228–9, 303, 349, 351, 402, 408–9; and totalitarian despotism, 229, 231, 319, 374; and Czechoslovakia, 232, 290, 349, 350; influence of fascism on, 275, 319, 324; knowledge of literature, 277, 514 n1, 523 n132, 532 n67; and the development of National Socialism, 287, 293, 315, 318, 365, 366–9, 371; early life and background, 287–8, 291, 516 n1, 518 nn, 519 n56; and World War I, 288, 304, 312, 313, 416, 423; development of his abnormal characteristics, 288–294, 316–17, 363, 517 n11; as a speaker, 292–3, 316, 318, 365, 367, 373, 374, 384–5, 524 n163, 526 nn; nature of his power, 293, 312–13, 367, 412; his political beginnings, 312–23, 333; and the German Workers' party, 317–18, 371; designated *Der Führer*, 319, 324; and the *Putsch* of 1923, 320, 333–4; his teachers and influences, 323–9, 333; as presented in Eckhart's *Conversations*, 329–33; his rise after 1930, 338–42; Communists and, 339, 359–60; his war in peacetime, 348 ff, 525 nn; his Four Year Plan, 349; his rapprochement with Italy, 349; and the attack on Austria, 349, 351; and the Munich agreement, 350, 352–3; implications of his rise to power, 351–4; and Poland, 353, 354, 413–14; and World War II, 354–9, 395, 423, 508 n433; and the USSR, 354, 357–8, 362, 522 n130; sole master of Europe, 355 ff; programme of annihilation, 358, 361, 364, 381, 398–401, 417; and the US, 360 ff, 527 n191; beginnings of his defeat, 361–4; his death, 364, 401, 423; nature of his assemblies, 367–9, 374, 382–6, 387, 412; his global struggle, 416 ff; his epochal nature, 423–4; studies of his doctrine, 535 nn; and Social Democrats, 518 n36, 524 n153; *Mein Kampf*, 246, 290, 298, 302, 303, 315, 329, 333, 365, 368–9, 406, 409, 411, 414, 419; *Hitler's Table Talk*, 288–9, 290, 325, 329, 331, 358, 367, 406, 409, 413, 415, 418
Hitler, Alois, 516 n1
Hobbes, Thomas, 36, 541 n7
Hoegner, Wilhelm, 367, 521 n83, 529 nn
Hofer, Walther, 526 n177, 528 n210
Hofmann, Hanns Hubert, 520 nn
Hoggan, David L., 526 n177
Hohlfeld, Johannes, 524 n146
Hölderlin, Friedrich, 334
Honegger, Hans, 465 n25
Hoog, Georges, 97
Horthy, Miklos von, 13–14
Höss, Rudolf, Commandant of Auschwitz, 399
Hossbach, Friedrich, 349; and Hitler's military plans, 526 nn
Hugenberg, Alfred, 14, 337, 341, 343, 345
Hughes, Emmet John, 465 nn26, 32
Hutten, Ulrich von, 331

Ideology, concept of, 24
Igliori, Ulisse, and the March on Rome, 213, 502 n329
Industry, and Action Française, 119; and fascism, 198, 203, 205, 217, 237–8, 261, 512 n26; and National Socialism, 324–5, 413, 524 n145; Hitler and, 403–4, 407, 412, 413, 537 n84

Jaspers, Karl, 7
Jaurès, Jean, 65, 72; Maurras and, 112, 113, 137, 482 n95
Jetzinger, Franz, *Hitlers Jugend*, 516 n1
Joan of Arc, 69
Jodl, Alfred, 350, 527 n199
Jörg, Joseph Edmund, 543 n34
Jouhaux, Léon, 180
Jung, Rudolf, 518 n35, 521 n97
Jünger, Ernst, 25

Kahn (Family), 328
Kahr, Gustav von, 320, 335, 348, 352
Kalbe, Ernstgert, 465 n24
Kaltenbrunner, Ernst, 400
Kant, Immanuel, 33, 60, 104, 434; Maurras and, 123, 139; his categorical imperative, 128, 219; his critique of reason, 432–3; and bourgeois society, 433, 438, 451; and transcendence, 540 n5, 541 n6
Kautsky, Karl, 162
Keitel, Wilhelm, 350
Kemal, Mustafa, 11, 461, 465 n23
Kepler, Johannes, 36
Kerenski, Aleksandr, 393
Klein, Fritz, 524 n145
Klemperer, Klemens von, 467 n1
Kluke, Paul, 529 n219
Knilling, Eugen von, 323
Koerber, Adolf-Viktor von, 536 n23, 537 nn
Krebs, Alfred, 523 n140

Kriebel, Hermann, 320; and the SA, 390
Kropotkin, Peter, 120, 170
Kruck, Alfred, 519 n49
Kubizek, August, and Hitler, 288, 291, 514 n1, 517 n25, 518 n37, 537 n67
Kuehnelt-Leddihn, Erik von, 466 n45, 537 n82
Kuhn, Käthe, 466 n40
Kun, Béla, 10, 522 n120
Künneth, Walter, 466 n41

Lagarde, Paul Anton de, 29, 277
Lagardelle, Hubert, 243
Lamenais, Hugues Félicité Robert, 59
Landauer, Karl, 465 n25
Lanz, Adolf (zu Liebenfels), Hitler and, 298, 406
Laschitza, Horst, 528 n210
Lassalle, Ferdinand, 88, 116, 543 n34
Lasserre, Pierre, 67-8; Le romantisme français, 473 n44
Latham, Hubert, 160
La Tour du Pin la Charce, René de, 52; Maurras and, 30, 48, 71, 116, 118; his radical conservatism, 49, 296; Vers un ordre social chrétien, 94, 470 n74 ff.
Laval, Pierre, 80, 81, 82, 83, 474 n72
Lazare, Bernard, 124
Lazzari, Costantino, 148, 193
Leibniz, Gottfried Wilhelm, 542 n32
Lemaître, Jules, 463, 467 n3
Lenin, Nikolai (Vladimir Ilich Ulyanov), 100, 105, 423; and the "workers' aristocracy", 5, 120, 157, 387, 446; trial of his veterans, 8; and automatism, 154; and idealism, 155, 161; and revolution, 156, 157, 452, 490 n48; compared with Mussolini, 157, 158; and an oppressed class, 158; accused of Blanquism, 164; and Marxism, 165-6; and the 1914-18 war, 167; Mussolini and, 176-7, 189, 215, 224, 228, 493 n155; and German imperialism, 306; said to be a Jew, 331; Hitler and, 406; and state capitalism, 545 n75; State and Revolution, 306
Leo XIII, Pope, 65
Leonhard, Susanne, 464 n15
Le Play, Frédéric, 30, 53, 118; his critical liberalism, 39-40, 41-2; his life, 40-1; his admiration for England, 41; La réforme social en France, 40, 469
Lerchenfeld, Hugo, Count, 319
Leviné, Eugen, 322
Lewien, Max, 322
Ley, Robert, 22, 384, 385
Liberalism, 5, 16; and Italian fascism, 17, 211, 215, 249; concept of, 31-2; challenged by revolution, 33; critical, 39-47; excluded by Maurras and Marx, 105, 115, 120, 126; the Risorgimento and, 147; and totalitarianism, 219; see also Doctrine of the, Enemy, Emancipation
Liebknecht, Karl, 165, 168; and the German revolution, 305, 307, 309
"Life-philosophy", Mussolini and, 159, 161,

162, 167, 220, 229, 234, 244, 246, 493 n167
Litvinov, Maksim, 352
Lloyd George, David, 175
Locke, John, 31, 541 n7
Loock, Hans Dietrich, 529 n220
Lösener, Bernhard, "race expert", 530 n30
Lossow, Otto Hermann von, 309, 320
Louis XIV (of France), 284, 414
Louis XVI (of France), 45, 67
Lucretius, 59, 102, 117
Ludendorff, Erich, 98, 305, 306; and the Republic, 309, 319, 320; influence on Hitler, 324, 325, 326-7, 334, 521 n100; Kriegführing und Politik, 325-6, 327, 333, 521 nn
Ludwig, Emil, 230, 505 n387
Lueger, Karl, 470 n83; his Christian Social People's party, 295-6; Hitler and, 298; his anti-Semitism, 518 n30
Lugan, Alphonse Marie, 477 n1
Lukács, Georg, and National Socialism, 7, 464 n12; and his rejection of history, 464 n13
Luther, Martin, 331, 332
Luxemburg, Rosa, 8, 165, 168; and the German revolution, 305, 307, 309
Luzzatti, Luigi, 230
Lyautey, Hubert, 484 n147
Lyons, Henri de, and the Camelots du Roi, 91

Macartney, Carlile Aylmer, and Hungary, 465 n22, 465 n30
Macaulay, Thomas Babington, Lord, 103
Macdonald, J. N., 496 n206
Mackinder, Halford J., 408
Maistre, Joseph Marie de, 40, 115, 126, 173, 244; Maurras and, 30, 121; and the French revolution, 34, 48; his conception of man, 34-5, 37, 485 n184; and Protestantism, 35; and the rule of Providence, 35-6, 37, 330; Considerations sur la France, 35, 468 n7 ff
Malaperte, Curzio, 249, 510 n15
Malatesta, Errico, and Italy's revolution, 187, 195, 497 n214, 499 n265
Malthus, Thomas Robert, 408, 434
Malvy, Louis-Jean, 73
Mann, Thomas, 192, 314; and the "complete victory" of fascism, 7, 464 n9; "Bruder Hitler", 464 n13
Manstein, Erich von, 357
Maraviglia, Maurizio, 496 n204
Marinelli, Giovanni, 494 n180; his death, 508 n446, 514 n64
Marinetti, Filippo Tommaso, 252, 264; and fascism, 488 n9, 494 n180
Marion, Paul, 474 n72
Maritain, Jacques, and Maurras, 77
Marsich, Piero, 511 n10
Martin, Claude, 456; Franco, 465 n32
Martow, L. (Zederbaum, J. Ossipovich), 493 n161
Marx, Karl, 26, 39, 99, 113, 485 n184, 516 nn, 541 nn; his precursors, 30, 47, 48;

Marx, Karl,—*continued*
and the proletariat, 42, 155, 156, 163, 192, 436, 440, 441; and capitalists, 48, 438; compared with Maurras, 64–5; his "union of theory and practice", 88, 89, 128; and democracy, 110; concept of liberty, 116, 127, 129; Maurras and, 119, 123, 128; and the importance of history, 136, 286; Mussolini and, 153, 177; and revolutionary evolution, 154–5; and the bourgeoisie, 157, 433, 434–41, 451, 490 n52, 541 n19; his image of the future, 160, 439; and idealism, 161; and the nature of revolution, 191–2, 322; Hitler and, 298; and the state, 435–6; concept of alienation, 436, 438, 440; and "division of labour", 437–8, 438–9; and the individual, 438–9; definition of communism, 439; and a classless society, 439–40; and religion, 440; and war, 481 n68; and nationality, 541 n10; and transcendence, 542 n32; *Das Capital*, 100, 156, 165, 286, 437, 439, 542 nn; *Communist Manifesto*, 165, 192, 434; *The German Ideology*, 436, 437

Marxism, fascism and, 20, 21, 29; Maurras and, 61, 115, 117, 119–20, 128, 135; Mussolini and, 89, 92, 116, 150, 151, 153–67, 174, 180, 223, 225, 231, 244, 424, 489 n13, 497 n223; Hitler and, 290–1, 293, 298, 302, 303, 315, 321, 408; *see also* Socialism

Massing, Paul W., 470 n83, 482 n114

Massis, Henri, 471 n8, 480 n28

Matteotti, Giacomo, 8, 209; murder of, 216, 260, 264, 499 n264, 503 n354, 504 n360

Matthias, Erich, 525 nn

Mau, Hermann, 525 nn

Maurras, Charles, 26, 35, 42, 150, 176, 356, 414, 471 nn–483 nn *passim*; his importance to a study of fascism, 30, 430; his forerunners and masters, 30, 39, 52, 60, 61, 78, 277, 467 n2; and the Dreyfus affair, 56–7, 58, 64, 65–6, 112, 287, 484 n147; his trial, 58, 84–5, 476 nn; background and early life, 58–60, 287, 288; growth of his political ideas, 60–5; literary achievements, 62, 68, 72, 73, 79, 85–6, 100–1, 116–17, 122; his monarchism, 64, 66, 68, 69, 81, 94, 102, 105, 108, 111–12, 115, 132, 133–5, 137; and Action Française, 65, 66, 67–8, 71, 72–3, 85–6, 91, 93, 94 ff, 467 n2; and war, 72–3; and the peace, 75; reply to the papal condemnation, 77; and fascism, 78–9, 86, 107, 112, 134; and National Socialism, 79, 333, 365; and Pétain's régime, 80–4; imprisonment and death, 85–7, 474 n77; his self-justification, 85–6; an unsystematic systematizer, 100–101; and fear, 101–3, 135, 139–40, 403; critique of democracy, 107–10, 117, 119, 120, 131, 134, 137; and the defence of the state, 110–12, 114, 118; critique of pacifism, 112–13, 162, 409; and class structure, 113–16; his reactionary social views, 117–19; and internationalism, 118–

119; critique of socialism, 119–20; attack on world finance, 121–2; and romanticism, 122–3; and Protestantism, 123–4, 138, 141; his idea of progress, 129–30; doctrine of the elite, 131–2; his vision of the future, 133–4; and Platonism, 136–7; and monotheism, 137–40; Mussolini and, 246, 249; Hitler and, 364, 365, 421, 424, 476 n101, 486 n195; and Renan, 469 n61; conception of France, 474 n58, 484 n155; and irrationalism, 483 n123; his provincialism, 483 n133; and the doctrine of social contract, 485 n185; *Le Chemin de Paradis*, 61, 62, 116, 137; *Kiel et Tanger*, 94, 111, 120, 478 n16; *Dictionaire politique et critique*, 100, 119, 474 nn, 479 n23

May, Karl, 290

Mayr, Karl, and Hitler, 316

Mazzini, Giuseppe, 146, 147, 167, 488 nn 2, 3; Mussolini and, 177, 248, 249

Megaro, Gaudens, 489 n27

Mehring, Franz, 491 n108

Meier-Benneckenstein, Paul, 522 n129

Meissner, Otto, 341

Meitner, Lise, 528 n217

Meletti, Vincenzo, 514 n2

Mendelssohn (Family), 328

Mercier, Auguste, and the Dreyfus affair, 65

Mazzasoma, Fernando, 508 n445, 509 n473

Michaelis, Meir, 507 n420

Michelet, Jules, 126

Michels, Robert, 489 n35, 498 n250

Militia (fascist), 212, 215, 235, 236, 256–7, 260–1, 266, 347, 369, 372, 393, 514 n60

Millerand, Alexandre, 97, 471 n2, 474 n72

Milton, John, 138, 542 n32

Mira, Giovanni, and the history of fascism, 459, 463

Mirabeau, Honoré Gabriel, 121, 146

Misiano, Francesco, 511 n3

Mistral, Frédéric, 57, 61

Modigliani, Giuseppe Emanuele, 230

Mohler, Armin, 467 n1

Molisch, Paul, 518 n31

Mommsen, Theodor, 515 n3

Monelli, Paolo, 489, n14

Monod, Gabriel, 129

Montard, Charlotte, 477 n6

Montesquieu, Charles de, 32, 42, 120, 123, 541 n7

Montesquiou, Léon de, 91

More, Thomas, 111

Moréas, Jean, 57, 63

Moreau, Lucien, 91

Moses, 406

Mosley, Sir Oswald, 12, 26, 455

Motza, Ion, 456

Mourre, Michel, 463; and Maurras' works, 471 n8

Müller, Adam, 29

Müller, Heinrich, 397

Mun, Albert de, 48

Murri, Romolo, 296

Mussert, Anton Adrian, 13, 456

Musset, Alfred de, 59, 123
Mussolini, Alessandro, 151, 194
Mussolini, Benito, x, 75, 100, 116; and the word "fascism", 3, 243; theory of the imminence of fascism, 6–7, 211; forms *Fasci di Combattimento*, 10, 251–2; his March on Rome, 11, 15, 17, 74, 210–14, 259, 502 nn, 503 nn; and the monarchy, 15, 205, 212, 219, 231; editor of *Avanti!*, 16, 152, 167, 169, 170, 171, 243; and interventionism, 16, 170, 171–4, 189, 231; and totalitarianism, 17, 217–19, 221, 231; documentation of, 22–3; presentation of his ideas, 23–4, 29, 244 ff; his war on Ethiopia, 79, 217, 226–7, 266, 267, 506 n405, 514 n63; his *Popolo d'Italia*, 150, 171, 190, 213, 226, 251, 252; his intellectual biography, 150 ff, 180–2, 188, 206, 211, 226, 231, 237, 239, 241, 243–6, 474 n72; family background and early life, 151–3, 164, 243, 287–8, 489 n18; as the *Duce*, 152, 208, 254, 255, 262, 263, 264, 501 n34; and class warfare, 153, 154, 155, 158, 160, 162, 165; and internationalism, 153, 162, 163–4, 166, 241, 461; use of violence, 153–4, 177; his "voluntarism", 154–5; use of propaganda, 155, 266; and the ideal, 159–60, 161; and the Libyan war, 161, 163, 164, 222; and faith, 161–2, 166, 211, 224; was he an orthodox Marxist?, 164, 165–7; his preoccupation with Nietzsche, 166, 189, 225, 240, 243, 497 n221; and World War I, 167, 168–78, 234, 287–8, 304, 306; expelled from the Socialist party, 171–2; and the Russian revolution, 175–7; and the Adriatic question, 181, 208, 233, 494 nn; his postwar position, 181–2, 251; and D'Annunzio, 185, 188, 190, 497 n216; his darkest year, 188–91; and the state, 188–189; and the development of fascism, 203–4, 205–6, 208, 209 ff, 243–4; and the army, 211–12; becomes Prime Minister, 214; his early government, 214–17; and Matteotti's murder, 216–17, 347; his new laws, 218–19; his form of dictatorship, 221, 222–3, 505 n388; faces towards the West, 225; on National Socialism, 225–6, 228; his rapprochement with Germany, 228 ff, 267, 349, 355–6, 455, 505 n400, 506 n401; and geopolitical ambitions, 229; becomes more undisciplined and arrogant, 231, 264, 505 n386; and Munich, 231; and the Steel Pact, 232, 507 n427; and World War II, 232–5, 236, 269, 270, 492 nn; and Yugoslavia, 233; his deposition and arrest, 235; his liberation, 236; and the *Republica di Salò*, 236; his socialization plans, 237–9, 508 n452; final statements, 241; his death, 242, 364; and the fascist state, 244; his awareness of history, 247–9; and the Bologna demonstration (1921), 254–5; his influence as a leader, 255, 258–9, 262, 269; takes second place to Hitler, 424; nostalgia for his youth, 491 n86

Mussolini, Vito, 267
Muti, Ettore, 269

Nanni, Torquato, 171, 243; and Mussolini's Marxism, 489 n13, 497 n221
Napoleon I, Maurras and, 11–12; and the revolution, 308
Napoleon III, 79, 130
Naquet, Alfred, 61
Nationalism, 20, 67; types of, 35, 52, 233, 460; Maurras', 63, 71, 83–4, 86, 103–7, 118–19, 140, 403; Mussolini and Italian, 145, 147, 150, 162–3, 178–9, 182–5, 190, 198–9, 204–6, 208, 209, 215, 221, 233, 259, 424, 493 n150, 503 nn; Hitler's, 277, 364, 397, 403, 410–11, 417, 424
National Socialism, 6, 7, 10, 13; a truly popular movement, 15, 410; its foundation in a threatened army, 57–8; and Action Française, 71, 86, 276, 365, 466 n51; structure, 95, 371, 410, 421–2; and Italian fascism, 181, 228, 275–6; founders of, 277, 328; German Workers' party and, 297, 317–18, 371, 518 nn; and bourgeoisie, 314, 322; nature defined, 314, 318, 387, 394, 412, 421, 422, 530 n37; first references to. 318; and the *Völkischer Beobachter*, 319; its growing power, 319–323; use of terror, 321, 322, 398; in N. Germany, 335–7, 371; its rise after 1930, 337–42; assumes power, 342 ff, 374, 525 n160; its uprising in Vienna, 348–9; use of propaganda, 368–9; style, 373–4, 394; state and, 394; and state, 373, 374, 378, 391, 411, 418; use of concentration camps, 398, 399; program of euthanasia, 398–400; concept, 417–19; pre-history, 467 n1; membership, 519 n59; and Zionism, 530 n37; songs and photographs, 533 n71; literary apologetics, 535 n92
National Socialism and Italian fascism (comparison), 15, 19, 22–6, 29–30, 57–8, 74, 225, 256, 260, 275–6, 466 nn, 486 n195, 504 n378, 521 n89; reaching for power, 320, 321, 322; seizure of power, 320, 321, 322–3, 343, 344–6, 347, 366; program, 318, 323, 341; chief intention, 314, 365, 369; before seizure of power, 314–15, 338–9, 366; race and population policy, 230, 353, 366, 376, 380, 412, 460–461; relationship to socialism, 320–1, 424, 460; organization, 338, 345, 371–2; party army, 345–6, 347, 369, 373, 393, 529 n12; policy, 346, 462; style, 356, 369–70, 387; development, 366; leadership principle, 369; structure, 375, 424; totalitarianism, 388–9; preconditions, 450, 467 n1; membership, 520 nn
Nature, Christian concept of, 37; Maurras' concept of, 102, 135–8; Hitler's concept of, 330, 408, 413, 419
Naumann, Friedrich, 5
Nenni, Pietro, 504 n378
Neumann, Franz, 466 n34
Neurohr, Jean, 467 n1

Neusüss-Hunkel, Ermenhild, and the SS, 532 n59
Newton, Sir Isaac, 36
Niekisch, Ernst, 466 n34
Nietzsche, Friedrich Wilhelm, 7, 26, 35, 43, 47, 126, 472 n23, 481 n51; and revolution, 61; and radical conservatism, 62–3, 140; his doctrine of "revolt of the slaves", 63, 116, 444; his lack of a system, 100; concept of the *Attentat*, 125, 442, 445; compared with D'Annunzio, 149; Mussolini and, 151, 153, 166, 244; and culture, 424, 441, 445; adversary of Marxism, 441, 442, 445, 449, 544 n57; his metaphysics of the glorification of life, 442–3; doctrine of the superman, 443, 444–5, 544 n57; and fascism, 445; and the bourgeoisie, 445–6, 451; Maurras and, 487 n202; and Marxism, 543 n34; his father, 543 n35; his cosmology, 543 n37; and the idea of destruction, 543 n42; his pupils, 544 n56; *Ecce Homo*, 444, 472 n31, 543 n36
Nitti, Francesco Saverio, 185, 210, 212, 504 n378
Nolte, Ernst, 467 n1, 488 n12, 493 n162, 522 n128, 544 n56

Ohlendorf, Otto, and the Security Department, 397–8
Olivetti, Angiolo Oliviero, *Pagine Liberare*, 243
Orano, Paolo, Mussolini and, 161, 243
Oriani, Alfredo, 24, 149, 488 n5
Orlando, Vittorio Emanuele, 17; and Mussolini, 214, 259
Ossietzky, Carl von, 531 n41

Paléologue, Maurice, 121
Panunzio, Sergio, 244, 510 n3
Papen, Franz von, 14, 341, 411; and Hitler, 524 n154
Papini, Giovanni, and *Leonardo*, 149; and *La Voce*, 150
Pareto, Vilfredo, 149; and the elite, 158; and Italian nationalism, 183
Paris, Count of, 77, 81
Parmenides, 138; and transcendence, 430, 431, 441, 540 n3
Parsons, Talcott, 466 n49
Pascal, Blaise, 60
Pasella, Umberto, 494 n180; and syndicalism, 511 n17
Pattee, Richard, 465 n32
Paul (the Apostle), 284, 331, 406
Pavelić, Ante, 13, 233, 355, 461
Pavolini, Alessandro, 508 n445, 509 n473, 514 n64
Péguy, Charles, 72, 243
Perrone-Compagni, Marchese Dino, 200–1; and the March on Rome, 213; and fascism, 499 n264
Perticone, Giacomo, 463, 508 n448
Pescatore, Martino, 508 n447
Pese, Walter Werner, 520 n80

Pétain, Philippe, 13; his régime, 80; Maurras and, 475 n84
Peter I (of Russia), 8
Pettinato, Concetto, 509 n456
Pfeffer von Salomon, Franz, 372
Philip (of Macedonia), 64
Picelli, Guido, 499 n258
Pichl, Eduard, 518 n31
Picquart, Marie-Georges, 55, 67, 72
Pieck, Wilhelm, 464 n2
Pilsudski, Józef, 11, 14, 460
Pinsker, Leo, 530 n37
Pittinger, Otto, 319
Pius X, Pope, and Action Française, 70, 71, 85; his *non expedit*, 146, 147
Pius XI, Pope, and Action Française, 76–7
Plateau, Marius, 85, 95; and the *Camelots du Roi*, 476 n101
Plato, 43, 108, 135, 136–7, 488 n11
Plekhanov, Georgi Valentinovich, 167
Pöhner, Ernst, 322
Poincaré, Raymond, 72, 97
Politics, integral, 64
Postiglione, Gaetano, 511 n10
Pottier, Eugène, 108
Pouvillon, Émile, 84, 137
Preziosi, Giovanni, 240, 507 n421
Prezzolini, Giuseppe, 157–8; and *Leonardo*, 149; and *La Voce*, 150, 170
Primo de Rivera, José Antonio, 15; and fascism, 465 n26
Principle of leadership (*Führerprinzip*), in Action Française, 95; in National Socialism, 366–9, 373, 375; Hitler and, 366–7, 373, 412; in Italian fascism, 369, 456
Proletariat, the enemy of the bourgeoisie, 5, 17, 192; Le Play and, 41; Maurras and, 120, 128; Marxist doctrines and, 153, 155, 156–7; its class warfare, 156, 297–8; Italian nationalism and, 183; and revolution, 191–2; Hitler and, 290, 411–12; *see also* Marxism, Socialism
Proudhon, Pierre Joseph, 67, 71; and war, 173, 424, 540 n154
Proust, Marcel, 78
Psichari, Erneste, 58
Pugliese, Emanuele, 502 n340
Pujo, Maurice, and Action Française, 66, 67, 69, 89–90, 91–2, 93; *Camelots du Roi*, 477 nn4, 7

Quint, Herbert A., 521 n98
Quisling, Vidkun, 13, 355, 456

Race doctrine, 21, 45, 285, 378; in Maurras, 53, 63–4, 131, 484 n155; and nation, 63, 283, 284; in Mussolini, 161, 209, 223, 226, 229, 240, 380, 495 n188, 501 n293, 505 n399; in National Socialism, 223, 328, 357, 359, 376 ff, 409; Hitler's 229, 240, 286, 298, 314, 316, 330–2, 362–3, 380–1, 384, 390, 393, 411, 415, 518 n39; character, 278; and anti-Semitism, 278, 280, 282, 283, 284, 285, 376 ff; and Christianity, 280, 281, 282, 283; and liberalism, 282,

Race Doctrine—*continued*
284; and socialism, 285; and the SS, 390, 392–3, 396, 417
Raeder, Erich, 526 n183
Ragionieri, Ernesto, 489 n15
Ramos, Ramiro Ledesma, 465
Rathenau, Walther, 98
Ratzel, Friedrich, 408
Rauschning, Hermann, *The Revolution of Nihilism*, 19, 466 nn44, 46; *Gespräche mit Hitler*, 289, 517 n7, 539 n137
Ravasio, Carlo, 235
Réal del Sarte, Maxime, and the *Camelots du Roi*, 91
Rebatet, Lucien, 82, 95
Redondo, Onesimo, and *Mein Kampf*, 465
Rée, Paul, 544 n56
Reich, Albert, 519 n57
Reichenau, Walter von, 340, 357
Rein, Gustav Adolf, 466 n50, 546 n1
Reinach, Joseph, 65, 471 n7
Reinhardt, Walther, 309
Reitlinger, Gerald, 528 n204, 532 n59
Rémond, René, 473 n46
Renan, Ernest, 26, 64, 78, 103, 311, 514 n1; Maurras and, 30, 47, 124; his critical liberalism, 42–3, 44, 126; and monarchism, 43; and aristocracy, 43–4; Mussolini and, 246; *Vie de Jésus*, 42, 124; *Oeuvres*, 42, 469 nn
Renner, Karl, 295
"Revolt of the Slaves", 7; Maurras' doctrine of, 62, 63, 116–17; Nietzsche's doctrine of, 63, 166, 444; rudiments in Mussolini, 166, 246
Revolution, its spread since 1789, 5; place of the French revolution in a total movement, 30–1; Maurras and, 30, 59, 61, 64, 105, 113, 123, 132–3; interpretations of, 31, 191, 308, 313; conservative concept of, 37, 53, 132–3, 432; Mussolini and, 133, 154, 168, 175, 193, 224; Hitler and, 133; its effect in Italy, 145–6; international aspects of, 157
Reuchlin, Johannes, 331
Rey, Etienne, 474 n59
Rhodes, Anthony, 496 n209
Rhodes, Cecil, 5, 303
Ricardo, David, 434, 543 n33
Ricci, Renato, 202, 500 n277, 508 n445
Richelieu, Armand-Jean, Cardinal, 111
Ritthaler, Anton, 525 n168
Robespierre, Maximilien de, 121, 146, 308
Rocca, Enrico, 230
Rocca, Massimo, 172, 488 n9, 511 n10
Rocco, Alfredo, 184; his *Leggi fascistissme*, 218, 345, 496 n201; biography, 496 n201
Rocque, François de la, 12; his *Croix de Feu*, 78
Röhm, Ernst, 26, 315, 323, 409, 455, 529 nn; and the German Workers' party, 317, 520 nn, 521 nn, 522 nn; influence on Hitler, 324, 327, 334; his death, 327; and National Socialism, 327, 333; and the SA, 347, 369, 390

Rolland, Romain, 474 n60
Roosevelt, Franklin D., 361, 415, 465 n18; compared with Mussolini, 8–9; and Hitler, 465 n20, 527 n191; and the atomic bomb, 528 n217
Roosevelt, Theodore, 5
Rosenberg, Alfred, 22, 240, 315, 328, 465 n21; and Catholicism, 333; and Soviet Russia, 336, 357, 363, 389; and the National Socialist revolution, 343, 466 n5; and anti-Semitism, 380, 400; and the Nuremberg rally, 383; his operational staff, 394; Hitler and, 464 n13, 523 n133; and Eckhart, 522 n116
Rosselli, Carlo, 230; and antifascism, 464 n14, 504 n378
Rossi, Cesare, 172; and Mussolini, 492 n133, 502 n343, 512 n22
Rossoni, Edmondo, 257; and syndicalism, 261, 488 n9, 495 n184
Rothbauer, Anton M., 465 n32
Rothfels, Hans, 464 n6, 528 nn
Rothschild (Family), 119, 328
Roudiez, Léon, 471 n16
Rousseau, Jean Jacques, Hitler his logical outcome, 19; his political ideas, 32–3, 35, 36, 43, 113, 187, 279, 468 nn5, 6; 481 n51; and democracy, 110; part of the romantic era in France, 122; Maurras and, 123, 430; and war, 481 n68; *Contract Social*, 110, 485 n184, 486 nn

SA, 335, 339, 342, 345–6, 347–8, 529 n9; its origin, 368, its character, 369, 370, 372, 373, 374, 393–4; and anti-Semitism, 377; and concentration camps, 398
Sainte-Beuve, Charles-Augustin, 467 n2
Saint-Just, Antoine de, 121
Saint-Simon, Claude Henri de, 16, 37, 116, 131, 166, 308; his pacifism, 112, 113; compared with Fourier, 541 n19
Salandra, Antonio, 17, 148, 206, 212, 259, 512 n26
Salazar, Antonio Oliveira, 14, 465 n31
Salvatorelli, Luigi, 17, 249, 511 n15, 546 n3; *Storia del fascismo*, 459, 463, 498 n253
Salvemini, Gaetano, 150, 170, 492 n131, 497 n230, 503 n349, 504 nn378, 380, 508 n452, 513 nn
Sand, George, 123
Sangnier, Marc, 72, 112; and Christian Democracy, 68, 70, 296; and the bourgeoisie, 115
Sansanelli, Nicola, 511 n10
Sarfatti, Margherita G., 230
Sauckel, Fritz, 528 n216
Sauer, Wolfgang, 525 n160, 530 n23
Sauro, Nazario, 508 n447
Schacht, Hjalmar, 524 n145, 537 n70
Schäfer, Dietrich, 313
Schäfer, Wolfgang, 530 n16
Schapiro, Leonard, 464 n15
Scheidemann, Philipp, 175, 309
Scheler, Max, 7, 519 n41
Schellenberg, Walter, and the Foreign Intelligence Service, 397

Schelling, Friedrich Wilhelm, 7
Schicklgruber, Anna Maria, 516 n1
Schieder, Theodor, 467 n1, 540 n153
Schinz, Albert, 468 n4
Schleicher, Kurt von, 339, 341, 348
Schlesinger, Walter, 519 n43
Schmeer, Karlheinz, 532 n56
Schmitt, Carl, 25
Schnabel, Franz, 467 n1
Schneider, Reinhold, 466 n40
Schönerer, Georg von, his Pan-German party, 296–7, 301; Hitler and, 298, 303, 402, 518 n37; his anti-Semitism, 518 n30
Schopenhauer, Arthur, 7, 116, 497 n221
Schrameck, Abraham, 95, 474 n63
Schreck, Julius, his Schutzstaffel, 390
Schreiner, Albert, 524 n145
Schüddekopf, Otto-Ernst, 464 n1, 523 n139
Schulz, Gerhard, 525 n160, 530 n23
Schuschnigg, Kurt von, 15, 350
Schwabe, Klaus, 519 n50
Schwarzschild, Leopold, 466 n47
Science, Maurras and, 63, 127, 129, 139, 430; Hitler and, 392, 404, 420, 421
Scorza, Carlo, 269
Seeckt, Hans von, 98, 308
Seraphim, Hans J., 527 n199
Serena, Adelchi, 269
Serrati, Giacinto Menotti, 197, 499 n256
Seyss-Inquart, Arthur, 350
Shakespeare, William, 138
Shirer, William, 467 n1
Siebert, Ferdinand, 507 n427
Sieyès, Emanuel Joseph, 121
Silone, Ignazio, 466 n48, 504 n378
Simmel, Georg, 7
Sismondi, Jean Charles de, 543 n33
Skalnik, Kurt, 518 n30
Smith, Adam, 434, 438, 541 n7
Socialism, 5, 16; Mussolini and, 16–17, 148, 150, 152, 159–64 passim, 170, 180, 189, 204, 206, 207–15, 239, 241, 461; in National Socialism, 96, 315, 317, 325, 335–7, 347; its final goal, 159–60; and World War I, 167; and interventionism, 179; its heyday in Italy, 182, 191, 193; its hostility to the state, 296; and revolution, 498 n242; see also Marxism
Socrates, 43, 441, 488 n11
Sombart, Werner, 523 n132; Die Juden, 536 n38
Sonnino, Sidney, 230
Sontheimer, Kurt, 467 n1
Sophocles, 103
Sordet, Dominique, and collaboration, 82, 83
Sorel, Georges, 71, 115, 162; Réflexions sur la violence, 69; Mussolini and, 153, 243; Révolution Dreyfusienne, 471 n1
South Tirol, 178, 223, 275, 334, 358, 501 nn, 505 n388, 539 n150
Sovereignty, doctrine of, 31, 110–11, 421; Rousseau and, 33; Maurras and, 104,

111–12, 113; Hitler and, 383, 393, 401, 407–9, 416, 418, 421, 539 n149
Speer, Albert, 364, 535 n92
Spengler, Oswald, 25
Spinosa, Antonio, 507 n420
SS, 236, 260, 266, 339, 346, 362, 363, 532 nn; and the SA, 348, 391; origins of, 368, 389; and the police, 374, 384, 391, 392, 394; Hitler and, 389–90, 391, 393; development of, 390 ff, 533 n70; its five pillars, 391–2; and the war, 394
Stalin, Josef, 20, 357, 388, 466 n47, 527 n200; and fascism, 8, 96; and Marxism, 166; and Hitler's rise to power, 352; his "revolution from above", 448
Stambolisky, Aleksandr, 12
Starace, Achille, and the Fascist party, 265 ff, 488 n9; and the Abyssinian war, 266, 267; his death, 509 n473, 513 n45; biography, 513 n45
Starhemberg, Ernst Rüdiger, 15
Stauffenberg, Claus Schenk von, 362
Stavisky, Serge Alexandre, 78
Stempfle, Fr Bernhard, 348
Stennes, Walter, 391
Stieff, Helmuth, 358
Stirner, Max, Mussolini and, 188, 497 n221
Stoecker, Adolf, 21, 296, 470 n83
Strasser, Gregor, 348, 390; and National Socialism, 335, 338, 371, 372
Strasser, Otto, 315, 364, 517 n27; and socialism, 335–6, 520 n62, 523 nn
Strauss, David Friedrich, 441
Streicher, Julius, 291, 318, 530 n22; and anti-Semitism, 315, 346, 376, 521 n97; Der Stürmer, 406
Stresemann, Gustav, 335
Stroop, Jürgen, and the Warsaw ghetto, 533 n71
Sturzo, Don Luigi, 210, 466 n39, 494 n176, 504 n378
Szálasi, Ferenc, 13, 14, 355, 456, 462
Szilard, Leo, 528 n217

Taine, Hippolyte, 26, 53, 78, 105, 126, 282, 311, 469 n65, 470; Maurras and, 30, 46–7; and the French revolution, 45–6; Origines de la France contemporaine, 45
Taittinger, Pierre, 12; his Jeunesses Patriotes, 78
Talleyrand, Charles Maurice de, 133
Tamburini, Tullio, 499 n264
Tasca, Angelo, 465 n34, 494 nn173, 179; 498 nn, 504 n378
Taylor, Alan J. P., 526 n177
Terracini, Umberto, 494 n173
Thalamas, François, 69, 85, 91
Thalheimer, Siegfried, 471 n7
Thälmann, Ernst, 341, 352
Thaon di Revel, Paolo, 214
Thibaudet, Albert, 471 n8
Thierack, Otto Georg, 398
Thiers, Adolphe, 70
Thimme, Anneliese, 523 n137
Thompson, Dorothy, 8

Thyssen, Fritz, 524 n145
Tilgher, Adriano, 501 n315
Tiso, Josef, 13
Tobias, Fritz, 525 nn
Tocqueville, Alexis de, 515 n7
Todt, Fritz, 384
Togliatti· Palmiro, 464 n2, 494 n173, 504 n378
Toller, Ernst, 322
Torre, Edoardo, 512 n22
Totalitarianism, concept of, 17–18, 219–21, 388, 456–7; in Italy, 17, 217–19, 221, 388, 460; in Germany, 17, 222, 374, 387–9, 460; in Russia, 222; communism and, 322, 388
Toussenel, Alphonse, 470 n83
Transcendence, Rousseau and, 33, 485 n184; Gaultier and, 139; Hitler and, 420–1; Maurras and, 421, 430, 487 n203; fascism and, 429, 434, 453; interpretations of, 430–4, 540 nn, 541 nn; and bourgeois society, 450–1
Treitschke, Heinrich von, 277, 515 n3
Treves, Claudio, 230, 489 n38, 502 n327, 504 n378
Trevor-Roper, Hugh R., 514 n1, 535 n1
Trotsky, Léon, 20, 105, 165, 466 n47, 480 n24, 493 nn155, 156; and the 1914–18 war, 167; and bureaucracy, 448
Tsankov, Alexandr, 12
Turati, Augusto, 265
Turati, Filippo, 148, 154, 177, 180, 189; and fascism, 181, 193, 315, 504 n378; Mussolini and, 206
Turgot, Anne Robert de, 37, 42

Vacher de Lapouge, Georges, his race doctrine, 280–2, 284, 286, 330, 515 nn
Vaihinger, Hans, 501 n315
Vaillant, Édouard, 170
Valentin, Veit, 323
Valois, Georges (Gressent, Georges), 12, 94, 466 n51; and Action Française, 71, 78, 90, 95, 115, 473 n54, 477 n8; his Faisceau, 78; and Maurras, 95–6, 97; compared with Mussolini, 473 n54
Vaugeois, Henri, and Action Française, 66, 67, 89–90; and National Socialism, 71
Vecchi, Ferruccio, 251
Verlaine, Paul, 59
Veuillot, Louis, 467 n2
Victor Emmanuel III (of Italy), 13, 146, 229, 240; and the March on Rome, 213, 214;

his lack of power, 219; and Mussolini's deposition, 235, 237
Vidussoni, Aldo, 269, 514 n61
Vigny, Alfred de, 487 n203
Vigo-Almereyda, Miguel, 73
Violence, as used by Camelots du Roi, 69–70, 72, 91–3, 98, 263, 270; nature of fascist, 98, 201–2, 511 n3; socialist use of, 182, 495 n191, 499 n259; a characteristic of class warfare, 153; as employed by Italian fascism, 197, 198, 499 n259, 500 n275; National Socialism and, 367–8
Vogelsang, Carl von, 296,
Vogelsang, Thilo, 524 n148, 525 n156
Vollweiler, Helmut, 504 n365
Volta, Alfredo Giovanni, 257–8
Voltaire, François-Marie, 34, 123, 127
Volz, Hans, 520 n73

Wagner, Richard, 290, 382, 386
Wagner, Winifred, 517 n25
Waldeck-Rousseau, Pierre, 66
War, Maurras and, 59, 111–13; Action Française and, 72–3; Lenin and, 162; Mussolini and, 162–3, 167, 168, 177, 224, 225, 239, 241, 245, 322; Marxism and, 173; Hitler and, 321–2, 352, 354 ff, 409–410, 417, 419–20, 423; no longer extolled for its own sake, 423; Proudhon and, 424
Weber, Eugen, 463 n1, 467 n1
Weber, Max, 7, 26, 299, 305, 452, 519 n52, 526 n188, 538 n88; his critique of Marxism, 446–50, 545 nn; and alienation, 448; and bureaucracy, 448–9; and class struggle, 449; Nationalist Revival in France, 473 n46
Weinberg, Gerhard L., 522 n121, 527 n199
Weisenborn, Günther, 528 n210
Whiteside, Andrew G., 518 n32, 546 n1
William, II (Emperor), 109, 300, 304, 480 n28
Wilson, Thomas Woodrow, 5, 175, 307, 423
Woltmann, Ludwig, 515 n18

Yorck von Wartenburg, Peter, Count, 18

Zamboni, Umberto, and the March on Rome, 213, 502 n340
Zanella, Riccardo, 494 n177
Zionism, 530 n37
Zola, Émile, "J'accuse", 55
Zoller, Albert (pseud.), 517 nn